THE STRUCTURE OF
HUMAN POPULATIONS

The Structure
of Human
Populations

EDITED BY

G. A. HARRISON

Reader in Physical Anthropology
University of Oxford

AND

A. J. BOYCE

Reader in Human Biology
University of Surrey

CLARENDON PRESS · OXFORD

1972

Oxford University Press, Ely House, London, W.1

GLASGOW NEW YORK TORONTO MELBOURNE WELLINGTON
CAPE TOWN IBADAN NAIROBI DAR ES SALAAM LUSAKA ADDIS ABABA
DELHI BOMBAY CALCUTTA MADRAS KARACHI LAHORE DACCA
KUALA LUMPUR SINGAPORE HONG KONG TOKYO

PRINTED IN GREAT BRITAIN AT THE PITMAN PRESS, BATH

FOREWORD

FRANK FENNER

FOR some millions of years man's ancestors struggled to produce enough offspring to ensure that the species survived, and many early hominids did not. Matters were not greatly different in the early millenia of man's history and prehistory. However, during the last two or three generations the situation has totally changed, for in technologically advanced human societies virtually every female now survives to reproductive age. This is a biologically novel situation to which man's breeding habits have not yet been adjusted, hence the human population explosion, which is the most striking and most important biological phenomenon of the twentieth century. Four great problems face man now and in the decades ahead, namely nuclear war, overpopulation or the threat of it, pollution and resource depletion, and the widening gap between the economic wealth of the rich and the poor countries. The last three are directly influenced by population growth, and as we have seen in the past, with cries of 'Lebensraum' and the 'greater East Asia co-prosperity sphere,' the likelihood of major war is not uninfluenced by population pressures.

It is only during the last few decades that we have become aware of these problems, because most men tend to think arithmetically and not in terms of exponential growth. As one consequence of this delay, we find that although there is now a spate of publications about 'the population problem', there are hardly any books that discuss human populations in the way that ecologists have long discussed the populations of other animals—there is as yet no equivalent of Andrewartha and Birch's *The distribution and abundance of animals* for the most important of all animals, man.

Just as the book, *Human Biology*, written by Harrison and his colleagues some eight years ago, pioneered the scientific consideration of the biology of man as an animal, like and yet unlike other animals, so this book, *The structure of human populations*, pioneers the integrative approach to the population biology of man; and it is necessarily an integrative study. Conceptually, it requires the capacity of systems analysts to build and modify models; for its numeration it requires the information and also the social insight of demographers, and for its interpretation it requires contributions from anthropologists and sociologists and from human biologists of diverse kinds, including some versed in environmental biology and others skilled in human genetics. This volume, the outcome of a Wenner–Gren Symposium in August 1970, encompasses all these disciplines, beginning with a statement of the conceptual bases of human population studies and then exploring man in relict hunter–gatherer communities, man in the tropics and man in the Arctic man in cities and in village communities, and most importantly man the social animal, regulating his fertility, undertaking deliberate small and large scale, migrations and planning, however imperfectly, for his future.

This book should become a milestone in the effort that man must now make to cope with the demographic results of his scientific and technological progress, for unless he understands and adjusts his population structure and thereby adjusts it to the world that is our only home, *Homo sapiens* will have no future, only a past.

Canberra, 1972

PREFACE

ALTHOUGH in so many ways educationally highly productive, the division of academia into discrete disciplines and policies which recognize these disciplines as the primary basis for learning and thus constantly reinforce their discreteness, has seriously limited the development of important areas of knowledge. Fortunately, many of the divisions are now breaking down and multidisciplinary and even interdisciplinary researches are being increasingly undertaken in a number of very different situations. The deeply entrenched division between arts and science, which in background, outlook, and attitude tends to separate the social scientist from the natural scientist is still, however, formidable and a number of fields of research have suffered from it. One of these concerns the nature of human populations—for knowledge of this depends upon genetics, demography, ecology, psychology, sociology and social anthropology, disciplines which until recently have rarely come all together in curricula. And an understanding of the way human populations are organized is today not only of academic interest but also of profound practical importance.

It is hoped that in some way this book will help remedy the situation. It is intended as a University text and was in fact devised very much with the new Honour School of Human Sciences at Oxford in mind—a School which represents a fundamental attempt to break down anachronistic disciplinary barriers. It is hoped, however, that it will be much more widely read in universities and outside.

It is doubtful if this book would ever have materialized without the help of the Directors of the Wenner–Gren Foundation who incorporated its theme in their Conference programme, and who invited all the contributors to their European Conference Centre at Burg Wartenstein to discuss not only the papers here presented but the much wider issues they raise. Those were for all participants stimulating, exciting, thought provoking, and happy days. On their behalf, but especially for ourselves, we would like to express here our deep gratitude and appreciation to Mrs Lita Osmundsen, Director of Research, of the Wenner–Gren Foundation and to her in every way superb staff, particularly Dr Karl Frey, Mrs Charlotte Frey, Miss Judith Webb, Miss Patricia Cassell, and Miss Arlene Sheiken.

G.A.H.
A.J.B.

January, 1972

ACKNOWLEDGEMENTS

GRATEFUL acknowledgement is made to the authors, editors, and publishers of the following works and journals for permission to use figures and tables. The appropriate reference is given in each caption.

American Journal of Physical Anthropology; Blau and Duncan, *The American Occupational Structure* (Wiley, New York); Bogue, *Principles of Demography* (Wiley, New York); *British Journal of Sociology*; *British Journal of Statistical Psychology*; Chagnon, *Yąnomamö: the Fierce People* (Holt, Reinhardt and Winston, New York); *Demography*; Drake, *Population and Society in Norway, 1735–1865* (Cambridge University Press); Glass, *Social Mobility in Britain* (Routledge and Kegan Paul, London); *International Congress of Anthropological and Ethnological Sciences*; *Proceedings of the National Academy of Science of the United States of America*; Schull and Neel, *Inbreeding in Japanese Schoolchildren* (Harper and Row, New York); Thompson and Lewis, *Population Problems* (McGraw-Hill, New York); *United Nations Demographic Yearbook*.

CONTENTS

CONTRIBUTORS

PAUL T. BAKER
Department of Anthropology, Pennsylvania State University

BURTON BENEDICT
Department of Anthropology, University of California, Berkeley

ANTHONY J. BOYCE
Department of Biological Sciences, University of Surrey

STEPHEN BOYDEN
Urban Biology Group, The John Curtin School of Medical Research, The Australian National University

NAPOLEON A. CHAGNON
Department of Human Genetics, The University of Michigan Medical School

JOHN I. CLARKE
Department of Geography, University of Durham

GORDON F. DE JONG
Department of Sociology, Pennsylvania State University

THEODOSIUS DOBZHANSKY
The Rockefeller University, New York

MICHAEL DRAKE
Faculty of Social Sciences, The Open University

JAMES S. DUTT
Department of Anthropology, Pennsylvania State University

A. H. HALSEY
Department of Social and Administrative Studies, University of Oxford

G. AINSWORTH HARRISON
Department of Human Anatomy, Anthropology Laboratory, University of Oxford

R. W. HIORNS
Department of Biomathematics, University of Oxford

PETER KUNSTADTER
Department of Epidemiology and International Health, School of Public Health and Community Medicine, University of Washington

WILLIAM S. LAUGHLIN
Department of Biobehavioural Sciences, University of Connecticut

FRANCISCO M. SALZANO
Departmento de Genetica, Instituto de Ciências Naturalis, Universidade Federal do Rio Grande do Sul

WILLIAM J. SCHULL
Department of Human Genetics, The University of Michigan Medical School

JAMES N. SPUHLER
Department of Anthropology, The University of New Mexico

MICHAEL S. TEITELBAUM
Office of Population Research, Princeton University

COLIN M. TURNBULL
Department of Anthropology, Hofstra University

JOSEPH S. WEINER
Medical Research Council Environmental Physiology Research Unit, London School of Hygiene and Tropical Medicine, University of London

1

INTRODUCTION
THE FRAMEWORK OF POPULATION
STUDIES

G. A. HARRISON *and* A. J. BOYCE

HUMAN beings like most other organisms are not distributed randomly over the surface of the earth, but tend to be grouped into clusters, or populations. Typically, these populations are themselves structured: they are organized with a definite form, and though the pattern of this form may change with time, it has continuity. In other words, populations are not merely conglomerations of individuals but rather, although to different degrees, ordered coherent systems, which have an entity greater than that of the sum of the individuals of which they are composed. The structure is manifest in a series of general biological and cultural characteristics and in a particular biological and cultural history. When seen in anything like its totality this structure is extremely complex even in the simplest situations, and each population is unique. This uniqueness inevitably arises from the uniqueness of all individuals but, apart from this, each population has an unrepeated structure. Of course, as with other types of variety, some structures resemble one another more than others and some populations, especially neighbouring ones, between which there tend to be high levels of biological and cultural relatedness and exchange, may be extremely similar in their structures. However, whilst classifications of certain components of structure have been attempted, nothing like an overall taxonomy has been made, partly because of the dearth of information, but mainly just because of the complexity of such an operation.

There are not only biological and cultural components of structure, but the innumerable determinants of this structure are also broadly classifiable as biological and cultural. Admittedly some factors, such as geographical and environmental conditions (which may profoundly affect population distribution and density) are not clearly ascribable to such categories; but even these can often be thought of as manifesting their effects through the inherent requirements for human life. On the other hand, cultural factors must be regarded as ultimately consequent upon biological ones. Social organization is a function of social behaviour and this is a biological property of the species. However, cultural factors, if not independent of the basic biology of man, can certainly be independent of biological variety in population structure. Indeed there are many, mainly sociologists, who believe that the limits set by biology are so wide that cultural variety is to all intents and purposes not in any profound way affected by these limits. The supposition here is that in any environment there are so many different types of social structure that are compatible with the biological existence of a population, that the particular structure found is from a biological viewpoint idiosyncratic. This, of course, does not deny that the parts of the social structure themselves may have very precise inter-determinations and that there is a strictly defined, overall functional social coherence which is adapted to the prevailing conditions. It does imply that the origins of cultural patterns are, within wide limits, chance events and that within these limits social change is self-generating and does not require a feedback from the biological structure. Whilst this view would seem to be by far the most widely accepted, it has been challenged, especially in rather extreme form by C. D. Darlington, who sees the whole course of historical development of human societies as arising from their genetic structure and composition. Even among those who believe that the importance of biological factors has been grossly underestimated, few would subscribe completely to Darlington's position, but the fact that this position is logically just as tenable or untenable as the completely environmentalist one indicates a crucial methodological problem. In science, the analysis of the relative contributions of a number of variables to the causation of a particular phenomenon depends on being able to randomize the effects of the set of variables with respect to one another. But in studying the history of human populations, the components of cultural inheritance can never be randomized with respect to those of biological inheritance. This situation is then often beyond formal analysis and intuitive judgements become the order of the day. Despite these difficulties there are instances where what are called cultural factors clearly affect biological structure, as for instance those that determine the choice of mate. And if examples of the converse are not so easily identified by observation there are certain situations where one can deduce that they must occur. Thus, although the analysis of particular situations presents complex problems and certain types of question are often beyond complete answer, it needs to be recognized that a complex interplay between biological and cultural factors can and probably does occur in the organization of human populations and that biological and social structures should not be seen as independent but as having a broad interface. In this sense it seems not misleading to draw an analogy with the structure of the individual, with a series of parts each of which differs in morphology and physiology but which are connected together in an interacting way to form an integrated whole.

So far we have referred to populations as though they were defined only in spatial terms; if not as clusters of people separated by relatively uninhabited areas from other clusters, at least as groups around which spatial boundaries can be drawn. These of course are the concepts of populations most commonly used. But for many purposes populations are defined in terms other than those of spatial continuity/discontinuity. In particular, there may well be structural heterogeneity within the population of any one place, such as the vertical units of social class, and people in different places may from certain points of view belong to a single population (as, for instance, those who share a common religion).

It is important to note here that most population concepts involve a hierarchical classification, in which units are defined in terms of the extent to which people are embraced by common characteristics. For example, in the simplest situation, the population of the world is made up of the populations of different countries, each themselves made up of the populations of states, counties, districts, and so on. Because there are many factors determining the ways populations are defined, hierarchies taking all factors into account must be multidimensional and in the overall viewpoint the situation may be much more like a continuum of overlapping categories than a series of clusters. However, whilst it is possible to conceptualize populations in these terms, in practical considerations populations are recognized according to some particular component which is of interest. And the major components on which interest focuses are demographic, genetic, social, and ecological.

The definition of a population for demographic purposes, in which concern is primarily directed to analyses of fertility, mortality, and migration, can be made entirely on arbitrary grounds. It need be no more than a group of individuals in which a demographer is interested, and whilst such a group often corresponds more or less to a genetic, social, or ecological population, it may have no real structural coherence, as, for instance, a group of individuals with some particular physical or age characteristic, or who have been exposed to some particular social experience. Demography, essentially, provides a methodology which can meaningfully be applied to many situations which are not primarily concerned with population definition. On the other hand, demographic structure, in terms of patterns of fertility and mortality, emigration and immigration and the effects of these on age and sex composition, are of vital concern when considering the dynamics of populations which have been recognized for other purposes.

Genetic, or Mendelian, populations are defined by the extent to which individuals share in a common gene pool. In other words, they are determined in terms of degrees of biological relatedness. The smallest Mendelian group consists of the parents and children within the nuclear family, as these show the maximal degree of relationship; and the largest the whole species, since all the members of a species potentially, at least, share in the same gene pool, whereas different species, because of their reproductive isolation from one another, have for ever different gene pools. Between the family on the one hand, and the whole species on the other, there are many intermediate categories of Mendelian population whose precise recognition often presents complex problems, since all the many factors determining relatedness have to be taken into account. However, the concept of a hierarchy of Mendelian populations is a vital prerequisite to understanding the nature of human variety, and much attention has been and will continue to be given by geneticists to those factors which determine the ways genes are organized into genotypes in human populations, i.e. genetic structure, *sensu stricto*, and the factors which determine which genes are present, i.e. genetic composition.

In many aspects of sociology and social anthropology, population units may be solely defined in terms of point of view, and workers in these fields can be as arbitrary as the demographer. However, there is certainly a social parallel to the genetic concept of population with people sharing to varying degrees common cultural heritages. And implicit in defining groups for many sociological and anthropological investigations is the concept of a hierarchy of socially defined populations such as band, clan, and tribe, or occupation and social class. Indeed, in some instances, the parallel with Mendelian populations may be even closer with populations being defined in terms of categories of relatedness, such as kin groups. However, whilst it is theoretically possible that such groups do in fact correspond to genetic populations, the social criteria for relationship may correspond only partially or not at all to biological genealogy, and the hierarchy of social populations can be very different from the genetic one.

From the ecological viewpoint, populations can be seen in terms of the extent to which people share in exploiting and developing the same environmental resources—to put the definition in similar form to that used for genetic and social units. This is not inconsistent with the more common viewpoint of an ecological population as a group of people interacting with one another, usually in some co-operative form in a particular habitat, and it more clearly indicates the potential, if not the real, hierarchical nature of ecological groups. Whichever viewpoint is taken, however, as with the other population categories problems arise in recognizing actual populations in the field. Habitats intergrade with one another, especially as they occur in the human context, and there are varying levels of interaction between individuals. Similarly, the extent to which people share in environmental resources is often an issue of infinite degree and there are difficulties in judging the extent to which such resources can be regarded as the same. Nevertheless, even if definition and recognition is imprecise, the concept of population in an ecological context is a valid and useful one.

Just as there can be an interrelation between a social population and a genetic population, so may each be interrelated with an ecological population. In fact a genetic population, which is primarily defined by mating pattern, is clearly determined on the one hand by the social factors which affect mate selection and which also define a social population, and on the other by environmental factors which affect population distribution, density, and movement and which help to define an ecological population. It can be argued further that social organization is to varying degrees affected by ecological conditions, both natural and man-made, and therefore that the definition of a social population is influenced by ecological conditions. Conversely, social factors determine the nature of habitats and available resources, and the levels of interaction between peoples, and to some extent genetic factors, may play a similar role. We might therefore expect a rather broad correspondence between populations defined for genetic, social, and ecological purposes, as many of the factors which determine each interact with one another. However, not all the factors determining one determine the others, or at least not to the same degree, and there is rarely, if ever, exact correspondence between genetic, social, and ecological populations. Sometimes indeed, a population defined singly for one purpose may embrace a number of populations when seen from other viewpoints. This is especially so for ecological situations, and it seems likely, for instance, that an ecologist looking at the interaction between man and his environment in relation to economics in many parts of the world, and especially in multiracial and class-structured societies, would define a population which from both the social and genetic points of view would be very heterogeneous and comprised of multiple populations. Because they are so intimately determined by social and ecological factors the units in a hierarchy of Mendelian populations are always likely to be no greater and often will be smaller than the units of social and ecological hierarchies.

It is hoped that these introductory remarks about the nature of populations, the factors influencing it, and the components of population structure, will afford a general framework for considering the contributions to this volume, which perhaps all too easily fall into the four categories: demographic, genetic, social, and ecological. For this, the editors must accept responsibility since authors were asked to write to a specific brief, but the form of the presentation does seem to be a necessary consequence of the existing limitations to our knowledge and of the fundamental divisions that still exist in human science. At the moment, there are few, if any, populationists, only various groups of demographers, geneticists, sociologists, and ecologists, interested in population problems, and under these circumstances it seemed right to anchor on the background disciplines. All the contributions, however, do relate directly or indirectly to the determinations or consequences of the demographic structure of populations. In demographic structure the interactions of the various determinants are most evident and many aspects of genetic, social, and ecological structure influence, and are influenced by, population size and distribution, movement, and patterns of fertility and mortality. In addition to this central role of demography all the contributions attempt to interlink aspects of other viewpoints, some provide integrated case studies, and the chapters on ecology deal with the interactions of man with his environment in a very wide context.

The ultimate framework for population studies is the whole population of the world, or seen in a more evolutionary viewpoint, the total human species. Compared with most species, man has a wide geographical distribution, and in his late evolutionary development has been remarkably successful. Though many other groups exceed him in numbers, none can compete in terms of the total biomass incorporated into the human species. However, this success, which of course is the cause for the profound changes which are now occurring in the world's environments, came quite late in human evolution. Until the end of the Palaeolithic, man was quite a rare animal, though by that time he had already developed a form which, so far as we can tell, is indistinguishable from that of present-day man. His success, then, would seem to be largely, if not entirely, attributable to his acquisition of a cultural organization and technology which allowed him to mould environments to his own needs. Certainly the colder regions of the earth, and probably the temperate ones too, could not have been colonized without substantial technology. Not all regions of the world, however, have yet been made equally favourable to human existence, and the distribution of the human species remains geographically very uneven. Regions of great cold or dryness have proved particularly inhospitable. The factors governing the present distribution of man are considered in this volume in the chapter by J. I. Clarke. He indicates the extent to which physical geographical factors have played a role in determining distribution, but also shows that many other considerations, especially economic history, have played and are likely to continue to play crucial roles.

Whatever its ultimate determinants, the distribution is the product of the demographic forces of fertility, mortality, and migration. G. De Jong is concerned with these, especially with the first two, on a global scale and introduces some of the methodology that the demographer uses for describing population characteristics and for making projections of the nature of future populations. He provides the background for the very real present concern for population growth with its consequent effects upon human environments, and therefore upon the whole ecological situation. Attention is given particularly to the heterogeneity in demographic structures of different national and regional groups, with their implications not only for social and economic development, but also for the future genetic composition of the human species, which will alter with changing and variable patterns of fertility and life expectancy.

The important question of the scale at which analysis of population problems is undertaken is raised in these first chapters; scale in this context relates to the levels in the hierarchical classification of populations that are abstracted for examination. The overall world situation arises from patterns in innumerable ecological populations, and it is by examination of situations on a very local basis that detailed interactions between determining factors are revealed most precisely. Increasingly, the study of human variation has turned from the general world or regional survey to examination of very particular situations.

From a biological viewpoint, the study of man, though often fraught with difficulties as compared with the study of animal populations, has one great advantage, in that through written records it is sometimes possible to give a historical time-depth to the structure of a population. This not only means that temporal patterns of change can be observed but also that information is available on the extent to which the structure at any one time is idiosyncratic, rather than conforming to a regular pattern. The perspective of the historical demographer, then, provides demographic information not only on a scale where it is most easily analysed in genetic, social, and ecological terms, but also gives the vital information about the representativeness of any situation. It is considered in this book by M. Drake, and although the approach is mainly developed in historical, economic, and social terms, which have been most explored, the biological implications are manifest.

The accumulated evidence of historical demographers indicates that, at least in Europe, practices of family limitation are a number of centuries old. And in many societies today, including those of simple and subsistence economy, there are customs which restrict fertility. It would seem, indeed, that few if any populations display maximum biological fecundity.† Carr Saunders was the first to develop the view that in societies which had had time to adjust to their environment and technology, fertility is regulated to afford the optimal population size for the resources available. The evidence for this is considered here by B. Benedict, who provides a world-wide comparative review of the social factors which may affect fertility patterns. This is one of the few areas in social anthropology where such large-scale comparative studies have been undertaken.

As all those concerned with consideration of population policy issues are aware, one of the major problems nowadays is understanding and altering the motivation of people in their family-building habits. How subtly social factors can operate is indicated by the case study of attempted fertility regulation in Mauritius which Benedict also provides.

A demographic variable of ramifying effect is the relative frequency of males and females in a population, not only overall, but in each age group. The sex ratio is clearly determined by the frequency of the sexes at conception and by their subsequent comparative mortality, and the latter, if not the

† In strict usage among demographers, the term fertility refers to realized reproduction and fecundity to potential reproductive capacity. Among biologists, however, these words are often used in the completely opposite sense.

former, is clearly subject to varying cultural, genetic, and ecological factors. Conversely, the sex ratio itself, especially in view of the comparative biological abilities of the two sexes, and the different roles afforded to the sexes in different cultures, can affect genetic, social, and ecological structure. It is itself a determinant as well as a characteristic of demographic structure. Most of the information available concerns the sex ratio at birth, which shows considerable variation between different spatial populations, and indeed in different vertical population units in the same place. In recent years these variations have been exposed to considerable analysis and innumerable factors have been claimed to be associated with or to determine the secondary sex ratio. The chapter by M. Teitelbaum can be regarded as a case study of the complexity of an apparently simple demographic character and the ways such characters have been analysed.

Even on the very local scale, the factors affecting demographic structure are inordinately complex. And in anything but a stable state, which over an extended period of time is rarely if ever found, the interplay of the demographic forces themselves, fertility, mortality, and migration, needs sophisticated mathematics for its analysis. This may be approached either by the computer simulation of particular situations, or by the construction of simplifying models of general situations which are algebraically soluble. Both approaches are of great value in understanding population dynamics. Simulation is particularly useful for revealing the effects of complex interactions, whilst models afford insight into how particular effects are brought about. Models also provide a framework against which the importance of various demographic factors can be measured and frequently indicate the way in which a real population problem should be approached. They are considered here by R. W. Hiorns in relation to various demographic parameters.

The chapters on the sex ratio and mathematical models act as links between the primarily demographic sections of this book and the five chapters dealing with genetic structure. These would seem to require the least general introduction as they follow a well established pattern for dealing with elements of human population genetics. Attention is given to the definition of genetic population units as affected by distribution and movement, in the chapter by the editors; to the effects of mating system, which determines genetic structure *sensu stricto*, in the chapters by W. J. Schull and J. N. Spuhler; and to selection as the prime force in determining the genetic composition of populations in the contribution by Th. Dobzhansky. The paper by F. Salzano affords a case study on a large scale of the interaction of these and other elements in considering the nature of genetic diversity among the indigenous inhabitants of the New World. All these contributions emphasize the importance of demographic, cultural, and ecological considerations in discussing genetic population units. Mate selection is obviously profoundly affected by many social factors and also by those demographic factors which influence mobility and population size. Population size is of critical concern in considering stochastic genetic processes, especially genetic drift, which operate in determining genetic composition. And it is important not to forget that natural selection operates through the daily lives of people, whose chances of survival and reproduction are affected by the genes they possess. It is in considering selection that the study of genetics and ecology come closest together. The environment, both natural and social, exerts the selection pressure on the gene pool, either to change it or to maintain its constancy, and although there is increasing evidence that factors of drift have been frequently underestimated, it is still generally believed that the genetic composition of human populations is determined by the action of differential selection. Population variety in gene frequency is to be seen, then, as the product of adaptation, currently or in the past, to different climatic, nutritional, disease, and similar natural environmental factors, and possibly also to different social and technological systems and ways of life.

Interpolated among the chapters on genetic structure, and following that on assortative mating, is a contribution by A. H. Halsey on social mobility. This is slanted primarily towards an interest in social structure, and may seem strangely placed among a series of genetic papers. However, social mobility affords an important example of selective movement which can have profound effects on the genetic structure of populations if there is a heritable element to the attributes which influence whether an individual moves up or down in the social hierarchy. Whereas non-selective movement tends to homogenize population units, selective movement can create population diversity; and social mobility, like assortative marriage, may itself be responsible for genetic stratifications in societies. It is for this reason that the social mobility chapter has been placed where it is and Halsey, in fact, devotes considerable attention to genetic implications of social mobility.

Another link between the genetic and other viewpoints is provided by the contribution of N. A. Chagnon. Whereas Salzano considered what light demographic and economic factors might throw on the genetic structure of Amerindian groups as a whole, Chagnon takes a particular small-scale situation in the same continent, the genetic heterogeneity among the Yąnomamö Indians of Venezuela, and shows how this is only explicable in terms of the detailed demographic and social history of the tribe. This chapter affords a most illuminating case study and indicates how dependent the population geneticist is upon social anthropology. It further exemplifies the increasing attention that geneticists have been giving to the detailed analysis of comparatively small population units. It is not surprising that these are often comparable to the units of sociological study because they tend to be socially defined; and as this paper indicates, although the components of structure looked at by social anthropologists and geneticists are very different, they are nowadays examined in comparable units and frequently are interrelated, especially in so far as both are determined by mating pattern.

The remaining six chapters present a primarily ecological viewpoint, especially as this relates to demographic structure. The first two, by C. Turnbull and P. Kunstadter, tend to have a social anthropological orientation whereas the last four by P. Baker and J. S. Dutt, W. Laughlin, J. S. Weiner, and S. Boyden are more biological. The distinction, however, is one of fine degree and Kunstadter, for instance, pays considerable attention to the effects of infectious disease, whilst Weiner is critically concerned with agricultural practice. The ecological approach is a totally synthetic one in which attention needs to be given to all components of the environment, both natural and man-made, and to their interactions with every aspect of the human population. Of course, ecological studies do vary according to purpose, with social anthropologists concentrating on those factors most directly and influentially determining economic and social structure and biologists more concerned with the environmental causes for genetic and phenotypic variety. With present knowledge and training this is as it should be. But seen in a holistic way, there probably are not even distinct sociological and biological foci, only a web of complex interactions between the environment and the human group which determine everything from the biological structure of the individual to traditions of philosophical thought. Just how pervading even the natural environment can be in a simple hunter-type of society is demonstrated by Turnbull in his consideration of the Congo pygmies. Indeed, it is through the effects of the environment on experience and beliefs and social structure that Turnbull sees the characteristic demographic patterns of the pygmies emerging.

Ecological studies reveal many chains of effects. The contributions by Kunstadter and Weiner show here how in tropical areas climate affects soils; soils, agricultural practices; agricultural practices, population distribution, density, and settlement patterns; and how these factors themselves influence other demographic characteristics and components of biological and social structure. Nor are such chains usually one way. In the above instance, social organization is related to technological level, technological level affects agricultural practices, and these have profound effects on soils. Soils determine vegetational cover, and such cover or lack of it have significant effects on climates. And so on. There is no end to ecological interactions, and quite subtle alterations in the environment or in the organization and activity of human populations can have ramifying ecological consequences. As has been frequently demonstrated, it is all too easy to upset the so-called 'balance of nature'. Ecosystems involving man have rarely been in anything like long-term balance since the end of the Palaeolithic, except, perhaps, in those cases where an economy of gathering and hunting still persists. Indeed, it may be doubted whether even simple agricultural economies are compatible with the long-term persistence of habitats capable of supporting human or other forms of life. Of course, what has happened is that man's advancing technology has so far more than kept pace with the destruction of natural environments; indeed, at least initially, such destruction in many areas actually increased the resources available. Because of this practically all of the world's populations have tended to show intermittent if not continual expansion. In most ecosystems economy and level of technology are by far the most important factors determining population growth and size. It is only in a few of the more inhospitable regions such as deserts, mountains, and arctic areas that natural factors still function as primary limiters. But at any one time, there are always some limits to a system and clearly these limits cannot be expanded indefinitely; at least not so far as the resources of this planet are concerned. Already many populations survive only because they can draw on resources far distant from the regions they inhabit. The present very real concern with the world's population growth arises mainly from the obvious ultimate limit to the earth's resources, which even scientific development cannot expand. But perhaps just as important is the fear that in attempting to support populations of even present-day size there will be irremediable and rapid destruction of environments. The problems of the 'population explosion' are not dealt with explicitly in this volume, but most of the contributions and especially those with an ecological viewpoint raise basic issues which are relevant to these problems.

By dealing with pygmy hunters, Thai cultivators in the tropics, Eskimos and Aleuts in the arctic, a variety of Amerindian groups including Quechua Indians at high altitude, and former temperate agriculturalists in Europe, the contributions already mentioned have considered in ecological terms a diversity of environments and economies. But a book of this nature would inevitably have failed in its purpose, had it neglected the situation which is rapidly becoming the one to which the majority of people are being exposed—the urban environment. It is dealt with in some detail here by S. Boyden. Urban conditions, so largely man-made, are clearly the most artificial of those to which human populations are exposed. Some of these conditions have been specifically designed to meet human needs or, as one should say, human needs in an urban environment; but others, like atmospheric pollution, noise, and crowding, are more or less concomitant consequences of urban structure —though, of course, they are subject to considerable modification. At the moment anyway, the urban way of life is very different from those which man, despite his diversity of environments, has in the past been practising and which determined, through evolution, his biological characteristics. One might well, therefore, expect problems of adaptation at the individual level, and strong selective forces operating at the population level. As we mentioned earlier, selection operates through the daily lives of people, in terms of genetically determined variation in fertility and mortality. It is true that post-natal mortality in many advanced industrial urban societies is small and, with sophisticated methods of contraception, there is a trend towards less variation in family size, but there is plenty of room still for evolution to occur through gametic selection, early zygotic selection, and varying generation times, as well as through variance in family size. Important also are the numbers of people who never marry and of those that do, those who have no children. Urban studies have so far been largely the preserve of sociologists, with some attention from medical viewpoints. But there are important general biological implications and a complete ecological approach to many of the problems presented by the urban environment and urban populations is required.

An ecological approach, whether it be in the study of simple gatherers or of urban industrialists inevitably raises the issue of the extent to which a population can be considered to be adapted to its environment, and how this can be measured. Most biological concepts of adaptation relate primarily to genes, characters, and individuals. Thus if a gene is spreading in a population under natural selection, it is said to have high adaptive value. Similarly, character variants which clearly increase the chances of survival and reproduction in the environment in which they occur may be termed adaptive whether they be of direct genetic determination or whether they arise from environmental modification of development. And such criteria are obviously extendable to the whole individual whose adaptedness to his conditions is biologically manifest in his probability of surviving and reproducing. It is important to remember that natural selection operates directly on the total phenotype of the individual and only indirectly on characters and genes.

Social attributes clearly can also be considered in these terms as equivalent to biological characters and even when their variation is entirely environmentally determined, they are relevant to a discussion of the comparative adaptedness of individuals. Traits such as specific intellectual and technical skills may affect mortality and the probability of reproduction in all societies and thus have biological relevance. But the concept of adaptation is also often applied to solely social considerations and measurements made against an exclusively social scale. Thus individuals are frequently referred to as being socially well or poorly adapted, implying variation in the extent of conformation to social norms and acceptance in the social system, and a value scale of what is socially desirable. No doubt some of the factors determining social adaptations are biological, and the scales may have biological consequences, but the objective in setting up the scales can be exclusively social. Scales, such as social and economic status, or 'standard of living' tend necessarily to be more arbitrary than biological ones but they have real adaptive meaning.

Some of these social scales are regularly extended from the level of comparative individual conditions to comparative population conditions. Indeed, others, such as degrees of technological advancement, are erected which, from a comparative viewpoint, can only be meaningfully considered at the level of whole populations. In a similar way biological standards such as health status are often extended from within-population comparisons to between-population ones. It does not, however, follow that because standards which are used for expressing individual adaptation can be transferred to the population level, it is possible to transfer also the concept of comparative adaptedness, or, at least, the concept in the same form as it is applied within populations. Darwinian fitness, the prime biological measure of adaptation, is assessed by relating the performance of individuals within a population to one another and is thus a function of the individuals who happen to be in that population and the way they compete with one another. More importantly, it is highly dependent upon the nature of the environment and an individual with a high capacity for survival and reproduction in one population in one environment may have a relatively low fitness in another population in another environment. Social performance obviously depends just as much upon the nature of the social environment, which clearly also varies from population to population. But even apart from the problems presented by this sort of relativity in cross-comparing individuals in different populations, it may be questioned whether attempting to translate population parameters to a scale of comparative adaptation adds anything to our understanding of the circumstances of a situation and the predictions we can make about it. Certainly populations differ markedly in, for instance, mortality rates, but in what sense can one say that a population with a high mortality rate is less well adapted to its environmental conditions than one with a low mortality rate is to its? Of course, if the conditions are the same the question immediately becomes meaningful, and if the two populations happen to be not only in the same conditions, but in the same place, the differences in mortality may have considerable relevance to predicting the futures of the populations. However, as Baker and Dutt point out here in their detailed analysis of the concept of population adaptation and the considerable methodological problems involved in measuring it demographically, even when two populations are in the same place, they are rarely if ever exposed to exactly the same conditions; if they were they would probably not represent separate populations. And populations in different places can never be exposed to exactly the same environments. Comparing the adaptive state of such populations is somewhat like comparing the adaptive state of different species in different niches—like asking which is the better-adapted animal, man or gorilla. Absurd as this question may appear, it nevertheless raises the possibilities of a scale against which population adaptation can, at least in principle, be measured—the scale of comparative ecological success. This view is developed in this volume by Baker and Dutt, who also show how difficult it is to test such theoretical propositions in a field context.

Using everyday standards of judgement, there would seem to be variation among existing populations in their success. Looking at the present-day distribution of man, few would say that the Australian Aborigine or the American Indian had been as successful as, for instance, the peoples of European, Asiatic, and African descent. But such judgements tend to be ones based on number, and population size alone is a very inadequate measure of success. Given the limited resources of the Arctic, it is doubtful if any population could be more successful even in terms of number than the Eskimo and Aleuts, yet numbers are perforce small. Clearly, as in the case of adaptation, comparative success can only be meaningfully discussed in terms of number if it can be discussed at all, by references to particular habitats and the resources which are directly or indirectly available to a population. Some environments have fewer resources than others and must carry smaller populations unless provision of the limiting resources can be made from other regions. And in these terms the favourability of an environment may be determined not by overall resources but by just one or a few which happen to be scarce in a particular region and which are critical for human existence.

It may be further noted here that resources which are necessary for some particular stage of technological development may not be required to anything like the same extent at a later stage of development. It is not coincidental that the industrial revolution was associated with regions of plentiful and high-quality coal, and peoples without such supplies were not likely to develop an industrial phase, but today coal is far less important to the maintenance of an industrial society. Similarly, early agriculturalists relied upon the replenishment of soil by alluvium carried by rivers, but now this is no longer a limiter of agricultural practices. It would seem that much of the comparative development of different societies can be explained in terms of resources and the sequence of their availability.

Whilst number alone is a poor indicator of ecological success it is a component, although not necessarily a large one, of a much more meaningful parameter: likelihood of persistence. Many populations have in the course of history become extinct, and a sad account is given in this volume by Turnbull of what must be the last years of the Ik people of Uganda. Other groups are bound to follow them, and by definition extinct groups were ecologically unsuccessful. However, such judgements are *post hoc*, and it is far more difficult if not impossible to make predictions about the future fate of populations. The most important consideration here is the way the environments of these populations change as change they must. And in considering such changes, one cannot view populations and environments independently of one another. Whilst some groups are more or less in balance with their habitats, many, as already mentioned, are not, and there is little doubt that the destruction they cause in their own environments will be extended to others. Because of these interrelationships it can be reasonably argued either that most present groups will survive or that none will, in which case the concept of ecological success in terms of likelihood of persistence is practically not very helpful. However, even if only of theoretical interest, the concept of probability of persistence is illuminating because it raises the issue of what variable factors occur in populations which facilitate their adaptive response to environmental change. Just as there has been an evolutionary premium in mammalian, and especially human, evolution on the adaptability of the individual, so those populations have persisted and may continue to persist, which because of their structure, biological and sociological, are adaptable and can respond to change or resist change. (There is a direct analogy here with adaptability and homeostasis in individual reaction to environmental variation.) The components of structure potentially concerned are manifold, ranging from breeding systems and genetic composition on the one hand through to the nature of economic and political systems on the other. Some attention has been given to the origin of biological structure in terms of the relationship between this structure and environmental change, and various theories have been proposed by sociologists to account for the nature of biological change. However, it would seem worthwhile to pay much more attention to these phenomena.

In discussing the concepts of adaptation and ecological success in terms of population persistence, it is perhaps worth noting that it is the population defined in genetic rather than ecological terms which one is considering. The ecological relationships, like the social structure, may be totally different from one time to another but if there is continuity of biological inheritance one can speak of population persistence. However, sharing in a common gene pool does not necessarily mean sharing the same genes, once the time factor is taken into account. Evolutionary factors may greatly change gene frequencies but such change does not necessarily alter the matrix of genealogical relationships and the continuing discreteness of these relationships which population persistence implies. Conversely, even though its genes may persist through being introduced into other populations by hybridization, a population which loses its discrete set of biological relationships will be regarded as having become extinct.

Our purpose in summarily considering the individual contributions to this book has been to show some of the main interlinking themes which relate to the overall structure of human populations. These at first sight may not be obvious, partly because it is difficult in any multi-authored book to achieve continuity of argument, but more so because in this complex field our knowledge and understanding is limited and patchy. There are important components of structure, especially of social structure, such as detailed kinship, political, and economic variety which have not been closely considered here because, at the moment their interrelations with biological elements have not been explored at all. This is not to say that such interrelations do not exist. It is quite possible for instance that biological variety in work capacity affects economic organization, and less-evident relationships are also possible. And even in these fields which are usually regarded as solely social, demographic considerations are of the greatest importance both as causes and as effects. We may perhaps then look forward to the day when all aspects of population structure can be seen with a wholeness which now eludes us. We hope that this book will contribute something to bringing that day nearer.

2

GEOGRAPHICAL INFLUENCES UPON THE SIZE, DISTRIBUTION, AND GROWTH OF HUMAN POPULATIONS

John I. Clarke

Geography and population

ALTHOUGH the scope and content of geography is a matter of perennial controversy, there is no doubt that geographers are principally interested in spatial distributions of elements which occur on the earth's surface and how these distributions vary in time. The approach of geographers to population study is therefore primarily distributional, although this approach is not exclusive to them. Demographers have generally given only limited attention to this approach, and have focused their main attention on the processes of population change. Obviously, geographers studying areal patterns of population must have some knowledge of these processes of population change, but there is much in demographic analysis which has little spatial significance and consequently little direct relevance to the geographer. Nevertheless, geographers do not confine themselves to an analysis of patterns of population numbers, but also look at areal patterns in the composition, growth, and migration of population.

Moreover, geographers are not merely interested in distributional patterns; the core of their subject lies in the complex spatial interactions between man, his manifold activities, and the physical environment, here defined as natural conditions† (Trewartha 1953). So in their study of population, they endeavour to relate the locational diversity of populations to the nature of places (Beaujeu-Garnier 1956–8 and 1966, Clarke 1965, George 1959, Trewartha 1969, Wilson 1968, Zelinsky 1966). It is, however, patently obvious that patterns of population cannot be explained solely in terms of the physical environment without recourse to socio-economic factors. It is true that some earlier geographers were guilty of attempting explanations from an excessively deterministic viewpoint, but the determinist or environmentalist attitude to geography has long been regarded by most geographers as too narrow and restrictive, although individual viewpoints have been subjectively influenced

† Like many other terms used in this volume, the term *physical environment* has varied connotations for geographers, anthropologists, urban planners, and others.

by personal experience of different environments, whose impact upon man varies markedly not only according to the severity of physical environments but also according to the level and type of technology of different peoples.

It is a pity that geographers have not been very successful in conveying the changing character of their discipline to the general public, which equates geography with the study of the physical environment as it affects man. Such a study is also obviously incomplete because it precludes analysis of the spatial relationships between different physical distributions or between different human distributions, and also precludes analysis of purely physical environments such as an uninhabited island or a man-made environment such as the central zone of a city. Unfortunately, this general view of geography is deeply rooted, and thus the term *geographical factors* is frequently interpreted as physical or natural factors, including relief, climate, water, soils, vegetation, and minerals as well as space relationships. Until recently, this connotation of the term was even current among geographers (Simons 1966), but it is no longer acceptable. Nevertheless, when asked to prepare a paper on the 'geographical factors determining the size, growth, and distribution of human populations' for an inter-disciplinary volume of this nature, I was conscious of being asked to consider the general influences of the physical environment upon these aspects of human populations, and as specialists are examining the influence of other factors, I am grateful to seize the opportunity of limiting my brief.

Before proceeding, it is perhaps worth reiterating that although the physical environment has a powerful influence upon populations, especially those living with limited technological ability in harsh physical conditions, patterns of population are not explicable in terms of the physical environment alone or any particular element of the environment. Theories such as climatic determinism offer biased explanations of the complexities of population patterns, as do theories based on stages of economic development or political stability. There are no simple or general explanations of the patterns of size, distribution, composition, or growth of human populations. In this essay, therefore, no attempt is made to explain patterns, but merely to show the influence of physical factors upon them.

In many ways this is an inadequate approach, because since the Industrial Revolution there has been a progressive weakening of the traditional ties between society and the land (Wrigley 1965). In agricultural, pastoral, and hunting and collecting societies, the population map is still greatly influenced by the physical environment, and even in industrial societies based on mineral resources this remains true, but the growth of tertiary industry (government service, retailing, wholesaling, transport and communications, banking and commercial services, the professions) and the market orientation of manufacturing have released large sections of populations from land-boundedness and have encouraged widespread urbanization. This process is particularly marked in developed countries, but is increasingly apparent in developing countries as well.

In the same way, population growth can no longer be simply explained in terms of social and economic evolution. The most important demographic feature of the world today is the abruptness of mortality decline in many of the less developed countries. This change is associated with some social and economic evolution, but not nearly enough, and certainly there is no significant correlation between levels of economic development and rates of population growth. Consequently, the practice of examining populations as the end of a Place–Work–People chain on a cause and effect basis is not justifiable. This old chain of analysis, so beloved of earlier human geographers concerned with the adaptation of 'modes of life' to the physical environment, is no longer so suitable as a framework of study. The coherence, harmony, and order between environment and human activities, which were found in the modes of life approach, have frequently been disrupted by the introduction of elements of modern economy such as mines, plantations, cities, roads, and railways. It may be much better to consider the distribution and growth of population and its economic activities by first examining the population itself.

Population is therefore gaining a more central position in the discipline of geography, and has been regarded by some as the touchstone of relevance for geography as a whole (Webb 1969). It has even been postulated that as geography has become so increasingly man-orientated the explanation of the areal distribution of population should become the central geographical problem, and that rather than concern ourselves with objective studies of place itself we should examine the ideas of man about place (Hooson 1960). Not all geographers would agree with this view of the subject, but it emphasizes the necessarily restricted scope of this essay.

The concept of scale

Geographers are in the habit of studying areas varying in dimension from a square mile to tens of millions of square miles, and in consequence the concept of scale is well known to them. One particular problem is that of overcoming the vast size of the earth's surface and generalizing about it: in doing so, many of us have resorted to classifications (e.g. races, modes of life, levels of economic development, stages of population growth) which have oversimplified reality.

Scale has special relevance in geographical studies of population size and change, for the relative significance of migration and natural increase/decrease varies according to the scale of the areas examined; this is largely because the volume of migration to or from a place appears to vary inversely with distance. The significance of migration increases when smaller areal units are used, and natural increase/decrease accounts for a smaller part of population change. At the world scale natural increase accounts for all population growth, and at the continental and national scales (except for a few micro-states) natural increase is much more important than migration, but at smaller scales, such as the county, parish, village, or street, migration becomes increasingly important so that it often outweighs natural change, and natural decrease may well replace natural increase. Therefore, conclusions derived from analysis at one scale should not be expected to apply to other scales.

It follows that factors influencing growth and distribution of population may change with scale. For example, site factors influencing the location of a village may differ substantially from local, regional, and national factors; climate plays only a small part in the location of population within a parish, but its influence is much greater upon the pattern of the ecumene, or permanently inhabited area of the earth's surface. Although each explanation fits into the next highest group of factors, there is a problem of linking results obtained at one scale to those obtained at another (Haggett 1965a). This scale-linkage problem is known to most of us who have pondered over the relevance of a large-scale sample study to the small-scale national or continental pattern.

One particular difficulty is the most suitable size of population units for analysis, not only in terms of validity of conclusions but also for definition as units. Populations rarely constitute discrete units or isolates, and therefore boundaries are not easy to draw between peoples unless there are sharp-edge densities and intervening no-man's-lands, as in the case of some political boundaries and marked physical barriers like coastlines and deserts. Gradual transitions are more common than abrupt transformations.

The scale of study of population is of course largely dependent upon the size of the areal units for which enumerations have been made: these may be administrative units or combinations of administrative units or special units devised for statistical purposes. But many of these units are not very suitable for the geographer, who is often more interested in areal units with some internal homogeneity or nodality than in administrative/political units. Moreover, administrative/political units vary enormously in demographic and areal dimensions. The gamut of state size ranges from a plethora of pocket or micro-states (e.g. Hong Kong, Singapore, Kuwait, Gambia, Luxembourg, and Guyana) to macro-states each with more than 100 million inhabitants. It is worth recalling that about 58 per cent of the total world population lives in seven large states: China, India, U.S.S.R., U.S.A., Pakistan, Indonesia, and Japan.

The range in the size of states is very significant from the point of view of population change, partly because the superimposition of an irregular net of political boundaries across the earth's surface has had a stabilizing influence upon population distribution during the twentieth century. International migrations have been restricted, especially by those countries (e.g. Australia, the United Kingdom, Canada) who have feared the evolution of plural societies. The reduction in the volume of international migration means that although it has little effect upon large states like India and China it has had a great effect upon the population growth of small states like Israel, Kuwait, and Hong Kong. In addition, rates of natural increase are not unaffected by population size, for in general it is easier to effect a rapid reduction in mortality (and probably also fertility) in small states than in large ones, where it is likely there are more complex ecological systems and cultures. In other words, small states are prone to demographic instability (Fosberg 1965, MacArthur and Wilson 1967). Islands are particularly prone to instability—Tristan ba Cunha and the Hebrides spring to mind—but the concept may also de extended to the village and tribe.

Population distribution and the physical environment

One other major difficulty facing geographers in their analysis of patterns of population is that, whether one takes a macroscopic or a microscopic view, human populations exhibit great unevenness of distribution and great diversity of composition.

According to recent estimates (Grigg 1969), although the average population density of the world is about 65 per mile^2, 64 per cent of the land area is very sparsely inhabited with densities below 5 per mile^2, and 35–40 per cent may be regarded as uninhabited. Such estimates should be accepted only with caution, for it is not easy to draw a line between inhabited and uninhabited areas, and the amount of land with a population density of less than 5 per mile^2 is considerably affected by the size of areal units for which data are available, but they indicate the approximate dimensions involved. The expansion of the ecumene (or inhabited area) over the last few centuries was principally due to the spread of European control over much of the world, including the so-called 'empty continents' of the Americas, Africa, and Australasia as well as parts of Asia. During this century intercontinental migrations have reduced in volume and, despite recent rapid population growth, the Americas, Africa, and Australasia still contain less than one-quarter of mankind in contrast with Eurasia which contains over three-quarters. Moreover, the limits of the ecumene have been more or less stabilized, at least for the time being, although there are local advances and retreats of the settlement frontiers.

Past expansion of the ecumene has therefore been much influenced by the spread of cultures and types of economy, but today the non-ecumene (sometimes called negative areas) is mainly composed of lands which are physically hostile to man, given his present technological ability. Although other physical factors are often directly hostile to man's presence, climate exercises the most powerful influence upon the distribution of the non-ecumene, and in particular three types of climate: cold, dry, and hot–wet, in that order of importance. These areas all pose difficulties to human existence, but this does not mean that they are committed to emptiness. Indeed, some arid lands (e.g. Egypt) and some hot–wet lands (e.g. Java) have population densities among the highest in the world, and the hot–wet lands in particular exhibit wide discrepancies in the density of human occupancy. Consequently, the relationships between population distribution and climatic types are not simple (Staszewski 1961), for elements of the physical environment do not act in isolation but in co-ordination. There are few obvious general correlations between population distribution and individual physical factors; tendencies occur but exceptions are common, and it is better to think of 'partially coincident sets of relationships which are not direct but are filtered through the medium of local cultures and economies' (Zelinsky 1966).

Whether difficult environments are inhabited or not depends upon the limitations they exert on human existence, the choice they offer to people, and the need to occupy them. Critical levels of temperature and of oxygen, fluid, and food supply impede human expansion horizontally and vertically, but the adaptation to hostile environments of primitive peoples and the ecological success of their modes of life has demonstrated that absolute environmental limitations to human survival are few, and cultural mechanisms have been so effective in shielding man from the direct impact of his physical environment that, in general, physiological difficulties in occupying harsh environments are less significant than problems of economic development. Problems of cultivation, livestock raising, water supply, route construction, and so on, differ substantially from those in the temperate lands where the great majority of mankind lives, and consequently harsh environments are less attractive and more expensive to develop, especially for large-scale settlement. Therefore they tend to be developed only when the need arises—such as through the push of population or political pressures or the pull of mineral resources or power supplies. Their environmental potential cannot be easily determined or quantified, for the attraction and habitability of an area change in time according to a host of cultural factors, including the technology and character of the society involved in settling the area; the vivid contrasts in the population and settlement of Japan and New Zealand, which have not too dissimilar physical environments, exemplify this point.

Different peoples perceive and utilize similar environments in different ways, and high environmental potential is not nearly enough to ensure human habitation. For example, merely the small size of an island or the remoteness and inaccessibility of a continental interior may be enough to detract settlement. Furthermore, just as the quantity and quality of resources tend to limit the population size of an area, so also does the size and quality of a population greatly affect the quantity of resources extracted or converted. So in one mountain massif in the Maghreb or the Middle East, it is possible to find several different peoples practising diverse types of economy ranging from pastoral nomadism to sedentary cultivation all under similar environmental conditions, the explanations being largely found in the origins and traditions of these peoples in other environments. In short, the interrelationships between population and environment are neither simple nor static; they are modified whenever there are changes in population, technological availability, and the resource base. This is one reason why population–resource ratios may not be very meaningful, except perhaps as a conservationist's measure of critical population densities among closed subsistence societies (Allan 1965) dependent upon land, and these are becoming a decreasing minority of the world's population.

There is no doubt that habitability increases in time and space as technology enlarges the resource base and overcomes physical obstacles, but difficulties are great in assessing potential habitability and productivity of any part of the earth's surface and they have caused contrasting views on the future expansion of the ecumene and the number of people who can live on earth. These views range from pessimistic gloom to optimistic visions. At present there is little advance into the negative areas, partly because in continents like Africa and South America there is insufficient population pressure and capital to encourage such advance and partly because the modern sectors of the economies of these continents and other parts of the underdeveloped world have been externally orientated and peripherally located (Clarke 1970). So it is not easy under present conditions to imagine more than localized settlement of the non-ecumene in places where there can be intensive production of power, minerals, water, industrial products, or crops.

Within the ecumene there are enormous variations in the density of population, and the influence of physical factors is more indirect. The principal influence is upon the types of economies which in turn greatly affect population density. Among subsistence economies population densities largely reflect the intensity of agriculture, which may often be fairly closely related to variations in the environment, but among more sophisticated exchange-based economies the importance of agriculture as a determinant of population density diminishes and consequently the influence of physical factors is attenuated. Among such economies, especially where the primary sector is small, concepts such as carrying capacity have little relevance; Hong Kong has more than 4 million people living at very great density which has little relationship to the availability of agricultural land. The number of people present in an area, their ways of life and standards of living are all related to their economy, their culture, and their past.

It must be stressed that the strong tendency to clustering of population, at continental and national levels, is not explicable by physical factors alone. It is estimated (Grigg 1969) that 76–9 per cent of the world's population live at densities exceeding 50 per square mile on 16 per cent of the land area, and 63 per cent live on 10 per cent of the area in four major clusters of very high density which fall into two contrasting pairs: east and south Asia, and

Europe and the north-eastern part of North America. While the two Asiatic clusters, with 42 per cent of mankind, are primarily agricultural and rural, the two Atlantic clusters, with 21 per cent of the world's population and 80 per cent of the world's wealth, epitomize the developed, industrialized, and urbanized world. The size of such clusters depends on how their limits are defined; in the above calculations an isoline of 50 persons per mile^2 was used, but other thresholds might be employed.

It must be obvious that whereas physical factors have largely conditioned the shape of the non-ecumene, the character of clustering on a continental scale owes much to cultural causes. With the exception of north-eastern North America, the smallest of the major clusters, these concentrations are areas of prolonged human occupation and civilization and until the eighteenth century contained a higher proportion of mankind than now. In about 1750, Eurasia contained some 84 per cent of the world's population (Durand 1967), and the persistence of such pre-industrial concentrations of population is a salient fact of present distributional patterns.

On the other hand, the massive clustering of people into cities, which is greatly intensifying the unevenness of population distribution, is a recent phenomenon. During the first sixty years of this century the proportion of the world's population living in settlements with 20 000 inhabitants or more rose from less than one in ten to more than one in four, and by the end of this century, the ratio may well be one in two. Furthermore, in 1960 nearly three-quarters of all city-dwellers lived in large cities with 100 000 or more inhabitants (Breese 1966), and by A.D. 2000 such cities will probably contain over two-fifths of mankind. Few countries, even among those described as underdeveloped or developing, are exempt from increasing urbanization, and in most countries the proportion of the urban population is rising, but this growth owes little to factors of the physical environment. While physical factors of site, situation, and resources have played a significant part in the location of urban concentrations, the growth of cities, though influenced by political, demographic, and other factors, is particularly dependent upon economic factors such as the existence of transport networks, the snowballing of diversified activities, and the high costs of relocation.

Although the distribution of cities is uneven, it is not wholly irregular. The regular relationships which exist between the size of cities and their rank were first noted as long ago as 1913 and have been examined many times since then, especially in regard to the rank–size rule (Berry 1961, Berry and Garrison 1958, Stewart 1958, Zipf 1949), which states that if cities in an area are ranked in order of population size $(1...n)$ then the population of the nth city will be $1/n$ the size of the largest city. Considerable attention has also been given to the existence of primate cities (Berry 1961, Ginsberg 1961, Linsky 1965, McGee 1967), which dominate their urban hierarchies. In addition, a large number of studies has been devoted to seeing how the spacing of cities is related to their size. In essence, research has demonstrated that urban centres do not exist in isolation but tend to establish themselves in interrelated patterns and networks, and, in the spatial analysis of such patterns, central place theory has proved a useful model (Christaller 1966, Haggett 1965b).

Population dynamics and physical environment

Three main demographic forces influence the patterns of population dynamics: natural increase/decrease, distributional inertia, and human mobility. There can be little doubt that on a world scale the first two forces are most powerful, but at a local scale the importance of human mobility has increased immensely.

Natural change of population has probably never offered more areal variations than at present, owing to declines in mortality and fertility at various times and rates during the nineteenth and twentieth centuries. In consequence, even at national level natural increase varies from about 0·0 per thousand (East Germany in 1968) to 55·2 per thousand (Kuwait), and within countries even wider differences occur. In countries like Britain and the United States, both experiencing overall natural increase, there are large areas suffering natural decrease, and even within an under-developed country there are wide regional and rural/urban discrepancies in natural increase arising particularly as a result of local conditions, notably the localized occurrence of diseases and the availability of medical facilities.

One consequence of the recent changes in the rates of population growth is that the small-scale world map of population distribution (Fig. 2.1) does not correlate with the world map of population growth (Fig. 2.2); in other words, present distributions are more reflective of past densities than present growth rates. But whereas the influence of physical factors is discernible in the density map, this is not so in the growth map or in the world maps of mortality and fertility. The spread of public sanitation and modern medicine has startlingly reduced the impact of environmental or exogenetic diseases in many parts of the world, especially endemic and epidemic infectious diseases like malaria, sleeping sickness, and yellow fever. It would be wrong to exaggerate the areal extent of this morbidity reduction in developing countries where it is principally confined to urban centres and accessible rural regions. In the tropics, in particular, sharp influences of the physical environment upon disease (e.g. river blindness, bilharzia, and trachoma) are still abundantly evident (May 1958–61). In developed countries, however, the role of environmental diseases is less and the relative impact of social influences (employment, industry, housing, etc.) upon degenerative diseases and mortality is much greater, although studies in medical geography of such countries (Howe 1963, Murray 1967, Stamp 1964a and b) have revealed persistent links between patterns of morbidity/mortality and the physical environment, particularly climate, as well as marked areal and seasonal variations.

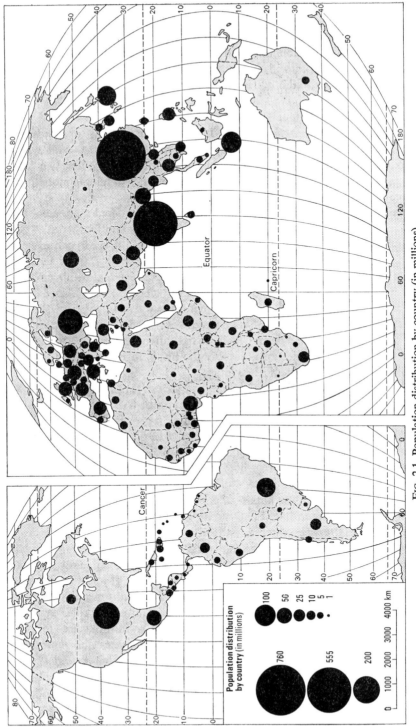

FIG. 2.1. Population distribution by country (in millions).

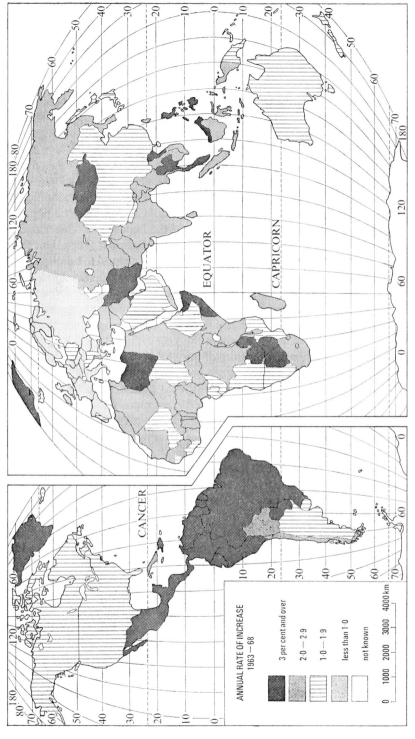

FIG. 2.2. Annual rate of population increase 1963–8.

The links between the physical environment and patterns of human fertility are much more tenuous, except perhaps among populations living in close contact with their environment in areas of climatic extremes where despite considerable human adaptation to difficult conditions there is evidence to suggest that reproductivity is affected. This is the case among populations living at high altitudes, as, for example, in the Andes. It is, however, always difficult to isolate one particular influence among the wide variety of influences upon human fertility, and this is even more difficult in regions where more moderate climatic conditions prevail and the influence of the physical environment is more restricted. Nevertheless, such influence exists and seasonal rhythms of fertility have been noted in many parts of the world, among highly urbanized populations practising birth control as well as agricultural populations knowing little about it. The argument of the importance of such influences should not be stressed too much, however, because it is apparent that the great range in human fertility from one part of the world to another owes more to the direct influence of family limitation than to the indirect influence of multitudinous factors of the social, economic, and physical environment.

Emphasis has been already given to the persistence of past concentrations of population and the restrictive influence upon human migrations exercised by political boundaries. At the moment the process of international migrations only effects minor redistributions of the world's population, and it seems unlikely that the pattern of major population concentrations will be affected substantially by them, at least while the present political structures prevail. On the other hand, human mobility is increasing rapidly through improved means of transport and has immensely important effects upon patterns of population distribution and growth within countries. Although migrations are extremely difficult to classify because they vary greatly in cause, course, duration, distance, size, selectivity, organization, and consequence, the pattern of migrations generally assists the concentration of population rather than its dispersal, and today the rural–urban and urban–urban flows usually exceed rural–rural flows.

The significance of the influence of the physical environment upon migrations is changing. Among hunting and collecting and pastoral societies the physical influence is paramount, and among agricultural societies the quality of the physical environment can strongly influence its colonization or depopulation. In an increasingly urbanized world, however, the attraction or repulsion of physical factors at the points of arrival and departure are rather less important, but still present as we see in the growth of migrations to retirement in sunnier climates. Moreover, the physical environment provides the framework for all human migrations, in particular the concept of space and its corollary distance, which acts as an intervening obstacle between the origin and destination of migrants (Lee 1966). The significance of such an obstacle obviously changes in time, especially according to the means of transport available but also according to the way that distance is perceived. An individual carries around a mental map which reflects his cultural and physical experience, his behaviour in space and his visual perception of space relationships (Gould 1966). The cost factor remains, and cost is related to distance. It is not surprising therefore that short-distance migration (Johnston 1967) is extremely important (in many countries it is associated with exogamy), and that there is a tendency for migration intensity to diminish with distance from a centre. But the size of a city influences its attraction and the strength and direction of migration. The *gravity model* of migrations states that the frequency of migration or interaction between two centres is directly proportional to the product of the two populations and inversely proportional to the distance between them (Stewart 1948, Zipf 1949, Carrothers 1956). The *inverse distance law* has been the subject of much study (Olsson 1965) and there are many difficulties in its application, because the rate of change in interaction over distance varies in time, according to place and according to the social composition of the population (Hagerstrand 1957). Distance is of course only one of the intervening obstacles to migration; others include the availability of intervening opportunities (Stouffer 1940) as well as the presence of physical barriers, cultural barriers (e.g. language, religion, customs), and migration quotas. Migration streams and their inevitable counter-streams are affected by many factors, but their analysis as linkages within complex networks has attracted much attention.

There can be little doubt that the increase in human mobility associated with the diversification of human activities causes increasing problems in our analysis of the ecological relationships of man with his environment, but systems analysis has proved a fruitful method of approach.

Conclusion

The one common theme of this paper has been that mankind is gradually extracting itself from the dictates of the physical environment and is estabishing its own environments which have increasing influence upon patterns of population distribution and movement. The stage of advance of this process varies greatly from one part of the world to another, and the contrasts in demographic systems are now very great. Whereas the process is extremely advanced in some developed countries, it is highly localized or incipient in many of the developing countries.

REFERENCES

ALLAN, W. (1965). *The African husbandman*. Oliver and Boyd, Edinburgh.
BEAUJEU-GARNIER, J. (1956–8). *Géographie de la population*. 2 vols. Presses Universitaires de France, Paris.
—— (1966). *Geography of population*. Longmans, London.
BERRY, B. J. L. (1961). City size distributions and economic development. *Econ. Devel. Cult. Change*, **9**, 573–88.

—— and GARRISON, W. L. (1958). Alternate explanations of urban rank–size relationships. *Ann. Ass. Am. Geogr.* **48**, 83–91.

BREESE, G. (1966). *Urbanization in newly developing countries.* Prentice-Hall, Englewood Cliffs.

CARROTHERS, G. A. P. (1956). An historical review of the gravity and potential concepts of human interaction, *J. Am. Inst. Plann.* **22**, 94–102.

CHRISTALLER, W. (1966). *The central places of southern Germany.* Transl. C. Baskin. Prentice-Hall, Englewood Cliffs. Originally published in 1933 as *Die zentralen Orte in Suddeutschland,* Fischer, Jena.

CLARKE, J. I. (1965). *Population geography.* Pergamon Press, Oxford.

—— (1970). *Population geography and the developing countries.* Pergamon Press, Oxford.

DURAND, J. D. (1967). The modern expansion of world population. *Proc. Am. phil. Soc.* **111**, 136–59.

FOSBERG, F. A. (ed.) (1965). *Man's place in the island ecosystem.* Bishop Museum Press, Hawaii.

GEORGE, P. (1959). *Questions de géographie de la population.* Presses Universitaires de France, Paris.

GINSBERG, N. (1961). *Atlas of economic development.* University of Chicago Press.

GOULD, P. R. (1966). On mental maps. *Mich. Int-Com. Math. Geogr.* No. 9.

GRIGG, D. (1969). Degrees of concentration: a note on world population distribution. *Geography* **54**, 325–9.

HAGERSTRAND, T. (1957). Migration and area. In *Migration in Sweden—a symposium* (ed. D. Hannerberg, T. Hagerstrand, and B. Odeving). *Lund Stud. Geogr.* Ser. B., **13**.

HAGGETT, P. (1965a). Scale components in geographical problems. In *Frontiers in geographical teaching* (ed. R. J. Chorley and P. Haggett). Methuen, London.

—— (1965b). *Locational analysis in human geography.* Arnold, London.

HOOSON, D. J. M. (1960). The distribution of population as the essential geographical expression. *Can. Geogr.* **17**, 10–20.

HOWE, G. M. (1963). *National atlas of disease mortality.* Nelson, London.

JOHNSTON, R. J. (1967). A reconnaissance study of population change in Nidderdale, 1951–61. *Trans. Inst. Br. Geogr.* **41**, 113–23.

LEE, E. S. (1966). A theory of migration. *Demography* **3**, 47–57.

LINSKY, A. (1965). Some generalizations concerning primate cities. *Ann. Ass. Am. Geogr.* **55**, 506–13.

MACARTHUR, R. H., and WILSON, E. O. (1967). *The theory of island biography.* Princeton University Press.

MAY, J. M. (1958–61). *Studies in medical geography* (3 vols.). American Geographical Society, New York.

MCGEE, T. G. (1967). *The south-east Asian city: a social geography of the primate cities of south-east Asia.* Bell, London.

MURRAY, M. A. (1967). The geography of death in the United States and the United Kingdom. *Ann. Ass. Am. Geogr.* **57**, 301–14.

OLSSON, G. (1965). Distance and human interaction: a migration study. *Geogr. Ann.* Ser. B. **47**, 3–43.

SIMONS, M. (1966). What is a geographical factor? *Geography* **51**, 210–17.

STAMP, L. D. (1964a). *Some aspects of medical geography.* Oxford University Press, London.

—— (1964b). *The geography of life and death.* Collins, London.

STASZEWSKI, J. (1961). Bevölkerungsverteilung nach den Klimagebieten von W. Köppen. *Petermanns geogr. Mitt.* **105**, 133–8.

STEWART, C. T. (1958). The size and spacing of cities. *Geogr. Rev.* **48**, 222–45.

STEWART, J. Q. (1948). Demographic gravitation: evidence and applications. *Sociometry* **11**, 31–57.

STOUFFER, S. A. (1940). Intervening obstacles: a theory relating mobility and distance. *Am. Sociol. Rev.* **5**, 845–67.

TREWARTHA, G. T. (1953). The case for population geography. *Ann. Ass. Am. Geogr.* **43**, 71–97.

—— (1969). *A geography of population: world patterns.* Wiley, New York.

WEBB, J. W. (1969). Population geography. In *Trends in geography* (eds. R. U. Cooke and J. H. Johnson). Pergamon Press, Oxford.

WILSON, M. G. A. (1968). *Population geography*. Nelson, Melbourne.

WRIGLEY, E. A. (1965). Geography and population. In *Frontiers in geographical teaching* (eds. R. J. Chorley and P. Haggett). Methuen, London.

ZELINSKY, W. (1966). *A prologue to population geography*. Prentice-Hall, Englewood Cliffs.

ZIPF, G. K. (1949). *Human behaviour and the principle of least effort*. Addison-Wesley, Cambridge, Mass.

3

PATTERNS OF HUMAN FERTILITY AND MORTALITY

GORDON F. DE JONG

THERE are no more important social or biological events in personal history than birth and death, and there are no aspects of human behaviour more significant for the survival of a society than fertility and mortality patterns. This statement summarizes the seminal character of demographic trends for scientific as well as political explanation and prediction. Fertility (used here as a synonym for natality) is, of course, the vital force which continuously replenishes the population from the attrition of mortality. To ascertain the forces which affect fertility and mortality is to increase the potential for human survival and progress.

Introduction

It is a fair assumption that the educated public is aware of the general nature of world population growth today—that there are now about 3·6 thousand million people on the earth; that the fertility rate is high in many countries; and that, since space is finite, the Malthusian menace may become a reality at some time in the shadowy future. However, past these general perspectives, an appreciation of world demographic structure and process is frequently absent, or based on tenuous projections of demographic trends for a given nation or set of nations with which one is familiar. The character of demographic change makes such a process a source of scientific quicksand.

The purpose here is to present major patterns of fertility and mortality which exist in different parts of the world. Within the framework of the demographic transition several generalizations will be presented concerning fertility and mortality and their relationships to age and sex structures of populations. These generalizations are part of the basic framework for subsequent detailed discussions of the interrelationships between ecological, social structural, and biological factors.

The demographic approach to explanation

Demography has as its main emphasis the explanation of spatio-temporal variations in population structure and process. A demographer seeks to explain population change in terms of the relative contribution of birth, death, and migration rates. If further explanation is desired, total birth, death, or migration rates can be decomposed into age-specific rates (e.g. birth rates for women aged 15–19, 20–24, etc.). Such a process permits the researcher to identify which sub-groups of the population contribute disproportionately to population distribution or change. Just as it is possible to calculate age-specific rates, it is also possible to decompose vital rates on several structural variables simultaneously (e.g. age-sex-race-education-specific birth rates). The variations among population sub-groups provide clues in the search for causes of population differentiation.

In relating demographic factors to social structural and biological variables, it is important to recognize two basic aspects of demographic explanation (Stinchcombe 1968).

1. The *number* of people to whom a particular factor is applied.
2. The *proportionality* between numbers of different kinds of people.

Most important social structural and many biological variables vary a great deal among different kinds and sub-groups of populations. Changes in the number or distribution of these sub-groups have a highly significant but theoretically different meaning from changes in the causal factor applied to the population. For example, it makes a great deal of difference theoretically whether or not a migration rate declines because of fewer people in the highly mobile young adult age groups or because the economic conditions have markedly improved in the area.

Demographic explanations are particularly valuable when the proportionality factors for sub-groups of the population are significantly different and when populations differ in their internal structure. A basic demographic investigative strategy, then, is to decompose demographic structure and process variables into sub-group units so that connections with variables in other social and biological systems are more apparent (Ford and De Jong 1970). This process facilitates the examination of more direct links which tend to be obscured by focusing only on the total population. It is unfortunate that the topical scope and brevity of this paper make it impossible to pursue this logic to a significant extent.

Basic fertility and mortality measures

Several possible measures of fertility and mortality can be used in comparative studies, and since each taps slightly different aspects of the problem, this paper will include alternate measures. Perhaps the most common indicator of fertility is the *crude birth rate* (CBR)—the yearly number of births per 1000 total population. However, as the name indicates, it is a gross measure of fertility and, for instance, is insensitive to alterations in the age and sex structure of the population. The *general fertility rate* (GFR), defined as the number of births that occur in a year per 1000 women of childbearing age, is superior to the crude birth rate because the denominator is more nearly restricted to those actually 'exposed' to the risk of childbearing. As a control for possible variations in the age structure, an indirectly standardized general fertility rate (Ind. Std. GFR) is also presented. This measure makes it possible to compare national rates with the age composition statistically controlled.

A more detailed analysis of fertility patterns by age is possible with the age-specific fertility rate—the number of births per year to 1000 women of a particular age. Typically, demographers group the data into five-year age groups rather than using single-year rates. The age-specific measure is important because the rate of childbearing is not uniform throughout all ages, and because it provides data for the calculation of the total fertility rate (TFR), one of the most sensitive cross-sectional measures of fertility. The total fertility rate is an estimate of the number of children which a cohort of 1000 women would bear if they all went through their reproductive years exposed to the age-specific fertility rates that were in effect at a particular time. It is computed by summing the age-specific fertility rates for all ages and multiplying by the interval into which the ages are grouped. If the total fertility rate for a country was 2000, for instance, this would mean the parents were very nearly replacing themselves (an average of two children per couple).

As with measures of fertility, a common measure of mortality is the crude death rate (CDR)—the annual number of deaths per 1000 total population However, this measure is insensitive to variations in age and sex structure of the population, thus making exact comparisons difficult. A much more precise basis for comparison of mortality differences consists of life expectancies which are derived from a life table—a mathematical model that portrays mortality conditions of a population at a particular time and provides a measure of longevity. It is based on age-specific mortality rates for a particular year or other short span of time and produces a measure which allows direct comparison between different populations and different time periods.

The infant mortality rate, defined as 'the number of deaths which occurred under one year of age per 1000 live births in the same period', constitutes the other demographic indicator discussed in this chapter (United Nations 1967). Unfortunately, it is most difficult to obtain valid statistics on infant mortality. Societal variations in legalities and customs concerning what is a live birth, how old the infant must be before its death is officially reported, or even whether the death of a newborn infant is worthy of official note contribute to considerable understatement and non-comparability of infant death rates.

Quality of data

The emphasis here is to compare national fertility and mortality patterns at a given time rather than through history. Table 3.1 presents the latest available crude birth and death rates and the infant mortality rates for the major nations for which data were presented in the 1967 United Nations

Demographic yearbook. Where available, data on expectation of life at birth are included.

TABLE 3.1

Vital statistics rates and expectation of life at birth:
latest available year†

Country	Year	Rate per 1000			Expectation of life at birth		
		Crude birth	Crude death	Infant mor- tality	Year	Male	Female
Northern Africa							
Algeria	1963	44·1	10·0	86·3	1948	—— 35	——
Libya	1964	25·1	——	——	——	——	——
Morocco	1962	46·1	18·7	149	1964	—— 47	——
Sudan	1956	51·7	18·5	93·6	1950	—— 40	——
Tunisia	1959	47	26	100	——	——	——
U.A.R.	1967	39·3	14·3	83·2	1960	51·6	53·8
Western Africa							
Dahomey	1961	54·3	26·0	109·6	1961	—— 37·3	——
Gambia	1963	38·7	21	——	1963	—— 43	——
Ghana	1960	47–52	24	156	1948	—— 38	——
Guinea	1955	62	40	216	1955	26	28
Ivory Coast	1961	56·1	33·3	——	1957–8	—— 35	——
Mali	1960–1	61	30	123	1957	—— 27	——
Mauritania	1964–5	45	28	187	1961–2	—— 40	——
Niger	1959–60	52	27	200	1959–60	—— 37	——
Nigeria	1952–3	53–57	——	——	——	——	——
Senegal	1960–1	43·3	16·7	92·9	1957	—— 37	——
Togo	1961	55	29	127	1961	31·6	38·5
Upper Volta	1960–1	53	35	182	1960–1	32·1	31·1
Eastern Africa							
Burundi	1965	46·1	25·6	150	1965	35·0	38·5
Kenya	1962	50	20	——	1962	—— 40–45	——
Madagascar	1966	46	25	102	1966	37·5	38·3
Malawi	1953	——	——	148	——	——	——
Mauritius	1967	30·4	8·5	64·2	1961–3	58·7	61·9
Mozambique	1965	——	——	90	1940	—— 45	——
Reunion	1966	40·9	10·2	78·9	1959–63	54·1	60·6
Rwanda	1957	52·0	13·7	137	——	——	——
Southern Rhodesia	1962	48·1	14·0	122	1962	—— 50	——
Tanzania	1957	46	24–25	190	1957	—— 35–40	——
Uganda	1959	42	20	160	——	——	——
Zambia	1963	51·4	19·6	259	1963	—— 40	——

† From Table 3, United Nations *Demographic yearbook* 1967. For most developing countries the vital rates and expectations of life are subject to deficiencies of varying degrees. In some cases the data are estimates of the United Nations Secretariat. The reader is encouraged to consult the original source for all data limitations.

TABLE 3.1—*continued*

| Country | Year | Rate per 1000 | | | Expectation of life at birth | | |
		Crude birth	Crude death	Infant mor-tality	Year	Male	Female
Middle and southern Africa							
Angola	1965	—	—	—	1948	— 35	—
Central African Republic	1959–60	48	30	190	1959–60	33	36
Chad	1963–4	45	31	160	1964	29	35
Congo (Brazzaville)	1960–1	41·1	24·4	180	1960–1	— 37	—
Congo (Democratic Republic)	1955–7	43	20	104	1950–2	37·6	40·0
Gabon	1960–1	35	30	229	1960–1	25	45
Lesotho	1956	40	23	181	—	—	—
South-west Asia							
Cyprus	1967	23·0	5·1	25·6	1961	63·6	70·0
Israel	1966	25·5	6·3	25·3	1965	70·5	73·2
Jordon	1959–63	47	16	36·3	1959–63	52·6	52·0
Kuwait	1966	51·6	5·7	37·0	—	—	—
Turkey	1966	43	16	161	1966	— 52·7	—
South central Asia							
Ceylon	1967	31·5	8·2	55·8	1962	61·9	61·4
India	1951–61	41·7	22·8	139	1951–60	41·9	40·6
Iran	1965	48	24·5	—	—	—	—
Nepal	1961	41·1	20·8	—	—	—	—
Pakistan	1965	49	18	142	1962	53·7	48·8
South-east Asia							
Burma	1955	50	35	—	—	—	—
Cambodia	1959	41·4	19·7	127·0	1958–9	44·2	43·3
Indonesia	1962	43·0	21·4	125	1960	47·5	47·5
Laos	1965	47	23	—	—	—	—
Malaysia (east)							
Sabah	1966	35·4	5·7	40·9	—	—	—
Sarawak	1966	28·9	4·8	40·3	—	—	—
Malaysia (west)	1966	37·3	7·6	50·0	1956–8	55·8	58·2
Philippines	1967	—	—	72·9	1946–9	48·8	53·4
Singapore	1966	29·8	5·5	25·8	—	—	—
Thailand	1964	46·0	12·9	31·2	1959–61	53·6	58·7
Vietnam, Republic of	1960	35	18	—	—	—	—
East Asia							
China (Mainland)	1957	34	11	—	—	—	—
China (Taiwan)	1967	28·5	5·5	20·2	1963	65·2	67·6
Hong Kong	1967	23·0	5·1	25·6	1961	63·6	70·5
Japan	1967	19·3	6·7	13·3	1965	67·7	73·0
Korea (North)	1960	38·5	10·5	—	—	—	—
Korea (South)	1955–60	44·7	16·0	—	1955–60	51·1	53·7
Mongolia	1965	40·0	9·7	—	—	—	—
Ryukyu Islands	1966	18·5	5·2	—	1960	68·0	74·7

TABLE 3.1—*continued*

| Country | Year | Rate per 1000 | | | Expectation of life at birth | | |
		Crude birth	Crude death	Infant mortality	Year	Male	Female
Northern America							
Canada	1967	18·0	7·3	23·1	1960–2	68·4	74·2
United States	1967	17·9	9·4	22·1	1966	66·7	73·8
Middle America							
Barbados	1960–5	29–32	9	47·7	1959–61	62·7	67·4
Costa Rica	1960–5	44–46	8–9	69·9	1962–4	61·9	64·8
Cuba	1960–5	34–36	8–9	44·7	1958–62	57·0	59·2
Dominican Republic	1960–5	45–48	14–16	80·7	1959–61	57·2	58·6
El Salvador	1960–5	47–49	14–16	62·0	1960–1	56·6	60·4
Guadeloupe	1966	34·1	7·7	42·4	1959–63	62·5	66·5
Guatemala	1960–5	46–48	18–20	91·5	1964	48·3	49·7
Haiti	1960–5	45–50	20–24	——	1950	—— 32·6	——
Honduras	1960–5	47–50	15–17	41·2	——	——	——
Jamaica	1960–5	39–40	8–9	35·4	1959–61	62·7	66·6
Martinique	1966	30·8	7·3	38·2	1959–63	62·5	66·5
Mexico	1960–5	44–45	10–11	62·9	1956	55·1	57·9
Nicaragua	1960–5	47–50	14–16	55·4	——	——	——
Panama	1960–5	41–42	10–11	45·0	1960–1	57·6	60·9
Puerto Rico	1967	26·2	5·5	36·7	1959–61	67·1	71·9
Trinidad and Tobago	1960–5	37–39	8	35·3	1964	63·9	68·0
South America							
Argentina	1960–5	22–23	8–9	58·3	1960–5	63·7	69·5
Bolivia	1960–5	43–45	20–22	86·0	1949–51	49·7	49·7
Brazil	1960–5	41–43	10–12	170	1940–50	39·3	45·5
Chile	1960–5	34–36	11–12	127·5	1952	49·8	53·9
Colombia	1960–5	41–44	12–14	80·0	1950–2	44·2	46·0
Ecuador	1960–5	47–50	13–15	90·4	——	——	——
Guyana	1960–5	40–41	9–10	39·9	1959–61	59·0	63·0
Paraguay	1960–5	42–45	12–14	40·3	——	——	——
Peru	1960–5	44–45	12–14	63·0	1961	51·9	53·7
Uruguay	1960–5	24–25	9	43·3	——	——	——
Venezuela	1960–5	46–48	9–10	45·5	——	——	——
Northern and western Europe							
Austria	1967	17·4	13·0	26·4	1966	66·8	73·5
Belgium	1967	15·2	12·2	23·7	1959–63	67·7	73·5
Denmark	1966	18·4	10·3	16·9	1964–5	70·2	74·7
Finland	1967	16·5	9·4	15·0	1956–60	64·9	71·6
France	1967	16·8	10·8	17·1	1965	67·8	75·0
West Germany	1967	17·3	11·2	23·5	1964–5	67·6	73·5
Iceland	1966	23·9	7·1	13·7	1961–5	70·8	76·2
Ireland	1967	21·1	10·7	24·4	1960–2	68·1	71·9
Luxembourg	1967	14·8	12·3	20·4	1946–8	61·7	65·8
Netherlands	1967	18·9	7·9	14·7	1961–5	71·1	75·9
Norway	1967	18·0	9·2	16·8	1961–5	71·0	76·0
Sweden	1967	15·5	10·1	12·6	1961–5	71·6	75·7
Switzerland	1967	17·7	9·0	17·8	1958–63	68·7	74·1
United Kingdom	1967	17·5	11·2	18·8	1963–5	68·1	74·2

TABLE 3.1—*continued*

Country	Year	Rate per 1000			Expectation of life at birth		
		Crude birth	Crude death	Infant mortality	Year	Male	Female
Eastern Europe							
Bulgaria	1967	15·0	9·0	32·9	1960–2	67·8	71·4
Czechoslovakia	1966	15·6	10·0	23·7	1964	67·8	73·6
East Germany	1967	14·8	13·2	21·2	1963–4	68·3	73·3
Hungary	1967	14·5	10·7	38·4	1964	67·0	71·8
Poland	1967	16·3	7·7	38·0	1960–1	64·8	70·5
Romania	1967	27·1	9·3	46·8	1963	65·4	70·3
Southern Europe							
Albania	1966	34·0	8·6	86·6	1960–1	63·7	66·0
Greece	1967	18·5	8·3	34·7	1960–2	67·5	70·7
Italy	1967	18·1	9·7	34·3	1960–2	67·3	72·3
Malta	1967	16·5	9·4	27·5	1964–6	67·5	71·1
Portugal	1967	21·1	10·0	59·3	1959–62	60·7	66·4
Spain	1967	21·1	8·7	33·2	1960	67·3	71·9
Yugoslavia	1967	19·5	8·7	61·3	1960–2	62·4	65·6
Oceania							
Australia	1967	19·5	8·8	18·2	1960–2	67·9	74·2
New Zealand	1967	22·4	8·4	17·7	1960–2	68·4	73·8
U.S.S.R.	1967	17·4	7·6	26·0	1964–5	66	74

The quality of these population statistics ultimately depends on the care and thoroughness with which census and vital statistic information is gathered at the local level. Many countries lack the resources to develop adequate vital statistic systems—for assessing births, deaths, marriages, and divorces—while census data is of dubious accuracy for many nations, even some of the most developed countries. And even though the United Nations statistical office exerts every effort to achieve comparability in the calculation of rates and ratios for all nations, idiosyncracies in definitions of concepts, data-collection systems, and presentation methods lead to numerous inconsistencies. (Since an adequate analysis of these problems is beyond the scope of this chapter, the reader is encouraged to consult appropriate sections of the *Demographic yearbook* and other technical studies prepared by the United Nations.) These considerations make it imprudent to generalize solely on the basis of crude statistics.

More refined estimates of basic fertility measures, prepared by Cho (1964), are reproduced in Table 3.2. Cho's basic estimating procedure was to make use of reliable fertility data from registration systems where they were available. For the remaining national estimates, he used multiple-regression equations developed by Bogue and Palmore (1964). Although subject to errors of estimations the measures provide a rather accurate collaborative picture of fertility differentials. These estimates are not the most recent data available; however, they are judged to present the most accurate basis for comparative analysis. Mortality data are less subject to seemingly erratic jumps than are fertility data, especially with the use of life expectancy information.

The theory of demographic transition

Although it is difficult to summarize the mass of data in Tables 3.1 and 3.2, the theory of demographic transition provides a frame of reference in which patterns of fertility and mortality can be considered. The theory states that as a nation industrializes, its mortality rate declines first, while the birth rate, through the application of the technology of birth and death control, is attenuated later. The lag in time between the decline in rates accounts for the extraordinarily rapid population growth in developing nations (Satin 1969). Before transition begins, there is an initial condition of high birth but also high death rates which yields a population in a state of stationary numbers or very slow growth. Typical of non-industrial societies, cultural patterns sanctioning high fertility do more than just offset high mortality; they also provide a large labour force to enhance production in the agrarian economic system.

As public health and medical technology bring a decline in mortality, the population grows more rapidly, because fertility remains at a relatively high level. In part this is because the desire to control death is nearly a universal value and can be greatly affected by public measures. Birth rates, however, are not as amenable to induced change, and the factors supporting high fertility tend to remain. Nations characterized by these demographic conditions tend to be in the process of urbanization and industrial development.

In developed societies a relative balance between fertility and mortality is typically re-established. However, unlike the earlier condition where birth and death rates were high, both rates are relatively low. The important difference, of course, is the decline in the birth rate which is indicative of a complex of personal and social factors that precipitate fertility control. There is now no nation on earth that has not already begun at least the early stages of this process, but there are also relatively few nations that have entirely completed it.

The stages in the demographic transition can be summarized as follows (Bogue 1969).

1. Pre-transitional—little regulation or control either of death rates or birth rates, with the consequence of high vital rates but almost zero growth.
2. Transitional—death rates and birth rates are in the process of being reduced.

      (a) Early transitional—death rates are being reduced but birth rates remain high and may even rise higher because of the improved health of the childbearing population.

TABLE 3.2

Estimated fertility rates for countries of the world, 1955–60[a]

Country	Class of estimate[b]		Summary fertility measures				Age-specific fertility rates						
			CBR	GFR	Ind. Std. GFR	TFR	15–19	20–24	25–29	30–34	35–39	40–44	45–49
Northern Africa													
Algeria[c]	II		46·5	195·0	191·1	6317	93·1	234·8	316·2	278·4	215·0	102·2	23·7
Sudan	III	H	54·9	234·8	228·9	7496	136·6	315·4	371·7	309·3	234·6	105·2	26·4
		L	50·9	212·2	206·5	6751	126·1	291·0	329·9	275·3	209·2	94·9	23·9
Tunisia	II		46·0	195·0	191·9	6244	132·2	305·2	301·6	240·1	174·8	76·1	18·6
United Arab Republic	II		42·3	180·7	177·7	5824	113·6	281·7	299·6	228·2	157·9	67·3	16·6
Tropical and South Africa													
Basutoland	II		49·5	206·1	203·0	6697	88·7	235·1	333·2	299·6	239·2	115·8	27·7
Congo (Brazzaville)	IV	H	47·7	189·7	182·4	5955	121·5	250·1	284·6	238·9	182·7	87·9	25·5
		L	46·9	186·9	179·5	5896	111·3	229·9	291·2	244·8	185·6	90·2	26·3
Congo (Leopoldville)	III		42·8	189·6	187·1	6077	132·3	290·0	300·9	233·7	165·8	72·8	20·0
Ghana	III	H	53·5	224·1	209·9	6860	155·6	306·9	336·3	270·6	194·8	84·7	23·1
		L	48·6	207·4	194·1	6297	165·3	338·4	306·6	227·1	150·0	57·4	14·6
Guinea	II		54·3	216·4	204·2	6605	187·1	315·8	292·7	239·3	177·6	81·9	26·6
Kenya	IV		49·7	205·7	198·5	6500	109·8	267·1	322·1	270·9	208·2	97·1	24·9
Ivory Coast	III		49·1	219·4	215·2	6987	167·5	324·1	333·5	268·7	195·2	84·9	23·6
Madagascar	III		42·8	178·5	170·7	5612	85·3	243·6	286·5	234·8	174·1	79·7	18·3
Mauritius	I		40·8	185·6	183·0	5907	131·7	301·4	295·4	231·0	154·7	59·3	7·8
Nigeria	IV	H	50·7	209·4	200·5	6510	156·9	308·0	305·2	247·8	181·7	80·3	22·1
		L	47·9	199·7	191·2	6213	154·8	311·3	300·2	230·3	159·8	67·2	19·0
Reunion	III	H	47·1	202·4	197·4	6831	62·9	251·2	341·8	329·6	240·1	124·5	16·1
		L	40·0	172·0	168·3	5499	72·6	203·7	282·3	253·3	191·3	83·1	13·6
Seychelles	II		38·8	167·7	164·2	5364	71·9	206·0	278·0	245·2	182·1	77·5	12·0

Country		H/L											
St. Helena	II	H	38·4	170·7	178·4	5786	94·1	269·9	299·6	239·6	171·9	69·4	12·7
		L	35·5	160·8	168·9	5469	92·5	275·2	289·4	220·7	150·6	56·5	8·9
Swaziland	IV	H	54·1	219·7	212·8	6970	110·3	255·2	323·1	301·3	249·5	123·6	30·8
		L	47·9	198·4	192·3	6290	107·0	266·4	301·1	261·0	203·9	96·0	22·7
Togo	IV		50·0	200·6	188·3	6156	103·1	261·4	293·3	250·8	199·5	97·5	25·7
Tanganyika	II		47·7	194·8	187·6	6117	110·5	258·1	299·3	250·8	192·0	89·2	23·4
Uganda	II		47·5	195·9	188·6	6174	99·4	256·7	309·4	257·6	196·9	91·6	23·2
Union of South Africa[d]	II	H	48·8	207·7	201·0	6636	89·5	253·0	338·6	292·5	225·4	104·7	23·4
		L	47·3	202·8	196·2	6478	88·7	255·7	333·5	283·1	214·8	98·3	21·5
Upper Volta	III		49·0	198·8	188·5	6128	142·1	287·2	289·2	233·9	172·4	78·3	22·4
Zanzibar and Pemba	III		42·0	167·9	161·4	5232	130·2	266·3	248·6	190·5	133·1	59·6	18·1
Northern America													
Bermuda	II		29·0	121·4	120·9	3932	68·2	213·3	210·8	153·0	96·9	38·0	6·2
Canada	I		27·8	119·4	124·6	4075	66·7	232·7	242·3	159·4	91·1	30·1	2·7
Greenland	II		40·9	177·7	171·4	5690	72·7	225·7	301·0	254·5	185·9	83·0	15·2
St. Pierre and Miquelon	II		29·7	121·5	123·5	4096	42·0	167·1	226·5	182·1	128·3	60·4	12·7
United States (white)	I		23·5	101·7	110·9	3674	76·8	252·1	211·5	121·4	57·0	15·2	0·9
United States (non-white)	I		34·3	145·4	151·3	4861	171·0	314·0	236·7	147·1	78·4	23·0	1·9
Middle America													
Barbados	II		31·4	125·8	130·0	4171	124·6	201·9	194·2	171·0	104·3	34·9	3·2
Costa Rica	I		49·7	223·8	215·2	7068	128·2	355·9	345·4	259·9	218·1	91·4	14·4
Cuba	III	H	33·9	139·2	137·4	4412	86·6	245·1	217·3	163·4	113·5	46·9	9·5
		L	32·4	133·5	131·7	4235	74·1	227·4	219·0	163·8	111·6	45·9	8·8
Dominica	II		47·0	212·1	214·5	6975	128·2	346·7	374·0	265·2	161·2	117·6	2·0
Dominican Republic	III	H	44·8	192·4	185·8	6085	100·5	260·8	307·8	257·8	190·6	82·9	16·7
		L	42·6	185·0	178·7	5847	99·3	264·7	300·1	243·6	174·6	73·2	13·8
El Salvador	I		46·5	199·7	193·3	6232	141·6	306·4	318·5	234·3	170·4	56·5	18·8
Guadeloupe	III		38·5	168·0	168·1	5662	69·7	208·5	278·3	265·0	187·5	93·9	9·8
Guatemala	I		49·5	204·3	197·0	6510	145·6	272·3	305·4	287·2	189·8	76·9	24·8
Grenada	II		45·7	204·3	204·3	6394	161·1	325·1	302·9	275·8	159·3	46·3	8·3
Haiti	II		42·7	175·5	167·4	5576	49·7	153·4	287·3	275·6	219·5	107·7	22·0
Honduras	II		50·8	220·9	215·7	6962	139·0	328·1	341·0	277·9	205·6	83·2	17·5
Jamaica	II		42·7	169·8	169·7	5494	148·0	316·2	284·1	190·5	111·4	41·7	6·8
Martinique	III		39·6	170·7	169·5	5746	62·7	212·0	246·8	291·9	192·8	100·2	12·2

TABLE 3.2—continued
Estimated fertility rates for countries of the world, 1955–60[a]

Country	Class of estimate[b]		Summary fertility measures				Age-specific fertility rates						
			CBR	GFR	Ind. Std. GFR	TFR	15–19	20–24	25–29	30–34	35–39	40–44	45–49
Mexico	I		45·0	196·7	189·7	6268	104·6	293·3	312·0	257·4	192·2	94·2	0·0
Montserrat	III		43·4	190·9	200·6	6555	106·5	268·7	321·0	282·4	216·7	96·6	19·1
Netherlands Antilles	III		39·4	173·8	173·5	5660	108·6	284·1	282·1	224·8	157·5	64·1	10·8
Nicaragua	II		44·8	194·3	190·2	6127	124·0	298·4	300·4	243·5	176·2	69·8	13·1
Panama	I		40·9	182·5	181·7	5667	147·6	319·9	304·9	190·9	126·3	36·0	7·9
Puerto Rico	I		33·7	148·4	153·0	4855	97·6	288·0	240·8	164·5	120·0	50·5	9·7
St. Kitts-Nevis and Anguilla	III		49·8	224·5	230·4	7531	127·2	326·5	383·8	315·7	234·0	98·4	20·6
St. Lucia	II		42·8	175·9	181·9	5809	134·0	280·1	283·0	235·4	165·8	53·8	9·7
St. Vincent	II		49·8	212·0	211·4	6594	182·3	343·7	278·6	241·4	151·8	81·0	9·9
Trinidad and Tobago	I		39·5	173·0	175·9	5536	139·3	303·1	281·7	211·3	126·5	39·9	5·3
Virgin Islands (U.S.)	I		35·2	163·4	169·5	5348	153·7	323·7	251·4	192·8	101·1	40·2	6·7
Virgin Islands (U.K.)	III		50·1	226·2	227·1	7385	147·1	342·5	353·2	301·3	224·8	92·4	15·7
South America													
Argentina	I		23·2	89·9	90·3	2962	59·3	132·6	180·8	116·3	70·5	26·3	6·7
Bolivia	III	H	43·6	177·8	170·6	5629	74·7	202·9	281·3	252·2	197·3	95·6	21·8
		L	41·5	170·7	163·8	5403	73·6	206·7	274·0	238·7	182·0	86·4	19·1
Brazil	II		44·6	183·7	176·7	5768	91·9	231·5	284·5	247·7	190·7	87·7	19·7
British Guiana	I		43·2	197·6	196·2	6174	164·0	349·0	303·9	229·2	136·6	48·5	3·6
Chile	I		35·4	138·8	135·4	4537	76·2	178·7	243·8	204·5	124·0	64·5	15·6
Colombia	III		42·1	178·7	174·5	5681	108·3	269·9	275·9	227·9	167·1	72·7	14·9
Ecuador	II		45·2	208·8	233·3	7598	133·5	329·4	382·7	316·7	236·3	99·7	21·4
Paraguay	II		39·8	162·5	158·5	5077	96·2	230·4	241·7	207·8	157·5	67·9	13·9
Peru	II	H	45·9	198·6	196·0	6392	111·2	276·4	316·1	268·6	201·4	87·2	17·4
		L	44·8	195·1	192·6	6279	110·6	278·3	312·5	261·9	193·8	82·6	16·1
Venezuela	II		45·8	199·7	194·8	6211	121·1	275·4	292·9	263·1	200·7	78·3	10·6

Region / Country		H/L											
South-west Asia													
Cyprus	II		25·8	105·3	104·9	3481	37·4	195·0	207·6	131·6	85·9	31·9	6·8
Iran	III	H	45·5	195·6	186·6	6803	133·6	315·7	300·3	229·3	158·4	64·7	14·5
		L	42·4	184·6	175·9	5744	120·3	300·8	296·6	219·6	145·1	56·8	11·8
Iraq	II	H	50·6	226·3	221·2	7243	145·8	347·8	366·8	286·9	202·0	81·7	17·5
		L	48·0	217·4	212·7	6960	144·4	352·6	357·7	270·1	182·9	70·2	14·1
Israel	I		27·9	121·0	126·1	4101	59·9	247·3	236·4	163·2	79·3	27·7	6·4
Kuwait	III		40·3	174·2	159·0	5207	115·2	294·0	272·4	191·3	117·7	42·7	8·1
Turkey	II	H	48·2	197·2	186·1	6098	114·4	266·0	301·0	245·9	183·9	85·5	22·8
		L	44·6	178·4	167·3	5482	105·1	245·0	270·5	217·8	160·9	75·9	21·0
South central Asia													
Afghanistan	IV	H	51·7	215·3	208·4	6789	159·4	314·5	324·1	260·9	190·6	84·6	23·8
		L	45·9	195·4	189·1	6178	144·7	304·3	311·3	234·4	158·2	65·2	17·7
Ceylon	I		40·0	172·0	168·5	5494	67·8	272·2	315·9	220·2	158·8	42·6	21·0
India	I		41·0	172·5	168·4	5424	151·6	275·7	255·5	197·0	133·8	51·9	19·2
Pakistan[e]	II	H	50·8	209·0	201·6	6520	184·6	337·7	298·6	230·5	162·1	69·1	21·4
		L	49·1	204·5	197·3	6377	184·7	344·3	295·4	220·9	150·0	61·2	18·9
South-east Asia													
Brunei	II		53·2	234·4	226·3	7391	152·0	354·0	369·5	290·7	207·8	85·0	19·1
Burma	III		43·0	171·4	163·6	5357	90·9	227·1	262·5	220·0	168·0	81·4	21·5
Cambodia	III		49·7	213·1	209·1	6895	98·6	267·5	350·6	300·3	230·9	106·6	24·5
Indonesia	III	H	47·9	197·3	187·3	6115	123·3	281·4	295·0	240·8	179·4	81·9	21·1
		L	44·0	184·1	174·6	5704	120·5	286·4	286·4	216·6	149·9	64·2	16·6
Federation of Malaya	II		43·6	192·6	189·6	6195	128·0	320·4	324·2	236·1	156·2	60·2	14·0
North Borneo	II	H	46·4	199·3	192·0	6288	123·2	301·0	322·3	247·3	173·0	72·9	17·8
		L	44·3	192·2	185·1	6061	122·1	304·8	315·0	233·9	157·8	63·6	15·1
Philippines[e,f]	II	H	48·5	206·2	200·0	6650	99·1	274·7	342·9	285·4	213·6	94·2	20·1
		L	44·4	189·5	184·8	6091	90·8	255·7	315·3	260·3	192·1	85·6	18·4
Sarawak	II	H	47·0	200·2	195·7	6409	121·0	290·2	323·3	258·0	187·1	82·0	20·3
		L	43·9	189·6	185·5	6070	119·3	295·9	312·3	237·8	164·2	68·2	16·2
Singapore	I		36·6	168·7	166·2	5541	64·0	257·9	295·9	253·0	161·1	66·6	9·7
Thailand	II		45·5	189·0	181·4	5963	96·5	254·2	296·3	248·4	188·3	88·1	20·9
South Vietnam	IV	H	45·0	187·4	179·5	5906	90·5	245·9	298·2	249·7	188·5	87·8	20·6
		L	43·0	180·3	172·7	5680	89·4	249·7	290·9	236·3	173·3	78·6	17·9

TABLE 3.2—continued

Estimated fertility rates for countries of the world, 1955–60[a]

Country	Class of estimate[b]	Summary fertility measures				Age-specific fertility rates						
		CBR	GFR	Ind. Std. GFR	TFR	15–19	20–24	25–29	30–34	35–39	40–44	45–49
East Asia												
China (mainland)[g]	IV H	39·3	156·6	149·7	4926	74·6	206·7	247·8	206·6	155·2	75·4	18·8
	L	37·5	150·2	143·3	4753	59·5	187·5	253·7	206·6	151·2	73·3	18·5
China (Taiwan)	I	39·5	179·7	172·1	5809	47·1	247·9	327·1	259·9	180·4	85·1	14·3
Hong Kong	II	35·6	159·4	158·1	5211	71·0	252·8	292·9	216·5	143·0	56·4	9·8
Japan	I	16·8	62·2	61·5	1978	4·3	102·7	162·3	85·0	32·4	8·4	0·5
South Korea[h]	II	40·6	169·8	167·1	5509	81·7	248·0	292·5	226·4	162·1	73·2	18·0
South Korea[i]	II	42·0	185·2	180·7	5987	71·2	261·5	330·9	256·8	182·0	78·5	16·5
Macau	II	30·0	129·5	134·1	4457	43·5	181·9	251·9	201·4	139·5	61·9	11·2
Mongolia	III H	37·0	150·1	151·6	4920	98·1	248·3	236·4	187·2	136·0	62·4	15·7
	L	35·9	146·9	148·7	4795	109·2	270·8	225·5	170·0	118·8	51·9	13·0
Ryukyu Islands	I	25·8	110·8	105·9	3600	12·7	127·4	201·0	179·5	135·7	56·5	7·2
U.S.S.R.[j]	II	23·9	99·1	96·5	3182	60·1	202·4	178·1	114·0	58·3	21·2	2·3
Northern and western Europe												
Belgium	I	17·0	75·3	78·3	2565	24·8	151·2	164·8	103·7	47·3	19·9	1·3
Denmark	I	16·8	70·8	78·2	2577	36·7	165·8	159·9	95·9	43·3	12·8	0·9
Faeroe Islands	III	25·5	112·0	115·9	3796	49·1	202·2	221·9	155·2	93·1	33·8	4·0
Finland	I	19·6	80·5	85·5	2810	28·4	155·2	167·0	111·4	66·5	30·5	3·0
France	I	18·4	83·9	85·7	2797	21·7	168·6	181·6	112·1	53·2	20·5	1·8
Iceland	I	28·1	127·0	130·8	4256	77·4	248·3	220·3	156·7	104·6	40·7	3·2
Ireland	I	21·1	95·5	103·8	3432	9·1	92·8	185·0	197·1	143·9	54·2	4·2
Luxembourg	I	15·9	65·6	67·7	2206	22·1	138·1	142·1	88·4	37·5	12·2	0·7
Netherlands	I	21·2	91·1	95·8	3174	15·0	116·2	210·2	162·0	91·6	36·6	31·0

Country	Group												
Norway	I		18·0	78·9	89·1	2961	24·7	156·5	183·6	129·6	70·1	25·3	2·4
Scotland	I		19·0	80·5	86·4	2832	29·2	167·8	181·8	113·3	56·8	16·5	0·9
Sweden	I		14·4	61·1	69·1	2296	31·8	128·5	145·8	93·9	44·8	13·4	1·0
England and Wales	I		16·1	68·9	75·7	2506	28·3	151·2	164·5	98·3	44·6	13·5	0·8
Central Europe													
Austria	I		17·2	69·9	77·2	2558	38·6	154·1	149·2	101·4	47·9	19·2	1·1
Czechoslovakia	I		18·0	76·7	80·7	2692	44·1	210·4	150·8	83·2	33·7	15·3	1·0
West Germany	I		17·0	67·2	71·0	2336	23·1	113·8	154·2	107·5	49·2	18·0	1·3
Hungary	I		17·3	69·1	72·3	2367	51·9	176·5	127·8	72·7	30·2	13·4	0·8
Poland	I		26·3	103·1	102·5	3324	44·0	204·8	185·2	123·2	78·7	20·0	2·9
Switzerland	I		17·5	70·0	71·4	2319	13·9	118·5	150·7	104·8	54·4	19·9	1·5
Southern Europe													
Albania	III		42·2	182·6	181·1	5967	83·9	248·4	321·5	256·5	184·4	80·4	18·3
Bulgaria	I		18·6	72·9	72·8	2412	68·2	200·0	124·9	57·9	20·7	9·2	1·4
Gibraltar	II		16·9	70·2	78·0	2519	39·6	171·6	152·6	90·5	39·6	9·9	0·0
Greece	II		19·3	73·7	69·7	2365	15·6	109·8	148·8	107·9	59·6	28·0	3·4
Italy	I		18·2	71·2	72·2	2362	21·2	103·8	150·3	111·6	56·4	27·1	2·0
Malta and Gozo	I		25·6	107·9	107·5	3559	22·2	192·0	195·0	149·4	106·9	41·4	4·9
Portugal	I		23·5	91·2	91·2	3020	27·1	145·2	162·1	127·4	89·2	48·0	4·9
Romania	I		22·3	82·6	83·1	2668	50·1	173·5	141·8	89·1	62·5	14·4	2·3
Spain	I		21·5	83·9	85·7	2796	9·1	115·3	184·1	138·9	77·7	30·2	3·9
Yugoslavia	I		24·6	97·9	92·9	3022	51·5	198·9	169·6	96·7	49·9	30·6	7·2
Oceania													
American Samoa	I		40·6	189·4	185·4	6267	44·0	290·2	381·7	260·2	180·2	76·1	21·0
Australia	I		22·6	97·6	105·2	3485	41·0	210·4	228·2	132·7	63·2	20·1	1·4
British Solomon Islands	II		41·2	179·5	172·6	5678	103·1	280·1	299·0	225·6	152·3	62·4	13·0
Cook Islands	II		53·0	230·1	226·8	7503	99·2	272·2	383·8	335·7	261·2	121·2	27·4
Fiji Islands	II		45·2	199·6	194·9	6386	122·7	313·7	331·5	251·7	172·8	69·6	15·1
Guam	III		35·2	191·4	177·6	5790	106·2	344·2	285·6	210·5	138·7	65·9	6·2
New Caledonia	II		35·2	150·2	150·7	4901	92·0	250·3	253·5	191·5	129·6	52·8	10·8
New Zealand	I		26·3	118·0	128·0	4239	39·4	249·4	285·6	166·8	81·8	23·1	1·7
Niue	II	H	48·7	221·4	214·9	7180	92·6	275·4	380·7	324·6	238·8	105·2	18·6
		L	46·1	212·6	206·4	6897	91·2	280·1	371·5	307·8	219·8	93·7	15·2
Pacific Islands	II		42·3	195·0	196·0	6418	106·8	322·6	349·8	256·9	171·8	64·2	11·7

TABLE 3.2—continued

Estimated fertility rates for countries of the world, 1955–60[a]

Country	Class of estimate[b]	Summary fertility measures				Age-specific fertility rates						
		CBR	GFR	Ind. Std. GFR	TFR	15–19	20–24	25–29	30–34	35–39	40–44	45–49
Tokelau Islands	II	H 45·9	203·7	199·5	6506	99·1	289·1	350·7	274·3	194·7	77·4	15·9
		L 43·9	196·9	193·0	6291	98·0	292·7	343·8	261·5	180·2	68·6	13·3
Tonga Islands	II	H 42·3	184·1	175·8	5840	90·3	237·6	296·6	256·6	188·0	84·6	14·8
		L 40·7	178·4	170·3	5659	89·4	240·6	290·3	245·8	175·9	77·2	12·6
Western Samoa	II	H 48·6	222·4	216·5	7127	120·3	339·5	379·3	290·7	201·2	79·6	15·0
		L 46·5	215·2	209·7	6901	119·1	343·3	372·0	277·2	186·0	70·3	12·3

a. From Cho 1964.
b. Class   I. Countries with good census data and vital statistics, and published fertility measures.
   Class   II. Countries with a relatively accurate census, but poor vital registration. Fertility measures presented are estimates except those of the few countries having published data of satisfactory quality.
   Class   III. Countries having data only on age composition. Fertility measures were estimated from available age data and supplementary indices.
   Class   IV. Countries with neither census or vital statistics. Fertility measures were based on estimated demographic characteristics. Estimated fertility measures in this class are most likely to be in error and therefore are presented to provide an approximate range.
c. For Moslem population only.
d. For coloured population only.
e. Based on population statistics by age groups and marital status of poor or uncertain quality.
f. Age data without supplementary indices were used to estimate the total fertility rate and the other rates were obtained in the regular way.
g. Based on age composition estimated by the U.N. and on other estimates of supplementary indices.
h. Based on 1955 Korean census.
i. Based on 1960 Korean census.
j. Based on recently published 1959 U.S.S.R. census.

(b) Mid-transitional—both death rates and birth rates are being re-duced, with birth rates remaining higher than death rates.

(c) Late transitional—death rates are low and unchanging or declining very slightly while birth rates are moderate to low and fluctuating or declining. Knowledge of contraceptive methods is widely diffused throughout the population.

3. Post transitional—both birth and death rates are low; contraceptive methods are almost universally diffused and used to keep vital rates in near balance; growth is quite low or approaching zero on a long-term basis.

A summary of world demographic transition

A useful summary measure of world demographic transition has been developed by Bogue (1969) (Fig. 3.1). He finds that the highest levels of

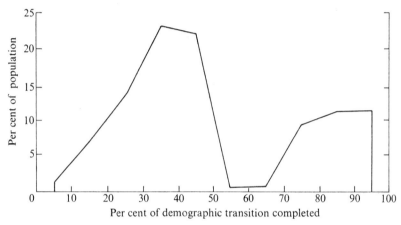

FIG. 3.1. Percentage of demographic transition completed by the world population: 1960. (Data from D. J. Bogue (1969) *Principles of demography*.)

fertility in any country of the world are a crude birth rate of about 55, a general fertility rate of about 235, and a total fertility rate of about 7500. These are taken as the parameters of a population whose fertility is nearly at a biological capacity, given factors of nutrition, health, and marriage as they exist in the world today. Corresponding values for low fertility are a general fertility rate of about 60 and a total fertility rate of about 2200. The transition of a nation from high to low fertility and mortality can be measured by tracing its stage between these two extremes. The stage of transition is esti-mated as the difference between the present general fertility and total fertility rates and the values for the biological maximum as a percentage of total possible change during transition. Since the data are 1960 estimates, it is obvi-ous that the picture would be different at another time period. For example, a country which in 1960 had a total fertility rate above 2500, and thus had not completed demographic transition by this measure, may have been below 2200 at some earlier time period. Further, a nation's entire population was put on the same step of fertility change whereas there is frequently a wide distribution within each nation. Thus the figure should be viewed as an approximation.

It is obvious from the bimodal distribution of Fig. 3.1 that the largest proportion of the world's population is still in the early to mid-transitional stage of demographic transition with moderately high birth rates. A minority of the world's population is nearing or has reached the post-transitional stage of relative balance with low and stable birth and death rates. Not only do these facts explain the extraordinarily rapid rate of current world population growth, but they also clearly indicate the relative number of the world's population to whom high and low fertility patterns can be attributed. As pointed out previously, this type of information is of critical importance in establishing links with other social structural and biological aspects of world population. Van Nort's (1956) formulation is perhaps a useful summary statement in this context.

> The transition from 'high' to 'low' levels of fertility represents, in first approximation, a transition from a *biological* model of fertility to an *economic* model of fertility. By a *biological* model of fertility we mean the ideal-type situation in which levels of fertility are determined by the more or less direct operation of biological factors, conditioned by a set of social and psychological factors specific to a preindustrial society. By an *economic* model of fertility we mean the ideal-type situation in which levels of fertility are determined by decisions based on the rational allocation of resources among competing wants of the type normally denoted economic, conditioned by a set of social and psychological factors specific to a modern industrial society. The transition in fertility represents, in terms of this particular formulation, the gradual limiting of biological determinants of fertility by a process of rational decision-making.

Within the transitional framework, several generalizations can be stated about patterns of fertility and mortality among nations of the world, and the interrelationships between fertility and mortality trends. For this paper, such a review must be highly selective and obviously cursory. The geographic variability in birth and death rates among world areas provides one criterion for developing useful generalizations concerning trends in vital rates.

Europe, the U.S.S.R., North America, Oceania, and Japan have populations in the latter phases of demographic transition. Death rates are low and crude birth rates are usually well below 20. Some of the Eastern European countries have exceptionally low birth rates and their populations are almost stable.

While the debate continues concerning the populating of the 'empty' continent of South America, vital rates for the temperate regions (the nations of Uruguay, Chile, and Argentina) are lower than for the remainder of Latin America. Birth rates tend to be moderate while death rates are quite low. Tropical Latin America includes both 'Middle' America and the tropical sections of South America. The lowest crude birth rate in tropical South America is 40–1 in Guyana (see Table 3.1). While birth rates are high throughout the region, death rates vary considerably in the low-to-moderate range from 10 to 20 per 1000 population.

In south and east Asia fertility remains generally high, while crude death rates are moderate to low. Japan is currently the only major nation which is an exception to this generalization about fertility. Japan is also the only major non-western country to achieve large-scale modernization and industrialization as well as an advanced stage of demographic regulation.

Birth rates for virtually all African nations are very high (crude rates primarily between 40 and 55) and death rates also remain moderately high (crude rates mostly between 20 and 30). Unfortunately, data for some African nations are either not available or of very poor quality. However, it appears that there are only a few countries where *both* birth and death regulation have made significant progress.

By way of summary, the following points can be made.

1. Every industrialized nation of the world now is in the low-mortality category, and future improvements in mortality can be expected to be very minor and gradual (Bogue 1969).
2. Very great reductions in mortality have been effected in Asia, Africa, and Latin America through campaigns against infectious diseases, especially malaria, smallpox, cholera, and plague. Where the conquest of these diseases has been accompanied by a rising level of living, the result has been a very sharp decline in mortality, such as Singapore, Taiwan, and Mexico (Bogue 1969).
3. Although mortality decline will continue, further reduction will come somewhat more gradually and more in proportion to societal socioeconomic improvements (Bogue 1969). Malnutrition, poverty, and illiteracy are major barriers to quick reduction of mortality in large segments of the population in south Asia, the Middle East, and Africa.
4. In general, industrialization is inversely related to fertility. Nevertheless, while every industrialized nation of the world now is in the low-mortality category, nations with the lowest fertility are not necessarily those that are the most industrialized, or the most urbanized, or have the highest level of educational attainment (Bogue 1969). The requisites for national fertility control are more diverse and difficult to determine than for mortality control.

Speculations as to why populations of the more developed nations tend to have an effectively implemented desire to control their number of births have included several possibilities (Coale 1967).

1. A decline in the death rate increases the proportion of children surviving, and reduces the number of births needed to achieve a given family size.

5

2. In an urban industrial society children are less of an economic asset and more of an economic burden than in a rural society. The economic disadvantage of children is increased by laws restricting child labour and making education mandatory.
3. Modernization raises the status of women, increases their relative educational level, and broadens the opportunities for employment outside the home. These changes compete with the continuation of uncontrolled fertility.
4. In rural agrarian communities where education is non-literate and transmitted within the family, behaviour is apt to be determined by custom, rote, and tradition; in urban industrial communities the forces of tradition are weaker and the influence of secular rationality stronger.

The relative contribution of these and perhaps additional hypotheses to the total explanation of fertility decline is one of the salient foci of social demographic research (De Jong 1968).

It must be emphasized that the theory of demographic transition is not a law of population growth but only an empirical generalization of the world's demographic history. Indeed there has been some variation between countries in the ways in which birth and death rates have changed in relation to each other over time. With the many questions of the applicability of transitional theory to newly developing nations, the theory may be '. . . only a general assertion of faith that ultimately every population must bring its birth and death rates into balance and that if it does not do this voluntarily, it will be done for it by external forces' (Bogue 1969).

If, however, the *long-range* trends do follow the transitional model, the population growth-rate curves for different areas of the world will vary significantly. For Europe, the U.S.S.R., North America, Oceania, and Japan, population growth rates are likely to be relatively small with a high degree of birth and death control. The moderate growth rates for nations in the temperate area of Latin America will continue to decline as birth rates are reduced to a level more consonant with current low death rates. For tropical Latin America, however, population growth rates may increase for a relatively short period of time as death rates continue to decline, but birth rates remain relatively stable before they also start to fall. In south and east Asia (with the exception of Japan, Singapore, Hong Kong, and Taiwan) and in most of Africa the potential for increased population growth rates is very great. The important parameter is the present potential for further reduction in mortality, particularly infant mortality. Unless there is an unusually rapid reduction in the birth rate, these areas may experience marked population growth. It is this possibility that has spurred a redoubling of the efforts of international agencies and national governments to hasten the development of effective fertility control policies and programmes. At present, family-planning programmes have had only limited success; however, some observers maintain that improvements could significantly alter the future relationship between fertility and mortality rates in many developing nations.

It is important to emphasize some basic generalizations which are relevant to the above data and discussion.

1. The primary cause of current rapid population growth (the 'population explosion') in many nations of the world is the decline in the death rate.
2. The basic logic is that under conditions of industrialization, there is a marked tendency for the technology of death control to be applied earlier and more extensively than the technology of birth control. Later, and less predictably, the technology of birth control may be employed to reduce the rate of growth and bring about a new condition of equilibrium (Cowgill 1963).
3. The technology of birth and death control is applied first and most extensively in the upper social and economic classes and only somewhat later is it applied with equal vigour within the lower classes. Thus, while birth and death rates manifest a secular decline, there tend to be differentials between social classes (Cowgill 1963).
4. Another general pattern has been for urban birth rates to decline first, resulting characteristically in a differential between urban and rural birth rates for the same region (Cowgill 1963).
5. However, with the recent advances in the control of infectious diseases, social class and geographic differentials in mortality rates are declining.
6. In fact, an important feature of a developing country today is that it can remain backward in many aspects and yet match the crude death rates of most advanced countries (Petersen 1969).

Mortality patterns and age and sex structure

The discussion now turns to some relationships between demographic process and basic aspects of demographic structure. Two of the more significant demographic variables affecting mortality patterns are the age and sex structure of a population.

The mortality curve by age has a U-shape: high in the first year of life, declining rapidly in the second and third years until age 9; remaining low until middle age; then increasing at a rapid rate during the older years (Bogue 1969). The character of the curve for developed and less-developed countries is much the same; however, the mortality rates at all ages are lower in developed nations. This is notably true for infant mortality rates. In fact, in high-mortality populations, infant deaths form the largest single age category for mortality (Bogue 1969). Even in low-mortality populations, the number of deaths during the first year of life may not be reached again until approximately age 65.

A significant part of the deaths during the first few hours of life are attributable to diseases and conditions to which the adult population is much less vulnerable. Further, infant mortality may be affected rather quickly and directly by health programmes specifically oriented towards the problems of infants; thus the infant mortality rate may be altered more rapidly than the general death rate. As a result, the infant mortality rate tends to vary more independently of mortality rates at older ages than the rates of older ages vary among themselves (Bogue 1969).

For the less developed countries the potential for continued mortality decline in most age categories is quite significant, due primarily to the extraordinary success of medical research and the application of medical programmes for the control of infectious, parasitic, and respiratory diseases. In the developed countries mortality from these causes, which primarily affect the population from ages 1 to 45, is approaching zero. Further progress in reducing the mortality rate must come in lowering the death rate of the population over 45 years of age. The significant causes of death in this age category are cancer and cardiovascular diseases. While further progress can be expected, the reduction of mortality with the resultant increase in life expectancy is likely to be slow and in small increments. Large increases in longevity will occur only as the result of a general breakthrough on the whole ageing front. As fertility rates decline and the age composition moves toward an increased proportion of the population in the older-age categories, the crude death rate in developed countries will rise, instead of decline, as age-specific death rates tend to remain relatively stationary (Bogue 1969).

Mortality patterns for males and females also differ between the more- and less-developed countries. The basic generalization is that males typically have higher age-specific death rates than females. The few cases of higher female death rates are in less-developed countries with high general mortality rates. As the death rate of a nation declines during demographic transition, the sex differential widens. In many of the more-industrialized nations the sex differential in life expectancy at birth is approaching eight years. The causes of this large and widening sex differential are not well known, and the biological superiority of women in regard to mortality, even with social factors controlled, is an important area of research (Madigan 1957).

Fertility patterns and age structure

No less dramatic are the comparative differences in national fertility trends by age (Table 3.2). As has been noted, fertility in the less-developed countries tends to be high, conforming more closely to a biological model of fertility than is the case in the developed countries.

In general, the fertility curve by age has an inverted U-shape: low but rising sharply in the mid-to-late teenage category; highest for women in their twenties; then declining slowly for women past thirty until menopause, which occurs normally between ages 45 and 50. Differences in marital and child-bearing practices, presence or absence of fertility control, and regulations about widowhood, divorce, and remarriage influence the magnitudes of age-specific fertility rates but do not alter the general pattern. However, less-developed societies tend to have higher fertility rates at all age levels than is the case in developed societies.

Before considering different patterns of the fertility curve, the impact of the gradual loss of fecundity (the ability to procreate as opposed to fertility which is the actual procreative performance) which accompanies ageing should be noted. At about age 50, almost all women have lost their fecundity, but the process of gradual deterioration begins well before this age. It is a phenomenon, involving both biological and social factors, which is difficult to measure and, at this time, a relatively unexploited field of research (Bourgeois-Pichat 1967).

A United Nations study (1965) has classified countries into three types according to the maximum or peak age of the fertility curve and according to the behaviour of the fertility curve around the peak. In the broad-peak types, typical of less-developed countries, age-specific fertility rates for women aged 20–4 and 25–9 differ only slightly; however, each of these rates is some-what higher than those of younger and older women. Only the onset of sterility and menopause appear to be associated with a dramatic fertility decline.

More typical of developed countries are the early-peak or late-peak types. These are differentiated by the attainment of maximum age-specific general fertility rates in the 20–4 age category or the 25–9 age category. Mitra (1967), pursuing the analysis with single year age-specific rates, has added to these basic patterns. He notes that voluntary fertility control has the effect of re-ducing the range of the effective fertility period. In societies which have largely completed their demographic transition, pregnancies do not occur in large proportions at very early or very late fertility ages, and a decline in fertility tends to be followed by a decline in the variance of age-specific fertility rates.

The major determinants of age-patterns of fertility appear to be age of marriage, the proportion of women married who are in the 20–9 age category, and the social and biological determinants of fertility control within marriage. Marriage is the first factor which regulates the production of offspring in the less developed societies (Bourgeois-Pichat 1967). Under conditions of minimal fertility control within marriage, age of marriage can be the key parameter of total fertility. However, where there is significant marital fertility control, age of marriage may be more significant in defining fertility timing (the early-peak or late-peak types) rather than total fertility. The importance of age of marriage in fertility patterns is demonstrated by the following generalization: in low-fertility nations marriage occurs almost five years later on an average than in high-fertility nations (Bogue 1969). The complex of factors determining patterns of nuptiality and marital fertility are still an unresolved mosaic.

Population ageing and patterns of fertility and mortality

Finally, let us turn to some of the ways in which patterns of fertility and mortality are related to the ageing of a population. Basic to this discussion is the finding that high fertility rates are associated with high infant mortality and vice versa (United Nations 1953). During the period of early demographic transition, infant mortality begins to decline (Heer 1966). Initially this may result in an increase in fertility under conditions of improving child and maternal care, although the long-range prospects are for fertility decline. As noted earlier, the dynamics of these fertility and mortality patterns produce significant population growth. The following are some of the consequences for the age-sex structure.

1. A population in which both birth and death rates are relatively uncontrolled will be a young population with an above-average proportion of males (Cowgill 1963, Satin 1969).
2. However, a population which is experiencing secular declines in both birth and death rates will manifest a marked ageing trend (Cowgill 1963, Satin 1969). Because of differences in male and female mortality, an ageing population tends to be predominantly female (Cowgill 1963, Satin 1969).

A succinct amplification of the demographic forces which produce the ageing of a population has been developed by Coale (1964).

Whether a national population is young or old is mainly determined by the number of children women bear. When women bear many children, the population is young: when they bear few, the population is old.

The effect of fertility on the age distribution is clearest when a population continuously subject to high fertility is compared to one continuously subject to low fertility. The high-fertility population has a larger proportion of children relative to adults of parental age as a direct consequence of the greater frequency of births. . . .

It is the small number of children born per woman that explains the high average age now found in industrialized western Europe, and the high birth rate of the underdeveloped countries that accounts for their young populations. The increase in average age and the swollen proportion of old people in the industrialized countries are the product of the history of falling birth rates that all such countries have experienced.

Most of us would probably guess that populations have become older because the death rate has been reduced, and hence people live longer on the average. Just what is the role of mortality in determining the age distribution of a population? The answer is surprising— mortality affects the age distribution much less than does fertility, and in the opposite direction from what most of us would think. Prolongation of life by reducing death rates has the perverse effect of making the population somewhat younger. Consider the effect of the reduction in death rates in the United States, where the average duration of life has risen from about forty-five years under the mortality conditions of 1900 to about seventy years today. Had the risks of death prevailing in 1900 continued unchanged, the other variables—rates of immigration and rates of childbearing per mother—followed the course they actually did, the average age of the population today would be greater than it is: the proportion of children would be less and the proportion of persons over sixty-five would be greater than they are. The reduction of the death rate has produced, in other words, a younger American population.

Some other demographic correlates of the dynamics of ageing now become apparent. The dependency load for children tends to be extremely high in the high-fertility populations, with an average of 44 per cent of the population under 15 years of age (Bogue 1969). This compares to a dependency load for children of about 24 per cent of the population in very low-fertility countries. However, the developed countries have a significantly greater proportion of their population in the older age categories. While there are great differences in extreme ages between the more- and less-developed countries, there are relatively small differences in the percentage of the population in the 20–45 age bracket—around 35 per cent. As a summary measure, it is not uncommon to find a median age of 16 or 17 years in many less-developed countries as compared to more than double this level for many more-developed countries. Under conditions of zero population growth, where the fertility rate equals the mortality rate, the median age of a population would be approximately forty years.

Summary discussion

This chapter has presented data on, and a series of generalizations about, fertility and mortality patterns for countries at different stages of demographic transition. It should be carefully noted that the demographic patterns presented can be generalized only to an aggregate unit of analysis—in this case, principally national units—and not to fertility and mortality patterns of individuals. Perhaps an example will make the individual/aggregate distinction clear. While it is obvious that individuals become older as death rates decline, it is surprising to discover that the main determinant of ageing in a population is the fertility rate. The significance of this distinction should not be lost since ecological studies frequently use *populations*, not individuals, as units of analysis. Unfortunately, the methodology of quantitative ecological analysis has been the concern of too few ecological researchers, and as a consequence research findings may be erroneously generalized. An analysis of methodology is important if the ecological approach is to be useful in research. In this matter, we benefit from political behaviourists (see, for example, Dogan and Rokkan 1969) in their efforts to synthesize electoral research findings from sample survey and geographical-ecological perspectives, and from geographers who have wrestled with the 'concept of scale' in studying areas varying in dimension from a square mile to tens of millions of square miles (see Clarke's discussion in the preceding chapter of this book).

As summarized in Fig. 3.1, one of the major findings concerning patterns of human fertility and mortality is that, at the present juncture in history, most of the world's population can be characterized as in either an early to mid-transitional stage (economically developing nations) or nearing the post-transitional stage (economically developed nations). These stages describe demographically significant patterns which are basic to theorizing about the social structure and biological components of current populations. Put another way, perhaps only 2–3 per cent of the world's population approaches the fertility and mortality patterns typically ascribed to 'primitive' populations. Again, the demographic patterns caution that the results of anthropological studies are not representative samples of current populations—but rather are illustrative of potentially significant types of ecological relationships which usually are far more difficult to isolate in the complexities of larger and more-developed societies.

By design, this chapter has focused only on the basic demographic patterns of fertility and mortality. Largely unexplored has been how demographic system structures and processes are linked to aspects of social and biological systems—a necessary next step toward an understanding of human adaptability.

REFERENCES

BOGUE, D. J. (1969). *Principles of demography*. Wiley, New York.

—— and PALMORE, J. A. Jr. (1964). Some empirical and analytic relations among demographic fertility measures, with regression models for fertility. *Demography* **1**, 316–38.

BOURGEOIS-PICHAT, J. (1967). Social and biological determinants of human fertility in non-industrial societies. *Proc. Am. phil. Soc.* **3**, 160–3.

CHO, L. J. (1964). Estimated refined measures of fertility for all major countries of the world. *Demography* **1**, 359–74.

COALE, A. J. (1964). How a primitive population ages or grows younger. In *Population: the vital revolution* (ed. R. Freedman). Aldine Press, Chicago.

—— (1967). The voluntary control of human fertility. *Proc. Am. phil. Soc.* **3**, 164–9.

COWGILL, D. O. (1963). Transition theory as general population theory. *Social Forces* **41**, 270–4.

DE JONG, G. F. (1968). *Appalachian fertility decline: a demographic and sociological analysis*. University of Kentucky Press.

DOGAN, M., and ROKKAN, S. (1969). *Quantitative ecological analysis in the social sciences*. Massachusetts Institute of Technology.

FORD, T. R., and DE JONG, G. F. (1970). *Social demography*. Prentice-Hall, Englewood Cliffs.

HEER, D. M. (1966). Economic development and fertility. *Demography* **3**, 423–44.

MADIGAN, F. C. (1957). Are sex mortality differences biologically caused? *Milbank meml Fund Q. Bull.* **35**, 202–23.

MITRA, S. (1967). The pattern of age-specific fertility rates. *Demography* **4**, 894–906.

PETERSEN, W. (1969). *Population*. Macmillan, London.

SATIN, M. S. (1969). An empirical test of the descriptive validity of the theory of demographic transition on a fifty-three nation sample. *Sociol. Q.* **10**, 190–203.

STINCHCOMBE, A. L. (1968). *Constructing social theories*. Harcourt, Brace, and World, New York.

UNITED NATIONS (1953). *The determinants and consequences of population trends*. Population Studies No. **17** (ST/SOA/Ser. A), 134–5.

—— (1965). *Population bulletin*. No. **7** (ST/SOA/Ser. N).

—— (1967). *Demographic yearbook*.

VAN NORT, L. (1956). Biology, rationality, and fertility: a footnote to transition theory. *Eugen. Q.* **3**, 157–60.

4

PERSPECTIVES IN HISTORICAL DEMOGRAPHY

MICHAEL DRAKE

SOCIAL scientists are becoming increasingly interested in historical data. Likewise, historians are becoming more sympathetic towards the aims of the social sciences. This coming together is nowhere more apparent than in population studies. Essentially, this is because population problems have a particular inter-disciplinary appeal since explanations, in terms of one discipline, are more unsatisfactory here than in most other areas, and because in demography the past is so obviously relevant to the present.

Sources

Despite this enthusiasm for historical demography and despite the very considerable efforts of the last twenty years or so, the pay-off remains relatively meagre. This is due primarily to the nature of the subject. Historical demography is the *statistical* study of past populations. And it is this essential statistical component that presents the major obstacle to the advance of the subject. Fig. 4.1 indicates schematically the core of the problem. Historical

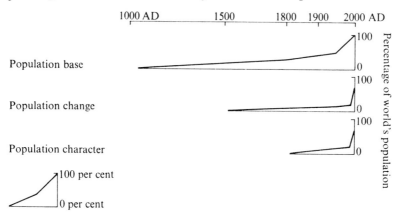

FIG. 4.1. Population statistics, A.D. 1000 to 2000.

demographers require base population figures (census statistics); totals of births, marriages, and deaths (vital statistics); and quantitative evidence of a variety of population characteristics, such as occupations, incomes, educational experience, religious affiliations, disease, household composition, geographical and social mobility. Reliable statistical material for all of these categories is still not available for the bulk of the world's populations and even for the most favoured is confined to but a few decades. Various 'guesstimates' have, of course, been made for a much longer period than this.

Take, for instance, one of the favoured countries—England. From Domesday (1086) to the first official census in 1801, there were large numbers of returns made for ecclesiastical, military, and revenue purposes (Hollingsworth 1969). The analysis of these gives a broad indication of the magnitude and geographical distribution of the country's population. But the findings tend to appear more impressive to the historian, wearing his traditional hat, than to the social scientist. One cannot fail to share the enthusiasm of the historian for the ingenuity needed to bring forth these findings. But to the social scientist they must often appear partial, non-testable, owing more to the inspired hunch than to the canons of scientific method.

At the beginning of each decade from 1801 to 1831 the British Government carried out a population census. These censuses represent a major advance. They appeared at regular intervals: they sought information of direct interest to the demographer, so that no elaborate computations were required (as in the case of hearth taxes, militia rolls, heriots, lists of communicants, etc.) to arrive at population totals; they were comprehensive and, in part, the results were published in such a way as to facilitate comparisons over time. But they suffered from a number of drawbacks, understandable in any new venture. The occupational and age data were rudimentary, different questions being asked at each census. Above all, the censuses were organized on a tally system. That is to say, local officials themselves aggregated the information for their localities. There is, therefore, no way of checking their accuracy, or of re-analysing the material (Drake 1972).

This latter drawback was rectified with the census of 1841. This was the first nominative census. Information was required of each individual and the analysis of the enumerators' books was done centrally. Beginning with the census of 1841, and even more so that of 1851, the historical demographer is provided with a surfeit of information which, even with the aid of the computer, he has barely begun to exploit.† Unfortunately, the Registrar-General's 100-year rule, which prohibits the use of this nominative data if less than a hundred years has elapsed since its collection, means that currently it is only possible to examine the four censuses from 1841 to 1871. The last three are

† Work in this field has been done by Dyos at the University of Leicester and by Armstrong, Pearce, and Drake at the University of Kent at Canterbury. Armstrong's work on York in the 1840s and 1850s is completed; that of Pearce and myself on Ashford, Kent, in the years 1840–70 is still in progress. For similar work in other countries see the files of the *Historical Methods Newsletter*, published by the Department of History, University of Pittsburgh, U.S.A.

the most valuable, giving for each individual the name, address, sex, age, position within the household, marital status, occupation, and place of birth.

Turning to the quantitative evidence of population change in England (vital statistics), we are faced with an even less satisfactory situation. Not until 1837 was there any civil registration of births, marriages, and deaths. Prior to that, one must rely upon the registers of baptisms, marriages, and burials, the most comprehensive of which were those kept by the Church of England, beginning in 1538. Though an enormous number of registers is still available, few are free from gaps and all, of course, suffer from the fact that they were intended not as the record of demographic events, but of religious experiences. The absence of any reliable figure of population makes the production of vital statistics from the material in these registers a hazardous enterprise. Nevertheless, attempts have been made over the last two decades and a considerable literature now exists (see Hollingsworth 1969). Changes in mortality have also been inferred from such evidence as the probate of wills (Fisher 1965) and the number of heriots (fines paid on the handover of a holding) (Postan and Titow 1959). Work of this kind is, however, subject to an even greater degree of error than the manipulation of the figures in ecclesiastical registers (Ohlin 1966).

From 1837 there exist the civil registers of births, marriages, and deaths. The information in these has remained substantially unchanged down to the present day so that comparative work is possible. (The *birth registers* contain the name of the child; whether or not he or she was legitimate; address, name, and occupation of father; maiden and christian name of mother. The *marriage registers* contain the names of the bride (maiden name) and bridegroom, their ages (if known), their address, whether or not they could sign their own name, the names and occupations of their respective fathers. The *death registers* contain the name, age, address, and sex of the deceased, the date of death, the cause of death (when known) and the occupation of the deceased, or where this inappropriate that of the husband, father or mother.) Unfortunately the Registrar-General has not felt able, with one or two exceptions, to allow historical demographers access to these registers. One must, therefore, make do with the aggregative data presented in the Registrar-General's annual reports.

Finally we come to the statistical evidence required by historical demographers if they are to explain population change in anything but purely demographic terms. Such evidence is extremely scarce and before the mid-nineteenth century can only be described as fragmentary. By that time, some of it is being provided by the census: for instance on such matters as occupation, birthplace, household size and composition. Other information can be culled from the civil registers, for example on literacy (marriage registers) or morbidity (death registers). Before this, one must fall back upon the eccentric endeavours of private individuals, often clerics, though their activities are usually local in extent and cover but a brief time-span. Close examination of these often shows them to be vehicles more of promise than performance. For example, in 1778 the Vicar of Birstall (a large parish in the woollen cloth manufacturing area of the West Riding of Yorkshire) decided, for no apparent reason, to enrich his burial registers. So instead of entering merely the name of the deceased and the date of burial he began to add the address, cause of death, age at death, marital status, and occupation of the deceased. Where the person buried had no occupation, then that of the father or husband was given. Unfortunately, this particular exercise was not repeated in subsequent years. We are thus left with the bane of the social scientist—a unique non-replicable set of data of limited extent.

From the middle of the nineteenth century, one finds an increasing amount of nominative data which can be linked with that provided by the census and vital registration systems. There are, for instance, workhouse admission and discharge sheets; school registers; trade directories; calendars of court cases; pay sheets and rate books. There is too an ever-increasing volume of aggregative information resulting from enquiries initiated by local or national authorities, or by individuals like Charles Booth (Booth 1902–3) into social and economic conditions.

In sum, this review of the sources available to the historical demographer has shown how limited they are over time and space, as well as in their range and quality. This is all the more obvious in that the discussion has been focused on England, one of the most favoured countries. One or two other countries excel in certain types of evidence. France, for instance, has more detailed parish registers than England (Fleury and Henry 1965); Sweden a richer and more reliable census and vital registration system (Gille 1949–50 and Swedish Central Bureau of Statistics 1955); Norway has the extensive socio-demographic studies of a pioneer sociologist, Eilert Sundt (1817–76), which add a great deal to our understanding of this mid-nineteenth century pre-industrial society (Drake 1969a). Certain non-Western societies, for instance China and Japan, appear to have voluminous population statistics for many centuries past, though their accuracy remains very much in doubt (Hollingsworth 1969). In spite of these instances, however, the conclusion at the beginning of this section still stands.

Methods

A somewhat jaundiced view of the historical demographer would be that what he lacks in material he has tried to make up in technique. That he has not always succeeded is apparent if one views the not inconsiderable literature in which historical demographers take each other to task. Some notable examples are Krause (1957) on Russell's (1948) attempt to calculate the average size of medieval households; Hollingsworth (1969), on Wrigley's family reconstitution work in the parish of Colyton in Devon (Wrigley 1966a,

1968); Krause (1967) on an aggregative study by Eversley (1957) of certain Worcestershire parishes from the mid-seventeeth to the mid-nineteenth centuries; and Drake (1963) on the use of literary evidence by Connell (1950) in the determination of the age at marriage in Ireland during the first half of the nineteenth century. (But see also Lee's (1968) reply to Drake.)

At the present time the main techniques used by historical demographers can be subsumed under the two heads of aggregative and nominative. (For some applications of these in an English context, see Wrigley 1966*b*.) Essentially, aggregative techniques are used when one is aiming for global figures of population, birth, deaths, marriages, household size, migrants, etc., with a view to producing relatively crude rates of one sort or another. Examples of such work in England include studies by Chambers (1957), Krause (1958, 1967), Eversley (1957), Sogner (1963), and Drake 1962). Each of these studies is based on the time-consuming aggregation of entries of baptisms, marriages, and burials in the parish registers kept by the Church of England. Works by Drake (1969*a*) on Norway; Utterström (1954) on Sweden, and Lassen (1965) on Denmark also include some findings based upon aggregative techniques.

By contrast, nominative techniques involve the linking together of various pieces of demographic information using the names of individuals as the linking device. Thus in England, Wrigley (1966*a*, 1968) has been able to calculate age-specific birth and death rates and marriage ages by drawing together the entries of baptisms, marriages and burials using a technique analogous to that of the genealogist. His work was foreshadowed by that of Gautier and Henry (1958) in France. The technique lends itself to computerization. Wrigley is currently developing computer techniques to this end with the Cambridge Group for the History of Population and Social Structure (20 Silver Street, Cambridge, England). Whilst the core of Wrigley's work rests on parish registers, other students are exploiting census enumerators' returns. These include Johansen (University of Odense, Denmark) who has worked on the Danish censuses of 1787 and 1801; Thernstrom (1964) (University of Harvard) who has used the U.S. censuses of Newburyport, Mass.; and Katz (Ontario Institute for Studies in Education) who is currently using a variety of nominative material, including censuses, in a study of Hamilton, Canada. Over the past four years, Carol Pearce and myself have been conducting a socio-demographic study of Ashford, a small town in Kent which expanded rapidly over the years 1840–1870 as a result of the decision by the South Eastern Railway Company to make it not only an important junction, but also the site of the Company's machine shops. This has involved the transfer onto some 50 000 IBM cards of information concerning named individuals from a variety of sources, including the censuses of 1841, 1851, and 1861; the civil registers of births, marriages, and deaths from 1837 to 1871; the poll books derived from the parliamentary elections of 1852, 1857, 1863, 1865, and 1868; the entries from several trade and professional directories (1839, 1851, 1855, 1867, and 1874) together with the return made to Parliament in 1874 of the owners of landholdings of more than one acre —this gives the name and address of the owner, the amount of land, and the rental derived from it. This study has also involved the production of general 'sort-and-merge' computer programmes which enable the various items of information to be combined. This permits us to do longitudinal studies of such matters as fertility, voting behaviour, household structure, social mobility, etc. This linking process also helps to improve the quality of the information. For instance, in a study involving the relating of age at marriage to birth intervals, it was discovered that the marriage registers often failed to give the precise age at marriage. Age, however, was very rarely omitted from the census returns. Thus, if only the marriage registers had been available the marriages used in the fertility analysis would have numbered but 329: using the census, we were able to increase the number to 534.

Our conclusion must be that the nominative method of analysis, especially when linked with computer technology, is emerging as the most valuable of the techniques available to the historical demographer. It is, however, subject to the caveat made at the beginning of this section, namely, that however refined and sophisticated the techniques, the historical demographer is subject to the limitations of his data.

Problems

The problems taken up by historical demographers would appear, at first glance, to be so diverse as to defy classification. It is, however, possible to set almost all of them into a framework which involves, in spatial terms, the contrasting of Western and non-Western demographic experience and, in temporal terms, the exploration of the similarities and dissimilarities between the industrial and the pre-industrial world. Once one recognizes this, it comes as no surprise that so much attention has been paid to the changes occurring in Western populations during the period of the Industrial Revolution, or more broadly from about 1650 to about 1850. I propose then to discuss the major findings of recent years within this framework.

The size and structure of households

In a recent article, Laslett (1969) has analysed the household structure of some 100 communities for which local censuses happen to be available. The period covered by these censuses is 1574–1821. Two striking conclusions are drawn by Laslett. The first is that the mean household size was only 4·77: the second that the deviations from this mean were slight. The figure is also very close to the one derived from my Ashford study, this being 4·85 in 1851. Indeed, the similarity persists when one dissects the households. Table 4.1, for instance, does this with regard to the distribution of households by size and Table 4.2 examines the social composition of the households. A further look at Tables 4.1 and 4.2 shows that the English pattern is somewhat different from that derived from my Norwegian study (Drake 1969a). The Norwegian communities were all rural, one being a west-coast parish (Herøy in Sunnmøre): two being mountain parishes (Ål and Nes in Hallingdal) and two being lowland parishes (Nes and Ringsaker in Hedmark). Mean household size in

TABLE 4.1

Distribution of households by size†

Number of members	100 communities 1564–1821, per cent	Ashford 1851, per cent	Norwegian communities 1801, per cent
1	5·7	6·0	0·1
2	14·2	13·3	8·1
3	16·5	16·2	12·9
4	15·8	17·1	16·3
5	14·7	14·1	16·5
6	11·8	10·6	13·4
7	8·0	8·3	10·9
8	5·4	6·1	7·6
9	3·1	3·4	4·9
10 and over	4·9	4·8	9·2

† *Sources:* 100 Communities: population 67 382, households 14 131 (Laslett 1969). Ashford 1851: population 4980, households 1028 (Drake and Pearce unpublished). Norwegian communities 1801: population 20 945, households 3663 (Drake 1969a).

TABLE 4.2

Component parts of mean household size†

Mean number per household	100 communities 1564–1821, per cent	Ashford 1851, per cent	Norwegian communities 1801, per cent
Heads	1·0	1·0	1·0
Wives	0·7	0·7	0·9
Children	2·1	1·9	2·3
Total nuclear family	3·8	3·6	4·2
Kin	0·2	0·4	0·4
Lodgers‡	0·0	0·7	0·6
Servants§	0·6	0·2	0·5
TOTAL	4·6	4·9	5·7

† *Sources:* as in Table 4.1.
‡ Ashford figures include visitors and living-in assistants.
§ Ashford figures include domestic servants only.

these Norwegian communities was somewhat higher than in the English ones, being 5·7 persons per household. The most marked difference, however, seems to be in the proportion of one-member households—virtually unknown in the Norwegian parishes—and in the proportion of households with ten or more members—much greater in Norway than in England.

Table 4.3 compares the marital status of the heads of households in the three areas. Again, the data for the 100 communities and for Ashford are very

TABLE 4.3

Distribution of households by marital status of head†

Percentage of households headed by:	100 *communities* 1564–1821, *per cent*	*Ashford* 1851, *per cent*	*Norwegian communities* 1801, *per cent*
Married couples	70·4	76·3	92·1
Widowers	5·2	4·3	2·4
Widows	12·9	9·2	2·8
Single males	2·1	5·7	1·9
Single females	1·1	4·2	0·1
Unspecified	7·3	0·2	0·6

† *Sources:* as in Table 4.1.

similar. And the most obvious conclusion to be drawn from them—that the overwhelming majority of households were headed by married couples—is even more marked in the case of the Norwegian material. The broad similarity of the findings in each of these tables, and for each of the three areas is all the more striking when one considers the very different sources from which the material is drawn. That for the 100 communities comes from a variety of household listings, or local censuses, the credibility of which is an open question. The Norwegian material is taken from the first nominative census in a country which was not to develop a major industrial sector for almost a century to come. Ashford in 1851 was, of course, in a society which in that very year was demonstrating its industrial hegemony in the halls of the Great Exhibition.

The significance of these tables, is, for the purpose of this paper, to be found in the common picture they paint of household structure: one which other studies appear to bear out (see the as yet unpublished papers presented to the International Conference on the Comparative History of Household and Family, organized in September 1969, at Cambridge by the Cambridge Group for the History of Population and Social Structure). The similarities to be noted here are three in number. First, that the mean household size was small—between 4·7 and 5·7. Second, that what might be termed the core family was a nuclear one headed by a married couple. Third, that the above-average households were larger not because they were extended households, but because they contained relatively large numbers of servants or lodgers. This household structure was, of course, both cause and effect of the demographic variables which have been the second main focus of attention of historical demographers.

Fertility

The discussion of fertility by historical demographers has taken place very largely within the context of a single debate: namely, what brought about the rapid rise of population in Britain during the late eighteenth and early nineteenth centuries. This debate has raged (the term for once is highly appropriate) for over twenty years (for a collection of the key papers, see Drake 1969b) and continues still. When the debate began it was assumed that Britain, in common with most societies, had 'high' fertility unrestricted by anything but changes in the age at marriage, which in turn were thought to be small. This view is no longer tenable. Variations in the age at marriage both over time and within any one pre-industrial Western society appear to have been not inconsiderable (Connell 1950, Wrigley 1966a, Drake 1969a). Furthermore, fluctuations in fertility appear much more marked than can be explained either by changes in the proportions married or in the age at marriage. The bottom line of Table 4.4, for example, suggests that fertility

TABLE 4.4

Births, deaths, and marriages per 1000 *mean population in the diocese of Akershus, Norway,* 1771–1776 *(from Drake* 1969a)

	1771	1772	1773	1774	1775	1776
Deaths	21	26	64	29	26	20
Marriages	7	6	6	9	10	9
Births	34	28	22	29	35	32

might well have been controlled in years of crisis. One can, of course, do no more than infer this. We know that the early 1770s witnessed acute food shortages throughout Scandinavia. This would seem to be the explanation of the trebling of the crude death rate in Norway's Akershus diocese between 1771 and 1773. Over the same period, the birth rate dropped by more than a third—though the marriage rate remained relatively stable. Of course, some of the fall in fertility must be ascribed to miscarriages and the deaths of pregnant women. It seems not unlikely, however, that some of the fall must also have been due to a conscious control of fertility within marriage.

Wrigley's (1966a) material from the Devonshire parish of Colyton is particularly interesting in this context. Since his method (the 'reconstitution of families') involves the relating of particular births to particular women over time, he is able to calculate birth intervals. As a result of his calculations, he asserts that in the late seventeenth and early eighteenth centuries there was a marked rise in the mean interval between the penultimate and the last birth, which is 'typical of a community beginning to practice family limitation. It rises in these circumstances, because even after reaching an intended final family size additions are nevertheless occasionally made either from accident (failure of whatever system of restriction is in use), from a reversal of an earlier decision not to increase family size, or from a desire to replace a child which has died'. This interval was much shorter in the period 1550–1650 and again in the period 1720–69 than in 1650–1720.

Nuptiality

Wrigley's findings are the most telling yet, in support of the view that birth-control within marriage was a feature of pre-industrial Western societies. That fertility was limited more than in many non-Western societies is, however, now in little doubt, though most scholars believe this to be due to a relatively late age at marriage, with the result that a high proportion (approximately 50 per cent) of the women in the fertile age group were unmarried at any one time. Hajnal (1965) talks of a 'European' marriage pattern which prevailed from the sixteenth century to the 1930s. In this, only some 20–30 per cent of women aged 20–4 were married as compared with some 80 per cent of women in many non-Western societies. The social and economic effects of this difference between Western and non-Western experience have no doubt been profound. Historical demographers, however, have been less concerned with working on this than on trying to ascertain the extent to which the age at marriage varied in pre-industrial Western societies and why. Again, the period of the British industrial revolution has been the focus of the debate. Unfortunately most of this period covers the years when, as noted earlier, the appropriate statistical information is lacking. Nevertheless, some statistics have been produced. Wrigley (1966a) has shown that in Colyton the mean age of women at first marriage moved from 27·0 years in the period (1560–1646) to 29·6 (1647–1719), 26·8 (1720–69), and to 25·1 (1770–1837). On the other hand, Razzell (1965), using a variety of sources from various parts of England, concludes that the mean age of women at first marriage moved little: being about 24 years. My own work in Norway (1969a) suggests a range in the years 1841–5 from 22·8 years (deanery of Vest Finnmark) to 26·5 years (deanery of Söndre Sunnmöre) for the median age of women at first marriage.

Explanations of the differences in marriage age lean heavily on the economic factor. In Britain a supposed fall in the age at marriage of men during the late eighteenth and early nineteenth centuries has been ascribed to such factors as an increase in employment opportunities resulting from the industrial revolution: with a particular expansion in jobs where maximum earnings came early, thus reducing the incentive to delay marriage. The decline in apprenticeship; the decrease in the number of farm servants living-in and therefore remaining celibate; the expansion of Poor Law conventions providing a basic subsistence for all, scaled according to family responsibilities, have also been put forward as possible causes. None of these factors directly affects the age at marriage of women, but it has been assumed that the earlier the age at marriage of men, the earlier that of women. Evidence from Norway (Drake 1969a) and to a lesser extent from England (Wrigley 1966a) indicates that this was not always so—though it does nothing to weaken the argument that the economic factor was the most important determinant of the age at marriage. Thus in Norway, cottars (who were paid for their labour on the farms partly in cash, but mostly by being allowed to cultivate small plots of land) not infrequently married women who were several years older. They did so partly because older women had more material possessions to offer (e.g. household equipment, the odd cow or goat); more experience in running a holding (female Norwegian farm servants did a lot of outside work); and even because older women were less fertile—'I thought that when I took such an old woman,' one cottar said, 'the crowd of young ones would not be so great for it is difficult for one who is in small circumstances to feed so many' (Drake 1969a).

Evidence from Norway also suggests that the primacy of the economic factor might have had a significant effect on the genetic structure of the population. For instance, there were considerable variations in the extent to which the population in a particular area participated in one or more marriage markets. In a study published in 1864, the Norwegian sociologist Eilert Sundt divided the population of the country into two classes which he called the propertied and the propertyless and which, Norway being a pre-industrial society, meant essentially farmers and cottars. He then divided the country geographically into fifteen areas. Sundt was able to show that over the country as a whole 76 per cent of the bridegrooms in the propertied class married brides from the same class, but that the range varied from 60 per cent in one area to 82 per cent in another. As for bridegrooms in the propertyless class, 82 per cent married girls from their own class; the range being from 60 to 92 per cent.

Two other instances might be cited as illustrations of the close tie between economic and marital fortunes. One was the custom of what might be termed 'swap marriages' in certain parts of western Norway (Drake 1969a). These occurred when a member of one family was only allowed to marry a member of another, if a reciprocal marriage could be arranged, so that in the property settlement between the two families no one would be the loser. Sundt (1858) also drew attention to conditions on the island of Vigren, remarkable even by Norwegian standards. Here the number of farms had remained constant from 1800 to 1855 at 53 and even in 1759 numbered only 60. More noteworthy even than that, for the population of the region had doubled, was the fact that the island had only six cottars. This was not because the farmers did not require farm labour over and above what they and their families could provide. On the contrary, in 1855 there were 118 male living-in farm servants, 27 of whom were sons of the farmers and 91 were hired. Of these 91, only 2 had been born on the island. Farm servants were unable to marry until they got a croft and most farmers allowed some cottars on their land in exchange for labour. But not on Vigren. When the 89 gave up being farm servants they had to leave the island.

I have discussed Norwegian conditions at some length partly because I am familiar with them. The discussion also illustrates, however, two important features of recent work in historical demography. One is that historical demographers do draw a great deal on the international discussion of population change. Another is that, as noted at the very beginning of this paper, reliable evidence of the sort which today would be generated by social surveys to explain population change is only rarely available to the historical demographer. When he discovers it he tends, as with the statistical findings, to try to adapt it to the society he happens to be studying.

Mortality

The study of mortality by historical demographers is highly indicative of the international character of the discipline. For no discussion of mortality in pre-industrial Europe could be considered complete unless one took into account the work of French historical demographers (e.g. Goubert 1960) on the 'crises of subsistence'. The French position is that demographic crises, in which mortality rose sharply and fertility fell, can be directly related to harvest failure. One must also take account of the work of Utterström in Sweden (1954) and of Lassen in Denmark (1965). The former demonstrated that, at least in Sweden, some of the most significant eighteenth-century peaks of mortality were not associated with bad harvests, but were the product of epidemics of smallpox, typhus, and dysentery: diseases which he suggested followed their own cycle of virulence unaffected by harvest conditions. Lassen has argued that even when major epidemics and harvest failures appear to be linked (as in 1710–11; 1741–3; 1756; 1763; 1771–3), the primary cause of the spread of disease was preparation for war, which in these years not only brought together large numbers of people in insanitary camps, but spread the diseases which flourished there as soldiers were sent out to collect the materials of war, particularly food.

That demographic crises were serious checks to population growth in some pre-industrial societies is indicated by Fig. 4.2. This shows the fluctuations in the crude death rate in two Norwegian dioceses over the period 1735–1865.

These dioceses covered large areas of the country and contained sizeable populations: that of Akershus rising from 262 000 in 1735 to 745 000 in 1865, and that of Bergen from 109 000 in 1735 to 266 000 in 1865. There are a number of interesting features about this graph, but for the purposes of this discussion the one to note is the difference between the pattern of mortality in the two dioceses. Akershus, the inland diocese, had demographic crises of a much greater magnitude than the coastal diocese of Bergen. This variation in the one country is mirrored between countries: eighteenth-century France, for instance, having much more serious crises than eighteenth-century England.

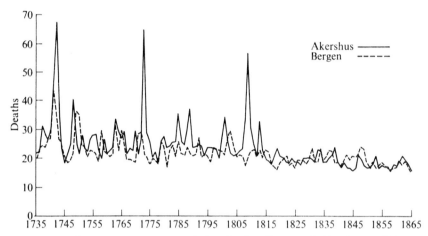

FIG. 4.2. Deaths per 1000 mean population in the dioceses of Akershus and Bergen 1735–1865 (from Drake 1969a).

The main contribution of English historical demographers to the discussion has centred upon the effect of preventive medicine on mortality in the period 1750–1850. In a famous article McKeown, a medical man, and Brown, a sociologist (1955), poured scorn on the idea that medical advances could have played any part in reducing mortality in the eighteenth century, or indeed for much of the nineteenth, with the possible exception of inoculation against smallpox. One of their oft quoted remarks is that 'the chief indictment of hospital work at this period is not that it did no good, but that it positively did harm'. This last point has been challenged (Sigsworth 1966), though it is still widely accepted. More challenging, however, is the work of Razzell (1965) who suggests that inoculation against smallpox became widespread from the 1760s onwards and it was this which, by cutting mortality from a major disease, caused the population to expand. There is much circumstantial evidence to support Razzell's position—though the absence of adequate quantitative material, as in so much historical demography, is a regrettable lacuna.

This makes the presence of a burial register, like that for Birstall in 1778 (see above), especially tantalising. For it happened that in 1778, of the 142 deceased for whom cause of death was stated (it was not stated in a further 40 cases), smallpox accounted for 53. Of these 53, only 6 were under one year of age (indicating a high level of congenital immunity). A further 39 were aged between 1 and 4 years, 2 were in the 5–9 age group, and 1 in the 20–4 year group. Age was not stated in a further 5 cases.

Migration

Migration is a particularly difficult population characteristic to measure. Few societies keep migration registers and although estimates can be made, from a combination of statistics, derived from vital registration and census systems, only *net* migration figures are obtained. Historical demographers have not surprisingly, therefore, done relatively little in this area. Deane and Cole (1967) have attempted to measure migration in eighteenth-century England and Friedlander and Roshier (1966) have done so for the nineteenth century. A number of local studies have also been made, for example by Buckatzsch (1951) and Laslett and Harrison (1962). In the main, however, historical demographers come across migration more as an obstacle in the path of their studies than as an object of study in itself. It is, of course, the biggest single stumbling-block to the success of studies based on the reconstitution of families. And even though most studies of migration, both historical and contemporary, show that the bulk of it is over short distances, its magnitude is sufficient to reduce sample sizes drastically.

Conclusion

In this paper, I have tried to look at the work of the historical demographer from three points of view. First, his sources. These, it must be emphasized, are deficient in many respects, particularly as regards quantitative evidence of the characteristics of population, though even the material for producing statistics of population size and change are difficult to come by. Second, his methods. With the advance of the subject, aggregative methods, which have served to indicate the broad changes in population, are giving way to nominative methods, facilitated increasingly by the computer. Third, his substantive interests. These have covered the whole gamut of the demographer's traditional interests in population size and structure, and the major variables of fertility, nuptiality, mortality, and migration. It has been suggested that two general conclusions can be drawn from the work of the last two decades. First that the demographic experience of the pre-industrial West was by no means homogeneous, considerable differences being discerned both between areas and over time. Secondly, despite these variations, a number of striking differences appear to justify the drawing of a line between the demographic experience of pre-industrial Western and non-Western societies. Compared with non-Western societies, the Western societies appear to have had smaller households that were nuclear rather than extended; much tighter controls on fertility and nuptiality, essentially economic in origin; and, partly resulting from this, populations that were limited more by 'preventive' than 'positive' checks, to use Malthusian terminology. The implications of these differences for the economic development of the two areas might well have been crucial.

REFERENCES

BOOTH, C. (1902–3). *Life and labour of the people in London*. Macmillan, London.

BUCKATZSCH, E. J. (1951). The constancy of local populations and migration in England and Wales before 1800. *Popul. Stud.* **5**, 62–9.

CHAMBERS, J. D. (1957). The Vale of Trent, 1670–1800. A regional study of economic change. *Econ. Hist. Rev.* Suppl. **3**.

CONNELL, K. H. (1950). *The population of Ireland 1750–1845*. Clarendon Press, Oxford.

DEANE, P. M. and COLE, W. A. (1967). *British economic growth, 1688–1959*. Cambridge University Press.

DRAKE, M. (1962). An elementary exercise in parish register demography. *Econ. Hist. Rev.* 2nd ser. **14**, 427–45.

—— (1963). Marriage and population growth in Ireland, 1750–1845. *Econ. Hist. Rev.* 2nd ser. **16**, 301–13.

—— (1969a). *Population and society in Norway, 1735–1865*. Cambridge University Press.

—— (ed.) (1969b). *Population in industrialization*. Methuen, London.

—— (1972). The census, 1801–1891. In *Study of the nineteenth-century society* (ed. E. A. Wrigley), Cambridge University Press.

EVERSLEY, D. E. C. (1957). A survey of population in an area of Worcestershire, from 1660 to 1850, on the basis of parish registers. *Popul. Stud.* **10**, 253–79.

FISHER, F. J. (1965). Influenza and inflation in Tudor England. *Econ. Hist. Rev.* 2nd ser. **18**, 120–9.

FLEURY, M. and HENRY, L. (1965). *Des registres paroissiaux à l'histoire de la population: Nouveau manuel de dépouillement et d'exploitation de l'état civil ancien*. I.N.E.D., Paris.

FRIEDLANDER, D. and ROSHIER, R. J. (1966). A study of internal migration in England and Wales, Part I: Geographical patterns of internal migration 1851–1951. *Popul. Stud.* **19**, 239–78.

GAUTIER, E. and HENRY, L. (1958). *La population de Crulai, paroisse normande. Étude historique*. I.N.E.D., Paris.

GILLE, H. (1949–50). The demographic history of the northern European countries in the eighteenth century. *Popul. Stud.* **3**, 3–65.

GOUBERT, P. (1960). *Beauvais et le Beauvaisis de 1600–1730, contribution a l'histoire sociale de la France du XVIIIe siècle*. S.E.V.P.E.N., Paris.

HAJNAL, J. (1965). European marriage patterns in perspective. *Population in history* (eds. D. V. Glass and D. E. C. Eversley), Arnold, London.

HOLLINGSWORTH, T. H. (1969). *Historical demography*. Hodder and Stoughton, London.

KRAUSE, J. T. (1957). The mediaeval household: large or small? *Econ. Hist. Rev.* 2nd ser. **9**, 420–32.

—— (1958). Changes in English fertility and mortality, 1781–1850. *Econ. Hist. Rev.* 2nd ser. **11**, 52–70.

—— (1967). Some aspects of population change, 1690–1790. In *Land, labour, and population in the Industrial Revolution* (eds. E. L. Jones and G. E. Mingay), Arnold, London.

LASLETT, P. (1969). Size and structure of the household in England over three centuries. *Popul. Stud.* **23**, 199–223.

—— and HARRISON, J. C. (1962). Clayworth and Cogenhoe. In *Historical essays, 1600–1750, presented to D. Ogg* (eds. H. E. Ball and R. L. Ollard), A. and C. Black, London.

LASSEN, A. (1965). *Fald og Fremgang: Træck av Befolkningsudviklingen i Danmark 1645–1690*. Universitets forlaget Aarhus.

LEE, J. (1968). Marriage and population in pre-famine Ireland. *Econ. Hist. Rev.* 2nd ser. **21**, 283–95.

MCKEOWN, T. and BROWN, R. G. (1955). Medical evidence related to English population changes in the eighteenth century. *Popul. Stud.* **9**, 119–41. (Reprinted in Drake, 1969*b*.)

OHLIN, P. G. (1966). No safety in numbers: some pitfalls of historical statistics. In *Industrialization in two systems: Essays in honor of Alexander Gerschenkron* (ed. H. Rosovsky), Wiley, New York.

POSTAN, M. M. and TITOW, J. (1959). Heriots and prices on Winchester manors. *Econ. Hist. Rev.* 2nd ser. **11**, 392–411.

RAZZELL, P. (1965). Population change in eighteenth-century England: a reappraisal. *Econ. Hist. Rev.* 2nd ser. **18**, 312–32. (Reprinted in Drake, 1969*b*.)

RUSSELL, J. C. (1948). *British mediaeval population.* University of New Mexico Press, Albuquerque.

SIGSWORTH, E. (1966). A provincial hospital in the eighteenth and early nineteenth centuries. *Coll. Gen. Practnrs, Yorkshire Faculty Journal*, 1–8.

SOGNER, S. (1963). Aspects of the demographic situation in seventeen parishes in Shropshire, 1711–1760. *Popul. Stud.* **17**, 126–46.

SUNDT, E. (1858). Harham: et exempel fra fiskeri distrikterne. *Folkevennen* **7**, 329–423.

—— (1864). *Fortsatte Bidrag angaaende Sædeligheds-Tilstanden i Norge.* Christiania.

SWEDISH CENTRAL BUREAU OF STATISTICS (1955). *Historical statistics of Sweden. 1. Population, 1720–1950.* Stockholm.

THERNSTROM, S. (1964). *Poverty and progress: Social mobility in a nineteenth-century city.* Harvard University Press.

UTTERSTRÖM, G. (1954). Some population problems in pre-industrial Sweden. *Scand. Econ. Hist. Rev.* **2**, 103–65.

WRIGLEY, E. A. (1966*a*). Family limitation in pre-industrial England. *Econ. Hist. Rev.* 2nd ser. **14**, 82–109. (Reprinted in Drake, 1969*b*.)

—— (1966*b*). *An introduction to English historical demography.* Weidenfeld and Nicolson, London.

—— (1968). Mortality in pre-industrial England: the example of Colyton, Devon, over three centuries. *Daedalus, Cambridge, Mass.* **97**, 546–80.

5

SOCIAL REGULATION OF FERTILITY†

Burton Benedict

A QUESTIONNAIRE recently administered to students and faculty at Cornell University showed that 84 per cent of the 1059 who responded agreed on the desirability of limiting family size. Yet 65 per cent said it wanted three children (39 per cent) or more (26 per cent); only 30 per cent wanted two children, and a mere 5 per cent wanted one or none. Even those whom the investigators expected to be most concerned about the population crisis, such as graduate students and young faculty in biology, included a minimum of 50 per cent who wanted three or more children (Eisner, van Tienhoven, and Rosenblatt 1970). Neither awareness of the population crisis nor knowledge of effective and available means of contraception were deterring a majority of this highly educated sample of people from increasing the world's population. Messrs. Eisner, van Tienhoven, and Rosenblatt are quite upset by the results of their questionnaire. I think this is somewhat naive of them. If there is one thing which experience with family planning has shown (apart from the unreliability of questionnaires to predict actual behaviour) it is that people are not motivated to limit their families by population statistics or even by the ease and availability of contraceptives, but by a whole set of social factors impinging on their personal lives and changing over their life cycles. In the vast majority of the societies of the world these factors serve to promote human fertility. In a few societies or parts of societies they serve to limit fertility.

In this short paper I shall undertake to review the various social factors which are believed to affect fertility. This necessarily will involve a tour of many societies and hence will introduce a certain distortion and lack of coherence as social customs are treated out of the social matrix of which they are a part. It must be stated at once that the information we have about population regulation in simple societies is extremely poor. Very few anthropologists have been concerned with this problem. Their interests have been in outlining the social structure, recording social customs, and examining the political, economic, and religious aspects of the societies they have studied. The quantitative data they have collected on population growth or decline have not been very systematic or complete, nor have the data been collected in such a way as to make comparisons from society to society possible.

---

† This article represents a revision and further development of my article in Allison (1970). It also incorporates some material from Benedict (1971).

Moreover, most anthropological studies have been synchronic, studying the society in question at a single period of time, the one or two years during which the anthropologist was in the field. Only a handful of anthropologists have been able to restudy the people among whom they did previous field-work (e.g. Firth 1959 and Mead 1956). Even fewer have followed up the work of a predecessor in the same area (e.g. Malinowski/Powell, Redfield/Lewis). For most of the societies studied there are no reliable historical records. Therefore, in most cases, it has not been possible to examine trends or changes in population growth.

A cross-cultural survey of factors affecting fertility

These limitations appear clearly in a cross-cultural survey of factors affecting human fertility in non-industrial societies published by Nag (1962). Over and over again the correlations he attempts between fertility and various social customs seem to lack significance because the data are inadequate, but they do enable us to divide the factors affecting fertility into at least three types.

1. Biological factors such as general health conditions, disease, sterility, and venereal disease (which are, of course, linked), diet, and length of fertile period. In general I shall not be dealing with these, though clearly they are affected by social factors. Improvements in health, education, nutrition, etc. are products of prevailing social, economic, and political conditions. The high priority that is given to the social services has been a major factor in the increase of world population. As health conditions improve, one may expect greater fecundity as well as a higher survival rate of children born.

2. Indirect social factors. These are factors deriving from social customs which affect fertility, but which are usually not primarily regarded by the people themselves as affecting fertility, such as age at marriage, the incidence of separation or divorce, absence of a spouse, widowhood and widow remarriage, polygamy, post-partum sexual abstinence, abstinence during certain seasons or ceremonies, and temporary or permanent celibacy by some members of the population.

3. Direct social factors affecting population growth such as voluntary sexual abstinence, contraceptive practices, abortion, and infanticide.

Indirect social factors affecting fertility

Let us now examine some of the indirect social factors. As previously mentioned, this is an unsatisfactory procedure, for it means removing certain customs or practices from their cultural matrix. What appears to be a similar practice may have very different meanings in different societies or be correlated with other factors which may negate or enhance its effect on fertility. In general, the evidence that these indirect social factors limit population growth is far from conclusive.

Age at marriage

Late marriage does appear to reduce fertility, the classic instance being Ireland. In Western Europe, until quite recent times, the age of marriage of women was high and many men and women never married. This had a marked effect on lowering fertility (Revelle 1968). In most other societies, the age at marriage does not seem to be significant in affecting fertility. In the large number of African societies reviewed by Mair (1953) marriage for women generally occurs at puberty or shortly thereafter. In nearly all societies men marry at a later age than women, but this would appear to have no affect on fertility. A number of societies are organized into age sets and this sometimes regulates sexual activity and marriage. Data on this subject are meagre in the otherwise extensive treatment of age groups by Eisenstadt (1956).

Age sets are more commonly found among males than females. In a number of warlike societies (e.g. Masai, Zulu) men in the warrior grade or set were forbidden to marry until the king gave his permission, when the whole age regiment could marry into an age regiment of girls (Gluckman 1940). It is not clear what effect this had on fertility.

In some societies, for example in India, marriage may occur before puberty, but sexual relations do not normally occur until after puberty. In others, for example in the West Indies, marriage occurs late, but regular sexual relations and the production of children may precede marriage. Mair's survey of African marriage and family life cites a trend in a number of societies for later marriage among both men and women in urban conditions, yet illegitimate births also increase under these conditions. Insofar as couples do not set up a household together, sexual relations may be at irregular intervals and lead to reduced fertility.

In most primitive societies marriage occurs early. Two types of explanation may be relevant here: the evolutionary and the social structural. Compared to most other animals, human beings reproduce slowly. They usually produce only one offspring at a time and this offspring is peculiarly helpless and needs a great deal of parental care before it reaches self-sufficiency. The infant mortality rate in many societies is extremely high, so that early unions insure that the female will conceive a maximum number of offspring during her years of fecundity. Not only is infant mortality high in such societies but mortality in general is high and the life span short. Thus, from an evolutionary standpoint, early marriage would seem to promote survival of the species.

Yet among humans evolutionary forces rarely work themselves out directly, and it would be an oversimplification to regard the early age of marriage as a simple evolutionary adaptation. Cultural behaviour almost always intervenes between biological needs and their satisfaction. That this is true for age of marriage can be seen by the variety of social structures that tend to promote it and, more significantly, by the far fewer cases which tend to discourage it.

From the point of view of the social structure, many societies are characterized by lineage, clan and/or joint family organization. Such social forms place great emphasis on continuing the line, and on producing heirs for property and succession to office. This concern motivates people to arrange early marriages for their offspring.

Polygamy

When anthropologists talk about polygamous societies, they mean societies in which polygamy (either polyandry or polygyny) is permitted, not that it is the statistical norm. Polygamous marriages are virtually always a minority of marriages.

Polyandry is so rare and the information about it so meagre, that we can say very little about its effect on fertility. The Toda and the Jaunsari, the two polyandrous societies listed by Nag, show no significant difference in the fertility levels of polyandrously and non-polyandrously married women.

Most investigators have thought that polygyny does reduce fertility, but Lorimer (1954) thinks the opposite. The great difficulty is to determine the extent of polygyny within a given society. Nag's data do not support an association between polygyny and reduced fertility, but he is comparing a whole society in which polygyny is practiced with one in which it is not. A better procedure, as he himself admits, is to compare fertility levels of polygynously and monogamously married women within a single society. Dorjahn (1958) did this for some African societies and claimed that polygyny does reduce fertility, but this conclusion is not confirmed by tests of statistical significance according to Nag. Factors which may reduce the fertility of polygynous union are: (a) lower frequency of coitus per wife. Many societies have rules about the number of nights a husband is required to spend with each wife; (b) age factors. In most polygynous societies it is only older men who have gained enough wealth, power, and prestige to take more than one wife. Second and subsequent wives are usually very young women. It is assumed that such older men are less sexually active than young men. At the same time, the wives are forbidden sexual relations with other men.

Separation and divorce

Nearly all societies make some provision for separation or divorce. To see how this affects fertility, one would need to know for each society: (a) frequency of separation; (b) age of spouses at separation; (c) frequency of remarriage after separation; (d) the length of the interval between separation and remarriage. Though the data are not conclusive, there does seem to be a correlation between a high rate of separation and a low level of fertility. In Jamaica, Roberts (1954) has shown that the fertility level is highest in legal unions, second highest in common law unions, and lowest in casual or visiting unions. Other factors such as abortion, sterility, or frequency of coitus may intervene. Ardener's (1962) data on the Bakweri of the Cameroons also corre-late low fertility with instability of marriage.

Widowhood

Variables affecting fertility are: (a) frequency of remarriage; (b) the age interval between the husband's death and remarriage; (c) the probabilities of women becoming widows at different ages. Social customs vary from absolute prohibition of remarriage and even the immolation of widows (as in *sati* in India), to compulsory remarriage (as in the levirate which obliges a man to raise seed in his brother's widow). In Upper Burma, widow remarriage is infrequent and this is correlated with the socially acceptable role of the un-married person in his family of orientation and the sanction afforded to the unmarried state by Buddhism (Nash and Nash, 1963). Widow remarriage appears to be correlated with the type of kinship and family structure and with economic factors including class. In general, marriage is more stable in patrilineal societies than in matrilineal ones. In the former a woman produces children for her husband's lineage. In the latter she produces them for her own, of which her brother or mother's brother is usually the head. Yet if this affects fertility negatively in matrilineal societies (and there is not very good evidence that it does) the effects may be counteracted by the higher incidence of widow remarriage in matrilineal than in patrilineal societies. This shows the danger of isolating such factors as separation, widowhood, polygamy, and age at marriage. Clearly, they are interrelated in their effects on fertility.

A more important factor than whether a society is matrilineal, patrilineal, or cognatic (without corporate lineages and tracing relationships through both parents) is economic class. In India and China, for example, widow celibacy is usually more strictly enforced among upper classes than in lower classes.

Post-partum abstinence

This varies from a few weeks to two or three years in some societies. A long period of abstinence (i.e. more than one year) does seem to be correlated with lower fertility according to Nag, but there are often other factors inter-vening such as a period of lactation and polygyny. Societies in which coitus is forbidden during lactation often have beliefs that it would harm the child.

Abstinence and menstruation

Belief that coitus should not occur with a menstruating woman is very widespread. A very few societies, such as the Marquesans, the Trukese, the Walapai, and the Maori do permit it (Ford and Beach 1952). Beliefs supporting abstinence vary from the idea that it is disgusting to notions about the danger and ritual impurity of menstrual blood. In some societies women retire to a special house during menstruation. Orthodox Hindus will not allow a menstruating woman to prepare food for the household. As ova are not released during menstruation, it is unlikely that abstinence during this period affects fertility.

Ceremonial abstinence

In many societies sexual abstinence is associated with religious fasts or rituals, for example, to ensure success in hunting or during periods of mourning. Their occurrence is irregular, but among Hindus it has been estimated that there are about 24 such days per year (Chandrasekaran 1952). It is difficult to estimate the effect that ceremonial abstinence has on fertility levels, but it would not seem to be great.

Celibacy

Obviously no society enjoins permanent celibacy on all its members. In most societies celibacy is to be avoided at all costs and no individual remains unmarried unless he is seriously physically disabled or a mental deviant. A number of societies have special roles for such deviants, who may become mediums or ritual specialists. In some societies, particularly warlike societies which are organized into age grades, sexual relations may be forbidden to young men in the warrior grade. Among the Zulus, as mentioned above, the king's age regiments were forbidden to marry and were required to live at his capital until, after a number of years, he gave them permission to marry and disperse. Similarly, the plains Indians of North America often went through a period of celibacy as warriors. Sometimes such celibate periods may be organized around religion. Thus, in Buddhist countries young men are expected to spend several years as novices during which they should not engage in sexual relations. The effect of such practices is to delay the age of marriage, so it is possible that they have some negative effect on fertility. Again, we simply do not have any figures to substantiate this.

Permanent celibacy for significant numbers of a population seems to be confined to complex societies. Permanent spinsterhood in Ireland or in Victorian England, for example, seems to be correlated with economic factors (see Davis and Blake 1956). Permanent celibacy for any considerable number of males seems to be confined to certain religious orders such as those found among Roman Catholics and Buddhists, but it does not appear to have occurred on a scale large enough to affect fertility levels.

Frequency of coitus

It is, of course, exceedingly difficult to obtain information about actual frequency of coitus. Easier to obtain are people's beliefs about frequency. What bearing these have on actual frequencies must remain an open question. A few societies such as the Yap of Micronesia and Juang of Orissa are reported to believe that excessive coitus is harmful, but there is no evidence as to how this affects frequency. The Crow Indians are reported to believe that it is weakening to have intercourse every night, but find it difficult to have it less frequently (Ford and Beach 1952)! In Nag's sample, only among the Yap does a low frequency of coitus appear to be correlated with low fertility. A study by Nag (1970) reports that average frequency of coitus among Indian women is less than among American white women of corresponding age but maintains that this results in a very small difference in fertility level. An important variable affecting frequency is age and this is rarely mentioned in ethnographic accounts about coitus. The evidence for frequency of coitus variables is so poor that no conclusions can be drawn. One can only guess that it is unlikely to be so low in the vast majority of societies as to affect fertility significantly.

Direct factors affecting fertility

Direct factors limiting fertility involve problems of motivation, so that it becomes even more important to examine the social context in which such actions are taken than was the case with indirect factors. Our information about the incidence of contraception, abortion, and infanticide in most societies is meagre. Nag reports contraception as having a high negative effect on fertility in only 5 of the 61 societies which he considers to have factors affecting fertility negatively. Abortion is reported as having a high negative effect in 13 societies, but there is no information for 22 of the 61 societies in the sample. Infanticide is not even listed because the data are so scanty.

Contraception

A fairly large number of simple societies are reported to use various plants to attempt to produce temporary or permanent sterility in males and females, but their extent and efficacy are not known. A post-coital douche is also reported in a number of societies. However, by far the most commonly reported contraceptive technique is *coitus interruptus*. As Glass (1963) has pointed out, this method was instrumental in the West before modern chemical and mechanical techniques became available, and only in the United States has it ceased to be one of the major techniques employed. Seppilli (1960), reporting on a rural community in central Italy, notes a 50 per cent drop in birth rate between 1930 and 1950 brought on entirely by increased abortion and contraception through the practice of *coitus interruptus*. It should be noted that this is almost invariably a male-initiated technique, though Schapera (1941) reports that among the Kgatla of Botswana the women sometimes initiate it by moving their hips or turning over as they feel the man nearing ejaculation. He also reports this leads to quarrels.

The patterns of relations between the sexes can be studied from at least two aspects which may be put as questions: With whom do sexual relations take place? With whom are sexual matters discussed? These rarely coincide. In many societies one can discuss sexual matters with people, even people of the opposite sex, with whom it would be unthinkable to have sexual relations, and it is often considered highly improper to discuss sexual matters with one's sexual partner, particularly if that partner is one's spouse. A Manus of the Admiralty Islands can make lewd jokes and even fondle the breasts of his female cross cousin, but he may not copulate with her. His relations with his wife are rather strained and formal if not actually hostile. Such attitudes are linked with other factors in the social structure; for example, he is heavily in debt to pay for his marriage, and he may be assisted by his cross cousin (Mead 1930). In investigating motivations for limiting fertility the patterns of communications between the sexes are major variables which have been too often neglected by family planners.

Abortion

Unlike *coitus interruptus*, abortion is almost invariably a female-initiated technique. It can often be done without the knowledge of the male. It is very widely reported in simple societies but is generally socially disapproved, and it is very difficult to say anything about its extent. A further difficulty lies in the failure by many investigators to distinguish between abortion and miscarriage. Abortion may be demographically important in some societies. Schneider (1955) reports it is widely practiced on Yap, where women are not expected to have children until they are in their thirties. Youth is defined as a period of sexual licence, when a woman should not be tied down with children. Frequent abortions by young women sometimes cause sterility. Yap is in fact becoming depopulated. A similar practice seems to prevail in Formosa where Devereux (1955) reports some women had as many as 16 abortions.

Infanticide

Infanticide allows for selection of personal characteristics of the offspring such as sex and physical condition. Motivating factors can be ritual or economic. In some societies twins are considered unpropitious and one or both may be killed. Other societies consider them a highly favourable omen. Unusual births, such as children born feet first or with teeth or whose mothers died at birth or who are born on unlucky days may be killed (Davis and Blake 1956). Except possibly for a very few societies like the Rendille of Kenya who kill boys born on Wednesday or after the eldest brother has been circumcised (Spencer 1965), infanticide for ritual reasons would not seem to have much effect in reducing fertility levels.

Infanticide for economic reasons seems to be closely linked with the food supply. It occurs among peoples living in very harsh environments, for example, the Eskimos (Balikci 1967), or in very restricted environments such as small islands, for example, the Tikopia (Firth 1936), or among those living in great poverty, for example, the Chinese (Fei 1939). In such societies, it is usually female infants who are killed, and this factor is closely linked to other aspects of the social structure. Thus the Netsilik Eskimos kill girl babies (usually by allowing them to freeze or smothering them) because women do not hunt, are not self-sufficient, and require years of care only to leave at marriage (Balikci 1967). The practice is so prevalent along the arctic coast that male children outnumber females by two to one, at least in four groups which were surveyed by Weyer (1932).

Among the Tikopia of Polynesia infanticide is at the discretion of the father who turns down the face of an unwanted child immediately after birth. Reasons given by informants usually had to do with potential food supplies, though sometimes illegitimacy was a cause. It is not clear from Firth's material whether male or female infanticide was more prevalent, but he quotes an informant who stated: 'The work of the women is to plait mats and fill the water-bottles, and when one or two girls have been born, that is enough! But men go out and catch fish and do other work' (Firth 1936).

Among the peasant cultivators of the Yangtze plain studied by Fei in the 1930s the smallness of individual holdings meant economic disaster if too many children were born. Abortion was frequently practised as was infanticide. Males were sometimes killed, but it was far more usual to kill females. Fei found a ratio of only 100 girls to 135 boys in the 0–5 age group. The Chinese kinship system is strongly patrilineal and patrilocal marriage is practiced. Thus, girls are an economic burden on their parents and leave the household as soon as they are mature. Moreover, they must take a considerable dowry with them on marriage. Patrilineality is strongly reinforced by ancestor worship; only a son can perform these rites for his parents and only a son can carry on the line.

Female infants may not be killed outright, but in families where food is short, sons are better fed. Even where girls do not actually starve, epidemics will be much more likely to carry them off than their better-nourished brothers (Lang 1946). The situation is similar for India.

This brief survey of direct and indirect factors affecting fertility has shown that for the vast majority of societies there are few social mechanisms for controlling fertility, and that those that exist, except in a very few societies, do not appear to be very effective. The fact is that in most societies people do not wish to restrict fertility. On the contrary, they desire to produce the maximum number of children.

Social factors and family size

It is often assumed that the availability of food supplies limits population. Yet the relationship is not a simple one. In an extensive review of the evidence Wynne-Edwards (1962) has shown that non-human animal populations do not expand to the absolute limits of the food supply. If this were so, one would find starving animals, but such conditions are the exception not the rule. There are intervening variables which limit population growth before starvation does. These intervening variables consist in the social behaviour of animals which limits the access of some members of the species to food and mates. Examples of such behaviour are territoriality, by which an animal or group of animals marks out a territory which he or they will defend against interlopers of the same species, and hierarchy, by which high-ranking animals have priority to food and mates. Wynne-Edwards postulates that these same processes apply or applied to *Homo sapiens*. A similar argument has been put forward by Stott (1962). Such theories lay great stress on indirect social factors for limiting population. As Douglas (1966) has pointed out, they really do not work for human societies. Though we can find both territorial and hierarchical behaviour among humans, this has conspicuously not led to a control of population. In animal societies, we find such social behaviours as territory and hierarchy intervening between the animal's basic needs for food and mates and their satisfaction. In human societies we find a whole host of behaviours intervening and these can be broadly described as culture. But cultural factors do not merely intervene, they tend to define needs. Human needs even in the simplest societies are not confined to food and mates or even territory. They have become elaborated, particularly by considerations of status and prestige. The Chinese killed girl babies not simply because there was a shortage of food, but because the status and prestige of the family is manifested in the dowry given to a daughter on marriage and because the lineage can only be perpetuated by males. The Tikopia, too, are patrilineal so that only males can carry on the line. Important ceremonies are performed by males and only males hold office. Even among the Eskimo, it is the males who carry the prestige of the domestic group.

When humans attempt to control their populations, individuals, except in the very extreme cases which I have cited, are not inspired by a concern for scarce basic resources but by a concern for scarce social resources, objects, or behaviours which give status and prestige, which are, of course, defined in terms of scarcity.

In so far as prestige factors are linked with family size, the emphasis in the vast majority of the world's societies is on the maximum production of children. Lorimer (1954) advanced the hypothesis that corporate kin groups, particularly unilineal ones, generate strong motives for high fertility. What evidence we have seems to confirm this. In societies where there is a strong emphasis on the male line of descent, barrenness in women or even the failure to produce a son may lead to the repudiation of a wife. The pressures on women to produce children do not cease after one or two children, and this is due to the high social value of children and the way the production of children is built into the political, economic, and social systems of the society. One of the reasons for this is the high infant mortality rate in primitive and peasant societies. High infant mortality is not only the fact in such societies, but also the expectation. Due to the spread of medical services in recent years, the facts have changed more quickly than the expectations.

In most simple societies the lines of kinship are the lines of political power, social prestige, and economic agrandizement. The more children a man has, the more successful marriage alliances he can arrange, increasing his own power and influence by linking himself to men of greater power or to men who will be his supporters. Considerable economic exchanges in cattle in Africa, in shell money, yams, and pigs in the Pacific, in produce, consumer goods, and money in peasant societies take place at marriages. The man with many children controls much wealth. In terms of economic production more children mean an increased food supply and perhaps the production of surpluses for trade. Most of the world's religions place great emphasis on the production of children. In many societies fertility cults, often linking human fertility with that of natural products, abound. These and many similar practices and beliefs place a high value on children. In primitive and peasant societies the man with few children is the man of minor influence and the childless man is virtually a social nonentity. Some of these customs and beliefs may have a high survival value where the mortality rate is high, as they keep the society well supplied with new members. But they are proving disastrous where the mortality rate is low and resources to maintain life are limited.

It is only in societies or sections of a society where status and prestige factors operate against large families that individuals attempt to limit the number of their offspring. To return to the example of the rural community in central Italy where the birth rate dropped by 50 per cent in twenty years (Seppilli 1960), we find this to be correlated with marked economic and social changes. In 1930 the community was chiefly engaged in farming. The extended patriarchal family was the norm. More children meant more help on the farm. The economy was basically a subsistence one. By 1950 the community had become almost a dormitory suburb of the nearby town of Rieti, where many men and some women worked in factories. Instead of living in large rural homesteads dependent on the produce of the land, many now lived in small houses or flats and were dependent on a wage. To have many children was now seen as an economic hardship dragging the whole family down. The emphasis was on conjugal family living with few children whom it was desired to educate. There was a greater desire for consumer goods.

A significant point to be derived from this and other studies is that it is upwardly mobile couples who tend to want to limit their families because they see that this mobility will be accelerated by having smaller families, and they have entered into a system in which prestige factors are not linked to children. The very poor even in industrial societies can often see no advantage in limiting their children. At the lowest levels, ten children are no more of a handicap than nine. The child as yet unborn may be the very one who will help his parents. If a man does not have dependents, on whom will *he* depend when he is old and ill? In countries, such as Britain, which pay family allowances, these act as a positive inducement to have children, especially in families where cash is chronically short.

The cognatic system of kinship with its stress on the nuclear family often accompanied by neolocal residence at marriage seems to adapt itself more easily to limiting the number of its offspring than do the unilineal systems of kinship. In Upper Burma, for example, there are important social and economic roles for unmarried children in the nuclear household, and little parental pressure to force them to marry. In Upper Burma there is a late age of marriage, a high percentage of bachelors and spinsters, and a low rate of widow and widower remarriage (Nash and Nash 1963). There is also a low rate of population growth. The European pattern of delayed marriage for women was, according to Revelle, very responsive to changing economic conditions. In periods of economic stress, marriages were postponed. When economic conditions improved, the number of marriages increased (Revelle 1968). Married couples also limited the numbers of their children. David Heer, following a scheme developed by Joseph Spengler, analyses the decision to have children as a function of a preference system having to do not only with income and the price system but with the system of social status. With economic development, he sees a shift from ascribed to achieved status. The latter, with its emphasis on conspicuous consumption means that people will forego extra children in favour of more consumer goods (Heer 1968). It should be born in mind, however, that particular behaviours or possessions which bring prestige are subject to rapid change. Large numbers of children have been indices of high status in many societies for many centuries. Economic development may diminish the desire for children temporarily, but affluence may rekindle it.

An attempt to regulate fertility in Mauritius

The interplay of social factors affecting fertility can be appreciated if we examine an attempt to regulate fertility on the island of Mauritius in the Indian Ocean. The newly independent nation of Mauritius has an area of 720 miles^2 and a population of 823 000 increasing at the rate of about 2·2 per cent per annum. Mauritius is a plural society. It had no indigenous inhabitants, but today is composed of 51 per cent Hindus and 16 per cent Muslims, both of Indian origin; 28 per cent Creoles of mixed African or Indian and European ancestry; 3 per cent Chinese and 2 per cent Europeans mostly of French descent (Benedict 1961, 1965). The population explosion is a post-World War II phenomenon and was brought on almost entirely by the eradication of malaria. By 1963 expenditure on public assistance had surpassed expenditure on education as the most costly item in the government budget.

In 1960 a commission headed by Professor R. M. Titmuss proposed a series of disincentives for large families which it was hoped would limit population growth while at the same time offering some help to the poorest families (Titmuss and Abel-Smith 1961). The plan proposed to pay a cash benefit to all families with three or more children under 14, provided the mother was over 21. No payments were to be given to families with fewer than three children nor would there be additional payments for more than three children. Parents with fewer than three children were to be rewarded by higher old age pensions. To encourage the spacing of children, a cash maternity payment would be made to women who had not borne children in the previous two years, again provided she had fewer than three children and was over 21. As an incentive to delay marriage, a payment would be made to the father of the bride provided she and her husband were over 21 at the time of marriage and that the girl had not previously borne children. All these provisions only applied to families in which the household head was not liable to income tax; that is to say, to the poor.

This plan was unlikely to work because it was based on assumptions which were not those of Mauritians. It assumed a degree of planning among poor Mauritians which they could not afford. Mauritians live in a cash economy; nearly all necessities can only be bought with cash. The demand for cash, particularly among the poor, is overwhelming (Benedict 1958). In these circumstances, it was likely that large numbers of couples would attempt to secure the cash benefit which is paid only on the birth of the third child by having three children as quickly as possible. Even if a woman delayed marriage and childbearing until she was 21 (thereby allowing her father to receive a payment) and spaced her children at two-year intervals (thereby qualifying for the maternity benefit), she could still have three children by the age of 25, leaving a considerable period of fertility before her.

The incentives to qualify for the three-child cash benefit would probably outweigh the incentives for the spacing of children, for the maternity benefit was not worth nearly so much as the three-child one. At the low economic levels at which most labourers live, a family which was receiving a cash benefit on the birth of the third child would probably not consider itself to be much worse off, and probably would not be much worse off on the birth of a fourth child. The fourth and possibly subsequent children were unlikely to be seen as diminishing opportunities for those who already existed. They might be the very ones who would succeed. Certainly the promise of a higher old age pension, which one might not live long enough to collect, was exceedingly unlikely to inhibit procreation. Such long-term planning is a luxury which is not available to the very poor.

Both Hinduism and Islam place a very high value on the production of children, particularly male children. Wives can be and are returned to their parents if they fail to produce children. A woman does not gain fully adult status until she is a mother, not just a wife. Her future depends not on an old age pension but on having sons. They are her social security. They win the respect of her husband and her mother-in-law. They assure her that she will be a mother-in-law herself. A man too must have some sons to carry on his lineage, to help him in his work, to bring him honour and status in the community. The pressures to marry early and to produce children and especially sons early are very strong. They operate against provisions for spacing children and for postponing marriage.

Postponing a girl's marriage until she is 21, runs counter to a whole range of Indian (both Hindu and Muslim) religious and social values. Moreover, from an economic point of view, no poor Indo-Mauritian family could afford it. It is well known that Indians favour early marriage for girls. A girl must be a virgin when she marries, but she has natural sexual desires and it is not only unkind to frustrate these by keeping her from marrying, but it becomes increasingly difficult to control her and keep her away from men as she gets older. Among Indo-Mauritians marriages are still arranged by the parents and it is a major religious duty for a man to marry off his daughters. The longer marriage is postponed the more difficult it becomes to arrange, for doubts are cast on the girl's character and that of her family. An unmarried girl must be protected and her reputation carefully guarded. She cannot be allowed to wander about or to go to work alone, but must be kept in the house. Poor Indo-Mauritians cannot afford to keep a girl in relative idleness until she is 21. A further difficulty arises when sons marry. Patrilocality is the rule among Indo-Mauritians, at least in the early years of marriage. A girl in her late teens or early twenties is not apt to get along very well with her brothers' wives. They resent her interference, particularly if she is not working as hard as they are. They have enough trouble with their husbands' mother, without having to deal with an adult unmarried sister's claims on their husbands. The newly-married man is put in a difficult position. Does he side with his wife or his sister when they quarrel?

A curious aspect of the Titmuss proposal was that the marriage benefit was to be paid to the father of the girl, not to the girl herself. This could hardly be an inducement for the girl to wait patiently at home for four or five years after the normal age of marriage in Mauritius. It also assumes that the father would be able to control his daughter. Even in Indo-Mauritian families, girls grow more independent as they grow older. Few fathers in Mauritius, particularly in poor families, could exercise such control. Few mothers would support the attempt. The whole notion is based on an idea of a very autocratic patriarchial family which hardly exists in Mauritius, particularly among the poor. Only the wealthy can be effectively autocratic; only the wealthy can afford late marriage for their daughters, but wealthy fathers would not be eligible to receive the marriage benefit. It is clear that the small marriage benefit could not outweigh the factors conducive to early marriage among Indo-Mauritians. Among Creoles, who tend to marry later, the marriage benefit might be more frequently paid, but there would be even less excuse for paying it to the girl's father. Many of the poorer Creoles live in consensual unions of varying duration. Illegitimacy is common. The husband/father is often a peripheral role as has been described for the West Indies. Under such circumstances, to pay a benefit to a girl's father could hardly affect the decision of a girl to postpone marriage to the age of 21.

A final difficulty with the proposals was a political one. The report stressed the need for determined government action. Mauritius was moving rapidly toward independence. The British Government wanted to help solve the population problem but they also wanted political stability. Many politicians in Mauritius wanted power. The problems of pluralism were ever present. The temptations to pluck the roses such as the payment of family cash benefits and avoid the thorns such as a vigorous birth control programme were very strong. Yet attempts were made. In April 1960 the Financial Secretary, a British Civil Servant, announced in the Legislature that Government had decided to implement a policy of planned parenthood based on the Titmuss proposals backed up with birth-control clinics and a massive publicity campaign. These proposals met a storm of opposition from the Catholic Church, from leading Franco-Mauritian politicians, from some Hindu and Muslim leaders, and even from some supporters of the Government. The opposition was so strong that the government, fearing defeat, adjourned debate for a year. In April 1961 the debate resumed. By this time, the Catholic opposition had agreed that the rhythm or safe period method of contraception could be used. This, of course, is a very inefficient method of birth control. The Legislative Council failed to set up an effective birth control programme, but it passed a family-allowance scheme granting Rs. 15 per month to non-taxpaying families with three or more children under the age of 14. In 1964 the Roman Catholic Church informed the Minister of Health that it would have no objection to government funds being used to subsidize voluntary family-planning agencies even where their methods differed from those approved by the Church. A voluntary family-planning association was already functioning in the island. (For information on the founding of this association and its subsequent history, see Benedict, 1971.) Aid was solicited from overseas organization and publicity campaigns were mounted in 1965–6.

It is probably too late to avoid demographic disaster in Mauritius, and the rest of the world may have to rescue this island people from the consequences of their overbreeding. Yet these consequences were clearly predictable in the 1940s. If birth control had been introduced then, would enough people have practised it to slow or halt population growth? One cannot be easy about the answer. Most Mauritians are too poor to plan their families. It is difficult to imagine what would have persuaded them to do so. In the 1950s most people in Mauritius were ignorant, misinformed, and/or hostile to birth control. These attitudes have changed, and some Mauritians are now practising birth control. The experience in Mauritius shows that birth control depends on a great many more factors than the availability of easily-used contraceptives. There must be an understanding of the social structure of the community. If family-planning concerns intimate relations between men and women, it also concerns political and economic relations within the whole community. Family planning succeeds or fails insofar as people see their own individual life chances in terms of more or fewer children. These estimates vary not only between groups and individuals but can change for a given individual over the course of his life. Governments can influence these attitudes and estimates, but not without a thorough understanding of the social milieu in which they are embedded.

Summary

In animal societies there are certain mechanisms of social behaviour which tend to control access to food and mates. In a sense, status is involved as it is chiefly the high-ranking animals which have this access. Such social behaviour in animals tends to limit population growth. Animals have developed anatomical structures and conventionalized forms of behaviour operating always within the same competitive framework of access to food and mates. Man lives in a highly adaptive social framework in which the objects for which he competes and the very rules of competition can change rapidly. Such social behaviour in man is not necessarily linked to population control. Douglas (1966) shows for a number of societies that population control is not related to subsistence but to competition for power and prestige. In most societies insofar as scarce social resources are connected with population, they emphasize the production of the maximum number of children. In some sections of industrial and urban societies and in a very few simple societies prestige factors may be linked with small family size. Except under the harshest ecological and economic conditions, human beings do not regulate their populations in relation to the food supply, but in relation to the prestige supply.

REFERENCES

ALLISON, A. (ed.) (1970). *Population control*. Penguin Books, Harmondsworth.
ARDENER, E. (1962). *Divorce and fertility: an African study*. Oxford University Press, London.
BALIKCI, A. (1967). Female infanticide on the Arctic coast. *Man: Jl. R. anthrop. Inst.* N.S. **2**, 615–25.
BENEDICT, B. (1958). Cash and credit in Mauritius. *S. Afr. J. Econ.* **26**, 213–21.
—— (1961). *Indians in a plural society*. H.M.S.O., London.
—— (1965). *Mauritius: Problems of a plural society*. Pall Mall, London.
—— (1971). Controlling population growth in Mauritius. In *Technological innovation and culture change* (eds. H. R. Bernard and P. J. Pelto). Macmillan, New York.
CHANDRASEKARAN, C. (1952). Cultural patterns in relation to family planning in India. In *Proc. III Int. Conf. Planned Parenthood*, Bombay.

DAVIS, K. and BLAKE, J. (1956). Social structure and fertility: an analytical framework. *Econ. Devel. cult. Change* **4**, 211–35.

DEVEREUX, G. (1955). *A study of abortion in primitive societies.* The Julian Press, New York.

DORJAHN, V. R. (1958). Fertility, polygyny, and their interrelations in Temne society. *Am. Anthrop.* **60**, 838–60.

DOUGLAS, M. (1966). Population control in primitive groups. *Br. J. Sociol.* **17**, 263–73.

EISENSTADT, S. N. (1956). *From generation to generation.* Routledge and Kegan Paul, London.

EISNER, T., VAN TIENHOVEN, A., and ROSENBLATT, F. (1970). Population control, sterilization, and ignorance. *Science, N.Y.* **167**, 337.

FEI, H. T. (1939). *Peasant life in China.* Routledge and Kegan Paul, London.

FIRTH, R. (1936). *We, the Tikopia.* Allen and Unwin, London.

—— (1959). *Social change in Tikopia.* Allen and Unwin, London.

FORD, C. S. and BEACH, F. A. (1952). *Patterns of sexual behaviour.* University Paperbacks, London.

GLASS, D. V. (1963). Fertility and birth control in developed societies: their relevance to the problems of developing countries. *Family Planning* **12**, 5–8.

GLUCKMAN, M. (1940). The Kingdom of the Zulu of South Africa. In *African political systems* (eds. M. Fortes and E. E. Evans-Pritchard). Oxford University Press, London.

HEER, D. M. (1968). Economic development and the fertility transition. *Daedalus, Cambridge, Mass.* **97**, 447–62.

LANG, O. (1946). *Chinese family and society.* Yale University Press, New Haven.

LORIMER, F., FORTES, M., BUSIA, K. A., RICHARDS, A. I., REINING, P., and MORTARA, G. 1954. *Culture and human fertility.* U.N.E.S.C.O., Paris.

MAIR, L. P. (1953). African marriage and social change. In *Survey of African marriage and family life* (ed. A. Phillips). Oxford University Press, London.

MEAD, M. (1930). *Growing up in New Guinea.* Morrow, New York.

—— (1956). *New lives for old.* Morrow, New York.

NAG, M. (1962). *Factors affecting human fertility in non-industrial societies: a cross-cultural study.* Yale University Publications in Anthropology No. **66**, New Haven.

—— (1970). Frequency of coitus as a factor affecting human fertility. *Curr. Anthrop. Letter to Associates* **51**, 540C.

NASH, J. and NASH, M. (1963). Marriage, fertility, and population growth in Upper Burma. *SWest. J. Anthrop.* **19**, 251–66.

REVELLE, R. (1968). Introduction to Historical Population Studies. *Daedalus, Cambridge, Mass.* **97**, 353–62.

ROBERTS, G. W. (1954). Some aspects of mating and fertility in the West Indies. *Popul. Stud.* **8**, 199–227.

SCHAPERA, I. (1941). *Married life in an African tribe.* Faber and Faber, New York.

SCHNEIDER, D. M. (1955). Abortion and depopulation on a Pacific island. In *Health, culture, and community* (eds. B. Paul and W. B. Miller). Russell Sage Foundation, New York.

SEPPILLI, T. (1960). Social conditions of fertility in a rural community in transition in central Italy. In *Culture, science, and health* (ed. V. Rubin). *Ann. NY. Acad. Sci.* **84.**

SPENCER, P. (1965). *The Samburu.* University of California Press, Berkeley and Los Angeles.

STOTT, D. H. (1962). Cultural and natural checks on population growth. In *Culture and the evolution of man* (ed. M. F. Ashley Montagu). Oxford University Press, New York.

TITMUS, R. M., ABEL-SMITH, B., and LYNES, T. (1961). *Social policies and population growth in Mauritius.* Methuen, London.

WEYER, E. M. (1932). *The Eskimos.* Yale University Press, New Haven.

WYNNE-EDWARDS, V. C. (1962). *Animal dispersion in relation to social behaviour.* Oliver and Boyd, London.

6

FACTORS ASSOCIATED WITH THE SEX RATIO IN HUMAN POPULATIONS

MICHAEL S. TEITELBAUM

Terminology

THE sex ratio, an indicator of the relative number of males and females in a population, is a basic measure in demography, genetics, and epidemiology. Unfortunately, however, the term *sex ratio* is often used imprecisely. Sometimes the proportion of a population which is male, i.e.

$$\left(\frac{\text{Males}}{\text{Males}+\text{Females}}\right)$$

is called the 'sex ratio'; the convention in demography, and the one to be employed here, is:

$$\text{Sex ratio} = \left(\frac{\text{Males}}{\text{Females}} \times 100\right)$$

According to either definition, a 'high' sex ratio implies a high number of males relative to the number of females.

By convention, sex ratios are calculated for three stages of human development, but these conventions too are imprecise. The *primary sex ratio* is defined as the sex ratio at either 'conception' or 'fertilization', although these two terms are not completely synonymous. The *secondary sex ratio* normally refers to the sex ratio of live births, but stillbirths are sometimes included. The *tertiary sex ratio* is even more indeterminate; it refers to the sex ratio of a cohort at some age after live birth, possibly at 'marriage age' or at age of 'independence'. It is not clear why there should be such terminological difficulty concerning the sex ratio. Instead of speaking loosely of 'primary', 'secondary', and 'tertiary' sex ratios, it would involve no great effort to specify exactly what is meant, e.g. 'live-birth sex ratio', 'stillbirth sex ratio', 'sex ratio at fertilization', etc. In this paper such specific nomenclature will be employed, with the understanding that 'sex ratio at birth' is equivalent to 'live-birth sex ratio', and that in the interest of brevity a simple reference to 'the sex ratio' may be used when its meaning is absolutely clear from the context.

Importance of the live-birth sex ratio to demographic models

Demographers have long recognized that the simple tabulation of live births per 1000 population (the crude birth-rate) is an inaccurate indicator of the true reproductive performance and potential of a population. Not only is it insensitive to changes in the age distribution of the population, but it likewise fails to take into account the total production of 'breeders' for the next generation. Since only the female can reproduce (the male acting more in the role of 'accessory'), the rate at which females are produced is of primary importance to demographic models. For example, even with an unchanging age distribution, it is possible to have an increase in the birth rate in conjunction with a decrease in the absolute numbers of females produced. This would involve an increase in the sex ratio. Hence, if the live-birth sex ratio is not a constant, as has often been assumed, it must be considered as a possibly significant factor in the reproductivity of a population or of parts of it.

Demographers have not, of course, been blind to this point; for example, the demographic measures *gross reproduction rate* and *net reproduction rate* were devised with the sex-ratio factor in mind, at least implicitly. These measures are used to show by what proportion a synthetic cohort of potential mothers following the current fertility schedule may be expected to replace itself, account being taken (net rate) or not taken (gross rate) of the proportions of female offspring expected to survive to the age of their mothers under the current mortality schedule. Despite this recognition that it is the replacement of *females* that is of importance to the reproductivity of the population, demographers often make a possibly unwarranted assumption that the sex ratio is a constant 105 or 106, considering that significant deviations from this constant are indicative of data deficiencies rather than of real variation.

For example, a common procedure for obtaining the net reproduction rate (NRR) is to calculate the number of total births expected according to given fertility and mortality schedules (total expected births = sum of the products of each current age-specific birth rate and the probability of women in this population surviving to the mid-point of this age interval), and then dividing by 2·05 (i.e., $(105+100)/100$) to account for the 'constant' sex ratio of 105. Such a procedure is taught in the most popular of the introductory textbooks (Thompson and Lewis 1965), as shown in Table 6.1. The net reproduction rate of this population, assuming a sex ratio of 105, is NRR = $348·524/205$ = 1·700.

The demographic significance of the assumption of a uniform sex ratio of 105 may be given a simplified and artificial illustration by considering the possibility that the above population P is composed of two sub-populations P_1 and P_2 of equal size and with identical age-specific birth rates and female mortality schedules, but with differing sex ratios.† Let us assume, for example, that while the aggregate sex ratio of P is 105, that of P_1 is 109 and that of P_2 is 101. (Sex ratio differences of this order of magnitude are indicated by data to be described later.) Hence P_1 and P_2 differ from each other only in

TABLE 6.1

Net reproduction rate, California, 1960
(from Thompson and Lewis 1965)

Age of mother	Number of years lived in age interval by a birth cohort of 100 000 females	Age-specific birth rates	Calculated number of births
15–19	484 208	0·1028	49·777
20–4	482 693	0·2673	129·024
25–9	480 803	0·1891	90·920
30–4	478 259	0·1034	49·452
35–9	474 665	0·0483	22·926
40–4	469 409	0·0130	6·102
45–9	461 537	0·0007	0·323
Total	—	0·7246	348·524

their sex ratios. In this situation, the net reproduction rates of P_1 and P_2 differ markedly:

$$\text{NRR}\ (P_1) = \frac{348 \cdot 524}{209} = 1 \cdot 6676$$

$$\text{NRR}\ (P_2) = \frac{348 \cdot 524}{201} = 1 \cdot 7340$$

Since NRR (P_2)/NRR$(P_1) = 1 \cdot 7340/1 \cdot 6676 = 1 \cdot 0398$, the net reproduction rate of P_2 is 3·98 per cent higher than that of P_1 solely by virtue of their differing sex ratios. The implications of such a difference in net reproduction rate on the intrinsic rate of increase r (the rate of increase of the stable population) may be calculated as follows, assuming that P_1 and P_2 have the same length of generation (T) as does P (where $T = 25 \cdot 86$):

$$r = \frac{\log_e \text{NRR}}{T}$$

† The primary artificiality of this situation is the assumption of identical age-specific birth rates and female mortality schedules for the two stable populations. The difference in sex ratio at birth would imply a subsequent difference in sex ratio at reproductive age, unless male mortality schedules differed substantially. Such differences in the relative numbers of marriageable males and females at each age would be expected to affect age-specific birth rates by influencing proportions married and/or age at marriage.

$$P_1 : r_1 = \frac{\log_e 1 \cdot 6676}{25 \cdot 86}$$

$$= \frac{0 \cdot 511\ 38}{25 \cdot 86} = 0 \cdot 019\ 77$$

$$P_2 : r_2 = \frac{\log_e 1 \cdot 7340}{25 \cdot 86}$$

$$= \frac{0 \cdot 550\ 43}{25 \cdot 86} = 0 \cdot 021\ 28$$

This is a difference in r of $0 \cdot 001\ 51$, a noteworthy difference given the small range of r. For example, calculations of the doubling time of these two populations show that P_1 would take $35 \cdot 1$ years to double, while P_2 would take only $32 \cdot 6$ years. Hence, two sub-populations differing only in their sex ratios have different intrinsic growth rates as a result, and the assumption of a uniform sex ratio of 105 or 106 may conceal such differences. The change in r implied by changes in the sex ratio will be of even greater interest if effective and easily used techniques of sex predetermination are ever developed (see below).

Importance of the sex ratio to biological models

Observations that the sex ratio of live births is almost always greater than 100 have affected biological models since the time of Aristotle, as the sex ratio of the various processes is a critical indicator of the nature of reproduction. Sex ratio is of interest to the study of at least the following reproductive processes.

Spermatogenesis. The sex of a foetus is known to be determined by the nature of the spermatozoon which fertilizes the ovum. It is possible that more male-producing (Y-carrying) spermatozoa are produced than are female-producing ones (X-carrying). Indeed, Shettles (1964) has claimed to have found two discrete populations of spermatozoa, the 'smaller, round-head' and the 'larger, elongate-head' present in normal seminal fluid in an overall ratio of 2:1 round-head to elongate-head. This, he suggests, could explain the preponderance of male foetuses, if the rounded sperm were Y and the elongated X.

Sperm access to ovum. It has been suggested that the Y sperm, whether due to innate properties or environmental conditions, is more likely to reach the ovum, thereby increasing the probability of a male conceptus (assuming that the process of fertilization is random). Such differential access could be due to a variety of factors, including the longevity, activity, or mass of the sperm itself, or various characteristics of the vaginal and uterine environment.

Fertilization. The process of fertilization is as yet little understood, and it is therefore possible that one type of sperm is favoured during the process.

Implantation. $4\frac{1}{2}$ to 7 days after fertilization, the zygote must be implanted in the uterine wall. It has been suggested that one type of zygote is favoured during this process (Kirby, McWhirter, Teitelbaum, and Darlington 1967).

Gestation. It has long been thought that the sex ratio of abortions and stillbirths is relatively high (Stevenson and Bobrow 1967), and it is therefore generally considered that there is differential wastage of male foetuses during the entire period of gestation. The sexing of early foetuses is difficult, and few data are available, but such differential wastage of male foetuses could be of great importance to the sex ratio at birth (Mikamo 1969).

Birth. It has been suggested that male babies are subjected to greater trauma at birth, possibly due to their larger size (Stern 1960). This is said to account for the reportedly high sex ratio of stillborn babies.

Knowledge concerning the sex ratio, therefore, is intimately connected with the understanding of the process of reproduction—a finding of a deviant sex ratio at a given stage of reproduction is a finding of importance, for it implies selective mechanisms which must be examined if the reproductive process itself is to be well understood.

Importance of the sex ratio to genetic models

Perhaps the most substantial literature on the live-birth sex ratio is in the discipline of genetics. In general, we may point to two broad areas of genetic interest in the sex ratio. The first area concerns the question of *genetic variability and heritability of the live-birth sex ratio* itself. The second area involves the use of live-birth sex ratio data as an *indicator of mutation rates*. In a sense, these two approaches are different ways of looking at the same phenomenon: the one considers the sex ratio as a normal genetic trait, subject to natural selection. The other implicitly assumes the sex ratio to be given, and deviations from the normal as indicators of other genetic changes. We shall deal with these two areas in turn.

The question of the heritability of the live-birth sex ratio has an extensive literature of its own. This literature has been reviewed in an excellent and complete manner by Edwards (1962b), and a repetition of his efforts is not necessary here. In general, the search for genetically-controlled variability and heritability of the sex ratio has not been fruitful. Very extensive analyses and re-analyses have been made to prove or disprove the heritability hypothesis, but often these have been applied to data of questionable accuracy, and on occasion even numerical inaccuracies of analysis have affected interpretation of results (Turpin and Schutzenberger 1948, Edwards 1959). At the conclusion of his extensive review of this literature, Edwards (1962b) notes that 'little progress has been made in establishing the heritability of the sex ratio', and that 'it must be concluded that, if genetic variability exists, it is of a very low order of magnitude'. The situation is apparently no different today, for Edwards has recently expressed similarly negative conclusions (Edwards 1970). There is therefore little to be gained here from an extensive consideration of the possible heritability of the sex ratio.

Before moving to the other area of genetical interest in the sex ratio, however, a brief comment should be made concerning Fisher's theory of the role of natural selection in determining the sex ratio (1958). Fisher was addressing himself to a problem posed earlier by Darwin as to whether the sex ratio was a genetic segregation subject to natural selection. Fisher's argument was essentially an economic one: The total parental 'expenditure' (effort, time, money, etc.) incurred by parents in raising children of each sex to reproductive age will be equal. Otherwise, those parents genetically inclined (assuming genetic control of the sex ratio) to produce the 'cheaper' sex (in total expenditure terms) would produce more reproductive value per unit expenditure. This would tend to increase the proportion of the 'cheaper' sex reared in future generations. Hence the sex ratio is subject to natural selection in the sense that it will adjust to the relative expenditure necessary to rear the two sexes to reproductive age.

The Fisherian theory is a very difficult one to test, as Shaw and Mohler (1953) have long ago pointed out. It is essentially a non-genetic argument, employing such a diffuse term as 'parental expenditure' as its critical variable. Only when this term is interpreted as implying simply 'survivorship' or 'reproductive value' does the concept become genetically meaningful (Bodmer and Edwards 1960). In this interpretation of the theory, Fisher is concerned with two sex ratio measures: live-birth sex ratio and differential mortality by sex after live birth (up to the age of reproduction). According to the Fisherian theory, selective pressures operate on the first of these according to the characteristics of the second. It should be noted, however, that the question of differential mortality by sex is an exceedingly complex one in demography. In general, mortality is higher for males than for females, but the nature of differential mortality by sex, not to mention its cause, is by no means well established. Indeed, it appears that the differential is not a constant, but varies with a number of environmental factors. In view of this lack of clarity, caution must be exercised in generalizing about the genetic implications of such mortality differentials.

Apart from their intrinsic interest to demographers and biologists, variations in the live-birth sex ratio have in recent years become of great significance to geneticists as indicators of mutation rates in man. It is not surprising that the sex ratio has come to be used in this manner. Data on mutation rates in humans are exceedingly difficult to obtain, while live-birth sex ratio data are recorded as a matter of course and/or law in virtually every study and in all vital registration systems. Such data have been employed to estimate both spontaneous and induced mutation rates, and have also been used as an index of the aggregate genetic damage resulting from various forms of radiation.

There is, of course, some theoretical support for the use of sex ratios in this manner. The argument (sometimes not explicitly stated) is generally as follows.

1. It is known that the sex ratio of foetal deaths is higher than that of live births.†

2. Recessive lethal mutations occurring on the X chromosome would cause the death of only a portion of the females with this allele (the homozygotes) while causing the death of all the hemizygous males.

3. Hence, X-linked recessive lethals could explain the claimed predominance of males in foetal mortality.

4. In the same way, an increase in the frequency of X-linked recessive lethals resulting from exposure to ionizing radiations should proportionally increase the mortality due to these lethals for each sex, resulting in a lower live-birth sex ratio.‡

It is not proposed to present a complete review and evaluation of the evidence relating to this tradition in genetics. At least five such reviews have already appeared, all written by highly respected population geneticists (Lüning 1962, Neel 1963, Schull 1963, Schull, Neel, and Hashizume 1966, Stevenson and Bobrow 1967). The conclusions of these researchers with regard to the use of the sex ratio as a genetic indicator are distinctly negative. Stevenson and Bobrow (1967) conclude that:

In view of the large number of factors associated with fluctuations in the sex proportions of foetuses *in utero* early and late in pregnancy in man, and the further evidence of specific modifying factors from experimental work, great care must clearly be taken in interpreting findings in respect of any group of births with unusual sex proportions (as in the offspring of irradiated parents) or fluctuations of the proportion over time, even if demonstrably associated numerically with other factors.

The conclusions of Schull, Neel, and Hashizume are summarized succinctly in the somewhat exasperated final paragraph of Schull *et al.* (1966).

We have repeatedly stressed the unsatisfactory nature of the sex ratio as a variable. It is apparently influenced by any number of factors, e.g. maternal age, paternal age, parity, etc. While the effects of these variables are generally small, adequate explanation of their origin has not been advanced despite the existence of bodies of data far larger than those pertinent to the radiation problem. Unfortunately, these unexplained perturbations are often lost sight of, and only the elegance of the genetic argument is seen. As matters stand—and we sincerely hope this is our last word on the subject—the Hiroshima–Nagasaki data

---

† This view has been challenged. See Stevenson and Bobrow (1967) and Mikamo (1969).

‡ Lest the empirical basis of propositions 2–4 be overstated, it should be noted that Stevenson and Bobrow (1967) argue that there is 'little evidence from experimental mammals or from man on the subject of harmful mutations on the X chromosome, and findings in *Drosophila* have dominated speculation as to the situation in man'.

fail to provide unequivocal evidence for an effect of radiation on the sex ratio, although they are consistent with a small effect in the early post-bomb years which has since disappeared.

In the light of the above, it is clear that several prominent geneticists consider the use of the sex ratio as an indicator of mutation rates unjustified at present. Nonetheless, papers have recently appeared in which such use is made of sex ratio data. It therefore seems worthwhile to present a brief review of the most recent literature in this area.

Verley, Grahn, and Leslie (1967) attempt to employ sex ratio data from experimental mice to estimate the rate of spontaneous mutation to X-linked lethal recessives. Under their experimental design, the 'dams of all families with a significant deficiency of males beyond random expectation would be arbitrarily classed as carriers of recessive sex-linked lethal mutations.' The authors conclude that the sex ratio is an insensitive indicator of incidence of X-linked recessive lethals. They do not, however, challenge the theoretical arguments on which their use of the sex ratio is based.

Havenstein, Taylor, Hansen, Morton, and Chapman (1968) accept the theoretical arguments and assumptions originally set out by Schull and Neel in 1958, and later put in doubt by these same authors in their 1966 review paper. In agreement with the first Schull and Neel paper, Havenstein *et al.* expect a significant effect of cumulative X-radiation on the sex ratio. They construct a linear regression model to estimate the mutation rate per chromosome per radiation dose, viewing the sex ratio as a wholly genetic trait completely determined by the incidence of X-linked recessive lethal mutations. Their expectations are borne out by their data on irradiated rats, and they point to the similarity of their results to those of Searle (1964) on the mouse. After further analysis of his data, however, Searle argued that sex-linked lethals were responsible for very little, if any, of the effects he reported. Havenstein *et al.* do not agree with the conclusions of Searle, arguing instead that their data demonstrate a real sex ratio change following spermatogoneal exposure. They further note, however, that they 'cannot ... rule out the possibility that the effect is arising from something other than sex-linked lethals.'

In addition to the above two papers, in which the sex ratio is employed as an indicator of genetic phenomena, a number of other recent papers are relevant to consideration of the use of the sex ratio in this manner. The interested reader is referred to Vorisek (1966), Schlager and Roderick (1968), Huang (1967), Sheridan (1968), Leonard and Schröder (1968), and Awa, Bloom, and Yoshida (1968).

To summarize very briefly, while the sex ratio is of considerable theoretical interest in genetics and has been extensively studied, both analysis of the sex ratio as a genetic trait and the use of the sex ratio as a genetic indicator have not proved to be fruitful. Heritability of the live-birth sex ratio, if real, appears

8

to be so small in magnitude as to escape unambiguous detection in data now available. The use of the live-birth sex ratio as a genetic indicator has stimulated considerable controversy among geneticists, and the consensus now appears to be that it is a dubious methodology at best.

Analyses of factors associated with the human live-birth sex ratio

Since the time of Aristotle, many factors have been believed to be associated with the human live-birth sex ratio (for a review of early theories, see Edwards 1962b). The elucidation of the mechanism of sex determination by McClung (1902) eliminated many of the early speculations, but new ones took their place. Had the normal live-birth sex ratio in Western Europe been 100 (i.e. equal numbers of male and female), it probably would not have commanded nearly the attention which it has. A ratio of 100 would have been in agreement with the predictions of a simple biological model positing equal numbers of X and Y spermatozoa, equal probabilities of their access to and successful fertilization of the ovum, and equal likelihood that the resultant conceptuses would survive to birth. Instead, the human sex ratio has been observed to vary with time and other factors, and generally to be in excess of 100. Since 1931, observations such as these have led to suggestions of many factors as affecting the human sex ratio at birth, and in some cases to refutations of such suggestions. The most parsimonious means of describing these is simply to list them, along with the appropriate references. It must be noted that the papers on a given factor are by no means in agreement as to that factor's importance.

TABLE 6.2

Suggested factors associated with the human live-birth sex ratio

Factor	References
Birth order	Russell 1936, Ciocco 1938, Lawrence 1941, Martin 1943, 1948, Jalavisto 1952a, MacMahon and Pugh 1953, Myers 1954, Novitski and Sandler 1956, Novitski and Kimball 1958, Pollard 1969, Teitelbaum 1970.
Family size	Russell 1936, Lawrence 1941, Thomas 1951, Jalavisto 1952b.
Sex of first-born	Lancaster 1950.
Maternal age	Martin 1943, 1948, Lowe and McKeown 1950, Jalavisto 1952a, b, Bernstein 1953, Novitski 1953, MacMahon and Pugh 1953, Takahashi 1954, Myers 1954, Pollard 1969, Teitelbaum 1970.
Paternal age	Russell 1936, Jalavisto 1952a, b, Novitski 1953, Bernstein 1953, Novitski and Sandler 1956, Novitski and Kimball 1958, Moran, Novitski, and Novitski 1969, Pollard 1969, Teitelbaum 1970.

TABLE 6.2—*continued*

Factor	References
Relative ages of father and mother	Ciocco 1938, Lawrence 1941, Bernstein 1953, Lejeune and Turpin 1957, Novitski and Kimball 1958.
General genetic factors	Slater 1944, Bernstein 1951, 1954, Bodmer and Edwards 1960, Edwards 1960b, 1962b, Trichopoulos 1967.
Race and colour	Ciocco 1938, Strandskov 1945, Visaria 1967, Teitelbaum 1970.
Inbreeding and outbreeding	Schull 1958, Kirby, McWhirter, Teitelbaum, and Darlington 1967, Schull and Neel 1965.
Radiation damage	Schull and Neel 1958, Lejeune, Turpin, and Rethore 1960, Lüning 1962, Scholte and Sobels 1964, Schull, Neel, and Hashizume 1966.
Ancestral longevity	Lawrence 1941, Jalavisto 1952b, Cavalli-Sforza 1961, Krehbiel 1966, Cann and Cavalli-Sforza 1968.
Physique and temperament	Heath 1954, Damon and Nuttall 1965.
Baldness of father	Damon and Nuttall 1965.
Cigarette-smoking	Damon, Nuttall, and Salber 1966, Fraumeni and Lundin 1964.
Coffee-drinking	Vogel, Kruger, Kürth, and Schroder 1966.
Blood groups	Cohen and Glass 1956, 1959, Allan 1958, 1959, Kirby *et al.* 1967, Jackson, Mann, and Schull 1969.
Birth control	Winston 1932a, Slater 1944, Gini 1951, Robbins 1952, Edwards 1958, Weiler 1959, Goodman 1961.
Artificial insemination	Jalavisto 1952b.
Frequency of intercourse	Jalavisto 1952b.
Time of conception during menstrual cycle	Lawrence 1941, Jalavisto 1952b, Hatzold, 1970.
Seasonal and monthly variation	Russell 1936, Ciocco 1938, Takahashi 1952, Slatis 1953.
Geographical and climatic conditions	Ciocco 1938, Lyster and Bishop 1965.
Illegitimacy	Ciocco 1938.
Parental occupation	Russell 1936, Bernstein 1951, 1954.
Socio-economic status and conditions	Winston 1931, 1932a, b, Russell 1936, Ciocco 1938, Lawrence 1941, Martin 1948, Bernstein 1948, 1954, Crew 1948, Fancher 1956, Teitelbaum 1970.
War and post-war periods	Russell 1936, Martin 1943, Myers 1949, MacMahon and Pugh 1953, 1954.
Urban/rural and other differences	Russell 1936, Ciocco 1938.
High-speed stresses	Snyder 1961.
Sex of last prior pregnancy	Turpin and Schutzenberger 1948, Edwards 1959, 1960a, 1961, 1962a, b, Renkonen 1956, 1964, Renkonen, Makala, and Lehtovaara 1962.

Unfortunately, the results of this great expenditure of effort and interest have been unsatisfactory. To the present day there is little agreement as to which factors, if any, are associated with the sex ratio at birth, and in what way. It is such difficulties, among others, which severely restrict the use of the sex ratio as a genetic indicator (see p. 94). In general, what have been lacking in most of these studies are data which allow the analyst to control for two or more of the suggested factors at once, and/or adequate methodology for studying certain factors while removing the confounding effects of others.

The consequences of analysing multiple factors simultaneously using an appropriate methodology may be illustrated by a brief summary of findings concerning the relationships between birth order, maternal age, paternal age, race, and socio-economic status. The relationships between the sex ratio and three of these factors—birth order, maternal age, and paternal age—have been extensively studied (Wicksell 1926a, b, Russell 1936, Ciocco 1938, Lejeune and Turpin 1957, Novitski 1953, Bernstein 1953, Novitski and Sandler 1956, Novitski and Kimball 1958, Moran, Novitski, and Novitski 1969, Pollard 1969). Overall, the results have been contradictory and confusing. The main difficulty has been that many of these studies suffer from inadequacies of data which make impossible the simultaneous analysis of the three study factors. Since these factors are highly intercorrelated, analysis of a single factor without controlling for the other two is a procedure open to question.

For the present purposes, the simultaneous tabulations of sex of live birth by birth order, maternal age, and paternal age obtained by Novitski and Kimball (1958) were analysed. Novitski and Kimball applied a multiple quadratic regression surface analysis to their data, and detected a significant negative birth-order effect, a significant negative paternal-age effect and no significant maternal-age effect. Unexpectedly, they also found a highly significant positive interaction effect between paternal age and birth order. Because of this interaction effect, their analysis indicated that at high paternal ages the negative birth-order effect becomes positive, and that similarly at high birth orders the negative paternal-age effect becomes positive. In their discussion, they noted that such an interaction is difficult to explain in biological terms, and suggested that it might be due to the confounding effects of other factors, or to inadequacies of their analysis. Such a conclusion is supported by the highly significant residuals resulting from their analysis. As it seemed likely that the regression methodology they employed was responsible, at least in part, for these anomalous findings, it was desirable to make use of a non-regression method which would still allow the determination of the independent effects of each factor after removing the confounding effects of the other factors. The method chosen stems from one originally presented by Mantel and Haenszel (1959) and subsequently extended by

Mantel (1963).† In effect, the Mantel–Haenszel procedure reverses the regression-type approach of Novitski and Kimball. Instead of being directed, for example, to how the male sex proportion changes with birth order, it is directed to how the average birth order differs for male and female children. If we are adjusting for paternal age, a comparison of birth-order averages is made for each paternal age, the separate comparisons then being combined into a summary comparison. Alternatively, adjustment can be made for maternal age alone, for both parental ages, or for neither.

Associated with each comparison of average differences between male and female children, whether of birth order or the age of either parent, the Mantel–Haenszel procedure calculates a chi square which permits assessment of the statistical significance of the observed difference. As a measure of the importance of the study factors, use was made of the measure R, the 'relative odds', which is here equivalent to the odds for a male child. This measure is defined in Table 1 of Mantel and Haenszel (1959), and used there as an approximate measure of relative risk of disease. In the present context, the 'relative odds' or odds for a male child corresponds to the ratio of two sex ratios. The results of the re-analysis of the Novitski–Kimball data by means of this method differed substantially from those obtained by Novitski and Kimball's regression procedure. The present results, to be reported in detail elsewhere, can be briefly summarized as follows.

The crude (unadjusted) analysis for the birth-order effect yielded a very highly significant χ^2 value ($\chi^2 = 53{\cdot}65$, d.f. $= 1$, $P < 0{\cdot}000\,01$). Even when adjustment was made for either or both of the other two variables, the birth-order effect remained very highly significant. Associated with this χ^2 value were odds for a male child at birth orders five-and-above that were about 2·6 per cent lower than that at the first birth order. Hence the birth-order effect was a small but clearly significant one. In contrast, neither the paternal-age nor the maternal-age effects were significant after adjustment was made for the birth-order effect. The crude (unadjusted) analyses of these parental-age factors yielded significant χ^2 values, but the χ^2 values which were obtained after providing adjustment for the confounding effects of birth order were small and insignificant.

Hence, the primary finding of this first analysis was that of a significant negative effect of birth order on the sex ratio—as birth order increased, the sex ratio declined. This effect, which showed up whether or not the confounding effects of parental ages were removed, was quite limited, however, and was reflected in a reduction of only 2·6 per cent in the odds for a male child among fifth and later births as compared to that of first births.

The results of this analysis seemed to explain some of the more contradictory results of this analysis reported in the literature on the sex ratio.

† The author is indebted to Mr. Nathan Mantel and Dr. Charles R. Stark for advice and assistance in adapting this procedure to the available data.

Analysis of paternal-age or maternal-age effects on the sex ratio without controlling for the birth-order effect would give rise to apparently significant parental-age effects. The confusion in the literature concerning *which* parental-age factor affects the sex ratio may have resulted from failure to take account of birth order. Similarly, while our analysis did detect the significant negative effect of birth order noted by Novitski and Kimball, we cannot confirm their report of a significant effect of paternal age after the confounding effects of birth order were removed. From these results, it would appear that the only 'real' effect in these data is that of birth order, and that this effect gives rise to other apparent effects when control is inadequate.

There remained the question of the anomalous, but highly significant, inter-action effect reported by Novitski and Kimball. A more detailed analysis of the paternal-age and birth-order factors did show some suggestion of a negative paternal-age effect at the first birth order but a positive effect in the highest birth-order group considered. This would appear to accord with the Novitski–Kimball finding of a significant birth-order × paternal-age interaction. However, further examination suggested that this reversal of effect was attributable not to an interaction effect as such, but rather to the exceptionally low sex ratios shown by high birth-order offspring of young fathers. In the United States, young fathers with large families tend to be either black or poor, and probably both. If either race or socio-economic status were associated with the sex ratio, such an association could result in the low sex ratios shown by high birth-order children of young fathers. Such effects could therefore be the source of the interaction effect reported by Novitski and Kimball, whose data were not controlled for either race or socio-economic status. This possibility indicated the need for analyses of the potential effects of race and socio-economic status upon the sex ratio.

For this purpose, vital statistics of the United States for the year 1955 (the same year as the Novitski–Kimball data) were obtained and analysed. These data allow assessment of any sex-ratio differences between white and Negro births occurring in that year, after controlling for the birth-order effect shown to be significant in the Novitski–Kimball data. In brief, these analyses showed a highly significant difference between the sex ratios of white and Negro Americans, even after adjusting for the significant birth-order effect ($\chi^2 = 116 \cdot 71$, d.f. $= 1$, $P < 0 \cdot 000\ 01$). The odds for a male child were 3 per cent lower for Negroes than for whites. A subsequent analysis of the birth-order effect, with adjustment being provided for the race effect, indicated that the birth-order effect was still significant, though substantially smaller in magnitude. This suggests that analysis of the birth-order effect in the presence of the effects of the race factor may lead to an overestimate of the strength of the birth-order effect.

It was possible to conclude at this point that: (1) the apparent effects of paternal age and/or maternal age on sex ratio were derivative from a real birth-order effect, and (2) that the apparent interaction between birth order and paternal age derived from a real racial difference which affected the distribution of male births in the Novitski–Kimball data. An important question still remained, however. It was whether either the birth-order effect or the race effect itself could derive from a socio-economic effect for which control could not be provided in the vital data being used.

The possibility of a socio-economic effect on the live-birth sex ratio has its own extensive literature (Winston 1931, Crew 1948, Russell 1936, Lawrence 1941, Bernstein 1948, 1954, Fancher 1956). Some of the reported findings are positive and some negative, but most of the above studies suffer from serious methodological problems. Unfortunately, analysis of socio-economic factors precludes the use of vital statistics, as very little information of a socio-economic nature is available on birth records. This forced us to rely upon data from survey samples or special studies. The data analysed here were taken from a large-scale study known as the *Collaborative study on cerebral palsy, mental retardation, and other neurological and sensory disorders of childhood* (hereafter referred to as the Collaborative Study). The Collaborative Study data contain extensive socio-economic information which allow the use of a highly refined indicator of socio-economic status known as the socio-economic index (Myrianthropoulos and French 1968). The Collaborative Study socio-economic index provides a ranking of individuals or families which simultaneously takes into account their standing on three dimensions of social stratification—occupation, income, and education. For the purposes of analysis, the study population was grouped into four categories of socio-economic index scores; adjustment was provided for race and for gravidity (the medical measure of the birth-order factor).

The results of this analysis can be summarized as follows: in general, the sex ratio at birth appeared to be significantly related to the socio-economic index ($\chi^2 = 13\cdot16$, d.f. $= 1, P < 0\cdot0003$). The relationship was a positive one —as the socio-economic index scores increased, the sex ratio increased. This was true even after the data were adjusted for the confounding effects of race and gravidity (adjusted $\chi^2 = 6\cdot17$, d.f. $= 1, P < 0\cdot015$). The calculations of odds for a male child suggested that this effect was not a linear one, however. Rather, it was characterized by an apparent 'diminishing-return' curve—a sharp increase in sex ratio as the socio-economic index went from low to moderate scores, but no further increase in sex ratio as the socio-economic index went from moderate to high. Overall, children born to families in the lowest socio-economic index category had approximately 8–9 per cent lower odds of being a male than those born to families in the moderate and higher socio-economic index categories.

However, this socio-economic effect did not appear to account for the race effect noted in the previous analysis. After adjusting for the confounding effects of the socio-economic factor, the difference between white and Negro sex ratios in the present analysis remained significant.†

Overall, then, the results of these analyses suggest a significant negative association between sex ratio and birth order, a significantly lower sex ratio for Negroes than for whites, and a significant negative association between sex ratio and socio-economic status. The remaining two study factors— paternal age and maternal age—are apparently not associated with the sex ratio.

Sex predetermination

In recent months there has been considerable discussion of the prospects for and implications of techniques for predetermining the sex of offspring. Indeed, a major popular journal has gone so far as to publish a cover story on a technique purported to predetermine the sex of offspring with high reliability (Rorvik and Shettles 1970).

Despite such popularization, biologically sound techniques of sex predetermination are not yet available on other than an experimental basis. Many methods operating before fertilization have been tested, including techniques of sperm centrifugation (Lindahl 1958), sperm electrophoresis (Gordon 1958), density gradients (Bhattacharya, Bangham, Cro, and Keynes 1966), timing of coitus during menstrual cycle (Shettles 1961), and even coital position (Rorvik and Shettles 1970). In no case has any of these methods been shown to be minimally reliable.

One post-fertilization technique has been reported to be reliable in experimental work on rabbits (Gardner and Edwards 1968). It involves abdominal surgery for removal of unimplanted blastocysts, microsurgery and nuclear sexing of the blastocyst, and innovulation of those blastocysts of the desired sex. The reliability of the technique has as yet not been demonstrated in humans. Another potentially successful technique would involve amniocentesis, nuclear sexing of foetal cells in the amniotic fluid, and selective abortion to eliminate foetuses of the unwanted sex. The complexity, dangers, and expense of both of these potentially available techniques makes their widespread adoption highly unlikely.

In view of these biological facts, the futuristic optimism of Etzioni (1968)

---

† It should be recognized that, despite the extensive efforts made to provide simultaneous control for all study factors, some confounding may still be present. For example, the socio-economic and race factors may still be confounded in the following sense: due to cultural differences and discrimination factors, Negroes and whites at the same socio-economic index level may still differ significantly in standards of prenatal care and nutrition. Alternatively, socio-economic status among Negroes may be associated with the degree of white admixture. To the extent that this kind of confounding is present, it is the result of differences in socio-economic and/or racial status which are not accessible by means of the standard indicators employed in this study. Far more elaborate (and perhaps more questionable) indicators such as 'style of life' or 'degree of blackness' would be required to resolve this kind of difficulty.

and Taylor (1968) hardly seems justified. Both predict the free availability of sex predetermination techniques before 1975. Such views are the explicit justification for two recent papers relating to the demographic implications of such techniques. Markle and Nam (1970) report a pilot survey of a non-representative sample of Florida college students regarding the ideal sex distribution of their families and attitudes towards sex predetermination. While the authors note that generalization from their data are unwarranted, it is instructive to note that of those initially indicating a favourable attitude to the idea of sex predetermination (with method unspecified), fully half defect from that view when it is specified that the technique would involve artificial insemination (only 16 per cent of the total sample remain favourable). Since the response to a method involving abdominal surgery and/or selective abortion is likely to be far less positive than that to a method employing only artificial insemination, these data suggest that currently available methods are not likely to be widely employed, at least by the Markle–Nam sample.

In another recent paper, Serow and Evans (1970) calculate alternative projections of the 1960 United States population 200 years into the future, modifying only the sex ratio of fertility. They keep constant the total fertility rate, assuming that a reduction in the male fertility rate (presumably at random throughout the age-specific fertility schedule) would be matched by an equal increase in the female fertility rate. Not unexpectedly, they find that such assumed sex ratio changes imply differences among the several resulting stable populations in population sizes, crude birth rates, crude death rates, rates of natural increase, age distribution, and sex ratios.†

Only limited conclusions can be drawn from the recent literature on the implications of sex predetermination. Most reports assume early access to simple means of sex predetermination, but, as has been noted, such developments in the near future are unlikely. The low participation rates in currently or potentially available methods implied by the Markle–Nam report make the Serow–Evans projections unrealistic, especially since they are based upon the fertility and mortality experience of 1960. By the time the simple and reliable methods anticipated by Serow and Evans are actually available, fertility and mortality schedules may bear little resemblance to those of 1960.

Conclusions

Due to its great importance to demographic, biological, and genetic models, the human sex ratio at birth has been the subject of many hypotheses and analyses. The findings summarized above are illustrative of the consequences of simultaneous analysis of multiple factors thought to be associated with the

† It should be noted that Serow and Evans's conclusion that the sex ratio 'has no influence on the intrinsic rate of increase' is not warranted, as has been shown in the present paper. Serow and Evans's statement is probably simply a miswording of their intended meaning.

sex ratio. Most of the numerous factors listed have been studied independently, without provision of any control for the possible effects of other variables. It seems likely that re-analysis of some of these suggested factors after controlling for at least the three factors shown to be significant in the present analyses would result in the elimination of spurious associations, such as those between the sex ratio and maternal age and paternal age.

A second result of the present findings is the addition of a further caveat to the use of the sex ratio as an indicator of mutation rates in man. In addition to recognizing the questionable theoretical basis of this procedure, the effects of such apparently significant factors as birth order, race, and socio-economic status must be taken into account. Unless such control is provided, sex ratio differences within or among populations are not amenable to clear genetic interpretation.

REFERENCES

ALLAN, T. M. (1958). Rh blood groups and sex ratios at birth. *Br. Med. J.* **2**, 248.
—— (1959). ABO blood groups and sex ratio at birth. *Br. Med. J.* **1**, 553–4.
AWA, A. A., BLOOM, A. D., and YOSHIDA, M. C. (1968). Cytogenetic study of the offspring of atom bomb survivors. *Nature, Lond.* **218**, 367–8.
BERNSTEIN, M. E. (1948). Recent changes in the secondary sex ratio of the upper social strata. *Hum. Biol.* **20**, 182–94.
—— (1951). Action of genes affecting secondary sex ratio in man. *Science, N.Y.* **114**, 181–2.
—— (1953). Parental age and the sex ratio. *Science, N.Y.* **118**, 448–9.
—— (1954). Studies in the human sex ratio: 4. Evidence of genetic variation of the primary sex ratio in man. *J. Hered.* **45**, 59–64.
BHATTACHARYA, B. C., BANGHAM, A. D., CRO, R. J., and KEYNES, R. D. (1966). An attempt to predetermine the sex of calves by artificial insemination with spermatozoa separated by sedimentation. *Nature, Lond.* **211**, 863.
BODMER, W. F. and EDWARDS, A. W. F. (1960). Natural selection and the sex ratio. *Ann. hum. Genet.* **34**, 239–44.
CANN, H. M. and CAVALLI-SFORZA, L. L. (1968). Effects of grandparental and parental age, birth order, and geographic variation on the sex ratio of liveborn and stillborn infants *Am. J. hum. Genet.* **20**, 381–91.
CAVALLI-SFORZA, L. L. (1961). Un metodo per la stima della frequenza de mutazione nell'uomo: risultati preliminari. *Atti. Ass. genet. ital.* **6**, 151–62.
CIOCCO, A. (1938). Variation in the sex ratio at birth in the U.S. *Hum. Biol.* **10**, 36–64.
COHEN, B. H. and GLASS, B. (1956). The ABO blood groups and the sex ratio. *Hum. Biol.* **28**, 20–42.
—— (1959). Further observations on the ABO blood groups and the sex ratio. *Am. J. hum. Genet.* **11**, 274–8.
CREW, R. A. E. (1948). *Measurements of the public health.* Oliver and Boyd, Edinburgh and London.
DAMON, A. and NUTTALL, R. L. (1965). Ponderal index of fathers and sex ratio of children. *Hum. Biol.* **37**, 23–8.
—— and SALBER, E. J. (1966). Tobacco smoke as a possible genetic mutagen: parental smoking and sex of children. *Am. J. Epidem.* **83**, 520–36.
EDWARDS, A. W. F. (1958). An analysis of Geissler's data on the human sex ratio. *Ann. hum. Genet.* **23**, 6–15.
—— (1959). Some comments on Schulzenberger's analysis of data on the human sex ratio. *Ann. hum. Genet.* **23**, 233–8.
—— (1960a). The human sex ratio. Ph.D. thesis, Cambridge.
—— (1960b). Natural selection and the sex ratio. *Nature, Lond.* **188**, 960–1.

—— (1961). A factorial analysis of sex ratio data. *Ann. hum. Genet.* **25**, 117–21.

—— (1962a). A factorial analysis of sex ratio data: a correction. *Ann. hum. Genet.* **25**, 343–6.

—— (1962b). Genetics and the human sex ratio. *Adv. Genet.* **11**, 239–72.

—— (1970). The search for genetic variability of the sex ratio. *J. biosoc. Sci.* Suppl. **2**, 55–60.

ETZIONI, A (1968). Sex control, science, and society. *Science, N.Y.* **161**, 1107.

FANCHER, H. L. (1956). The relation between the occupational status of individuals and the sex ratio of their offspring. *Hum. Biol.* **28**, 316–22.

FISHER, R. A. (1958). *The genetical theory of natural selection.* 2nd ed. Dover Publications, New York.

FRAUMENI, J. F. and LUNDIN, F. E. (1964). Smoking and pregnancy. *Lancet* **1**, 173.

GARDNER, R. L. and EDWARDS, R. G. (1968). Control of the sex ratio at full term in the rabbit by transferring sexed blastocysts. *Nature, Lond.* **218**, 346–8.

GINI, C. (1951). Combinations and sequences of sexes in human families and litters. *Acta genet. Statist. med.* **2**, 220–44.

GOODMAN, L. A. (1961). Some possible effects of birth control on the human sex ratio. *Ann. hum. Genet.* **25**, 75–81. Also in *Readings in mathematical social science* (eds. P. F. Lazarsfeld and N. W. Henry). Science Research Associates, Chicago.

GORDON, M. J. (1958). The control of sex. *Scient. Am.* **199** (Nov.), 87–94.

HATZOLD, O. (1970). Zur Sexual Proportion der Geborenen—Sohn oder Tochter nach Wunsch—Eine methode zur willkürlichen Geschlechtsbestimmung. Vortrag, gehalten auf der Konventsitzung der Deutschen Akademie für Bevölkerungswissenschaft in Kirkel, 1969. 'Mitteilungen' für die Mitglieder und Freunde der Deutschen Gesellschaft für Bevölkerungs-Wissenschaft E.V., 1970 Heft 1, Januar, 8–11.

HAVENSTEIN, G. B., TAYLOR, B. A., HANSEN, T. C., MORTON, N. E., and CHAPMAN, A. B. (1968). Genetic effects of cumulative X-radiation on the secondary sex ratio of the laboratory rat. *Genetics, Princeton* **59**, 255–74.

HEATH, C. W. (1954). Physique, temperament, and sex ratio. *Hum. Biol.* **26**, 337–42.

HUANG, C. C. (1967). Induction of high incidence of damage of the X-chromosomes of *Rattus* (*Mastomys*) *natalensis* by base analogues, viruses, and carcinogens. *Chromosoma* **23**, 162–79.

JACKSON, C. E., MANN, J. D., and SCHULL, W. J. (1969). Xg^a blood group system and the sex ratio in man. *Nature, Lond.* **222**, 445–6.

JALAVISTO, E. (1952a). Sex ratio at birth and its dependence on birth order and parental age. *Annls Chir. Gynaec. Fenn.* **41**, 129–37.

—— (1952b). Genealogical approach to factors influencing the sex ratio at birth. *Annls Chir. Gynaec. Fenn.* **41**, 182–96.

KIRBY, D. R. S., McWHIRTER, K. G., TEITELBAUM, M. S., and DARLINGTON, C. D. (1967). A possible immunological influence on sex ratio. *Lancet* **2**, 139–40.

KREHBIEL, E. L. (1966). An estimation of the cumulative mutation rate for sex-linked lethals in man which produce fetal deaths. *Am. J. hum. Genet.* **18**, 127–43.

LANCASTER, H. O. (1950). The sex ratios in sibships with special reference to Geissler's data. *Ann. Eugen.* **15**, 153–8.

LAWRENCE, P. S. (1941). The sex ratio, fertility, and ancestral longevity. *Q. Rev. Biol.* **16**, 35–79.

LEJEUNE, J. and TURPIN, R. (1957). L'influence de l'âge des parents sur la masculinité de naissances vivantes. *C. R. hebd. séanc. Acad. Sci. Paris* **244**, 1833–5.

—— and RETHORE, M. O. (1960). Les enfants nés de irradiés (cas particuliers de la sex ratio). *Proc. XIX Int. Congr. Radiol.*, Munich, 1959, 1089.

LEONARD, A. and SCHRÖDER, J. H. (1968). Incidence of XO mice after X-radiation of spermatogonia. *Mol. gen. Genet.* **101**, 116–19.

LINDAHL, P. E. (1958). Separation of bull spermatozoa carrying X and Y chromosomes by counter-streaming centrifugation. *Nature, Lond.* **181**, 784.

LOWE, C. R. and McKEOWN, T. (1950). The sex ratio of human births related to maternal age. *Br. J. Soc. Med.* **4**, 75–85.

LÜNING, K. G. (1962). Sex-ratio: an unreliable method for estimations of radiation hazards. U.N. Documents A/AC82/G/L671. United Nations, New York.

LYSTER, W. R. and BISHOP, M. W. (1965). An association between rainfall and sex in man. *J. Reprod. Fert.* **10**, 35–47.

McCLUNG, C. E. (1902). The accessory chromosome—sex determinant? *Biol. Bull.* **3**, 43–84.

MACMAHON, B. and PUGH, T. F. (1953). Influence of birth order and maternal age on the human sex ratio at birth. *Br. J. prev. Soc. Med.* **7**, 83–6.

—— (1954). Sex ratio of white births in the United States during the Second World War. *Am. J. hum. Genet.* **6**, 284–92.

MANTEL, N. (1963). Chi-square tests with one degree of freedom: extensions of the Mantel-Haenszel procedure. *J. Am. statist. Ass.* **58**, 690–700.

—— and HAENSZEL, W. (1959). Statistical aspects of the analysis of data from retrospective studies of disease. *J. Cancer Inst.* **22**, 720–48.

MARKLE, G. E. and NAM, C. B. (1970). The impact of sex predetermination on fertility. Paper presented at the annual meeting of the Population Association of America, 18 April 1970.

MARTIN, W. J. (1943). Sex ratio during war. *Lancet* **2**, 807.

—— (1948). The sex ratio. *Med. Offr.* **79**, 153–6.

MIKAMO, K. (1969). Female preponderance in the sex ratio during early intrauterine development: a sex chromatin study. *Jap. J. hum. Genet.* **13**, 272–7.

MORAN, P. A. P., NOVITSKI, E., and NOVITSKI, C. (1969). Paternal age and the secondary sex ratio in humans. *Ann. hum. Genet.* **32**, 315–17.

MYERS, R. J. (1949). War and post-war experience in regard to the sex ratio at birth in various countries. *Hum. Biol.* **21**, 257–9.

—— (1954). The effect of age of mother and birth order on sex ratio at birth. *Milbank meml Fund Q. Bull.* **33**, 275–81.

MYRIANTHROPOULOS, M. C. and FRENCH, K. S. (1968). An application of the U.S. Bureau of the Census Socio-economic Index to a large, diversified patient population. *Social Sci. Med.* **2**, 283–99.

NEEL, J. V. (1963). *Changing perspectives on the genetic effects of radiation.* C. C. Thomas, Springfield.

NOVITSKI, E. (1953). The dependence of the secondary sex ratio in humans on the age of the father. *Science, N.Y.* **117**, 531–3.

—— and KIMBALL, A. W. (1958). Birth order, parental ages, and sex of offspring. *Am. J. hum. Genet.* **10**, 268–75.

—— and SANDLER, L. (1956). The relationship between parental age, birth order, and the secondary sex ratio in humans. *Ann. hum. Genet.* **21**, 123–31.

POLLARD, G. N. (1969). Factors influencing the sex ratio at birth in Australia, 1902–1965. *J. biosoc. Sci.* **1**, 389–404.

RENKONEN, K. O. (1956). Is the sex ratio between boys and girls correlated to the sex of precedent children? *Ann. Med. Exp. Fenn.* **34**, 447–51.

—— (1964). Problems connected with the birth of male children. *Acta genet. Statist. med.* **14**, 177–85.

——, MAKALA, O., and LEHTOVAARA, R. (1962). Factors affecting the human sex ratio. *Nature, Lond.* **184**, 308–9.

ROBBINS, H. (1952). A note on gambling systems and birth statistics. *Am. math. Mon.* **59**, 685.

RORVIK, D. M. and SHETTLES, L. B. (1970). You can choose your baby's sex. *Look* **34** (8), 88–98.

RUSSELL, W. T. (1936). Statistical study of the sex ratio at birth. *J. Hyg., Camb.* **36**, 381–401.

SCHLAGER, G. and RODERICK, T. H. (1968). Secondary sex ratio in mice. *J. Hered.* **59**, 363–5.

SCHOLTE, P. J. L. and SOBELS, F. H. (1964). Sex ratio shifts among progeny from patients having received therapeutic X-radiation. *Am. J. Genet.* **16**, 26–37.

SCHULL, W. J. (1958). Empirical risks of consanguineous marriages: sex ratio, malformation, and viability. *Am. J. hum. Genet.* **10**, 294–343.

—— (1963). Heredity effects. *Nucleonics* **21**, 54–7.

—— and NEEL, J. V. (1958). Radiation and the sex ratio in man. *Science, N.Y.* **128**, 343.

—— (1965). *The effects of inbreeding on Japanese children.* Harper and Row, New York.

SCHULL, W. J., NEEL, J. V., and HASHIZUME, A. (1966). Some further observations on the sex ratio among infants born to survivors of the atomic bombings of Hiroshima and Nagasaki. *Am. J. hum. Genet.* **18**, 328–38.

SEARLE, A. G. (1964). Genetic effects of spermatogonial X-radiation on productivity of F_1 female mice. *Mutat. Res.* **1**, 99–108.

SEROW, W. J. and EVANS, V. J. (1970). Demographic effects of pre-natal sex selection. Paper presented at the annual meeting of the Population Association of America, 18 April 1970.

SHAW, R. F. and MOHLER, J. D. (1953). The selective signifigance of the sex ratio. *Am. Nat.* **87**, 337–42.

SHERIDAN, W. (1968). The effects of acute single or fractionated X-ray treatment on mouse spermatogonia. *Mutat. Res.* **5**, 163–72.

SHETTLES, L. B. (1961). Conception and birth sex ratios: a review. *Obstet. Gynaec.* **18**, 122–30.

—— (1964). The great preponderance of human males conceived. *Am. J. Obstet. Gynec.* **89**, 130–3.

SLATER, E. (1944). A demographic study of a psychopathic population. *Ann. Eugen.* **12**, 121–37.

SLATIS, H. M. (1953). Seasonal variation in the American live birth sex ratio. *Am. J. hum. Genet.* **5**, 21–33.

SNYDER, R. G. (1961). The sex ratio of offspring of pilots of high performance aircraft. *Hum. Biol.* **33**, 1–10.

STERN, C. (1960). *Principles of human genetics*, 2nd edn. W. H. Freeman, San Francisco and London.

STEVENSON, A. C. and BOBROW, M. (1967). Determinants of sex proportions in man, with consideration of the evidence concerning a contribution from X-linked mutations to intrauterine death. *J. med. Genet.* **4**, 190.

STRANDSKOV, H. H. (1945). Birth sex ratios in the total, the 'white' and the 'coloured' U.S. populations. *Am. J. phys. Anthrop.* **3**, 165–75.

TAKAHASHI, E. (1952). Notes on Japanese birth statistics. *Hum. Biol.* **24**, 44–52.

—— (1954). The sex ratio of neonatal deaths in Japan. *Hum. Biol.* **26**, 133–42.

TAYLOR, G. R. (1968). *The biological time bomb.* World Publishing Co., New York.

TEITELBAUM, M. S. (1970). Factors affecting the sex ratio in large populations. *J. biosoc. Sci.* Suppl. **2**, 61–71.

THOMAS, M. H. (1951). Sex pattern and size of family. *Br. med. J.* **1**, 733–44.

THOMPSON, W. S. and LEWIS, D. T. (1965). *Population problems.* McGraw-Hill, New York.

TRICHOPOULOS, D. (1967). Evidence of genetic variation in the human sex ratio. *Hum. Biol.* **39**, 170–5.

TURPIN, R. and SCHUTZENBERGER, M. P. (1948). Recherche statistique sur la distribution du sexe à la naissance. *C. r. hebd. Acad. séane Sci. Paris* **226**, 1845–6.

VERLEY, F. A., GRAHN, D., and LESLIE, W. P. (1967). Sex ratio of mice as possible indicator of mutation rate for sex-linked lethals. *J. Hered.* **58**, 285–90.

VISARIA, P. M. (1967). Sex ratio at birth in territories with a relatively complete registration. *Eug. Quart.* **14**, 132.

VOGEL, F., KRUGER, J., KURTH, M., and SCHRODER, T. M. (1966). On the absence of a relation between coffee-drinking in parents and the sex ratio of children. (In German). *Humangenetik* **2**, 119–32.

VORISEK, P. (1966). Effect of continuous intrauterine irradition on sex ratio and birth weight. *Strahlentherapie* **129**, 448–55.

WEILER, H. (1959). Sex-ratio and birth control. *Am. J. Sociol.* **65**, 298.

WICKSELL, S. D. (1926a). Sex proportion and parental age. *Acta Univ. Lund.* M.F., Avd. 2, 22, Nr. 6 (cited in Russell 1936).

—— (1926b). *K. fysiogr. Sällsk. Lund Förh.* N.F., 37, Nr. (cited in Russell 1936).

WINSTON, S. (1931). The influence of social factors upon the sex ratio at birth. *Am. J. Sociol.* **37**, 1–21.

—— (1932a). Birth control and the sex ratio at birth. *Am. J. Sociol.* **38**, 225–31.

—— (1932b). Some factors related to differential sex ratios at birth. *Hum. Biol.* **4**, 272–9.

7

MATHEMATICAL MODELS IN DEMOGRAPHY

R. W. HIORNS

ALMOST three hundred years have elapsed since Graunt (1662) and Halley (1693) performed calculations which can be recognized as those leading to the construction of a life table. There has been some dispute concerning which of these two men really did construct the first life table (Glass 1950, Sutherland 1963). From the present viewpoint, however, the distinction between them is clear. Graunt, having constructed the first sample survey, using parish bills of mortality for several English regions (and, incidentally, identifying an important problem, which remains a current one, of heterogeneous response rates), may be properly accredited 'the first statistician'. Halley, with his intensive background in what is now called 'physical science', prompted Newton to write the *Principia* (which would not have been published without financial support from Halley), and was conversant with thinking in terms of mathematical models. Graunt was not. It is Halley then who may add to his other achievements, the first use of a mathematical model in demography. Later in this account the importance of population structure will be seen to have been emphasized in recent model approaches. Both Graunt and Halley appreciated structure and the differential mortality operating in their day.

But the needs of a demographer are wider than the mere consideration of mortality as depicted in the life table. It would seem that he has two principal needs.

1. To make comparisons in terms of certain parameters between populations whose structures may be different with respect to many variables such as age, sex, occupation or social class, marital systems, economy.
2. To undertake projection of population size within one country, state, or other population unit.

Mathematical models should then be considered in the light of these two needs.

The first of these needs is traditionally met by standardization procedures. For example, if two populations are to be compared with respect to their mortality and their age structures are markedly different, the populations must first be standardized for the age difference. This may be achieved directly by means of a standard population whose age distribution is used to adjust the observed mortality of each of the two populations being compared. Alternatively, reference may be made to some theory of population growth based upon a mathematical model which will, in its simplest form, incorporate three fundamental characteristics of each population:

(a) the age distribution,
(b) the age-specific mortality rates,
(c) the age-specific fertility rates.

The general theory for population growth as presented independently by Lotka (1925), Volterra (1931), and Nicholson and Bailey (1935), considered in deterministic terms the growth of a population whose age structure remained constant. Such a stable population will, in theory, always emerge under the long-term action of constant fertility and mortality rates. In the *stochastic population theory*, which was initiated by Feller (1939), although allowing for random variation of the rates, the most elementary models, called by him 'birth and death processes', do not consider any structure of the population by age, sex, etc. Solutions in mathematical terms may be found from such models for the mean, variance, and other moments of the distribution of the population size even when the birth and death rates are general functions of time (Kendall 1949). Although obtained from such a crude and over-simplified model, the variability of population size is of particular importance, as it gives information on the probability of extinction or of reaching a certain critical size. The distributions of the expectation of life and other life table quantities are described by Chiang (1968) and Hoem (1970). Such detailed information on the distribution of population size for the more difficult models incorporating structured populations may not be obtained in mathematically general terms, but numerical solutions and simulation results are in principle possible without difficulty for any population structure, in the stable population case.

The rather restrictive stable population model, despite its apparent simplicity, provides more than enough mathematical sophistication in its stochastic treatment. There would seem to be little point, therefore, in hoping for any contribution of any value to practical demography from the mathematical theory which deals with populations whose age distributions are not stable. The so-called *quasi-stable theory* which allows the vital rates to change slowly with time here offers some consolation. This theory arose in the form of a generalization of the classic stable population theory, and was motivated by the requirement to make that classic theory more practically relevant. Coale (1957) and Lopez (1961) were primarily responsible for demonstrating that the initial age distribution of a population will be changed into quasi-stable ones determined by the slowly changing vital rates over time. This mathematical property known as *weak ergodicity* depends upon a general theorem (see Kemeny and Snell 1960) and the quasi-stable theory is attractively described and justified by McFarland (1969).

Arising from the needs of the demographer, as identified above, a considerable problem emerges when the population units are identified as breeding units and the biological aspects of the populations are the subject of concern. This is the problem of definition of the population units themselves. The size of unit, in particular, would be of utmost importance from the point of view of population genetics or epidemiology. In specific cases, the homogeneity within groups of individuals or families may be maximized by an appropriate choice of groups which will then also maximize the heterogeneity between the groups. This is the fundamental object of *cluster analysis* or *taxonomic classification*; reference is made to the discussion by Sokal and Sneath (1963).

The function and variety of mathematical models

It is of some value in an attempt to assess the importance of mathematical models in demography to consider the purpose or role of such models. This is the only satisfactory basis for classification of models since the nature of the situation in which the model is derived will usually determine the type of the model. On the one hand, a model which expresses almost perfectly the behaviour of population size under the influence of biological, economic, and social variables and the constraints which a particular environment imposes upon such variables may be of little value for short-term predictions in a fluctuating environment; on the other, an empirical model which in no way portrays the underlying mechanisms may well be optimal as a predictor of short-term behaviour. This kind of difference is typified by the presence of periodicities in data from observed populations when the complex causes for the oscillations cannot be analysed but the overall behaviour can be characterized perfectly well for predictive purposes by means of a mathematical model.

In some ways, the division between models in this way is unsatisfactory. Unless a predictive model and all its parameters are capable of interpretation in terms other than mathematical ones, the application is bound to be the subject of considerable suspicion. For example, the principal harmonic which represents the main period of oscillation in some demographic series (such as generation length) must have, as its origin, some complex interaction of factors. If such factors cannot be identified or, what is worse, if when they are identified the interaction between them seems unlikely in practical terms, then the application of such models puts too much trust in the hands of the mathematician. The considerable lack of understanding involved is a little disturbing, yet for short-term behaviour of such series, this would often seem to be the situation.

A mathematical model may be of no practical value but of fundamental interest for its sheer generality and simplicity. A most striking example of such a model would be that representing the growth of world population over the last four or five millennia, as depicted in Fig. 7.1. In this model, P, the population size at any time t, is a simple exponential function of time which would imply that the increase in population over any short period is a constant fraction of the population at the beginning of that period. On a time-scale of

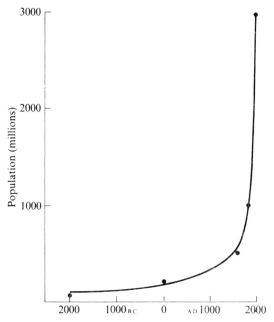

FIG. 7.1. The growth of world population. The points plotted are estimated values of the population of the world at various times and the curve represents an asymptotic regression model fitted to these values.

several millennia, this constant proportional increase would seem to apply if the period considered was a single millennium. It would not apply, because of short-term fluctuations, when the period was taken to be a decade.

This model may be expressed in the form

$$P = a + be^{ct}$$

where the constant a represents the original population of *Homo sapiens* generally supposed reasonably constant until the Neolithic revolution which brought agriculture and settlement with a consequent increase in population size. From some rather rough and clearly not uncontestable estimates of population size at various times, the above model when fitted gives the values $a = 196\cdot4$, $b = 3\cdot57$, and $c = 0\cdot0017$ and the fitted curve is drawn in Fig. 7.1. It must be noted, however, that the estimate of a depends upon what assumption is made concerning the time over which the population size was constant.

9

The environment, influencing human behaviour in the widest sense, imposes severe limitations upon population growth at certain times after which technological innovation allows either territorial expansion through the colonization of previously uninhabitable lands or more people to be sustained by the same lands. Such innovations may take many forms, e.g. improved communications, economic conditions, or medical care. This phenomenon clearly produces bursts of growth in world populations which are countered in the classical Malthusian theory by the forces of war, famine, and epidemic, and in addition by man's ability to control his environment. Such fluctuations are of a short-term nature and clearly it would be most inappropriate to employ a long-term model of the simplicity of that described above for short-term projection.

In a medium-term situation, it is possible to represent the expansion and limitation which a newly created population might experience. This would be done most effectively by some sigmoid model incorporating the growth increase and decrease, both being exponential in character.

For example, McKendrick and Pai (1911), in their description of the growth of a bacterial colony in a test tube took the initial growth rate of the bacillus to be proportional to the number, so that

$$\frac{dP}{dt} = aP$$

But the supply of food to the colony in the test tube will be limited and the growth rate must also be proportional to some such quantity as $b-P$, where b is the size at which the population growth rate begins to diminish.

Hence
$$\frac{dP}{dt} = aP(b-P)$$

or, after integration,
$$P = \frac{L}{(1+e^{-mt})}$$

where t is the time measured from b, $m = ab$ and L is the ultimate limit to the population size. This curve is shown in Fig. 7.2. The well-known *logistic curve* (Verhulst 1847) derives from a model of this type and has been found to describe accurately the growth of the population of the United States. Such curves may be fitted quite easily in practice using a technique due to Stevens and described by Hiorns (1965).

More detailed long-term growth models for population size incorporate the structure of a population with respect to one or more variables such as age, sex, marital state, occupation, or education. Of these, age is the structure most often considered.

In a simplified treatment of age structure, the population may be considered through its female reproductivity alone. For purposes of illustration of the

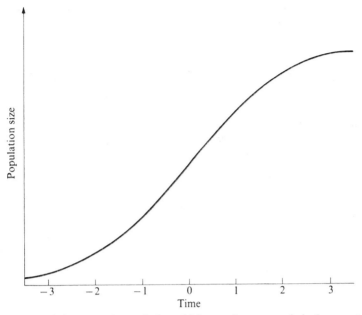

FIG. 7.2. The logistic curve. A population which experiences a period of unconstrained growth followed by constrained growth for a further period will tend to have a size of the form shown.

stable population theory, the life span may be divided into six equal fifteen-yearly periods, ages 0–14, 15–29, 30–44, 45–59, 60–74, and 75–90 (assuming that no one survives beyond the age of 90). A survivorship matrix S and a fertility matrix B are then defined by

$$S = \begin{pmatrix} 0 & 0 & 0 & 0 & 0 & 0 \\ p_1 & 0 & 0 & 0 & 0 & 0 \\ 0 & p_2 & 0 & 0 & 0 & 0 \\ 0 & 0 & p_3 & 0 & 0 & 0 \\ 0 & 0 & 0 & p_4 & 0 & 0 \\ 0 & 0 & 0 & 0 & p_5 & 0 \end{pmatrix} \text{ and } B = \begin{pmatrix} f_1 & f_2 & f_3 & 0 & 0 & 0 \\ 0 & 0 & 0 & 0 & 0 & 0 \\ 0 & 0 & 0 & 0 & 0 & 0 \\ 0 & 0 & 0 & 0 & 0 & 0 \\ 0 & 0 & 0 & 0 & 0 & 0 \\ 0 & 0 & 0 & 0 & 0 & 0 \end{pmatrix}$$

where the p values are survival or transition probabilities, so that p_i is the probability that an individual in the ith age-range at one instant survives to appear in the next age range fifteen years later; furthermore, f_1, f_2, and f_3 are the fertility rates. These latter rates represent, for a given age range, the average number of daughters produced in the next fifteen years by all women now in that age range. From this definition, only the first three age-ranges will have attached to them fertility rates which are non-zero.

The matrix $M = S + B$ is a female replacement matrix and, if the vector $\mathbf{v}$ has elements equal to the numbers of females in the six age groups in one time period, then the product $M\mathbf{v}$ will be the numbers in those groups in the following period. After t such periods, with $\mathbf{v}_0$ initially

$$\mathbf{v}_t = M^t \mathbf{v}_0.$$

According to the stable population theory of Lotka, the limit of $\mathbf{v}_t$ as t tends to infinity is $\mathbf{v}_\infty$ which has the property that $M\mathbf{v}_\infty = \lambda \mathbf{v}_\infty$, where λ is the *intrinsic rate of growth of the population* and $\mathbf{v}$ the 'stable or eventual age distribution'. Mathematically, λ is the eigenvalue of largest modulus of the matrix M and $\mathbf{v}_\infty$ is the eigenvector corresponding to it. These values are found readily by powering the matrix using a computer. There is, in principle, no difficulty in extending within the matrix notation the number of age groups, or the structure by introducing sex, social class, and migration within and between populations. An illustration is given in Table 7.1. Once this stable age distribution has been reached, the population growth will be exponential in a continuous or discrete manner as shown in Fig. 7.3 and the proportions of individuals in the age groups will thereafter be constant as in Fig. 7.4.

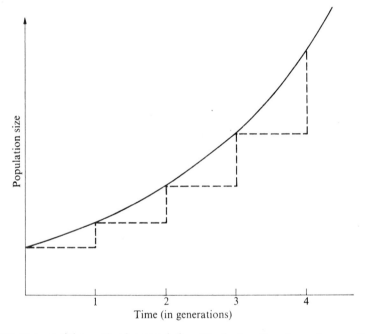

FIG. 7.3. Exponential growth of a population. The broken line shows the growth of a population which increases by a constant proportion of its size at the end of each generation, where generations are of equal length and non-overlapping. The curve represents this growth in continuous time. A closed population experiencing constant birth and death rates where the births are more numerous will grow according to this model according to the stable population theory.

TABLE 7.1

Age composition of females in two populations under the effects of migration and differential fertility and mortality

Population	Age range	Number of females (thousands) after time (years)					Eventual composition (per cent)	
		0	15	30	...	300	(i)	(ii)
I								
	0–14	100	104·0	106·1	...	530·7	33·9	14·6
	15–29	100	98·8	109·0	...	527·9	33·7	14·6
	30–45	100	99·9	98·4	...	506·2	32·4	14·0
Total	0–45	300	302·7	313·5		1564·8	100·0	43·2
II								
	0–14	100	136·0	144·6	...	811·2	39·3	22·4
	15–29	100	97·2	125·9	...	668·4	32·4	18·4
	30–45	100	99·8	97·3	...	582·4	28·3	16·0
Total	0–45	300	333·0	367·8		2062·0	100·0	56·8
Total I+II		600	635·7	681·3		3626·8	—	100·0

In this illustration, only females, in three age ranges up to and including reproductive ages, are considered since only their vital rates affect the growth of the two populations. In Population I, females in these ranges are assigned probabilities 0·25, 0·5, and 0·25 of producing a female live birth in the next fifteen years, and probabilities 0·99, 0·999, and 0 of surviving that period. The corresponding probabilities for Population II are 0·35, 0·7, and 0·35 and for survivals 0·97, 0·998, and 0. These values are applied to non-migrants and migrants are presumed to have values equal to the average of their origin and destination values; the probability of migration between I and II in either direction is taken here to be independent of age and equal to 0·2.

Although described in terms of two populations, this illustration may be thought of in the context of two social classes within a single closed population. Very roughly, the vital rates above correspond to two occupational groups, which may be termed non-manual and manual, but the migration or mobility rate is set too high for any actual population such as England and Wales, 1969. Despite the high mobility, there are sizeable differences between I and II in the overall eventual age and class distributions, shown in columns (i) and (ii). II is a larger and younger population (55 per cent of total; mean age of females specified, 19·95) than I (45 per cent of total; mean age 22·24). The intrinsic rate of growth is 1·0973 per fifteen-year period or 1·006 per year, approximately.

On the supposition that knowledge of a population consists of age-specific birth and death rates, certain statements may be made concerning the behaviour of this population assuming that the rates remain constant. In particular, as has been shown, the birth and death rates determine directly an 'intrinsic rate of growth' for the population. Whether this rate of growth is realized in the short term will of course depend upon the present age structure of the population. As well as the growth rate itself, an 'eventual age distribution' for the population will be determined by the birth and death rates. The degree of similarity between this eventual distribution and that in the present age distribution will principally decide two things: firstly, the closeness of the actual short-term growth of the population to its intrinsic growth rate, and secondly, the time taken before the actual age structure corresponds to the eventual one, which will not then change further. Equivalently, it is the time which must pass before the actual rate of growth becomes the intrinsic rate of growth. An important observation at this stage is that

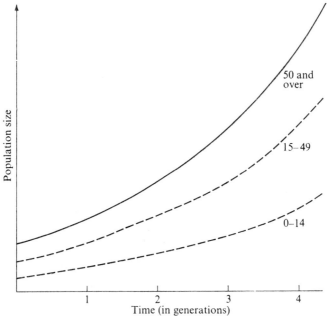

FIG. 7.4. Population growth with stable age distribution. In each of three age groups, the proportions remain constant and the numbers grow at the same rate. This is the limiting situation ultimately to be attained over a sufficiently long period by a population which experiences constant birth and death rates.

except in trivial situations of no demographic interest the eventual age distribution in no way depends upon the present age distribution of the population.

In the above discussion, the stability of the age structure of a population has been the central feature. This stable population will be achieved eventually assuming that the birth and death rates remain constant. When these rates change with time for any given population, and when they differ for several populations, the stable population for each set of rates may serve respectively as a basis for comparison of the given population at different times or several populations at the same time.

The notion of using the stable population for making comparisons of actual populations has been extended by Keyfitz (1968). He considers, for a stable population with the observed mortality and fertility, changes in the value of a population parameter (for example, the mean age of the population) and by means of a factorial approach he decomposes a change in the parameter into parts due to changes in the birth rates, death rates, and the interaction between birth and death rate changes. This kind of use of models, although referring to the unreal stable population, represents a valuable aid to understanding population phenomena. A particular finding of some interest is the alternating pattern in the England and Wales population and other Western European populations whereby changes in the mean age are in one generation due to a change in mortality and in the next to a change in fertility with this sequence repeating every two generations for a period of somewhat more than a hundred years.

All analyses of this kind, it must be borne in mind, are in terms of the stable population, and changes in rates may be regarded as causing the actual population to steer a new course in its progress to some new stable rate. That such analysis is capable of misinterpretation is clear when it is realized that the actual mean age of a population (or, of course, any other population parameter) may change dramatically even though the mortality and fertility it experiences remain constant. As has already been indicated, this would be due to an initially unstable age distribution in relation to the prevailing mortality and fertility.

These remarks remain true for models with more highly structured populations. Recent developments, in particular the work of Goodman (1969) and Bartlett (1970), have increased enormously the complexity of population structures as represented in mathematical models. The intrinsic rate of growth and reproductive capacity of a population which have been investigated in earlier models through the female line only, are now extended to include consideration of the direct effects of sex ratio, male fertility, parity, marriage duration, etc. However, the increasing adoption of matrix models (Bernadelli 1941, Leslie 1945, Keyfitz 1964) has enabled structures of the hierarchical or nested type, such as parity, marriage duration, or social class, to be incorporated as well as crossed structures such as sex, or years at school.

Of all possible structures of a population, one which has been widely recognized as important in studies of differential fertility and mortality in populations is the occupational or social class structure. In considering the effects upon demographic parameters, social mobility is likely to be an important factor because of the differential fertility and mortality in the social classes. Particularly where this mobility affects class sizes and perhaps, as a consequence, the overall rates in the population, the mobility may change the rates within the classes, without necessarily changing class sizes. There have been many sociological studies of intra- and inter-generation mobility and a few (notably Goodman 1962, Hodge 1966, and Matras 1961, 1967) have been concerned with the treatment by mathematical models in the form of stochastic processes. In particular, Matras has shown the developing occupational distributions with time for several nations on the assumption that the inter-generation mobility may be represented by a first-order Markov process with constant transition probabilities. An unsatisfactory aspect of such work using stochastic processes is the lack of information from actual data which would validate the Markovian assumption, i.e. that the probability of mobility at any time depends only upon the class occupied at that time, though in a limited way the evidence of Hodge (1966) shows that this is sometimes a reasonable approximation. It would be less acceptable to assume that social mobility and differential fertility were independent factors.

Although constituting an important class of models, those which consider population growth as a function of specific rates of mortality and fertility according to some structure of a population are not the only ones. Other types of model may consider the relationship between demographic variables within populations and describe the pattern of migration between populations. It is a matter of some conjecture whether these further types of model are in reality of even more importance to the anthropologist. Whereas population size is clearly of profound significance to him through its effect upon genetic constitution through drift, migration is of similar genetic importance as was developed in matrix terms by Roberts and Hiorns (1962). As a means of stratification of patterns of human behaviour, the social structure is para-mount and this is clearly likely to change with age structure (Moser and Scott 1961) but may equally be changed by repeated selective migration (Harrison, Hiorns, and Küchemann 1970), i.e. where migrants are not a random sample from the population but one in which the higher classes are over-represented. Models which crystallize human behaviour with respect to fertility may relate, for example, birth interval to completed family size and birth order (Küchemann, Boyce, and Harrison 1967) or again mortality to population size (Farr 1885).

Where models containing demographic variables are limited by the statisti-cal distributions of those variables, there is clearly a need to investigate these distributions in some detail. Whereas the form of the distribution may in some instances be general, particular populations will characterize themselves by different parameters. In the case of completed family size, the mean and variance of family size of an English rural population in 1700 would be expected to differ from corresponding parameters in a comparable present-day population even though a modified geometric distribution may correspond closely to observed data from both populations. Such distributions, of course, can never be employed to determine the mechanisms of human behaviour whether at the individual or population level. Their purpose is to summarize data by means of a few parameters which then offer a basis for comparison, between populations or between the fluctuating environments which a given population may experience.

From the genetic and demographic point of view, an important set of distributions are those for marriage distance, which have been discussed by several research workers (e.g. Ravenstein 1889, Cavalli-Sforza 1962, Boyce, Küchemann, and Harrison 1967).

Populations whose structures are simple and constant with time, as was seen in the case of the matrix model, may be investigated in terms of their chief characteristics with recourse only to straightforward direct calculation. When structures become more complex, the mathematical analysis which would lead to the setting up of formulae for such direct computation is inevitably more difficult, and even for simple structures, few such formulae are possible. In these situations, the technique known as simulation is used. The basis of the procedure is to conduct a large number of realizations using random numbers to arrive at random samples from intrinsic probability distributions, in particular, concerning fertility and mortality relating to specific groups of individuals. From a detailed recording of events in the lives of the simulated individuals, derived distributions emerge, for example that of time between live births for women of a certain marital status who are using a particular contraceptive technique and have some specified desired family size. In computer simulations, a great amount of detail of this kind may be incorporated both describing the structures and the transitions between them which individuals undergo during their lives. Furthermore, the accumulated effects may be calculated of vital rates which change with time in response to environmental change due to wars, improved technology (including birth control devices) or other factors (Hyrenius and Adolfsson 1964).

The effect upon population size of mortality caused by epidemics has been studied by many distinguished mathematicians. In the eighteenth century, Daniel Bernoulli and D'Alenbert both considered the probabilities of attack and consequent death by smallpox and the modification of a life table to take account of deaths from the disease. The first epidemic curve, however, is believed to have been produced by Farr about one hundred years ago (Greenwood 1948). Epidemic theory contains the earliest of the stochastic process models (McKendrick 1914) as well as the most fully developed of all such models having demographic interest (Bartlett 1955, 1966, Bailey 1957). A useful review is given by Irwin (1963).

Models for contagious diseases have been derived and used for predicting the time interval between the appearance of subsequent cases. The lengths of the latent and infectious periods are parameters of such models and these may be estimated using data from households containing several susceptibles. Originally applied to measles, one model has also been used for infectious hepatitis (Bailey 1957 and Bailey and Alff-Steinberger 1970). Further applications of this type of model which have hitherto been prevented by the difficulty of the estimation procedure, may be expected in the future from the more widespread use of electronic computers.

Analysis of demographic time-series and the use of models for projection

Models for demographic parameters involving time may portray one or more variables and the correlations of these variables as well as their dependence upon time. In the case of a single variable, the description of data takes the form of a time-series in which observed values of the variable are plotted against time. It is common to many such series that three components in a model may be isolated; these are the trend and seasonal components and the residual or error component. Furthermore, the first of these components, the trend, is often representable by a low-order polynomial and if this can be estimated and removed the seasonal component may be estimated separately. Stepwise estimation of these components using the traditional moving-average technique is well known but these techniques inevitably introduce bias in the estimation. To overcome this bias the simultaneous efficient estimation of trend and seasonal components is necessary and this may be described in terms of an analysis of covariance as shown by Hiorns (1967). A model for live births recorded quarterly might take the form

$$y_t = q_i + ct + e_t$$

where t is the time measured in quarter years, y_t the number of births at time t, q_i the effect of the ith quarter of a year, ct the trend term taken here to be linear, and e_t the random error term. Using the estimation procedure mentioned and applying the model successively to short sequences of the data for England and Wales from 1955 to 1969 produces the predicted values shown for comparison with the actual values in Fig. 7.5. It turns out that little is gained in this situation by introducing into the above model a term on the right-hand side in the previous observation, thus producing an autoregressive model. The error term in the model will be correlated from one observation to the next and this can be taken into account by certain forms of moving average.

The use of moving-average techniques in a demographic context, in connection with models for projection, is difficult to justify because of the fundamentally weak property of all traditional moving averages. This is the lack of precision of the average which is most marked at the ends, one of which concerns the most recent part of the time series. The reason for this is the repeated use which a moving average makes of the middle values of the series, the values towards the ends being used less frequently. More appropriate therefore are averages, or measures of trend, which somehow accumulate information concerning a process while retaining the most recent information and attaching greatest weight to it. These will gradually discard 'historic' information which may have no relevance to the present behaviour of the process. One such average is the exponentially weighted moving average first described by Holt, Modigliani, Muth, and Simon (1960) that attaches observation weights which, as the name implies, decline exponentially from the most recent to the earliest observation.

Exponential smoothing may also be applied to remove the similar but quite separate weakness of regression used to estimate underlying trends in demographic series. In this situation the precision of regression is known to be greatest at the centre of the range of the observed values, not at the right-hand

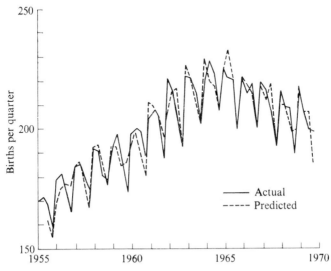

FIG. 7.5. Live births in England and Wales, 1955–69. The actual quarterly recorded births are drawn as the continuous line graph and the broken line represents a prediction made quarterly using the model given in the text. (Data taken from the Registrar General's Quarterly Return.)

end, the region of interest for projection purposes. Exponentially weighted moving averages based initially upon polynomial regression coefficients and modified by differencing of currently observed values serve to describe the current demographic trends as accurately as possible using the most recent history of the population. How recent this history is depends upon the smoothing constant for which suitable values may be found by trial and error, and a compromise has to be found between a value which causes the model to follow all short-term erratic movements and one which causes the model to disregard important effects by its too static behaviour. The choice of this constant depends fundamentally upon the appropriate period of recent history which is relevant to a specific projection. This problem was discussed briefly by Hiorns (1967) using an approach which lends itself to a further investigation of this period. There seems no reason why this period should not become an additional parameter of the model being employed. But this important problem has not received a full mathematical consideration in these terms.

The nearest approaches so far are the model investigations in which the order of an autoregressive sequence is estimated, or their counterparts in terms of spectral theory, and these are of limited value in short-term projection owing to the need for a long base series from which to estimate autocorrelations or the spectrum (Jenkins and Watts 1968).

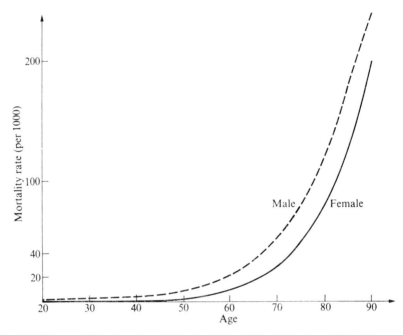

FIG. 7.6. The mortality of males and females in the United Kingdom, 1969. The curves shown are of the Gompertz-type and were fitted to age-specific rates, taken from the Annual Abstract of Statistics, Central Statistical Office.

Models for population projection may be divided into two broad categories: those which seek to determine, having selected appropriate population structures, age- or other structure-specific rates from raw data, and those which employ these rates to make projections. The component method which is employed by demographers embraces two stages corresponding to these two categories of model. In the first category, regression models will be found which relate, for example, mortality to time, or alternatively smooth or graduate a life table. The Gompertz law may be applied for the latter purpose and this particular model has some mathematical affinity with the logistic model (Hiorns 1965).

Mortality curves for adult males and females in the United Kingdom in 1969 are depicted in Fig. 7.6 and these were obtained by fitting Gompertz-type models. For males, the resulting curve for mortality m_x at age x, represented as a rate per thousand, has the equation

$$m_x = (0 \cdot 296) \cdot (1 \cdot 078)^x$$

and for females, $\qquad m_x = (0 \cdot 035) \cdot (1 \cdot 101)^x$

The constants in these equations indicate that the male mortality is always greater over the range of ages for which the curves are fitted but that the mortality rates increase at approximately the same rate (as adjudged by the similarity of the exponents). This latter feature accounts for the 'parallelism' of the curves over the upper part of the age range.

The fitting of curves of some specified mathematical form to fertility rates has employed mainly the Pearson-type distributions, the Hadwiger exponential function (Gilje 1969), as well as the Brass polynomial functions of the form

$$b_x = (x - \alpha + 1)(\beta - x)^2 (a + bx + cx^2 + dx^3)$$

where b_x is the probability of childbearing for a woman age x and a, b, c, and d are constants. The parameters α and β are the limits of the fertile period for women and may be estimated, together with the constants, from observed rates (Brass 1960).

In the second category of projection models, matrices of the type described in detail in the last section are used, in which the rates for fertility, mortality, and migration are entered as elements. The procedure for projection is described by Keyfitz (1964).

Further applications of projection models to particular specially structured populations have been made. In applications to the manpower or workforce projection for an organization, the projection models have to take into account the special differences between birth and immigration in populations and recruitment in the context of an organization and similarly between death and emigration on the one hand and retirement and resignation on the other. One important modification of the population models in organizational contexts deals with the hierarchy of occupations and promotion which represents, in population terms, unidirectional selective migration. Similar modifications are needed to the models for considering the projection of university student populations (Gani 1963). The importance of these manpower applications would seem to be that highly structured communities with special behaviour patterns are becoming the subject of increasing analysis using mathematical models.

To return to the problem of definition of population units, whilst reiterating the enormous difficulty of this task in general, one situation where some solution is possible may be mentioned. This concerns the spatial distribution of populations. If population density is treated as continuous over a two- or three-dimensional map, a spectral analysis may be performed to study the tendency towards clustering (Tobler 1969). This type of analysis may be applied to population systems in which the structures affecting biological or social characteristics are not determined solely by spatial separation.

In conclusion, the development of demographic theory has clearly been very rapid in recent years. The increasing knowledge about populations which has become available in the form of raw data from more refined data-collection procedures has led to demands for improved techniques of analysis. Fortunately, the pace of development of mathematical models upon which to base this analysis has been equally rapid. The introduction of the matrix into more fields of application, the creation of a formal theory of stochastic processes and the innovation of electronic computers are the three major causes for improved model-based investigation of demographic phenomena.

REFERENCES

BAILEY, N. T. J. (1957). *The mathematical theory of epidemics*. Griffin, London.
—— and ALFF-STEINBERGER, C. (1970). Improvements in the estimation of latent and infectious periods of a contagious disease. *Biometrika* **57**, 141–53.
BARTLETT, M. S. (1955). Deterministic and stochastic models for recurrent epidemics. *Proc. III Symp. Mathematical Statistics and Probability, Berkeley*, **4**, 81–109.
—— (1966). *An introduction to stochastic processes with special reference to methods and applications*, 2nd edn. Cambridge University Press.
—— (1970). Age distributions. *Biometrics* **26**, 377–85.
BERNADELLI, H. (1941). Population waves. *J. Burma. Res. Soc.* **31**, 1–18.
BRASS, W. (1960). The graduation of fertility distributions by polynomial functions. *Popul. Stud.* **14**, 148–62.
BOYCE, A. J., KÜCHEMANN, C. F., and HARRISON, G. A. (1967). Neighbourhood knowledge and the distribution of marriage distances. *Ann. hum. Genet.* **30**, 335–8.
CAVALLI-SFORZA, L. L. (1962). The distribution of migration distances: models and applications to genetics. In *Les déplacements humains* (ed. J. Sutter). *Entret. Monaco Sc. Hum.I*, 139–58.
CHIANG, C. L. (1968). *Stochastic processes in biostatistics*. Wiley, New York.
COALE, A. J. (1957). How the age distribution of a human population is determined. *Cold Spring Harb. Symp. quart. Biol.* **22**, 83–9.
FARR, W. (1885). *Vital statistics*. Memorial volume (ed. N. A. Humphreys). Office of the Sanitary Institute, London.
FELLER, W. (1939). Die Grundlagen der Volterraschen Theorie des Kamfes ums Dasein in wahrscheinlichkeitstheoretischer Behandlung. *Acta biotheoret.* **5**, 11–40.
GANI, J. (1963). Formulae for projecting enrolments and degrees awarded in universities. *Jl. R. statist. Soc.* A **126**, 400–9.
GILJE, E. (1969). Fitting curves to age-specific fertility rates: some examples. *Statistik tidskrift* **2**, 118–34.
GLASS, D. V. (1950). Graunt's life table. *J. Inst. Actuar.* **76**, 60–4.
GOODMAN, L. A. (1962). Statistical methods for analysing processes of change. *Am. J. Sociol.* **68**, 57–78.
—— (1969). The analysis of population growth when the birth and death rates depend upon several factors. *Biometrics* **25**, 659–81.
GRAUNT, J. (1662). *Natural and political observations made upon the Bills of Mortality by John Graunt*. (ed. W. F. Wilcox) Reprinted by Johns Hopkins Press, Baltimore (1939).
GREENWOOD, M. (1948). *Medical statistics from Graunt to Farr*. Cambridge University Press.
HALLEY, E. (1693). An estimate of the degrees of mortality of mankind drawn from curious tables of births and funerals at the City of Breslaw; with an attempt to ascertain the price of annuities upon lives. *Phil. Trans. R. Soc.* **17**, 596–610.
HARRISON, G. A., HIORNS, R. W., and KÜCHEMANN, C. F. (1970). Social class relatedness in some Oxfordshire parishes. *J. biosoc. Sci.* **2**, 71–80.

HIORNS, R. W. (1965). *The fitting of growth and allied curves of the asymptotic regression type by Stevens's Method*. Tracts for Computers Series, Vol. XXVIII. Cambridge University Press.

—— (1967). Seasonal adjustment and forecasting in the presence of trend. *Comput. J.* **10**, 143–9.

HODGE, R. W. (1966). Occupational mobility as a probability process. *Demography* **3**, 19–34.

HOEM, J. M. (1970). Probabilistic fertility models of the life table type. *Theoret. Popul. Biol.* **1**, 12–38.

HOLT, C. C., MODIGLIANI, F., MUTH, J. F., and SIMON, H. A. (1960). *Planning production, inventories, and workforce*. Prentice-Hall, Inc., Englewood Cliffs, N.J.

HYRENIUS, H. and ADOLFSSON, I. (1964). *A fertility simulation model*. Almquist and Wiksell, Göteburg.

IRWIN, J. O. (1963). The place of mathematics in medical and biological statistics. *Jl. R. statist. Soc.* A **126**, 1–45.

JENKINS, G. M. and WATTS, D. G. (1968). *Spectral analysis and its applications*. Holden-Day Inc., San Francisco.

KEMENY, J. G. and SNELL, J. L. (1960). *Finite Markov chains*. Van Nostrand, Princeton.

KENDALL, D. G. (1949). Stochastic processes and population growth. *Jl. R. statist. Soc.* **11**, 230–65.

KEYFITZ, N. (1964). Matrix multiplication as a technique of population analysis. *Milbank meml Fund Q. Bull.* **42**, 68–84.

—— (1968). Changing vital rates and age distributions. *Popul. Stud.* **22**, 235–51.

KÜCHEMANN, C. F., BOYCE, A. J., and HARRISON, G. A. (1967). A demographic and genetic study of a group of Oxfordshire villages. *Hum. Biol.* **39**, 251–76.

LESLIE, P. H. (1945). On the use of matrices in certain population mathematics. *Biometrika* **33**, 183–212.

LOPEZ, A. (1961). *Problems in stable population theory*. Princeton, N.J. Office of Population Research.

LOTKA, A. J. (1925). *Elements of physical biology*. Williams and Wilkins, Baltimore.

MATRAS, J. (1961). Differential fertility, intergenerational occupational mobility, and change in occupational distribution: some elementary relationships. *Popul. Stud.* **15**, 187–97.

—— (1967). Social mobility and social structure: some insights from the linear model. *Am. sociol. Rev.* **32**, 608–14.

McFARLAND, D. D. (1969). On the theory of stable populations: a new and elementary proof of the theorems under weaker assumptions. *Demography* **6**, 301–22.

McKENDRICK, A. G. (1914). Studies on the theory of continuous probabilities with special reference to its bearing on natural phenomena of a progressive nature. *Proc. Lond. math. Soc.* **13**, 401–16.

—— and PAI, M. K. (1911). The rate of multiplication of micro-organisms: a mathematical study. *Proc. R. Soc. Edinb.* **31**, 649–55.

MOSER, C. A. and SCOTT, W. (1961). *British towns*. Oliver and Boyd, Edinburgh.

NICHOLSON, A. J. and BAILEY, V. A. (1935). The balance of animal populations. *Proc. zool. Soc. Lond.* **3**, 551–98.

RAVENSTEIN, E. G. (1889). The laws of migration. *Jl. R. statist. Soc.* **52**, 241–305.

ROBERTS, D. F. and HIORNS, R. W. (1962). The dynamics of racial intermixture. *Am. J. hum. Genet.* **14**, 261–77.

SOKAL, R. R. and SNEATH, P. H. A. (1963). *Principles of numerical taxonomy*. Freeman, London.

SUTHERLAND, I. (1963). John Graunt: A tercentenary tribute. *Jl. R. statist. Soc.* A **126**, 537–56.

TOBLER, W. R. (1969). Geographical filters and their inverses. *Geogr. Anal.* **3**, 234–53.

VERHULST, P. F. (1847). Deuxième mémoire sur la loi d'accroissement de la population. *Nouv. Mem. Acad. Roy. Sci. et Belles-Lettr. de Bruxelles* **20**, 1–32.

VOLTERRA, V. (1931). *Leçons sur la théorie mathematique de la lutte pour la vie*. Gautier-Villars, Paris.

8

MIGRATION, EXCHANGE, AND THE GENETIC STRUCTURE OF POPULATIONS

G. A. HARRISON *and* A. J. BOYCE

THE human species is remarkable in its wide geographical range and there are few areas of the earth's surface which are not permanently inhabited by at least some people. Few other species, especially among mammals, can match this extensive distribution and many of those that do, owe their range directly or indirectly to that of man. Until the middle of the Pleistocene, hominids appear to have been confined to what were then tropical and sub-tropical regions of the Old World, but, taking the usual view that at least since the end of the lower Pleistocene there has never been more than one extant species of hominid, even this limited earlier geographical distribution was considerable. And since that time, and especially during the Upper Pleistocene, there has been constant expansion into the colder regions of the world. Clearly this latter expansion depended upon the acquisition of cultural traits which encapsulated man in an environment of his own making, but it was largely completed before the advanced technology associated with the neolithic was achieved, and at a time when man was still a comparatively rare animal. The wide range, rapid expansion in that range, and the unity of the human species in its recent evolutionary history imply characteristics of great mobility both of the species as a whole, and of the individuals who compose it. Indeed, it seems very likely that migration and other forms of movement have been one of the main factors maintaining the integrity of the human species in its wide geographical range. Gene flow, which occurs only through some form of movement, is the great homogenizing influence in evolution.

At no time in human evolution, however, have individuals been distributed at all evenly in space. Quite apart from differences in the favourability of ecological conditions and in levels of technical sophistication which produce marked variations in population density in different parts of the world, people, for social and economic reasons, tend to live in clusters in all types of environment. These clusters may be more or less permanently sited in one place as are villagers in many modern agricultural societies, or may be transitory in their situation, as in nomadic settlements, but typically in either case, the people themselves tend to be grouped together and to be separated by space, which though exploited by one group or another, can be regarded as being largely uninhabited. Despite high levels of individual mobility, the spatial separation of clusters tends to act as a barrier to reproduction, and typically, though not invariably, mating within spatially separated clusters tends to occur more frequently than between them—or at least between any pair of them. When this is so, the clusters are frequently the smallest units in the hierarchy of Mendelian populations which make up the human species. A Mendelian population has been defined by Dobzhansky (1955) as 'a reproductive community of individuals who share in a common gene pool'.

In recent times, with rapid population growth and advancing technologies, there has been an increasing tendency, especially in industrial societies, for people to have become more or less evenly and densely distributed over quite considerable areas. Small clusters have expanded and coalesced, and though the resulting conurbations still tend to be separated from one another by relatively uninhabited space, they have generated a different type of genetic structure within themselves. Although none are so large as to prevent individuals from moving in their own lifetime over the whole of their area, especially since the population growth has coincided with the development of mechanical transport, people usually do not move at all evenly over the range. In particular, they tend to take their mates from within some limited part of the distribution. When this is so, the demographic population is not the basic genetic unit, and the genetic structure can best be viewed as a series of overlapping neighbourhoods—a concept which will be developed further later.

Space and distance can clearly be seen to be prime determinants of genetic structure, but of course many other factors, especially social, cultural, and religious ones, affect human mate selection. Often what appears to be a single demographic unit may be composed of a number of smaller Mendelian populations and people who are geographically separated may interbreed more commonly than people in the same locality. We shall return later to the problems this poses, but recognizing the importance of social factors in determining genetic structure in no way invalidates the view that patterns of human movement are critical in determining the way the human species is organized.

There are clearly many components to human movement, but the only ones of genetic concern are those which lead to an individual of one population contributing his genes to another. From the point of view of population surveys of genetic composition, non-reproducing immigrants may be of concern, but typically gene flow implies the production of offspring in a population other than that in which either one or other or both parents were themselves born. Also of interest, since it affects geographical distribution of genes, is the case where a population maintains itself as a single unit, but transfers itself by migration from one place to another. The two types of movement can of course occur synchronously.

Long-range movement

It may also be convenient to distinguish between long-range movement and short-range movement, though the distinction is clearly only one of degree, and again it is possible for both to occur at more or less the same time. Long-range movement is, however, of special concern in considering the broad evolutionary prospectus of a species, whilst short-range movement is of paramount importance in determining local genetic structure and differentiation. Long-range movement can itself occur either by the migration of a group of people during their own lifetime over some considerable distance, or by the continual movement of a population through many generations over an equivalent distance. The former has been particularly frequent in historical time, and of course is ever increasing. In many cases, though by no means all, the migrants are initially characterized by a disturbed sex ratio, which leads particularly to miscegenation with local populations en route and on arrival. It is difficult to know how extensive such far-ranging individual mobility was in prehistoric and early historic times. Clearly, the distances covered were much less before the advent of advanced technology, but there is evidence that in conquest and in the activities of itinerant traders and craftsmen, individuals moved over some very considerable distances. However, until quite recently it seems likely that most long-range movement occurred by the constant small movements of whole populations or parts of them. That this can produce very rapid expansion is indicated by the spread of populations of modern skeletal type throughout Europe following the retreat of the Würm I glaciations, and even more so by the colonization of the New World by Amerindian populations some of whom must have moved the length of the Americas in a few thousand years. More generally, the rapid spread of archaeological cultures and industries might suggest extensive movement. However, ideas and techniques can clearly move much faster than genes, though often the expansion of a particular culture in the past has been definitely associated with the movements of people. Overall, the evidence suggests that long-range movement in one form or another has been a widespread phenomenon throughout the later phases of human evolution, certainly since the origin of *Homo sapiens*. Such movement, however, except in most recent times is usually difficult to quantify in amount and effect, and tends not to follow any simple pattern, or show adherence to rigid migration laws.

Short-range movement

This is far less true of short-range movement, which is broadly dictated by routine daily activity patterns. Those aspects which are here of main concern, because of their genetic implications, are the movement of individuals which directly or indirectly lead to the choice of a mate, and the subsequent movement of pairs, which determines into which populations the offspring are introduced. Since children are usually born within some form of 'wedlock', the former can conveniently be referred to as marital movement. It is one important component of parent–offspring movement—the matter of critical genetic concern—post-marital movement being the other. Much of the data available relates to marital movement, at least in Europe, where marriage-records, especially for non-contemporary populations, provide the most generally available information; but from census-type records, it is often possible to establish directly parent–offspring movement. With increasing mobility it is becoming progressively more important to take account of post-marital movement, but in the past it would appear that by far the greatest contribution to parent–offspring movement came from marital movement. Marital movement can be thought of as having four possible components: magnitude, distance, orientation and direction, and we shall first consider these separately.

Magnitude is typically measured in terms of the amount of spatial exogamy. Because they are isolated by distance, demographic units such as villages or parishes are usually taken as Mendelian populations and the extent to which both marriage partners come from within one of these compared with the extent to which one partner comes from outside, provides an endogamy/exogamy ratio or the exogamy rate. Clearly in an exogamous union only one person moves, and allowance for this is made in calculating the genetic effects of exchange. In most societies, it is typically the woman who moves into her husband's population; but even when this is so, it is common for the marriage actually to take place in the bride's population. When using records of marriages such as parish registers as sources of information on exogamy, one is therefore usually making an indirect estimate of the proportion of mates coming into a population from outside, but one would expect, and one usually finds, that exchanges through marriage between any two populations are symmetrical.

The extent of spatial exogamy is influenced by many factors, and varies from place to place, time to time, and society to society. Most of the quantitative information comes from agricultural European communities. Alström and Lindelius (1966), for Swedish parishes, found exogamy rates varying in the first half of the nineteenth century from 40 per cent to nearly 90 per cent. In the Parma villages studied by Cavalli-Sforza (1958) the rates averaged over the last three centuries ranged from 23 to 66 per cent. A number of estimates have been made for various English rural populations (Buckatzsch 1951, Chambers 1957, Eversley 1957, Sogner 1963) which show considerable regional and temporal differences, and examples from other European countries show the same phenomena (see Beckman 1961). Despite this heterogeneity, if the same populations are examined for different historic periods, there is, as one would expect, a general tendency within the recent past for exogamy rates to increase. Thus Küchemann, Boyce, and Harrison (1967) found in a group of Oxfordshire villages a progressive increase in exogamy from rates of around 40 per cent in the early seventeenth century to 64 per cent during the last fifty years. Data for the past are not so available for non-European societies, but that spatial exogamy is in general a quantitatively important demographic and genetic phenomenon is shown, for instance, by the observations of Tindale (1953) that in Australian Aborigines tribal exogamy occurs, with a range of 7 to 21 per cent. The causes for exogamy are varied: among a group of rural Dorset villages in mid-nineteenth century England, Perry (1969) found by multiple regression analysis that variations between the villages in exogamy were related principally to village size and density, regional location with respect to geology and, therefore, type of agriculture, literacy rate, and distance from neighbouring towns and railways. However, in other types of situation, quite clearly, totally different factors are concerned.

Local genetic structure is determined not only by the amount of gene flow into a population, but also by the size of the geographical area over which the genes are flowing. The area of flow, which arises from marital movement, can be derived from the distance between the birthplaces of spouses. Such marital distances have sometimes been averaged only over the exogamous unions, but in other cases, endogamous unions regarded as representing a marital distance of nought, have also been included in the average. As indicated earlier, when parent–offspring distances can be established, they provide a better measure of the movement of genetic importance, since they take into account post-marital movement. Parent–offspring distance has sometimes been measured as father–offspring distance, in other cases as mother–offspring distance, but most commonly as the mean of the distances between the birthplaces of both parents and the birthplace of their offspring. Unless otherwise stated, the term will be used here in this sense only. If movement tends to occur throughout the life of parents, the birthplaces of sibs obviously may differ from one another. In such cases, the distance between birthplaces of parents and of the last-born child is likely to provide the best estimate of the genetic movement. At least until quite recently, however, it would appear that children tended to be born in the birthplace of one or other parent, i.e. there was little post-marital movement. When this is so, the parent–offspring distance clearly equals half the marital distance. Cavalli-Sforza (1962) found for the Parma villages he studied that the mean marital distance was approximately 10 miles, and the average parent–offspring distance 6 miles. Alström and Lindelius (1966) did not present figures for marital distance, but calculated parent–offspring distance in a Swedish parish during the mid-nineteenth century as 4·8 miles. This figure corresponds exactly to that found during much the same period in Oxfordshire villages for father–offspring distance, when mean marital distance was 9·7 miles.

When information is available for the same population over a period, there tends to be systematic variation over time in marital distance. Thus, for instance, Küchemann *et al.* (1967) found in Oxfordshire villages that whilst there was little change in mean marital distance during the seventeenth, eighteenth, and early nineteenth centuries when it never exceeded 10 miles, around the mid-nineteenth century there was a dramatic rise to between 20 and 30 miles. This rise was associated with the advent of mechanized forms of transport in the region.

Whilst average data on marital distance are usually presented as means of observed distances, such means can be very profoundly affected by occasional marriages contracted over very large distances. The frequency of such marriages has been ever increasing, but inclusion of them in estimates of marital distance has effects on means which are out of all proportion to their genetic effects. Various methods have been used to obviate this problem, including transformation of the distance scale, but perhaps the most satisfactory for most purposes is to use median distances rather than means. This average was used by Spuhler (1961) in analysing recent marital movement into Ann Arbor, Michigan, where many of the marriages were contracted over great distances. Spuhler found in this highly mobile society that the median marital distance was 160 miles.

Not only are average marital and parent–offspring distances important in determining genetic structure, but the distributions of these distances are also of concern. These distributions are affected not only by mobility but also by the way the interchanging populations are arranged in space. In the simplest situation, one can envisage a series of population clusters distributed evenly in space. Clearly, the number of populations situated within a given radius of any one population is a function of the area determined by that radius. And since the radius which determines marital distance increases as a linear function, the area increases as the square of that function. It follows that, with an even distribution of populations in space, the number of populations lying within unit increments of distance away from any one population increases linearly. Such a relationship is bound to affect distributions of marital distances, though allowance can obviously be made for it. Its effects can also be ignored, if the contributions made by a series of surrounding populations to a central one are each considered separately of one another. Thus, one can plot the frequency of marital movement between pairs of populations as a function of their distance apart. This was done by Boyce, Küchemann, and Harrison (1967) in considering the local marriage movement within Oxfordshire villages (Fig. 8.1). Such a distribution can be regarded as an *average* curve of marital distance.

More commonly, and especially when all marital movement is taken into account, the contributions from all populations within particular distance classes are added together and the distribution represented in histogram form (Fig. 8.2). Such a distribution can be regarded as representing an *aggregate* curve of marital distance and is affected by the relationship between population number and distance. The type of effect produced by representing marital movement in these two forms can be seen by comparing the average curve (Fig. 8.1) with that part of the aggregate curve (Fig. 8.2) referring to movement within the five-mile limit. It will be noted in this instance, that although

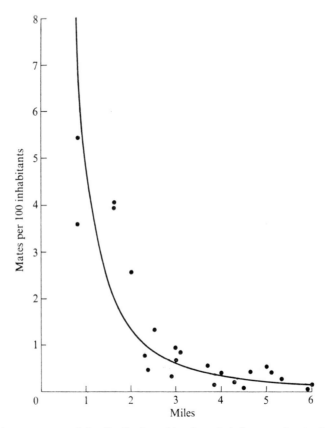

FIG. 8.1. Average curve of the distribution of local marital distances for the Oxfordshire village of Charlton-on-Otmoor in the mid-nineteenth century (exogamous marriages only).

there is an exponential decline with distance in the contribution that any one population makes to another, the contributions from all populations within a three-mile radius do not differ very much from the contributions made by the populations lying between the three- to five-mile limits. In other words, the decline with distance within five miles occurring when populations are considered separately is offset by the increase in the number of populations with distance.

In presenting both average and aggregate curves one is, as it were, 'rolling up' the two-dimensional distribution of populations, and presenting their contributions to one another as though they lay on a single line. It is thus being assumed that there is no orientation to the movement, though evidence of simple asymmetry in contributions would appear in the average distribution where the position of points on the graph might for instance suggest that one was dealing with two curves rather than one.

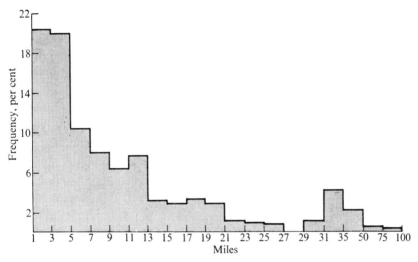

FIG. 8.2. Aggregate curve of the distribution of marital distances for the Otmoor region of Oxfordshire in the mid-nineteenth century (exogamous marriages only).

Little attention appears to have been paid to spatial orientations in marital movement, though in considering the contributions made by a series of Oxfordshire villages to a central one, Boyce, Küchemann, and Harrison (1968) by drawing 'contours' around populations making identical contributions, did find that distinct orientations were introduced by differences in population size, roadway patterns, and uninhabited land. Whilst such factors affecting marital movement must be commonplace, they probably usually act only on a very local scale. Whether this is so or not, it would be difficult to allow for orientation in some of the models of population structure which will be considered later, and it is usually assumed that marital movement is isotropic, i.e. has no orientation.

Although marital movement can have orientation, one would not expect it to show additional direction, and the exchange between any two populations may be expected to be symmetric. Where it has been tested, this expectation seems to be more or less realized. However, there is clearly no necessary expectation of symmetric exchange in post-marital movement, and here cases of directional movement are common. Thus, for instance, in the study of Oxfordshire villages made by Boyce *et al.* (1968) there was clear evidence from census data of an overall directional movement of people along a north-east–south-west axis, probably generated by the active attraction of the City of Oxford during its main growth period.

Despite the tendency, which is no doubt increasing, for overall movement to show direction, father–offspring, mother–offspring, and parent–offspring distances for those few societies which have been studied show similar distributions to marital distance. This can be seen for the Oxfordshire village

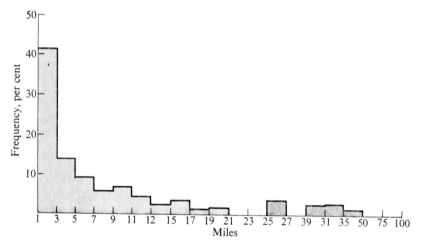

FIG. 8.3. Aggregate curve of the distribution of parent–offspring distances for the Otmoor region of Oxfordshire in the mid-nineteenth century (exogamous marriages only).

situation by comparing Fig. 8.2 with Fig. 8.3 which indicates again that for these populations in the mid-nineteenth century, post-marital movement had little effect on the area of gene flow.

The forms of the distributions of marital and parent–offspring distance have been subjected to considerable analysis (e.g. Cavalli-Sforza 1962). In attempting to explain the average type distribution of marital distance for very local movement, Boyce *et al.* (1967) invoked the concept of neighbour-hood knowledge. This model derives from the facts that agricultural communities have a more or less permanent home base to which people tend to return each night; that daily mobility before the advent of mechanized transport was limited to a few miles; and that people travelling on foot or horse-back do not travel blindly and in moving to any distant place pass through the intermediate places both as they travel out and back. They may, therefore, be expected to come to know their immediate neighbourhood particularly well. On this basis, it was possible to construct a model in which the frequency of marriages with the inhabitants of a village at a particular distance from the home base, when allowance is made for the number of inhabitants, is given by an expression of the form $ar^{-b}/2^b(b-1)$ where r represents distance and b the exponent in the relationship between frequency of journeys and distance. The model was fitted to the observed average marital distance distribution for an Oxfordshire village and produced a derived value for the b coefficient of nearly 2 which suggests that the frequency of journeys of a particular distance is inversely proportional to approximately the square of that distance.

In considering the aggregate distributions of marital distance, particularly as observed among Parma villages in Italy, Cavalli-Sforza (1958) has applied models both of diffusion and gravitational attraction. The first of these he derived from the theoretical curve for normal diffusion of the form

$$f(x, y) = \frac{1}{\pi v} e^{-(x^2 + y^2)/v}$$

where f is the frequency of marriages, v the mean square distance from the origin, and x and y the distances in rectangular co-ordinates from the origin. This model provided a poor fit to the observed distributions, but it seems that diffusion may play some role in determining marital distance, since the older the spouses at marriage, the greater are the distance between their birthplaces.

In the gravitational model, Cavalli-Sforza envisaged populations attracting people to them according to their size and distance away. If such attraction conformed to the physical laws of gravity, one would expect the probability of an individual taking a marriage partner from some population to be directly proportional to the number of people in that population and inversely proportional to the square of the distance between the population and the birthplace of the individual 'seeking' a partner. Thus the frequency of marriage at distance r will be equal to kAr^{-2} where A is the number of people living at distance r. The gravitational model fits quite well the distribution of marital distances over shorter distances among Parma villages, a Swedish village, and the city of Philadelphia, but does not account for the longer range marital movement. It shows certain similarities with the neighbourhood knowledge approach.

These models derive from theories about the causes of human movement and are clearly important in understanding aspects of human behaviour. However, from the point of view of the effect of movement on the genetic structure and relatedness of populations, all that matters is that the movement can be described accurately and in summary form. Empirical approaches are therefore just as useful and all types of functions have been used for representing the distributions of marital distance and parent–offspring distance. Those which have been most frequently used are linear, logarithmic, normal, exponential, and gamma functions (Morrill 1962) and, with varying degrees of success, these can be fitted to observed distributions. Because these distributions tend to be both comparatively regular in form and of similar pattern in different populations, at least among sedentary communities, they would seem to represent some general migration law, but clearly the expression of this law is not uniform, and one would not expect it to be so.

Population models

Exchange and movement, as already indicated, are critical determinants of the genetic structure of populations and have to be taken into account in considering such important genetic parameters as effective population size, inbreeding and consanguinity, and genetic variance within and between populations; whilst outbreeding and hybridization are largely functions of movement alone. All models of population structure must therefore take movement into account. The prime aim of these models is usually, though not invariably, to present the framework in which the causes for the ubiquitous genetic variation between populations can be sought. Many models of varying levels of sophistication have been proposed, starting basically with the original isolate concept of Dahlberg (1929). Most of the recent work, however, derives from the pioneering work of Sewall Wright (1943 and 1951). Wright presented two types of model structure—the *island model* and the *diffuse model*.

In the first of these he considered a series of spatially separated populations —the so-called islands—between which there is exchange, and defined the structure in terms of the effective sizes of the populations and the effective amount of gene flow into each of these populations, including systematic migration from outside the cluster which is assumed to be qualitatively the same into all of the separate islands. It is further assumed that there is no qualitative heterogeneity between populations inside the system in the nature of the contributions they receive from each other. However, the outside and inside flows may themselves differ. Under these circumstances Wright showed that an equilibrium state is reached in which the genetic variance between islands is independent of the migration pattern between them and depends only on the effective population sizes of the islands (which he took to be the same) and on the rate of immigration from outside the system. The genetic variance at equilibrium is

$$\frac{\bar{q}(1-\bar{q})}{4N_e\,m+1}$$

where $\bar{q}$ is the frequency of a gene in the total cluster, N_e the effective population size, and m the magnitude of migration from outside, but this only applies where m is relatively small. What is termed outside immigration in this model as in others can be taken also to include the effects of differential genetic selection, and mutation. From the model Lasker and Kaplan (1964) extracted the two parameters N_e and m whose product they used as a measure of isolation among Peruvian populations and termed the *coefficient of breeding isolation*.

The second model proposed by Wright caters for the demographic situation in which people are not arranged in clusters, but are both widely and diffusely distributed in space. As already mentioned, with limited local mobility, mating is typically not at random within such populations. Wright defined their genetic structure in terms of the concept of *neighbourhood* which mathematically is the inverse of the probability of self-fertilization. This probability is determined on the one hand by the population density and on the other by the amount and nature of the mobility. It was assumed that the mobility was of normal diffusion form and could be characterized by the standard deviation of the difference in the birthplaces of parents and offspring. Thus, neighbourhood size N can be calculated as $4\pi\sigma^2 d$, where d is population density and σ^2 the variance of parent/offspring distance (i.e. along an axis, as in the 'rolled up' form of average distributions). As with the island model, Wright went on to show the relationship between the size of the neighbourhood and the expected genetic variance. The diffuse model has been applied by Alström and Lindelius (1966) who, for Swedish parishes during the period 1800–1824, for instance, found neighbourhood diameters ranging from 12 to 20 kilometres and neighbourhood sizes from 600–4400 individuals. For Japanese populations Spuhler (personal communication) estimated neighbourhood sizes to be of the order of 2×10^6. The importance of the two models of Wright cannot be overestimated, but they were primarily designed for consideration of the possible effects of genetic drift, and only indirectly for analysing the effects of movement on the genetic similarity between neighbouring populations. In fact, in the island model, the form of local movement and heterogeneity within the system are not taken into account and in the diffuse model, the assumption that movement is governed by the laws of normal diffusion, as indicated earlier, is highly questionable.

In recent years more direct attention has been devoted to the causes of genetical covariance between different populations and greater concern has been given to the actual form of movement and the way this affects the development and levels of between-population similarity. The two main analytical approaches are due to Kimura and Weiss (Kimura and Weiss 1964, Weiss and Kimura 1965) and Malécot (e.g. 1948, 1959, 1962, 1966). The Kimura–Weiss models consider directly the covariance of gene frequencies in a number of neighbouring populations, subject to inter-exchange and systematic pressures such as long-range migration. They were developed initially with rather simple organizations for population sizes and patterns of migration, e.g. a rectangular lattice of populations of equal size with single-step migration between these populations—hence the so-called stepping-stone model. But it was shown that the models could be extended to more complex situations, and that in each case, if long-range migration is not excessive, an equilibrium is established in which there is generally an exponential decline in covariance with distance. These models are mathematically complex and appear not as yet to have been applied to any practical situation. Further, though they can be more generalized, they are derived initially, as in Wright's island model, from the assumption that human populations are organized into discrete clusters.

The work of Malécot broadly parallels that of Kimura and Weiss, but was based on developing an integro-differential equation for a continuum, and is thus more applicable to a diffuse population structure. Furthermore, similarity is defined in terms of relatedness, the coefficient of kinship, rather than expressly in correlation. The coefficient of kinship between two individuals is defined as the probability that one locus chosen at random from the two loci of one individual and one locus chosen at random from among the homologous loci of the other individual are identical (Malécot 1966). Less exactly, but more briefly, it can be said to be the probability that at any particular locus, two individuals will have a gene in common, identical by descent. When the two individuals are mates the coefficient of kinship between them equals the coefficient of inbreeding of their children. Clearly, the coefficient of kinship tends to decline with increasing distance between the birthplaces of individuals, since the probability of common ancestry decreases with distance. And the rate of the decline depends upon the form of the migration law, that is on those probabilities which determine the distribution of parent–offspring distances and which we have previously considered. If one knows the spatial distribution of the coefficient of kinship in any one generation then its distribution in the next is determined by parent–offspring distances and a recurrence relationship can be established. Assuming that parent–offspring distances are normally distributed, i.e. that they decrease exponentially with the square of distance, Malécot showed that an equilibrium level is reached when the coefficient of kinship between individuals distance d apart equals $a\mathrm{e}^{-bd}\,d^{-c}$ where a is the mean coefficient of kinship of local populations and c is related to the dimensionality of movement and equals $1/2$ for isotropic movement in two dimensions. The coefficient b equals $\sqrt{2\mu}/\sigma$, where σ is the standard deviation of parent–offspring distance and μ is the measure of systematic pressure, such as long-range migration or selection. The relationship, further, is not confined to the situation where parent–offspring distances are normally distributed, but holds also for other exponential and K-functions.

To apply the Malécot approach to real situations, one needs to know the distributions of phenotypes and birthplaces over a region; one can then attempt to fit the curve of expected spatial variation, as predicted from the formula for the coefficient of kinship, to the observed variation. This has been done by Azevêdo, Morton, Miki, and Yee (1969) for populations in north-eastern Brazil and by Morton, Yasuda, Miki, and Yee (1968) in

Switzerland. Using the similarity between pairs of individuals in polymorphic systems, anthropometric characters, and isonomy (surname concordance) in relation to the distance apart of their birthplaces, Azevêdo *et al.* found that they could fit the predicted variation to the observed variation in Brazil, particularly well over mid-range distances. Similar results were obtained for Swiss ABO blood group data and it was further shown that in this blood-group system it was possible to detect in the coefficient for systematic pressure, selection effects of the same order as those thought to be operating. Yasuda and Morton (1967) conclude that the Malécot approach is validated by these studies.

There is no doubt that the coefficient of kinship is a most elegant and powerful tool for defining genetic structure and for determining the causes for genetic variation between populations. It is, however, worth noting some of the assumptions on which its application is based. First, as with the other models mentioned, it is taken that relatedness and spatial genetic variety are in an equilibrium state; this is an important matter to which we will refer again later. Secondly, it depends on knowledge of the migration law governing short-range movement and determining the distributions of marital and parent–offspring distances. Though the relationship holds for a number of different functions for this law, as has been indicated earlier, no precise descriptions of these distributions have yet been made. Further, the nature of the law may change from time to time and place to place, and certainly recent technological changes affect human movement patterns qualitatively as well as quantitatively. Finally, it is assumed that the systematic pressures, which include long-range migration, are acting uniformly over all the populations being considered. Thus, if one is unable to fit the expected distribution to the observed distribution of genetic variation, it may be because the populations are not in equilibrium, or because the wrong form of migration law has been applied, or because there are non-uniform systematic pressures. Just as important is the converse situation where there is concordance between expectation and observation. It is quite possible that there is internal compensation for some of these factors, and the extracted coefficients could be seriously misleading.

An alternative type of approach has recently been put forward by Bodmer and Cavalli-Sforza (1968), Hiorns, Harrison, Boyce, and Küchemann (1969), and Smith (1969) to which at least some of these difficulties do not apply. The feature common to the models proposed by these workers is that the actual exchanges between all the populations in a cluster are measured. These exchanges are then compounded in the form of a migration matrix and their effects accumulated by powering the matrix. Because observed values of exchange are the basic inputs into the models no assumption is made about the orientation of movement or about the form of migration laws. Further, the long-range movement can be separately identified and its effects determined. Account can also be taken of differences in population size within the clusters.

The models of Bodmer and Cavalli-Sforza, and of Smith, like the ones already discussed, are primarily aimed at predicting the amount of spatial gene frequency variation in terms of the covariance between the populations in the system, and incorporate stochastic elements in their formulation. Bodmer and Cavalli-Sforza, for instance, show that the covariance between the gene frequencies in populations i and j in the nth generation is given by

$$\text{Cov}\,(\theta_i^{(n)}, \theta_j^{(n)} \mid \theta^{(o)}) = \frac{1}{8} \sum_{l=1}^{k} \frac{1}{N_l} \sum_{r=1}^{n-1} (m_{il}^{(r)}\, m_{jl}^{(r)})$$

where $\theta_i^{(n)}$ is the vector of angular transformations of gene frequencies in the ith population, $\theta^{(o)}$ is the vector of initial transformed gene frequencies of the k populations, N_i is the effective size of the ith population and $m_{ij}^{(r)}$ is the ijth term of the rth power of the migration exchange matrix.

The approach of Hiorns et al., though basically similar, is developed in terms of the relatedness of populations to one another rather than in terms of gene frequency variation and interest is focused more on the pattern in which relatedness develops, and the time it takes to reach an equilibrium state, than on the nature of that state. Relatedness is measured by the extent to which populations share a similar distribution of common ancestors, and since the occurrence of ancestors is a fixed condition, the model is developed deterministically rather than stochastically. At equilibrium, in this viewpoint, there is no spatial heterogeneity in relatedness. Whether or not there is corresponding genetic heterogeneity depends on stochastic elements and systematic pressures causing divergence. Bodmer and Cavalli-Sforza show that with effective population sizes of 100, stochastic processes can have quite marked effects on gene frequency variation even when the exchange between populations is quite large. In fact, they conceive of populations diverging from original identity under these processes, whereas Hiorns et al. envisage populations running, under the observed exchange pattern, from a state of heterogeneity to one of homogeneity in relatedness, and in genetic similarity too, if the stochastic forces could be ignored.

One of the disadvantages of the matrix approach, as compared for instance with that of Malécot, is that it is most clearly applicable to the situation where people are grouped into a finite number of discrete clusters. In principle, it can be applied to more diffuse population distributions but this would require the preparation of exchange matrices of very large order. Its advantages, however, are that, as already mentioned, it makes no assumptions about migration laws, and also it is possible to determine whether or not the populations are likely to be in that state, since under any particular exchange pattern a maximal time to equilibrium can be calculated. Of course, in practical terms, every model is dependent upon the reliability of the data with which it is supplied and although the matrix model does not assume any particular pattern of movement, the results obtained from it depend on the magnitude of the inter-population exchanges that are introduced into it. The magnitude of these exchanges clearly varies from society to society and from time to time. Hiorns *et al.* showed in theoretical terms just what a constant rate of temporal change in exchange would produce in the pattern of developing relatedness between a group of populations which exchanged symmetrically with one another. They also applied their model to a group of Oxfordshire villages for which it was possible from marriage records to establish the actual exchanges over a 300-year period. As it happened, under these exchanges it took not much longer to move from maximum heterogeneity to a state where 95 per cent of ancestors were distributed evenly over the populations, than the period encompassed by the records. However, in general, it seems very unwise to assume that human populations are in an equilibrium state. As indicated earlier, throughout human history populations have been constantly affected by long-range movement in no systematic way, population sizes have been constantly varying and though the evidence is less clear, selective forces have probably been constantly changing.

Attention has here been focused mainly on spatial movement and its effects on geographical heterogeneity. It was earlier noted that social factors affect not only the pattern of the movement but also the way demographic populations are structured genetically. In fact, it is often possible to recognize a vertical differentiation of populations as well as a horizontal one, because of the more or less distinct breeding boundaries which arise from social heterogeneity. Some of the models of structure which have been discussed, especially those based on an exchange matrix, can be applied to considering the effects of social movement. Thus, for instance, Harrison, Hiorns, and Küchemann (1970) applied the relatedness model to examine the effects of both social mobility and social marriage exchange on social class heterogeneity in Otmoor villages in Oxfordshire. In this case, they found that under the average social mobility patterns which characterized the area, the different classes would come to share 95 per cent of their ancestry in sixteen generations; the marriage exchange would produce the same levels of relatedness in twenty generations, and the combined effects of social mobility and marriage would produce homogeneity in nine generations. Subsequent analysis (Harrison, Hiorns, and Küchemann 1971) showed distinct historical trends, relationships between population size and social class distributions and differential spatial movement according to class, but, in this instance, they concluded that one would not expect the social stratification to affect geographical relatedness. However, class structure clearly can influence effective population sizes and therefore stochastic processes, and where social barriers are stronger than geographical ones, their presence may delay the establishment of equilibrium.

Further, whilst genes which do not affect social mobility and marriage movement are not likely to show stratification in the Otmoor populations, genes affecting behavioural traits may well be heterogeneously distributed. It would seem to us that much more attention needs to be given to behavioural variation, in considering population genetic structure and that imprecise models which take it into account are more practically useful than sophisticated ones that do not.

REFERENCES

ALSTRÖM, C. H. and LINDELIUS, R. (1966). A study of the population movement in nine Swedish subpopulations in 1800–49 from the genetic-statistical viewpoint. *Acta genet. Statist. med.* **16**, 1–44.

AZEVÊDO, E., MORTON, N. E., MIKI, C., and YEE, S. (1969). Distance and kinship in north-eastern Brazil. *Am. J. hum. Genet.* **21**, 1–22.

BECKMAN, L. (1961). Breeding patterns of a north Swedish parish. *Hereditas* **47**, 72–80.

BODMER, W. F. and CAVALLI-SFORZA, L. L. (1968). A migration matrix model for the study of random genetic drift. *Genetics, Princeton* **59**, 565–92.

BUCKATZSCH, E. J. (1951). The constancy of local populations and migration in England and Wales before 1800. *Popul. Stud.* **5**, 62–9.

BOYCE, A. J., KÜCHEMANN, C. F., and HARRISON, G. A. (1967). Neighbourhood knowledge and the distribution of marriage distances. *Ann. hum. Genet.* **30**, 335–8.

—— (1968). The reconstruction of historical movement patterns. In *Record linkage in medicine* (ed. E. D. Acheson). E. & S. Livingstone, Edinburgh.

CAVALLI-SFORZA, L. L. (1958). Some data on the genetic structure of human populations. *Proc. X Int. Congr. Genet.* **1**, 389–407.

—— (1962). The distribution of migration distances: models, and applications to genetics. In *Les déplacements humains* (ed. J. Sutter). *Entret. Monaco Sc. Hum. I*, 139–58.

CHAMBERS, J. D. (1957). The Vale of Trent 1670–1800. A regional study of economic change. *Econ. Hist. Rev. Suppl.* **3**.

DAHLBERG, G. (1929). Inbreeding in man. *Genetics, Princeton* **14**, 421–54.

DOBZHANSKY, T. (1955). A review of some fundamental concepts and problems of population genetics. *Cold Spring Harb. Symp. quant. Biol.* **20**, 1–15.

EVERSLEY, D. E. C. (1957). A survey of population in an area of Worcestershire from 1600 to 1850 on the basis of parish registers. *Popul Stud.* **10**, 253–79.

HARRISON, G. A. HIORNS, R. W., and KÜCHEMANN, C. F. (1970). Social class relatedness in some Oxfordshire parishes. *J. biosoc. Sci.* **2**, 71–80.

—— (1971). Social class and marriage patterns in some Oxfordshire populations. *J. biosoc. Sci.* **3**, 1–12.

HIORNS, R. W., HARRISON, G. A., BOYCE, A. J., and KÜCHEMANN, C. F. (1969). A mathematical analysis of the effects of movement on the relatedness between populations. *Ann. hum. Genet.* **32**, 237–50.

KIMURA, M. and WEISS, G. H. (1964). The stepping-stone model of population structure and the decrease of genetic correlation with distance. *Genetics, Princeton* **49**, 461–76.

KÜCHEMANN, C. F., BOYCE, A. J., and HARRISON, G. A. (1967). A demographic and genetic study of a group of Oxfordshire villages. *Hum. Biol.* **39**, 251–76.

LASKER, G. and KAPLAN, B. A. (1964). The coefficient of breeding isolation: population size, migration rates, and the possibilities for random genetic drift in 6 human communities in Northern Peru. *Hum. Biol.* **36**, 327–38.

MALÉCOT, G. (1948). *Les mathématiques de l'hérédité.* Masson et Cie., Paris.

—— (1959). Les modèles stochastiques en génétique de population. *Publ. Inst. Stat. Univ. Paris* **8**, 173–210.

—— (1962). Migration et parenté génétique moyenne. In *Les déplacements humains* (ed. J. Sutter). *Entret. Monaco Sc. Hum. I*, 205–12.

—— (1966). Identical loci and relationship. In *Proc. V Symp. Mathematical Statistics and Probability, Berkeley* (eds. L. Lecam and J. Neyman), **4**, 317–32.

MORRILL, R. L. (1962). The development of models of migration and the role of electronic processing machines. In *Les déplacements humains* (ed. J. Sutter). *Entret. Monaco Sc. Hum.* I, 213–30.

MORTON, N. E., YASUDA, N., MIKI, C., and YEE, S. (1968). Population structure of the ABO blood groups in Switzerland. *Am. J. hum. Genet.* **20**, 420–9.

PERRY, P. J. (1969). Working-class isolation and mobility in rural Dorset, 1837–1936: a study of marriage distances. *Trans. Inst. Br. Geogr.* **46**, 121–41.

SMITH, C. A. B. (1969). Local fluctuations in gene frequencies. *Ann. hum. Genet.* **32**, 251–60.

SOGNER, S. (1963). Aspects of the demographic situation in 17 parishes in Shropshire, 1711–1760. *Popul. Stud.* **17**, 126–46.

SPUHLER, J. N. (1961). Migration into the human breeding population of Ann Arbor, Michigan, 1900–1950. *Hum. Biol.* **33**, 223–5.

TINDALE, N. B. (1953). Tribal and intertribal marriage among the Australian aborigines. *Hum. Biol.* **25**, 169–90.

WEISS, G. H. and KIMURA, M. (1965). A mathematical analysis of the stepping-stone model of genetic correlation. *J. appl. Probab.* **2**, 129–49.

WRIGHT, S. (1943). Isolation by distance. *Genetics, Princeton* **28**, 114–38.

—— (1951). The genetical structure of populations. *Ann. Eugen.* **15**, 323–54.

YASUDA, N. and MORTON, N. E. (1967). Studies on human population structure. In *Proceedings of the third international congress of human genetics* (ed. J. F. Crow and J. V. Neel) John Hopkins Press, Baltimore.

9

GENETIC IMPLICATIONS OF POPULATION BREEDING STRUCTURE

WILLIAM J. SCHULL

CUSTOMARILY the forces which contribute to the persistence, spread, or loss of a mutant gene, that is, to changes in gene, genotype, and phenotype frequencies are divided into two groups, namely, those whose effects are directional or systematic, and those whose effects cannot be predicted in a directional sense but whose magnitudes are estimable, the so-called dispersive or stochastic forces. Among the former are mutation, gene flow (migration), and selection; among the latter are genetic drift, a function of population size, and the random variability which may occur either spatially or with time in the directional forces. There exists one other important factor which is generally numbered among the systematic forces and that is the mating formula of the population in question, the limitations placed upon mate selection such as number, age, and propinquity (biological as well as geographic).

It is the purpose of this presentation to describe some of the genetic implications of various systems or patterns of mating. The approach will be historical for several reasons. First, this will provide an insight into the tempo of development and the growth in sophistication of our knowledge. Second, it will afford some notion of the relevance of past efforts to present attempts to understand the impact upon man's evolution of his long existence in small isolates, social as well as geographic, which were intermittently broken down by forces with which he could not then cope, such as a technologically superior enemy. Subsequent presentations will consider the effect of these events upon local differentiation. Finally, it will expose our indebtedness to a small number of investigators whose ingenuity in isolating problems of moment which were mathematically tractable, warrants wider recognition.

Systems of mating

Some seventy years ago, A. E. Garrod called attention to the fact that more than a quarter of the then recorded cases of alkaptonuria, a recessively inherited biochemical abnormality in the metabolism of homogentisic acid, were the offspring of unions of first cousins. Shortly thereafter, William Bateson in a Report to the Evolution Committee of the Royal Society (1902) commented on this observation as follows: 'Now there may be other accounts possible, but we note that the mating of first cousins gives exactly the conditions most likely to enable a rare and usually recessive character to show itself. If the bearer of such a gamete mate with individuals not bearing it, the character would hardly ever be seen; but first cousins will frequently be bearers of similar gametes, which may in such unions meet each other, and thus lead to the manifestation of the peculiar recessive characters in the zygote.' This was a perceptive explanation of Garrod's data, but equally it was important in that it represented the first clear recognition that the rate of manifestation of an inherited characteristic could be influenced by mating patterns.

The next essential abstraction was the behaviour of genes and genotypes in a randomly mating population. Castle (1903) appears to have grasped the fundamentals of the issue, but it remained for G. H. Hardy (1908) and Wilhelm Weinberg (1908), working independently, to record unequivocally the conditions for equilibrium of gene and genotype frequencies under random mating, namely, infinite population size and the absence of selection and mutation. Their proofs tacitly assumed two alleles and non-overlapping generations, i.e., a discrete time scale, but the extension to multiple alleles and to continuous time is not formidable (see Ewen 1969). The importance of their contribution cannot be overstated; the Hardy–Weinberg Law, as their results are commonly termed, is the central theorem of population genetics. As Ewen has stated, rarely indeed is the central theorem the first to be proved in an area of mathematics, and even more rarely is that theorem fully accessible to the beginning student.

Succeeding years saw an active and widespread interest in systems of mating and their effects upon gene, genotype, and phenotype frequencies. Many of these efforts focused on inbreeding (see, for example, Pearl 1913, 1914a, b, Jennings 1912, 1914) presumably stimulated in part by the work of Shull and East on heterosis in corn following inbreeding and outcrossing. But there were also more general investigations of changes in the frequencies of the parameters adverted to under diverse systems of mating with and without selection. Jennings (1916, 1917), for example, explored in some detail the numerical results of a number of systems of breeding with respect to one and two pairs of characters, linked as well as independent. He stressed the recurrence relationships by which one might compute the phenotypic proportions to be expected in a particular generation given a system of mating; rarely did he derive the limiting population, and one can only presume from his own self-deprecatory remarks that his mathematical talents were not equal to the occasion. However, he clearly recognized that the random mating of zygotes gives the same results as the random mating of the gametes which they produce, and he utilized this principle to derive the recurrence relationships which characterize the various mating systems that he chose to analyse. This device of finding the proportion of the various sorts of gametes derivable from zygotes differing with respect to k characters and, from these gametic proportions, the frequencies of the different kinds of zygotes for the next generation is still commonly used.

Robbins (1917, 1918a, b) brought to the study of systems of mating an elegance of technique not apparent in the work of his predecessors. His proofs were by repetition and induction, rather than exhaustion; he was continually concerned with compact formulations and the limiting population. He was one of the first to recognize and state that inbreeding invariably results in a decay in heterozygosity. On an early occasion, he asserted that '*any method of breeding* (emphasis mine) which gives A and a gametes equal chances of mating and which tends to eliminate heterozygous individuals will in successive generations give populations which approach a stable condition in which the two types of homozygous individuals appear in the same proportions as were their types of gametes in the original population', and therein acknowledged that positive assortative mating produces the same general results as inbreeding. We also owe to Robbins (1918a) a neat demonstration that for a sex-linked character the proportions are not generally fixed after one generation of random mating, an exception exists when the proportion of dominant males, i.e., the AY phenotype, equals the proportion of A gametes in females. He noted, however, that as the number of generations increases, the population will approach a fixed composition except in very special cases. He clearly recognized too that with random mating the effect of incomplete linkage between two factors is only temporary, and with continued random mating the distributions of the two sets of factors will be orthogonal.

Robbins (1918c) also examined the rather interesting case of random mating with the exception that brothers and sisters did not mate. He has shown that if each family has exactly two offspring, the proportion of heterozygotes in the limiting population is greater than for complete random mating; whereas if more than two offspring exist, the limiting population will be the same as if mating had been completely random. This observation has interesting evolutionary implications. Most human societies have proscribed the union of siblings even when they have condoned other consanguineous marriages. Thus, throughout the many centuries when man's number was increasing slowly, when the mean number of surviving offspring in a family was very nearly two, the avoidance of close inbreeding could have been an important force in maintaining genetic variability. In fact, MacCluer and Schull (1970a), in a study of an age-structured population through Monte Carlo simulation, have recently shown that the avoidance of matings of siblings and half-siblings can increase the effective size of a population as much as two-fold. And more recently, Jacquard (1971) has examined the effect of exclusion of brother-sister mating upon genetic drift, that is, the variability in gene frequencies introduced through the sampling of gametes from one generation to the next.

Developments of the nature we have just described were capped by Sewall Wright (1921) in a series of articles utilizing his method of path coefficients. The device of analysing a mating system in terms of the determination of each individual by others and expressing the correlations which arose as chains of path coefficients offered a compact, and certainly in his hands, an uncommonly powerful technique. He was able to examine systems of mating, such as the obligatory mating of octuple third cousins (the most remote matings possible in a closed population of 16), too cumbersome to be attacked by the methods of Jennings and Robbins. Among the more important findings to emerge or be reaffirmed were the following:

1. In the absence of selection (that is, a differential rate of reproduction for whatever reasons), random mating, inbreeding, and assortative mating do not alter gene frequencies, and one generation of random mating is sufficient to restore the composition of the original population. Selection alone effects a permanent change in the average composition of the population.

2. Most systems of inbreeding lead to the breaking up of a population into non-interbreeding lines; subsequent random mating within one of these lines will not necessarily restore the original population composition.

3. The correlation between relatives within a single non-interbreeding line approaches zero in the absence of non-genetic causation; whereas the correlation between members of a single line when a random group of the possible inbred lines are combined approaches one with continued inbreeding.

4. Perfect homozygosis is not an inevitable consequence of all systems of inbreeding; in fact, perfect homozygosis will not be achieved in an indefinitely large population for matings more remote than single first cousins. Limitation of the breeding population to some small number, say less than 100, is a more important means of achieving homozygosis than inbreeding relatives more remote than first cousins.

5. Perfect homozygosis is achieved with assortative mating only if the latter is perfect and the somatic characteristics on which assortment occurs are completely determined by heredity. If assortative mating is based on a single factor and is perfect, homozygosis is approached at the same speed as in a system of self-fertilization.

6. Combinations of inbreeding with assortative mating bring about an increase in homozygosis which is approximately equal to the sum of their separate effects, if the latter are small.

7. Inbreeding or assortative mating without selection leads to increased variability in a population as a whole. Intuitively, this is clear since both processes lead to polarization of the population. Disassortative mating diminishes the variability as contrasted with a randomly breeding population.

As stated, inbreeding leads to the subdivision of a population, and thereby contributes to the structure of the latter. It is important to distinguish in this context, however, between two components of inbreeding, namely, that which arises out of random mating in finite populations and that which arises as a consequence of the preferential mating of relatives. Intuitively, one recognizes that in very large populations the probability of selecting at random a relative as a spouse is vanishingly small, and thus all consanguineous marriages reflect preferential mating. But it is also clear that as population size diminishes the chance probability of selecting a relative increases; the precise nature of the increase will depend upon such variables as family size, matrimonial radius, etc. Sewall Wright (1951, 1965) has proposed three parameters for describing the process and the properties of hierarchically subdivided natural populations. These parameters, the so-called F-statistics, are defined as follows:

1. F_{IT} is the correlation between gametes that unite to produce the individuals within a population relative to the gametes of the total population.
2. F_{IS} is the average over all subdivisions of a population of the correlation between uniting gametes relative to the gametes of their own subdivision.
3. Finally, F_{ST} is the correlation between random gametes within subdivisions relative to gametes of the total population.

It should be noted that F_{IT} and F_{ST} are necessarily positive; however F_{IS} can be negative if there is systematic avoidance of consanguineous marriage within the subdivisions. This approach has been applied with some success to the analysis of variability in breeds of livestock, but its worth in the analysis of human population structure remains to be established. Crow and Mange (1965) have shown that these parameters can be estimated from the occurrence of isonymous (same-name) marriages and a knowledge of the frequencies of surnames in the pertinent population. Specifically, it can be shown that

$$F_{IT} = I/4 \text{ and } F_{ST} = I_r/4$$

where I and I_r are, respectively, the frequency of isonymous marriages observed, and the frequency expected through random matching of surnames. Finally,

$$F_{IS} = \frac{F_{IT} - F_{ST}}{1 - F_{ST}}$$

Yasuda and Furusho (1971) have utilized this approach to demonstrate the constancy of the random component in a city in north-eastern Japan at a time when preferential consanguineous marriages were on the decline.

Selection and patterns of mating

Most of the effects of inbreeding we have cited are predicated on the assumption that all genotypes have equal selective values, and this is generally not true. Haldane recognized this and in a series of papers (Haldane 1924a, b, 1926, 1927, 1932) examined the effect of slow selection for a fully dominant gene in a large population mating randomly, completely inbred, and partially inbred. He was able to demonstrate that in a randomly mating population selection is not very effective if only a small proportion of recessives exist; whereas with self-fertilization or obligatory sib mating the number of generations required to produce a given change is inversely proportional to the intensity of selection. As could be anticipated, partial inbreeding leads to intermediate results, that is, even a small amount of inbreeding will enable selection to act on rare recessives. On the other hand, assortative mating has no appreciable effect. Inquiries of this nature reached full flower in Fisher's Fundamental Theorem of Natural Selection, which states that the rate of increase in fitness of a population at any time is equal to its genetic variance in fitness at that time (Fisher 1930b). This can be shown to hold for any system of mating where $Q^2 = \beta PR$, and Q, P, and R are the frequencies of the Aa, AA, and aa genotypes respectively. Since $\beta = 1$ in the case of random mating, the latter is merely a special case of this more general formulation. Suffice it to say that the validity of the argument on which this conclusion rests is strongly dependent upon the underlying assumptions. One of these assumptions is, of course, a single genetic locus, and it is questionable whether there exists a valid extension of the fundamental theorem to the two-locus situation.

Two further developments in this general area of research warrant mention at this point. First, Haldane and Waddington (1931) solved an important issue raised by Jennings (1917), namely, the conjoint effects of linkage and inbreeding in the absence of selection. They derived formulae for the amount of crossing-over which is to be found in the final population when individuals heterozygous for linked genes are inbred according to various systems. Second, Bartlett and Haldane (1935) introduced the use of generation matrices into the analysis of mating systems; a technique enlarged and further developed by Fisher (1949). While it is moot whether this approach has contributed insights not foreseen by Wright or deducible through the use of path coefficients, it has an elegance which appeals to the mathematician. The matrix approach does provide a more complete analysis than do path coefficients, and will, for example, give the proportions of completely fixed matings, i.e. $AA \times AA$, $aa \times aa$, etc., not obtainable by path analysis. However, extremely complicated systems of mating, say, linked factors with selection, can be intractable to this method because of the sheer sizes of the generation matrices which result. The rate of progress to homozygosity is measured by the largest (non-unit) latent root or eigenvalue of the generation matrix defined by a particular system of breeding.

Among the more imaginative uses of this method is the work of Hayman and Mather, and Reeve and his colleagues on inbreeding with selection (see Reeve 1955, 1957, Reeve and Gower 1959). Hayman and Mather (1953) examined the effects of various systems of inbreeding when homozygotes are at a disadvantage. They assumed that selection operated both within lines where the homozygotes produced fewer surviving progeny, and between lines where the more homozygous lines were more likely to be extinguished by chance (or discarded in an experimental breeding programme). They found a critical survival rate of homozygotes for each inbreeding system below which homozygosity is never attained; thus, for example, in a system of obligatory brother–sister mating where homozygosity would ultimately obtain if all genotypes were selectively equal, if homozygotes have a survival value of less than 76 per cent homozygosis is not achieved (Haldane 1956, Hayman and Mather 1956).

Reeve (1955) examined the case where selection occurs only within lines, and found that within systems of inbreeding such as sib mating or double first-cousin mating homozygosity is ultimately achieved for all finite survival values but as the latter are reduced there is a marked slowing down of progress. His study and that of Hayman and Mather (1953) were directed toward a single pair of alleles. Clearly, however, many characteristics are of a more complicated nature and depend upon segregation at more than one locus. This prompted Reeve (1957) to examine the effect of selection when linkage of loci obtains which had previously been considered only by Bartlett and Haldane (1935) for the special case of forced heterozygosis. Reeve considered two cases, selfing and sib mating (see also Reeve and Gower 1959), and from these it appears that severe selection against homozygotes at a few points on a chromosome can markedly reduce the rate of progress towards homozygosity. At the moment, the effect of linkage with or without selection is again under active study (see, for example, Ohta and Kimura 1969, Watterson 1970, Karlin and Feldman 1970).

Elegant proofs of a number of the statements of the preceding paragraphs are to be found in Karlin's (1969) *Equilibrium behavior of population genetic models with non-random mating.* Two other recent, and more measured accounts of some of the consequences of differing population breeding structures are Wright's (1969) *Evolution and the genetics of populations: the theory of gene frequencies* and Crow and Kimura's (1970) *An introduction to population genetics.*

Consanguineous marriages and rare recessive traits

The avenue of research briefly cited was patently not the only one under attack in these years, and moreover must have seemed particularly unpromising to the contemporary human geneticist. Most of the systems of inbreeding studied rarely, if ever, occur in man, and the relevance of the work was less conspicuous than some other developments. Thus, Lenz (1919) had seized upon the principle so clearly seen by Bateson, and calculated the frequency of consanguineous marriages that is to be expected among the parents of recessive-trait bearers at various frequencies of the character in the general population. These calculations established without compromise the importance of consanguineous marriages in the diagnostic criteria associated with rare, recessive autosomal inheritance. Dahlberg (1929) pursued this general issue, and derived a procedure for the calculation of the frequency of chance consanguineous marriages. He further showed that given the frequency of chance consanguineous marriages, one could estimate the size of the breeding population. His approach has been roundly criticized in recent years (Morton 1955), and possibly somewhat unfairly Dahlberg has been tarred with a brush which should have been directed at those who applied his argument to circumstances which were inappropriate. Be this as it may, he saw and stated the issue with respect to consanguineous marriages in human populations quite clearly, that is, 'From the point of view of the population, consanguineous marriage has very little importance for the occurrence of recessive character bearers. From the point of view of the character bearers, on the other hand, it has great importance, in the case of recessivity, and if the character is rare.'

The decay of genetic variability

Advances possibly more important than those just enumerated were set in motion by an exceptional book published in 1921 by the Hagedoorns entitled *The relative value of the processes causing evolution*. These Dutch geneticists observed:

> The group of organisms chosen by fate to become the parents of the next generation is usually, but always occasionally, considerably smaller than the number of individuals of their species. Every case in which rare individuals, having genes not present in the majority, or in which rare individuals, being impure for or lacking in genes common property of the majority, happen to be excluded from the number of procreating individuals, the total variability is lowered.
>
> Reduction of potential variability, in other words purity of species, is automatic, and not dependent upon any sort of selection. (Chapter 5, p. 120.)

Somewhat similar thoughts were earlier expressed by Gulick (1905), a missionary to Hawaii.

Homozygosity is the inexorable fate of all finite populations. This was undoubtedly a startling thought to those who had searched so diligently to explain the selective value associated with the most minute of characters. The Hagedoorns did not quantify this march to uniformity, but Fisher (1922, 1930a) and Wright (1929) have done so. The importance of the phenomenon, which Fisher termed the 'Hagedoorn Effect' but is more widely known now as genetic drift, continues to be a matter of lively debate. This issue concerns us here, however, only insofar as the rate of approach to homozygosity may depend upon the mating structure of the population.

Wright (1939) as well as Kimura (1955) have considered the rate of decay in variability in a randomly mating population; Kimura obtained an exact solution for the model to which Wright's solution was approximate. The rate is, of course, a function of population size. More recently, Moran (1959) has examined this issue when generations are overlapping but mating is still random. However, Watterson (1959a, b) has been able to show that assortative mating may either increase or decrease the decay in variability depending upon the nature of the assortative mating and the divergence of the numbers of males and females from equality. He considers three models of birth–death behaviour. In the first, ascribed to Wright (1939), all members of the population die simultaneously and are replaced by a new generation with gene frequencies dependent upon those of the previous generation. In the second, attributed to Moran (1958), individuals are assumed to have a negative exponential lifetime distribution, and to die singly at random. In the third which he advances (Watterson 1959b), births occur in succession, but each birth entails the death of one parent. Population size is assumed to be constant in all three instances. With random mating, the approach to homozygosity is the same in Wright's and Watterson's models, but twice as fast in Moran's; with complete assortative mating, Watterson's model results in a very rapid elimination of heterozygotes while the other two drift slowly to complete homozygosity. The latter drift is, however, twice as fast as that which obtains with random mating if the sexes are equally frequent. Patently none of these models closely resembles the human situation, and since the rate of approach to homozygosity is obviously dependent upon the birth–death model, extrapolations to man are hazardous.

Age-specific models of birth, death, and nuptiality

It is uncertain how much of the work we have described can be applied to man. Intuitively, one is apprehensive although prepared to accept these studies as indicative of the bounds of the behaviour of human populations. Most of the models assume that all unions within the population occur at one instant in time, and that a male chosen at random will select his spouse from a fixed universe of women every one of whom he has equal probability of marrying. This is clearly at variance with the human experience. Many also assume that a new individual born into the population is an immediate potential parent, a somewhat unrealistic premise if the model is to be applied to human beings. The effect of a time-lag due to the maturation when genetic diversity exists has been poorly investigated. Norton (1928) is one of the few who have attempted to introduce age-specific birth and death rates into a diploid model. Even here, though, the model is somewhat contrived. Generations overlap, as in truth they do, but selection is presumed to operate through differential mortality, whereas the bulk of current evidence suggests differential fertility to be the more important. Norton also assumes the distribution of ages of mating couples to be independent but, in fact, they are correlated.

In so far as the system of mating is concerned, a closer correspondence to reality would presumably occur if the model used were to incorporate limitations of choice based upon age, propinquity, and the cultural and traditional mores which are observed to be involved in mate selection in man. Considerable attention has been directed, therefore, to the formulation of a definition of random mating more in keeping with human behaviour than the conventional one previously stated (see Hajnal 1963, Cavalli-Sforza, Kimura, and Barrai 1966, Schull and MacCluer 1968). Much of this effort has been focused on explaining the observed frequencies of consanguineous marriages when it is assumed that the probability of a particular consanguineous marriage is a function of the age limitations imposed upon the choice of a spouse, of the distance over which spouses are commonly drawn, and of the abundance of one's relatives of the appropriate kind and age within this common distance. Clearly numeric specification of these probabilities requires knowledge of three distributions, namely, (1) age-specific probabilities of nuptiality, (2) marital distances, and (3) the number and ages of specified relatives within marital distances. The first of these is a common demographic statistic in all developed countries, and is generally readily accessible. The second and third are not routinely available. *Ad hoc* censuses have, however, provided data to test a variety of different distributional forms, and moreover, if one's attention is focused on a single community or a relatively small area, the marital distance is, in a sense, fixed. Concern then centres on the distribution of ages of relatives of a specified class. The latter is, as previously stated, not routinely available, but Hajnal (1963) and Cavalli-Sforza, Kimura, and Barrai (1966) have suggested that this distribution can be satisfactorily approximated by a linear function of the differences in age between siblings and a weighted sum of the mean age at paternity and the mean age at maternity. The weights are merely the number of males and female ancestors intercalated between the relatives in question and the siblings through whom relationship passes. It should be noted that the age distribution which is computed is the distribution of the differences in ages at birth and the substitution of this for the distribution of ages at nuptiality can be justified only if survivorship is not correlated between relatives. Though the latter seems unlikely on prior grounds, a weak correlation would not necessarily impinge seriously on the argument.

These linear functions have been shown to predict reasonably well the 'true' mean and variance for a given category of relatives in Italy (Cavalli-Sforza, Kimura, and Barrai 1966) and Japan (Schull and MacCluer 1968). In the first instance, the observed frequencies of consanguineous marriages are wholly explicable in terms of the age and propinquity constraints. This is not true for Japan, however. Some further elaboration of the model is clearly necessary, one which incorporates other social and traditional values.

Illustrative of these latter values is the increased frequency of consanguineous marriages involving first sons as contrasted with subsequent sons.

The models we have just described are aimed at large populations and assume these populations to be demographically stable, that is, their vital rates are presumed to be constant over time. It is natural to wonder whether these models are applicable to small populations where the stochastic element may be large. Alternatively stated, how inappropriate are these constructs when applied to small populations? MacCluer and Schull (1970a, b) have attempted to examine this issue as it applies to one small, isolated island population of Japan, Takushima. The necessary demographic parameters to fit the Hajnal model are known. It has thus been possible to contrast the predictions from this model with the results of a Monte Carlo simulation of a population, never larger than 800, with the same vital rates. Briefly, we find that slight variations in demographic characteristics, such as those which can readily occur by chance in a small population even under constant vital rates, can produce significant differences in Hajnal predictions. But it can also be shown, by comparing the Hajnal model with an artificial population of known size, that reasonably accurate estimates of isolate size can be obtained. Somewhat parenthetically, computer simulations of the kind under consideration provide a useful means of estimating from demographic information alone the probable level of inbreeding and the importance of remote consanguinity. This should be a boon to investigators interested in economically primitive, pre-literate populations or in populations with poorly or inadequately developed systems of vital records, for it is generally possible in these instances to obtain the requisite demographic data through surveys.

The observed consequences of inbreeding in man

Thus far, we have limited this presentation to some of the theoretical consequences of various systems of mating, and to models which seek to determine the randomness or non-randomness of occurrence of certain mating types. It is important to recognize, of course, that a single population of individuals can be simultaneously randomly mating with respect to certain attributes and non-randomly with respect to others. Most large populations appear to mate at random insofar as the inherited red blood cell antigens are concerned even though mating assortatively with respect to stature and intelligence, for example. But what, now, are some of the consequences of different patterns of mating as measured empirically? Since a subsequent presentation will examine the results of phenotypic assortative mating, our attention will be restricted to consanguineous marriages, and more specifically to studies in Japan which provide, in aggregate, the largest and most comprehensive body of data presently available. Most of these studies were undertaken either as a consequence of the relatively high frequency of consanguineous marriages throughout Japan (some representative values are given in Table 9.1) and the opportunity to appraise the results of such marriages empirically, or from a belief that such investigations would contribute importantly to the estimation of the roles of segregation and mutation in the maintenance of genetic variability in the face of selection, or both. Evidence on the effect of inbreeding is available for rural and urban populations, and from most of the major geographic areas, specifically from Kyushu, Chugoku, Kinki, Kanto, Tohoku, and several more. Ascertainment of the various samples has involved such

TABLE 9.1

Some representative frequencies of consanguineous marriages in Japan†

Place	Number of couples studied	Proportion of marriages known to be consanguineous	First cousins	Relationship 1–1/2 cousins	Second cousins	Other	Not related
Cities							
Nagoya	9569	0·0262	205	10	36	—	9318
Hiroshima	27 934	0·0592	944	317	392	—	26 281
Nagasaki	33 319	0·0801	1602	414	651	—	30 652
Tokyo	1708	0·0914	68	——51——		37	1552
Villages							
Shigajima	627	0·1707	71	14	21	1	520
Inawashiro	196	0·3113	14	2	2	43	135
Ohama	487	0·1541	49	10	15	1	412
Itadori	993	0·1320	102	6	23	—	862
Ubagai	1279	0·0587	61	3	11	—	1204
Shiiba	1246	0·2408	189	47	64	—	946

† See Schull and Neel (1965) for references.

disparate techniques as pregnancy registrations, hospital admissions, questionnaires distributed to school children, and complete censuses of sharply delimited areas. The individual studies vary from a few hundred observations to tens of thousands.

Interest has converged on three broad areas of observation, namely, the effects of inbreeding and consanguinity upon (1) mortality, (2) other characteristics of the offspring from such marriages, and (3) fertility. Here, and in the remarks to follow, we shall attempt to distinguish between inbreeding and consanguinity effects. The latter expression will be restricted to the effect of a consanguineous marriage on the number and kind of offspring born to such a marriage; whereas the term inbreeding effect will be limited to those effects on offspring number and kind which results from a parent being the product of a consanguineous marriage.

The greatest concordance in the data available is to be seen in observations on mortality between conception and maturity (here arbitrarily taken to be

21 years of age). Illustrative of the magnitude of the effect of consanguinity are the following observations: Schull, Furusho, Yamamoto, Nagano, and Komatsu (1970) have recently examined the reproductive performances of some 10 530 marriages on Hirado (Nagasaki Prefecture) of which some 15 per cent were consanguineous. They found that among all marriages contracted in the years 1920–39 the increase in pre-reproductive mortality (expressed in percentage) per percentage maternal inbreeding is $0 \cdot 4836 \pm 0 \cdot 2257$, and per percentage foetal inbreeding (consanguinity) is $0 \cdot 7703 \pm 0 \cdot 1620$ (these figures are for the regression coefficient and its standard error). No effect of paternal inbreeding was observed, and neither parental inbreeding nor consanguinity could be shown to exert a significant effect upon the frequency of stillbirths. In somewhat earlier studies in the cities of Hiroshima, Nagasaki, and Kure, Schull and Neel (1965, 1966) found the increased risk of death to be somewhat smaller, approximately $0 \cdot 5$ per cent per percentage inbreeding (consanguinity). These studies did not contribute to our appraisal of parental inbreeding effects, for attention was centered solely on the effects of consanguineous marriage. Yanase and his colleagues in Fukuoka find some heterogeneity with time in the effect of consanguinity, but report an increase of approximately $0 \cdot 6765$ per cent (increased risk of death in the first twelve years of life), on the average. Yanase's summary (1966) of studies of isolated populations, principally in Kyushu, is in accord with the values cited. Viewed in terms of the regression coefficients, values reported varied from $0 \cdot 0405$ to $1 \cdot 4074$, but cluster in a neighbourhood slightly above $0 \cdot 5000$; to a close approximation, then, mortality in the first twenty years of life increases about $0 \cdot 5$ per cent per percentage foetal inbreeding (consanguinity), and by a lesser amount as a function of maternal inbreeding. A brief summarization of the absolute and relative risks of occurrence of death and certain morbid conditions among the offspring of unrelated parents and of first cousins is given in Table 9.2 (a more detailed accounting will be found in Schull and Neel 1965).

Only two large studies exist which relate attributes other than survival of the child to consanguinity and parental inbreeding. These are the studies in Hiroshima and Nagasaki (Schull and Neel 1965), and Hirado (see Neel, Schull, Yamamoto, Uchida, Yanase, and Fujiki 1970 and Neel, Schull, Kimura, Tanigawa, Yamamoto, and Nakajima 1970) to which reference has already been made. No clear effect of parental inbreeding on such diverse indicators of possible effects as: (1) physical development, (2) systolic and diastolic blood pressure, (3) tapping rate, (4) notable disease of the eye and ear, (5) visual accommodation, (6) visual acuity, (7) auditory acuity, (8) I.Q., and (9) school performance emerged. Consanguinity did, however, exert a significant effect on several of these indicators. Somewhat simply stated, all of the metrics of physical and mental growth and development were depressed with consanguinity. The effects though demonstrated were small, amounting

TABLE 9.2

The absolute and relative risks of occurrence of death and certain morbid conditions among the offspring of unrelated parents and of first cousins[1]

Characteristic	Offspring of unrelated parents per cent	Offspring of first cousins per cent	Relative risk per cent
Congenital defects in the newly born[2]	1·02	1·69	1·6
Simple cleft palate			5·0
Some congenital cardiac defects			3·0
Atresia ani			4·0
Anophthalmos/Microphthalmos			3·0
Oligodactyly			7·0
One or two major defects[3]	8·5	11·7	1·4
One or more minor defects	7·9	9·8	1·2
Hearing impairment[4]	10·5	13·9	1·3
Organic defect of eye	0·45	0·99	2·2
Severe visual loss without organic defect[5]	1·01	1·43	1·4
Mortality[6]	5·5–16·0	11·6–24·1	1·4–3·4

1. Where data are available from more than one study, the ranges of the various risks are recorded.

2. These figures include only those congenital defects recognizable by physical means alone at or very shortly after birth; thus they do not include many congenital heart defects or retardations of motor and mental development.

3. These values include only those defects which are incompatible with life, life-threatening, or seriously impinge upon normal functions; all such diagnoses in the first eight years of life, on the average, are included.

4. Defined as loss of at least 10 decibels in one or both ears at one or more of three frequencies, 128, 1024, and 2048 Hz.

5. Defined as vision of 20/400 or worse in one or both eyes when tested with a Snellen chart.

6. The differences to be noted here stem both from the numbers of years at risk of death and changes in mortality with time. Most recent studies suggest a relative risk closer to 1·4 than to 3·4.

to at most a few per cent of the mean of the outbred children. The data in Table 9.3 are illustrative of the magnitudes of the effects seen. When socioeconomic differences which obtained in this study are controlled, the inbreeding effects are diminished somewhat although the contrast between the offspring of unrelated parents and first cousins remains a statistically significant one. Morbidity was also increased and particularly with regard to the sensory organs, the eye and ear. The picture is one of small but pervasive effects, detectable only with large numbers of observations.

The findings with respect to fertility are more unexpected, and consequently the more interesting (see Schull *et al.* 1970). On Hirado, total pregnancies and

TABLE 9.3

A comparison of some selected findings in a cohort of control children and in a cohort of children born to first cousin marriages studied in Hiroshima and Nagasaki (after Schull and Neel 1965)†

Characteristic	Sex	Control children	Offspring of first cousins	Inbreeding effect per cent	Change with inbreeding, per cent
Mean performance on W.I.S.C. Intelligence Test (Hiroshima)					
Verbal score	Male	58·67	55·34	2·76	4·7
	Female	57·01	53·46	2·76	4·8
Performance score	Male	57·37	54·94	2·06	3·6
	Female	55·10	52·52	2·06	3·7
School performance (average grade Hiroshima)					
Language	Male	3·09	2·95	0·10	3·2
	Female	3·28	3·10	0·10	3·0
Mathematics	Male	3·21	3·04	0·13	4·0
	Female	3·19	2·99	0·13	4·1
Physical development (Hiroshima)					
Weight (kg)	Male	26·59	26·31	2·34	0·9
	Female	26·35	25·99	2·34	0·9
Height (cm)	Male	129·7	129·1	0·47	0·4
	Female	129·8	129·1	0·47	0·4

† Sexes are indicated separately only when there is a significant difference between males and females. All differences are statistically significant. For the continuously distributed characteristics, the percentage by which the depression due to consanguinity would have been overestimated through failure to consider socioeconomic concomitants has been shown. The average age of the children at the time of study was approximately 98 months in Hiroshima and 105 months in Nagasaki. The physical measurements have been standardized to age 120 months. Inbreeding effects have been computed from a regression based on the findings for both sexes.

total livebirths were significantly increased with consanguinity, but 'net fertility', defined as total livebirths minus non-accidental deaths prior to age 21, was not significantly increased when allowance was made for the role of socioeconomic factors, and religious affiliation was ignored. Among Buddhists, the only religious group large enough to warrant separate analysis, total

pregnancies, total livebirths, and 'net fertility' were all significantly and positively associated with parental relationship. However, the regression coefficient associated with 'net fertility' is less than half the value associated with
either total pregnancies or total livebirths in this instance. There is thus some
evidence for reproductive compensation in association with the excess
mortality due to inbreeding in the foetus; in this context, reproductive
compensation implies no more than the replacement of a child dying young.
Admittedly, other interpretations of these observations are possible; it has
been suggested, for example, that in India where a similar fertility effect has
been observed that the lessened social stress associated with the marriage of
relatives rather than increased infant mortality is the basis for the increased
fertility. However, if 'social stress' is inversely proportional to parental
relationship, a ponderable proposition, the genetic effect remains the
same.

Extrapolations from the findings so briefly summarized in the preceding
several paragraphs to man's past evolution and specifically to the calibre of
the 'inbreeding bottleneck' through which he is presumed to have passed
involve numerous assumptions which are difficult to justify. We shall enlarge
on only one, namely, the frequency of consanguineous marriages which has
obtained in the past. It is commonly assumed that the frequency of consanguineous marriages has decayed more or less steadily over the past several
centuries partly as a consequence of man's increasing number and a wider
choice of spouses, and partly as a consequence of his increasing mobility.
Those few efforts, notably in Italy, Belgium, and France, to record the changes
in frequency with time suggest that this picture is incorrect, and that, in fact,
consanguineous marriages may have increased fairly steadily in number until
the second half of the nineteenth century and then declined rather sharply.
This phenomenon is understandable in demographic terms, for an increase
in man's number also brought an increase in the number of relatives of an
individual and hence an increase in the probability that at least one relative
would be of the appropriate sex and age to be selected as a spouse. In Japan,
the evidence is more equivocal, and suggests geographic heterogeneity. Data
from some of the larger cities lead one to believe that consanguineous
marriages are on the wane, but this does not appear to be universally true
in the rural areas (Schull, Komatsu, Nagano, and Yamamoto 1968). But
then the one need not imply the other for the sociological forces motivating
unions of related individuals are apparently different in farm families as contrasted with non-farm families. Suffice it to state that facile references to
inbreeding bottlenecks to account for exceptional bodies of data are unlikely
to give insight.

As we have seen, there exists a large and impressive literature of a theoretical nature on the genetic implications of a variety of systems of mating. Much
of this work has been prompted by the needs of animal and plant improvement

12

programmes and the tractableness of the problem or problems under investigation. As a consequence, its relevance to man is debatable save possibly through the specification of limits to population behaviour. Otherwise stated, present genetic models are incapable of providing the guides to conduct and prediction which are or will soon be so desperately needed. These limitations of theory can not as yet be offset, either through an appeal to empiricism alone, as our data are insufficient, or through an appeal to the computer, the *deus ex machina* of our age.

REFERENCES

BARTLETT, M. S. and HALDANE, J. B. S. (1935). The theory of inbreeding with enforced heterozygosis. *J. Genet.* **31,** 327–40.

CASTLE, W. E. (1903). The Laws of Galton and Mendel and some laws governing race improvement by selection. *Proc. Am. Acad. Arts Sci.* **35,** 233–42.

CAVALLI-SFORZA, L. L., KIMURA, M., and BARRAI, I. (1966). The probability of consanguineous marriages. *Genetics, Princeton* **54,** 37–60.

CROW, J. F. and MANGE, A. P. (1965). Measurement of inbreeding from the frequency of marriages between persons of the same surname. *Eugen. Qu.* **12,** 199–203.

DAHLBERG, G. (1929). Inbreeding in man. *Genetics, Princeton* **14,** 421–44.

EWEN, W. J. (1969). *Population genetics.* Methuen, London.

FISHER, R. A. (1922). On the dominance ratio. *Proc. R. Soc. Edinb.* **42,** 321–421.

—— (1930a). The distribution of gene ratios for rare mutations. *Proc. R. Soc. Edinb.* **50,** 205–20.

—— (1930b). *The genetical theory of natural selection.* Clarendon Press, Oxford.

—— (1949). *The theory of inbreeding.* Oliver and Boyd, Edinburgh.

GULICK, J. (1905). Evolution, racial and habitudinal, controlled by segregation. *Publs Carnegie Instn Washington.*

HAGEDOORN, A. L. and HAGEDOORN, A. C. (1921). *The relative value of the processes causing evolution.* Martinus Nijhoff, The Hague.

HAJNAL, J. (1963). Random mating and the frequency of consanguineous marriages. *Proc. R. Soc.* B **159,** 127–77.

HALDANE, J. B. S. (1924a). A mathematical theory of natural and artificial selection. Part I *Trans. Camb. phil. Soc.* **23,** 19–41.

—— (1924b). A mathematical theory of natural and artificial selection. Part II. *Proc. Camb. phil. Soc. biol. Sci.* **1,** 158–63.

—— (1926). A mathematical theory of natural and artificial selection. Part III. *Proc. Camb. phil. Soc.* **23,** 363–72.

—— (1927). A mathematical theory of natural and artificial selection. Part IV. *Proc. Camb. phil. Soc.* **23,** 607–15.

—— (1932). *The causes of evolution.* Longman, Green and Co., London.

—— (1956). The conflict between inbreeding and selection. I. Self-fertilization. *J. Genet.* **54,** 56–63.

—— and WADDINGTON, C. H. (1931). Inbreeding and linkage. *Genetics, Princeton* **16,** 358–74.

HARDY, G. H. (1908). Mendelian proportions in a mixed population. *Science, N.Y.* **28,** 49–50.

HAYMAN, B. I. and MATHER, K. (1953). The progress of inbreeding when homozygotes are at a disadvantage. *Heredity* **7,** 165–83.

—— —— (1956). Inbreeding when homozygotes are at a disadvantage: a reply. *Heredity* **10,** 271–4.

JACQUARD, A. (1971). Effect of exclusion of sib-mating on genetic drift. *Theoret. Popul. Biol.* **2,** 91–9.

JENNINGS, H. S. (1912). The production of pure homozygotic organisms from heterozygotes by self-fertilization. *Am. Nat.* **45**, 487–91.

—— (1914). Formulae for the results of inbreeding. *Am. Nat.* **48**, 693–6.

—— (1916). The numerical results of diverse systems of breeding. *Genetics, Princeton* **1**, 53–89.

—— (1917). The numerical results of diverse systems of breeding, with respect to two pairs of characters, linked or independent, with special relation to the effects of linkage. *Genetics, Princeton* **2**, 97–154.

KARLIN, S. and FELDMAN, M. W. (1970). Linkage and selection: two locus symmetric viability model. *Theoret. Popul. Biol.* **1**, 39–71.

KIMURA, M. (1955). Solution of a process of random genetic drift with a continuous model. *Proc. natn. Acad. Sci. U.S.A.* **41**, 144–50.

LENZ, F. (1919). Die Bedeutung der statistisch ermittelten Belastung mit Blutverwandtschaft den Eltern. *Münchner med. Wochenschr.* **66**, 1340–2.

MACCLUER, J. W. and SCHULL, W. J. (1970a). Frequencies of consanguineous marriages and accumulation of inbreeding in an artificial population. *Am. J. hum. Genet.* **22**, 160–75.

—— —— (1970b). Estimating the effective size of human populations. *Am. J. hum. Genet.* **22**, 176–83.

MORAN, P. A. P. (1958). Random processes in genetics. *Proc. Camb. phil. Soc.* **54**, 60–71.

—— (1959). The rate of approach to homozygosity. *Ann. hum. Genet.* **23**, 1–5.

MORTON, N. E. (1955). Non-randomness in consanguineous marriages. *Ann. hum. Genet.* **20**, 116–24.

NEEL, J. V., SCHULL, W. J., YAMAMOTO, M., UCHIDA, S., YANASE, T., and FUJIKI, N. (1970). The effects of parental consanguinity and inbreeding in Hirado, Japan. II. Physical development, tapping rate, blood pressure, intelligence quotient, and school performance. *Am. J. hum. Genet.* **22**, 263–86.

—— ——, KIMURA, T., TANIGAWA, Y., YAMAMOTO, M., and NAKAJIMA, A. (1970). The effects of parental consanguinity and inbreeding in Hirado, Japan. III. Vision and hearing. *Hum. Hered.* **20**, 129–55.

NORTON, H. T. J. (1928). Natural selection and Mendelian variation. *Proc. Lond. math. Soc.* **28**, 1–45.

OHTA, T. and KIMURA, M. (1969). Linkage disequilibrium due to random genetic drift. *Genet. Res., Camb.* **13**, 47–55.

PEARL, R. (1913). A contribution towards an analysis of the problem of inbreeding. *Am. Nat.* **47**, 577–614.

—— (1914a). On the results of inbreeding a Mendelian population: a correction and extension of previous conclusions. *Am. Nat.* **48**, 57–62.

—— (1914b). On a general formula for the constitution of the nth generation of a Mendelian population in which all matings are brother × sister. *Am. Nat.* **48**, 491–4.

REEVE, E. C. R. (1955). Inbreeding with homozygotes at a disadvantage. *Ann. hum. Genet.* **19**, 332–46.

—— (1957). Inbreeding with selection and linkage. *Ann. hum. Genet.* **21**, 277–88.

—— and GOWER, J. C. (1959). Inbreeding with selection and linkage. II. Sib mating. *Ann. hum. Genet.* **23**, 36–49.

ROBBINS, R. B. (1917). Some applications of mathematics to breeding problems. *Genetics, Princeton* **2**, 489–504.

—— (1918a). Applications of mathematics to breeding problems. *Genetics, Princeton* **3**, 73–92.

—— (1918b). Some applications of mathematics to breeding problems. III. *Genetics, Princeton* **3**, 375–89.

—— (1918c). Random mating with the exception of sister by brother mating. *Genetics, Princeton* **3**, 390–6.

SCHULL, W. J., FURUSHO, T., YAMAMOTO, M., NAGANO, H., and KOMATSU, I. (1970). The effect of parental consanguinity and inbreeding in Hirado, Japan. IV. Fertility and reproductive compensation. *Humangenetik*, **9**, 294–315.

——, KOMATSU, I., NAGANO, H., and YAMAMOTO, M. (1968). Hirado: Temporal trends in inbreeding and fertility. *Proc. nat. Acad. Sci. U.S.A.* **56**, 671–9.

—— and MacCluer, J. W. (1968). Takushima: Some of the statics and dynamics of a small Japanese island. In *Haldane and modern biology* (ed. K. J. Dronamraju). Johns Hopkins University Press, Baltimore.

—— and Neel, J. V. (1965). *The effect of inbreeding on Japanese Children*. Harper and Row, New York.

—— —— (1966). Some further observations on the effect of inbreeding on mortality in Kure, Japan. *Am. J. hum. Genet.* **18**, 144–52.

Watterson, G. A. (1959a). Non-random mating, and its effect on the rate of approach to homozygosity. *Ann. hum. Genet.* **23**, 204–20.

—— (1959b). A new genetic population model, and its approach to homozygosity. *Ann. hum. Genet.* **23**, 221–32.

—— (1970). The effect of linkage in a finite random mating population. *Theoret. Popul. Biol.* **1**, 72–87.

Weinberg, W. (1908). Über den Nachweis der Vererbung beim Menschen. *Th. Ver. vaterl. Naturk. Württ.* **64**, 368–82.

Wright, S. (1921). Systems of mating. I, II, III, IV, and V. *Genetics Princeton* **6**, 111–78.

—— (1929). Fisher's theory of dominance. *Am. Nat.* **63**, 274–79.

—— (1939). Statistical genetics in relation to evolution. *Actualités Scientifiques et Industrielles*, No. 802. Herman Cie., Paris.

—— (1951). The genetical structure of populations. *Ann. Eugen.* **15**, 323–54.

—— (1965). The interpretation of population structure by *F*-statistics with special regard to systems of mating. *Evolution, Lancaster, Pa.* **19**, 395–420.

Yanase, T. (1966). A study of isolated populations. *Jap. J. hum. Genet.* **11**, 125–61.

Yasuda, N. and Furusho, T. (1971). Random and non-random inbreeding revealed from isonymy study in a small city of Japan. *Am. J. hum. Genet.* (in press).

10

BEHAVIOUR AND MATING PATTERNS IN HUMAN POPULATIONS†

J. N. Spuhler

THE pattern of mating is one determinant of how genes are combined in genotypes in human and other bisexual populations. Mutation, gene flow, selection, and genetic drift are usually considered to be a complete list of the systematic modes of change of gene frequencies in such populations. Given the gene frequencies for a generation and knowledge of the pattern of mating, we can in principle predict the distribution of genotypes for that generation.

Thus different patterns of mating may have different behavioural consequences in a breeding population to the extent that differential behaviour is in some part a result of differences in genotypes. The causes of differential patterns of mating in human populations are not understood in any detail, although it is certain that the causes involve a complex interplay of biological, demographic, social, and cultural factors (Ford 1945, Lorimer 1954).

The paths between biology and behaviour may run in both directions and circle back; we know that cultural differences operating on the pattern of mating may result in changes in the distribution of genotypes in a breeding population and that these genetic changes may lead to differences in the acquisition and performance of at least some items in the cultural repertory by individuals.

We will consider three general patterns of mating: random, inbreeding, and assortative mating.

In no human population is the mating perfectly random. If a breeding population has N males, and if a given female has a first child by a given father, the probability under strictly random mating that her next child will have the same father is $1/N$. The observed frequency of this event is closer to unity than to $1/N$ in all known human populations. However, in many cases where the theory of population genetics is used to interpret observed genotype frequencies, the departures from randomness in mating are small enough to be negligible. This is true, for instance, of the distribution of blood-group genotypes in several hundred known populations (Mourant 1954).

† This article is essentially as published in *Genetic Diversity and Human Behaviour* edited by J. N. Spuhler, published by Aldine Publishing Co., 1967. Grateful acknowledgement is made to the Wenner–Gren Foundation for Anthropological Research for permission to reprint the article.

The idea of random mating as used in the Hardy–Weinberg equilibrium (where the array of genotypes in a randomly mated population is given by the square of the gene frequencies when these are expressed as a binomial or multinomial summing to unity) provides a convenient reference point for analysis of changes in the distribution of genotypes resulting from inbreeding or assortative mating.

Inbreeding

Inbreeding is the mating of individuals who have one or more biological ancestors in common.

The two most important observed consequences of inbreeding in experimental and farm animals are (1) the reduction of the mean phenotypic value shown by characters connected with reproductive capacity or physiological efficiency, and (2) the increase in uniformity, or reduction in the variance, about the mean phenotypic values within inbred lines. The reduction in fitness, termed *inbreeding depression*, may decrease the mean fertility of *Drosophila* (per pair per day) by as much as 1·25 per cent for each 1 per cent increase in inbreeding; in mice, litter size at birth may be decreased by 0·8 per cent, and female weight at six weeks of age by 0·3 per cent per 1 per cent increase in inbreeding (Falconer 1960). As will be shown in the material to be reviewed below, inbreeding depression is well established for morphological, physiological, and behavioural characters in human populations.

Both inbreeding depression and uniformity within inbred lines find a fully verified genetic explanation in the increased homozygosis consequent upon inbreeding. Thus, as Wright (1921) first suggested, it is desirable that an inbreeding coefficient should run on a scale from 0 to 1 while the percentage of homozygosity is running from 50 to 100 per cent (50 per cent being the proportion of homozygosis for two alleles with equal frequency in a randomly mated population), and the coefficient should measure as directly as possible the consequences of inbreeding to be expected on the average from any given regular or irregular pedigree.

In the sections to follow, the properties of Wright's coefficient of inbreeding (which he named 'F' because intense inbreeding results in the 'fixation' of genes in homozygous genotypes, that is, it brings about the complete absence of heterozygosis) will be explored in sufficient detail to interpret some observed results on inbreeding in human populations. Attention also will be called to inbreeding effects on genotypic variance and on the genetic correlation of biological relatives.

The methods used by anthropologists and biologists to measure the degree of inbreeding before Wright (see Pearl 1915) were based on the intuitively reasonable idea of 'ancestor loss', the fact that an inbred individual possesses fewer different ancestors in some particular generation than the maximum possible number, which is 2^n for the nth ancestral generation. This method is defective and sometimes quite misleading because the same degree of 'ancestral loss' is found for certain patterns of mating known to have radically different inbreeding consequences and to result in different degrees of homozygosis.

The operation of a pattern of mating gives a lineage of breeding populations a structure in time consisting of a complicated network of parent–child relationships. The net (Fig. 10.1) consists of individual organisms (father, mother, son,

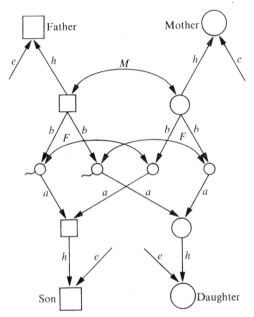

FIG. 10.1. Path diagram showing determinants of parent–parent, parent–child, and sib–sib correlations (after Wright 1921). For explanation see text.

daughter, sperm, egg, zygote) connected by paths of two sorts. A single-headed arrow (Fig. 10.2) indicates the direct effect along the path of one variable upon another. For example, the genotype of a zygote is completely determined by the sperm and the egg that unite to form it. A double-headed arrow indicates residual relations going back to factors not included in the diagram. For example, in Figure 10.1, $\overset{M}{\longleftrightarrow}$ stands for the correlation between mates, and $\overset{F}{\longleftrightarrow}$ for the correlation between uniting gametes. These two correlations are of great importance in the study of mating patterns, for M is used to measure the degree of assortative mating and F to measure the degree of inbreeding. F and M will be considered in greater detail below. Their full evaluation requires the tracing of paths more remote than those shown in Figure 10.1.

Method of path coefficients

The method of path coefficients, an invention of Sewall Wright, is perhaps the most convenient tool for the genetical analysis of such networks; Wright (1921, 1969) used this method to develop a major portion of the genetic theory of systems of mating. We will consider here only those parts of the theory needed to introduce Wright's conclusions on the genetic consequences of inbreeding and assortative mating.

If $\bar{V}_o$ is the mean and σ_o is the standard deviation of the variable, V_o, the standardized form, X_o, of that variable is $X_o = (V_o - \bar{V}_o)/\sigma_o$. Assume that X_o is a linear function of known variables X_1, X_2, ... X_m, and that the causal network is made formally complete by addition of statistically independent hypothetical or unanalysed variable, X_n. Single-headed arrows in the network may be indicated by path coefficients, p_{oi}, representing the path from X_i to X_o. The relations between X_o and the known and hypothetical variable may then be written $X_o = p_{o1}X_1 + p_{o2}X_2 + \ldots p_{om}X_m + p_{on}X_n$.

The correlation, r_{oq}, between two standardized variables, X_o and X_q, is defined as their mean product $r_{oq} = \sum\limits_{i=1}^{n} p_{oi}r_{iq}$. The correlation of a variable with itself, $r_{oo} = 1$, leads to the equality $\sum\limits_{i=1}^{n} p_{oi}r_{oi} = 1$, which may be parti tioned into a component $\sum\limits_{i=1}^{m} p_{oi}r_{oi}$ expressing the portion of the variance (σ^2_o) due to known factors—in other words, the squared coefficient of multiple correlation—and a component $p_{on}r_{on} = r^2_{on}$, the portion of the variance due to unknown factors.

The paths for genes passing along the network of biological descent are represented in Fig. 10.1. Variation in the phenotypes of individuals are

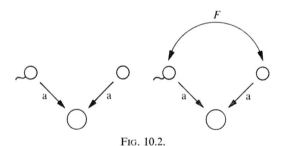

FIG. 10.2.

assumed to be determined by the additive effects of a hereditary (h) and an environmental path (e) so that $e^2 + h^2 = 1$. Variation in the genotypes of individuals is determined completely by the gametes (over paths a) that unite to produce them. The path coefficient a relates zygotic genotype to one of these gametes. The genotypic value is assumed to be the sum of the values of the two gametes that produce it. For each of these gametes, we add the two paths aa and aFa so that $2a(a+aF) = 1$ and $a = \sqrt{[(1/2)/(1+F)]}$. Variation in gametes formed by individuals is determined over path b, which relates a gamete to the genotype that produced it. This path coefficient b is also the correlation between the gamete and the genotype, since the two are connected by a single path. With regard to the alleles at a specific locus, that correlation expressed by b is equal to the correlation between that genotype and one of the gametes a generation back that produced that particular genotype. Using primes to indicate the preceding generation, $b = a'+a'F' = \sqrt{[(1+F)/2]}$.

With these definitions, we may now find the correlation between parent and parent, r_{pp}, between parent and offspring, r_{po}, and between brother and sister, r_{oo}; these correlations are of great importance to behaviour genetics because they can be estimated directly from observations on family members. A single correlation, M, connects parent and parent. There are two paths connecting parent and offspring; $habh+habMh = h^2ab(1+M)$. Four paths of two kinds connect brother and sister: $2\,(habbah)+2(habMbah) = 2h^2a^2b^2 (1+M)$. It should be noted that $M\ (= F/b^2)$ is taken to add up all possible connections between the parental genotypes. Under panmixia $M = F = 0$ and r_{po} and r_{oo} reduce to $0 \cdot 5\,h^2$.

The h_2 in the above path equations measures the 'heritability' of a trait with reference to a specific population and environment. In this context, it is the ratio of the additive genetic variance to the total phenotypic variance: the term is used with a variety of other statistical meanings, especially in twin studies.

Much biological variation of interest to behaviour genetics is likely to involve non-additive connections between genotype and phenotype due to gene interaction within (called dominance) and between (called epistasis) loci. And in human behavioural traits there are nearly always some non-additive relations between genotype and environment. The complexities due to non-additivity are difficult to handle and are discussed in works on quantitative genetics (Wright 1969, Kempthorne 1957, Falconer 1960).

Calculation of F *from pedigrees*

The value of F can be obtained by tracing the parent–child paths that connect an inbred individual to all ancestors common to his two parents. The method is illustrated in Fig. 10.3 showing the matings of: (a) brother and sister, and (b) single first cousins.

Starting with Fig. 10.3(a), consider the transmission of the four genes A^1, A^2, A^3, A^4, at some autosomal locus in the two common ancestors, that is, the parents of X and Y. The probability that gene A^1 will reach the inbred child, Z, over parent–child steps 1 and 2 is $(1/2)^2 = 1/4$; the probability that the same gene will reach Z over steps 3 and 4 is also 1/4. Steps 1 and 2 together with steps 3 and 4 form one of two inbreeding loops connecting Z with his two common ancestors. The probability that A^1 will reach Z over both sides of one inbreeding loop is 1/16, which is the probability that Z will be homozygous A^1A^1 for two genes identical by descent. The same argument holds for genes A^2, A^3, and A^4. Thus the probability that Z will be homozygous for genes identical by descent, that is, for any one of the four genes in question, is by definition the inbreeding coefficient of offspring of brother × sister matings; this probability is $4 \times 1/16 = 1/4$.

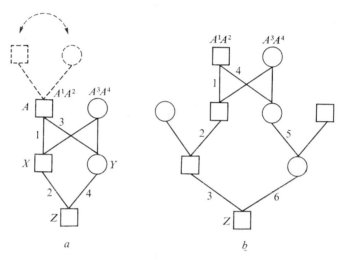

FIG. 10.3. Pedigrees of an inbred child from (a) brother × sister mating, and (b) mating of single first cousins. One of the common ancestors in pedigree (a) is inbred.

In the case of the child whose parents are single first cousins, Fig. 10.3(b), the probability that gene A^1 will reach the inbred child Z over parent–child steps 1, 2, and 3 is 1/8. Thus the probability that Z will be homozygous A^1A^1 is $(1/8)^2$ and that of homozygosity for any one of the four genes present at an autosomal locus in the two common ancestors is $4(1/8)^2 = 1/16$.

If a common ancestor is inbred, as indicated by the dashed pedigree in Fig. 10.3(a), the two genes A^1 and A^2 in that common ancestor may be identical by descent from a more remote ancestor common to his parents; the probability of this is, by definition, the inbreeding coefficient of the more proximate common ancestor, say, F_A. The fact that A is inbred increases the probability that X and Y will receive genes identical by descent from A by a factor $F_A/2$, and all inbreeding loops connecting to an inbred common ancestor require multiplication by the factor $(1+F_A)$.

By extension of these procedures, the contribution of any common ancestor, A, to the inbreeding coefficient of a descendant individual, Z, is $(1/2)^n (1+F_A)$ where n is the number of individuals in the loop leading from one parent to the common ancestor and back through the other parent. An inbred individual may have more than one common ancestor, and more than one inbreeding loop may connect an inbred individual and the same common ancestor. The contribution of all common ancestors to the inbreeding coefficient of a descendant is the sum of the contribution of all inbreeding loops connecting all common ancestors:

$$F = \Sigma[(1/2)^n(1+F_A)]$$

where n is the number of individuals in the inbreeding loop not counting Z.

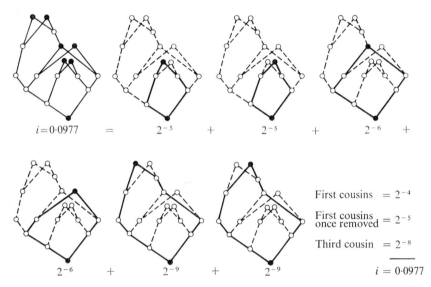

FIG. 10.4. Calculation of the inbreeding coefficient of a child whose parents are related as first cousins, first cousins once removed, and third cousins. (From Spuhler and Kluckhohn 1953.)

If the genes being considered are sex-linked, only female offspring may be inbred (since, barring non-disjunction, males get a Y chomosome from their fathers and are hemizygous for sex-linked genes), only females in the inbreeding loop are counted—omitting the inbred females whose inbreeding coefficient is desired—and any loop containing a father–son step is omitted entirely.

The above formula allows us to find the inbreeding coefficients of individuals, sibships, members of a generation, or members of a breeding population. It may be extended to pedigrees of any degree of complexity, as suggested in Fig. 10.4, the pedigree of the most inbred sibship in the Ramah Navaho Indian population (Spuhler and Kluckhohn 1953).

For comparatively highly inbred, natural, and enduring human populations, application of the formula given above for F is tedious because of the difficulty of finding and counting all of the inbreeding loops once and only once. Wright and McPhee (1925) found a sampling method for approximating the inbreeding coefficient of a population. Kudo (1962) and Kudo and Sakaguchi (1963) suggested an exact method for calculating inbreeding co-efficients which is easily adapted to machine programming.

F as the correlation of uniting gametes

The above results suggest an increase in the proportion of homozygotes among autosomal loci is, on the average, an expected population consequence of inbreeding, and we can use these results to explore a second definition of the inbreeding coefficient, that is, F = the correlation between uniting gametes. The array of genotypes for two autosomal alleles in a breeding population may be written in terms of the gene frequencies (where p is the frequency of A and $(1-p)$ that of the other allele, a) and the proportion of heterozygotes, H:

$$[(p-H/2)AA+HAa+(1-p-H/2)aa].$$

The correlation, F, between the gametes that united to form this array of genotypes is given by the formula for a four-fold table

$$F = \frac{(p-H/2)[(1-p)-H/2]-(H/2)^2}{\sqrt{[p^2(1-p)^2]}} = \frac{H_o-H}{H_o}$$

where H_o [$= 2p(1-p)$] is the proportion of heterozygotes under panmixia. Thus F may be used to measure the deviation of genotype frequencies in an inbred population from that expected under panmixia.

Panmixia and fixation

Now, if we define a coefficient of panmixia, P, as $P = (1-F)$, we can summarize in compact form the results to this point in Table 10.1 which gives the frequencies of genotypes from two autosomal alleles under three patterns of mating: (1) random mating or panmixia, where $F = 0$ and $P = 1$, (2) an intermediate degree of inbreeding, where $F>0$, $P<1$, and (3) complete fixation, where $F = 1$, $P = 0$, and heterozygotes are completely absent from the population. The intermediate condition of mating may be expressed in three equivalent ways: (1) deviation from panmixia, (2) a compound of pan-mictic and fixed components, and (3) deviation from fixation. It is important to note these changes in genotype frequency take place without change in gene frequency; they may be reversed by changes in the pattern of mating.

Recurrence Relations for F

We have considered the F values for isolated cases of brother × sister and single first-cousin mating. Recurrence equations can be obtained in cases where regular patterns of mating occur over several or many generations. These equations have been obtained for regular patterns of close inbreeding

TABLE 10.1

Genotype frequencies under three patterns of mating for autosomal alleles with frequencies p, q

Mating pattern		Genotype			
		AA	Aa	aa	Totals
Panmixia $F = 0$		p^2	$2pq$	q^2	1
Intermediate $0 < F < 1$	Deviation from panmixia	$p^2 + Fpq$	$2pq - 2Fpq$	$q^2 + Fpq$	$1 + 0$
	Panmictic and fixed components	$Pp^2 + Fp$	$2Ppq$	$Pq^2 + Fq$	$P + F = 1$
	Deviation from fixation	$p - Ppq$	$2Ppq$	$q - Ppq$	$1 - 0$
Complete fixation $F = 1$		p	—	q	1

by working out in algebra the consequences of every possible type of mating and giving each type its proper weight in each generation. For example, Jennings (1916) showed the decrease in heterozygosis (H) for a regular system of brother × sister mating is given by the terms of the Fibonacci series.

$$\frac{1}{1}, \frac{1}{2}, \frac{2}{4}, \frac{3}{8}, \frac{5}{16}, \frac{8}{32}, \frac{13}{64}, \ldots$$

where the numerator is the sum of its preceding two terms and the denominator doubles every term, giving the recurrence equation $H_{n+2} = (1/2)H_{n+1} + (1/4)H_n$.

Any method of working out all possible mating types is not practical for more complex systems of mating; for example, the case of double first-cousin matings with autosomal linkage involves the consideration of 10 000 different pairs of mating types. However, Wright's method of path coefficients leads quickly to results identical with the tedious, if more elegant, algebraic methods (Wright 1921, 1933, 1951).

The regular practice of continued sib-mating breaks a population into separate and branching lines of descent consisting, at any given generation, of 'isolates' whose members are a sibship. Since only brothers and sisters are mates, the correlation M (see Fig. 10.1) between mating individuals in generation n is that between full sibs in generation $n-1$; that is, $r_{pp} = r'_{oo}$, or

$$M = 2a'^2(b'^2 + b'^2 M')$$
$$= 2a'^2(b'^2 + F').$$

Substituting the values of a'^2 and b'^2, we find

$$M = \frac{1+2F+F''}{2\,(1+F')}$$

or

$$F = b^2 M = (1/4)(1+2F'+F'').$$

Since $H = H_0(1-F)$, the recurrence equation for H is

$$\begin{aligned}
H &= H_0(1-\tfrac{1}{4}-\tfrac{1}{2}F'-\tfrac{1}{4}F'') \\
&= \tfrac{1}{2}H_0(1-F')+\tfrac{1}{4}H_0(1-F'') \\
&= \tfrac{1}{2}H'+\tfrac{1}{4}H''
\end{aligned}$$

which is identical with the recurrence relation $H_{n+2} = \tfrac{1}{2}H_{n+1}+\tfrac{1}{4}H_n$ obtained from the Fibonacci series.

If we assume the decay of heterozygosis process has reached equilibrium by $H/H' = H'/H''$ then $H/H' = (1/4)(1+\sqrt{5}) = 0\cdot809$, indicating heterozygosis decreases about 19·1 per cent per generation under continued brother × sister mating. Wright has shown the heterozygosis decrease rate in a population of size N with random mating (union of gametes) is $1/2N$ per generation.

By using the method of path coefficients, the effects of continued regular systems of inbreeding may be obtained for single first and second cousins and other mating patterns of anthropological interest shown in Fig. 10.5.

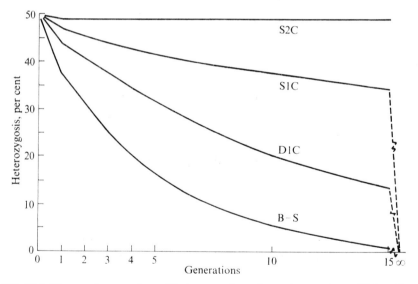

FIG. 10.5. Changes in percentage of heterozygosity under various systems of inbreeding: single second cousins (S2C), single first cousins (S1C), double first cousins (D1C), and brother × sister (B–S). (Data from Wright 1921.)

The genetic consequences of inbreeding implied by some particular F value must be taken as relative to some reference population; the statement that the coefficient of inbreeding is x per cent in population A at time t_1 implies that heterozygosis is x per cent less than expected from random mating within the founding or base population of, say, time t_0 to which the pedigrees trace. If we let the subscript I refer to individuals, S to groups, strains, isolates, or other sub-divisions of the population, and T to the total, base, or founding population, then F_{IT} is the inbreeding of individuals with reference to the total population, F_{IS} that of an individual relative to a group within the comprehensive population, and F_{ST} that relative to the base population that would persist if random mating within the subpopulations were initiated. The mating structure of populations may be analysed by application of the formula $(1-F_{IT}) = (1-F_{IS})(1-F_{ST})$, where F_{ST} and F_{IT} are necessarily positive but F_{IS} can be negative.

Degree of inbreeding in human populations

The mean F values for known human populations occupy only a small part of the theoretical range from 0 to 1. The Samaritans, with $F = 0.043$, have the highest degree of inbreeding reported for a human group (Bonné 1963). The highest F value reported for a human individual, 0.4270, was calculated by Rasmuson (1961) for Cleopatra-Berenike III—an aunt of the Cleopatra we associate with Caesar and Antonius—on the basis of the unreliable pedigree drawn up by Strak in 1897, which probably mistakes unrelated women given the term of address and reference 'sister' after marriage for biological sisters.

The mean F for the general population of France in the period 1926–45 was $0.000\,66$ (Sutter and Tabah 1948) and that of England and Wales in the period 1924–9 was $0.000\,28$ (Bell 1941). Bunak (1965) suggests many contemporary rural populations of Europe, North America, and Negro Africa are composed of demes numbering 1500 to 4000 individuals, with about 80 per cent endogamy, and with a preponderant part of the deme members related to one another as third cousins, that is, with $F = 0.0039$. A number of human geneticists take the maximum value commonly observed in isolated populations, about 0.006, as the probable long-term F value for the human species (see, for example, Neel, Kodani, Brewer, and Anderson 1949). Morton, Chung, and Mi (1967) used data from a study of interracial crosses in Hawaii to estimate the inbreeding coefficient due to remote consanguinity in large populations at about 0.0005. Wright (1950) arrived at a value of 0.02 for the long-term inbreeding coefficient in human populations by considering random mating for a neutral gene within local breeding populations of 200 mated couples. The available ethnographic data suggest this is an underestimate of the upper limit to the inbreeding coefficient in primitive human populations, for it is improbable that human bands exceeded a total of 200

to 300 persons of all ages (or 50 to 75 breeding pairs) during the history of
the species before agriculture. Known food-gathering people without domestic animals other than the dog rarely live in groups of over fifty or sixty individuals (Linton 1955). If this is indeed the general case, various enduring
local populations of our species passed through an 'inbreeding bottleneck',
after a very long time in transit, from a few to not more than 300
generations ago.

Inbreeding and behaviour

Hundreds of investigations on the consequences of inbreeding for behaviour, especially for the defective and gifted extremes of the behavioural spectrum, appeared prior to the development of population genetics in the first
third of this century. Huth (1875) compiled the earlier studies, Westermarck
(1903) brought together the data from the last quarter of the nineteenth
century, and East and Jones (1919) surveyed the information from the opening
decades of the twentieth century. Holmes (1924) gave an extensive bibliography of these inquiries, nearly all of them now lacking other than historical
interest.

Despite extended statistical scrutiny, the behavioural outcome to be
expected on the average from the marriage of near kin remained controversial—some experts were for and others against it. The following explanation for this lack of agreement is quoted here from East and Jones (1919)
because it is still widely accepted in anthropological circles.

The impossibility of a correct statistical answer to the problem is clear if one works back
from the answer given by research on heredity: 'Inbreeding is not in itself harmful; whatever effect it may have is due wholly to the inheritance received.' It is not to be wondered,
therefore, that examination of the pedigree record of one family led to one conclusion,
and of another family to exactly the opposite (pp. 243–244).

East and Jones' *Inbreeding and Outbreeding*, appeared two years before
Sewell Wright's *Systems of Mating*, 1921, the starting-point of modern population genetical studies on inbreeding.

Inbreeding and behaviour in Japanese children

A study of Japanese children is up to now the most elaborate attempt to
measure the behavioural consequences of inbreeding in a human population.
The study was organized by the Human Genetics Group at the University
of Michigan under the direction of Neel in collaboration with a number of
Japanese workers and carried out by the Child Health Survey, Hiroshima
and Nagasaki, in 1958–60 (Schull and Neel 1962, 1965). I had the pleasure
of being field director for the survey in 1959 but did not take part in the
analysis of the data by Schull and Neel.

I will give a brief account of the Hiroshima results. Schull and Neel (1965) may be consulted for full details on the study in both cities. The sample numbers of inbred and control boys and girls available for neuromuscular and psychometric observation in Hiroshima were:

	Males	Females	Totals
Inbred ($F > 0$)	552	959	1511
Controls ($F = 0$)	621	987	1608
Totals ($F \geq 0$)	1173	1946	3119

The behavioural variables observed in Hiroshima under the direction of Drew were:

1. and 2. 'Age when walked' and 'Age when talked' are two behavioural criteria of common use in paediatric and parental appraisals of child development. They are, of course, subject to errors of parental recall and may be biased by cultural norms.
3. A dynamometer was used to measure strength of grip in kilograms in the right and left hands. The handle of the instrument was adjusted to fit the hand size of each child, who was allowed several practice tries.
4. Tapping rate is the average number of taps with the index finger on a telegraphic-type key over five periods, each of 10 seconds duration. The rate is recorded separately for the two hands.
5. The Colour Trail is a paper-and-pencil test with five pairs of simple geometric figures (triangles, circles, and so forth), each pair of two different colours, the same colour being present in one member of two different figures in the case of three pairs and one colour being unique to one of the other two pairs. The object of the test (which is easier to do than to describe) is to connect a figure of one colour to the same shape of another colour, and so on. Each child had a practice run on a simplified version. A maximum of 120 seconds was allowed. The score is the number of seconds taken for completion.
6. The maze test has five pencil mazes of the Porteus type that are included in the Japanese version of the Wechsler Intelligence Scale for Children (W.I.S.C.). Three maze trails were available for practice. Each maze must be completed in a specified time; if more mistakes than a specified number are made, the score is zero points; if the maze is completed with exactly the allowable number of mistakes, the score is 1 point. Scores of 2 or 3 points are given for fewer mistakes. The overall score is the sum of the points on the five mazes, and the fewer the mistakes the greater the total score, the maximum being 21 points.
7. The Japanese version of the W.I.S.C. (Kodama and Shinagawa 1953) was administered to children at their regular schools by the staff of the Department of Psychology, Hiroshima University. The W.I.S.C. consists

of verbal and performance subgroups, each with six parts as listed below with their maximum raw scores:

Verbal		Performance	
General information	30	Picture completion	20
General comprehension	28	Picture arrangement	57
Arithmetic	16	Block design	55
Similarities	28	Object assembly	34
Vocabulary	80	Coding (A or B)	50 or 93
Digit span	26	Mazes	21

The maze section of the W.I.S.C. furnished a measure of reliability as it was given both in the survey clinic and in the schools. In general, the Digit Span test was not administered.

The W.I.S.C. raw scores are converted into scaled scores yielding a verbal I.Q., a performance I.Q., and, when these are summed, a full-scale I.Q. These I.Q.s are obtained by comparing each subject's test results with the standard scores for each four-month age group. Within each group the expected full-scale I.Q. is 100 and the standard deviation is 15.

8. School Grades. The boys and girls in school years 1–4 in the Hiroshima elementary schools are taught Japanese language, social studies, arithmetic, science, music, fine arts, and physical education; beginning with the fifth year, a course on domestic science is added. The student's school performance is scored from 1 to 5 in unit steps. Score '1' is the mark of the lowest 5 per cent, '2' that of the next 20 per cent, '3' of the middle 50 per cent, '4' of the next higher 20 per cent, and '5' of the highest 5 per cent.

Parental migration away from Hiroshima accounted for a 19 per cent loss between the time of establishment of the cohort of children at birth and the time of examination in the Child Health Survey. There is no evidence for systematic difference between the children who left the city and those who stayed and were available for examination as regards parental age, birth rank, or recognized perinatal morbidity.

Table 10.2 sets out comparative data on the average control child and the average child of single first cousins (whose $F = 1/16$), with reference to the eight classes of behavioural variables. Where appropriate, observations have been standardized to age 120 months.

In each case, the mean of the inbred children is significantly depressed compared with the mean of the control children. The observed inbreeding depression is remarkably similar in the psychometric and the school performance variables. Schull and Neel suggests that this concordance would seem to imply a high correlation between potential and achievement in these Japanese school children.

TABLE 10.2

Effects of inbreeding on the behaviour of Japanese children†

Characteristic	Sex	Average control child	Average offspring of first-cousins	In-breeding effect	Per cent change with inbreeding	Potential inflation effects of socio-economic variation	
						In-breeding effect	Magnitude, per cent
Age when walked	M	14·06	14·19*	0·13	0·9	—	—
(months)	F	13·62	14·07**	0·45	3·3	—	—
Age when talked	M	11·81	12·60**	0·79	6·7	—	—
(months)	F	10·38	10·82**	0·44	4·2	—	—
Dynamometer grip,							
right hand (kg)	M	14·04	13·71**	0·29	2·1	0·04	12·1
	F	12·35	12·02**	0·29	2·3	0·04	12·1
left hand (kg)	M	13·23	13·01**	0·20	1·5	0·02	9·1
	F	11·43	11·20**	0·20	1·7	0·03	13·0
Tapping rate/10s.							
right hand	M	28·02	27·62**	0·31	1·1	0·09	22·5
	F	26·28	25·85**	0·31	1·2	0·12	27·9
left hand	M	26·11	25·66**	0·38	1·5	0·07	15·6
	F	24·90	24·42**	0·38	1·5	0·10	20·8
Colour Trail	M	20·54	22·33**	0·68	3·3	1·11	62·0
test score	F	21·76	23·27**	0·68	3·1	0·83	55·0
Maze tests score	M	17·92	17·50**	0·34	1·9	0·08	19·0
	F	16·98	16·52**	0·34	2·0	0·12	26·1
W.I.S.C. verbal	M	58·67	55·34**	2·76	4·7	0·57	17·1
score	F	57·01	53·46**	2·76	4·8	0·79	22·3
W.I.S.C. performance	M	57·37	54·94**	2·06	3·6	0·37	15·2
score	F	55·10	52·52**	2·06	3·7	0·52	20·2
School grade:							
language	M	3·09	2·95**	0·10	3·2	0·04	28·5
	F	3·28	3·10**	0·10	3·0	0·08	44·4
social studies	M	3·17	3·04**	0·09	2·8	0·04	30·8
	F	3·14	2·98**	0·09	2·9	0·07	43·8
mathematics	M	3·21	3·04**	0·13	4·0	0·04	23·5
	F	3·19	2·99**	0·13	4·1	0·07	35·0
science	M	3·29	3·11**	0·13	4·0	0·04	23·5
	F	3·16	2·95**	0·13	4·1	0·08	38·1
music	M	2·94	2·78**	0·12	4·1	0·04	25·0
	F	3·34	3·14**	0·12	3·6	0·08	40·0
fine arts	M	3·09	2·95**	0·10	3·2	0·04	28·6
	F	3·40	3·23**	0·10	2·9	0·07	41·1
physical	M	3·28	3·13**	0·13	4·0	0·05	13·3
	F	3·27	3·09**	0·13	4·0	0·05	27·8

** Significant at the 1 per cent level.
* Significant at the 5 per cent level.

† From Schull and Neel (1965).

The inbreeding effect, computed by regression analysis, is based upon a regression coefficient common to the sexes if these could not be shown to differ. The percentage change with inbreeding varies from 0·9 to 6·7, both extremes falling in the classes 'Age when walked' and 'Age when talked'. It is interesting to note that the per cent effect of inbreeding on these imprecise measurements is roughly the same as that for the more precise psychometric tests. The per cent change due to inbreeding tends to be greater for the psychometric and school performance than for the neuromuscular scores. The inbreeding effects are greater for the behavioural variables in general than for the measurements of body size which show a small, consistent, and significant inbreeding depression of about 0·5 per cent.

Compared with the controls, the inbred children as a whole come from families of lower socio-economic status as measured by parental occupation and education, density of persons in the household, and food expenditures per person per month. The effects of socio-economic status were removed by the use of a socio-economic score. In boys, about 23 per cent of the apparent inbreeding depression is attributable to socio-economic variation in the case of neuromuscular tests, 16 per cent for psychometrics, and 25 per cent for school performance. The corresponding percentages for girls are 26, 21, and 38.

Assortative mating

When mates in a breeding population have more phenotypical characters in common than would be expected by chance, that is, by random mating, the pattern is called positive assortative mating; when they have fewer than would be expected by chance, it is called negative assortative mating. Usually, the degree of assortment is measured by an association statistic that runs from $+1$ for perfect positive assortative mating to -1 for perfect negative assortment. The product moment correlation coefficient is used below for continuous traits and the tetrachoric correlation for discrete traits.

We saw that under inbreeding the percentage of heterozygosis in a breeding population is independent of the number of gene loci involved and of their dominance relations. This is not the case under phenotypical assortative mating. The analysis of assortative mating is complicated by the fact that the same phenotype may be due to genotypes of different gene constitution, and the complication increases with the number of loci involved. If dominance is present, a constant correlation $(0 < r_{pp} < 1)$ between the phenotypes of mates $(h^2 = 1)$ in a series of assortative mating results in a changing correlation between their genotypes. Assortative mating acting by itself, like inbreeding, does not change gene frequencies in a breeding population.

First, consider perfect positive assortative mating $(r_{pp} = +1)$ for three phenotypes (2, 1, 0) determined by two autosomal alleles (A, a) without dominance. The frequencies of the three possible kinds of homogamous matings and their offspring are:

	Mating		Offspring		
Phenotypes	Genotypes	Frequency	AA	Aa	aa
2×2	$AA \times AA$	r	r	—	—
1×1	$Aa \times Aa$	$2s$	$s/2$	s	$s/2$
0×0	$aa \times aa$	t	—	—	t
Totals		1	$r+s/2$	s	$s/2+t$

In the initial generation, the frequency of gene $A = p_n = r+s$ and that of gene $a = q_n = s+t$; in the offspring generation, their frequencies are

$$p_{n+1} = r+s/2+s/2 = r+s = p_n,$$
$$q_{n+1} = s/2+s/2+t = s+t = q_n,$$

showing that the gene frequencies are not changed by this system of assortative mating. The genotype frequencies for the nth generation are

$$r(AA)_n+2s(Aa)_n+t(aa)_n = 1,$$

but for generation $n+1$ we have, as given above for the offspring,

$$(AA)_{n+1} = r+s/2$$
$$(AA)_{n+1} = s$$
$$(aa)_{n+1} = s/2+t.$$

Thus, in general,

$$(AA)_n = (AA)_o+(1/2-1/2^n)(Aa)_o$$
$$(Aa)_n = 1/2^n(Aa)_o$$
$$(aa)_n = (aa)_o+(1/2)-1/2^n)(Aa)_o.$$

Accordingly, the frequency of heterozygotes is halved in each generation and the homozygotes tend toward the following limiting values:

$$\lim (AA)_n = (AA)_o+1/2(Aa)_o = p_o,$$
$$\lim (aa)_n = (aa)_o+1/2(Aa)_o = q_o.$$

This result was first obtained by Jennings (1916). Geppert and Koller (1938) applied the direct method to obtain sequence equations for several other modes of inheritance, including dominance and multiple alleles. If the dominant and recessive alleles are of equal frequency in the population, the percentages of heterozygosis in a system of assortative mating involving two alleles run:

No dominance: 1/2, 1/4, 1/8, 1/16, 1/32, . . .
Dominance: 1/2, 1/3, 1/4, 1/5, 1/6, . . .

The direct method, which considers the outcome of all possible assortative matings, requires too much space to be given in detail here in the case of perfect assortative mating for phenotypes controlled by genes from more than one locus and for all cases where the phenotypical correlation is $0 < r_{pp} < 1$. Wright (1921) carried the work of the direct method to the fourth generation for perfect positive assortative mating for five phenotypes (4, 3, 2, 1, 0) determined by two pairs of equally frequent autosomal alleles (A, a and B, b) lacking dominance and epistasis and assumed to be in equilibrium before the start of assortative mating: the percentages of heterozygosis in successive generations form the series 1/2, 3/8, 10/32, 17/64; the correlations between gametes produced by an individual form the series 0, 1/3, 1/2, 53/87; and the correlations between uniting gametes form the series 1/2, 2/3, 3/4, and 70/87. Fortunately, the method of path coefficients obtains without difficulty general recurrence equations for the genetical consequences of perfect or imperfect assortative mating involving any number of loci with or without dominance.

Fig. 10.6 is a path diagram showing the phenotypes and genotypes of two mated individuals as determined by genes at three autosomal loci lacking dominance and as correlated through correlations among these loci. The path coefficients are defined:

i = the path measuring the influence of the gene pair at a given locus on the genotype—the sum of the effect of these gene pairs.

a_u = the path from A^1 to $A^1 A^2$, the subscript indicating the path measures the effect of a unit factor—the genes at one locus.

e and h are defined as for inbreeding to measure the degree of environmental and of genetic determination of the phenotype.

The correlations shown in Fig. 10.6 are defined:

r_{pp} = correlation between phenotypes of mated individuals (father–mother), the coefficient of assortative mating based on phenotypical resemblance.

M = the correlation between genotypes of mated individuals.

f = the correlation between uniting gametes, as defined for inbreeding. (Not to be confused with f_u.)

f_u = the correlation between genes of the same set of alleles, in different individuals (such as A^1 and A^3).

g_u = the correlation between two genes of the same set of alleles that separate in gamete formation (for example A^1 and A^2); since these genes united at fertilization in the preceding generation, $g_u = f'_u$.

j_u = correlation between genes from different loci that act on the same phenotypical character (such as A^1 and B^3). It is assumed $j_u = f_u$.

k_u = the correlation between genes of different sets of alleles (such as A and B) in the same individual.

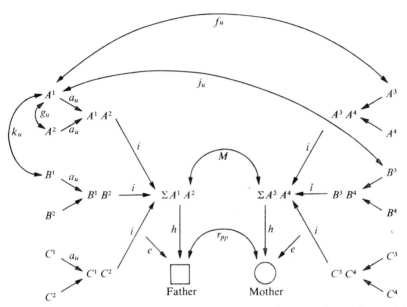

FIG. 10.6. Path diagram showing determinants of phenotypic correlations (after Wright 1921). For explanation see text.

On the basis of these definitions and the path diagram, if we are given n = number of loci (gene pairs), r_{pp} = correlation between the phenotypes of mates (coefficient of assortative mating), and h^2_0 = initial heritability at the start of assortative mating, the following equations may be used to find the effect of any degree of positive or negative phenotypical assortative mating for any number of loci:

$$M = h'^2 r_{pp}$$
$$f_u = (M/2n)[1+f'_u+2(n-1)k_u]$$
$$k_u = (1/2)(f'_u+k'_u)$$
$$H = (1/2)(1-f_u)$$

Negative values of M are used in the case of negative assortative mating $(0 > r_{pp} > -1)$.

When equilibrium is reached $f_u = (M)/[2n-M(2n-1)]$, $H = [n(1-M)]/[2n(1-M)+M]$.

Now we can see that the above equations reach the same results for the effects of assortative mating as those obtained by the direct enumeration of all possible mating pairs. In the case of perfect positive assortative mating for three phenotypes (2, 1, 0) determined by two autosomal alleles (A, a) lacking dominance, we have $n = r_{pp} = h^2{}_o = 1$,

$$f_u = (1/2)[1+f'_u+0]$$
$$H = (1/2)(1-f_u) = (1/2)H'$$

and one half of the heterozygosis is lost in each generation as found by the direct method.

In the case of perfect positive assortative mating for five phenotypes (4, 3, 2, 1, 0) determined by two pairs of independent autosomal alleles (A, a and B, b) lacking dominance and epistasis, where equilibrium is assumed to have been reached before the beginning of assortative mating, the change in percentage of heterozygosis is given by

$$f'_u = (1/4)[1+f_u+2k_u]$$
$$k'_u = (1/2)(f'_u+k_u).$$

Starting with $f_u = k_u = 0$, the above equations yield the following series:

$$f_u = 0,\ 1/4,\ 3/8,\ 30/64,\ 35/64,\ 157/256,\ \ldots,\ 1$$
$$k_u = 0,\ 1/8,\ 1/4,\ 23/64,\ 29/64,\ \ldots,\ 1$$

Thus, beginning with $H = 1/2$, since $H = (1/2)(1-f_u)$, we have $H = 1/2$, $3/8$, $5/16$, $17/64$, $29/128$, which agrees with the fractions obtained by the direct method.

Wright (1969) should be consulted regarding other results of assortative mating, including the effect of dominance, imperfect assortative mating, the consequences of these patterns of mating for the correlation between parent and offspring and between siblings, and the joint effects of inbreeding and assortative mating on the distribution of genotypes in breeding populations. The results for those degrees of positive and negative assortative mating of most anthropological interest are plotted in Fig. 10.7.

In general, population consequences of positive assortative mating are similar to those for inbreeding, since the proportion of heterozygous genotypes is reduced and that of homozygous genotypes increased, in comparison with the proportions expected under random mating. The consequences for multiple gene modes of inheritance differ from those with inbreeding in that fewer of the homozygous genotypes are preserved. For example, if five phenotypes (4, 3, 2, 1, 0) are controlled by two pairs of genes at independent autosomal loci (A, a; B, b) as follows: 4—$AABB$; 3—$AaBB$, $AABb$; 2—$AAbb$, $AaBb$, $aaBB$; 1—$Aabb$, $aaBb$; 0—$aabb$; close inbreeding will result in a genotype distribution with all homozygous classes ($AABB$, $AAbb$, $aaBB$, $aabb$)

preserved, while one of perfect positive assortative mating will preserve only two homozygous classes (*AABB, aabb*). Negative assortative mating leads to an increase in the proportion of heterozygosis. With perfect assortative mating, no dominance, and complete heritability, equilibrium is not reached until heterozygotes are entirely absent. This triple condition probably never holds for human populations (excluding the uninteresting case of the negative correlation in sex and some sex attributes between mated pairs). In fact, as we will see in the next section, phenotypic correlations above $r_{pp} = 0.5$ are

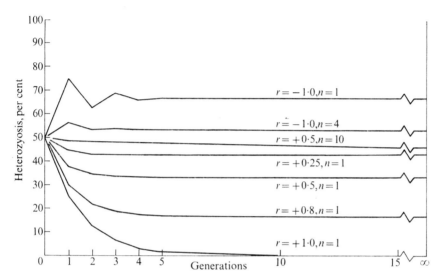

FIG. 10.7. Changes in heterozygosis in various gene systems under various degrees of assortative mating. r = phenotypical correlation between mates, n = number of pairs of genes. A condition of no dominance is assumed. (Data from Wright 1921.)

rare in human populations. Thus, in general, assortative mating in human populations may be expected to lead to a condition of genetic equilibrium without fixation of extreme types. A correlation of 0·50 between genotypes would be towards the high end of the range. With one pair of genes involved, heterozygosis is reduced only from 0·500 to 0·333 in an infinite number of generations of assortative mating; with ten pairs, H is reduced to 0·476. Assortative mating, like close inbreeding, leads to increased variability of the population as a whole. For those phenotypes of complete heritability, assortative mating of +0·50 results in a doubling of the genetic variance of the whole population if an indefinitely large number of gene pairs is involved. The effect is less for a smaller number of gene pairs. With perfect assortative mating, the population reaches equilibrium with completely homozygous genotypes concentrated at the two extremes. Negative assortative mating reduces the genetic variance of the population for phenotypes with high heritability (Wright 1921).

Assortative mating and behaviour

The volume of reliable recorded information on assortative mating in human populations is considerably less than that on inbreeding; and of studies on assortative mating, those concerned with behavioural variables considerably outnumber those on morphological or physiological traits. Table 10.3 gives an unsystematic selection of 25 studies based on samples of 100 mated pairs or more. Many, if not most, traits investigated probably have low heritability; for some of the traits, the observed correlation probably developed or increased after marriage rather than prior to it. The unweighted mean of the 21 product–moment correlations in this table rounds to 0·25

TABLE 10.3

Assortative mating for intelligence-test scores, personality ratings, and miscellaneous characteristics

Item	Source	N pairs	r ± s.d.†
Intelligence scores			
Stanford–Binet	Burks (1928)	174	0·47±0·04
Otis	Freeman, Holzinger, and Mitchell (1928)	150	0·49±0·04
Army Alpha	Jones (1928)	105	0·60±0·04
Progressive matrices	Halperin (1946)	324	0·76
Various tests	Smith (1941)	433	0·19±0·03
Vocabulary	Carter (1932)	108	0·21±0·06
Arithmetic	Carter (1932)	108	0·03±0·06
Mental grade	Penrose (1933)	100	0·44
Personality ratings			
Neurotic tendency	Hoffeditz (1934)	100	0·16±0·07
Neurotic tendency	Terman and Buttenwieser (1935)	126	0·11±0·06
Neurotic tendency	Terman and Buttenwieser (1935)	215	0·22±0·04
Neurotic tendency	Willoughby (1928)	100	0·27±0·05
Self-sufficiency	Hoffeditz (1934)	100	0·09±0·07
Self-sufficiency	Terman and Buttenwieser (1935)	215	0·12±0·04
Self-sufficiency	Terman and Buttenwieser (1935)	126	0·02±0·06
Dominance	Hoffeditz (1934)	100	0·15±0·07
Dominance	Terman and Buttenwieser (1935)	126	0·24±0·06
Dominance	Terman and Buttenwieser (1935)	215	0·29±0·04
Introversion–extroversion	Terman and Buttenwieser (1935)	126	0·02±0·06
Introversion–extroversion	Terman and Buttenwieser (1935)	215	0·16±0·04
Miscellaneous			
Temperament	Burgess and Wallin (1944)	316	0·22
Insanity	Goring (1909)	1433	0·06
Criminality	Goring (1909)	474	0·20

† Tetrachoric correlations are shown without standard deviations.

and the range goes from r-values not significantly different from zero to 0.62 ± 0.05.

A number of highly capable, statistically oriented biologists, not motivated by any particular political outlook, have expressed concern about the possible decline in intelligence in the general population deduced from the negative correlation between the measured intelligence scores of children and the size of the families they represent. Several large-sample projects have established small, negative correlations (in the range -0.3 to -0.2 and of unquestioned significance) between the number of sibs and the intelligence scores of school-age children in various countries, including France, New Zealand, Scotland, and the United States.

The decline argument goes this way: test results are obtained for a sample of school children, say, of age 11. It is assumed that the tested child's score may be taken as an estimated score of his untested siblings. A mean score is calculated for children of each sibship size. The mean score of the untested *parental generation* is estimated from the mean scores of each sibship size class weighted by the number of subjects in that class.

The mean score of the *offspring generation* is estimated by weighting the number of subjects in a sibship size class by the size of the sibship. Given the negative correlation between intelligence scores and sibship size, the estimated mean score of the offspring generation is necessarily lower than the estimated mean score of the parental generation and the difference is taken as a measure of the decline in average intelligence scores in one generation (Giles-Bernardelli 1950).

The argument for a decline in the average level in intelligence is accepted with little question by some workers despite the fact that test scores on school children are observed to be higher than those of about a decade earlier.

Higgins, Reed, and Reed (1962) and Bajema (1963) identified a serious defect in the decline argument insofar as it is based on the negative correlation between intelligence scores and sibship size ascertained from school children. That part of the population that does not reproduce (as much as 20 per cent in Bajema's Michigan study) is not represented in a sample drawn from school children. The relationship between the intelligence of an individual and the size of the family from which he comes is biased in a negative direction because as intelligence decreases the probability of childlessness increases, as a result of either differential marriage rates or differential child-bearing rates.

Using a life-table analysis to calculate the intrinsic rate of natural increase, Bajema found the Kalamazoo, Michigan, population was either very close to equilibrium with respect to genetic factors favouring high intelligence or, more likely, had experienced a recent slight increase in the frequency of such factors, despite the fact that the observed correlation between intelligence score and completed family size is -0.26 (significant at the 1 per cent level).

Penrose (1949) produced a hypothetical model demonstrating that perfect positive assortative mating for intelligence (assumed to depend on a single pair of autosomal alleles) leads to an equilibrium with respect to the distribution of the genotypes concerned with intellectual ability, if the birth rate of the heterozygous inferior group is twice that of the homozygous superior group and if the inferior group just replaces their numbers, because one-quarter of their offspring go into the superior group, one-half stay in the inferior group, and one-quarter are subnormal and infertile.

An obvious improvement in the design of studies on the supposed decline of the population in intelligence would correlate the tested intelligence scores of *both* parents with the number of their children. I will conclude this report by presenting the results of two cognitive tests carried out in a study of assortative mating in the population of Ann Arbor (Spuhler 1962), together with heritability estimates for these tests based on a one-egg and two-egg twin sample from the area centering about Ann Arbor.

The first test is the Progressive Matrices (Raven 1946), which is described as 'a non-verbal test of a person's capacity at the time of the test to apprehend figures presented for his perception, see relations between them, and conceive the correlative figures completing the system of relations presented.' When used with a time limit, the Progressive matrices constitute a 'test of intellectual capacity'. The present analysis of the test scores is based on the total number correct with a possible range from 0–60.

The second test is the 'Verbal meaning' part of the Chicago Tests of Primary Mental Abilities (Thurstone and Thurstone 1941). The present analysis is restricted to the scores on the 'Sentences' part of the test, which involves selection of one of four words that best completes the meaning of each of forty sentences. Three minutes were allowed for practice and five minutes for the test. The maximum score is 40. The present analysis considers: (1) the total number of right answers, and (2) the proportion of right answers.

Table 10.4 indicates the observed correlations between spouses for the three test results are all significant beyond the 1 per cent level.

The heritability of these test scores is not known for the general population of Ann Arbor but their general magnitude may be inferred from results based on the Ann Arbor twin sample:

	Twin pairs	h^2	P
Progressive matrices, total right	76	0·94	$< 0·05$
Sentences, total right	82	0·45	$< 0·05$
Sentences, proportion right	82	0·40	$0·05 < P < 0·1$

The correlation between fertility and intelligence scores of the married couples in our sample may be obtained by use of a fertility index. Many of these couples had not completed their reproductive period. A square root

TABLE 10.4

Assortative mating for three scores on two intelligence tests†

Statistic	Progressive matrices	Chicago verbal	
	Total right	Total right	Proportion right
Number of couples	180	151	148
Father's mean	35·60	22·21	0·93
Mother's mean	34·99	20·86	0·91
Correlation	+0·399**	+0·305**	+0·732**

** Significant at the 1 per cent level.

† From Spuhler (1962).

transformation of months of exposure to pregnancy plotted against the number of live-born children showed a strong, approximately linear relationship between exposure and fertility. From this relationship a score was obtained giving the difference between observed and expected fertility for each couple. The range of this fertility score was from −2·57 to +3·49, with a mean of +0·0003 and a standard deviation of 1·06. The distribution of the fertility scores was found to be satisfactorily close to a normal distribution. The correlation between the test scores and the fertility indices are given in Table 10.5.

TABLE 10.5

Correlation of intelligence test scores and fertility indices†

Subject	Progressive matrices		Chicago verbal			
	Total right		Total right		Proportion right	
	N	r	N	r	N	r
Mother	180	+0·148*	151	+0·128	148	+0·234*
Father	180	+0·032	151	−0·010	148	+0·038

* Significant at the 5 per cent level.

† From Spuhler (1962).

The correlations are positive and significant at the 5 per cent level between mother's fertility index and her score on two of the three tests. The correlations are not significantly different from zero for father's fertility index and test scores.

Just where the population of Ann Arbor falls in the distribution of all possible samples from human populations is, of course, unknown. With regard to the evidence from our small sample, we may conclude that there is significant positive assortative mating for intelligence as estimated by scores on three cognitive tests; that one of the tests shows strong, another moderate, and the third no heritability; and that there is a positive correlation between tested intelligence of mothers and their reproductive performance.

REFERENCES

BAJEMA, C. J. (1963). Estimation of the direction and intensity of natural selection in relation to human intelligence by means of the intrinsic rate of natural increase. *Eugen. Q.* **10**, 175–87.

BELL, J. (1941). A determination of the consanguinity rate in the general hospital population of England and Wales. *Ann. Eugen.* **10**, 370–91.

BONNÉ, B. (1963). The Samaritans: a demographic study. *Hum. Biol.* **35**, 61–89.

BUNAK, V. V. (1965). Der Verwandtschaftsgrad der Bevölkerung kleiner ländlicher Gemeinden. *Acta Genet. Med. Gemmell.* **14**, 174–81.

BURGESS, E. W. and WALLIN, P. (1944). Homogamy in personality characteristics. *J. abn. soc. Psychol.* **39**, 475–81.

BURKS, B. S. (1928). The relative influence of nature and nurture upon mental development. *Yb. Nat. Soc. Stud. Educ.* **27**, 219–321.

CARTER, H. D. (1932). Family resemblances in verbal and numerical abilities. *Genet. Psychol. Monogr.* **12**, 1–104.

EAST, E. M. and JONES, D. F. (1919). *Inbreeding and outbreeding.* Lippincott, Philadelphia.

FALCONER, D. S. (1960). *Introduction to quantitative genetics.* Oliver and Boyd, Edinburgh.

FORD, C. S. (1945). A comparative study of human reproduction. *Yale University Pub. Anthrop.* No. 3.

FREEMAN, F. N., HOLZINGER, J., and MITCHELL, B. C. (1928). The influence of the environment on the intelligence, school achievement and conduct of foster children. *Yb. Nat. Soc. Stud. Educ.* **27**, 103–217.

GEPPERT, H. and KOLLER, S. (1938). *Erbmathematik.* Meyer Verlag, Leipzig.

GILES-BERNARDELLI, B. M. (1950). The decline of intelligence in New Zealand. *Popul. Stud.* **4**, 200–8.

GORING, C. H. (1909). Studies in national deterioration. *Draper's Company Research Memoir,* 5. Dulau, London.

HALPERIN, S. L. (1946). Human heredity and mental deficiency. *Am. J. ment. Defect,* **51**, 153–63.

HIGGINS, J., REED, E., and REED, S. (1962). Intelligence and family size: a paradox resolved. *Eugen. Q.* **9**, 84–90.

HOFFEDITZ, E. L. (1934). Family resemblance in personality traits. *J. soc. Psychol.* **5**, 214–27.

HOLMES, S. J. (1924). A bibliography of eugenics. *Univ. Calif. Publs Zool.* Vol. 25.

HUTH, A. H. (1875). *The marriage of near kin.* Longmans Green, London.

JENNINGS, H. S. (1916). The numerical results of diverse systems of breeding. *Genetics, Princeton* **1**, 53–89.

JONES, H. E. (1928). A first study of parent–child resemblance in intelligence. *Yb. Nat. Soc. Stud. Educ.* **27**, 61–72.

KEMPTHORNE, O. (1957). *An introduction to genetic statistics.* Wiley, New York.

KODAMA, H. and SHINAGAWA, F. (1953). *The W.I.S.C. intelligence test.* Nihon Bunka Kagakusha, Tokyo. (In Japanese.)

KUDO, A. (1962). A method for calculating the inbreeding coefficient. *Am. J. hum. Genet.* **14**, 426–32.

—— and SAKAGUCHI, K. (1963). A method for calculating the inbreeding coefficient. II. Sex-linked genes. *Am. J. hum. Genet.* **15**, 476–80.

LINTON, R. (1955). *The tree of culture*. A. A. Knopf, New York.

LORIMER, F. (1954). *Culture and human fertility*. U.N.E.S.C.O., Paris.

MORTON, N. E., CHUNG, C. S., and MI, M. P. (1967). Genetics of interracial crosses in Hawaii. *Monographs in Human Genetics*, Vol. 3. Karger, Basel.

MOURANT, A. E. (1954). *The distribution of the human blood groups*. Blackwell, Oxford.

NEEL, J. V., KODANI, M., BREWER, R., and ANDERSON, R. C. (1949). The incidence of consanguineous matings in Japan with remarks on the estimation of comparative gene frequencies and the expected rate of appearance of induced recessive mutations. *Am. J. hum. Genet.* **1**, 156–78.

PEARL, R. (1915). *Modes of research in genetics*. Macmillan, New York.

PENROSE, L. S. (1933). A study in the inheritance of intelligence. The analysis of 100 families containing subcultural mental defectives. *Br. J. Psychol.* (Gen. Sec.), **24**, 1–19.

—— (1949). *The biology of mental defect*. Grune and Stratton, New York.

RASMUSON, M. (1961). *Genetics on the population level*. Svenska Bokförlaget, Stockholm.

RAVEN, J. C. (1946). *Progressive matrices*. H. K. Lewis, London.

SCHULL, W. J. and NEEL, J. V. (1962). The Child Health Survey: a genetic study in Japan. In *The use of vital and health statistics for genetic and radiation studies*. United Nations, New York.

—— —— (1965). *The effects of inbreeding on Japanese children*. Harper and Row, New York.

SMITH, M. (1941). Similarities of marriage partners in intelligence. *Am. sociol. Rev.* **6**, 697–701.

SPUHLER, J. N. (1962). Empirical studies on quantitative human genetics. In *The use of vital and health statistics for genetic and radiation studies*. United Nations, New York.

—— and KLUCKHOHN, C. (1953). Inbreeding coefficients of the Ramah Navaho population. *Hum. Biol.* **25**, 296–317.

SUTTER, J. and TABAH, L. (1948). Fréquence et répartition des marriages consanguins en France. *Population, Paris* **4**, 607–30.

TERMAN, L. M. and BUTTENWIESER, P. (1935). Personality factors in marital compatibility. *J. soc. Psychol.* **6**, 143–71, 267–89.

THURSTONE, L. L. and THURSTONE, T. G. (1941). *The Chicago tests of primary mental abilities, V*. Science Research Associates, Chicago.

WESTERMARCK, E. A. (1903). *The history of human marriage* (3rd ed.). Macmillan, London.

WILLOUGHBY, R. R. (1928). Family similarities in mental test abilities. *Yb. Nat. Soc. Stud. Educ.* **27**, 55–9.

WRIGHT, S. (1921). Systems of mating. *Genetics, Princeton* **6**, 111–78.

—— (1933). Inbreeding and recombination. *Proc. natn. Acad. Sci. U.S.A.* **19**, 420–33.

—— (1950). Discussion on population genetics and radiation. *J. cell. comp. Physiol.* **35** (Suppl. 1), 187–210.

—— (1951). The genetical structure of populations. *Ann. Eugen.* **15**, 323–54.

—— (1969). *Evolution and the genetics of populations. Vol. 2, The theory of gene frequencies*. University of Chicago Press.

—— and McPHEE, H. C. (1925). An approximate method of calculating coefficients of inbreeding and relationship from livestock pedigrees. *J. agric. Res.* **31**, 377–84.

11

SOCIAL MOBILITY

A. H. HALSEY

SOCIAL mobility is of more than academic interest. The question of what opportunities are available to individuals in society will clearly have implications for both the satisfaction of individuals' needs and aspirations and for the attachment which individuals have to their society. Social mobility rates also tell us something about the openness of a society and therefore contribute to political, philosophical, and moral discussion of fairness, justice, and efficiency in social arrangements. For the sociologist, these aspects of social mobility are an important background but not the substance of the subject. Sociologically, the problem is first to define, then to measure, and then to investigate and explain the causes and consequences of variations in social mobility. Our purpose in this chapter is to introduce the reader to the present state of knowledge from these sociological points of view.

The definition of social mobility

If societies are conceived of as networks of social relationships, i.e. interactions between individuals in various social positions, then it would make sense to conceive of social mobility as movement of a given individual from one position in the network to another. In this sense, a change of job, a bereavement, a change of address, a change of religious adherence or of trade union membership, an elevation to the peerage, or indeed any movement of an individual from one position to another *vis-à-vis* his fellows could be thought of as social mobility. But in fact the concept is not so generally applied in sociological writing: it is restricted to movements from one position to another in a system of social stratification.

Hence, the first problem in the study of social mobility is to define the system of stratification in which it takes place. Social stratification refers to the arrangement of individuals in society in groups or strata such that general standing within groups is equal and between groups is unequal or hierarchical. The relations between strata are relations of superordination and subordination involving differential deference, prestige, power, and influence. Systems of stratification may be broadly classified as follows: caste, estate, class, and status. (For a general introduction to the types of stratification, see Bendix and Lipset 1966.) Castes are hereditary, endogamous, occupational groups arranged in a hierarchy indicated by ritual distance from the topmost or dominating caste. The estate system, which was widespread in Europe from the time of the decline of the *pax Romana* through the mediaeval period, was a hierarchical system of strata based on rights and duties in relation to land tenure. A class system is most clearly defined in Marxist terms as an arrangement of groups with different relations to the means of production. (This is, of course, a simplified classificatory definition of class. The concept of class as used by Marx is in fact dynamic, being based on a theory of historical evolution in which the struggle between conflicting classes propels society through progressive epochs of social development. For an account of classes in modern society, see Bottomore 1955.) Status groups are distinguished from classes as groups the members of which have common relations to the means of consumption. Status groups form a hierarchy of styles of life to which differential social prestige is attached. In the long run, as Max Weber pointed out, the maintenance of a status position is determined by class. But the two variables are partially independent and interact with each other in complex ways.

It must, of course, be appreciated that the stratification system of any given society is likely to contain elements of more than one of the four main types which we have distinguished. For example, in considering modern Britain, the concept of caste is not wholly irrelevant to the study of coloured minority groups; there are vestigial remains of the estate system in honours, titles, and public ceremonials; there are classes based on different relations to the means of production and varying degrees of class consciousness, and there are different levels of social prestige attaching to different styles of life which are expressed in differentially evaluated forms of speech, manner, dress, and habits. Class and status form the more important dimensions of stratification in modern industrial societies, and mobility studies concentrate on these two aspects, though class mobility and status mobility are seldom clearly distinguished either from each other or from power mobility which has little or no place in the sociological literature.

The unit of social mobility

Mobility may be thought of as an attribute of the biography of individual persons. However, it is usually more realistic to think of the nuclear family as the appropriate unit, i.e. parents and their dependent children. But it is also possible to think in terms of larger units, i.e. to consider the movement of whole strata, for example the rise of the gentry in Britain in the fourteenth century, or of other groups, for example sub-castes. There is similarly the question of what time-span is considered to be appropriate for problems of social mobility. In most societies mobility is possible within the life-span of the individual. However, for family or larger units, longer time-intervals may be considered, extending over many generations.

Dichotomizing these two variables, we can distinguish four types of mobility as follows:

Types of social mobility

Time unit	Social unit	
	Individual	*Group*
Intra-generational	1	3
Inter-generational	2	4

Each type will, of course, be further differentiated according to the dimension of stratification which is treated. The great majority of social mobility studies have focused on types 1 and 2; for example, Glass (1954), Blau and Duncan (1967), and Svalastoga (1965). Intra-generational group mobility would include studies of the rise or decline of occupational groups or possibly of revolutionary class movements. Where, as in type 4, such studies extend over longer time periods they merge into the study of changes in the stratification system as such. On the whole, the study of group mobilities (types 3 and 4) belong more to the province of the historian than to the work of modern empirical sociologists.

The measurement of social mobility

Given a definition of types of strata and types of movement between them, we can now concentrate our attention on individual inter-generational mobility. The first problem which arises here is that of deciding on an indicator which locates individuals in defined strata. Some sociologists have used multiple indices of class, status, or social class, including occupation, education, source and type of income, home address, etc. A classic example of this approach is the series of studies by W. L. Warner (1952) and his associates of social stratification in American communities; but most studies have used occupation as the index of stratum position. This device is sensible, first because occupation is highly correlated with the determinants of social class and status, including income, education, styles of life, and social attitudes. Second, a large number of studies have shown consensus about the ranking of occupations in a hierarchy of desirability or 'goodness' of jobs which is similar in many different kinds of industrial country. Third, it is a convenient and more or less objective attribute of adult males. There are, however, difficulties. Occupational mobility has to be distinguished from the different types of social mobility. They are not the same phenomenon, and indeed it is an urgent sociological task to investigate the relations between them. It is possible for 'upward' occupational mobility to be subjectively experienced as 'downward' social mobility and vice versa. For example, although the traditional demarcation between manual and non-manual work remains of considerable importance (Runciman 1966), it has been shown in the recent studies of affluent workers by a Cambridge group of sociologists (Goldthorpe, Lockwood, Bechnofer, and Platt 1970) that movement from white-collar to manual employment may be a means of maintaining a middle-class style of life, i.e. deliberate choices for 'downward' occupational mobility are here exemplified as a means of maintaining a middle-class status.

Occupational scales vary in their relation to the structure of class and status. The so-called occupational prestige scales, of which the Hall–Jones scale in Britain and the N.O.R.C. scale in America have been widely used, can only dubiously be held to represent a consensus concerning the structure of occupational prestige. (For a discussion of occupational prestige, see the two articles by Robert W. Hodge in Bendix and Lipset 1966.) There is more certain evidence of an agreed hierarchy of occupations in terms of desirability. If, therefore, the occupational index is used as one of occupational mobility we are on safe ground. If, however, the further step is taken of interpreting occupational mobility as social mobility with the underlying assumption that there is an order of status groups and classes which is faithfully reflected in the occupational scale, we are on dangerous ground. Unfortunately, most of the large-scale studies of social mobility make precisely this assumption. Though the consequences may not be misleading in respect of the overall patterns of social mobility, there is no means of knowing at what points and in what ways the relation between occupational and social mobility may vary in reality.

Bearing these limitations in mind, we may now examine the way in which mobility is typically measured in the large-scale studies. (The two most important studies of this kind are those by Glass (1954) in Britain and by Blau and Duncan (1967) in the United States. A new study of social mobility in Britain, replicating the Glass study and designed to be comparative with the Blau and Duncan study, is at present in progress in Oxford.) For the purpose of constructing the basic mobility table, two questions are asked of a random sample of the adult male population. The first question is what is your present occupation, and the second, what was your father's occupation. This question may be vague or it may be age-specific in order to make the inter-generational comparisons more precise. Notice that in the once-for-all survey the sample has to represent the last generation (fathers) as well as its own (sons). Errors are accordingly introduced through fertility and mortality as well as through changes in occupational structure. The answers to the first question (present occupation of sons) give us a distribution of occupational or social destinations. The answers to the second question tell us the pattern of social origins. Both answers together can be arranged as a matrix linking origins to destinations. A hypothetical example is shown in Table 11.1, where it is assumed that the total population of adult males is 1000, distributed between three social or occupational classes, the upper class numbering 160 in the filial generation, the middle class 440, and the lower class 400. In the paternal generation, these numbers were assumed to be 100, 400, and 500, i.e. an 'upward' shift in occupational structure has been built in to this illustrative model.

TABLE 11.1

Social mobility between fathers and sons (numbers)

Class of fathers	Class of sons			
	1	2	3	*Total*
1	60	30	10	100
2	80	240	80	400
3	20	170	310	500
Total	160	440	400	1000

The columns show the *inflow* to given destinations of sons from the three possible origins. This inflow analysis is shown in percentage form in Table 11.2. The rows show the *outflow* from given origins to the three possible destinations. This outflow analysis is shown in percentage form in Table 11.3.

TABLE 11.2

Social mobility—inflow analysis (percentages)

Class of fathers	Class of sons		
	1	2	3
1	37·5	6·8	2·5
2	50·0	55·6	20·0
3	12·5	37·6	77·5
Total	100·0	100·0	100·0

It should be noticed that the two analyses focus on two different aspects of the same process. For example, 60 per cent of sons from fathers in class 1 have entered class 1 (Table 11.3); but of all those recruited to class 1, only 37·5 per cent have class 1 origins (Table 11.2). The difference is accounted for partly by the increase of class 1 between the two generations and partly by the fact that some class 1 sons have experienced downward mobility into classes 2 and 3 to be replaced by others having origins in these classes. Another way of stating this pattern is to say that the influence of social origin on occupational destination is expressed not in the absolute proportion of men

with the same origin who end up at a given destination, but in the relative
proportion. If, however, we take the Total row in Table 11.3 (which gives us

TABLE 11.3

Social mobility—outflow analysis (percentages)

Class of fathers	Class of sons			
	1	2	3	*Total*
1	60·0	30·0	10·0	100·0
2	20·0	60·0	20·0	100·0
3	4·0	34·0	62·0	100·0
Total	16·0	44·0	40·0	100·0

the present distribution of the occupational structure) as the standard against
which all other percentages in the table are to be compared and we divide
each row by the total row percentage, we arrive at a ratio which is called in
the Glass study the *index of association*. This ratio, which is shown in Table
11.4, measures the extent to which mobility from one occupation to another
in the course of the generation has surpassed or fallen short of chance. A
value of 1·0 would indicate that the observed mobility is equal to that expected
on the assumption of statistical independence. The values determined by
statistical independence, i.e. where all the numbers in the table would be
1·0, are those used in the so-called model of 'perfect' mobility. The numbers
in Table 11.4 show the degree to which the pattern of mobility in our hypothetical example departs from perfect mobility.

TABLE 11.4

Social mobility—indices of association

Class of fathers	Class of sons		
	1	2	3
1	**3.75**	0.68	0.25
2	**1.25**	**1.36**	0.5
3	0.25	0.77	**1.55**

Four cells in the matrix have values in bold type. These are the ones in which
the observed value is greater than the value to be expected from an assumption
of random relation between parental and filial status, i.e. where the index of
association is greater than 1·0. These high values tend to cluster in the diagonal

cells, indicating systematic tendencies towards status inheritance or occupational self-recruitment. The values are reduced in the off-diagonal cells on both the lower left, which show upward mobility, and even more so on the upper right, which show downward mobility, because, as we have seen in this particular example, there is net upward mobility in the society as a whole.

But the example in Tables 11.1 to 11.4 is hypothetical. In Tables 11.5 and 11.6 we show matrices of the index of association for two empirical cases. Britain in 1949 (Glass 1954) and U.S.A. in 1962 (Blau and Duncan 1967). The British study used an occupational prestige scale (Hall–Jones) to divide its sample into seven social strata. The American study has seventeen occupational categories ordered according to income and length of education among the members of each occupational group.

TABLE 11.5

Significant differences between indices of association for
total male sample, Britain 1949 (from Glass 1954)

Father's status	Subject's status category						
category	1	2	3	4	5	6	7
1	13·158						
2	*	5·865					
3	*	*	1·997				
4	*	*	‡	1·618			
5	*	*	*	*	1·157		
6	*	*	‡	‡	*	1·841	
7	*	*	‡	†	*	‡	2·259

Notes: * significant at 1 per cent level.
       † significant at 5 per cent level.
       ‡ not significant.

With respect to Table 11.5, the pattern may be summarized as follows. The closest association between parental and filial status for British men in 1949 was to be found in the top two status categories (professional and high administrative) and was loosest in status category 5 (skilled manual and routine grades of non-manual). There is, again, a higher intensity of association among the unskilled workers. This means that caste-like conditions of social heredity of jobs or status are most closely approximated at the top of the social stratification system. In other words, as Glass and Hall put it, 'if ... we were to draw a profile over the whole status hierarchy, we should find the category of skilled manual and routine non-manual workers constitutes a kind of valley, with the really important peaks rising on the upper status side, culminating in the professional and high administrative occupations, which show the highest ratios of actual to expected self-recruitment' (Glass 1954).

TABLE 11.6

Mobility from father's occupation to occupation in 1962, for males 25 to 64 years old: ratios of observed frequencies to frequencies expected on the assumption of independence, U.S.A. 1962 (from Blau and Duncan 1967)

Father's occupation	Respondent's occupation in March 1962																
	1	2	3	4	5	6	7	8	9	10	11	12	13	14	15	16	17
Professionals																	
1 Self-employed	11·7	3·1	1·2	3·0	0·6	0·7	0·9	0·3	0·3	0·5	0·3	0·2	0·3	0·2	0·5	0·4	0·5
2 Salaried	2·3	3·1	1·6	1·9	0·7	1·2	1·1	0·5	0·6	0·2	0·7	0·7	0·6	0·5	0·1	0·2	0·1
3 Managers	2·5	2·2	2·5	2·0	1·1	1·2	0·7	0·8	0·7	0·6	0·4	0·3	0·3	0·5	0·2	0·1	0·1
4 Salesmen, other	2·9	1·7	2·7	4·1	1·3	0·9	2·2	0·4	0·8	0·4	0·3	0·5	0·3	0·0	0·2	0·2	0·2
5 Proprietors	2·6	1·3	2·3	1·9	2·3	1·0[a]	2·1	0·5	0·7	0·8	0·5	0·5	0·5	0·2	0·3	0·2	0·2
6 Clerical	1·6	2·3	1·4	1·9	0·7	1·4	0·8	0·9	1·0[a]	0·4	0·4	0·6	1·0[a]	0·5	0·4	0·2	0·0
7 Salesmen, Retail																	
Craftsmen	0·5	1·3	1·8	2·8	1·6	1·0[a]	1·7	0·8	0·5	0·6	0·9	0·7	0·8	0·1	0·7	0·4	0·0
8 Manufacturing	0·7	1·5	1·1	0·8	0·9	1·0	1·1	2·1	0·9	0·9	1·1	0·8	0·8	0·8	0·6	0·1	0·1
9 Other	0·6	1·1	1·2	1·2	0·9	1·2	1·0	1·1	1·7	0·9	0·8	1·2	0·8	0·6	0·6	0·2	0·2
10 Construction operatives	0·6	0·7	0·9	0·8	1·2	1·3	0·5	1·4	1·1	2·8	0·8	0·8	0·9	0·5	1·0	0·2	0·4
11 Manufacturing	0·7	0·8	0·7	0·9	0·8	1·0	0·9	1·7	1·0[a]	0·6	1·8	0·9	0·9	1·9	0·8	0·2	0·4
12 Other	0·4	1·1	0·6	0·8	0·9	1·0[a]	0·9	1·0	1·3	1·0	1·0[a]	1·7	1·1	1·0	1·0	0·2	0·7
13 Service	0·5	0·9	0·9	1·1	0·9	1·5	1·2	1·1	0·9	1·1	1·2	1·1	1·9	1·3	0·8	0·2	0·1
Labour																	
14 Manufacturing	0·0	0·6	0·7	0·2	0·5	0·7	0·5	1·5	0·8	0·6	1·8	1·2	1·7	3·3	1·4	0·3	0·5
15 Other	0·3	0·5	0·4	0·8	0·5	1·4	1·1	1·1	1·1	1·2	1·3	1·4	1·5	1·6	2·3	0·2	0·7
16 Farmers	0·4	0·4	0·5	0·4	0·9	0·7	0·7	0·8	0·9	1·2	1·0[a]	1·1	0·9	1·1	1·3	3·2	2·3
17 Farm labourers	0·1	0·2	0·4	0·2	0·6	0·6	0·8	0·9	0·9	1·2	1·3	1·4	1·4	1·5	2·1	1·1	5·5

[a] Rounded to unity from above (other indices shown as 1·0 rounded to unity from below).

With respect to Table 11.6, Blau and Duncan summarize the American pattern as follows:

First, occupational inheritance is in all cases greater than expected on the assumption of independence; note the consistently high values in the major diagonal. Second, social mobility is nevertheless pervasive, as revealed by the large number of values in bold type off the diagonal. Third, upward mobility (to the left of the diagonal) is more prevalent than downward mobility (to the right), and short-distance movements occur more often than long-distance ones.

If occupational inheritance and fixed careers were dominating the stratification system, all excess manpower would be concentrated in the 17 cells in the major diagonal and the values in all other cells would fall short of theoretical expectation. In fact an excess flow of manpower is manifest in 101 cells of the father's-to-1962-occupation matrix, also 101 cells in the father's-to-first-job matrix, and 78 cells in the first-to-1962-job matrix. This indicates much movement among occupational strata. A rough indication of the prevailing direction of mobility is the number of such cells lying on either side of the major diagonal. For the inter-generational flow of manpower, as [Table 11.6] shows, the values in bold type to the lower left of the diagonal, which indicate disproportionate upward mobility, outnumber by more than three to one (64:20) those to the upper right, which indicate disproportionate downward mobility.

Short-distance movements exceed long-distance ones. Most of the values in bold type are concentrated in the area adjacent to the major diagonal, denoting short-distance mobility, and there are few in the areas surrounding the upper right and the lower left corners, which would be evidence of long-distance mobility. The values of the mobility ratios tend to be highest in the diagonal and decrease gradually with movement away from it. In general, the closer two occupations are to one another in the status hierarchy the greater is the flow of manpower between them. (Blau and Duncan 1967.)

The pattern shown in the British and American enquiries, though with numerous exceptions in detail, appears to be common to the advanced industrial societies. In an attempt to summarize the results of studies from many countries, Lipset and Bendix (1960) had to use the crude device of measuring movement across the manual/non-manual line between generations. In the industrial sector of many countries the upward movement varied around one-third (U.S.A. 31–5 per cent, France 35 per cent, Sweden 29 per cent, Japan 33 per cent) and downward movement similarly, though with greater variation. In short, social mobility in industrial society is fairly high and apparently fairly uniform.

Causes of social mobility

Having defined and measured social mobility, the next step is to explain its variations. Four sociological factors may be identified as determining the rate of social mobility, and these are interrelated in such a way as to distribute societies along a range from complete self-recruitment of strata to perfect mobility. These sociological factors are:

(1) the definition of social roles (structure of opportunities),
(2) the occupational structure,
(3) differential fertility,   and
(4) the socialization process.

But, in addition to and also in interaction with these social determinants, there is the genetic structure of the population, i.e. the distribution of genetic potential for social mobility as between individuals.

Definition of social roles (structure of opportunities)

The four types of stratification system (caste, estate, class, and status) are partially defined in terms of the rate of mobility which they permit. From this point of view, caste and class may be conceived of theoretically as polar cases. Allocation to social roles is entirely by ascription at one end of the continuum and entirely by 'achievement' or tests of competence to perform the role at the other end. Caste systems proscribe mobility: class systems are intrinsically open to individual inter-generational and intra-generational mobility through success or failure in the labour or capital markets. Estate systems imposed legal restrictions on mobility, but at the same time in practice permitted it through the Church and through military service. Status systems exercise restraint on market forces in the sense of delaying translation of class mobility into social prestige: this is the meaning of such concepts as *arriviste* or *parvenu*. Caste may be thought of as an extreme case of status.

Occupational structure and differential fertility

Given that stratification systems, from one point of view, are a social mechanism structuring the labour supply, caste is most viable in economies with an unchanging and relatively simple division of labour. The labour supply depends only on the fertility and mortality patterns of sub-castes. But in industrial economies there is both a changing and increasingly complex division of labour as well as the possibility of fluctuating fertilities. It is characteristic of modern industrial societies that as economic development takes place there is an associated shift in the occupational structure resulting in a relative increase in the proportion of white-collar highly-paid jobs and a diminution of unskilled and low-paid work. All other things being equal, this will result in net upward mobility between generations as illustrated in Tables 11.1–11.4. It is also well known that there has been, in the recent history of industrial societies, i.e. between the middle of the nineteenth century and the middle of the twentieth century, an inverse relation between class and fertility. All other things being equal, such a fertility pattern also results in net upward mobility between generations.

These two structural factors together have reinforced each other. In the American case, they have been linked to a pattern of immigration from Europe and migration of Negroes from the rural South to the urban North. They have produced a widespread experience of social escalation between the generations which, in part, accounts for the widespread feeling that American society is more open than European society despite the fact that rates of mobility measured in the way we have described do not differ essentially as between America and the European countries.

The socialization process

In caste societies, socialization takes place through familial institutions, occupational skills are handed down from father to son, and the systems of beliefs (strongly reinforced by religious indoctrination) discourage social ambition. By contrast, industrialism permits and encourages aspirations towards upward social mobility. This is the meaning of 'the American dream'. The advancing division of labour of industrial societies also generates elaborate systems of formal education and tends to produce a tightening bond between education and occupation. To the degree that education determines occupation in modern society, the character of educational selection becomes an important causative variable in the determination of rates of social mobility. Many sociological commentators interpret modern trends as approximating to meritocracy, i.e. a system in which education acts as a selective device to place individuals socially according to their innate ability. We shall return to the social determinants of mobility through education. But meanwhile, the meritocracy question opens up the problem of the relation between social mobility and genetic distributions between different social strata.

The distribution of innate abilities

If occupational placement is linked to intelligence, whether or not through education, and if intelligence is partially inherited, then social strata may be or may not be becoming distinct genetic groups. This is the question we must now explore. On the evidence, especially of correlation coefficients derived from studies of twins, siblings, and foster children, it may be concluded that there is a genetic component in the intelligence-test performance of individuals, and hence it is reasonable to postulate a genotype of innate intelligence which we may call, following Hebb, I_A (Hebb 1949). As P. E. Vernon (1966) puts it, 'the really convincing evidence of genetic determination is: first, the correlation between the intelligence of orphans or foster children and that of their true parents who have had nothing to do with their upbringing; and second, the fact that children in the same family often differ so widely in intelligence from their parents or from one another'.

The actual manifestation of intelligence, which we may call I_B, is a social product of adaptive behaviours within the framework laid down by I_A. Vernon describes I_B as the set of behavioural characteristics correlative to Hebb's 'phase sequences' or patterns of discharge in the association areas of the brain. Phase sequences, and their counterparts in adaptive behaviour, are dependent for their formation on experience of appropriate environmental stimuli. 'We *learn* to perceive, to imagine, to reason, to judge; ... we learn how to learn just as much as we learn how to ride a bicycle or learn spelling and arithmetic. . . . I_B, which we observe in a person's behaviour and thinking, is the product of the interaction between I_A and environment.' (Vernon 1966.)

I_A is non-observable and non-measurable. Our present knowledge of factors in intelligence is derived from intelligence tests. Again following Vernon, we may call performance in intelligence tests I_C. Any of the many measures of intelligence (I_C) consists of a *sample* from the set of behaviours which constitute I_B. It is a biased sample because intelligence tests have been developed for educational selection and their validation has been predominantly in terms of educational success. The factors derived from analysis of intelligence tests are determined by the content of the tests and this in turn by the requirements of prediction of educational performance in given educational systems.

The exact relation between I_A and I_C through I_B is not known. We cannot dismiss the problem of genetic and environmental determination of intelligence simply by attributing so much variance to genetic and so much to environmental components. As has often been pointed out, phenotypic variation is a product not only of genetic and environmental factors but also of the interaction between them. The variation in environmental conditions determines the degree to which genetic influences can work and vice versa.

We do, however, know that there is a positive relation between class and I_C. This has been shown many times in many countries and may be illustrated from Table 11.7, which is taken from a paper by Burt (1961).

TABLE 11.7

Mean I.Q.s of parent and child according to class of parents

	Parent	Child
Higher professional	139·7	120·8
Lower professional	130·6	114·7
Clerical	115·9	107·8
Skilled	108·2	104·6
Semi-skilled	97·8	98·9
Unskilled	84·9	92·6
Average	100·0	100·0

On the basis of this correlation and on Galton's 'law of regression', namely, that the children of parents towards the extreme show a regression from the extreme towards the mean of the general population, Young and Gibson (1963) have put forward the suggestion that social mobility is a cybernetic mechanism whereby something like a 'steady state' is maintained in each occupational class by means of constant movement into and out of it. Given the fact of regression and the positive correlation between class and intelligence, they argue 'that there must have been mobility upwards of more intelligent children to take the place of the less intelligent, who move down from the higher classes. Had such mobility upwards and downwards not occurred, the mean I.Q.s for the parents in the upper classes would not be as high as appears in Table 11.7, but would be at least as low as the means for the children, or indeed, if the regression had continued without compensation for a series of generations, they would by now have reverted to the general average; and the distribution of intelligence in each class would have become much more like the distribution in the general population than it actually is. A rough stability can only be maintained within each class by a continuous interchange between them.'

In exploring the distribution of innate intelligence (I_A) we must recognize that genetic variations in distributions are limited and partially controlled by variations in social structure, especially the size of populations, the degree of endogamy and exogamy in their mating systems, and the ease of geographical migration and social mobility between groups within them. We may then explore the postulated character of I_A through a series of simple models.

We begin with an assumption of single gene determination of I_A. This is a gross oversimplification but nonetheless instructive because, in any given social structure, it gives the maximum weight to genetic factors in the selection progress which we are about to discuss. The following section is taken from Halsey (1958).

Let it be assumed that I_A is produced by inheritance through a gene A such that the homozygote AA has the value of 120, the heterozygote Aa the value of 100, and the homozygote aa the value of 80.

Case 1. A caste system

We may begin consideration of the effect of variations in social structure on the social distribution of innate intelligence (I_A) by imagining a society having a population of 1000 divided into two castes—a low caste numbering 900 and a high caste numbering 100. Castes are by definition endogamous and let us further assume that there is random mating within them and equal fertility between them.

Looked at genetically and ignoring mutation and genetic drift (genetic drift could not, of course, be ignored in a complete analysis of such small populations) this society consists of two separate gene pools, each in Hardy–Weinberg equilibrium (see Moody 1953), the Hardy–Weinberg formula $[p^2+2p(1-p)+(1-p)^2]$ being a mathematical statement of the frequency of genotypes in a random mating population in successive generations. Thus if the frequency of the gene for high intelligence (A) in the low caste is 0·3 ($p_A{}^L = 0·3$) and in the high caste is 0·7 ($p_A{}^H = 0·7$) the following equilibrium results:

	Low caste			High caste		
Proportions:	0·49aa	0·42Aa	0·09AA	0·09aa	0·42Aa	0·49AA
Numbers:	441aa	378Aa	81AA	9aa	42Aa	49AA
Means:	Low caste $I_A{}^L = 92$					
	Total population $I_A{}^T = 94$					
	High caste $I_A{}^H = 108$					

In other words, the result under these genetic and social conditions is that:

(1) The high caste has the higher mean (108 compared with 92).
(2) The high caste has a much higher proportion but a much lower number of individuals with high intelligence (49 compared with 81).

(3) There is a considerable overlap between the castes in the distribution of I_A, and, genetically, this means that there are many more A genes in the low than in the high caste, most of them in heterozygous condition.

The situation described would remain stable between generations. It should, however, be noticed that the means of I_A are a function of the frequencies (p_A) chosen in the example. We could, for instance, have shown equal p_As in the two castes and in that case the mean values of $I_A{}^L$, $I_A{}^T$, and $I_A{}^H$ would have been equal.

Case 2. A class system

The assumptions made in the caste model could not be found in any actual society and are certainly very far from representing the kind of social structure to be found in modern Britain. We may move closer to the latter by imagining a society in which social position is determined by selection according to I_A. In the example which follows we continue to ignore mutation and genetic drift, we retain our assumption that innate intelligence is determined by a single gene but we introduce new migration (or mobility) assumptions. We postulate a low class of 900 and a high class of 100 with, in each generation before marriage, mobility upward of the 10 most intelligent members of the low class and mobility downward of the 10 least intelligent members of the high class. Mating is again assumed to be random within classes and fertility equal between classes.

The process begins at generation F_0 with gene frequencies p_A and p_a equal (i.e. 0·5) in both classes. Then the proportions of aa, Aa, and AA individuals are 0·25, 0·50, and 0·25 respectively in both classes and the corresponding numbers of individuals are 225aa, 450Aa, and 225AA in the low class and 25aa, 50Aa, and 25AA in the high class. Mobility then takes place to alter the distribution of individuals so that there are 235aa, 450Aa, and 215AA in the low class and 15aa, 50Aa, and 35AA in the high class. The gene frequencies become, at the same time $p_a{}^L = 0·5111$ and $p_a{}^H = 0·4000$ so that, after mating, the distribution of individuals in generation F_1 is for the low class 235aa, 450Aa, and 215AA and for the high class 16aa, 48Aa, and 36AA. This distribution gives the low class a mean intelligence ($I_A{}^L$) of 99·56 and the high class ($I_A{}^H$) 104. A summary of the process, continued for subsequent generations is given in Table 11.8.

The trend of the distribution I_A has the following characteristics:

(1) The mean $I_A{}^L$ decreases at a decreasing rate to 98; the mean $I_A{}^H$ increases at a decreasing rate to 120 and the mean $I\hat{A}^T$ is constant at 100.
(2) The class distributions continue to overlap, the majority of people with high in-intelligence still remaining in the low class.
(3) Only over seven generations would low intelligence (a) be bred out of the high class. High intelligence would never be bred out of the low class. At the eighth generation the social distribution of I_A stabilizes with a constant rate of 'circulation' of AA between the classes.
(4) The number of homozygotes in the total population increases in each generation (from F_1 to F_7), i.e. there are more people of high intelligence *and* more people of low intelligence, i.e. the standard deviations increase in each generation.
(5) In other words, the heterozygotes form a reservoir of both high and low ability which, in this case, is drained high to high class and low to low class up to the eighth generation.

Thus the general effect of selective migration through intelligence, other things being equal, is to increase the frequency of homozygotes and to decrease heterozygotes, i.e. to increase the incidence of both high and low intelligence and to reduce the incidence of middling intelligence.

These results have been obtained from a very simple model of society. If we wish to move still nearer to reality, many more complex assumptions as to both social structure and the genetics of intelligence must be considered. However, these complications do not alter the basic features of the simple model and they can be treated summarily. What we want to know of each complication is its effect on the rate of social class differentiation in

TABLE 11.8

Social distribution of intelligence (I_A) *in a class society with single-gene inheritance of intelligence*

| | Low class | | | | | | | High class | | | | | | | Mean intelligence of total population |
| | Gene frequency | | Number of persons | | | Mean intelligence | | Gene frequency | | Number of persons | | | Mean intelligence | | |
Generation	p_a^L	p_A^L	aa	Aa	AA	I_A^L		p_a^H	p_A^H	aa	Aa	AA	I_A^H		I_A^T
F_0	0·500	0·500	225	450	225	100·0		0·500	0·500	25	50	25	100·0		100
F_1	0·511	0·489	235	450	215	99·6		0·400	0·600	16	48	36	104·0		100
F_2	0·522	0·478	245	449	206	99·1		0·300	0·700	9	42	49	108·0		100
F_3	0·533	0·467	256	448	197	98·7		0·205	0·795	4	33	63	111·8		100
F_4	0·541	0·459	263	447	190	98·4		0·134	0·866	2	23	75	114·6		100
F_5	0·547	0·453	270	446	186	98·1		0·075	0·925	1	14	86	117·0		100
F_6	0·553	0·447	275	445	180	97·9		0·022	0·978	1	4	96	119·1		100
F_7	0·556	0·444	278	444	178	97·8		0·000	1·000	0	0	100	120·0		100

I_A. We may therefore divide them according to whether they speed up or slow down the differentiation process.

Among the accelerating factors must be included a higher rate of social mobility and the differentiation of more social classes. It may be noted, parenthetically, that a uniform increase of mean I_A with social class need not be assumed. An interesting case of this kind is suggested by the recent British social mobility inquiry in which the index of association (i.e. the degree to which caste conditions are approximated) rises sharply at the highest occupational levels (Glass 1954). If the high caste in our Case 1 were allowed to remain a caste while selective migration for I_A were allowed to produce a middle class out of the former low caste, then the middle class would inherit a mean I_A higher than that of the high caste, largely by recruitment from the heterozygote pool in the low class.

A more formidable array of decelerating factors comes into play as the model is modified to take account of real conditions. Of these the first is the assumption of polygenic determination of I_A—and the trend in psychology toward the recognition of more factors in measured human abilities implies a more complex genetic structure determining intelligence. In fact it is difficult to conceive of anything as elaborate as human intelligence being determined by as few as (say) 10 genes. Yet if we add only one other gene B in Case 2, with all other assumptions, both genetic and social, remaining the same the result is that the high class does not become 'pure' before the passage of 9 generations. (However, for the addition of each further gene there is a smaller increase in the number of generations required to reach purity.) This process is summarized in Table 11.9.

Second, on the side of social structure we have to recognize the existence of determinants of social mobility which are wholly unconnected or only partially connected with intelligence —for example, sexual beauty or ugliness, good or evil fortune in business, military prowess or timidity, etc. Though precise estimates are impossible, we can be confident that selection other than for I_A has been of great relative importance especially before the rise of the educational system as an agency of social selection in the last two generations. This type of social mobility or any increase in its incidence would have decelerating effects on the process of differentiation in the I_A composition of the classes. Moreover, any reduction in mobility based on selection for I_A would have a similar effect.

Putting the accelerating and decelerating factors together it seems reasonable to conclude that the net effect would be to slow down the process of differentiation described under the simple assumptions of Case 2. If this be so, then we are justified in concluding that what little we know of the history of social stratification in Britain would hardly yield an expectation of social class differences in innate intelligence of the order arrived at in Case 2.

Accepting the hypothesis of an innate intelligence (I_A) we have drawn up a simple model of society designed to show the relation between variations in social structure and the distribution of genotypes.

In the extreme case of a caste society each caste has to be seen genetically as a separate gene pool and therefore, provided there is random mating within castes and equal fertility between them, the distribution of I_A is stable.

When a caste society is transformed into a class society, the classes may still be seen as gene pools but with migration between them. The question now becomes one of determining the relation between social mobility and genetic migration. In our model of the class society we assumed that the rate of social mobility was such as to replace the 10 per cent of the high class with the least intelligence with an equal number of the most intelligent members of the low class. Under these conditions and assuming innate intelligence to be determined by a single gene it took seven generations to produce a 'pure' high class. Even so, it is important to notice that, with a high class constituting one-tenth of the total population, the effect of draining off a pure high-intelligence high class from the reservoir of the low class scarcely affected the mean I_A of the latter and still left it with a heavy preponderance of the total number of available genes for high intelligence.

The model may be elaborated in order to approximate more closely to the real conditions of contemporary society. For example its fertility assumptions may be modified in order to throw light on the question of trends in the national intelligence. The central focus of our attention has been on the rate of genetic purification in the high class. From this point of view the refinement of our assumptions has to be considered in terms of acceleration and

TABLE 11.9

Social distribution of intelligence (I_A) in a class society with two-gene inheritance of intelligence

	Low class								High class							
	Gene frequency		Number of persons						Gene frequency		Number of persons					
Generation	p_a^L and p_b^L	p_A^L and p_B^L	aabb	aAbb or aaBb	AAbb or aaBB	AABb or aABB	AABB		p_a^H and p_b^H	p_A^H and p_B^H	aabb	aAbb or aabB	AAbb or aaBB	AABb or aABB	AABB
F_0	0·500	0·500	56	225	338	225	56		0·500	0·500	6	25	38	25	6
F_1	0·510	0·490	61	234	337	216	52		0·409	0·591	3	16	35	34	12
F_2	0·519	0·481	65	242	337	208	48		0·327	0·673	1	9	29	40	21
F_3	0·528	0·472	70	250	335	200	45		0·250	0·751	0	5	21	42	32
F_4	0·535	0·465	74	256	334	194	42		0·186	0·814	0	2	14	40	44
F_5	0·541	0·459	77	262	333	188	40		0·130	0·870	0	0	8	34	57
F_6	0·547	0·454	80	266	332	184	38		0·082	0·918	0	0	3	25	71
F_7	0·550	0·450	83	270	331	180	37		0·047	0·953	0	0	1	16	82
F_8	0·553	0·447	84	273	330	177	36		0·019	0·981	0	0	0	7	93
F_9	0·556	0·444	86	274	329	176	35		0·000	1·000	0	0	0	0	100

deceleration of the process of purification: and what we know of the genetics of I_A and the history of social mobility in Britain leads us to doubt the hypothesis of innate class differences in mean intelligence.

Education and social mobility in Britain

This is not to say, however, that, through a meritocratic education system tightly linked to occupational placement, it would be impossible to form strata which were genetically distinct. The question may therefore usefully be asked, does the educational system in Britain now operate in this fashion? That it should do so has been official policy since the passing of the 1944 Act. Thus when Lord Boyle was the Conservative Minister of Education he wrote a foreword to the Newsom Report (Central Advisory Council for Education 1963). In it he said: 'The essential point is that all children should have equal opportunity of acquiring intelligence, and of developing their talents and abilities to the full'. We may conclude this discussion of social mobility by exploring the implications for educational and social policy of the aims formulated by Lord Boyle.

In order to explain these implications, it is necessary to begin with two generalizations about British society and its educational system. First, like all advanced industrial societies, Britain lives by applying science to the process of production. This means that a large supply of educated people is necessary for efficiency and economic growth. Second, equality of educational opportunity in Britain does not exist and this is essentially because families and schools have unequal shares of money, prestige, power, and influence which are used to give some children better educational opportunities than others irrespective of their native capacity to profit by them.

The first generalization is not in dispute. It is a common characteristic of all the modern industrial countries that they tend to suffer from shortages of scientifically and professionally qualified people, they all have programmes of rapid educational expansion, and they all try more or less effectively to identify potentially able children whatever their social origin and to educate them beyond the primary and secondary schools to fill the ever-increasing number of jobs for scientists, engineers, managers, and other professions. The result is that all these countries have a high rate of social mobility; as we have noted about a third in each generation cross the line one way or the other between manual and non-manual work compared with their fathers. In these societies social mobility is increasingly a function of the school. In traditional societies, before modernization, sons followed fathers in their occupations, and they received their education and training largely through the family or the para-familial institution of apprenticeship. In modernized societies entry to occupation is typically controlled through qualifications obtained in the formal educational system. The underlying forces here are primarily economic, but politically the movement is often expressed as the right of an individual to have been educated to the limit of his capacities.

15

The second generalization is more disputable. But there is a wealth of evidence in favour of it (e.g. Little and Westergard 1969). For Britain, an official source of evidence is the Robbins Report (1963). In their study of children born in 1940–1 the authors of the Robbins Report looked at the chances of entering full-time higher education of children who at age 11 had been found to have intelligence quotients of 130-plus. Two findings emerged. First, children of this very high level of ability had more than twice as much chance of going to university if they came from a middle-class rather than a working-class home. But, second, what is less often noticed, only about a third of the middle-class children at this level of ability did in fact go to university. This is a salutary warning against assuming too close a connection between mobility through formal education and measured intelligence. (But see Gibson 1970.)

There are two inferences to be drawn from this set of statistical facts. First, it is clear that there remain differential chances between social classes, irrespective of the social distribution of natural ability. Second, it also indicates that our schools and universities continue to be extremely inefficient from a meritocratic point of view, i.e. in turning natural ability into educational achievement.

From the point of view of social policy, there is an underlying conflict here between the school and the family. The problem can be put in an over-simplified way by saying that the school can represent the principle that each person has an equal opportunity with every other person to compete for educational achievement and hence a higher or lower occupation. The family, on the other hand, represents the moral principle that a parent does his best for his own child, and this includes, among other things, giving his child the best educational start in life that he can give whether or not this is to give his own child an advantage over the next child in the competition for rewarding and well-paid work. The principle also works negatively to disadvantage children from poor families.

In some ways the conflict is a simple one in that the British educational system is divided between a small minority who have parents able and willing to purchase educational advantages in the private sector which has smaller classes and usually better qualified teachers while the majority go to state schools in which the type of education given to the children and the resources spent on them are largely determined by public decision and by school teachers rather than parents. This divided system gives greater opportunities to acquire intelligence and to develop talents and abilities to a minority. It is an arrangement which guarantees inequality rather than equality of opportunity and while it exists Lord Boyle's 'essential point' cannot be met.

However, the conflict is by no means confined to a division between private and state schooling. Within the state system the conflict still goes on in a very large number of complicated ways. The better off and the more highly-educated parents can understand and support the purposes of the school and therefore make it easier for their children to perform well more effectively than the poorer and less well-educated parents. The development of a child's capacities is the product of a partnership between the family and the school. The family is a more or less effective school itself, teaching children basic literacy and inculcating attitudes to work, authority, and achievement which directly affect the response that a child will make when he encounters the formal teaching of the school classroom.

The strength of the influence of the family and social class on the educational achievements of children is again illustrated by the findings of the Robbins Report 'that the proportion of children who reach full-time higher education is about six times as great in the families of non-manual workers as those of manual workers: the chances of reaching courses of degree level are about eight times as high'.

Given the strength of the family and assuming that, for widely accepted reasons, there are severe limits of the degree to which the state intrudes on family autonomy, it follows that public policy can only be concerned with a rather weak version of the notion of equality of opportunity. The practical question here is how weak. Thus, political debate tends to centre on the question of what proportion of funds should be allocated to the raising of educational standards in those districts where the influence of family and neighbourhood results in a depression of the performance of children below their native capacities.

Thus, as with so many issues in social life, public action is at root concerned with a moral dilemma. In this case, the pursuit of equality of opportunity in the name of the rights of individuals to have equal chances of mobility has to be set against the right of parents to bring up their own children in their own way. The human sciences can lay bare the character of such dilemmas. But solutions carry us beyond the realm of science into that of moral decision.

REFERENCES

BENDIX, R. and LIPSET, S. M. (1966). *Class, status and power*, Revised edn, Part I. Free Press, New York.

BLAU, P. M. and DUNCAN, O. D. (1967). *The American occupational structure*. Wiley, New York.

BOTTOMORE, T. B. (1955). *Classes in modern society*. Allen and Unwin, London.

BURT, C. (1961). Intelligence and social mobility. *Br. J. statist. Psychol.* 14, 3–25.

GIBSON, J. (1970). Biological aspects of a high socio-economic group: I.Q., education and social mobility. *J. biosoc. Sci.* 2, 1–16.

GLASS, D. V. (1954). *Social mobility in Britain*. Routledge and Kegan Paul, London.

GOLDTHORPE, J., LOCKWOOD, D., BECHNOFER, F., and PLATT, J. (1970). *The affluent worker in the class structure*. Cambridge University Press.

HALSEY, A. H. (1958). Genetics, social structure and intelligence. *Br. J. Sociol.* 9, 15–28.

HEBB, D. O. (1949). *The organisation of behaviour*. Wiley, New York.

LIPSET, S. M. and BENDIX, R. (1960). *Social mobility in industrial society*. Heinemann, London.

LITTLE, A. and WESTERGARD, J. (1969). *Trend of class differentials in educational opportunity in England and Wales. Br. J. Sociol.* **15**, 301–15.

MOODY, P. A. (1953). *Introduction to evolution.* Wiley, New York.

NEWSOM, SIR J. (1963). *Half our future.* Report of the Central Advisory Council for Education (England), 1963. H.M.S.O.

ROBBINS, LORD (1963). Report of the Committee on Higher Education (1963). H.M.S.O.

RUNCIMAN, G. (1966). *Relative deprivation and social justice.* Routledge and Kegan Paul, London.

SVALASTOGA, K. (1965). Social mobility: the Western European model. *Acta sociol.* **9**, 172–9.

VERNON, P. E. (1966). Development of current ideas about intelligence tests. In *Genetic and environmental factors in human ability* (eds. J. E. Meade and A. S. Parkes). Oliver and Boyd, Edinburgh.

WARNER, W. L. (1952). The structure of American life. The Munro Lectures delivered at Edinburgh University, April/May 1950. *Edinburgh University Publications: Demography and Sociology, No. 1.*

YOUNG, M. and GIBSON, J. (1963). In search of an explanation of social mobility. *Br. J. statist. Psychol.* **16**, 27–36.

12

NATURAL SELECTION IN MANKIND

Theodosius Dobzhansky

Historical sketch

FOR more than a century, the role of natural selection in the evolution of man has been a controversial subject. In *The descent of man* (1871) Darwin wrote: 'a crowd of facts—all point in the plainest manner to the conclusion that man is a co-descendant with other mammals of a common progenitor'. Natural selection was an important factor in human evolution: 'I have now endeavoured to show that some of the most distinctive characters of man have in all probability been acquired, either directly or more commonly indirectly, through natural selection.' A. R. Wallace, the co-discoverer with Darwin thirteen years earlier (1858) of natural selection as the key factor in the evolution of the living world, thought differently. In 1869, Wallace questioned whether natural selection could have brought about the emergence of man's mind with its reasoning faculties and its ethics. To this, Darwin retorted with some exasperation (1871): 'I cannot, therefore, understand how it is that Mr. Wallace maintains, that "natural selection could only have endowed the savage with a brain a little superior to that of an ape".'

Yet Darwin himself (1871) was 'baffled in all our attempts to account for the differences between the races of man'. Natural selection can hardly explain race differences, because 'beneficial variations alone can be thus preserved; and as far as we are enabled to judge (although always liable to error on this head) not one of the external differences between the races of man are of any direct or special service to him'. Sexual selection seemed to Darwin a more likely explanation: 'For my own part I conclude that of all the causes which have led to the differences in external appearance between the races of man, and to a certain extent between man and the lower animals, sexual selection has been by far the most efficient.' But even so, 'I do not intend to assert that sexual selection will account for all the differences between the races. An unexplained residuum is left . . .'

Biologists and anthropologists who followed Darwin not only shared but exaggerated his bafflement. Thus Hooton, for many years the leading figure in physical anthropology in America, made the assertion that race differences are 'principally unadaptive' a part of his definition of race (1926). The eugenic movement started by Galton, at the turn of century, was based on two related premises. First, natural selection has become relaxed under conditions of civilized living, and no longer efficiently eliminates deleterious genetic variants. Second, with advancing knowledge of biology and particularly genetics, natural selection can and should be replaced by artificial selection of variants which the eugenists consider desirable.

Some proponents of eugenics and popular writers worked themselves up to a state of panic. If civilization and natural selection are really incompatible, mankind is headed for biological twilight and eventual extinction. To escape this calamity, eugenic crash programmes are needed. Even so outstanding a scientist as the late H. J. Muller felt these fears to be justified and drastic remedies in order. In one of his many essays on this topic (1963) he reasoned as follows. Under primitive conditions in which our pre-human and early human ancestors lived, natural selection worked to enhance such traits as mutual aid, co-operation, communication, and general intelligence. There was positive feedback from cultural to genetic evolution. 'Thus culture itself provided a basis for more effective natural selection in favour of the very traits that advanced that culture.' This happy state exists no longer because of modern social organization and technology. Indeed civilized society now aids and enables to survive those 'who for whatever reason, environmental or genetic, are physically, mentally, or morally weaker than the average'.

Muller estimates that, in order to prevent genetic deterioration, at least 20 per cent of the human population must in every generation 'fail to live until maturity or, if they do live, must fail to reproduce'. This supposed biological necessity is no longer met in developed countries, chiefly owing to improved hygiene and medical care. The mortality in infancy and childhood is depressed to a small percentage, and the genetically defective individuals who reach adulthood not only do not refrain from reproduction but actually out-reproduce the genetically better-endowed ones. Therefore, 'selection is today working actively in reverse, so as to decrease fitness'. We do not need to consider here in detail the remedies advocated by Muller, which begin with artificial insemination of women by the sperm of eugenically approved donors.

In recent years attention has been drawn increasingly to the complexity of the phenomena of natural selection. Natural selection is really a common name for several processes of rather diverse biological significance. This is true of selection in the living world as a whole, as well as in the human species. It is most essential to distinguish between these processes as they occur in mankind. It then becomes very clear that natural selection has neither ceased to operate in modern mankind, nor is likely to do so in the predictable future. Natural selection is, however, not acting in our species as we, men, would like it to operate.

Fitness

Darwin's beautifully simple and clear definition of natural selection was 'preservation of favourable variations and the rejection of injurious variations'

(1859). Natural selection is a sequel to the struggle for existence. This struggle includes 'not only the life of the individual but success in leaving progeny'. The stress is nevertheless on mortality. Darwin acknowledges the doctrine of Malthus as the source of his own: 'There is no exception to the rule that every organic being naturally increases at so high a rate that if not destroyed, the earth would soon be covered by the progeny of a single pair.' We must 'keep steadily in mind that each organic being is striving to increase at a geometric ratio; that each at some period of its life, during some season of the year, during each generation or at intervals has to struggle for life and to suffer great destruction'. If this makes one feel squeamish, 'we may console ourselves with the full belief that the war of nature is not incessant, that no fear is felt, that death is generally prompt, and that the vigorous, the healthy, and the happy survive and multiply'.

The emergence of genetics has shifted the attention of evolutionists to the transmission of genes from one generation to the next. Selection occurs when the carriers of some gene variants leave more or fewer surviving descendants relative to the carriers of other variants. Or to put it differently, natural selection is differential perpetuation of genetic variants from generation to generation. The carriers of a certain variant may be more viable, or more fecund, or sexually more active, or reach sexual maturity earlier, or have a longer reproductive period than do the carriers of another variant. Any one, or any combination, of these advantages may influence the contribution of the carriers of a given genotype in one generation to the gene pool of the next generation. The magnitude of the contribution of the carriers of a given genotype relative to those of other genotypes in the same population is the Darwinian fitness of the genotype. Adaptive value or selective value are alternative terms used synonymously with Darwinian fitness. Natural selection takes place when a population contains two or more genotypes with different Darwinian fitnesses, in the environments in which this population lives.

Darwinian fitness should not be confused with fitness in everyday language. This is why 'Darwinian' is added. Darwinian fitness is reproductive fitness. In principle, natural selection could take place without differential mortality. Imagine a population in which all the children born survive to maturity. However, some prospective parents may remain celibate, others produce few children, and still others many children. If the numbers of the children born are correlated with the genetic constitutions of the parents, differences in Darwinian fitness are present, and selection is taking place. Or else, suppose that everybody is married and has the same number of children, all of whom survive. Selection could still operate, if some people would have children at a younger and others at a later age, and if the age of childbearing is a function of the genetic constitution.

Of course, selection can also operate with differential survival of the children born, regardless of whether genetic variations in fecundity or in the childbearing age are present or not. Crow has proposed a very simple measure of 'the opportunity for selection'. This is $I = V/\bar{W}^2$, where V is the variance of the numbers of children born per couple, and $\bar{W}$ the mean number of children. The greater is I the more opportunity there is for selection to operate. The value, I has two components, I_m due to differential mortality, and I_f, due to differential fertility. As expected, the values of I are diverse in different human populations. What is however, interesting and rather surprising is that, by and large, the Is are greater in populations with small average numbers of children per couple than in those with many children. This is so because the variances of the numbers of children per family grow relatively less rapidly than do the squares of the average numbers of children. In other words, large families are by no means necessary for natural selection to occur. Variations in the numbers of children per family are sufficient, provided, of course, that they are genetically conditioned (Spuhler 1963).

It must be stressed that Darwinian fitness is a relative measure. A genotype may have a higher or a lower Darwinian fitness than other genotypes. For example, colour-blind or myopic individuals were probably at some disadvantage compared to those with 'normal' vision in tribes of hunters and food gatherers. Diabetics are at a disadvantage in modern well-fed societies, notwithstanding the ministrations of modern medicine. It is certain that colour-blindness, and some forms of myopia and diabetes are genetically conditioned. Since these defects reduce the Darwinian fitness of their carriers in certain environments, natural selection did, and probably still does, discriminate against them, and favours what we call 'normal' eyesight and carbohydrate metabolism.

Imagine, however, that in mankind everybody is myopic, or colour-blind, or diabetic. It is at least conceivable that a human species consisting entirely of myopic, or colour-blind, or diabetic individuals could have survived. It would then be meaningless to say that these characteristics reduce the Darwinian fitness of their possessors, because we would have nothing to compare them with. Nobody would even suspect that he is a carrier of a genetic defect. If a person with what we call normal vision appeared by mutation in a colour-blind mankind, he would be regarded a possessor of an extraordinary ability or possibly a sorcerer. If his progeny inherited his vision, their Darwinian fitness might be higher than that of most of their conspecifics, and natural selection would increase their incidence from generation to generation.

Adaptedness

Every living species or population is adapted to live in certain environments. This statement is almost tautological: a species without adaptedness would be extinct. But it is not quite a tautology, because there are different degrees of adaptedness. For example, California condor and whooping crane have very narrow ranges of adaptedness, as manifested by their being reduced to small numbers of individuals. By contrast, the Norway rat and house-sparrow are flourishing in a variety of climates and on a variety of foods. The human species has an unequalled adaptedness, owing to the ability to control the environments and to devise new environments by means of culture and technology. Since the ability to develop and to maintain culture has a genetic basis, the adaptedness must be considered a product ultimately of the human genetic constitution.

It seems intuitively obvious that the adaptedness of modern mankind is superior to that of mankind of palaeolithic times, or of the australopithecine ancestors. One can also surmise that uncontrolled population growth and despoliation of the world environments may seriously lower man's adaptedness. The difficulty with the concept of adaptedness is that there are thus far no good methods for its quantification. However difficult it is in practice, the measurement of the Darwinian fitness of human genotypes is theoretically straightforward. Data must be obtained on the reproductive performance (including, of course, the survival of the progeny) of the carriers of the genetic variants under study, in relation to the performance of other genotypes at the same time and in the same environment. Thus, the Darwinian fitness of achondroplastic dwarfs in Denmark is roughly $0 \cdot 1$ of that of the non-dwarfs (Mørch 1941, Popham 1953). This value may, of course, change with time, and it may be different in different social and physical environments.

As to the adaptedness of a population or a species, the numbers of individuals and the biomass are clearly relevant. On these criteria, California condor and whooping crane are far below the house-sparrow and the rat, and these are below man. But this is not the whole story. A statistic called the Malthusian parameter or innate capacity for increase has been proposed to measure the rate of the population growth in an environment in which the living necessities are not limiting (Andrewartha and Birch 1954). This statistic, denoted r_m, tells us, in essence, how rapidly the number of individuals of a species can increase in a certain environment before its carrying capacity becomes insufficient.

The innate capacity for increase is vastly greater in many lower organisms, such as insects and micro-organisms, than in man. It can, however, be argued that for such very different organisms, living in quite different environments, comparison of the r_m values is really not informative. It is more meaningful for populations of the same species or closely related species. Thus, the rate of growth and the doubling time of human populations has speeded-up in recent centuries, particularly since the industrial revolution, and it is still becoming more rapid. Furthermore, not all human populations and races have been growing equally rapidly. Some have, in fact, declined. It is reasonable to say that the adaptedness of the human species, and particularly of the populations living in technologically advanced environments, has increased. This is not contradicted by the fact that the runaway population growth will be a calamity—any environment is bound eventually to become limiting for any species, no matter how excellent its adaptedness.

Adaptation and adaptability

Adaptation is a process whereby the state of adaptedness is achieved. 'Adaptation' is used also as an abbreviation for adaptive trait, i.e., for a structure or a function which contributes to the adaptedness. This double meaning is unfortunate, but it is probably too firmly rooted in the biological vocabulary to be rectified easily. Adaptation as a process may be physiological or genetic. An individual adapts physiologically to low oxygen pressure by some changes in the composition of his blood, and to sunlight exposure by deposition of more skin pigment. Genetic adaptation of a plant population to the presence of parasitic fungi, or the presence of salts of heavy metals in the soil, takes place by selection favouring the genotypes which confer immunity to these noxious agents. Similar selective processes have presumably occurred in human evolution in response to pathogens of various sorts.

Natural selection results in adaptation when genetic variants which confer superior adaptedness have a Darwinian fitness higher than do variants of lesser adaptedness. As a rule, superior Darwinian fitness goes together with superior adaptedness, and vice versa. This statement is by no means trivial. Exceptions are known when greater Darwinian fitness turns out to be the property of genotypes which give rise to maladaptive traits. A striking example are some of the alleles at the complex t locus in mice, extensively studied by Dunn and his collaborators (Dunn 1964 and other works). These t alleles are lethal to homozygotes, and yet males heterozygous for t produce many more sperms carrying t than its normal allele. This makes t have a superior Darwinian fitness, and yet a population with high frequencies of t suffers heightened embryonic mortality. Another example is the 'sex ratio' condition, carried in many X chromosomes in natural populations of several species of *Drosophila*. A male with such an X chromosome transmits it to his entire progeny, instead of to half the progeny as in normal males. If not counteracted by some other factor, the 'sex ratio' condition would spread in the population, until the latter becomes unisexual, which in an organism incapable of parthenogenesis means extinction. Though not known with certainty, genetic variants like the t alleles in mice or the 'sex ratio' in *Drosophila* may exist also in man.

Neither the Darwinian fitness nor the adaptedness are immutable attributes of a genotype. They depend on the environments, and consequently may shift upwards or downwards at different times and in different places. By and large, the Darwinian fitness and the adaptedness are positively correlated; if they were uncorrelated, life on earth would probably have become extinct long ago. Yet even apart from the rather exceptional situations mentioned above, there is a fundamental constraint on the ability of natural selection to conserve or advance the adaptedness of a population or of a species. This is simply that natural selection has no foresight. It selects what is advantageous, and has a high Darwinian fitness where and when the selection operates. In short, natural selection is opportunistic.

While it brings a short-term advantage, opportunism may be disadvantageous in the long run. It entails the risks of failure of adaptedness and of eventual extinction. After all, extinction is the commonest destiny of most evolutionary lines, from local populations to species and classes. Why is this so? The reason is simply that a peerless adaptedness forged by natural selection in yesterday's and today's environments may turn out to be deficient in future environments. One can hardly imagine a more striking example than the runaway population growth of the human species. It may be the greatest hazard to the adaptedness and even to survival of our species. And yet, the ability of a living population to increase its numbers is, as pointed out above, one of the measures of adaptedness!

Thoday (1953) defined the 'fitness of a unit of evolution' as 'its probability to leave descendants after a given long period of time. Biological progress is increased in such fitness'. He also wrote that 'The fit are those who fit their existing environments and whose descendants will fit future environments.' He is speaking obviously neither of Darwinian fitness nor of adaptedness, but of adaptability. Adaptability is the capacity to become adapted to changes in the environments. The persistence, or durability, of a unit of evolution in time depends, in the long run, on its adaptability. Some so-called 'living fossils', such as the horseshoe crab, have survived apparently unchanged for long geological epochs, presumably because the ecological niches which they inhabit have also persisted without major changes. But these are exceptions; most organisms evolved to occupy ecological niches different from those of their ancestors. Surely, human environments created by culture and civilization are quite different from those of our pre-human ancestors. When challenged by altered environments, a species with high adaptability evolves genetically (or in the case of man also culturally) to fit into the new environments. A species lacking adaptability becomes extinct or, at best, persists as a relic.

Whence comes adaptability? It might seem that natural selection cannot be its source, because selection is concerned with what is, and not with what will be. This is, however, not the whole story. Every organism has an adaptedness to live in a range of environments. Adaptedness to only a single constant environment would lead quickly to extinction, because environments are not constant. Therefore, every living species is made by natural selection adaptable to the range of the environments which it encounters regularly, or at least at frequent intervals, in its natural habitats. Inhabitants of the temperate zones have to survive winters as well as summers, and of the tropics rainy and dry seasons. A child, a youth, and an adult man live in different social environments and have different roles to play.

Adaptability is obviously of several kinds. There exist physiological and genetic adaptive processes. Physiological homeostasis enables life to go on, and the essential physiological processes to proceed undisturbed, in the face of changes in the environment. Maintenance of constant body temperature and of the pH of the blood are standard examples. Developmental homeostasis, plasticity, or flexibility are less easily reversible within an individual's lifetime than are physiological homeostatic reactions. The dependence of stature on the nutrition during the growth period is an illustration. The ability to learn, and the consequent flexibility of behaviour, are however most important forms of individual adaptability in human societies. Genetic adaptability is due, on a given time level, to the presence of genetic variability and genetic polymorphisms, particularly in populations of sexually reproducing organisms. Diversity of environments can be exploited best by a population that contains diverse genotypes, with optimal adaptedness in different environments. It is less likely that there will appear an all-purpose genotype which will be optimal in all environments.

Physiological and genetic adaptability are certainly not alternative but complementary. Every genotype which occurs regularly in a population must be at least tolerably adapted to some range of environments, but different genotypes may have different ranges of adaptedness. The genetic adaptability in time, i.e. the genetic flexibility when the environment changes in the course of evolution, is probably a function in part of the genetic diversity available on a given time level. Suppose that a population consists of genetically identical individuals, as clones of micro-organisms sometimes do. If an environmental change exceeds the tolerance of the genotype, a genetic adaptation can occur only if there appears a mutant with a more favourable tolerance range. A sexual population is likely to contain a variety of genotypes with different optima and tolerances. Some of them may be selected for in new environments. One need not, however, suppose that genotypes adapted to all possible contingencies will always be available ready made. Unless the environmental change is very sudden (in terms of the numbers of generations), the selection may gradually compound new genotypes adapted to new environments from genetic building-blocks present in the population.

It is sometimes said that a species on a certain time level was 'pre-adapted' to the environment or to the ways of life which it met or chose at a later time level. For example, erect posture developing in our remote ancestors preadapted our less remote ancestors to rely for survival on tool-making and tool use; the versatile hands of these less remote ancestors were pre-adapted for driving automobiles and piloting aircrafts today. Now 'pre-adaptation' is not some sort of a prophetic gift of natural selection. Whatever the selection promoted in our ancestors was favoured because it was useful to these ancestors, not because it is even more useful to us today. Erect posture, versatile hands, tool-using and tool-making abilities, evolved not one after the other, but gradually and together. There was a positive feedback between these morphological and psychological traits. The more the life of our ancestors depended on using and making tools, the more natural selection advanced the versatility of the hands which held the tools. Conversely, the more skilful became the hands the better became the tools which they made. In Washburn's (1968) words, 'human biological abilities are the result of the success of past ways of human life. Through the feedback relation between behaviour and biology, the human gene pool is the result of the behaviours of times past. From the short-term point of view, human biology makes cultures possible. It poses problems and sets limits. But from the long-term evolutionary point of view it was the success of social systems that determined the course of evolution'.

As mentioned above, A. R. Wallace questioned the power of natural selection to endow 'the savage man' with a brain much superior to that of his ape-like ancestors. What conceivable advantage could men of palaeolithic times derive from mental abilities which in their remote descendants resulted in the inventions of calculus, physics, and metaphysics? The problem would be insoluble if there existed independent genes for each of these abilities. But this is not so—these abilities are outgrowths of the more basic capacities of abstraction, conceptual thinking, and communication by means of symbolic language. These capacities were useful since the beginning of the process of hominization, and their usefulness to all human beings has been increasing ever since. This is not to say that everybody can be an outstanding mathematician or metaphysician. Natural selection has been, and continues to be, a powerful evolutionary agent in the human species precisely because human populations contain ample stores of genetic variants on which the selection works. Though all non-pathological representatives of the human species do possess certain basic abilities, there is still room for individual variation.

Normalizing natural selection

Teissier (1945) and Schmalhausen 1949) independently pointed out the need to distinguish two kinds of natural selection. One is directional selection (*sélection novatrice*) that changes the gene pool of the population on which it acts, and the other is stabilizing or normalizing selection (*sélection conservatrice*) that keeps the gene pool constant.

Failure to make this distinction is responsible for a confusing episode in the history of the selection theory. Darwin acknowledged that the key insight leading to his theory was derived from reading the work of Malthus on populations. The tendency of populations to expand geometrically is counteracted by shortage of food or other resources; a part of the progeny is eliminated; the incidence of favourable genetic constitutions is greater among the survivors than among the victims, and hence increasing in succeeding generations. Eiseley (1959) has, however, uncovered papers of Edward Blyth, published in the Magazine of Natural History between 1835 and 1837, i.e. more than two decades before Darwin's *The origin of species*. Blyth quite explicitly describes natural selection (of course, not so named). This selection operates to eliminate variations which deviate from the perfectly adapted status characteristic of species living in their natural environments. It thus preserves the boundaries between species, and prevents these species from becoming too variable. Although Darwin was almost certainly familiar with Blyth's writings, he nowhere acknowledges the relatedness of his concept of selection to that of Blyth. Certain authors saw fit to accuse Darwin of plagiarism, something utterly out of keeping with all that is known of Darwin's personality.

The explanation is probability much simpler and not at all sinister. Darwin looked for a selection that changes species and gives rise to evolution, while Blyth wrote about selection that keeps species unaltered and thus prevents evolution. Having the advantage of hindsight, we see that these processes are basically kindred, although their outcomes are the opposite of one another. Darwin was not conscious of the similarity.

In point of fact, normalizing selection is only one of several forms which may act to keep the gene pool of a population constant in composition. Another such form is balancing selection due to heterosis, i.e., to superior fitness of heterozygotes. Others are frequency-dependent selection and selection in populations which inhabit a variety of ecological niches in the same territory.

Mutations occur in man, as they do in all living species. The mutation process is adaptively ambiguous, in the sense that mutations arise regardless of whether they can be useful where and when they appear, or anywhere. In fact, most newly arisen mutants are harmful to their carriers, at least in the environments in which the species usually lives. Uncontrolled accumulation of mutants would therefore lower the adaptedness of the species.

The control is realized through normalizing natural selection. Suppose that a gene A mutates to a recessive state a at a rate u per generation; u is generally small, say of the orders of 10^{-5} or 10^{-4}, so that about 1 in 100 000 or 1 in 10 000 sex cells carry a newly arisen a. Suppose further that Darwinian fitness of AA and Aa individuals is 1, and of aa is $1-s$; s is the selection coefficient, which measures the reproductive disadvantage of being aa. In every generation some a genes are introduced in the population by mutation, and some are eliminated because of the lower Darwinian fitness of aa. An equilibrium state is reached when the numbers of a eliminated by the selection become equal to those arising by mutation. It can be shown that the frequency of a deleterious recessive gene a in a population at equilibrium will be approximately $\sqrt{u/s}$.

Consider the situation when aa individuals are lethal (do not survive) or sterile (do not reproduce). Their Darwinian fitness is 0, and the selection co-efficient is 1. If the mutation rate, u, is 0·0001, the equilibrium frequency of a in the population will be $\sqrt{0·0001} = 0·01$. In other words, about 1 per cent of the sex cells produced in the population will carry a, and about 0·01 per cent of the individuals will be homozygous aa; some 2 per cent of the individuals will be the heterozygotes Aa, healthy carriers of the gene a concealed in heterzygous condition. If a deleterious mutant is dominant to the ancestral condition, the equilibrium frequency of the deleterious mutant gene in the population will be lower, namely u/s. For a dominant lethal (such as retinoblastoma without surgical treatment) the value of s is unity. Hence, the number of cases appearing in a population in every generation will be $2u$, twice the mutation rate (because it takes two sex cells to produce an individual, and a dominant mutation in either will cause the disease to appear).

Unfortunately, very few estimates of the Darwinian fitness of human genotypes are available; not unexpectedly, these concern almost entirely hereditary diseases and malformations, because they produce such appreciable changes in fitness that the depression is easily perceptible. The labour and expense needed to obtain fitness estimates for non-pathological traits are so great that few investigators have ventured into this field. The following estimates are taken from the review by Spuhler (1963).

Trait	Fitness
Retinoblastoma (without surgery)	0
Infantile amaurotic idiocy	0
Achondroplastic dwarfism	0·09–0·10
Haemophilia	0·25–0·33
Dystrophia myotonica	0·33
Marfan's syndrome	0·5
Neurofibromatosis, males	0·41
females	0·75
Huntington's chorea, males	0·82
females	1·25

It should be noted that these estimates are valid, even if based on large population samples, only for the places and times where and when they were made. Retinoblastoma is no longer lethal, if the affected eyes are surgically removed or given certain other treatments. The low fitness of achondroplastic dwarfs is in part due to their appearance deviating from the popular canons of sexual attractiveness, making some of them unable to find mates. Since the onset of Huntington's chorea occurs usually in middle age, the Darwinian fitness of the choreics will be higher if marriages and childbearing occur early than if they occur later. Discovery of more effective medical treatments increases the Darwinian fitness of the 'defective' genotypes, and, with unchanged mutation rates, permits these genotypes to accumulate in the populations.

The problem of normalizing selection can also be approached by recording the total incidence of genetically conditioned disability of all kinds found in human populations. The data of Stevenson (1959, 1961) for the populations of Northern Ireland and of some districts in England are probably the best available. Between 12 and 15 per cent of pregnancies that continue longer than 4 weeks end in abortion by 27th week, and about 2 per cent end in still-births. Miscarriages in earlier stages of pregnancy are not recordable. A considerable, though not exactly known, proportion of the miscarriages and stillbirths are due to genetic defects. About 26·5 per cent of hospital beds are occupied by genetically handicapped persons; 7·9 per cent of consultations with medical specialists and 6·4 per cent of those with general practitioners involve such persons. According to the extensive review by Kennedy (1967) congenital anomalies of various sorts are found the world over in between 1 and 5 per cent of live births, the figures depending largely on the criteria used in the records. During the 1960s a large amount of literature has accumulated on the chromosomal aberrations in man. Duplication of chromosome 21 of the normal set gives the so-called Down syndrome, presence of two X chromosomes and a Y chromosome is responsible for the Klinefelter syndrome, and presence of a single X without a Y chromosome for the Turner syndrome. Though they are not lethal, the Darwinian fitness of the afflicted individuals is very low, or zero, because of the sterility. Mental diseases and mental retardations are often genetically conditioned, although the modes of inheritance are mostly unclear or under dispute. Insofar as these infirmities decrease the reproductive success of the individuals affected, they are acted upon by normalizing selection.

Balancing selection

Some genetic variants cause heterosis, a Darwinian fitness of heterozygotes superior to that of homozygotes. The consequences of this are quite interesting. Suppose that the frequencies of the gene alleles A_1 and A_2 in a population are p and q, and that the fitness of the genotypes is as follows:

Genotype	A_1A_1	A_1A_2	A_2A_2
Frequency	p^2	$2pq$	q^2
Fitness	$1\text{-}s_1$	1	$1\text{-}s_2$

It can be shown that heterotic balancing selection will act to retain both alleles in the population, with frequencies at equilibrium $p = s_2/(s_1+s_2)$ and $q = s_1/(s_1+s_2)$. This will happen even if one of the alleles causes, when homozygous, a lethal hereditary disease. For example, if A_1A_1 dies before reproduction ($s_1 = 1$), and A_2A_2 suffers a 10 per cent reduction of fitness ($s_2 = 0·1$), the stable equilibrium frequencies will be $p = 0·09$ and $q = 0·91$; about 0·8 per cent of the fertilizations will have the lethal disease ($p^2 = 0·09^2$). If the heterozygote has only a slight advantage, say, 1 per cent, over both homozygotes ($s_1 = s_2 = 0.01$), the equilibrium will be established at $p = q = 0.5$, and the population will consist of about 50 per cent of heterozygotes and 25 per cent of each of the two homozygotes.

The superior fitness of heterozygotes for a gene which in double dose causes a usually lethal sickle-cell anaemia is most often cited as the example of heterotic balancing selection in man. This should not be taken to mean that this form of selection is rare in human populations, only that selection phenomena in man have been astonishingly little studied. In homozygous condition, SS, the gene causes a disease resulting in death, usually at between 3 months and 2 years of age, although a minority survive even to adolescence. The heterozygotes, Ss, not only live but are more resistant, relative to the 'normal' homozygotes ss, to a form of malaria widespread in the tropics (*falciparum* malaria).

Allison (1964) carried out experiments, infecting volunteer Ss and ss individuals with this malaria. The results were dramatic; only 2 of the 15 Ss, and 14 out of 15 ss individuals contracted the disease. Since the superior Darwinian fitness of Ss is a function of the prevalence of *falciparum* malaria in a given territory, the incidence of the gene S is highest where this malaria is pandemic (up to 40 per cent of Ss persons in the population), while the gene is rare or absent where malaria does not occur. Studies in various parts of Africa indicate that the fitness of Ss persons may be as much as 30 per cent higher than that of ss; the fitness of SS remains close to zero. When a population with a high frequency of S moves to a country free of malaria, the superior Darwinian fitness of the heterozygotes disappears, and the incidence of S decreases after some generations. This is apparently happening in the United States in populations of African descent. Good, though not quite conclusive, data indicate that several other genetic variants may also be maintained by heterotic balancing selection because of the protection they confer upon their carriers against malaria or other diseases. Here belong the genes for haemoglobins C and E, the Mediterranean anaemia (thalassaemia), perhaps that for deficiency of the red-cell enzyme, glucose-6-phosphate dehydrogenase, and certain others.

The Darwinian fitness of a given genotype relative to others may evidently change when the environment changes. Reference has been made above to the disappearance of the heterotic advantage in Ss heterozygotes in countries free of malaria. The Darwinian fitness may also depend on how frequent are certain genotypes in a given population. A gene may increase the fitness of its carriers when they are a minority, but decrease the fitness when they become a majority. If so, a frequency-dependent balancing selection may work to increase the incidence of a gene when it is rare, but decrease it when it is too common. A balanced equilibrium is reached when the carriers of that gene have neither an advantage nor a disadvantage compared to non-carriers.

No instance of frequency-dependent selection is established in man, although such selection may be quite common. Neel and Schull (1968) give the following imaginative but not implausible example.

A primitive, polygynous society in which each male was highly aggressive might so decimate itself in the struggle for leadership that it was non-viable. At high frequencies of aggressiveness, the non-aggressive male who could keep aloof from the sanguine struggle might stand a better chance of survival and reproduction than the more aggressive, with his chance a function of the amount of aggressiveness in the group. But at low frequencies of the same traits, the aggressive male who assumed leadership (and multiple wives) would be the object of positive selection, and the more passive the group, the greater his reproductive potential. There would thus be an intermediate frequency at which this phenotype (and its genetic basis) would tend to be stabilized.

Diversifying (called disruptive by some authors) selection is related to but not identical with frequency-dependent selection. Any human population and, indeed, any animal or plant population faces not a single environment but a variety of environments. Different variants in the gene pool are likely to possess greatest fitness in these environments. Theoretical and experimental studies of Mather (1955), Thoday (1959), Levins (1968), and others have shown that selection favouring multiple goals may result in the population becoming polymorphic; it will then contain two or several arrays of genotypes having maximum fitness in different sub-environments which the population inhabits. Another possible outcome of selection in diversified environments may be the establishment of 'all-purpose genotypes', which do at least tolerably well under the entire range of the environments.

Diversifying selection may be an important agency in the human species, although only speculative examples of its action can be given. All human societies, and technologically advanced more than primitive ones, have a multiplicity of occupations, tasks, professions, and vocations to be filled if the society is to function properly. How is this need satisfied? It is satisfied in two ways. Any non-pathological human genotype enables its carrier to be trained for the performance of the functions which a given individual elects or is designated to perform. In this sense, *Homo sapiens* has an 'all-purpose genotype' as its species characteristic. It can produce phenotypes suited to many cultural environments in which people may find themselves.

The adaptive flexibility of the human development pattern, particularly as it concerns the processes of learning and acquisition of social competence, is not at all inconsistent with the existence of genetic variability. To put it simply, it is easier to teach some things to some individuals and other things to others. Almost anybody can be trained as a soldier, or an agriculturist, or a mechanic. But soldiering seems to be more congenial to some, and tilling the soil to others. It is quite likely, though there is no definitive proof of this, that genes contribute towards differentiation of human tastes and preferences.

An even stronger case can be made for genetic conditioning of some special abilities. Outstanding musical, mathematical, artistic, poetic talents, superior prowess in sports or acts of physical endurance, are almost entirely not within the realm of possibilities for most of us. Historical examples are many, in which individuals endowed with such outstanding abilities fared badly at the hands of their more ordinary contemporaries, *les hommes moyens sensuels*. And yet, it is probable that, statistically considered, outstanding achievements in most fields carry now, and have always carried, advantages in survival of the achievers as well as of their families. If this is so, then a variety of geno-types predisposing their carriers towards different occupations and different roles in the society may be favoured by diversifying selection. This selection will tend to establish balanced equilibria; the incidence of the genes, and of the abilities which they are most likely to produce will, in at least a rough way, correspond to what a society needs or admires.

Directional selection

We have discussed the forms of selection which, given enough time to act in a reasonably unchanging environment, conduce towards genetic steady states. In normalizing selection, the steady state is due to an opposition of a mutation pressure generating variants of low fitness, and a selection removing them from the gene pool. With balancing selection, the steady state is due to an opposition of selection processes acting on different genotypes or in different environments in the same population.

Directional selection is, in a sense, the simplest form of selection, which must have occurred on a grand scale in evolutionary history. A change in the environment may confer upon one gene allele, or a chromosomal variant, a fitness superior to that which it had before the change. Given enough time, the new favoured allele is substituted for, and displaces entirely the previously prevalent allele. The spread of melanic varieties of moths in polluted districts in England (industrial melanism), of insect pests resistant to insecticides, and of variants of rust fungi able to attack the most frequently planted varieties of wheats, are classical examples of directional selection.

Directional selection has certainly operated in the evolution of man and his ancestors. Does it still continue to operate in modern mankind? Geneti-cists and anthropologists must admit their inability to give even a single well authenticated example of a directional selective process having been observed in operation. The most widely publicized instance in which such selection was supposed to be taking place was the alleged trend towards decreasing intelligence. A higher average fertility of people with lower intelli-gence, compared to that of more intelligent people (as measured by I.Q. tests), has been repeatedly found in several studies in different countries. There is also evidence that a considerable fraction of the variance in the I.Q. scores is genetic. Therefore, one could have reasonably expected to observe a gradual drop in the intelligence averages, at least in the populations for which differ-ential fertility seemingly favouring lower intelligence has been recorded. And yet, the famous surveys conducted by the Scottish Council for Research in Education in 1932 and 1947 failed to verify the expectation. There are several possible reasons why the expectation was unfounded, which cannot be discussed adequately in the present article. In brief, the surveys did not include families with no children attending schools; people with severe mental retardations seem to have quite low fertility.

An idea has gained credence, chiefly among social scientists but also among some biologists, that the biological evolution of mankind came to a halt when our species developed culture. Since then, mankind evolves culturally, but is allegedly stable biologically. Confronted with this assertion, a biologist is in an embarrassing position. As stated above, no fully reliable evidence of directional genetic changes has been secured in human populations. Does this prove that man is no longer evolving biologically? It is appropriate to be reminded at this point that Darwin did not claim to have observed natural selection actually taking place. He adduced instead abundant evidence which showed that natural selection must be taking place. As we see this matter at present, there are two necessary and sufficient conditions for natural selection to operate. These are, first, presence of genetic variation of certain morphological, physiological, or psychological traits; and, secondly, this variation affecting the Darwinian fitness of the possessors of these traits.

The environments and the ways of life of people change with extraordinary rapidity, within time intervals of the order of a human lifetime, not to speak of centuries or millennia. True enough, people become adapted to these changes principally by means of cultural rather than genetic transformations. The dichotomy of 'environmental' versus 'genetic' is however invalid, and so is the dichotomy of 'cultural' versus 'genetic'. Cultural and genetic changes always were, and continue to be, connected by feedback relationships.

Genetic death

Consider again the action of normalizing selection which counteracts the accumulation of deleterious mutants in a population. A steady state is achieved when the average number of mutants arising per unit time (e.g. per generation) equals the number eliminated by selection. The elimination has been called by Muller (1950) 'genetic death'. This emotion-laden phrase has taken root in the literature, although a genetic 'death' need not produce a cadaver. For example, a gene for achondroplasia is removed by genetic 'death' when a dwarf carrying this gene fails to find a mate. A sort of genetic 'half-death' occurs when a couple of parents has, for genetic reasons, a single child instead of two.

The numbers of genetic deaths that must occur for natural selection to operate were investigated theoretically by Haldane (1937) and by Muller (1950). With normalizing selection at equilibrium, the number of deleterious genes arising by mutation must be equal to the number eliminated. Therefore, the number of genetic deaths that must occur will be equal to the mutation rate (for recessive deleterious mutants), or will be twice the mutation rate (for dominants that are eliminated chiefly in heterozygous carriers). What seems paradoxical at first sight, is that the numbers of genetic deaths are independent of the degree of harm a mutant produces, from complete lethals to slight diminutions of fitness. The degree of harm caused by a mutant will, of course, influence its frequency in a population, and also the average number of generations which will elapse between the origin of a mutant and its elimination. The sum total of the genetic deaths will, however, be determined only by mutation frequencies. Even if the mutation rates of genes considered one by one are low (say, of the order of 10^{-5}), with tens or hundreds of thousands of genes subject to mutation, there will be hecatombs of 'genetic deaths'.

The heterotic balancing selection has to be paid for by still more genetic deaths. If the homozygotes are less fit than the heterozygotes (as in the case of the sickle-cell condition discussed above), there will in every generation take place some genetic deaths among the former. Let the frequencies of the homozygotes A_1A_1 ('normal' non-carrier of the sickle-cell gene) and A_2A_2 (the anaemic condition) be p^2 and q^2 respectively, and their selective disadvantages s_1 and s_2 (see above, page 224). The heterozygotes, A_1A_2, enjoy the highest fitness (in malarial countries). A population consisting entirely of heterozygotes would be the fittest, but such a population produces some homozygotes, A_1A_1 and A_2A_2 in the progeny. Compared to such an 'ideal' population, a population consisting of the three genotypes at equilibrium will suffer a loss of fitness amounting to $s_1p^2+s_2q^2$. Suppose that the anaemic homozygote dies before sexual maturity ($s_2 = 1$), and the non-carrier has a 20 per cent disadvantage ($s_1 = 0.2$). The loss of fitness will then be 0.168, almost 17 per cent of 'genetic deaths'!

The problem of genetic loads imposed on a population by genetic polymorphisms maintained by balancing selection has attracted much attention of population geneticists. In recent years, many studies of such polymorphisms have been carried out, especially with the aid of techniques of separation of enzymes and other protein variants by their electrophoretic mobility. These techniques have revealed that a surprisingly high proportion of genes is polymorphic in natural populations. Estimates for human populations are based on the works of Harris (1970) and Lewontin (1967); at least a quarter of the genes examined proved to be polymorphic; an individual is heterozygous for approximately 16 per cent of his genes. Assuming that these estimates are not grossly in error, and assuming that a human sex cell contains some 100 000 genes, an average individual turns out to be heterozygous for some 16 000 genes.

If an appreciable fraction of these polymorphisms is maintained by heterotic balancing selection, the genetic load would seem to be intolerable. Indeed, suppose that the two homozygotes A_1A_1 and A_2A_2 have fitness only 2 per cent lower than the heterozygote, A_1A_2 ($s_1 = s_2 = 0{\cdot}02$). The loss of fitness caused by this polymorphism will, according to the formula given above, be 1 per cent; the fitness of the population will then be $0{\cdot}99$ of what it would have been if the population consisted solely of heterozygotes. This may not seem very grave; in point of fact, a loss of this magnitude would probably go undetected, given the present state of human population genetics. Suppose however, that there are 1000 such polymorphisms, and that the losses of fitness which they produce are multiplicative. The fitness of the population will then be $0{\cdot}99^{1000}$, or about two-thousandths of 1 per cent of that of a population consisting entirely of heterozygotes. If the loss of fitness means increase of genetic deaths, then no human population, and probably no other living population, can sustain such a loss.

A still more serious difficulty was pointed out by Haldane (1957), and following him by Kimura and others (see Crow and Kimura 1970). Adaptive changes by directional selection, i.e., by substitution of gene variants of superior fitness for those of inferior fitness, entails a 'substitutional load' of genetic deaths. This 'load' may, according to the theory, be so heavy that it will slow down very materially the rate of adaptive genetic changes. To understand this paradox, suppose that there arises in some population a novel favourable mutant. Let the mutant be symbolized as a change of a gene A_1 to a superior allele A_2. The new mutant will be present originally in a single heterozygous individual, A_1A_2, in a population in which all other individuals are A_1A_1. Since A_1A_2 is superior in fitness to A_1A_1, the origin of a favourable mutant means that the population suddenly acquires a genetic load of inferior A_1 genes. Directional selection will then start working to increase the frequencies of A_2 and to decrease those of A_1. The process can be viewed as causing many genetic deaths, owing to differential mortality of the carriers of A_1.

Evolutionary changes often involve reconstructions of the genetic endowment of a species by substitution of relatively more favourable alleles at many gene loci. A calculus of genetic deaths needed to achieve the substitutions shows that the adaptive improvement can only be achieved very slowly, over many generations, and at the cost of tremendous numbers of genetic deaths. Has 'Haldane's dilemma' driven the theory of evolution by natural selection into a blind alley? Two ways of escape have been suggested.

The more radical one is to suppose that most, or at any rate many, evolutionary changes are 'non-Darwinian' (King and Jukes 1969). It is postulated that many, or most, mutations which occur in the genetic material are adaptively neutral, i.e. do not change the fitness of their carriers either in positive or in negative directions; that the unfixed, polymorphic, genes found in natural populations are mostly neutral variants; and that a majority of the allelic substitutions that occur in evolution is also neutral. Adaptively neutral changes make no genetic loads and cause no genetic deaths. They merely drift in the population gene pool; their frequencies go up or down by chance alone. This drift, or 'random walk', eventually results in loss of some of the variant genes, while others, on the contrary, become more frequent and supplant their competitors. The amplitude of the fluctuations, and the probabilities of loss and fixation, are functions of the population size; they are greater in small than in large populations (Crow and Kimura 1970).

The fundamental assumptions on which the 'non-Darwinian' theory rests are adaptive neutrality of many or most genetic variants, and consequently their irrelevance to adaptive evolution. A critical analysis of these assumptions cannot be given in the present article. It can only be stated that the assumptions lead to construction of mathematical models describing the expected behaviour of genetic variants in populations. Fortunately, the models lead to some predictions that can be tested by observations and experiments on natural and experimental populations. Such tests occupy the attention of many workers at present.

There is another way to escape Haldane's dilemma that must be mentioned here. Sved, Reed, and Bodmer (1967), King (1967) and Wallace (1968, 1970) have considered so-called 'truncation' models of the action of natural selection. To assume, as classical theorists habitually did, that every gene is selected and produces its genetic deaths independently of other genes and of the ecological factors that govern the population size is obviously unrealistic. Of course, a mutant gene which results in a lethal hereditary disease will kill its carrier no matter what other genes the latter may carry. But this 'hard' or 'rigid' selection need not be universal. The selection may also be 'soft' or 'flexible'; it may remove the carriers of some genetic endowments when the population is crowded or exposed to ecological stresses, and let them survive and reproduce when the environment is more permissive. Likewise, the genetic endowments removed by genetic death may be those having combinations of several or many deleterious genes, while the carriers of any one of them without the others may survive. The numbers and kinds of deleterious genes which tip the balance towards survival or towards death are again likely to depend on environmental and ecological situations.

A genetic death will, then, remove from the population not single unfavourable genes but more or less large groups of them. The number of polymorphisms maintained by heterotic balancing selection if that selection acts according to a truncation model is much larger than it can be if each gene is selected independently of the others (see above). Truncation models, like the 'non-Darwinian' ones, lead to some experimentally testable predictions. All that can be said about these predictions here is that investigations aiming to test them are under way.

Concluding remarks

Natural selection in mankind is a formidable topic. This review is of necessity brief, incomplete, and perforce superficial. Genetic technicalities have, with few exceptions, been omitted in order to make the review comprehensible to readers who are not at home in population genetics.

The present understanding of how natural selection operates, especially in man, is far from satisfactory. One can infer from circumstantial evidence that various forms of natural selection act on human populations, but only in a few exceptional instances has conclusive direct evidence become available. Normalizing selection is the simplest, and to an evolutionist perhaps the least interesting, form of selection; there is no doubt that it occurs in human populations and yet its quantitative aspects are much less well known than they ought to be. The view that the biological evolution of mankind became arrested when the cultural evolution began is uncritically accepted by many non-biologists. The invalidity of this view is demonstrable on the ground of theoretical inferences but not, it must be admitted, on the basis of concrete observations.

This is a really shocking state of affairs: scientifically and technologically advanced countries have seen fit to expend huge amounts of effort and money to perfect means for self-destruction and to fly to the moon, but not to learn the most basic facts about the state and the possibilities of mankind's own biological endowment. Nevertheless, important advances in our knowledge have been achieved, especially during the last decade or two. They concern mostly matters of conceptualization and theoretical analysis; collection of factual data in human population has progressed on the whole little, because of the expenses involved. We do realize, however, more clearly than in the past that 'natural selection' is a common name for several rather distinct biological processes which play different roles in the evolutionary process. Normalizing selection, different forms of balancing selection, and directional selection may be taking place separately or simultaneously in different populations and at different times. The distinctions between them must always be made in observational and experimental studies.

REFERENCES

The following list contains references to books and papers mentioned in the text of the article. Further references and discussion can be found in author's recent book: Th. Dobzhansky (1970) *Genetics of the evolutionary process*, Columbia University Press, New York and London.

ALLISON, A. C. (1964). Polymorphism and natural selection in human populations. *Cold Spring Harb. Symp. quant. Biol.* **29**, 137–50.

ANDREWARTHA, H. G. and BIRCH, C. L. (1954). *The distribution and abundance of animals.* Chicago University Press.

CROW, J. F. and KIMURA, M. (1970). *An introduction to population genetics theory.* Harper and Row, New York.

DARWIN, C. R. (1859). *Origin of species.* John Murray, London. (Facsimile edn., Harvard University Press, Cambridge, 1964).

—— (1871). *Descent of Man.* John Murray, London.

DUNN, L. C. (1964). Abnormalities associated with a chromosome region in the mouse. *Science, N.Y.* **144**, 260–3.

EISELEY, L. (1959). Charles Darwin, Edward Blyth, and the theory of natural selection. *Proc. Am. phil. Soc.* **103**, 94–158.

HALDANE, J. B. S. (1937). The effect of variation on fitness. *Am. Nat.* **71**, 337–49.

—— (1957). The cost of natural selection. *J. Genet.* **55**, 511–24.

HARRIS, H. (1970). *The principles of human biochemical genetics.* North-Holland, Amsterdam and London.

HOOTON, E. A. (1926). Significance of the term race. *Science, N.Y.* **63**, 75–81. (Reprinted in E. W. Count (1950) *This is race*, Henry Schuman, New York.)

KENNEDY, W. P. (1967). Epidemiologic aspects of the problem of congenital malformations. *Birth defects. Orig. Series* **3**, No. 2.

KING, J. L. (1967). Continuously distributed factors affecting fitness. *Genetics, Princeton* **55**, 483–92.

—— and JUKES, T. H. (1969). Non-Darwinian evolution. *Science, N.Y.* **164**, 788–98.

LEVINS, R. (1968). *Evolution in changing environments.* Princeton University Press.

LEWONTIN, R. C. (1967). An estimate of average heterozygosity in man. *Am. J. hum. Genet.* **19**, 681–5.

MATHER, K. (1955). Polymorphism as an outcome of disruptive selection. *Evolution, Lancaster, Pa.* **9**, 52–61.

MØRCH, E. T. (1941). Chondrodystrophic dwarfs in Denmark. *Opera ex Domo biol. hered. hum. Univ. Hafniensis* **3**, 1–200.

MULLER, H. J. (1950). Our load of mutations. *Am. J. hum. Genet.* **2**, 111–76.

—— (1963). Genetic progress by voluntarily conducted germinal choice. In *Man and his nature* (ed. G. Wolstenholme). Little Brown, Boston.

NEEL, J. V. and SCHULL, W. J. (1968). On some trends in understanding the genetics of man. *Perspect. Biol. Med.* **11**, 565–602.

POPHAM, R. M. (1953). The calculation of reproductive fitness and the mutation rate of the gene for chondrodystrophy. *Am. J. hum. Genet.* **5**, 73–5.

SCHMALHAUSEN, I. I. (1949). *Factors of evolution.* Blakiston, Philadelphia.

SCOTTISH COUNCIL FOR RESEARCH IN EDUCATION (1953). *Social implications of the 1947 Scottish mental survey.* University of London Press.

SPUHLER, J. N. (1963). The scope for natural selection in man. *Genetic selection in man* (ed. W. J. Schull). University of Michigan Press, Ann Arbor.

STEVENSON, A. C. (1959). The load of hereditary defect in human populations. *Radiat. Res.* Suppl. **1**, 306–25.

—— (1961). Frequency of congenital and hereditary disease. *Br. med. Bull.* **17**, 254–9.

SVED, J. A., REED, T. E., and BODMER, W. F. (1967). The number of balanced polymorphisms that can be maintained in a natural population. *Genetics, Princeton* **55**, 469–81.

TEISSIER, G. (1945). Mecanisme de l' évolution. *La Pensée* **2**, 5–19.

THODAY, J. M. (1953). Components of fitness. *Symp. Soc. exp. Biol.* **7**, 96–113.

—— (1959). Effects of disruptive selection. I. Genetic flexibility. *Heredity, Lond.* **13**, 187–203.

WALLACE, A. R. (1869). *Contributions to the theory of natural selection.* London.

WALLACE, B. (1968). *Topics in population genetics.* Norton, New York.

—— (1970). *Genetic load.* Prentice-Hall, Englewood Cliffs.

WASHBURN, S. L. (1968). Behavior and the origin of man. *Rockefeller University Rev.* (Jan.) 10–19.

13

GENETIC ASPECTS OF THE DEMOGRAPHY OF AMERICAN INDIANS AND ESKIMOS†

Francisco M. Salzano

Genetics and population structure

To the demographer population structure means the age and sex composition of a certain group. These two variables may change as a consequence of births, deaths, and selective migration, the basic demographic parameters. But as was indicated by Schull and MacCluer (1968), geneticists use this expression somewhat differently, including the population's system of mating and its size. According to these authors, all of those variables which shape the biological destiny of a population and contribute to its genetic diversity are a part of its structure.

The size of a group is no doubt important, since the complexity of structure which a population can maintain is ultimately determined by its size. Equally important are the patterns of mating: these are influenced by a series of factors—limitations of choice occur due to age, kinship, religion, caste, tribe, and the occurrence of polygamy. No less restrictive are the distances over which spouses are commonly drawn; and the influence of assortative mating with respect to phenotypes should be considered as well.

Genetic diversity depends also on the patterns of reproduction and mortality of a given group. Several different fertility measures have been developed by demographers, but some of them have no application to genetic models. Important parameters are achieved family size at the completion of the reproductive span and age-specific probabilities of maternity. Still lacking are measures of reproductive performance of individuals of specified genotypes or phenotypes, as well as an assessment of the influence of reproductive compensation on genetic variability. Also little explored is the question of the effect of inheritance of fertility on these variables (Nei and Murata 1966).

Natural selection can be partitioned into two components, one due to fertility and the other to mortality. Crow (1958) developed an index of potential selection in which these two components can be estimated using only demographic data. Mortality influences the genetic composition of a given

† The support of the Conselho Nacional de Pesquisas, Conselho de Pesquisas da Universidade Federal do Rio Grande do Sul, Coordenação do Aperfeiçoamento do Pessoal de Nível Superior, Fundação de Amparo à Pesquisa do Estado do Rio Grande do Sul, and the Wenner-Gren Foundation for Anthropological Research is gratefully acknowledged.

group in two ways: directly, through differential survival of genotypes or phenotypes; and indirectly by changing the demographic characteristics of the total population and thus affecting patterns of mating and reproduction, age structure and population size. Since the patterns of mortality and morbidity are greatly influenced by a series of environmental and social factors, it is important to develop an ecological approach in the analysis of such patterns (Salzano 1970).

Selective migration is a major factor in the determination of the genetic variability of a group. Numerous theoretical models of population movement and its genetic consequences have been suggested. If a population is subdivided into distinct, partially isolated groups, it can be studied using the island model of Wright (1943) or the stepping-stone model of Kimura (1953). Migration within a large, uniformly distributed population can best be investigated using the isolation by distance model of Wright (1943) or the analytical approach of Malécot (1966). Details of these models can be found in Chapter 8 of this book. Neel and Salzano (1967) have shown that the genetic structure of groups of hunters and gatherers may differ in important aspects from the above indicated population models and suggested that this structure follows a pattern designated as the fission-fusion model. At any one time, the bands into which populations of hunters and gatherers are subdivided may appear endogamous. However, as social tensions accumulate, a fission may take place. These fissions generally occur along kinship lines, leading to a highly non-random migration effect. The smaller product of this fission, numbering about 40–60 persons, may join another village, rejoin the original one after some time, or form a new village. Whenever a fusion of groups occurs, interbreeding between members of the original bands happens. This behaviour has important consequences. Instead of individuals, the unit of diffusion is a group of related individuals. Since these are nomadic populations, the geographic distances separating them at a given moment are not very important. And over a period of several generations there should be so much exchange between groups that the entire tribe should be considered as the breeding unit. In the formation of new tribes the composition of the founder group increases the probability that new combinations of gene frequencies will be explored, but, since the entire tribe will be the ultimate breeding unit, the effective population size will usually become such that over a sufficient interval of time deterministic rather than non-deterministic genetic events will control subsequent developments. This structure appears in general to correspond to that visualized by Wright (see, for instance, 1966) as most compatible with rapid and effective evolution.

A fundamental assumption in the Sewall Wright models of population genetics is that the islands in the island model, and the neighbourhoods in the distance model, are of uniform size. This certainly disagrees with the situation in human groups. Roberts (1965) applied three types of distribution to the community sizes observed among the Shilluk of southern Sudan and Hausa-speaking communities of northern Nigeria. The results show significant departures from the negative binomial and Neyman type A contagious distributions, but no appreciable deviation from the log-normal curve. Therefore, it may now be possible to reformulate Sewall Wright's mathematical model of gene frequency change taking into account the logarithmic form of the variation in island size.

Bodmer and Cavalli-Sforza (1968) have developed a theory aimed at predicting the amount of variation to be expected between gene frequencies of a finite number of colonies of different sizes and the correlations between them, with a general migration pattern given in the form of a migration matrix. The major advantage of using migration matrices is that it makes it possible to employ observed migration data in the model, without trying to force the migration pattern into a somewhat inflexible and usually inappropriate model (for further discussion, see Chapter 8 of this book). Going a step further, Ward and Neel (1970) suggested a new index of genetic migration by combining the values obtained through these matrices and the genetic distance between the village of origin of parents and the village of birth of a given child, as estimated by the method of Edwards and Cavalli-Sforza (1964).

A working hypothesis

We can visualize three stages in human evolution: *Stage A* would be represented by hunters and gatherers with incipient agriculture; *Stage B* by more advanced agriculturalists and fishers; and *Stage C* by pastoralists and populations living in densely inhabited areas and industrialized centres. The information available about the population structure of groups living in Stage A is scarce. But, as was indicated in the previous section, this structure may follow the pattern designated by Neel and Salzano (1967) as the fission–fusion model. The structure of populations in Stage B can be better described using the island model of Wright (1943), the stepping-stone model of Kimura (1953), or modified forms of them. They are generally settled, relatively small groups, separated from each other by large areas of unoccupied land. Migration is largely accomplished by individuals or small family units. The relative isolation of these populations should encourage local endogamy to a much larger extent than was possible in Stage A. As population sizes increase and the means of exploiting the environment improve, the isolation among groups diminishes and the tendency is towards a uniform density over a large area. This situation approaches the isolation by distance model of Wright (1943). Although this structure can be considered more typical of groups living in industrialized regions, it is by no means confined to them. The large African tribal populations can probably be best described using this model, as was demonstrated by Roberts (1956, 1965). And it may also have been typical of the great civilizations of the past, such as the groups living under the Inca,

Aztec, and Maya empires. The migratory movements of pastoralists have some peculiarities that set them somewhat apart, but since at least in Africa they group together in large units once a year (see Chapter 15) their genetic structures most closely resemble those of groups in Stage C.

In what follows I will first try to review the archeological and historical information about American Indian and Eskimo populations and then examine the demography of their contemporary groups. The latter are classified, for comparative purposes, into two categories: group A consists predominantly of hunters and gatherers with incipient agriculture, and group B of agriculturists, fishers, and tribes somewhat acculturated. The idea is to verify to what extent the available information permits the differentiation of demographic features typical of these two groups and to determine whether these patterns follow the scheme formulated above.

The demography of American Indians and Eskimos

Archeological and historical data

It is estimated that present-day American Indians and Eskimos number approximately 18 577 000 persons, distributed as follows: 27 000 unmixed Eskimos and Aleuts (Tax, Stanley, Thomas, MacLachan, and Rosenberg 1960; Pericot y Garcia 1962); 550 000 North American Indians (Officer 1965); 8 000 000 Middle American and 10 000 000 South American Indians (Salzano 1968). It is certain that Asiatic populations who came to this continent through the Bering Strait have contributed to a large extent to the formation of this population. The evidence for other routes of entry is inconclusive. There is considerable room for disagreement in relation to many phases of the origin and dispersion of these groups. To Laughlin (1963) the emerging picture for the immediate origin of the Eskimos and Aleuts is that of a Bering platform inhabited by contiguous populations stretching from Hokkaido around to what is now Umnak Island, probably some 10 000 to 15 000 years ago. By that time Palaeo-Indians were already clearly established in South and Middle America. Their separation from the Aleuts and Eskimos was probably ensured by differences in economic adaptation which caused different routes of migration into the New World. The land bridge that connected Siberia and Alaska during early Wisconsin time (some 30 000–11 000 years ago) was more than 1000 miles wide. The ancestral Indians, with their land-based economy, could have crossed the bridge without coming in contact with the Aleuts and Eskimos, mainly adapted to a fishing subsistence pattern.

Despite some uncertainties, we can establish the following tentative time-table for Palaeo-Indian man in America (Cruxent 1968): North America, 15 000–30 000 years; northern South America, 10 000 to 20 000 years; western and southern South America, 8 000 to 14 000 years. The figures for North America are still in doubt, but the experience from South America leads one to believe that new studies will uncover earlier dates.

There is wide divergence in the estimates of the native population of the Americas at the Conquest period. Kroeber (1939) estimated 8 400 000 for the hemisphere; Rosenblat (1945) 13 385 000; Rivet (1924) 40–45 000 000; Sapper (1924), 40–50 000 000; Spinden (1928) 50–70 000 000; and Dobyns (1966) 90 000 000. These differences are due first to distinct opinions about the accuracy of the historical documents available and second to the different methods employed by the authors to obtain their figures. A full discussion of this subject is presented in Dobyns (1966), Thompson (1966), and the pages of *Current Anthropology* following these two articles. Of considerable biological interest are the estimates of depopulation ratios following contact. These ratios vary from place to place and one of the criticisms made in relation to Dobyns' (1966) estimate is that he used a hemisphere-wide historic depopulation rate of 20 to 1, without regard to the completely different ecology of Indian populations located in the various regions of the continent. It is doubtful, for instance, if we can use the same depopulation ratios for tribes in tropical South America and for the technologically much more advanced populations of the Inca empire. Further discussion of these questions can be found in Lipschutz (1966).

Contemporary populations

Age distribution and sex ratio

Table 13.1 presents the data available on Eskimo and American Indian populations concerning these variables. Only seven groups, with 2643 individuals, could be classified in group A, while 33 other populations, with 402 959 persons, were included in group B. Also listed in Table 13.1 are the results of two national censuses, of the Indian populations of Panama and the U.S.A., with a total of 369 012 individuals.

The age interval shown in the table is the one related to persons who have not yet reached the age of reproduction (0–14 years). In the two national censuses the percentage of individuals in this category was respectively 46 and 41 for the Indian populations of Panama and the U.S.A., the combined figure for the two being also 41 per cent. The variability of these percentages in group A tribes ranged from 32 per cent (Yąnomamö) to 52 per cent (Juruna). Pooling the samples from the seven tribes of hunters and gatherers gives an average percentage of 39. In the group B tribes, the variability is even wider. The lowest value, 16 per cent, was observed among a group of 50 Bororo and the highest (55 per cent) among the Galibi and Arawak. Combining the 33 populations, we arrive at a figure identical to the one obtained for the national censuses: 41 per cent. Therefore, if there is a difference between the tribes of groups A and B in relation to this variable it should be small, with the agriculturalists presenting slightly more individuals in this age category than hunters and gatherers.

Information about the sex ratio of all groups is also presented in Table 13.1. The Indian populations of Panama and the U.S.A. show a sex ratio of 103 and 109 respectively, the combined value for the two being 108. This excess of males is expected in populations with a low average age, since more male than female births occur and the differences in mortality favouring the women express themselves more evidently only at older ages. In the seven group A tribes the sex ratios are distributed between 83 (observed among the Kuben-Kran-Kegn) and 120 (obtained among the Kuikuro). It is interesting to mention that the two populations with a sex ratio below 100 are from Cayapo Indians. The overall value, using data from the seven tribes, is 103. As for the 33 group B populations, the sex ratio varied from 81 (obtained among 87 Caingang from São Paulo and 47 Yabarana) to 180, found among 143 Piapoco. Two other populations show a large excess of males: the Muñangong, with a sex ratio of 150 and the Karluk Eskimos with 155. In the latter case Taylor (1966) suggested that the deviation may have been due to differential emigration, especially the marriage of Karluk women to whites. Combining all data of the 33 group B populations gives an overall sex ratio of 108, exactly the same as obtained in the two national censuses mentioned above. The finding of a higher sex ratio among agriculturists as compared to hunters and gatherers is surprising, especially if we consider earlier reports about the value that the latter give to male births, as well as the frequent accounts of the practice of female infanticide among them.

Endogamy and inbreeding

Three populations of hunters and gatherers are listed in Table 13.2 and three in Table 13.3. They are characterized by relatively low rates of admixture (12–16 per cent) and high inbreeding coefficients (0·0037–0·0220). There is a wide variation in the rates of admixture of agriculturalists, fishers, and tribes somewhat acculturated (4–46), at least nine of the eighteen listed showing lower values than those found among the former. The six inbreeding coefficients obtained from group B populations also vary widely (0·000 05–0·0143), showing numbers equivalent to those encountered among hunters and gatherers. The Eskimos, in accordance with their tradition of exogamy, show particularly low inbreeding coefficients (Table 13.3).

Fertility and mortality

Table 13.4 presents the number of livebirths per female over the age of 15 in the populations which are being compared. The average number varied between 3·1 and 4·2 in four populations of hunters and gatherers and between 3·0 and 6·8 in nine groups of agriculturalists, fishers, and tribes somewhat acculturated. The corresponding value obtained from the national census of the Indian population of Panama is 4·4. As can be seen in the table, five of

TABLE 13.1

*Age and sex distribution in one Eskimo and several
American Indian tribes*

Population and source	Per cent aged 0–14	Overall sex ratio	Estimated average age ($\bar{x}\pm s$)	
Group A†				
Yąnomamö, southern Venezuela	32	100	♂	20·8±15·3
(Neel and Chagnon 1968)			♀	23·4±16·4
Urubu, Maranhão, Brazil	41	109		
(Ribeiro 1956)				
Kuben-Kran-Kegn, southern Pará, Brazil	40	83		
(Ribeiro 1956)				
Caiapó, southern Pará and northern Mato	41	88	♂	20·1±15·5
Grosso, Brazil			♀	20·4±16·4
(Salzano, unpublished)				
Juruna, Upper Xingu, Mato Grosso, Brazil	52	107	♂	19·1±16·3
(De Oliveira and Salzano 1969)			♀	16·2±12·4
Kuikuro, Mato Grosso, Brazil	42	120		
(Ribeiro 1956)				
Xavante, Mato Grosso, Brazil	39	115	♂	17·4±13·1
(Neel, Salzano, Junqueira, Keiter, and			♀	18·3±14·2
Maybury-Lewis 1964, Salzano, Neel, and				
Maybury-Lewis 1967)				
Group B‡				
Karluk Eskimos, Kodiak Island, Alaska, U.S.A.	37	155		
(Taylor 1966)				
Papago, southern Arizona, U.S.A.	38	100		
(Niswander, Brown, Iba, Leyshon and				
Workman 1970)				
Seri, Tiburon Island, Mexico	60	96		
(Mazzotti 1934)				
Galibi and Arawak, Littoral, French Guiana	55	101		
(Hurault 1966)				
Oyampi and Emerillon, Oyapok region,	42	109		
French Guiana				
(Hurault 1966)				
Yabarana, Território Amazonas, Venezuela	47	81		
(Fuchs 1967)				
Curipaco, Território Amazonas, Venezuela	40	92		
(Fuchs 1967)				
Piapoco, Território Amazonas and Bolivar,	53	180		
Venezuela				
(Fuchs 1967)				
Makiritare, Bolivar and Território Amazonas,	41	111		
Venezuela				
(Fuchs 1967)				
Muñangong, Bolivar, Venezuela	34	150		
(Fuchs 1967)				
Taurepan (*Pemón*), Bolivar, Venezuela	53	96		
(Fuchs 1967)				
Camaracoto (*Pemón*), Bolivar, Venezuela	54	85		
(Fuchs 1967)				
Arecuna (*Pemón*), Bolivar, Venezuela	47	108		
(Fuchs 1967)				
Shirianá (*Yąnomamö*), Bolivar, Venezuela	40	119		
(Fuchs 1967)				

TABLE 13.1—*continued*

Age and sex distribution in one Eskimo and several American Indian tribes

Population and source	Per cent aged 0–14	Overall sex ratio	Estimated average age ($\bar{x} \pm s$)	
Sapé, Bolivar, Venezuela (Fuchs 1967)	41	120		
Piaroa, Território Amazonas, Bolivar and Apure, Venezuela (Fuchs 1967)	44	122		
Warao, Território Delta Amacuro, Monagas and Sucre, Venezuela (Fuchs 1967)	45	103		
Cariña, Anzoategui, Venezuela (Fuchs 1967)	47	111		
Parintintin, Amazonas, Brazil (Ribeiro 1956)	20	115		
Canela, Maranhão, Brazil (Ribeiro 1956)	35	111		
Tenetehara, Maranhão, Brazil (Ribeiro 1956)	45	103		
Gorotire, southern Pará, Brazil (Ribeiro 1956)	41	107		
Carajá, Mato Grosso, Brazil (Ribeiro 1956)	44	95		
Bororo, Mato Grosso, Brazil (Ribeiro 1956)	16	121		
Terena, southern Mato Grosso, Brazil (Salzano and De Oliveira 1970)	45	108	♂ ♀	21·6±20·1 19·3±17·2
Kadiweu, southern Mato Grosso, Brazil (Ribeiro 1956)	39	124		
Caingang, São Paulo, Brazil (Ribeiro 1956)	45	81		
Xokleng, Santa Catarina, Brazil (Ribeiro 1956)	46	110		
Caingang, Rio Grande do Sul and Santa Catarina, Brazil (Salzano 1961, 1964)	39	101	♂ ♀	22·7±18·5 21·0±16·4
Quechua, Hacienda Vicos, Peru (Alers 1965)	40	89		
Cashinahua, southeastern Peru (Johnston, Kensinger, Jantz, and Walker 1969)	29	112		
Macá, Fray Bartolomé de las Casas, Paraguay (Salzano, Moreno, Palatnik, and Gershowitz 1970)	28	115	♂ ♀	27·5±20·8 26·3±19·5
Yámana, Ona, and Alacaluf, Tierra del Fuego, Chile (Damianovic 1948)	45	107		
General				
Mainly *Guaymi, Cuna, and Chocó*, Panama (National census 1950)	46	103		
Several, U.S.A. (National census 1950)	41	109		

† Predominantly hunters and gatherers with incipient agriculture.

‡ Agriculturalists, fishers, and tribes somewhat acculturated. Some populations of the tribes listed by Fuchs (1967) which live in more inaccessible places could be placed in Group A, but since his results are based on Venezuela's 1950 census it is believed that only relatively acculturated Indians have been included.

TABLE 13.2

Rates of admixture in several American Indian and one Eskimo population

Population	Source	Rate of admixture[a] per cent	Sample of breeding population
Group A[b]			
Cubeo, Uaupes River, Colombia[c]	Goldman (1948)	12	80
Xavante, Mato Grosso, Brazil	Salzano, Neel, and Maybury-Lewis (1967)	16	304
Juruna, Mato Grosso, Brazil	De Oliveira and Salzano (1969)	16	64
Group B[d]			
Karluk Eskimos, Kodiak island, Alaska, U.S.A.	Taylor (1966)	29	52
Clallam, Washington, U.S.A.[c,e]	Hulse (1955)	46	114
Havasupai, Arizona, U.S.A.	Lasker (1954)[f]	8	134
Apaches, Arizona, U.S.A.[c]			
Eastern Band (1800–1936)	Kraus and White (1956)	20	188
Eastern Band (1930–54)	Kraus and White (1956)	19	266
Western Band (1800–1936)	Kraus and White (1956)	12	450
Western Band (1930–54)	Kraus and White (1956)	11	188
Cibecue (1930–1954)	Kraus and White (1956)	11	64
Ramah Navaho, New Mexico, U.S.A.	Spuhler and Kluckhohn (1953)	6	634
Totonac, Tajín, Mexico	Lasker (1954)[f]	29	354
Warao, Delta Amacuro, Venezuela[c]	Osborn (1964)	14	118
Aymara, Peru[c]			
Town of Chucuito proper	Tschopik (1946)	6	366
Qota ayllu, Chucuito	Tschopik (1946)	8	52
Town of Ichu	Tschopik (1946)	5	140
Cashinahua, Coronel Portillo, Peru[c]	Johnston, Kensinger, Jantz, and Walker (1969)	7	152
Macá, Fray Bartolomé de las Casas, Paraguay	Salzano, Moreno, Palatnik and Gershowitz (1970)	4	182
Terena, Mato Grosso, Brazil	Salzano and de Oliveira (1970)	30	354
Caingang, Rio Grande do Sul and S. Catarina, Brazil	Salzano (1961, 1964)	16	933

a. Ratio of the number of immigrants to the total breeding population (Lasker 1952).

b. Predominantly hunters and gatherers with incipient agriculture.

c. It is not known if all marriages listed were fertile; if they were not this would introduce a source of error in these estimates.

d. Agriculturalists, fishers and tribes somewhat acculturated.

e. Marriages contracted during the five generations preceding 1924.

f. Only the populations listed by Lasker (1954) for which numerical data were obtained and could be interpreted with some degree of assurance are presented here. Mestizo groups were excluded.

TABLE 13.3

*Mean inbreeding coefficients in two Eskimo and several
American Indian populations*

Population	Source	Inbreeding coefficient[a]	Number of matings
Group A[b]			
Wayana, Upper Maroni, French Guiana	Sutter (1966)	0·0108	39
Juruna, Upper Xingu, Mato Grosso, Brazil	De Oliveira and Salzano (1969)	0·0220	22
Xavante, Mato Grosso, Brazil	Salzano, Neel, and Maybury-Lewis (1967)	0·0037	257
Group B[c]			
Eskimos, Thulé, Greenland	Sutter and Tabah (1956)	0·0002–0·0030[d]	
Karluk Eskimos, Kodiak island, Alaska, U.S.A.	Taylor (1966)	0·00005	72
Ramah Navaho, New Mexico, U.S.A.	Spuhler and Kluckhohn (1953)	0·0066	316
Hopi, Arizona, U.S.A.	Woolf and Dukepoo (1969)	0·0080	388
Emerillon, Oyapok region, French Guiana	Sutter (1966)	0·0143	81
Caingang, Rio Grande do Sul and S. Catarina, Brazil	Salzano (1961, 1964)	0·0050	630

a. The coefficient of inbreeding of one individual (F) may be defined as the probability that a person is not only homozygous at a given locus, but that the two alleles are 'identical' in the sense that they were both derived from an allele present in a certain ancestor. The mean coefficient of inbreeding of a population is obtained by averaging the value for non-inbred individuals ($F = 0$) with the values for groups of different degrees of relatedness.

b. Predominantly hunters and gatherers with incipient agriculture.

c. Agriculturalists, fishers, and tribes somewhat acculturated.

d. Minimum and maximum estimates after an analysis through a mecanographic method of all relationships of the 302 members of this population.

the nine values observed among group B tribes are higher than those of hunters and gatherers.

Average numbers of liveborn offspring in completed sibships are also shown in Table 13.4. The three values of group A tribes varied between 2·6 and 5·3, while the seven from agriculturalists, fishers, and tribes somewhat acculturated ranged from 2·1 to 8·8. The figure obtained in the national census of the Indian population of Panama was 6·2. More than half of the averages obtained among group B tribes are again higher than those of populations of hunters and gatherers. Noteworthy are the high variances observed by Taylor (1966) among 12 Karluk Eskimo and by Erickson, Nerlove, Creger, and Romney (1970) in 52 Tzeltal women.

Table 13.4 also shows the average number of surviving offspring per female over the age of 15. The four means observed in group A tribes varied between

TABLE 13.4

Fertility and mortality information from one Eskimo and several American Indian populations

Population	Source	Fertility												Mortality	
		Offspring per female over 15						Offspring per completed sibship						Deaths before 15	
		Livebirths			Surviving			Livebirths			Surviving				
		N	x̄	s_x̄	N	x̄	s_x̄	N	x̄	s_x̄	N	x̄	s_x̄	N	Per cent
Group A[a]															
Yąnomamö, southern Venezuela	Neel and Chagnon (1968)	—	—	—	—	—	—	64	2·6	0·24	64	2·2	0·23	?	15
Xingu Indians, Mato Grosso, Brazil	Ranke (1898)	86	4·2	—	86	1·6	—	24	5·3	—	—	—	—	360	62
Kuikuro, Mato Grosso, Brazil	Ribeiro (1956)	30	3·7	0·5	30	1·5	—	—	—	—	—	—	—	109	58
Juruna, Upper Xingu, Mato Grosso, Brazil	De Oliveira and Salzano (1969)	13	3·2	0·8	13	2·9	0·7	—	—	—	—	—	—	42	9
Xavante, Mato Grosso, Brazil	Salzano, Neel, and Maybury-Lewis (1967)	170	3·1	0·2	160	2·0	0·1	60	4·7	0·32	60	3·1	0·26	606	35

Group B[b]

Location	Reference														
Karluk Eskimos, Kodiak Island, Alaska, U.S.A.	Taylor (1966)	31	5·0	—	—	—	—	—	12	8·8	1·40	—	—	—	—	—
Seminole, Florida, U.S.A.	Pollitzer, Rucknagel, Tashian, Shreffler, Leyshon, Namboodiri, and Elston (1970)	113	3·7	—	119	2·9	—	—	—	—	—	50	3·9	—	—	—
Ramah Navaho, New Mexico, U.S.A.	Spuhler (1962)	—	—	—	—	—	—	?	2·1	—	—	—	—	—	?	27
Seri, Tiburón Island, Mexico	Mazzotti (1934)	35	6·8	0·5	35	2·7	0·3	—	—	—	—	—	—	—	239	61
Tzeltal, Aguacatenango, Mexico	Erickson, Nerlove, Creger, and Romney (1970)	—	—	—	—	—	—	52	6·9	0·52	—	—	—	—	—	—
Cashinahua, Coronel Portillo, Peru	Johnston, Kensinger, Jantz, and Walker (1969)	35	4·0	—	58	2·2	0·2	—	—	—	—	—	—	141	41
Macá, Fray Bartolomé de la Casas, Paraguay	Salzano, Moreno, Palatnik, and Gershowitz (1970)	106	3·4	0·2	102	2·2	0·1	53	3·6	0·23	51	2·4	0·15	376	36
Fulnió, Águas Belas, Pernambuco, Brazil	Vianna (1966)	90	5·9	—	90	3·1	—	52	7·0	—	52	3·4	—	533	47
Bororo, Mato Grosso, Brazil	Baldus (1937)	28	3·0	0·5	28	2·1	0·3	11	3·5	0·71	11	2·4	0·53	85	32
Terena, Mato Grosso, Brazil	Salzano and De Oliveira (1970)	182	4·8	0·2	182	3·8	0·1	81	5·5	0·33	81	4·2	0·24	1009	21
Caingang, Rio Grande do Sul and S. Catarina, Brazil	Salzano (1961, 1964)	531	4·5	0·1	503	2·8	0·1	—	—	—	—	—	—	2563	39
General Indian population of Panama	National Census (1950)	9324	4·4	—	—	—	—	940	6·2	—	—	—	—	—	—

[a] Predominantly hunters and gatherers with incipient agriculture.
[b] Agriculturalists, fishers, and tribes somewhat acculturated.

1·5 and 2·9, and in eight group B populations the extreme numbers were respectively 2·1 and 3·8. In general, hunters and gatherers may have lower means, since only the Juruna average can be included in the range of group B values. As was mentioned by De Oliveira and Salzano (1969) that tribe may be atypical in this regard, since they are recovering from a previous extreme reduction in population size and therefore putting a premium on high fertility and low mortality. As far as surviving offspring in completed sibships are concerned the two means of hunters and gatherers are also at the lower end of the range of group B tribes.

There is wide variation in the percentage of individuals dying before the age of reproduction not only in group A tribes (9–62 per cent) but in populations of agriculturalists, fishers, and somewhat acculturated tribes as well (21–61 per cent—see Table 13.4). With the exception of two values observed among the Juruna and Yạnomamö the two ranges overlap.

Breeding size, effective size, and selection intensity

The relative proportions of the breeding and effective sizes to the total population seem to be similar in the two groups of tribes which are being compared (breeding sizes: 38–46 per cent, effective sizes: 21–46 per cent—see Table 13.5). As for the index of potential selection (Crow 1958) the two populations of hunters and gatherers studied show values around one. More variation is observed in the numbers obtained among agriculturalists, fishers, and tribes somewhat acculturated. The Terena show a very low index (0·63), the Caingang a number a little higher than one (1·29), and the Ramah Navaho an extreme value of 2·53. This latter high index is mainly due to fertility differences.

Discussion

Before considering if the data reviewed here are in accordance with the working hypothesis presented above, it is important to reiterate the need for new theoretical and empirical studies. A whole book has recently been published about hunting and gathering populations (Lee and De Vore 1968). It gives a wealth of data on economics, social and territorial organization, marriage rules, and other behavioural traits, as well as a section on prehistoric hunters and gatherers. But the kind of quantitative demographic information needed for biological interpretations is unfortunately very small. The question of range size and population density, for instance, is critical in any treatment of genetic problems by the isolation-by-distance approach. It is difficult, however, to assess the reliability of previous estimates and there are practically no recent attempts to calculate these variables in a rigorous way among American tribes.

Ward and Neel (1970) have recently emphasized the problems which arise

TABLE 13.5

Some genetic parameters derived from the demographic data

Population	Source	Breeding size[a] N	Per cent	Effective size[b] N	Per cent	Selection intensity[c] I_m	I_f	I_f/p_s	I
Group A[d]									
Yąnomamö, southern Venezuela	Neel and Chagnon (1968)	—	—	—	—	0·22	—	0·66	0·88
Xavante, Mato Grosso, Brazil	Salzano, Neel, and Maybury-Lewis (1967)	304	46	270	41	0·49	—	0·41	0·90
Juruna, Mato Grosso, Brazil	De Oliveira and Salzano (1969)	22	38	12	21	—	—	—	—
Group B[e]									
Ramah Navaho, New Mexico, U.S.A.	Spuhler (1962)	—	—	—	—	0·37	1·57	2·16	2·53
Cashinahua, Coronel Portillo, Peru	Johnston, Kensinger, Jantz, and Walker (1969)	87	42	68	33	—	—	—	—
Macá, Fray Bartolomé de las Casas, Paraguay	Salzano, Moreno, Palatnik, and Gershowitz (1970)	182	39	214	46	0·56	0·21	0·32	0·88
Terena, Mato Grosso, Brazil	Salzano and De Oliveira (1970)	362	39	222	24	0·27	0·28	0·36	0·63
Caingang, Rio Grande do Sul and S. Catarina, Brazil	Salzano (1961, 1963, 1964)	955	40	597	25	0·69	0·35	0·59	1·28

a. Breeding size = The number of individuals who leave progeny.

b. Effective size = An ideal population with N individuals who mate at random, half males and half females, in whom the variance of the random deviation of the gene frequencies is $q(1-q)/2N$ and the rate of decay of heterozygosis is $1/2N$. The size of the effective population is, therefore, a parameter of great genetic value since it permits comparisons between communities with different demographic structures in the context of population genetics theory.

c. $I_m = p_d/p_s$, where p_d = premature deaths and p_s = proportion surviving or $1-p_d$; $I_f = V_f/\bar{x}^2$, where V_f = variance in offspring number in completed sibships and $\bar{x}$ = mean number of livebirths per woman who completed her reproduction; $I = I_m + I_f/p_s$ = Index of opportunity for selection or potential selection; its genetic significance and usefulness are proportional to the genetic component in the phenomena on which it is based (see Crow 1958).

d. Predominantly hunters and gatherers with incipient agriculture.

e. Agriculturalists, fishers, and tribes somewhat acculturated.

when we equate geographic distance with genetic migration. Important limitations of present models were also mentioned by Morton (1969). Despite possible errors, however, Roisenberg and Morton (1970) calculated the mean coefficient of kinship of Central and South American Indians using blood-group data. They arrived at a figure of 0·0253, similar to the estimate of the mean coefficient of inbreeding (0·02–0·03) that Neel and Salzano (1967) supposed would give the best approximation to the situation among the Xavante. It is important to point out, however, that the family histories in this tribe provided a much lower figure (0·0037). The whole question of obtaining estimates of population inbreeding coefficients from raw field data has been thoroughly discussed in Allen (1965) and Morgan and Spuhler (1965).

The present genetic diversity of American Indians and Eskimos is a result of several factors. In the first place, the number and nature of the founder populations are no doubt important. We should, therefore, be aware of the uncertainties which exist concerning the groups that first arrived at our continent and the time of their arrival. Present 'reasonable' estimates differ by a factor of two. Wider divergence exists concerning the number of our native population at the Conquest period. Here the estimates vary by a factor of ten! These discrepancies are in part due to differing calculations of the depopulation ratios that followed contact, an important factor also in explaining the present level of genetic diversity.

The present review clearly shows the scarcity of data presently at hand for American Indian hunters and gatherers. While for the simpler tabulation of age and sex we have information on seven populations, for other comparisons the data available are restricted to two to five groups. However, the results suggest that populations of agriculturalists may perhaps contain a larger number of individuals who have not yet reached the age of reproduction; they are more isolated and show higher fertility. No distinction can be made in relation to the mortality indices, although agriculturalists show on average a higher number of surviving offspring in complete and incomplete sibships. The relative proportions of the breeding and effective sizes compared to the total populations seem to be about the same in the two groups. At least two of the four indices of total selection intensity calculated are higher among agriculturalists. These results, in a general way, are in accordance with the working hypothesis presented earlier in this paper.

The data on the sex ratio are, as was indicated before, surprising since *a priori* one would expect a higher sex ratio among hunters and gatherers than among agriculturalists, fishers, and tribes somewhat acculturated. In this connection, it is interesting to mention that eight of the fifteen Central Australian tribes listed by Meggitt (1968) showed a sex ratio lower than 100.

A final word should be said as a warning against easy generalizations. The fact that two groups rely on the same subsistence pattern and may have other demographic features in common does not necessarily mean that they are being subjected to similar selective agents. Dunn (1968) has recently prepared a list of the epidemiological factors which are acting in simple and complex ecosystems. Differences can be observed in the number of species of animals and plants available to a given individual, the kind and number of parasitic and infectious diseases that may afflict it, the number of potential vectors, intermediate hosts, and alternative hosts for parasites and infectious agents, factors of transmission and immunity, etc. The hunter and gatherer is an element in an ecosystem and cannot isolate himself from his environment. His relationship to the land, its flora and fauna, and other members of his species is intimate. Therefore, even if their populations present several characteristics in common, we should avoid considering them as a homogeneous cultural-genetic-ecologic unity. The same would apply, of course, to groups relying on other subsistence patterns, such as agriculturalists, fishers, or pastoralists. Even if they became more independent from their environment, their social and cultural features could be sufficiently different to warrant separation in distinct categories.

REFERENCES

ALERS, J. O. (1965). Population and development in a Peruvian community. *J. Int.–am. Stud.* 7, 423–48.

ALLEN, G. (1965). Random and non-random inbreeding. *Eugen. Q.* 12, 181–98.

BALDUS, H.(1937). *Ensaios de Etnologia Brasileira.* Companhia Editora Nacional, São Paulo.

BODMER, W. F. and CAVALLI-SFORZA, L. L. (1968). A migration matrix model for the study of random genetic drift. *Genetics, Princeton* 59, 565–92.

CROW, J. F. (1958). Some possibilities for measuring selection intensities in man. *Hum. Biol.* 30, 1–13.

CRUXENT, J. M. (1968). Theses for meditation on the origin and distribution of man in South America. In *Biomedical challenges presented by the American Indian.* Pan American Health Organization Scientific Publication No. 165, Washington, D.C.

DAMIANOVIC, J. (1948). Realidad sanitaria de la población indígena de la zona austral antártica. *Rev. chil. Hig. Med. prev.* 10, 3–17.

DE OLIVEIRA, A. E. and SALZANO, F. M. (1969). Genetic implications of the demography of Brazilian Juruna Indians. *Social Biol.* 16, 209–15.

DOBYNS, H. F. (1966). Estimating aboriginal American populations. 1. An appraisal of techniques with a new hemispheric estimate. *Curr. Anthrop.* 7, 395–416.

DUNN, F. L. (1968). Epidemiological factors: health and disease in hunter-gatherers. In *Man the hunter* (eds. R. B. Lee and I. De Vore). Aldine Press, Chicago.

EDWARDS, A. W. F. and CAVALLI-SFORZA, L. L. (1964). Reconstruction of evolutionary trees. In *Phenetic and phylogenetic classification. Publs Systematics Ass.* 6, 67–76.

ERICKSON, R. P., NERLOVE, S., CREGER, W. P., and ROMNEY, A. K. (1970). Comparison of genetic and anthropological interpretations of population isolates in Aguacatenango, Chiapas, Mexico. *Am. J. phys. Anthrop.* 32, 105–20.

FUCHS, H. (1967). Urgent tasks in eastern Venezuela. *Bull. int. Comm. Urgent Anthrop. Ethnol. Res.* 9, 69–98.

GOLDMAN, I. (1948). Tribes of the Uaupes-Caqueta region. In *Handbook of South American Indians* (ed. J. H. Steward), Vol. 3. Smithsonian Institution, Bureau of American Ethnology Bulletin No. 143, Washington, D.C.

HULSE, F. S. (1955). Blood-types and mating patterns among Northwest Coast Indians. *SWest. J. Anthrop.* 11, 93–104.

HURAULT, J. (1966). La population des indiens de Guyane Française. Troisième article. *Population, Paris* 21, 333–54.

JOHNSTON, F. E., KENSINGER, K. M., JANTZ, R. L., and WALKER, G. F. (1969). The population structure of the Peruvian Cashinahua: demographic, genetic and cultural interrelationships. *Hum. Biol.* **41**, 29–41.

KIMURA, M. (1953). 'Stepping-stone' model of population. *Ann. Rep. natn. Inst. Genetics Japan* **3**, 62–3.

KRAUS, B. S. and WHITE, C. B. (1956). Micro-evolution in a human population: a study of social endogamy and blood type distribution among the western Apache. *Am. Anthrop.* **58**, 1017–43.

KROEBER, A. L. (1939). *Cultural and natural areas of native North America.* University of California Publications in American Archeology and Ethnology No. 38, Berkeley.

LASKER, G. W. (1952). Mixture and genetic drift in ongoing human evolution. *Am. Anthrop.* **54**, 433–6.

—— (1954). Human evolution in contemporary communities. *SWest. J. Anthrop.* **10**, 353–65.

LAUGHLIN, W. S. (1963). Eskimos and Aleuts: their origins and evolution. *Science, N.Y.* **142**, 633–45.

LEE, R. B. and DE VORE, I. (eds.) (1968). *Man the hunter.* Aldine Press, Chicago.

LIPSCHUTZ, A. (1966). La despoblación de las Indias después de la Conquista. *Am. Indígena* **26**, 229–47.

MALÉCOT, G. (1966). *Probabilités et hérédité.* Institut National d'Études Démographiques, Presses Universitaires de France, Paris.

MAZZOTTI, L. (1934). Informe general sobre las condiciones sanitarias de la tribu Seri o Kunkaak. *Salubridad* **5**, 23–39.

MEGGITT, M. J. (1968). 'Marriage classes' and demography in Central Australia. In *Man the hunter* (eds. R. B. Lee and I. De Vore). Aldine Press, Chicago.

MORGAN, K. and SPUHLER, J. N. (1965). Inbreeding in small human populations. *Eugen. Q.* **12**, 204–8.

MORTON, N. E. (1969). Human population structure. *Rev. Genet.* **3**, 53–74.

NEEL, J. V. and CHAGNON, N. A. (1968). The demography of two tribes of primitive, relatively unacculturated American Indians. *Proc. natn. Acad. Sci. U.S.A.* **59**, 680–9.

—— and SALZANO, F. M. (1967). Further studies on the Xavante Indians. X. Some hypotheses-generalizations resulting from these studies. *Am. J. hum. Genet.* **19**, 554–74.

—— —— JUNQUEIRA, P. C., KEITER, F., and MAYBURY-LEWIS, D. (1964). Studies on the Xavante Indians of the Brazilian Mato Grosso. *Am. J. hum. Genet.* **16**, 52–140.

NEI, M. and MURATA, M. (1966). Effective population size when fertility is inherited. *Genet. Res. Camb.* **8**, 257–60.

NISWANDER, J. D., BROWN, K. S., IBA, B. Y., LEYSHON, W. C., and WORKMAN, P. L. (1970). Population studies on south-western Indian tribes. I. History, culture and genetics of the Papago. *Am. J. hum. Genet.* **22**, 7–23.

OFFICER, J. E. (1965). The role of the United States government in Indian acculturation and assimilation. *Anuário Indig.* **25**, 73–86.

OSBORN, H. (1964). Estructura familiar de un clan de guaraunos. *Antropológica* **13**, 11–29.

PERICOT Y GARCIA, L. (1962). *America Indigena. I. El Hombre Americano—Los Pueblos de America.* Salvat Editores, Barcelona.

POLLITZER, W. S., RUCKNAGEL, D., TASHIAN, R., SHREFFLER, D. C., LEYSHON, W. C., NAMBOODIRI, K., and ELSTON, R. C. (1970). The Seminole Indians of Florida: morphology and serology. *Am. J. phys. Anthrop.* **32**, 65–82.

RANKE, K. E. (1898). Beobachtungen über Bevölkerungsstand und Bevölkerungsbewegung bei Indianern Central-Brasiliens. *Korresp Bl. dt. Ges. Anthrop.* **29**, 123–34.

RIBEIRO, D. (1956). Convívio e contaminação. Efeitos dissociativos da depopulaçào provocada por epidemias em grupos indígenas. *Sociologia, São Paulo* **18**, 3–50.

RIVET, P. (1924). Langues americaines. In *Les langues du monde* (eds. A. Meillet and M. Cohen). Societé de Linguistique, Paris.

ROBERTS, D. F. (1956). Some genetic implications of nilotic demography. *Acta genet. Statist. med.* **6**, 446–52.

—— (1965). Assumption and fact in anthropological genetics. *Jl. R. anthrop. Inst.* **95**, 87–103.

ROISENBERG, I. and MORTON, N. E. (1970). Population structure of blood groups in Central and South American Indians. *Am. J. phys. Anthrop.* **32**, 373–6.

ROSENBLAT, A. (1945). *La Poblacion Indígena de América desde 1492 hasta la Actualidad.* Institución Cultural Española, Buenos Aires.

SALZANO, F. M. (1961). Studies on the Caingang Indians. I. Demography. *Hum. Biol.* **33**, 110–30.

—— (1963). Selection intensity in Brazilian Caingang Indians. *Nature, Lond.* **199**, 514.

—— (1964). Demographic studies on Indians from Santa Catarina, Brazil. *Acta Genet. Med. Gemell.* **13**, 278–94.

—— (1968). Survey of the unacculturated Indians of Central and South America. In: *Biomedical challenges presented by the American Indian.* Pan American Health Organization Scientific Publication No. 165, Washington, D.C.

—— (ed.) (1970). *The ongoing evolution of Latin-American populations.* Thomas, Springfield.

—— and DE OLIVEIRA, R. (1970). Genetic aspects of the demography of Brazilian Terena Indians. *Social Biol.* **17**, 217–23.

—— NEEL, J. V., and MAYBURY-LEWIS, D. (1967). Further studies on the Xavante Indians. I. Demographic data on two additional villages: genetic structure of the tribe. *Am. J. hum. Genet.* **19**, 463–89.

—— MORENO, R., PALATNIK, M., and GERSHOWITZ, H. (1970). Demography and H-Le[a] salivary secretion of the Macá Indians of Paraguay. *Am. J. phys. Anthrop.* **33**, 383–88.

SAPPER, K. (1924). Die Zahl und die Volksdichte der indianischen Bevölkerung in Amerika von der Conquista und in der Gegenwart. *Proc. XXI Int. Congr. American.* **1**, 95–104.

SCHULL, W. J. and MCCLUER, J. W. (1968). Human genetics: structure of population. *A. Rev. Genet.* **2**, 279–304.

SPINDEN, H. J. (1928). The population of ancient America. *Geogr. Rev.* **18**, 641–60.

SPUHLER, J. N. (1962). Empirical studies on quantitative human genetics. In: *Proc. U.N. W.H.O. Seminar on the use of vital and health statistics for genetic and radiation studies.* United Nations, New York.

—— and KLUCKHOHN, C. (1953). Inbreeding coefficients of the Ramah Navaho population. *Hum. Biol.* **25**, 295–317.

SUTTER, J. (1966). Étude sur la consanguinité des indiens Emerillon et Wayana. *Population, Paris* **21**, 355–6.

—— and TABAH, L. (1956). Méthode mécanographique pour établir la généalogie d'une population. Application à l'étude des esquimaux polaires. *Population, Paris* **11**, 507–30.

TAX, S., STANLEY, S., THOMAS, R. K., MACLACHAN, B., and ROSENBERG, M. (1960). *Map of the North American Indians. 1950 distribution of descendants of the aboriginal population of Alaska, Canada, and the United States.* Department of Anthropology, University of Chicago.

TAYLOR, K. I. (1966). A demographic study of Karluk, Kodiak island, Alaska, 1962–4. *Arctic Anthrop.* **3**, 211–40.

THOMPSON, H. P. (1966). Estimating aboriginal American population. 2. A technique using anthropological and biological data. *Curr. Anthrop.* **7**, 417–49.

TSCHOPIK, H., Jr (1946). The Aymara. In *Handbook of South American Indians* (ed. J. H. Steward), Vol. **2**. Smithsonian Institution, Bureau of American Ethnology Bulletin No. 143, Washington, D.C.

VIANNA, M. DE C. (1966). *Aspectos sócio-econômicos e sánitarios dos Fulni-ô de Águas Belas-Pernambuco.* SUDENE, Recife.

WARD, R. H. and NEEL, J. V. (1970). Gene frequencies and microdifferentiation among the Makiritare Indians. IV. A comparison of a genetic network with ethnohistory and migration matrices; a new index of genetic migration. *Am. J. hum. Genet.* **22**, 538–61.

WOOLF, C. M. and DUKEPOO, F. C. (1969). Hopi Indians, inbreeding and albinism. *Science, N.Y.* **164**, 30–7.

WRIGHT, S. (1943). Isolation by distance. *Genetics, Princeton* **28**, 114–38.

—— (1966). Polyallelic random drift in relation to evolution. *Proc. natn. Acad. Sci. U.S.A.* **55**, 1074–81.

14

TRIBAL SOCIAL ORGANIZATION AND GENETIC MICRODIFFERENTIATION†

NAPOLEON A. CHAGNON

Introduction

WITH the development of agriculture some 10 000 years ago in the Old World, and even more recently in the New, many human populations were dramatically transformed from tribal society to more advanced forms of social organization such as the chiefdom, confederacy, city, nation, and ultimately, the empire. Small communities of farmers, those who had taken the first halting and uncertain steps towards an agricultural way of life, were irresistably swept up by the powerful forces of the Agricultural Revolution and their population structure was transformed forever. From that time onward, the adaptability of their cultural system in a field of competing cultural systems would shape their biological destinies in a way that the tribal design could not. Their numbers and significance thereafter hinged as much on cultural inventions and chance association with these inventions as on natural selection. Irrespective of their biological attributes or adaptedness, time after time, place after place, millennium after millennium, more advanced forms of society replaced, absorbed, exterminated, or transformed the myriad of cultural congeners on their periphery, peoples who represented the attenuated socio-biological systems whence they themselves evolved. So powerful and encompassing were these socio-cultural events on human biology that it is estimated that the present racial composition of the world's major population blocs developed in the last 1 per cent of human history (Hulse 1955). That is to say, because of a chance association of *some* populations with major technological advance, these populations grew at a rate vastly higher than that characterizing the growth of those who were not at the foci of such technical developments.

For 500 000 years or longer, humans everywhere organized themselves and reproduced within the context of a tribal society. The tribal social design is perhaps the most successful—and certainly the oldest—form of human organization known. Much of our present biological nature as populations emerged in the Tribal Epoch of man; yet we know precious little about its directive

† The field research on which this article is based was sponsored by N.I.M.H. (1964–66), A.E.C. (1967, 1968, 1969), Wenner-Gren Foundation (1969), and N.S.F. (1970).

influence on the biological processes. So successful was the tribal design that it persists to this day in many remote areas and in some cases holds its own against the competitive pressures of politically organized States. But it is soon to pass, and with it, any hope of estimating its effect on man's biological evolution. Those tribesmen left today reflect in varying ways the cultural condition of man prior to and during the formative stages of the Agricultural

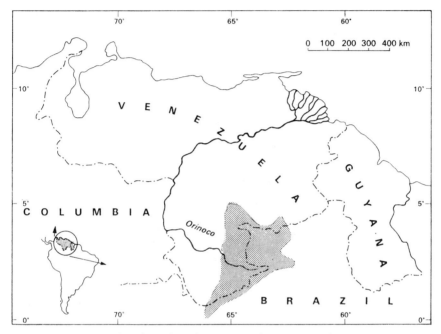

FIG. 14.1. Location of Yạnomamö in South America.

Revolution. Some, while maintaining their cultural and social characteristics intact, are no longer suitable for study from a biological or demographic perspective. But there are others, located in wild, remote, and unpenetrated parts of the world, where it is yet possible to study the relationship between perhaps man's most enduring social type and some of the biological consequences of it. In a few areas, it is still so successful that tribesmen continue to expand into unpopulated regions, oblivious of the changed state of nature elsewhere, unaware that their adaptation is soon to come to an end.

This communication is an attempt to explore some of the relationships between selected aspects of the tribal design and the systematic effects they have on human genetic variability, using the Yạnomamö Indians of Venezuela and Brazil as an example (Fig. 14.1). The Yạnomamö, like tribesmen everywhere, are organized into small communities, in this case, villages. But unlike most remaining tribes, the Yạnomamö are still a sovereign people and retain their aboriginal warfare pattern. This is particularly important, for most tribal institutions are structured in such a way that they make sense only in a political milieu that includes, if not actual warfare, the threat thereof. Marshall Sahlins has developed this point effectively and persuasively in his excellent booklet on tribal culture (Sahlins 1968). I will focus on those sociocultural processes that lead to village fissioning and migration, showing how they may lead in some cases, to genetic microdifferentiation.

The Yąnomamö

The Yąnomamö Indians, a group of tropical forest slash-and-burn cultivators, number some 10 000 to 15 000 people. They are divided into approximately 125 widely scattered villages in southern Venezuela and northern Brazil. Many of their villages have yet to be seen by outsiders and are located in the remote branches and headwaters of essentially unexplored rivers.

There is considerable variation in the tribe, in a cultural, linguistic, and biological sense. Linguistically, they are not yet convincingly identified as being related to any of the well-studied linguistic stocks of South America, although there are tentative classifications based on the existing and inadequate data (Greenberg 1960). Their language is subdivided into at least five dialects as shown in Fig. 14.2. This map is tentative and based as much on my subjective reaction to the relative linguistic difficulties I ran into as I moved from area to area as it is on the few meaningful linguistic publications (Migliazza and Grimes 1961, Borgman and Cue 1963, Borgman, Cue, Albright, Seeley, and Grimes 1965, Albright 1965, Migliazza 1967). Extensive discussions with Ernest Migliazza, a linguist familiar with this language, also served as a guide. As is apparent in this map, the distribution of the population is not continuous. Some groups of Yąnomamö, those on the east and north-east extension of the tribe, are geographically separated from the main body of the tribe and are presumably differentiating biologically as a consequence. How this process of geographical separation works will be shown below.

Materially, the Yąnomamö are rather uniform in terms of actual culture-content—and rather poor (Zerries 1964, Becher 1960). On the other hand, there is considerable social variation, an apparent response to the intensity of inter-village warfare (Chagnon 1968a, b, c). Briefly, the warfare pattern is most intense at the tribal centre and gradually lessens as one approaches the periphery (Chagnon 1968a, c). However, the intensity of warfare does not seem to diminish at a constant rate in all directions from the centre: villages on the south and south-western periphery seem to be more involved in warfare than do those on the north and north-eastern periphery. I suspect that this cline reflects the fact that the former villages have migrated from the more warlike centre in very recent times and still have not readjusted to their new situation. At the south-western periphery, many groups are so far away from old enemies that they must travel for up to a week to attack them.

Before turning to the observed biological diversity and genetic micro-differentiation among the Yạnomamö, I will first sketch the nature of the effects of warfare on village size, settlement pattern and political strategy. As a consequence of the warfare pattern, villages at the tribal centre tend to

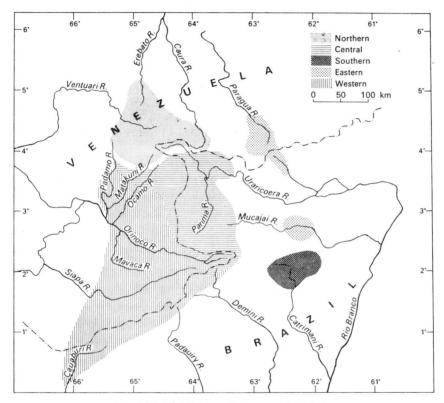

FIG. 14.2. Distribution of Yạnomamö dialects.

be much larger. They average close to 90 inhabitants compared with about 50 for villages at the periphery (Chagnon 1968c and unpublished data). Again, the range in village size is significantly different: central villages rarely fall below 40 individuals and occasionally reach as many as 250. Minimal village size seems to be determined by warfare as well: villages that are smaller than 40 have great difficulty organizing and conducting raids with efficiency and consistency. There is considerable variation in the structure of village popu-lation and occasionally one finds villages of less than 40 in number, but very rarely. Villages of this order of magnitude are usually so vulnerable that they invite predation on the part of larger groups that would steal their women.

Very small villages, therefore, have some difficulty fending for themselves and, unless they have strong allies, they are either driven out of the area or forced to amalgamate with others. The recent advent of missions in this area is changing the situation somewhat, since villages located near missions tend not to be subjected to the rigours of intensive raids. Thus, their populations occasionally fall below 40.

At the tribal periphery, on the other hand, villages are often as small as 25–30 people and rarely reach 100 (Chagnon 1968c). The distance between settlements seems also to be greater at the periphery, and groups here prefer to avoid their neighbours by migrating further and further away from them. To be sure, central groups also migrate away from enemy villages, but they are limited both in terms of distance and direction; they have no unoccupied lands into which they can colonize, so wherever they move they have neighbours. Still, the distance between villages is so great, even at the tribal centre, that inter-village warfare cannot be explained in terms of land-shortage or competition for other resources.

The overall settlement picture, then, is one of a cluster of some 125 villages, slightly more highly concentrated and numerically larger at the centre. At the periphery, especially at the north and east, the villages are smaller and more widely spaced. The general pattern of coming to grips with neighbours also differs from centre to periphery. Small villages at the periphery tend to live in isolation and adapt to the threats of neighbours by moving away from them (Chagnon 1968c). Villages at the centre do not have this option. Here, there has developed a rather elaborate system of inter-village alliances based on trading, feasting, and mutual ceding of marriageable women. As can be seen in Fig. 14.2, there is some evidence that this process is leading to the geographical separation of a few groups. Microdifferentiation at the socio-cultural level is evidenced by the fact that there are already distinct dialects here. Attendant genetic microdifferentiation is presumed to parallel this and, as we will show in a moment, actually does.

Village movements are shown in more detail in Fig. 14.3. Where villages have split into two or more groups, the splits are indicated by the ✳ symbol. Fig. 14.4 shows the same seven clusters of villages and their migrations along general phylogenetic lines. These population movements, when translated into behavioural terms, indicate that the residents of Yąnomamö villages fear and distrust their neighbours: they fear them for reasons having to do with super-naturally-caused death and because of the chronic warfare that obtains in this area, especially among the clusters designated as C, D, E, F, and G. They distrust them because it is not uncommon for Yąnomamö groups to treacher-ously turn upon their closest friends, kill the men, and abduct the women (Chagnon 1967, 1968a). Since the population is growing (Chagnon 1968a) and since the native social system is incapable of organizing more than 150–200 people successfully, there is a constant process of village fissioning as groups reach this order of magnitude. Population fissioning after a period of growth is characteristic of tribal populations.

Ideally, the villagers prefer to live in smaller groups, say 50–75 people, but warfare pressure is such that it is unwise for them to subdivide. This will be discussed later. Thus, the villages grow upwards of 250 people in some instances and split only when internal friction and fighting can no longer be contained by the norms of kinship and the authority of the headmen. When

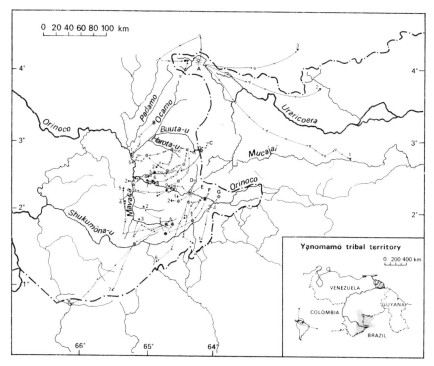

FIG. 14.3. Recent movements of selected Yąnomamö villages.

villages reach this order of magnitude, the events that lead to the actual fissioning are often violent and occasionally end in one or more deaths, such as during a club-fight within the village. The groups that result from the fissioning then enter into hostilities with each other, and at least one group moves to a new, distant location and establishes its garden there. Thus, the process of population growth in a milieu of chronic warfare generates a 'centripetal' settlement pattern, maximizing the possibility that genetically and historically related populations will separate from each other, at least geographically. That is to say, the social features inherent in this (and presumably many other) tribal systems of population expansion seem to maximize

18

the possibility that biological microdifferentiation will take place along the periphery of an expanding population.

This is clearly seen in Fig. 14.3, where the groups involved in particular fissions on the periphery move great distances away from each other. Even at the centre there is a tendency toward this pattern. In most cases, mutual hostility and inter-village raiding affects subsequent moves as well, further enhancing the possibility that closely related groups will be widely separated. I will examine the genealogical and marital analogues of this settlement pattern in a moment. The existence of an unoccupied periphery appears to act as a magnet for those groups located at a distance from the centre.

Mortality

To underscore the fact that warfare exercises a profound influence on Yạnomamö population movements, Table 14.1 gives mortality statistics for 610 adult Yạnomamö and represents pooled data published elsewhere (Chagnon 1968a) and recently collected data (1970) previously unpublished. The sample is drawn from the several villages in the central area comprising

TABLE 14.1

Cause of 610 adult Yạnomamö deaths

	Males	Females
1. Violent (21·8 per cent)		
Raids or duels	109	14
Within-group homicide	4	6
2. Magical (13·6 per cent)		
Sorcery, general	39	16
Spirits sent by enemies	11	13
Magic sent by foreigners	3	1
3. Epidemics	74	120
4. Malaria	40	67
5. Hayaheri (pains in abdomen)	3	4
6. Respiratory infections	3	8
7. 'Old age'	12	6
8. Diarrhoea	23	9
9. Snakebite	5	4
10. Miscellaneous	11	5
Total	337	273 = 610

clusters D and F of Fig. 14.4. Cause of death is based on Yạnomamö diagnoses. As is obvious, warfare accounts for a remarkably high mortality among both males and females (21·8 per cent). What is more staggering is the fact that 33 per cent of all *adult males* in this sample die violently, the overwhelming majority being killed by raiders from enemy groups. There is ample reason for the Yạnomamö to avoid their neighbours.

Equally significant are the deaths attributable to magic, for the Yąnomamö consider most of these in the same vein as they do actual homicide. Whenever someone dies from otherwise unexplainable sickness, his death is usually attributed to the malevolent actions of shamans in enemy villages. Indeed, the shamans in every Yąnomamö village daily take hallucinogenic drugs and attempt, through the agency of their spirits (*hekura*), to kill men, women, and

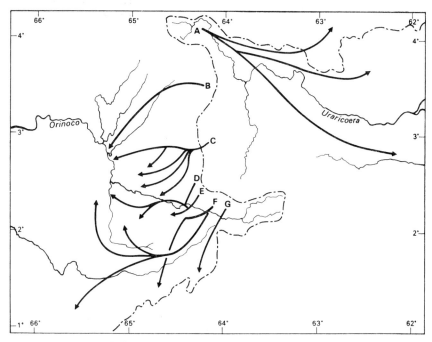

FIG. 14.4. General direction of macro-movements of selected Yąnomamö villages.

especially children in enemy villages. It is not surprising, therefore, that these same men attribute natural deaths in their own group to the malevolence of their competitors. Like homicide, deaths resulting from magic invite revenge at both the magical and military level. The net effect is that even in the absence of active military contests, Yąnomamö groups constantly generate mutual hostility and create reasons for avoiding each other.

Yąnomamö warfare, paradoxically, creates some interdependency between independent villages, especially at the tribal centre. As I mentioned above, one social response to the military threats impinging on villages is the creation of inter-group alliances based on trading, feasting, and inter-marriage. The basis for these alliances is as much economic as military, for one of the primary obligations allies have is to tender refuge in times of crisis, as when one group is driven from its garden by the incessant raids of one or more hostile neighbours. The process of settlement movement itself often requires such assistance, for it is impossible to abandon one's producing garden one day and create another garden tomorrow. Instead, the migrating group turns to an ally for refuge. An attempt is usually made to outlast the enemy by merely living with one's allies until raiding ceases, as it usually does in the wet season over most of the area. In hilly regions where drainage is good, there appears to be a much less marked seasonal impediment to inter-village travel. In most areas, however, the rains and subsequent flooding permit the

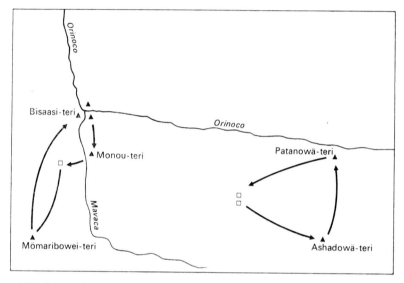

FIG. 14.5. Schematic plan of the movements of the villages Monou-teri and Patanowä-teri during 1965–6.

group to move back into its producing garden and continue life in the normal fashion. If there is some reason to suspect that the enemy will resume his raids in the dry season, then the group elects to establish a new garden else-where. This is an arduous, time-consuming process, for in addition to felling the timbers and burning the trees, plantain cuttings (often weighing 3 or 4 kilogrammes each) from the old garden, as well as food, must be transported to sustain the workers until their new garden begins producing.

A common response to this situation is to move into the village of an ally to avoid attacks from the enemy, thence to the new garden site to work for several weeks (carrying food from the ally's garden), and then back to the old garden. This cycle is continued until the new garden is established, a process requiring about a year. Fig. 14.5 shows, in schematic form, how two villages established new gardens (represented by squares) in 1965–6 by follow-ing essentially the pattern described here.

The Yạnomamö need allies but fear and mistrust them. This has resulted in a peculiar set of inter-village political relationships. Since it is appropriate to take advantage of the weak, no village can afford to seek alliances by asserting that it is weak. Instead, it confronts its neighbours rather aggressively and boisterously, attempting to show that it is strong and without need of allies. The Yạnomamö achieve this deception by actually creating artificial shortages of specific manufactured items, such as cotton hammocks and clay pots (Chagnon 1968a, b). While each group is able, technically, to produce the items, it chooses to rely on neighbours for them. In this fashion there is a 'neutral' cause for their reciprocal visits: each group is able to justify its interest in the other by citing the fact that they do not need allies for protection in time of crisis, but only clay pots, dogs, cotton hammocks, or arrows.

Reinforcing this peculiar interrelationship is the set of trade-related practices that insures that each presentation calls forth another. When members of Village A give items to Village B, they request—and are promised—different items at a later time. Thus, one trade calls forth another, and a modicum of mutual trust and interdependency is forged. At this point a second form of inter-group alliance can emerge: mutual, reciprocal feasting. Trade continues, but additional solidarity is forged by sharing food. Like trading, feasts are reciprocal. Finally, after two groups begin feasting, they are at a point where they are willing to exchange women in marriage. Alliances then usually break down, for the stronger of the two groups attempts to coerce more women out of its ally than it is willing to cede in return, and arguments and bickering begin. Over the short term, alliances serve to limit inter-village warfare, but the alliances are so tenuous and so easily broken that they are constantly in flux. This year's ally is next year's enemy. While the allies begin their shaky friendship by focusing attention on trade items, one of their ultimate goals is to acquire women, a preoccupation that makes sense when the sex ratio is considered (see below).

It is against this political milieu that the specific socio-cultural practices and their peculiar effects on the populations are to be seen. The point I am making is that the directly relevant tribal customs dealing with marriage and reproduction do not exist in a socio-political vacuum. Marriage, for example, responds to the political needs of the group and is not merely an independent social institution guaranteeing that mating takes place. It serves both reproductive and political functions, but it is the latter that determine its systematic nature.

Genetic microdifferentiation and systematic aspects of Yanomamö marriage

There is considerable genetic microdifferentiation found in Yạnomamö villages. Table 14.2 presents the gene frequencies found for 15 systems in 10 villages sampled in 1966 (published originally in Arends, Brewer, Chagnon, Gallango, Gershowitz, Layrisse, Neel, Schreffler, Tashian, and Weitkamp

TABLE 14.2

Gene frequencies observed in 10 *Yąnomamö villages*

Genetic system	Number tested	Allele in system	A	B	C	D	E	F	G	H	I	J
Rh	567	*CDe*	0·80	0·86	0·77	0·83	0·76	0·59	0·75	0·77	0·85	0·79
		CDE	0·09	0·05	0·17	0·16	0·12	0·24	0·21	0·23	0·14	0·11
		cDE	0·11	0·09	0·06	0·01	0·11	0·03	0·00	0·00	0·00	0·11
		cDe	0·00	0·00	0·00	0·00	0·00	0·03	0·00	0·00	0·00	0·00
		cDe*cde* }	0·00	0·00	0·00	0·00	0·20	0·12	0·04	0·00	0·01	0·00
MNSs	567	*MS*	0·04	0·06	0·00	0·02	0·05	0·24	0·04	0·09	0·05	0·21
		Ms	0·60	0·49	0·63	0·77	0·50	0·47	0·58	0·65	0·67	0·64
		NS	0·08	0·00	0·10	0·07	0·02	0·00	0·03	0·11	0·10	0·05
		Ns	0·28	0·45	0·27	0·14	0·43	0·29	0·35	0·15	0·18	0·10
Duffy	485	*Fy^a*	0·63	0·68	0·77	0·58	0·67	0·74	0·62	0·60	0·60	
P	565	*P*	0·63	0·60	0·53	0·34	0·51	0·26	0·49	0·38	0·53	0·70
Kidd	565	*Jk^a*	0·43	0·39	0·57	0·84	0·40	0·36	0·43	0·80	0·38	0·75
Erythrocyte phosphoglucomutase 1	299	*PGM^1*	0·83	0·92	0·96	1·00	0·99	0·95	0·92	0·91	0·89	0·95
Erythrocyte acid phosphatase	324	*B*	1·0	1·0	1·0	1·0	1·0	1·0	1·0	1·0	1·0	0·93
6-phosphogluconic dehydrogenase	283	*A*	1·0	1·0	1·0	1·0	1·0	1·0	0·97	1·0	1·0	1·0
Group component (Gc)	555	*Gc^1*	0·92	0·97	0·97	0·95	0·93	0·97	0·97	0·74	0·95	0·88
Serum protein Lp	381	*Lp^a*	0·0	0·0	0·0	0·18	0·0	0·02	0·04	0·05	0·0	0·10
Serum protein Ag	395	*Ag^a*	0·01	0·09	0·01	0·12	0·05	0·11	0·07	0·22	0·0	0·04
Haptoglobins	422	*Hp^1*	0·92	0·96	0·82	0·73	0·95	0·83	0·94	0·68	0·90	0·73
Transferrins	429	*Tf^c*	1·00	1·00	1·00	1·00	0·98‡	1·00	1·00	1·00	0·98‡	1·00
ABH-secretor	274	*Se*	0·88	1·00	1·00	1·00	—	—	—	0·86	—	—
Lewis-secretor	274	*Le*	0·68	0·77	0·40	0·56	—	—	—	0·53	—	—

† Five specimens in village E exhibited an abnormal phosphoglucomutase band in the presence of normal patterns for phosphoglucomutase 1 and 2.

‡ In both villages E and I, a single specimen was found to have a slowly migrating fraction which, however, migrated more rapidly than *Tf D*$_{chi}$.

1967). These villages are not independent. Villages A, B, and C were, in 1954, a single village. Villages D and H separated from each other in 1960, whereas villages E, F, and I were one village in about 1956; prior to this by about two generations, village G was also a part of the ancestral group. Finally, village J is a composite of people from two distinct groups, but a significant fraction of that village traces descent back to some of the ancestors of the A, B, and C group. As is apparent, there is considerable diversity at the genetic level, even among those groups that are known to be historically and biologically closely related. Ward (1970) has recently examined the genetic distances and contrasted the genetic relationships with the stated historical relationships.

Table 14.3 gives the genetic distances (based on six loci) for seven of the villages shown in Table 14.2 above. In particular, I wish to draw attention to the genetic distances between villages A, B, and E. The distance between A and B is 0·227, whereas the distance between B and E is only 0·144; that is to say, on the basis of the genetic data alone, village B looks to be more closely related to village E, but it in fact separated from village A a mere six years before our study was conducted. On the face of it, therefore, the genetic data seems to conflict with the known history of the two groups. However,

TABLE 14.3

Matrix of genetic distances, based on six loci, between seven Yąnomamö villages (from Neel and Ward 1970)

Village	B	C	D	E	H	I
A	0·227	0·228	0·385	0·157	0·416	0·243
B		0·367	0·506	0·144	0·537	0·360
C			0·298	0·295	0·346	0·297
D				0·464	0·154	0·364
E					0·486	0·296
H						0·350

when the genealogical data are examined, and the marriage practices taken into consideration, there is indeed a demonstrably close genetic relationship between villages B and E, one that would not be detected by ethnographic and/or linguistic comparisons. Two notions of 'relatedness' are involved here, culture–historical and biological. The two generally coincide (Ward 1970): villages that have the same origin in the past but, through village fissioning, have become distinct social entities tend also to be genetically similar. However, there are situations, to be described below, where culturally indistinguishable villages with a common history are genetically dissimilar.

To explain this otherwise curious finding, we must bear two things in mind. On the one hand, Yąnomamö marriage practices are very systematic (under certain definable conditions) and are, therefore, capable of amplifying and exaggerating initial genetic peculiarities. On the other hand, the initial irregularities are often as much a product of chance events as they are of deterministic and predictable aspects of the social system. The genetic similarity of village B and village E, in this case, results from a socially predictable event—intermarriage between two distinct villages for the purpose of establishing alliance—and largely unpredictable genetic events—the genotypes of particular individuals involved in the marriages.

Given this particular marriage, the systematic nature of Yąnomamö marriage practices can explain the genetic similarity between the two villages (B and E) in question. To the extent that genetic microdifferentiation exists among all Yąnomamö villages, these differences must be viewed, as in this case, as the outcome of both directive, systematic marriage practices and the often unpredictable way in which particular genotypes are combined in inter-group marriage. Let us therefore examine Yąnomamö marriage practices in the light of this example, and extrapolate from it.

Marriage practices

The Yąnomamö have what is called in the anthropological literature a prescriptive bilateral cross-cousin marriage rule. The term 'prescriptive' refers to the fact that males must marry a woman of a specific kinship category: they have no choice with respect to category (Needham 1963, Leach 1965). All the female relatives of a man fall into six primary kinship categories, but it is incestuous to marry women who fall into five of the six categories. However, within the single marriageable category there is some option as to which specific 'cross-cousin' a man will marry. Within the marriageable category, two of the genealogically specified relatives, in our own kinship system, would be mother's brother's daughter (MoBrDa) and father's sister's daughter (FaSiDa), i.e. biological first cross-cousins. But in the Yąnomamö kinship system more remote relatives (second, third, fourth, etc. cousins) are included. Any marriage outside this single kinship category is, by Yąnomamö definition, incestuous and is generally avoided. In addition to this marriage rule, there is clearly an understood obligation to reciprocate a woman in marriage, phrased anthropologically as brother-sister exchange: when a man obtains a wife from one kinship group, his group is expected to give another in return. For a people who have no numerical concepts beyond 'more than two', they keep fairly accurate track of marriage exchanges and attendant reciprocal obligation. Thus, six patrilineal lineages, the group to which all individuals belong and must marry out of, in four villages over four generations behaved as shown in Table 14.4 with respect to the women each gave and received.

TABLE 14.4

Numbers of women exchanged by six patrilineal lineages in four villages over four generations

Lineage	Gave to other five lineages	Received from other five lineages
A	74	79
B	61	60
C	16	17
D	8	4
E	16	11
F	6	10
Total	181	181

The combination of cross-cousin marriage rule, rule of descent and ex-ogamy, and reciprocal exchange enables us to represent their social system in an ideal model as shown in Fig. 14.6.

This model is the simplest one that can be drawn to illustrate the way in which marriage is ideally contracted in Yąnomamö society. It is the social anthropologist's equivalent to the non-existent phenomena of 'infinite popu-lation size' and 'random mating' used by geneticists in their gene-frequency

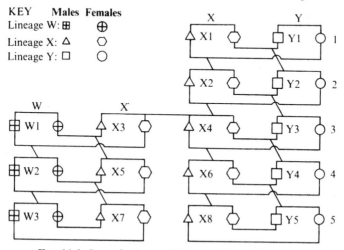

FIG. 14.6. General scheme of Yąnomamö social structure.

calculations. Like the assumptions of the Hardy–Weinberg formula, it is merely an approximation to a real and imperfect world.

Fig. 14.6, therefore, shows what might happen if everybody followed all the rules all the time and had only two children, one of each sex, except in generation 3, when it was foreseen by individual X_2 that lineage W wanted to join the village, whereupon he conveniently sired an additional son and daughter.

Fig. 14.6 can also be taken to represent an ideal Yąnomamö village over five generations. Everybody marries outside his patrilineage (males indicated as triangles for lineage X, squares for lineage Y, and crossed squares for lineage W). All males marry women who are simultaneously MoBrDa and FaSiDa, i.e. double (first) cross-cousins. All children belong to the lineage of their father. Finally, all men give their sisters in exchange for a wife, i.e., there is 'brother-sister' exchange. Technically, the term 'children exchange' would be more accurate, since it is the senior generation members who arrange marriages.

Ignoring the left half of the diagram for a moment, it can be clearly seen that if this represents a Yąnomamö village, we should then expect to find the average village to be composed of two patrilineages. In fact, most villages usually are composed of two patrilineages, if not in actual composition, then in terms of political groups—plus a fraction of 'outsiders'. These may be (1) people who have married into the group for purposes of alliance, (2) people, mostly women, who have been abducted from other villages, or (3) disgruntled fractions of other groups that have temporarily joined the village; many of these ultimately stay on and are absorbed by the local group. A large measure of the genetic diversity among related villages comes from the inclusion of people such as this. The degree to which any particular village exhibits 'dual composition' is largely determined by its current size and, therefore, its needs to create military alliances by marriage. Table 14.5 gives the composition by patrilineage of four villages. At one time the four villages were a single, large village before separating into distinct groups (Chagnon 1968*b*).

It should be noted that the lineages extend from one village to the next, reflecting the fact that villages are genealogically as well as historically inter-related. The dual nature of the largest village, Patanowä-teri, underscores the fact that larger villages are less compelled to make alliances and therefore approximate more closely to the ideal model shown in Fig. 14.6 above: 75 per cent of the residents of Patanowä-eri are members of the two largest and politically dominant lineages.

Returning to Fig. 14.6, the dual nature of the ideal villages is interrupted in generation 3 when members of lineage W join the group. Events such as this happen regularly in every village: individuals are constantly joining the group from the outside. In the idealized diagram, individual W_1 and his sister joined the group and married into lineage X. Thereafter, lineage X has a 'cadet' branch, indicated as X′ and distinguished by virtue of the fact that its members intermarry with lineage W, again following the traditional marriage rules. The fact that its social fate is intimately tied to that of lineage W is shown by its incipient separation from lineage X. In generation 5, the village is in fact divided into four patrilineages: X, X′, W, and Y. Since marriage bonds are extremely significant in this society, a village split would separate lineage X and Y away from X′ and W.

Fig. 14.7 shows how this process takes place (Chagnon 1968*b*): village A is comprised of two lineages, X and Y. It fissions to form villages B and C, each composed of lineages X and Y. Finally, village B fissions to produce villages D and E, while village C continues unchanged.

For comparison, Fig. 14.8 shows how four actual villages are related to each other. All four of these villages were one village in approximately 1940, when it split into two groups: Patanowä-teri and what today are Bisaasi-teri (upper and lower) and Monou-teri. Only the genealogical links of the adult males are shown in Fig. 14.8, but it is clear that the lineages, as in the ideal pattern shown in Fig. 14.7, extend through the present villages. The migration pattern of these villages is shown in Fig. 14.9.

TABLE 14.5

Village composition by lineage membership

Lineage	Males	Females	Total
A. Lower Bisaasi-teri			
Sha	9	7	16
Tom	9	3	12
Hor	1	2	3
Kio	2	4	6
Shamatari	3	9	12
Other	1	1	2
Total	25	26	51
B. Upper Bisaasi-teri			
Sha	11	14	25
Hor	8	5	13
Kio	5	11	16
Kah	5	3	8
Shamatari	3	7	10
Other	5	8	13
Total	37	48	85
C. Monou-teri			
Sha	11	9	20
Hor	15	8	23
Kio	3	3	6
Shamatari	3	9	12
Other	2	3	5
Total	34	32	66
D. Patanowä-teri			
Hor	58	33	91
Sha	39	29	68
Kah	17	8	25
Kar	1	3	4
Shamatari	2	6	8
Other	5	11	16
Total	122	90	212

We are now in a position to interpret the genetic data presented earlier in Tables 14.2 and 14.3. At the time when Lower Bisaasi-teri (village B of Tables 14.2 and 14.3) was a part of the larger, ancestral village then located at Patanowä-teri (Fig. 14.9), alliances between their group and the Mahekodo-teri developed (village E of Tables 14.2 and 14.3). Specifically, a man by the name of Tomorowä, a member of one of the larger Mahekodo-teri lineages, married into the (ancestral) village of Patanowä-teri and sired several children. He married a woman from the Sha lineage (Table 14.5) and, following the

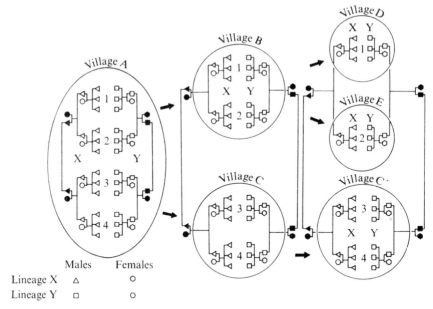

FIG. 14.7. The process of village fissioning.

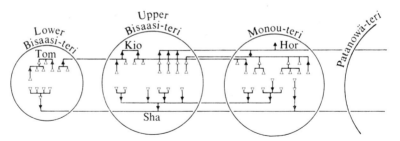

FIG. 14.8. Relationships of adult males in four villages.

customary marriage rules, his descendants entered into reciprocal marriage alliances with that (cadet) lineage in succeeding generations (Chagnon 1966 gives the complete genealogy). After the larger group fissioned in the fashion shown in Fig. 14.8, and ultimately moved to the mouth of the Mavaca River (Fig. 14.9), his descendants remained exclusively with the Lower Bisaasi-teri fissioned in the 'upper' and 'lower' fractions, Tomorowä's descendants again remained exclusively with the Lower Bisaasi-teri, and, by then, amounted to a significant fraction of the village (shown as 'Tom' in Table 14.5). Thus, the 'ideal' pattern shown in Fig. 14.6 is approximated by the actual events: Tomorowä is, in terms of the ideal model, the individual W_1, and his descendants constitute lineage W. Lineage X and X' represent parallel branches of the Sha lineage indicated in Table 14.5 above.

What appears, then, as an apparent paradox or conflict between genetic data (Table 14.2) and actual histories as given by Yąnomamö informants (Fig. 14.9) can be resolved by a careful examination of the genealogies of the villages in question, the inherent features of the marriage system, and the genealogical basis of village fissioning. Whereas Tomorowä's genetic contribution to the ancestral population was overwhelmed in that he and his

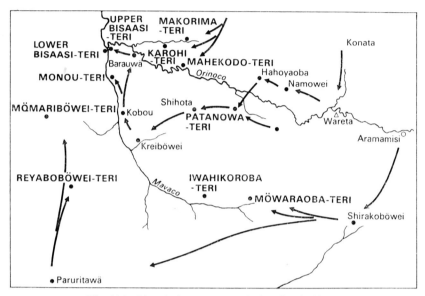

Fig. 14.9. Historical movements of Bisaasi-teri village.

descendants constituted only a minor fraction of the total, he and his descendants amount to a very significant fraction of Lower Bisaasi-teri, enough to make that village genetically more similar to the Mahekodo-teri than to Upper Bisaasi-teri from which they in fact separated. Culturally and historically, just the opposite is true. Although he and his offspring initially amounted to few people, over time and with the reciprocal marriage obligations his descendants have been concentrated into a single, small village where their genetic significance is much greater. Thus, the apparent conflict not only disappears, but it is seen as a logical outcome of the social rules that regulate marriage, village fissioning, and kinship ties in Yąnomamö society.

Yąnomamö demography as related to microdifferentiation

As was apparent in the section describing Yąnomamö warfare, there is also variation at the demographic level. Just as a pooled gene frequency report would gloss over significant genetic microdifferentiation as seen in genetic data reported village by village, so also does pooled demographic data conceal meaningful variation. Fig. 14.10 gives the age and sex pyramid for 2618 individuals from 29 villages. The ages are my own estimates—largely guesswork—since the Yąnomamö do not count and therefore do not know their ages. Redistributed into the categories 0–14, 15–30, and 31 upwards, the villages show a surprising variance about the mean, as can be seen from Fig. 14.11 (cf. Neel and Chagnon 1968).

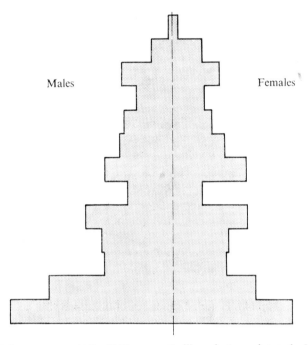

Males   Females

FIG. 14.10. Sex–age pyramid for 29 Yąnomamö villages in 4-year intervals. $N = 2618$.

Kunstadter (Chapter 16) draws attention to the fact that demographic characteristics of particular populations vary over time. Data from the Yąnomamö indicate that there is likewise considerable variation village by village at any given point in time. There is substantial reason to suspect that there is also considerable variation within each village over short periods of time, due largely to migration and localized sicknesses, such as diarrhoea and respiratory infections, which can dramatically alter the demographic properties of small villages. Child mortality in particular is very sensitive to village settlement pattern: as groups are compelled to move their gardens from one area to another more distant area, there seems to be an excessive mortality rate brought about by the physical rigours involved in the move. The death rate among new-born and recently-weaned children under these circumstances seems particularly high. Long camping trips in the jungle also lead to excessive child mortality. Statistics on mortality are very difficult to obtain from the Yąnomamö because of their extreme reluctance to discuss the recently deceased, and their anger with the anthropologist who persistently attempts to pry into such matters. In not a few cases, I have had my personal safety compromised in attempts to get such data.

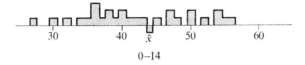

0–14

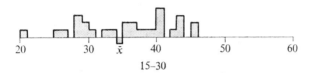

15–30

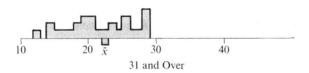

31 and Over

FIG. 14.11. Age distribution (in percentages) in 28 Yąnomamö villages.

The data from Fig. 14.11 are difficult to interpret unless particular social circumstances are considered. For example, a village with an excessive number of children but few adults in the 15–30 age category could not consider moving to an area where there were no neighbouring villages unless its population were rather large, as they would be extremely vulnerable to raids. Again, the distribution of the population within the group in terms of patrilineage is particularly important: chance alone might result in a village largely composed of adults from a single lineage within which marriage is forbidden by the incest prohibitions. In some cases, however, this can be circumvented by a few strategic but incestuous marriages. Yąnomamö headmen enjoy many prerogatives that their peers do not. There is a very high correlation between incest and headmanship, for headmen, being fierce, are feared and fearless, and as a group marry their sisters, daughters, and nieces with surprising regularity. Incestuous marriages play an important role in the social history of every Yąnomamö village and in themselves exhibit systematic tendencies. In general they tend to redefine the social category of large fractions of villages and generate new marriage possibilities that then follow traditional rules. In this fashion, matrimonial 'blind alleys' are avoided—that is to say, villages that might otherwise have disproportionately few individuals of one category, *vis-à-vis* a second group of individuals, can alleviate this by a few strategic incestuous marriages. Finally, it can not be assumed that each village is a biological entity of and by itself. Yąnomamö alliances and inter-group marriages are such that the breeding population is substantially larger than the figures given for any particular village. Probably a truer estimate of the significant demographic properties would come from grouping villages into the breeding populations that their current, albeit temporary, political alliances place them. The precise configuration and extent of such biological–political blocs is not, however, independent of the demographic properties of the several constituent villages, particularly its size and its sex ratio in the 15–30 age category. While the Yąnomamö ideal is to marry within the village, political necessity in smaller villages dictates that exogamic marriages must take place to ensure that the village has reliable allies. Thus, only the larger, militarily strong groups approach the desired ideal. Table 14.6 reflects the relationship between village size and frequency of endogamic marriages (from Chagnon 1968*a*, and *b*).

TABLE 14.6

Frequency of marriage types in two Yąnomamö villages

Marriage type	Patanowa-teri ($n = 212$)	Lower Bisaasi-teri ($n = 51$)
1. Prescriptive	37 (71 per cent)	7 (41 per cent)
2. Incestuous	4	1
3. Alliance/abduction	8 (15 per cent)	9 (53 per cent)
4. Unexplained	3	0
Total	52	17

Of the marriages in the larger village, 71 per cent followed the prescriptive cross-cousin marriage rule whereas only 41 per cent did in the smaller village, which had entered into marriage alliance with other groups.

To the extent that the demographic properties of populations are relevant to an explanation of their genetic possibilities, these data show that even within rather small populations such as Yąnomamö villages there is surprising demographic variation. While it is possible that thus far undetected natural catastrophes could account for some of these variations, it seems unlikely they could explain all of the observed variation, particularly in the younger age categories.

Perhaps one of the most startling facts of Yąnomamö demography is the peculiarities of the sex ratio. For the pooled 2618 individuals (representing 100 per cent or nearly 100 per cent census figures of 29 villages), the tertiary sex-ratio is 1·20. Given the Yąnomamö reluctance to discuss recently deceased individuals—children and adults alike—and their rather poor recollection of precisely how many livebirths a particular woman had, it is almost impossible to estimate reproductive performance with any accuracy. Their genealogical memory is rather good when it comes to individuals who reach puberty; it is rather poor when it comes to children who die before acquiring a name and a 'social personality'. It is almost impossible, therefore, to get an accurate estimate of sex ratio at birth.

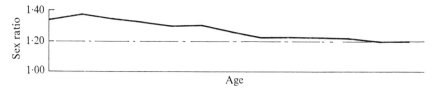

FIG. 14.12. Cumulative sex ratio in the pooled sample of 2618 individuals.

Fig. 14.12 shows the cumulative sex ratio in the pooled sample of 2618 individuals. What emerges is that the post-partum sex ratio of approximately 1·40 gradually approaches the level of 1·20, the figure for the entire population. This gradual reduction of male-excess is a consequence of the rather high male mortality in warfare mentioned earlier (see Table 14.1). The initial excess of males appears to be caused by differential female infanticide, also a direct reflection of the intensity of warfare: in areas where inter-village warfare is intense, the sex ratio for the age category 0–14 is 1·57. Where warfare is less intense, at the tribal periphery, the sex ratio for this category is 1·21 (Chagnon 1968c).

The relationship between warfare intensity and differential female infanticide is as follows: males grow up to become warriors and defenders of the village. Females, on the other hand, are considered to be less valuable and are often destroyed at birth: a common explanation for female infanticide is simply, '. . . she was female and not valuable, so we killed her.' The net result is that in order to have a male child as the eldest member of the sibship, or a sibship of predominantly males, a rather large number of female babies are killed at birth. Males are also killed at birth if the mother already has a nursing child, or if it is malformed, and, occasionally, if it is one of twins. Needless to say, the bias towards killing female children has an effect on the intensity of inter- and intra-village hostility: most Yąnomamö warfare and intra-village fighting is directly attributable to competition over women. Remarkably enough, this demographic fact helps account for the rigour with which the marriage rules are followed: in a situation where there are few females, the best way to ensure that your group acquires the maximum number possible is to follow the brother-sister exchange rule. That is, you give women only to those groups that will reciprocate them. In this competitive milieu it is not surprising that most of the polygyny is confined to the dominant males of the dominant lineages, usually the headmen of the village.

In addition to infanticide, the Yąnomamö also practice abortion and proscribe sexual intercourse during lactation. While reducing the livebirth average (Neel and Chagnon 1968), it also increases competition for sexual partners. Women nurse their children for up to three years, during which time they are not supposed to have sexual intercourse. In general the taboo is followed. I have heard even the most aggressive of men complain of their wive's lack of interest in their sexual advances. Since warfare calls forth aggressive behaviour in the males, and the greatest shortage of women is to be found where warfare is most intense, life for the adult male in villages at the tribal centre is nothing less than rigorous. He who is less than awesome is frequently obliged to remain a bachelor, whereas the aggressive and fierce tend to acquire multiple wives. One consequence of this is that the variance in completed male reproduction is very high compared to the variance in female reproduction (Neel and Chagnon 1968). This can be seen in Table 14.7, where the distribution of grandchildren reflects the political and therefore biological success of particular men.

While there is a large element of chance in the survival of children, the fact that the four men who had, respectively, 41, 42, 46, and 62 grandchildren were headmen or co-headmen of their villages argues that there is, on the basis of this limited data, an apparently strong correlation between headmanship and biological success. (I am currently collaborating with Dr. Jean MacCluer in an attempt to simulate the Yąnomamö population with her Monte Carlo programme. One of the many interesting facts that has emerged so far is that the reproductive success of males is very strongly associated with the status of their fathers. Men who acquire multiple wives tend regularly to be sons of polygamous headmen). The data shown in Table 14.7 were calculated on only one of the two large populations for which my demographic data is adequate: preliminary analysis on the second population suggests that headmanship confers even more advantage, in a biological sense, than is revealed in these figures. Finally, two of the men with large numbers of grandchildren were fathers of the other two.

While it is possible only to collect genealogical data for four or five generations from Yąnomamö informants, the amount of inbreeding detectable from such genealogical data, while substantial, is only an estimate, and perhaps a very low estimate, for the total amount of inbreeding that takes place. Dr. MacCluer has modified her Monte Carlo simulation programme to take account of specific demographic parameters peculiar to the Yąnomamö and

TABLE 14.7

Distribution of number of grandchildren living and dead for males in one Yąnomamö population presently composed of 425 people divided into four villages

Number of grandchildren	Men with that number
1	28
2	11
3	11
4	7
5	10
6	9
7	5
8	5
9	1
10	7
11	3
12	2
15	1
16	2
19	1
20	1
21	1
22	1
24	1
25	1
28	1
41	1
42	1
46	1
62	1

has made a number of simulation runs based on the genealogical and demographic input I provided. The preliminary results, subject to revision when the input data are updated to incorporate new information, presented in Fig. 14.13, imply that the inbreeding coefficient in these small, isolated populations exceeds, by a substantial margin, the 0·02 level that Wright (1950) suggested as the upper limit for most human populations. That is, the increment of relatedness added by counting the accumulated inbreeding out to third, fourth, and fifth cousins in this type of population is very substantial. Figs. 14.3 and 14.4 show that most of the Yąnomamö populations with which

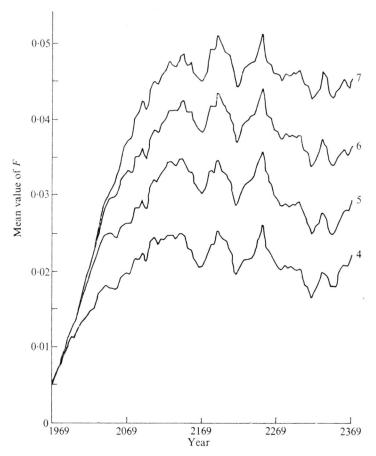

FIG. 14.13. Mean inbreeding coefficient (*F*) based on four, five, six, and seven ancestral generations.

I am dealing originated in the same general area, and there is no reason to suspect that they did not interbreed substantially in the past, beyond the genealogical recall of my informants. Indeed, the linguistic similarity of the groups with which I am currently working argues that this is most probably the case. The two populations, while historically separated for some 100 years of village migration (except for periodic abductions of women), nevertheless speak very similar dialects. I have no communication problem moving from one group to another between the dialect areas (shown as the central and western dialects of Fig. 14.2). In addition, members of both groups specifically state that they come originally from the same general area, as shown on Figs. 14.3 and 14.4 (populations D and F) and their ancestors knew each other.

To conclude this section, I will summarize a small case-study involving the flow of genes from the Makiritare Indians to the Yąnomamö population at the village of Borabuk (Chagnon, Neel, Weitkamp, Gershowitz, and Ayres 1970). The distribution of both tribes is given in Fig. 14.14.

In 1967 we visited Borabuk, the village of Yąnomamö separated from the main tribal population by several days journey. Their recent settlement

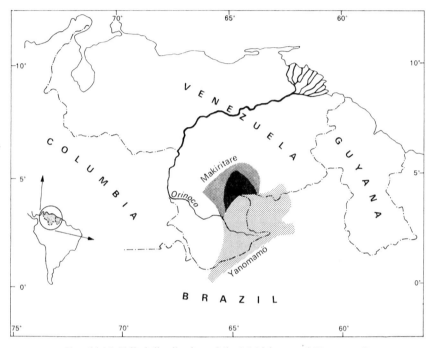

FIG. 14.14. Tribal distribution of the Makiritare and Yąnomamö.

pattern, shown in Fig. 14.15, as well as genealogical data, clearly showed that some 75–100 years prior to our study their ancestors had lived in a mixed village with Makiritare Indians in the headwaters of the Auaris River. Some intermarriage took place at this time, but because the Makiritare constantly seduced their women, a serious fight led to their separation. The Yąnomamö moved away downstream, and migrated far to the east. Their headman was a half-breed: his father was Makiritare and his mother was Yąnomamö. During the course of their migration to the east, they fissioned into three distinct groups, only one of which, Borabuk, has been included in this study.

Two events worthy of mention happened subsequent to their separation from the Makiritare, but prior to our study. They were hit by an epidemic in which a large number of men were killed, presumably a hunting party or a group of visitors separated from the women and children. The headman of the group acquired several of the widows of the men killed in the epidemic, a common prerogative of Yąnomamö headmen. He had a large number of children by these women. In addition, the Yąnomamö entered into hostilities with the poorly-known Maku tribe and exterminated all but a few individuals (Weitkamp and Chagnon 1967). They abducted a Maku woman, who subsequently had a large number of children by a Yąnomamö husband.

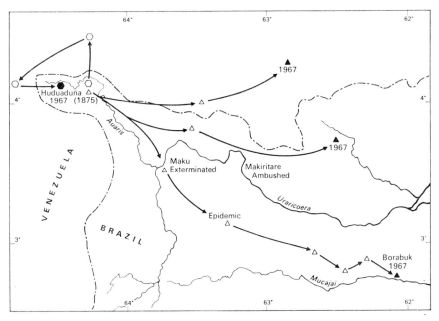

FIG. 14.15. Migration of the Borabuk village.

In about 1930–35 the Makiritare group, from which the Borabuk population separated earlier, sent a party of people down the Uraricoera River to make canoes. The Yąnomamö, who blamed them for the epidemic and who had old grievances to settle, attacked them and killed several of the men. They abducted four women and fled to the Mucajai River. These women ultimately had a greater than usual number of children, largely because they failed to practise infanticide and because they were shared around a great deal by the men who captured them (see Chagnon *et al.* 1970).

The results of our blood analysis confirmed what we already knew from village histories and pedigrees collected from informants: there was evidence of mixture with the Makiritare. However, we were surprised to find that the frequencies of two genes (Diego A positive and acid phosphatase A positive), known in the Makiritare population but not found in the Yąnomamö population (acid phosphatase A positive was found in low frequency in one other

Yąnomamö village, also known to have been intimately associated with Makiritare) were higher in the Borabuk population than they were in the Makiritare population from which they were derived. Also, a rare albumin type subsequently called Albumin Maku (Weitkamp and Chagnon 1967) was found in the abducted Maku woman and some of her progeny. The pedigree, Fig. 14.16, shows the distribution of these genes in the population of Borabuk.

Extrapolating from this vignette, the population of Borabuk is, at present, the easternmost village of Yąnomamö. It is already geographically isolated

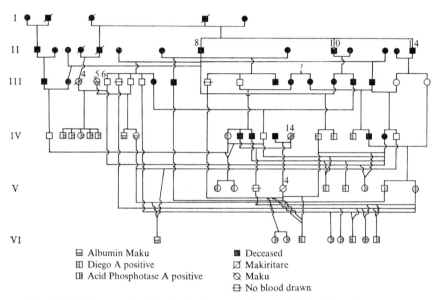

FIG. 14.16. Pedigree of the Borabuk village, showing the distribution of phenotypes.

from the main group of Yąnomamö (see Fig. 14.2) and its population speaks a very distinct dialect of Yąnomamö, perhaps influenced by Makiritare. Its settlement pattern implies that, should it migrate further, it will move eastward and become even more removed from the main body of the tribe. Genetically it is the most distinct Yąnomamö village studied by us to date. I believe that the reproductive advantages of headmen and the lower status of captive women and their subsequent forced higher reproductive performance has amplified and exaggerated the rather random introduction of three new genes to the population. In this case, it appears that the forces inherent in the Yąnomamö social organization has led to a certain amount of genetic microdifferentiation. Should Borabuk become a new 'tribe', whatever that implies, it would begin with somewhat unusual genetic characteristics.

Conclusions

At the end of a paper such as this, one wonders if an apology rather than a summary is more in order. As a social anthropologist attempting to communicate with human biologists I am the first to admit that what I study is not easily quantified and therefore must of necessity be understood in largely subjective, qualitative terms. On the other hand, I am the last to admit that only quantifiable phenomena can be understood or appreciated. I believe that it is possible for social anthropologists, in collaboration with population geneticists, to work out broad guidelines that will permit us to gain a better understanding of the biological consequences of some tribal social practices. In particular, I believe that meaningful reproduction models based on tribal demographic properties and systematic marriage practices can be formulated. Such models could take, initially, the form of mathematical statements that reflect the *observed* marriage types found in specific kinds of tribes as opposed to the *stated* marriage preference. This may require: (a) a more intensive effort in the field on the part of social anthropologists to pursue genealogical links more vigorously than is necessary for their own purposes or (b) the publication of such data where it already exists. My own field experience is such that I collected far more genealogical information—at an enormous cost in time—than was necessary to understand the Yąnomamö social system *as a social system*. However, I did so with the anticipation of using such data to define the population as accurately as possible as a biological system. I believe that my understanding of the social system improved as a consequence of this additional effort, although at the time the actual field work was conducted I had reservations.

The mathematical analysis of tribal marriage practices can only take us so far. As has been apparent in this paper, there are many, essentially non-quantifiable parameters that have an effect on tribal dynamics, composition, and structure. I am convinced that the only way to apprehend the nature of these variables is to turn to population simulation.

Yąnomamö social customs represent the most commonly found practices in the primitive world: Iroquois kinship system, bilateral cross-cousin marriage, patrilineal descent, village size ranging from 40 to 250, village fissioning, sororal polygyny, reciprocal marriage between definable kinship groups, sex ratio greater than 1·00, reproductive advantages for headmen, absence of female sterility, and a host of others. Thus, when Dr. MacCluer (MacCluer 1967, MacCluer and Schull 1970a, b) has her programme worked out to her satisfaction, it will be generally applicable to the great majority of tribal populations. To be sure, modification will have to be made for the purpose of analysing specific tribes whose particular social and demographic characteristics deviate from the estimated Yąnomanö values, but the general relationships should remain the same. The greatest differences should come at the demographic level as tribes are compared with tribes, or sub-populations within the same tribe contrasted.

The Yąnomamö represent a tribal population that is growing numerically and expanding geographically. Their warfare pattern and the failure of their political system successfully to organize more than 150–200 people in village units has led to a settlement pattern that seems to ensure that the groups at the periphery are maximally distinct genetically. Systematic aspects of marriage regulation are capable of ensuring a high degree of detectable genetic similarity among villages known to be historically related but at the same time can lead to genetic variability as new genetic materials are incorporated and confined, by marriage practices, to small segments of the total population. These genes can come from either culturally related groups within the tribe or from different tribes.

Presumably this pattern was common throughout the Tribal Epoch of man. We can only speculate about the relationship between tribal social practices and the observed genetic variability in present human populations. At the very least, it is safe to say that the tribal design is compatible with some of the observed variation in non-industrialized populations and can probably account for some portions of it. Chance, however, seems equally relevant. There is no demonstrable relationship between the genetic systems employed by human biologists to measure this variability and the development of cultural processes that have a profound effect on the survival and growth of culturally organized populations. Thus, what the tribal design can create it cannot, and did not, preserve. The variations that were preserved had little, if anything, to do with their biological adaptability, for the selection was more a function of political and technological evolution of the cultural groups.

REFERENCES

ALBRIGHT, S. (1965). Aykamteli higher-level phonology. *Anthrop. Ling.* **7**, 16–22.

ARENDS, T., BREWER, G., CHAGNON, N., GALLANGO, M. L., GERSHOWITZ, H., LAYRISSE, M., NEEL, J., SHREFFLER, D., TASHIAN, R., and WEITKAMP, L. (1967). Intratribal genetic differentiation among the Yąnomamö Indians of southern Venezuela. *Proc. natn. Acad. Sci. U.S.A.* **57**, 1252–9.

BECHER, H. (1960). *Die Surara und Pakidai: Zwei Yanomami-Stämme in Nordwest-Brasilien.* Musem für Volkerkunde, Hamburg, Vol. **26**.

BORGMAN, D. and CUE, S. L. (1963). Sentence and clause types in Central Waica (Shiriana). *Int. J. Am. Ling.* **31**, 222–9.

—— —— ALBRIGHT, S., SEELEY, M., and GRIMES, J. E. (1965). The Waican Languages. *anthrop. Ling.* **7**, 1–4.

CHAGNON, N. A. (1966). Yąnomamö warfare, social organization, and marriage alliances. Ph.D. thesis, University of Michigan.

—— (1967). Yąnomamö: the fierce people. *Nat. Hist., N.Y.* **71**, 22–31.

—— (1968a). Yąnomamö social organization and warfare. In *War: the anthropology of armed conflict and aggression* (ed. M. Fried, M. Harris, and R. Murphy), Natural History Press, New York.

—— (1968b). *Yąnomamö: the fierce people.* Holt, Rinehart, and Winston, New York.

—— (1968c). The culture-ecology of shifting (pioneering) cultivation among the Yąnomamö Indians. *VIII Int. Congr. Anthrop. Ethnol. Sci.* **3**, 249–55.

—— NEEL, J. V., WEITKAMP, L., GERSHOWITZ, H., and AYRES, M. (1970). The influence of cultural factors on the demography and pattern of gene flow from the Makiritare to the Yanomama Indians. *Am. J. phys. Anthrop.* **32**, 339–49.

GREENBERG, J. (1960). The general classification of Central and South American languages. *Sel. Pap.V Int. Congr. Anthrop. Ethnol. Sci.* (ed. A. F. C. Wallace).

HULSE, F. S. (1955). Technological advance and major racial stocks. *Hum. Biol.* **27**, 184–92.

LEACH, E. R. (1965). Letter. *Man* **65**, 12.

MACCLUER, J. (1967). Monte Carlo methods in human population genetics: a computer model incorporating age-specific birth and death rates. *Am. J. phys. Anthrop.* **19**, 303–12.

—— and SCHULL, W. J. (1970a). Frequencies of consanguineous marriage and accumulation of inbreeding in an artificial population. *Am. J. hum. Genet.* **22**, 160–75.

—— —— (1970b). Estimating the effective size of human populations. *Am. J. hum. Genet.* **22**, 176–83.

MIGLIAZZA, E. (1967). Grupos lingüisticos do Territorio Federal de Roraima. *Antropologia* **2**, 155–73.

—— and GRIMES, J. E. (1961). Shiriana phonology. *Anthrop. Ling.* **3**, 31–41.

NEEDHAM, R. (1963). Some disputed points in the study of prescriptive alliance. *SWest. J. Anthrop.* **19**, 186–207.

NEEL, J. V. and CHAGNON, N. A. (1968). The demography of two tribes of primitive, relatively unacculturated American Indians. *Proc. natn. Acad. Sci. U.S.A.* **59**, 680–9.

—— and WARD, R. H. (1970). Village and tribal genetic distances among American Indians, and the possible implications for human evolution. *Proc. natn. Acad. Sci. U.S.A.* **65**, 323–30.

SAHLINS, M. D. (1968). *Tribesmen.* Prentice-Hall, Englewood Cliffs.

WARD, R. H. (1970). Micro-differentiation and genetic relationships of Yąnomamö villages. Ph.D. thesis, University of Michigan.

WEITKAMP, L. R. and CHAGNON, N. A. (1967). Albumin Maku: a new variant of human serum albumin. *Nature, Lond.* **217**, 759–60.

WRIGHT, S. (1950). Discussion on population genetics and radiation. *J. cell. comp. Physiol.* **35**, (Suppl. 1), 187–205.

ZERRIES, O. (1964). *Waika: Die Kultur-geschichtliche Stellung der Waika-Indianer des Oberen Orinoco im Rahmen der Völkerkunde Sudamerikas.* Klaus-Renner,Verlag,Munich.

15

DEMOGRAPHY OF SMALL-SCALE SOCIETIES

Colin M. Turnbull

THIS paper must necessarily take a limited form for two major reasons. Firstly, there simply is no adequate information upon which to base any detailed conclusions, and secondly, the data, such as they are, are not easily, if at all, quantifiable and are subject to a wide diversity of social forces that vary from society to society. While some answer is possible to the first problem, the second is inescapable and the best that can be done here is to point to the broad types of consideration that must be taken into account before any accurate assessment can be made of demography in small-scale societies.

The lack of reliable data does not mean, unfortunately, that there is also a lack of unreliable data. Assessments have too frequently been made without regard for the complex social forces at play, based on the surface appearance of populations and accepting too readily information provided by informants. Unfortunately, those in the best position to obtain more reliable data, based upon observation over a longer period of time and upon a deeper understanding of the various demographic forces at work, namely social and cultural anthropologists, have not traditionally seen much need for acquiring such data. As a social anthropologist myself I am very aware that our interests have led us in other directions, and that our time in the field tends to be occupied in trying to grapple with problems more directly related to those interests, and that it simply is not possible to devote the time to the kind of minute detail and data collection that would be required for effective demographic study. Happily, we are now increasingly aware of the intricate interplay between biological and social structure, and are more willing to cooperate and devote the time necessary for interdisciplinary work, without which our knowledge and understanding of human populations must remain, at best, partial. A few notable anthropologists are in fact devoting a major part of their energies in this direction, and it should be possible to encourage more. The major problem, then, remains the very nature of the data, and the complex social factors affecting demography in small-scale societies.

The term 'small-scale', though not entirely satisfactory, is greatly preferable to 'primitive', which not only has pejorative connotations but which also, even more seriously for us, has connotations of evolution and progress that, from a social standpoint, are often difficult or impossible to justify. The term is of particular importance here because of the implications of population size upon social structure. 'Pre-literate', equally if not more pejorative, indicates another facet of small-scale societies of importance to demographers, for in the absence of written records one has to gather the necessary information from census data, where available, from informants, and from on-the-spot observation. There are difficulties at every turn here, for among such populations there are frequently good reasons for avoiding giving accurate information to any census-taker, informants are notoriously willing to give the kind of answers that will please, and quick to discover just what that is, and even where this is not so, are nearly always under certain restrictions, arising from their own culture, that prevent them from providing certain classes of information. Further, with informants, there is the exceptionally difficult problem of translation, for terms such as are of the utmost significance to the demographer, and unequivocal in nature, often have no exact counterpart in the language of a small-scale society but may translate into a term representing a superficially similar category that, in fact, is radically different. Even such terms as 'family', and kinship terms such as 'father', 'mother', 'brother', and 'sister' will vary widely from society to society in the classes of people covered by such terms. Frequently they are not related at all, for in small-scale societies such terms primarily indicate social relationships rather than actual kinship relationships, the family (as we could conceive of it) merely serving as a model. In this way it is perfectly common for an informant to count several fathers, of whom some may even be female. The likelihood is, that in this case they would all be relatives on his father's side, and share the same kind of mutual obligations with him as his father. Similarly with nearly all kinship terms, they are essentially classificatory. To spell out the difference between different kinds of fathers or brothers or sisters or mothers would often either be forbidden, or considered the grossest breach of etiquette. Similarly, mention of names of the dead often is forbidden; even the fact of death in some cases may not be referred to. Thus trying to elicit, by mere question and answer, whether a women has given birth to children that died during infancy or adolescence is frequently futile, and is likely to be worse, for in order to stop this undesirable line of questioning the woman, or the informant, will probably provide any figure that is likely to satisfy.

Families range, in the concepts of small-scale societies, from nuclear families to whole tribes, and in segmentary systems any individual will clearly define his family at three or four different levels according to the context, resolutely rejecting any other definition until the context changes. Marriage is another institution with wide variability in significance. For some, it takes place simply, as it does with us, by virtue of a ritual act. But often this act is prolonged over a period of days, weeks, months, or even years, and the marriage is not then considered final until the ritual is over, though the casual observer might consider it to have taken place on the first day if he judges just by outward appearances. With such passage of time divers rights are transferred from one group to the other, including rights to sexual intercourse, rights over children, and rights over property. Under some circumstances, a woman may address any of her husband's family as 'husband', for in the event of his death another will take his place, and perhaps even father children in the dead man's name. Sometimes a marriage is not considered effective until a child has been born and has lived beyond a certain period of time. Frequently a birth does not, so to speak, result in a child until, again, that child has shown that it has come to stay. He is then named, and assumes a social identity for the first time. If he were to die before naming there would be no way of remembering him, and no need to remember, for he had no identity. This custom of delaying the naming of a child, sometimes elaborated into the giving of a succession of names at different intervals, might in fact be of the utmost importance to a demographer as it is probably a fairly accurate gauge of the level and nature of infant and child mortality.

These, then, are some, and only a very few, of the kinds of problems to be faced in obtaining reliable demographic data, problems associated with the garnering of what, in other societies, would be the simplest and most unequivocal of facts. But when we come to consider the powerful social forces at work in affecting the structure of such a population then we face another kind of problem. Not only is there a great deal of variability from one society to another, as stated before, but there is the inescapable difficulty in any kind of quantitative assessment. How does one quantify belief, love, hate, hunger, or fear? These are just a few of the factors that come to mind as having potential significance in determining the demography of any small-scale population. Even to expect a simple rank-ordering may be asking too much, but the first step is plainly to set out what factors, as social anthropologists, we see as affecting population structure, leaving the issue of quantification for later study.

I propose, having attempted to give a broad outline of the nature of the problems, to illustrate in more detail a few of the major social factors involved, repeating only that there is an almost infinite variety of such factors. Having done this, I will then briefly sketch one small-scale society rather more completely, to show how even in one society, allegedly one of the simplest in terms of social structure, there is great complexity. I have chosen the Mbuti pygmies for this, partly because they are best known to me, partly because as one of the few remaining viable hunting and gathering groups left in the world, and at the simplest end of the technological scale, they present not only the simplest form of social structure, but are exceptionally intimately connected with their physical environment, a factor I suggest of supreme importance with regard to the demography of almost any small-scale society, though in the case of the Mbuti we have an extreme (for references, see Turnbull 1965a, b, and c). I also mention, in less detail, a second society, that of the Ik of northern Uganda, who until recently were hunters and gatherers but became caught up in political change, including an enforced change of environment which has led to their decimation to the point where, once again, they are able to maintain a precarious balance with their new ecological setting.

From such sketchy information it would be presumptuous to draw conclusions, so none are drawn. The objective is merely to point to some of the factors involved, and to the very real need for much closer co-operation than has hitherto been fashionable between members of different disciplines. While mentioning other aspects, I will concentrate on environmental factors and on the problem of mobility, both social and spatial. Professor L. L. Cavalli-Sforza and his colleagues have done by far the most intensive and significant, and the most recent, physiological and genetic studies among African pygmies and neighbouring populations (see, for example, Cavalli-Sforza, Zonta, Nuzzo, Bernini, De Jong, Meera Khan, Ray, Went, Siniscalco, Nijenhuis, Van Loghem, and Modiano 1969). Similarly, Lee and De Vore have been working intensively among the South African Bushmen, also hunters and gatherers. For the Ik, unfortunately, there is no published information available at all, and my own study is not likely to be in print for over a year yet. (For descriptive analyses of other African tribal groups see Gibbs 1965.)

Environmental considerations

Any experience of small-scale societies creates a strong sense of an intimate and dynamic interplay between the two (physical and social) aspects of life, with a good deal of adaptiveness on both sides. This is partly a function of population size, and partly, perhaps even more directly, a function of the limited technology. Such societies tend to be adaptive rather than dominant, and react sensitively to even minute environmental changes. While this is particularly true for hunters and gatherers, it is almost equally true for pastoralists, and is still of prime importance among the technologically more advanced cultivators.

A general observation might be made here concerning the influence of environment on small-scale population structure. At the relatively simple technological level of such societies there is a close response to environmental influence in terms of domestic (including kinship) organization, economy, political and religious structure, and systems of beliefs and values. It is a widespread fact among such societies that the totality of human experience is closely integrated into a single system of thought and the objective of that system, if one can properly talk of objective, is survival of the society as such. Among many pastoral peoples, for instance, dispute resolution ranks equally and is closely integrated with care of and consideration for cattle, with the whole value system which pivots around cattle and pasture and water, with the consequent pattern of domestic organization, and is ultimately sanctioned by a system of religious belief that encourages the most all-round satisfactory utilization of the environment, including among the fauna and flora the neigh-bouring human populations and their lands and produce.

The Mbuti pygmies are perhaps one of the clearest examples of the environ-mental potential, but rather than being considered as an exceptional example their case might well serve as a basis for an examination of similar potential elsewhere. While they can survive, in a physical sense, outside their forest environment, that is about all they can do, if even that. The psychological shock, for some, can be fatal, as can the inadequacy of a sense of hygiene that was perfectly adequate in the forest. But equally significant for the demographer, surely, is the almost total breakdown of a morality that in the forest context contributed strongly towards an effective form of birth control, maintaining the population size in sensitive response to environmental con-siderations. But this morality, like all aspects of social life, was closely inter-woven with the other aspects, and centred around the clear recognition by the Mbuti of their dependence upon, and intimate relationship with, the forest. Thus their forest morality had for them no significance the moment they stepped into one of the cleared enclaves cut from the forest by the village farmers. Any permanent settlement of pygmies in or near such enclaves, as being constantly proposed by divers governments, would have immeasurable demographic consequences.

Similarly with the Ik, whose relationship with their environment is different but none the less intense and intimate, their environmental conditioning has led them, in one generation, to the verge of total extinction despite a remark-able versatility and adaptability and willingness to change in all respects except in the one respect of location in their mountain environment. This was brought on by what seemed at the time an insignificant restriction on their nomadic pattern, coupled with a psychological inability to support life in the flat plains below their homeland.

Simplistic environmental determinism and the reaction against it has unfor-tunately obscured the subtle realities of man's relationship with the world around him, and examples of extreme cases, such as these, could well be used as springboards for the examination of urban, suburban, or rural environ-ments in other, more complex societies, with every likelihood of discovering forces at work affecting the demography of such populations. With a more complex technology, obviously, man is able to alter and control his environ-ment and adapt it to his will to a very great extent. This does not necessarily minimize his relationship with that environment, and it certainly does not remove the environment as a factor of major importance.

The absence of a complex technology brings other, perhaps more profound, skills into play, and calls for a flexibility of social organization perhaps only possible in small-scale societies. Above all, it encourages maximal use of the environment, and frequently causes systematic redistribution of populations and, I suspect, necessitates divers forms of population (size) control. One of the prime factors in many small-scale societies is mobility, in its widest sense. This is essential for economic reasons as well as political ones, and of course is of major concern to any demographer. I shall deal with mobility in more detail when discussing the Mbuti pygmies, but here it is worth pointing to certain forms of spatial population movement characteristic of different types of primitive society, each with different demographic implications.

Spatial movement among small-scale societies

For the demographer, as for the social anthropologist, it is not so much the quantity of movement but rather its quality that is important. Movement of any kind creates specific problems of social organization, and any changes in nomadic patterns result in changes in organization. Sometimes, as with the Ik, a slight change can result in a major shift in social organization and have drastic demographic consequences (Turnbull 1972). Movement is an essential part of nearly all small-scale societies, even of cultivators, though if measured in mere terms of distance it may seem insignificant. It creates, amongst other problems, problems of social control, and may well result in division of labour along lines of sex and age that have obvious demographic significance. I will give a brief example of the age factor but first wish to mention two types of population movement most characteristic of small-scale societies, leaving aside the shifting pattern of many cultivators which is dealt with elsewhere in this volume. The two types of movement referred to are nomadism and trans-humance, and with regard to the latter I should say that the usage of the term by social anthropologists does not exactly correspond to its usage by geogra-phers, but in essence remains the same. It is a form of seasonal migration of a population (or part of it) with its flocks or herds, in response to a variety of environmental conditions. But whereas for the geographer, altitude is of special importance, transhumance, for the anthropologist, also takes place horizontally, as with the Nilotic cattle herders, and the Fulani cattle herders of West Africa. The significance of transhumance remains in its essentially seasonal nature.

Nomadism is by no means the free, unpredictable, spontaneous form of movement it is sometimes said to be. A characteristic of hunting and gathering populations, nomadism obviously occurs within restricted areas, is frequently cyclic (particularly where there are marked seasonal variations), and even where it appears to be most haphazard can sometimes be shown not only to have a logic of its own, but to correspond to relatively predictable and limited movements of game. An area that contains a nomadic population might be exploited evenly by the total population, or it might be divided into territories each of which has its own nomadic cycle and contains its own nomadic sub-population. In the latter case, however, the sub-population is not necessarily stable in composition; it may be the territory that is fixed rather than the population, which may move from territory to territory as the bands undergo the process of fission and fusion. These are plainly different forms of nomadism each with different significance for the demographer as for the social anthropologist. The Mbuti pygmies whom we shall be considering, exemplify the greatest degree of mobility, each band being in a constant state of flux. Yet this fact could only be ascertained by living in one small hunting territory throughout a continuous period of twelve months and observing not only the nomadic pattern of the band, but the ever changing composition of the population. At any given moment it would have presented to an acute observer a picture of much greater stability than was in fact the case and we may suspect the same is true of other hunting-and-gathering peoples.

Transhumance, a pattern of movement characteristic of cattle herders, is more fixed in that there is generally a given starting place and a given finishing place for each leg of the back-and-forth movement. It is more predictable in that it usually corresponds to seasonal fluctuations in the availability of water and pasture. It is more stable in that while transhumant populations are often divided into sub-groups which, like the hunting band, are subject constantly to the process of fission and fusion, the process follows a lineal pattern of segmentation, and is associated with a unilineal kinship system unlike that of most hunters. During the annual cycle, then, while there is a waxing and waning of the size of the herding units, the social horizons are only temporarily altered, returning eventually to the same point. Just as the Mbuti are a clear example of the extreme flux to be found amongst hunters, so are the Nuer, of the southern Sudan, a clear example of the segmentary system and transhumance associated with cattle herding (Evans-Pritchard 1968). While during the wet season the Nuer live in isolated villages, with communications sometimes reduced to nil by flood waters, the people of these villages, linked in innumerable associations, come together in ever increasing numbers as they herd the cattle further and further away during the dry season. At the height of the dry season the Nuer are grouped together, not in isolated villages, but in a series of large cattle camps, the composition of which, each year, is almost as predictable as that of the villages during the wet season.

The Fulani of West Africa have a similar transhumant pattern, though for them the wet season is the time for assembly in maximal groupings (Stenning 1959, 1965). But the Fulani also exhibit another form of movement, which Stenning calls '*migratory drift*'. The Fulani movement is a north/south one, and is relatively stable from one year to the next, but a diversity of conditions, ecological and political, sometimes cause a sideways shift to east or west of the total transhumant population. While this does not affect relationships within the population, it does affect relationships between that population and neighbouring ones. The drift may also, though less often, be northward or southward. Under extreme conditions the Fulani transhumant population migrates in a single, dramatic shift. Again, at any given moment, or even over

20

a respectable period of time, say a whole year, it would be easy to misinterpret the situation as being much more stable than it actually is. Since many field studies cover only a single year, and few are conducted for a continuous period of more than two years, added to which there is not always an opportunity for remaining throughout with one single sub-group (a method that has its obvious disadvantages just as it has obvious advantages), it is plain that we do not have the facts we need. Small-scale societies that practise agriculture have on the whole been much better studied, and the data of demographic significance are more likely to be reliable. Such populations are, of course, more stable still, though by no means always as sedentary as might be expected. In the absence of the clear ecological forces that demand population movement, other forces come into play achieving at least something of the same effect.

One important corollary of the agricultural level of organization in small-scale societies is that, due to its semi-sedentary nature, a much more complex form of social control is necessitated resulting in the division of the population into a diversity of sub-groupings which may be domestic (kinship), economic, political or religious. These sub-groupings may be associated with rules of either exogamy or endogamy, the most common examples being the various lineal descent groups, class and caste groups such as nobility, which is usually hereditary, or specialized occupational castes such as black-smithing, wood-carving, ivory-working, judgement-giving, which may also be hereditary. Marital mobility, in such a relatively complex society may further be restricted by religious and political sub-groupings and, a prime factor much neglected, residential or territorial groupings (which are sometimes so important as to override other considerations, the spatial relationship plainly being more important than that of kinship which in any case is frequently hypothetical or fictional).

Spatial movement and age grouping

While in nearly all small-scale societies age is an important and vital subdivision of the population, its importance being witnessed by the elaborate rites of entry and exit, age grouping assumes special significance when related to population movement. The necessarily fissile, segmentary nature of transhumant populations calls for some kind of mechanism for balancing the tendency to fission with some kind of tendency to fusion. This is essential for social purposes, and is sometimes also necessary for military purposes (defence), though this aspect has probably been overplayed. None the less, the social, economic, political, and religious needs, any one of them, are enough to bring about the phenomenon of age grouping. The clearest examples known to me may be found among the East African cattle herders where social horizons are, to a great extent, sealed at or near puberty, having to all intents been predetermined by the date of birth. This is of particular significance for demographic purposes when it is ordained that mates shall be found within specific age-sets, or sub-sets (i.e. those who have been initiated during a given year or period), or taken from specific age-levels (i.e. youth, adolescence, early adulthood). The number of levels (or grades or groups, as they are sometimes called) varies from tribe to tribe, as does the duration of the initiation period during which individuals become age-mates in the same set. Once the set is closed, the horizons are sealed, just as the individual family is when the

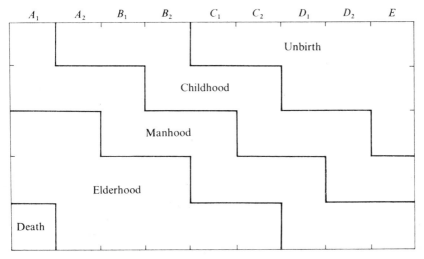

FIG. 15.1. Scheme of a system of age-sets in which each set is divided into two sub-sets. There are three age levels. Time is shown along the horizontal axis in five-year periods.

parents no longer produce (or adopt) children. In such societies this social age (for there is sometimes a fair degree of flexibility designed to allow for the precocious child as well as for the backward one) becomes a major factor, in conjunction with territory, in determining the approved direction of marriage.

A generalized example is here offered, of a type of age-set system that, while it rigidly divides the population into sets, each of which is subdivided into two sub-sets, still takes care to allow for an overlapping of age levels so that each set is allowed a brief period of fraternization (and possibility of intermarriage) with the set on either side of it. There are three basic age levels: childhood, manhood, and elderhood. Initiation marks the entry to manhood, a period which lasts from ten to fifteen years, and during which fraternization with the senior and junior sets may take place according to the scheme shown in Fig. 15.1. The horizontal scale, for simplicity, is in five-year periods; the vertical scale simply denotes the passage from childhood, through manhood, into old age. Thus, when the first subdivision of A age-set, A_1, is initiated, they enter manhood and live as age-brothers for five years before the second half of the set, A_2, is initiated. During those five initial years they were the junior men (*moran* is a common East African term) sharing the responsibilities of manhood with the previous set, who instructed them, and dropped out into elderhood as soon as A_2 was initiated. Thus, members of A_1 shared the same quarters as members of the previous set, and had access to their sisters, but A_2 did not. After a further five years, however, B_1 are initiated, and both A_1 and A_2 fraternize with that sub-set until they jointly drop out, as a unified set A, on the initiation of B_2.

During manhood the men live in special quarters, attended by their sisters, who become the lovers of other men whom they marry when the set passes into elderhood. Women are sometimes initiated into parallel sets, similarly organized.

A less formal variant is found among the Nyakyusa of Zambia, where at puberty boys leave their natal village and begin building villages of their own, into which they introduce their girl-friends as wives, 'closing' the village after a given period. It is not clear, however, along exactly what lines boys choose their village mates, male or female, but we have the clear establishment of what Wilson calls 'age villages'.

One more type of age-set system should be mentioned, which is cyclic rather than linear. In the linear system, when an age-set dies out, its name and identity die with it. In the cyclic systems the names recur, sometimes almost immediately (in which case those of age-set A who are in the old-age level, and are about to die, see children being born who, at puberty, they known will be initiated into a new A set, or into a 'shadow A' set) or sometimes after a generation has passed. In any case, the members of sets in such a system believe in a form of re-birth, and although once again the data are inadequate it would be reasonable to suppose that this might have demographic consequences. A man might, for instance, desire to have children that will be born into or initiated into a specific set or sets. Such a system is shown in Fig. 15.2.

Even in the much less complex societies, such as those of hunters and gatherers, age and residence are major factors in social organization, ranking equally and sometimes more importantly than kinship, and notions of relative age frequently are linked with mating patterns in sometimes unexpected ways. In northern Nigeria, for instance, among some of the non-Muslim tribes, there is the unusual situation in which biological motherhood is of such little significance (in organizational terms) that few men know who their mothers are. Very shortly after giving birth women leave their husbands, who have a plurality of wives in succession. The children are left with the father, and know only their foster-mothers. There is marked unconcern about the possibility of incest, which is recognized as being perfectly possible, and against which the only operative rule is an indirect one which discourages but does not prevent sexual relations between young men and older women. Such liaisons, however, are considered by some as rather dashing. When questioned as to whether it would be more or less dashing if the woman turned out to be her lover's mother, the men's reaction is 'only if she is older' . . . in other words the criterion is solely one of age, even in the face of possible mother/son incest.

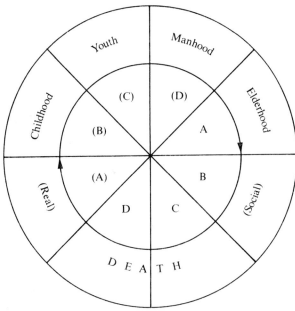

FIG. 15.2. Scheme of a cyclic system of age-sets. Outer circle denotes fixed levels; inner circle, revolving sets.

Another example of practised mother/son incest, known to me in my limited experience, can be found in northern Kenya and northern Uganda. Women anxious to acquire supernatural powers attempt to do so by forcing their own sons to have sexual intercourse with them. Brother/sister incest of the kind practised in ancient Egypt is relatively widespread in sub-Saharan Africa among people with comparable systems of kingship. Under those same conditions political considerations frequently compel the royal line to marry out into neighbouring populations. In some cases marriage boundaries are fixed (and followed) for the total population, in other cases they may be fixed only for a segment of the population, and in many cases, whether they are geographical, linguistic, religious, social, or kinship boundaries, they are, even within the same population, essentially flexible, serving as little more than temporary conveniences. What a population practises today is by no means necessarily an example of what it practised yesterday.

Birth control

There are many social factors affecting and controlling birth rate, some directly, some indirectly. Some, by their bizarre appearance or more obvious, superficial purpose, are not always recognized as such mechanisms. The marriage of young girls to old men, which may have a diversity of functions, may also have the effect of keeping a potential child-rearer out of action for a number of years. It may be as well to mention the fact, well enough known by now, but again perhaps of wider extent than is sometimes supposed, that polygyny does not always by any means involve childbirth; as an institution, it is frequently a way of taking care of widows, of barren women, or of young women whom it is desired to secure for the younger generation (in which case it is more a form of betrothal, via the prospective groom's father or older brother, rather than of marriage). Unfortunately, the term 'marriage' does not have the same connotations in all societies, yet is frequently used without adequate clarification as to the function of the union, which may be quite other than the rearing of children.

Similarly little discussed is homosexuality as a means of birth control which is practised among small-scale societies, usually in conjunction with various ritual taboos on sexual intercourse with women. The clearest examples of this, perhaps, come from South America, where among many of the Indian tribes the living quarters are divided into male and female sections, the women with their young children living apart from the men, and the men being subdivided into small groups of half a dozen or so who are, in a sense, endogamous—that is, adult males of each sub-group, within its own sleeping quarters, practise homosexual intercourse with each other, but not across the partitions that divide them either from the other males or from the females. It is only when weaning is complete (again, as among the Mbuti, frequently a lengthy period of up to three years) that a man may again have sexual intercourse with his wife, until she becomes pregnant, when he rejoins his homosexual sub-group. These sub-groups act as hunting units and as divisions of warring parties, and are considered as held together by this bond, which also binds them together by strong affective bonds, and makes for a tightly knit overall society. The Mbuti do not practise this form of homosexuality, though youths and men frequently sleep together around a camp fire and openly derive mild erotic satisfaction from the physical contact. In purely affective terms, probably most African societies, if not indeed most small-scale societies, may be said to be strongly homosexual, men looking to other men for companionship, and women to women, without precluding a different quality of affective relationship between men and their wives. The close bonds between men, the often vigorous activities they undertake together (particularly drinking and dancing), and the festivals they must attend that exclude women, all contribute to a reduction in the amount of sexual intercourse that can take place between man and wife, and life in a small-scale society is frequently full of such activity. One may suspect that among some peoples institutionalized warfare or raiding serve a similar function, frequently being accompanied by periods of a month or longer during which sexual intercourse is taboo, 'to make the men strong'.

The Ituri population

In many instances, it is even difficult to decide just what constitutes a 'population' in either biological or sociological terms. Even where neighbouring populations appear to be distinct by every criterion, including physical type, we should be careful in drawing our population boundaries, for each may prove to be part of a more complex network of interconnected (and interbreeding) populations. Such is the situation in the Ituri Forest, an area of some 50 000 square miles in the north-east corner of the Congo (Kinshasa), with a total population of some 100 000.

This population, which sees itself as an interacting group of sub-populations, and feels a common identity at least by virtue of its common occupation of a distinctive territory, consists of about 40 000 Mbuti pygmies, who are nomadic hunters and gatherers, and some 60 000 semi-sedentary slash-and-burn non-pygmy African farmers and fishers, to whom I refer generally as 'villagers'. The figures are very approximate; they refer to pre-independence times, and recent civil disturbances have resulted in a reduction of the population by anything up to 50 per cent. At first sight the total population seems to be further subdivided, both the pygmy and the villager segments, into smaller discrete sub-populations, each separated from the others in terms of territory, history, culture (including major linguistic divisions), and physical type. The pygmies are apparently physically homogenous, but are differentiated in terms of economy, nomadic pattern, language, and in the nature of their relationship with their villager neighbours; their territories are similarly distinct.

The villagers are similarly divided, but into many more groups, distributed as if in a vast circle which, apart from its southern sector, runs around the periphery of the forest. The distribution is strictly linear, with one or two minor exceptions, each tribal group having only two neighbours, one at each extremity, but all of them sharing in common the total pygmy population which occupies the central forest proper. To the south lies a vast stretch of allegedly uninhabited forest (certainly there are no farmers there, and there are no signs of any substantial pygmy population); to east, west, and north the forest thins out rapidly or changes abruptly into grassland. Some of the villagers are Bantu-speaking, others are Sudanic-speaking; correspondingly some of them do circumcise and some do not, and on that count alone there should be no interbreeding and no gene flow. Some came in from the north-west, some from the south, some from the east, some from the north-east; some arrived in the approximate area almost as much as 1000 years ago, but the bulk (in the south, east, and north-east) are recent immigrants, dating back perhaps not much more than 200 years, with a few stragglers still arriving. The Mbuti are the original inhabitants, beyond doubt, and can be dated back as far as nearly 5000 years by the historic documentation of the ancient Egyptians.

Other barriers than size, such as cultural and linguistic, at first sight should also in themselves be enough to prevent interbreeding, and the economic situation is such that each group is self-sufficient so there is no need for trade, just as there is ample land so there is no need for aggression. In the midst of this heterogeneity the Mbuti seem to preserve a remarkable homogeneity. They adopt many of the outward customs of their neighbours, but not the rules that go with them. Thus, those in the north-east do not circumcise, whereas those in the south and west do, but that does not prevent inter-marriage between those pygmies. And while there is a limited amount of intermarriage with all the villager groups, it maintains a single outward direction, village males taking pygmy females, the offspring of which are said (and seem) to never to return to the forest, but remain, with their offspring, as villagers. Thus the pygmy population contributes to the village gene pools, but is not itself affected. By their central location, their high degree of mobility, and the extremely fluid nature of their band composition, the pygmies actually create political links between village populations that are not adjacent, and effectively enlarge social horizons in a way that, to my certain but again limited knowledge, leads to some intermarriage 'across' the forest.

The diagram (Fig. 15.3) represents the general manner in which the village populations are distributed, and in which intermarriage within these technically endogamous tribal units takes place; the noteworthy thing being that at the extremities, as might be expected, the marital horizons are more limited than in the centre, but at the extremities certain overlappings of a cultural nature (shared initiations, for instance) are matched by overlapping pygmy bands, and by inter-tribal marriage. Thus the circle is complete, and not divided into truly discrete segments, and instead of a number of isolated populations we get a series of overlapping populations. In terms of distance, marital horizons are limited to market horizons; villages sharing markets share initiations and share wives. This is usually about five villages, but although village 1 does not market at village 9, its horizons extend as far as that, since both market, and may meet, at village 5. One of the prime functions of markets, in an area where each village is economically independent, is to provide for courtship.

The diagrams, of course, are an over-simplification of the actual situation, but represent accurately enough the system which pertained until the post-colonial disorders in the north-eastern Congo. Although the villagers all practised a method of cultivation that necessitated their shifting their plan-tations every three years, and their villages every nine years, their relative position on the circumference of the circle remained the same, and each village could be regarded as a patrilineage since marriage was patrilocal (the wife taking up residence in her husband's village) and descent patrilineal (the children inheriting clan membership, status, and wealth mainly from their father). Each village of any size, however, while still retaining its lineal character,

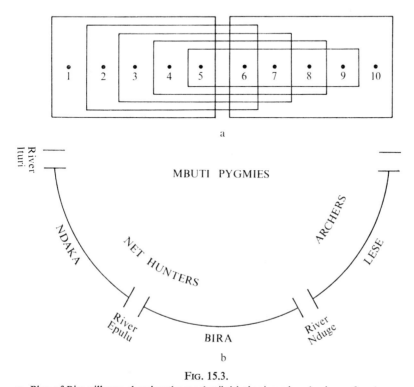

Fɪɢ. 15.3.
a. Plan of Bira villages, showing the market/initiation/marriage horizon of each one.
b. Plan of the Ndaka/Bira/Lese segment of the village circle.

tended to incorporate several other subordinate (in that village) lineal groupings, introduced either by marriage for purposes of economy or politics, or by necessity (such as the need for a blacksmith or some other specialist), in this latter case marriage with someone from the dominant lineage nearly always sealing the arrangement. Such accretions were seldom permanent, or significant in terms of marital mobility, for members of a small subordinate lineal group tended to continue to participate in the initiations and marital circles of the village where their lineage was dominant.

By contrast with this regularity, the Mbuti pygmies, who live within the circle, are in a constant state of flux. At first sight, their organization corresponds to that of the villagers, for radiating outwards from a central neutral territory are the various hunting territories of the 250 or so bands into which the total population of about 40 000 is evenly divided. The appearance is heightened by the system, which I have described elsewhere (Turnbull 1965*a*), whereby the pygmies deliberately lend credence to the villager belief that each hunting territory is populated by a patrilineal band, constituted under the kind of patrilineal/patrilocal organization practised by the villagers. This deception is an integral and vital part of the mechanism by which the two potentially hostile populations maintain a well ordered and peaceful relationship.

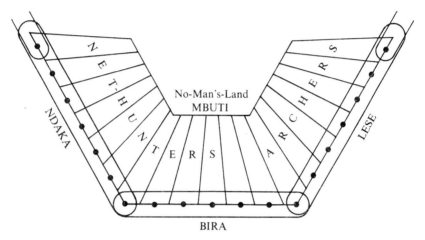

FIG. 15.4. Schematic relationship of hunting territories to villages. Each village and territory marked represents about five. Whereas each segment represents a marriage circle for the villagers, it has no such significance for the Mbuti. The diagram similarly defines the spatial mobility of the villagers, but not of the Mbuti.

The reality, however, is that only the territorial boundaries are fixed (and I really have no certainty that even these are fixed beyond the limits of my own experience, which covers three field trips to the same area between 1951 and 1958). The population within each territory is very definitely bilateral, a system that allows for maximum mobility, and changes with every monthly shift of camp, and even within the duration of any one camp. Figs. 15.4 and 15.5 give an idea of the territorial divisions of the Mbuti, and how they correspond to the village distribution, and of the internal fluctuations that take place within any one territory during the course of a year.

With reference to Fig. 15.5, although this is the typical pattern for a net-hunting group, an almost identical pattern of fission and fusion pertains for the archers. The major difference is that whereas for the bulk of the year the net-hunters live in relatively large-sized bands or sub-bands (six or seven nets, which is to say six or seven nuclear families, is a minimum for a successful net hunt, thirty is a maximum), splitting up into smaller units only for the honey season, the reverse is true of the archers, who for the bulk of the year live in small sub-bands, the total population for the territory uniting only during the honey season.

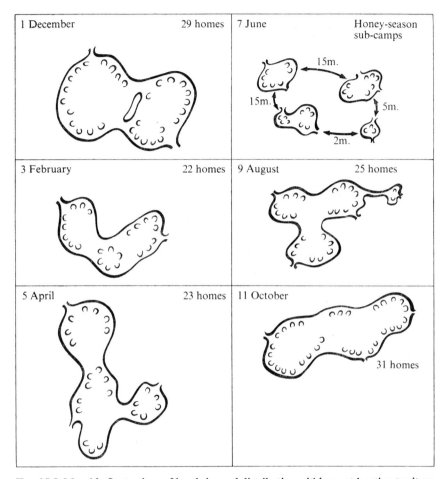

FIG. 15.5. Monthly fluctuations of band size and distribution within a net-hunting territory over a period of twelve months. The evident clusterings of homes within any camp do not necessarily correspond to kinship ties, but rather to bonds of friendship and co-operation.

The change in the size of the camps is about all that can be predicted, the composition of the population is entirely unpredictable, since one major function of this process is dispute resolution, and such movement is spontaneous, responding to political as well as economic needs of the moment. However, men in particular come to regard certain territories (two or three) as 'theirs'; a very few spend the major part of their life in one or other of these 'home' territories. There is a sentimental attachment, but also the practical consideration that these are areas that they know best, in all the intimate ecological detail so vital to successful hunting and gathering. They are usually areas in which they grew up as children. There is, then, a slight tendency to patrilocality, for hunting conditions are more particular than gathering, which is largely the province of women. It is no more than a slight tendency, however, and it should be mentioned that gathering is of greater importance than hunting from the point of view of general sustenance. Such economic and political considerations are coupled to a tendency for men to marry women from bands other than their 'home' bands, and the stated preference is for 'marrying far', meaning spatial distance, but also implying kinship distance.

Demography of the Ituri Mbuti

Out of the total area of 50 000 square miles, about 10 000–15 000 can be said to be a no-man's-land in the centre of the overall hunting circle, in which hunting seldom takes place, but which is neutral territory and can be used by any band at any time. Thus the population, which lies between 35 000 and 40 000 Mbuti, is distributed one per square mile of recognized hunting territory. The area occupied by the villages on the periphery of the circle is insignificant, each village being a tiny, tightly packed enclave usually no more than one or two square miles in extent, including the plantations.

Each hunting territory is populated by a band whose composition is not likely to retain much more than a 40 per cent continuity from one month to the next, hunting camps shifting their position within the territory approximately at monthly intervals. Within the brief life of any one camp, there are several factors influencing population mobility. If the camp is near (within a day's return walk) to the village, individuals or families might well move radially out and back, sometimes staying overnight or even a few days. This is of little demographic significance, since the only other Mbuti they are likely to meet in that village at that time are those who constitute the band from which they came, at that moment. Mbuti may, but seldom do, move from a given hunting territory directly to a village associated with another hunting territory. If they wish to do that, they first move laterally from their own hunting territory to the other, joining that band, as a member of which they then visit the new village. However, it is during these individual visits to villages that courtship leading to mating between a village male and a pygmy female may take place, rather than when an entire band descends and settles for a week or so on the edge of the village, as it may do two or three times each year.

Any move, individual or group, from hunting camp to village may be prompted by a variety of factors. The simple desire for trade is one, though not as important as has been supposed, for any interdependence between village and forest is voluntary, a question of convenience rather than necessity. More frequently Mbuti simply feel the need of a holiday from the rigours of hunting, and when weather is bad and hunting poor then the whole band may decide to give up hunting for a week and visit the village *en masse*. During such mass visits, however, they fraternize less with the villagers than during the individual visits. Another cause may be disputation within the camp, which is most commonly resolved, if it reaches major proportions, by one party or the other leaving, either going to another territory or to the village. Sometimes if an entire camp is torn by dispute (though this generally coincides with bad weather) it will decide to take its 'noise' to the village, which is considered a proper place for 'noise' whereas 'quiet' is the ideal value associated with the forest.

Apart from moves to and from the village, the band moves about month to month within its territory, changing its composition each time. There is a basic economic necessity for this, since after a month the game gets scared away from the vicinity of a camp, the vegetable foods are gathered out and have to be fetched from an inconveniently great distance, and Mbuti sanitation is such that much longer in any one camp would tend to be unhealthy. The moves are all within the territory, and usually each camp is a full day's march from the last, that being adequate to ensure ample supplies of game and vegetable produce.

As seen in Fig. 15.5, the size of a net-hunting camp remains fairly constant throughout the bulk of the year, but towards the honey season it begins to break up into smaller sub-camps which at the height of the season may be 15 miles from each other (an easy day's march). The total population within the territory, however, remains basically unaffected in terms of size.

If an adjacent or nearby territory for some reason becomes unfavourable to hunting, the band there will reduce itself in size to whatever size can be supported, the others going to join other bands. Similarly, a territory where the hunting is particularly good is likely to attract more members. Such fluctuations are temporary, the game and vegetable supply throughout the forest is remarkably even from one end of the year to the next. However, net hunting requires a minimum of 7 nets, and above 30 nets the hunt becomes cumbersome. Only married men may have nets, so a net may be said to correspond to a nuclear family, and the size of a net-hunting band must be between 7 and 30 families. A 'family' seems to average out at about 5 and may comprise parents and unmarried children, and sometimes visiting children, and sometimes widowed grandparents.

Archer bands undergo essentially the same process, but since they can hunt best in small numbers, remain fragmented into small sub-bands for most of the year, coming together at the honey season for the communal *begbe* hunt which requires maximum strength, usually about 30 families, never less than 20.

The honey season is said to be a time of year when vegetable produce is most plentiful, though in fact it is abundant throughout the year. The net-hunting ban takes advantage of this one seasonal event, the availability of honey, to split up into tiny groups and so get relief from all the tensions that build up in the larger, tightly co-operative camps. It is noteworthy that sibling unity seems to have little value for the Mbuti, and the honey season as frequently as not sees brothers go in opposite directions. Food-gathering compatibility is a much stronger factor in determining residence, far above kinship in importance.

The archers evidently feel the need to assert their unity, having been split up for the bulk of the year, and all those in a given territory join together during the honey season for the *begbe* hunt, a beat which requires the men and youths to form a tight but large semi-circle while the women and children beat the game into the arc, hence the necessity for large numbers. But again kinship plays little part, it is rather those that happen to be in any territory at the time of *begbe* who are expected to participate; in other words it is the territory that is considered of importance, rather than the population it contains. This is seen in other realms of Mbuti life, even the most sacred festivals, *elima* and *molimo*, demand participation (in the latter case under threat of death for failure to participate) on grounds of presence within the territory where the girl's initiation or the death ceremony is being held, quite regardless of any kinship consideration.

Movement from one territory to another is plainly of more importance. To some extent this is associated with the monthly displacements of each camp within its own territory, for this is the moment at which individuals decide to go and visit another band, either to escape the 'noise' of a dispute, or simply for the sake of seeing old friends and relatives, or, if a youth, for courtship. Trespass, brought on by pursuing game across territorial boundaries, occurs but is of no demographic significance. Families often exchange visits (sometimes simultaneously, so that the total number of nets is not affected, amongst net-hunters) and generally for purely personal reasons. This serves the same function as the market does for the villagers, it enlarges social horizons and gives youths a chance to find suitable mates. Marriage with someone whose home territory is adjacent is generally discouraged, since it limits rather than expands the social horizons. A gap of several territories is preferred, though not too frequently across the central neutral area (possibly due to the different hunting techniques, spear to the north, net west and south, bow and arrow in the east).

The only stated marriage restriction is against marrying anyone 'related on either side', but given the short genealogical memory of the Mbuti this only effectively excludes first cousins. The only stated preference is equally general, for 'marrying far', meaning several territories distant. There is a fairly widespread custom of sister-exchange, whereby a man is expected to provide a classificatory sister for his wife's classificatory brother, but the classification is so general that the custom has little significance other than as yet another mechanism for setting up a complex system of inter-familial and inter-territorial relationships that can be utilized or ignored according to the needs of the moment. The net result, however, is that almost any Mbuti can find one such relationship to invoke in almost every other territory, should it suit him to move there, temporarily or permanently. It is habitual for each hunter, with his wife and possibly with his unmarried children, to exercise their rights in at least four or five other territories ranging up to ten territories on either side of his home territory, and sometimes across the neutral area. But whereas the net hunter is versed in archery, and can readily join an archer band in the east, the archer, not possessing a net, is at a disadvantage in net-hunting territory unless there is a net (or a sick man, for instance) for him to use, or unless he is content with a junior role. Youths, male and female, frequently travel on their own for purposes of courtship, though there is nothing to prevent courtship and marriage within any one camp, since there are nearly always a number of 'stranger' families present, perhaps specifically with the purpose of effecting a marriage.

Life crises: birth, adolescence, marriage, and death

The villagers state categorically that Mbuti women are more fertile than their own women, and give this as one reason for seeking intermarriage. Other reasons, economic and political, can be suspected in addition, but there is the undoubted fact that venereal disease is rampant amongst the villagers and almost totally absent among the Mbuti, so there may be some truth to the belief. It may also be that the infant mortality rate is lower among the Mbuti, resulting in an appearance of higher birth rate. On the other hand, the Mbuti practise birth control, whereas to the best of my knowledge the villagers do not.

Birth

There is no anxiety, among the Mbuti, over birth; it is treated as a normal event. Each woman will follow her own inclinations as to food restrictions and hunting restrictions, but most continue to hunt and gather with the band until the day of delivery, and it is not uncommon for woman to give birth while on the hunt, pausing only for a couple of hours before returning to camp with the infant. It is not possible here to go into details of childbirth and child care; my knowledge is in any case limited, but I have observed great attention paid to post-natal care and my general impression certainly confirms the belief shared by the villagers and Mbuti that Mbuti children have a far better chance of survival than villagers. There are no reliable data on fertility or fecundity, nor on sex ratio. But there is definitely no evidence of infanticide, except in the case of monsters; stillbirths are evidently extremely rare, and yet according to Patrick Putnam, who lived in the Ituri for a quarter of a century and ran a hospital there, the population shows no signs of increase. This implies very clearly that there is some indigenous form of birth control.

The husband comes under important restrictions immediately following the birth of a child to his wife. Until that moment, he has been under no restrictions concerning sexual intercourse; some hold that during pregnancy it hurries matters along, and that towards the end it merely becomes 'uncomfortable'. Immediately following birth, the husband comes under the stated prohibition against intercourse *with his wife* until the child is weaned, a period of three years. It is, of course, difficult to be sure of what does and does not go on under cover of night in the huts of recent parents, but Mbuti leaf-huts being as flimsy and as close to each other as they are, one can occasionally hear signs of illicit activity. I suspect much of this is intentional, in the nature of a bawdy joke: only on one occasion was it taken by the Mbuti to be for real, and then it caused a major dispute on the grounds that such activity would be injurious to the health of the child. The Mbuti are much concerned about motherhood, and about lactation, for which they have several herbal medicines in case of deficiency. The women keep to the three-year weaning period, which means they do not become pregnant for three years, though I do not for a moment believe this is due to total abstinence from sexual intercourse. During this time their husbands may flirt around, everyone turning a blind eye to such flirtations provided they are discreet. Discretion is a simple matter. Only married couples have sexual intercourse inside huts, others like to have it outside, in the forest. During the weaning period the mother takes her child to introduce it to friends and relatives in other bands, while the husband may accompany her but frequently takes advantage of the occasion to go off on his own on special hunting expeditions, such as elephant hunting, on which women are not taken. The net effect is that a married women only produces one child (twins are almost unknown; I suspect that one is allowed to die at birth) every four years. It is difficult to arrive at any reliable figure for the number of children who survive into adulthood; the critical period, from a health point of view, is up to the age of eight or nine. I know a few young families with as many as six children alive, but I know of few families where more than four siblings are themselves parents.

Adolescence

As children grow up in the intimacy of their family hut, where nothing is concealed from them, and in a band within which among their age-mates they can find many a legitimate partner, and where pre-marital sexual intercourse is considered as a healthy and indeed a delightful pastime, it is remarkable that in some four years of close contact and intimate living among the Mbuti, I know of not a single case of pre-marital pregnancy. There are potions taken by youths of both sexes to avert conception, abortion is known and,

I am told, occasionally practised by unmarried girls and by married women, but more important perhaps are simpler restrictions on the ways in which an unmarried couple may lie and embrace each other. I found it difficult to obtain exact details, but it is certain that such restrictions cause certain difficulties (which are the subject of much mirth among the youths) and may very well effectively prevent conception. The Mbuti themselves indicate this is so, though they assert that intercourse is complete and satisfying to both partners. At adolescence there is a major religious festival, the *elima*, which in a sense is a joint puberty festival for youths of both sexes, but which is triggered by 'the first blood' of a young girl. There is a curious and highly significant difference of opinion and attitude concerning menstruation, between villagers and Mbuti. The former regard it with horror, as a sign of moral and ritual uncleanliness. Sexual intercourse is rigorously prohibited at this time, and the girl or woman is segregated, under strict taboos against handling food or fire. The 'first blood' among villagers is said to have been caused by her rape, and they demand that the girl (shut off from the entire community) name her aggressor. This is an opportunity for her to name her would-be spouse, whether or not he raped her. He then can either accept the charge, whereupon he pays the cleansing fine and is 'forced' to marry the girl. Or else (if he does not want to marry her) he denies the charge, pays a similar fine, and the girl is asked to think again. In any event, it leads to marriage almost immediately.

Among the Mbuti the attitude is quite different. The news is broadcast to the world with joy, for a mere girl has now become, they say, a potential mother. She is the object of pride and envy. Within the band, as constituted at that moment, there may be other girls about 'to see the blood', or who have recently seen it, and the girl who has seen it can nominate friends amongst these others and all jointly enter the *elima* hut, built specially for them. There they are taught the arts of motherhood, such as they do not already know, and they openly court the young men who flock to the camp when they hear the news of the *elima*. The young men, invited by the girls, also enter the hut, and sleep with the girls. It is a free-choice arrangement, but in order to enter the hut the youth has to display considerable courage and do battle with the mothers (prospective mothers-in-law) who surround the hut and have all the power needed to prevent any youth they dislike from entering the hut, by sheer physical force. It is expected that during the *elima* (usually a month in duration, i.e. one camp's duration) the girls will settle on their future life partners, but there is no compulsion to do so, and it may be only several years later that they enter marriage. It is said that restrictions on sexual intercourse inside the *elima* hut are rigidly enforced, along the lines mentioned earlier, for the girl is in particular danger of becoming pregnant at this time. This leads us to the possibly significant belief among the Mbuti, an odd one for a people so knowledgeable about animal life, that when a woman is menstruating, sexual intercourse has the most chance of causing pregnancy. Among youths it is a question of taste; some say that intercourse is more pleasurable at this time, some say it is less so; in itself it involves no restrictions. But during married life, if a couple want to have children, they concentrate their efforts on this monthly period. The effects of this upon birth rate might be worth considering.

Marriage

For the Mbuti this is a simple matter, depending almost entirely on the desire of the partners concerned. The question of locality is determined in part by the groom's knowledge of certain hunting territories, and in part by the strength of the bands in those territories at that time. The tendency is for patrilocality; but it is by no means universal, and if the couple has encountered any opposition to their marriage they are likely to go to a remote territory where, after all, they can learn speedily enough all they need to know about the new environment. Marriage takes place when the couple are about 16 or 17 years old, seldom earlier, sometimes later. The only qualification is that the young man should have proven himself capable of supporting a family, which he does by killing one of the larger antelopes from his position on the periphery of the hunt, or by single-handed tracking.

It is plain that economic and political considerations are paramount. In my own experience I know of only two cases in which kinship was raised as an issue, and only one of those involved a potential marriage, the other was merely a mildly incestuous affair. It is considered important that both partners should be approximately the same age; thus again age and residence are prime factors, superceding those of kinship. Companionability is a factor, and brothers and sisters who have grown up in the same territory, as usually happens, are often loath to be parted at marriage. Sister-exchange marriage, with both couples settling in the same territory, moving together as hunting companions, makes separation unnecessary, and is said to create the strongest bonds and make for the best hunting.

Polygyny occurs, but is relatively rare (perhaps one in thirty). It usually occurs by chance rather than design, for a couple of newly-weds who have not produced children are not considered as fully married, and do not have full marital status. If, after a year of living together, the girl has not shown signs of pregnancy, the couple usually separate, and seek new partners. It sometimes happens that after the boy has settled down with a new girl, which he has to do almost immediately in order to be able to operate as a net hunter (the alternative being to give up his net and rejoin the youths), his former bride finds that she is, after all, pregnant, and comes to rejoin him. I only know of one case where a man, by design, took three wives. This was considered as an invitation to 'noise', and held in disfavour. Sociological parenthood is of much more importance than biological parenthood; if a woman is so unfortunate as to bear no children, friends or relatives who already have four children will give their next child to the childless couple. It is extremely difficult, even by the most diligent enquiry, to know for sure when this has happened, and this is (though sometimes to a lesser extent) true of all the small-scale societies known to me. Even clan membership of the wife, in a patrilineal society, is often concealed, and it may be considered indelicate to enquire too closely into her lineal origins since this implies distance between her and her husband. There are societies where she is formally adopted into her husband's lineage, thus giving her security and status in a society in which she would otherwise remain a foreigner. This is perhaps a little unusual, though even where there is no such adoption a woman may well give her husband's clan when asked for hers. Even in a classical segmentary society, where lineage plays so dominant a role, sociological membership is the vital concern, although this usually coincides with biological descent in such a society. The Mbuti present an extreme example of wide-range marital mobility, yet I suspect that the range is much wider than is often supposed in many other more formally and tightly organized small-scale societies.

Death

As with other demographic factors, for the Mbuti little is known of morbidity and mortality. Accidental death is rare; pygmies are seldom injured during the hunt, and very rarely fall from trees or fall victim to attack by animal or snake. One of the few forms of accidental death that can be expected to repeat itself, infrequently, arises from the habit of waking at night and sitting close to a fire for warmth. On such occasions the Mbuti are likely to smoke, and to inhale with extra depth, and they have been known to fall unconscious as a result and fall into the fire and die as a result of their burns. There is no warfare or murder or feud, either amongst themselves or between themselves and the villagers. Disease is minimal, since on the forest floor there are neither flies nor mosquitoes to carry disease, and the nomadic life ensures sanitary living conditions. Mbuti associate the village with premature death, and with good reason, for in the villages they are subject to heat stroke and they have little resistance to various diseases against which the villagers have immunity. The villagers similarly associate the forest with premature death, and this reciprocal fear in itself is an effective demographic force encouraging the continued separation of the two populations.

The Mbuti recognize that the first 8 or 9 years of life are relatively hazardous, but having passed that period they can look forward to living a healthy life into their sixties. They accept death with equanimity as a natural if regrettable event. The ensuing festival in itself is part of the overall birth-control mechanism, while its symbolism clearly indicates a recognition of the necessity for regeneration of life. The *molimo*, or death festival, is accompanied by certain restrictions on sexual intercourse, and in any case is a period (of a month at least) of such intensive nocturnal activity, allowing the married men a mere one hour, just before dawn, when they can try and snatch some sleep before getting ready for the next day's hunt, that most men admit that sexual intercourse is just about unthinkable. Even the youths (who in any case would not produce children) find their ardour dampered. The ritual, significantly enough, is a dramatic symbolization of Mbuti notions about life and death, and the role of men and women in procreation, and their power to create, preserve, and destroy life. The sexual conflicts of interest are openly manifest, and there is a ritual dance performed at this time in which ritual reversal takes place, the men dressing and behaving as women, the women as men, culminating in an imitation of the act of copulation, each sex playing the opposite role. I confess I do not clearly see how this dance, *ekokomea*, is associated with population control or other demographic issues, but in conjunction with the rest of the *molimo* festival symbolism it may give us a clue as to attitudes that do lead to effective control.

Environment, identity, and population

By way of summary I use another population, the Ik of northern Uganda, as an example of the fundamental and dynamic yet potentially disastrous interplay between these three elements. The potential for disaster cannot be dealt with here, other than to point to the Ik as a clear example of such disaster arising from the interference by technologically more advanced peoples in the delicate balance of life among a technologically limited people until then living satisfactorily in an extremely restrictive environment. It would not be correct to blame the technological limitations of the Ik, for until such interference in their life they evidently had no difficulty in surviving, though their population size probably waxed and waned according to contextual changes. The point being made is sharpened, perhaps, by referring to the clear indications in our 'civilized' world that technology itself is directly inviting even greater disaster by making even greater disruption of this vital relationship possible. And again, the ultimate fault is not with technology *per se*, but rather with this dislocation that it encourages and causes, and with us for assuming that our technological mastery (limited as it is) over the environment, our highly individualistic and independent sense of identity, and our arbitrary and artificial and essentially politico-economic division of the world into 'national' populations, are all beyond question right and proper. However we might define 'ecological success', it would be difficult to consider the modern nation as ecologically successful, and it is significant that success seems further removed in proportion to the increasing size of the 'population', or nation.

Survival is surely a major component of ecological success, as is a reasonable anticipation of continued survival given similar ecological circumstances, and given a technology that can adapt to predictable changes in such circumstances. Small-scale societies, by such definition, are demonstrably far more successful than the larger more complex societies, and in analysing such success the interplay between the three elements under consideration is most evident. The intimate relationship of man to his environment we have already discussed, and obviously his identity is involved with it. It is not a romantic invention of the anthropologist that the pygmies refer to themselves as 'children of the forest', and that the Ik similarly refer to themselves as *kwarikik*, or 'mountain people'. And the identification itself is more than a mere intellectual exercise; it is real and full, for such people make themselves a living, responsive part of the environment they identify with, one might almost say a parasitic part, and therein lies the secret of their success.

One of the problems that the anthropologist, as also the demographer, has to face is how to define 'population', where to draw the boundaries between one population and another. Obviously, boundaries can be drawn at will, for purposes of analysis, but if we think again in terms of ecologically successful populations, we find that they tend to be those defined by common identity of this kind. Thus for the Mbuti it is not a question of size, colour, language, or culture that separates them from their village neighbours, it is their conscious identification with the forest, just as the villagers' conscious rejection of the forest provides them with *their* identity. Yet in so far as all live within the same overall forest they all perceive a wider identity, as different forms of parasites living off the same host. This corresponds, as has been seen, to both the anthropological and demographic facts.

Looking at the larger nations in the same way, we might be tempted to say that they do not form populations let alone societies in any meaningful sense, they are merely administrative or governmental conveniences at best. They have lost their intrinsic viability and are held together by man's fallible artifice. Yet by analysis we could perceive viable societies and populations within such nations, very often overlapping the artificial boundaries. Environment and identity again provide valuable clues.

It seems that among small-scale societies the individual sees himself differently than among large-scale societies, and that this must be understood before we can properly comprehend their thoughts or their actions, or, perhaps, their demography. The so-called kinship systems prove, on close inspection, to be by no means as closed and inflexible as they appear when stated. Kinship terms are a great deal broader (more classificatory) than our own, and designate social relationships rather than actual kinship. Among hunters and gatherers such as the Mbuti, such terms designate age levels, specifically, utterly ignoring kinship, so that all individuals of the same age regard each other and address each other as brother and sister, and all those younger as child, all those of a generation higher as mother or father, and those older still as grandparent. Even the sex differentiation only occurs in the parental terms, a single term equivalent to sibling (or, perhaps better, 'friend') being used rather than brother or sister. The terms are as follows:

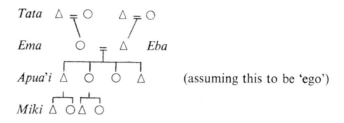

This clearly shows the sociological orientation of the people. They are concerned with the society as a whole, rather than with individuals. And just as these terms of address and reference indicate this concern, so do personal names and lineages and clan names. The individual only exists as part of a complex interlocking system of social relationships, by himself he has no identity and no value. Good and bad are judged by what is good and bad for the society as a whole. It was therefore perturbing for me, at first, when I found myself working amongst a group of hunters-turned-cultivators (the Ik of northern Uganda) whose only stated value was *ngag*, or food; whose only notion of goodness (*marangik*) was the individual possession of food in the stomach; and whose definition of a good man (*yakw ana marang*) was 'a man who has a full belly'. The Ik are barely surviving under conditions of extreme starvation, in an environment they refuse to leave and which is incapable of supporting them at their previous population size. Individualism was cultivated, it seems, in response to this situation, as a mechanism for reducing the population to a reasonable size, by making the frequency of death, and the fact of death, perfectly acceptable to the survivors. Neighbouring African tribes look on the Ik with horror, and denied that they were human, and said they were more like Europeans. This was no mere insult, it was a perceptive comparison between two peoples who practised the essentially un-African (and un-small-scale society) custom of allowing people to grow up as individuals, without any social consciousness (which is how Europeans appeared to these Africans, at least). Villages were still built, as a symbol of social solidarity, but the nuclear family, as a viable institution, simply ceased to function, in all but the most general way. Children, born with reluctance, maintained by reluctant mothers with even less grace until weaned at three (unless the mother has managed to leave the infant where it would be eaten by a leopard, an occasion for much rejoicing), had to find their own way in life from 3 years old onwards. They grow up, reasonably enough, without any great sense of filial devotion, and were as amused to see their parents die as their parents would have been to see them die, for after all, death by definition was a good thing, it meant more *ngag* for the others. Couples get married only in case there should be need for co-operation (the same reason that mothers bother to feed their children until weaned), in the unlikely event of the hunt or the fields ever being productive enough to require co-operation. But for the most part, food-getting for adults is an individual affair, and any tactics are justified by the supreme (because it is solitary) value of goodness, the individual possession of food in the stomach. One sees children opening the mouths of old people to extract food, should the old people manage to find any. Certainly nobody would give them any. Younger children get beaten up by older children if found with food. Food must be transferred to the stomach as rapidly as possible, so it is frequently not cooked, since the smoke from the fire would give the game away. The result of eating uncooked grains (rounded off with smooth pebbles and tree bark) is not unfrequently fatal.

Sexual activity is minimal, few have the energy. The breeding group (that is the teenagers, for in the early twenties one begins to age rapidly) is the healthiest and takes food from adults, elders and children alike, and indulges in limited sexual activity. It is considered as a chore, however, and likened, as only the Ik could liken it, to the mildly pleasurable chore of defaecation. Rather than intercourse, which is more tiring and leads to demands of payment in food (even between wives and husbands) by the female who knows she can sell what energy she has among the neighbouring herders, masturbation is practised. It is sometimes combined with a more important activity, such as keeping an eagle eye open for tell-tale signs of food—smoke, circling vultures, and so forth. The lesser activity is immediately abandoned.

In times of extreme shortage (such as the 18 months I spent among the Ik) these sad but functional practices are most obvious. But the situation being of over 30 years duration now, it has become established so that even in times of plenty, which I witnessed on a subsequent visit, the individual good is still the only good.

It is a remarkable achievement that the Ik have found a way of surviving *as a society*, in such abnormal situations. It is significant that their technique involves the retention of their 'environmental identity' even at the cost of their social consciousness. This would seem to be a last resort, for as little as two generations ago the Ik were, as far as we can tell, hunters and gatherers organized very similarly to the Mbuti. Both societies, in their extremes of abundance and insufficiency exhibit the same intensely sensitive adjustment to the environment, a characteristic, I suggest, of all small-scale societies, and perhaps more a characteristic of our own large-scale industrial societies than we might suppose; the comparison between ourselves and the Ik being uncomfortably close.

REFERENCES

CAVALLI-SFORZA, L. L., ZONTA, L. A., NUZZO, F., BERNINI, L., DE JONG, W. W. W., MEERA KHAN, P., RAY, A. K., WENT, L. N., SINISCALCO, M., NIJENHUIS, L. E., VAN LOGHEM, E., and MODIANO, G. (1969). Studies on African Pygmies. I. A pilot investigation of Babinga Pygmies in the Central African Republic (with an analysis of genetic distances). *Am. J. hum. Genet.* **21**, 252–74.

EVANS-PRITCHARD, E. E. (1968). *The Nuer.* Clarendon Press, Oxford.

GIBBS, J. L. (1965). *Peoples of Africa.* Holt, Rinehart, and Winston, New York.

LEE, R. B. and DE VORE, I. (eds.) (1968). *Man the hunter.* Aldine Press, Chicago.

STENNING, D. J. (1959). *Savannah nomads. A study of the Wodaabe Fulani of Western Bornu Province, Northern Region, Nigeria.* Clarendon Press, Oxford.

—— (1965). The pastoral Fulani of northern Nigeria. In *Peoples of Africa* (ed. J. L. Gibbs). Holt, Rinehart, and Winston, New York.

TURNBULL, C. M. (1965a). The Mbuti Pygmies: an ethnographic survey. *Anthrop. Papers, Am. Mus. Nat. Hist.* **50**, 139–282.

—— (1965b). The Mbuti Pygmies of the Congo. In *Peoples of Africa* (ed. J. L. Gibbs). Holt, Rinehart, and Winston, New York.

—— (1965c). *Wayward servants. The two worlds of the African pygmies.* Natural History Press, New York.

—— (1972). *The mountain people.* Simon and Schuster, New York.

16

DEMOGRAPHY, ECOLOGY, SOCIAL STRUCTURE, AND SETTLEMENT PATTERNS

Peter Kunstadter

Introduction

MY attempt in this paper is to deal with factors relating to demography, ecology, social structure, and settlement patterns. In speaking of demography I refer to conditions of birth, death, and migration, and the resulting age and sex distribution within a defined population. By communities, I refer to the groupings in which people live; by settlement patterns, I refer to the spatial distributions of communities relative to one another and relative to geo-graphical features. By ecology, I refer to the interrelationships between man and his environment, including his social environment, in particular the effects of man on the environment, and the limitations on man's activities imposed by the environment at a given level of technology and given relationships with other societies. By social organization, I mean the patterned interrelationships between men. Most of the data in this paper were gathered in north-western Thailand during research supported by National Science Foundation, National Institute of General Medical Sciences, Princeton University, and the University of Washington.

Basic differences are often overlooked between prehistoric man and people living in the underdeveloped parts of the modern world, where life has been heavily influenced by the social organizations and technologies of modern societies, despite superficial appearances. A trip to present-day India or rural Mexico is not a 'step backwards in time' although many aspects of material culture and social organization may have survived. Contemporary 'primitive' communities may not provide an adequate model for understanding man prior to modern public health and medicine, prior to the wide-reaching tech-nical and social innovations (including economic relationships) which have come to involve almost the entire world's population, and the major effect of these: the population explosion.

Non-modern men are men in non-literate, non-civilized societies, with small concentrations of populations, living in semi-isolation, having limited contacts with other such groups, limited economic and political differentiation. Such men have economic systems confined to single villages, although they may have occasional networks of trade between essentially equal units. These units are essentially self-sufficient, dependent mainly on resources within their own control. They are dependent not at all, or only rarely, on fossil fuels. Such societies have had relatively stable or slowly changing material culture for exploiting their natural environment, and relatively unstratified simple social systems for governing relations between individuals or between groups. Modern societies and their precursors have increasingly large populations and large population concentrations (cities), highly differentiated and inter-dependent segments, relatively rapidly changing technologies of environ-mental exploitation. By contrast with non-modern societies, they are not even theoretically homeostatic over the long run, as they have depended extensively on fossil fuels and other non-renewable resources.

One basic fact of the modern world is the population explosion, which is the result of relatively sustained interruption of many of the normal 'pre-historic' causes of mortality, or an interruption in wide swings of mortality rates, combined with relatively slow changes in prehistoric patterns of natality (or perhaps an increase in natality). Despite Malthus (1798) we have only begun to become aware of this condition, although it has been with us for a hundred years or more; we have not yet devoted our attention to the syste-matic study of the effects of development of modern demographic conditions on social structure, ecology, and settlement pattenrs. Despite the work of historical demographers (Drake, in this volume) and the recent work of anthropologists and geneticists with isolated, primitive populations (Chagnon, Schull, and Salzano, in this volume) we may now be too late to collect the type of data required for a world-wide evaluation of these changes.

Classic transition theory of demographic change

The classic 'transition' theory of population growth (Notestein, Taeuber, Kirk, Coale, and Kiser 1944) describes three periods or types of demographic structure as determined by relationships between birth and death rates. The first is supposed to have been characteristic of the vast majority of populations for the bulk of prehistory and history of mankind. This type has a high birth rate and a balancing death rate, with a consequent absence of population growth. The high birth rate gives these populations a high potential growth rate; many children are born, but few survive to reproduce. This condition accounts for the observed fact that *on the average* human population grew at an extremely slow rate from the time of the origin of the species until a few hundred years ago. The second, or 'transitional' stage occurs when death rates fall as a result of improved economic and health conditions, while birth rates remain high. This imbalance causes 'transitional growth' of populations as a higher proportion of children survive to the age of reproduction. In Europe the balance was restored in the third stage by a fall in birth rates, apparently as people came to recognize the economic disadvantages of large numbers of surviving children. Associated with the third stage is an increase in the average age of the population, and a decrease in the proportion of young dependent children.

The description of the first two stages in long-term, large-scale *averages* of population growth due to changes in relationships of birth and death rates is probably correct, but may be very misleading with regard to the operation of birth and death rates within individual communities. The European (and also Japanese and perhaps Taiwanese) pattern of transitional growth followed by lower fertility may not be the only one, and may not even be the usual one. Transitional growth resulting from the removal of one of the causes of mortality cannot go on indefinitely: sooner or later if fertility does not decrease, mortality will increase because of lack of resources. This would lead to a picture of high fertility and high mortality which is not the same as the classic European post-transition stage, nor the same as the pre-transition stage, since the causes and distribution of mortality are probably different.

Small populations, that is, the populations of communities in which most people have lived prior to extensive urbanization, do not behave in the same way as large statistical aggregates. Because of the effects of epidemic diseases on the population of small semi-isolated communities, and the application of random processes in small populations, the model is probably incorrect and misleading when applied to small communities on an annual or even a generation basis. Until relatively recently, most people have lived and evolved their social organizations (as well as their genetics) in small communities.

Demography of small communities

A more nearly accurate model of demographic conditions in the small hunting and gathering or agricultural communities within which most non-modern men have lived may have been high fertility (beyond the level needed for replacement in normal years) with low-to-medium death rate, with occasional or periodic variations in death rates due to natural disasters (floods, earthquakes, climatic fluctuations disrupting the normal environmental relations, insect plagues, crop failures, epizootics, etc.), and probably more recently, epidemic diseases. Chronic food-shortages must also have been a limiting factor on population growth, but we will deal first with the acute conditions. We do not know enough about the effects of acute environmental disasters on human populations to generalize. The effects may or may not be random. We can speculate, however, on the effects of epidemic diseases: these are unlikely to have random effects on demographic and social structure, but the effects would vary depending on the nature of the disease, mode of transmission, degree of virulence, period of contagion or transmissibility, period of immunity, non-human hosts or vectors, and so forth.

Measles is the best-known and best-worked-out disease model of epidemics. It may not be typical because of its special characteristics of high contagion, short, clearly-defined period of contagion, person-to-person spread by aerosol, life-long immunity to survivors, probably highly adapted stable agent, and variable virulence depending on general health and nutrition of the victims. Apparently measles will die out in an isolated population of limited size. There is no intermediate non-human host, and no natural storage of the disease agent. Bartlett (1960) has indicated that 'the critical community size for measles (the size for which measles is as likely as not to fade out after a major epidemic until reintroduced from outside, corresponding to a mean time to fade-out of about two years) is found for the United States to be about 250 000 to 300 000 . . . These figures agree broadly with English statistics . . .'

Measles is probably not a typical disease (there probably is no such thing for these purposes) but it does offer a handy example to allow speculation on the effects of epidemic disease or even periods of acute food stortage on demographic structure, if we assume that it may have had a sizeable mortality rate in non-modern populations. Two models of the demographic effects of epidemic disease are possible for discussion. Both assume high birth rates and high long-term average death rates for the population. One model assumes repeated, frequent passages of the diseases through the population; the other model assumes infrequent passages. Because of the characteristic size and distribution of non-modern populations, the second model is more likely to be correct. In the first model, the number of susceptible individuals would tend to be small at any one time, limited to the cohort which escaped the previous epidemic due to chance, due to the presence of maternal antibodies, or due to being born after the last epidemic. This would be a young group; the disease, even if it were highly fatal to susceptible individuals, would have relatively little disruptive effect on the social structure, since most of the victims would be infants and young children. The effect on demographic structure would be to reduce the rate of population growth. Age structure would remain relatively stable despite the repeated epidemics. Average annual birth and death rates would offer a good approximation of this process. The demographic consequences of this model resemble the first stage, 'high growth potential', in the classic transition theory of population growth.

The second model may be more likely for diseases of this type in non-modern populations. It postulates infrequent epidemics. These would probably have a much more disruptive effect, even if the disease were not very virulent, because the number and proportion of susceptibles in the population would be much greater, and their age distribution would be much more widespread. Family and village structure would be disrupted, and children might die if their parents died, even though the children themselves might not be mortally infected. By contrast with the first model, some aspects of the demographic structure would be quite variable. During non-epidemic periods, the proportions of children in the population would grow rapidly. As this cohort reached reproductive years, the crude birth rate would increase and the population growth would accelerate. After the epidemic the 'normal' age structure would be disrupted, the crude birth rate would drop, and the population growth would not accelerate until a new expanded cohort reached reproductive age. The exact effects would depend on the periodicity of the epidemics and the age distribution of mortality. Long-term average annual rates would give no clue to these effects. More subtle effects of this model on social structure are discussed below.

Effects of disease and disaster in a small semi-isolated community can be drawn from the recent history of Ban Pa Pae, a Lua' village of approximately 200 people in north-west Thailand. Modern medicine has not been available to this population until recently. The first measles epidemic in about 20 years struck Ban Pa Pae in about August 1966. Everyone under the age of 20 was reported to have come down with the disease. No one died, but many families (especially those with young children) had partial crop failures because they were unable to weed their fields while the children were ill. About 20 years previously, the villagers reported a smallpox epidemic; many people died, including children who had no one to care for them when their parents were sick. Following the smallpox epidemic, a fire destroyed about one-third of the houses in the village and destroyed stored grain and rice seed just before planting. No one was killed in the fire, but many families moved temporarily or permanently to the valley. In contrast with nearby villages which did not suffer so badly from the smallpox epidemic, Ban Pa Pae showed a relatively slow rate of population growth, and a somewhat higher than average median age, an older than average age at marriage, lower than average reproduction rates, and high rate of infant and child deaths in the epidemic. As time passes, the age distribution comes to resemble that of other nearby villages. The village population recovered slowly at first, and growth has accelerated in recent years, as the cohort born since the epidemic and fire reaches the age of reproduction (see Table 16.1 and Fig. 16.1).

This example suggests the demographic vulnerability of small isolated communities, and their resilience under conditions of high birth rate. I suspect this situation is common, but lack the data to prove it on a wide scale. The situation described for Ban Pa Pae resembles that of the second model, high birth rate with relatively low death rate and periodic epidemics or disasters (see Fig. 16.1). McArthur (1961) describes a similar fluctuation of demographic structure due to disease in the Pacific Islands, where a decline in crude birth rates associated with a period of colonial administration was not due to the 'psychological factor' or loss of will to reproduce, but rather resulted from the disastrous effects of a smallpox epidemic on the cohort in the reproducing age. When, through the passage of time, the age distribution became normalized, the crude birth rate returned to its normal high level.

As a result of considerations of this type, we can expect three types of demographic variability to appear when we examine small communities: variation of population structure within a given community over time;

TABLE 16.1

Reconstruction of mortality patterns (age at death)† from two upland villages in Mae Sariang District

Estimated age at death	Estimated date of death								Date unknown	Total	Percentage
	1964–1968	1959–1963	1954–1958	1949–1953	1939–1948	1929–1938	1919–1928	1909–1918			
Lua', Ban Pa Pae											
Under 1 month	2	4	3	2	6	0	5	2	7	31	27·4
1–12 months	1	5	3	6	4	4	0	0	0	23	20·6
1–4 years	2	1	2	1	15	4	7	0	1	33	29·2
5–9 years	0	1	0	0	2	1	0	0	1	5	4·4
10–14 years	0	0	0	0	3	2	2	0	1	9	8·0
15–19 years	0	0	0	0	0	0	0	0	1	1	0·9
Over 20 years	0	2	5	1	2	1	0	0	0	11	9·7
Total	5	14	13	10	32	12	14	2	11	113	
Karen, Laykawkey											
Under 1 month	4	3	1	2	2	0	0		1	13	18·9
1–12 months	2	7	6	1	1	3	1		0	21	30·5
1–4 years	5	2	2	2	3	2	2		0	18	26·1
5–9 years	0	0	1	0	3	2	0		1	7	10·2
10–14 years	0	0	0	0	0	0	0		0	0	0·0
15–19 years	1	0	0	1	1	1	0		1	5	7·3
Over 20 years	3	0	0	0	1	0	0		1	5	7·3
Total	15	12	10	6	11	8	3		4	69	

† This is a tabulation of results of questions relating to age at death and time of death for children born to mothers living in the censused populations. These figures should be interpreted with some caution since they are subject to several types of errors: no *rates* can be established because the base population is unknown for all dates; deaths are reported only for living mothers, and it is possible that mortality patterns for children of mothers who died before the census may be different; there may be errors of recall, especially for children born many years before the survey. Despite these cautions, Lua' and Karen mortality patterns appear to differ: the high rate of mortality for children at Ban Pa Pae during the period of the 1939–48 period. Laykawkey reported no smallpox deaths at this time, apparently as a result of a strict quarantine which closed the village to outsiders. When the extraordinary mortality of that period is removed, the Karen child mortality is probably at a higher rate (the village is smaller), and mortality hits Karens harder in the 1–4-year age category.

variation between communities with the same basic social system when observed at the same time; and variations between families within any given community at any time. Pooled averages, even with appropriate standard deviations, will not indicate the effects of these variations on social structure, demographic structure, or genetic structure of the populations.

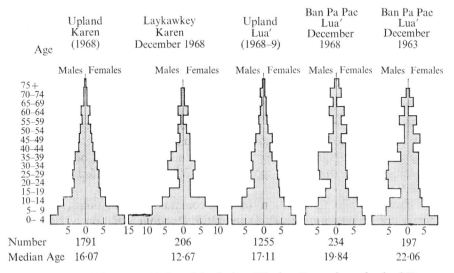

FIG. 16.1. Population pyramids from Mae Sariang District. Comparison of upland Karen and upland Lua' populations shows that the upland Karen population is younger and growing more rapidly, probably as a result of higher birth rates. Small villages may show marked variation from the pooled results of censuses in the villages shown in Fig. 16.2. Laykawkey, one of the hamlets of Mae Umlong Noi, has the youngest and fastest growing population of the Karen hamlets surveyed. Ban Pa Pae has been the oldest and slowest growing Lua' population, but is recovering rapidly from the effects of a smallpox epidemic and fire in the mid 1940s, about 20 years before the census. Laykawkey had no smallpox deaths during the epidemic, but evidently suffered a reproductive decline during the same period.

Effects of random variation in small populations

Regardless of the disease picture, man's social structures must always have had to have flexibility in order to survive the 'random' demographic variations which occur in small populations: that is, either growth or decline of the local community's population due to chance. For example, chance effects the sex of offspring, and thus the availability of appropriate mates at any one time within the community. The chance that the number of eligible boys will equal the number of eligible girls at an appropriate age for marriage is smallest in small communities. By chance, even if birth and deaths were, on the average, balanced within the community so as to allow exchange of marriage partners, some communities would increase in size while others would decrease (Kunstadter, Buhler, Stephan, and Westoff 1963).

Levy (1952) is correct in pointing to adequate sexual reproduction as the basis for recruitment as a functional prerequisite for any society, but he has taken a narrowly pronatalist view. Adequate *control* of population size is also a requisite for the survival of any society, since increase in community size is a threat to its continued existence, especially given the nature of primitive economic systems. It is a characteristic of non-modern economic systems that increase in population ordinarily will not give more than a marginal increase in productivity, and, in the case of some systems, may lead to ecological degradation and decrease in productivity (see below and Weiner's chapter for discussion of the effects of population growth on swidden agricultural systems).

Implications of demographic models

Two kinds of modifications in the usual model of prehistoric populations have been suggested: the likelihood of medium to low 'normal-year' mortality (implying a high 'normal-year' growth rate) and the likelihood of important random variations in small populations. What are the effects of these conditions?

Effects of random fluctuations in small community populations (sampling error) can be seen most easily in sex ratio. Random variation will appear regularly in the sex ratio, which can be expected to oscillate around a mean of about 1:1, with the degree of oscillation in a cohort dependent on the size of the population and its birth rate. The effect of such oscillation on social relationships may be to cause great variation from one cohort to the next in the modes of relationships between sexes (between the situation, for example, when women are scarce and when women are extremely plentiful in comparison with the supply of men) as has been observed in some small Pacific Island populations (Carroll, personal communication). Predictable oscillations of this type are another reason why small populations must have normal birth rates at above the replacement value, in order to assure that each generation will have an adequate supply of mated couples. Under predictable variation of this type, it is surprising, and worthy of detailed study, that human social systems can maintain stable ideals of marriage apparently irrespective of sex ratios in given cohorts. How do societies preserve stability in their ideals of marriage (absolute and relative age of marriage partners, preferential marriage choices, rules of plural marriage) in the face of continual local variation in demographic structure? Chagnon, in this volume, gives a good illustration of how ideal preferences may structure the society while depending on, and perhaps creating, demographic variability.

The verification and quantification of demographic models applicable to prehistoric and modernizing populations has many theoretical implications: for example, reconstruction of the details of human genetic evolution. The genetic effect of chance (genetic drift) in small populations is well recognized, but what were the effects of diseases of different types likely to have been, given various assumptions about community size, settlement pattern, and demographic structure in prehistoric populations? The effects of this type of demographic model on social evolution are not well understood. What are the typical demographic variations which a community is likely to suffer, given certain assumptions about disease, community size, and so forth, and what are the social structural effects of these variations? A classic 'transition-theory' model underlies many family-planning programmes. Contemporary family-planning theorists often state that motives for high birth rates in developing nations result from the common observation of parents that many of their children are liable to die, and their conclusion that they must bear a large number of children in order for a few to survive. Is this an accurate reconstruction of demographic facts in non-modern communities? How much do we know about the parents' subjective estimate of the probability of children surviving? If the subjective estimate is *not* dependent on high continual mortality rate for children, it is unlikely that lowering the mortality rate of children will have any direct effect on motives for family planning. The theory of evolution of diseases in relation to the evolution of human community structure also depends on a model of non-modern populations. It is likely that human diseases have evolved in response to changes in the characteristic distribution of host populations (Polgar 1964).

Quantified consideration of these points is beyond the scope of this paper, except to suggest that the relevant features of many of the important diseases are understood, and models might be constructed for computer simulation of their effects on human populations of defined demographic characteristics. We might predict from these considerations that many diseases (those dependent on human hosts, with short periods of contagion and conferring immunity) could not have reappeared frequently in human populations during most of prehistory, because population concentrations and numbers of susceptible individuals would have been too small to sustain frequent repeated passages of the disease agent. Other diseases (such as, perhaps, malaria) might not have been able to exist at all without a substantial concentrated human reservoir.

Primitive economic limits on community size

Several characteristics of primitive economic and ecological systems are relevant to a consideration of community structure and settlement pattern. Although the systems may be labour intensive, increase of labour beyond a certain point yields marginal gains, or may lead to a decline in productivity (examples: overgrazing leads to degradation of the range, soil erosion, and succession to noxious plants; overhunting may wipe out the supply of game animals by reducing their population to the point where they can no longer reproduce; overgathering may wipe out the supply of clams or roots or fish in a particular locality; planting swiddens too frequently, with insufficient fallow period for recovery of soil fertility, leads to degradation of soil and fallow cover and succession to grass which cannot be utilized under primitive swiddening techniques). With these technologies, it is uneconomic to concentrate human population in large communities in bounded, limited environments beyond a certain point. It leads either to destruction of the resources on which the population depends, or expenditure of inordinate amounts of time and energy in travelling to and from economic activities and in transporting the produce back to the village.

The interests of the individual or the household productive unit and those of the community may not coincide, especially where access to productive resources is in the hands of individuals or families. In these circumstances, large size may give a temporary advantage to the household by concentrating productive labour and power. Constraints on household size include the economic drain of dependent children before they became economically productive, the ambitions of family members to 'go it alone', and the limitations of resources within the household's grasp. Strongly developed traditions of exchange labour may alleviate the need for labour concentrated within the household, but this implies a constraint on competition between households for productive resources, as well as a minimum size for each household in order to make labour exchange effective. Systems in which land resources are viewed as unlimited probably favour large households over exchange labour between household units. While this strategy is successful it probably always leads to community growth, territorial expansion, and eventual community fission under primitive economic conditions. Examples are discussed below.

Limitation of land resources needed to produce food has often been viewed as the determinant of size and density of settlement (Carneiro 1961), but these limits do not automatically limit population growth. There are cases where the population does not reach its theoretical maximum (Bender 1971; Chagnon, this volume), as well as cases where it approaches or temporarily surpasses the food-producing limits of the environment–technology combination. We do not know in detail what keeps populations below the maximum set by food production (disease and a variety of crowding phenomena have been suggested). Birth rates do not always fall, nor do death rates rise to balance the food production–population density equation. Migration is also a solution to local overpopulation, and may allow high birth rates to be maintained without increasing local death rates. Migration may be either to areas of less dense population, or to areas of more intensive economic activities.

Until the environment-and-technology niche is filled, people can move elsewhere within the niche and produce a similar community with similar economic–ecological constraints, thus leading to the characteristic settlement pattern of particular human ecotypes. In isolated hunting-gathering societies, these settlements tend to be distributed systematically with size and location determined by access to limiting environmental conditions (e.g., water for Australian Aborigines, see Yengoyan 1968). In pure agricultural societies within uniform terrain, communities may be evenly distributed over the landscape with distances between communities determined primarily by convenience of access to fields. In more complicated systems there may be heavier investments in permanent features (markets, transport networks) which govern the settlement pattern (Skinner 1964). Where the niche is limited and there is no social differentiation in the surrounding area, communities must limit their populations. Prehistoric Eskimos are a good example of economic and ecological isolation, but are atypical of the situations of most societies known to anthropologists. Many societies, especially in recent historic times, have been able to introduce social innovations in response to population pressure (Harner 1970) the effect of which has been to allow greater population concentrations. The option of migration to areas of more intensive economic activity now exists for most agricultural populations, though the choice may not be a happy one. Similar choices have been available for thousands of years for peasants living on the margins of civilized societies.

Another limitation in primitive economies is the lack of effective storage facilities (in the form of vermin-proof or spoilage-proof food storage), and the inability to convert surplus production or labour into money or credit. These conditions make it difficult or impossible to accumulate and use surpluses in the future during years of scarcity, or to increase productive capacity. There are no markets in which surpluses can be sold and later converted to foodstuffs; there is no formal credit system, and no place to borrow when in need. The production systems are often characterized by rapid swings from surplus to scarcity, and the times of scarcity are the limiting factors in the annual or multi-annual cycle.

Problems of dealing with periodic fluctuations of population size are not limited to humans. A somewhat analogous situation and its solution with respect to the size of pig herds in New Guinea is discussed by Rappaport (1967). Permanent storage of surplus and unlimited accumulation of wealth in the form of pigs is impossible. The pig population can be built up to an unstable high level, and then slaughtered in a large feast as a means of accumulating credit for human use in a non-money economy.

Community mechanisms of population control

All societies have developed methods of dealing with their problems of underpopulation and overpopulation (Davis 1949, Davis and Blake 1956). In general, the first problem (avoidance of extinction due to reproductive failure) is handled by having annual reproductive rates on the average higher than values required for replacement. The second problem, that of overpopulation of the local community, is handled by a number of mechanisms affecting not only birth but also death and migration factors in the demographic equation. These mechanisms include such things as delay in age at marriage by requirement of bride price (as economic conditions decline, marriage will be further delayed, thus increasing spread between generations, decreasing the number of childbearing years for the average married woman, and slowing the annual rate of population growth), selective morbidity (infanticide, geronticide, suicide—the Eskimo case being the best documented; also, perhaps, head-hunting and warfare in general), non-reciprocal post-marital residence rules (especially situations in which women leave the village and are not replaced by equal numbers entering), village fission, expulsion of village members (e.g., for witchcraft, violation of taboos, etc.). The problem may also be handled by culture change, when increased population pressure leads to innovations which increase productivity (as in Boserup's (1965) theory of agricultural change). Each of these mechanisms has implications for settlement patterns and for the pattern of ecological adaptation of the population. Culture change (including both technical change and social change such as change in the scope of the marketing system) in effect changes the ecological niche to which the population is adapted, and may allow further concentration of the population, either through increase in village size, or increase in the density of the settlement pattern. Examples of some of these processes will be discussed below.

Non-modern and contemporary demographic patterns

Consideration of the causes and effects of epidemic diseases and recognition of their importance as a source of mortality makes it likely that there has been considerable secular variation in demographic structure in non-modern communities and perhaps large variation in overall demographic patterns of primitive peoples, depending on sizes of communities and their relationship to epidemic diseases. The New World was apparently completely isolated from some major epidemic diseases including smallpox and perhaps malaria until the age of exploration and colonization; the same may have been true for various Pacific islands, Australia, and New Guinea, and even for some of the more isolated populations on the Asiatic–African land mass. Such areas may have had a more serious problem of developing controls for *chronic* problems of population overgrowth than areas in which epidemics normally or occasionally appeared. Their social structures may have been adapted to an *average* condition of stability in population size and demographic structure, once the niche to which they were adapted was filled, with expected fluctuations in cohort structure less wide than in areas with epidemic diseases.

Other areas which were incompletely isolated from the concentrated population and epidemic disease centres of the world must have experienced regular or occasional epidemics of major proportions. In most years their populations would have to grow rapidly in order to make up for the large losses of epidemic years. Most years in the communities of these areas must have seen growth; population limitation devices might not have to be employed regularly, except in the event of a sustained period without epidemics, when the limits of the carrying capacity of the niche were reached—this condition was unlikely to be as chronic as it was in the more isolated communities.

By contrast, another type of situation exists in parts of the developing world today, where some of the major epidemic diseases have been eliminated or reduced, and population has grown rapidly, perhaps beyond the level of the carrying capacity given the technology available in these areas. With the usual epidemic limits removed, food resources are strained, and the burden of hardship apparently falls most heavily on young children and their mothers. Diets of children and nursing mothers are deficient in animal protein; the synergy between protein malnutrition and infectious diseases leads to extremely high mortality rates among young children from diseases which are usually non-fatal among well nourished children (Dubos 1965, Scrimshaw and Gordon 1968, Scrimshaw, Taylor, and Gordon 1968, Welbourn 1955). This may be a relatively new syndrome, related to the overgrowth of human population and the consequent scarcity or absence of game animals to supplement the diet. The disease is unlikely to develop in hunting-and-gathering communities while they can still rely on hunting (during the past 5000 years, these communities are likely to have been the most isolated and the most conservative with regard to population growth); nor is the condition likely where agricultural or pastoral populations have not grown so large as to require the elimination of domestic animals from the human food-chain due to direct competition for calories. The syndrome is likely to develop where old food customs break down and there are inadequate economic resources to provide substitutes for the traditional small protein supplement (e.g., in urbanization of formerly agricultural people who have been forced off the land; see Jelliffe 1962, Welbourn 1958), or among dry-farming agriculturists whose density has reached the point where game animals or domestic animals cannot survive. In irrigated areas fish is often available as a protein supplement.

It is the post-weaning children who die at very high rates in this situation (Early 1970 a, b). This may lead to an extremely dysfunctional relationship between motivations for fertility, child mortality, and economic activities for women. The effects on demographic structure of the population may be roughly similar to the effects of frequent repeated epidemics of contagious diseases with fairly high mortality, but the social, psychological, and economic effects are much worse than conditions in prehistoric society since the mothers are chronically undernourished, nursing and pregnant, and unable to work effectively. Also, children who survive this sort of childhood malnutrition may never reach adequate levels of mental or physical development (Scrimshaw and Gordon 1968).

Although undernutrition may have been common throughout human prehistory and history, I doubt that this type of malnutrition has been common and chronic until relatively recently, largely because of the change in the protein situation implied by the concentration of human population. This is, in fact, a post-transitional-growth pattern of demography, and is characteristic of many of the 'developing' areas of the world. The heavy burden of mortality placed on the very young in this situation may not be typical of demographic structures in the prehistoric and non-modern world (Neel 1970).

If this hypothetical reconstruction is correct, the selective forces operating on human populations at different points in history, and under different economic and socio-geographic conditions must have been very different. Contemporary conditions in Africa, for example, may be highly selective for ability to withstand chronic protein malnutrition while enjoying carbohydrate sufficiency; selective pressure on hunters and gatherers may have been highly selective for ability to withstand periodic acute food shortages (or to utilize large quantities of food whenever they were available); in other areas, major selective forces involved ability to withstand diseases (for example, malaria). Such pressures are obviously subject to cultural modification (Livingstone 1958).

Effects of demography on settlement pattern and social structure

What difference might all this make as regards settlement pattern and social structure? Let us assume that in some societies there is a very high birth rate, plus a medium death rate with no specially high mortality of children, yielding a high 'normal-year' rate of growth, coupled with periodic disasters or community fission, which combine to keep the overall rate of community growth low. One of the consequences of this model is to allow what we now think of as quite high rates of population growth to be quite normal for the short run of small communities, that is, for perhaps 80 to 95 per cent of the years in the experience of the village's population. These vital rates will produce a young population with high growth rate, and communities with populations of this type must either have a mechanism to dispose of the surplus population, or to reduce the rate of growth when necessary.

The resulting age distribution has some interesting social consequences. Students of kinship will be pleased to note that in a rapidly growing population with large numbers of young people, it is much more likely that a higher proportion can adhere to cross-cousin marriage prescriptions (Kunstadter, Buhler, Stephan, and Westoff 1963) or to unilineal extended family prescriptions, or to polygamous marriage rules, than in a population of the same size which has a low proportion of people in the lower age cohorts and is not growing. This conclusion is contrary to the figures and conclusions of the demographic argument in Coale, Levy, Fallers, Schneider, and Tomkins (1966), that actual family composition throughout prehistory must have been similar and must have resembled the nuclear family despite differences in ideals of family structure. My difference with this argument is my disagreement with the assumption that populations until recently have 'normally' not been characterized by growth. If Levy (in Coale *et al.* 1966) were correct in his conclusion that most people for most of the time in human history have lived in nuclear family-like units, and if there is a relationship between demographic condition and kinship systems we might expect to find the 'Eskimo kinship system' to be much more widespread. I believe that the Eskimo kinship system, which implies non-extended nuclear family structure, is an accurate reflection of Eskimo demographic–ecological conditions, which I have already suggested are atypical for human societies. Other kinship systems imply extended family structures, and these, in turn, imply population growth as a chronic condition. Levy (1966) evidently feels that average population figures are sufficiently representative to allow his conclusion which is mentioned above. The issue is probably best resolved by population simulation based on better data regarding village birth and death rates.

Because their proportions in the population are different the relative position of the aged will also be different in a growing population (in which they will form a relatively small cohort) or a non-growing one (probably a relatively large cohort). It is difficult to predict the effect of this difference, other than to say that it may be difficult or impossible to expect to have large numbers of leadership roles based on old age in a population where there are ordinarily few aged people.

We would also expect to find highly developed systems for handling the surplus population problem, which could be expected to recur repeatedly. Many such mechanisms are possible which affect directly or indirectly the birth, death, or migration rates, and thus influence community size. Cross-cousin marriage, or the 'circulating connubium' may be interpreted in this fashion, and perhaps an examination of this possibility might lead to more effective functional interpretation of symmetrical versus asymmetrical, circular versus non-closed systems of marriage exchange regardless of assumptions about intended or unintended consequences of the exchange. One of the quickest ways of reducing population growth in a community is to get nubile women out of the community and fail to replace them promptly. The point here is that exchange of brides not only relates to exchanges of bride wealth and extension of political ties, it also relates to movement of presumably fecund women between communities, and may directly affect the demographic composition of communities.

Other institutions which have been interpreted in political or economic terms may also be interpreted demographically. In order for segmentary lineage systems to segment (Sahlins 1961), there must be two or more 'brothers', and each must have a sizeable number of followers for segmentation to be a relevant issue. This situation will not develop unless the population is increasing. Similarly, the closed corporate community (Wolf 1957) may be seen as a community response to chronically increasing population, in the face of a geographical and social distribution of resources which makes fission impractical (filling of the ecological niche combined with political rules beyond the community level which govern settlement patterns). Communities which have achieved a rough balance between birth and death rates need not deal with these problems as frequently, and could not be expected to develop customs in response to them.

Contacts between cosmopolitan and isolated communities have many implications for demographic conditions and settlement patterns. These include changes in disease (introduction of new diseases to previously unaffected and therefore non-immune populations), and introduction of improved food technologies. In the early period of the age of exploration, the net effect of these changes was the decline of 'native' populations, as a result of newly introduced diseases, but this trend has long since been reversed due primarily to development of immunity within the population (Dubos 1965), and perhaps due to reasonably effective public health measures with regard to diseases such as cholera, smallpox, and malaria.

With regard to famine as a limit of population, perhaps as important at the introduction of new food technologies has been the introduction of social changes. The effect of these is to cushion the temporary fluctuations in availability of foods. Money, credit, markets, and wage-labour opportunities have meant the expansion of economic activities far beyond the bounds of primitive community ecosystems. Wage-labour supplements subsistence economic activities, cash cropping may provide money (or credit) to convert into foodstuffs during the non-productive period of the year or to increase productivity. The intensified economic systems which have resulted from these innovations have allowed the perpetuation of semi-isolated peasant communities, which though they are nominally independent entities depend on outside sources for employment, credit, markets, and a few essential manufactured goods. They may appear to be relics of a bygone era, but their demographic and economic condition depends on the outside world. Under these modern conditions, the settlement pattern of the 'isolated' areas can become more dense, and birth and death rates can be sustained in some of these peasant communities which yield continued high growth.

Apparently, there is considerable flexibility within even a fairly narrowly defined ecosystem, allowing choice among a variety of community population-control mechanisms. These can be illustrated by examples drawn from a relatively limited area of north-western Thailand.

Alternative patterns of adaptation in north-western Thailand

Lua' and Karen are two of the many minority peoples in north-western Thailand (for details of materials summarized here see Kunstadter 1965, 1966a, 1966b, 1967, 1969a, 1969b, 1970, 1971). Demographic surveys indicate

TABLE 16.2

Reproductive histories of women aged 15 and over

Location	Total women	Per cent ever married	Live births			Children surviving to time of census			
			Total	Mean for married	Mean for all women	Total	Mean for married	Mean for all women	Survival†
Incomplete reproduction									
Upland Karen	388	77	1285	4·28	3·31	934	3·11	2·41	0·727
Upland Lua'	243	72	675	3·86	2·78	517	2·95	2·13	0·766
Lowland Karen	211	78	547	3·33	2·59	453	2·76	2·15	0·828
Lowland suburban	1049	69	2555	3·51	2·44	2174	2·90	2·07	0·851
Lowland urban	367	59	701	3·26	1·91	641	2·98	1·75	0·914
Completed reproduction									
Upland Karen	136	99	927	6·87	6·82	601	4·45	4·42	0·648
Upland Lua'	120	97	576	4·97	4·80	348	3·00	2·90	0·604
Lowland Karen	89	100	485	5·45	5·45	311	3·49	3·49	0·641
Lowland suburban	356‡	97	1724	4·98	4·84	1207	3·49	3·39	0·700
Lowland urban	123	97	444	3·73	3·61	354	2·97	2·88	0·797

† Number of children surviving to census divided by total number of live births.
‡ Does not include three women of unknown reproductive experience.

that the populations of both groups are growing rapidly, as indicated in the reproductive histories summarized in Table 16.2. Village histories confirm the rapid growth of the population for the past 100 years or so, far earlier than any public health or modern medical changes could have influenced the pattern, and in spite of at least one major smallpox epidemic. The Lua' and Karen have participated to different degrees in this population growth, and have responded to it in different ways. The Lua' response approximates that of the 'closed corporate community' (Wolf 1957) while in the hills the Karen response has been similar to that of segmentary lineages (although they do not have a strongly unilineal kinship system).

Relatively unassimilated villages of Lua' are found in north-western Thailand in the hills of Chiang Mai and Mae Hongson provinces (see Fig. 16.2). Villages of Lua' who have largely assimilated the Northern Thai way of life are located in the valleys of the Yuam and the Ping. Settlements of recent Lua' migrants from the hills are found around the valley town of Mae Sariang, and individual Lua' have settled elsewhere in the lowlands after leaving the hills. There are over 10 000 of the unassimilated Lua' living in the hills, and many thousands in the lowlands, uncountable in their present condition, who have become assimilated. Karen villages are found on the western side of Thailand, from the Malay Peninsula north to Mae Hongson and Chiang Ria provinces, where they are an extension of the large Karen population in Burma. There are scattered Karen settlements in most of the northern provinces of Thailand. The total Karen population in Thailand is at least 125 000, most of whom have maintained their cultural distinctiveness whether they live in the hills or in the lowlands. The Karen pattern of adaptation described in this paper is characteristic of Mae Sariang District, but not of Thailand as a whole, where Karen patterns are quite variable.

Lua' and Karen hill villages in Mae Sariang District are found at altitudes of up to 1000 metres. The villagers practise subsistence swidden rice agriculture, usually on a regular field-rotation system, cropping for no more than one year, and fallowing as long as they can, for at least five or more years.

FIG. 16.2. A portion of Mae Sariang District and Mae La Noi Sub-District, Mae Hongson Province, Thailand. Communities covered in demographic survey:

Lowland urban
1. Mae Sariang town

Lowland suburban villages into which some migrants have moved from the hills
2. Ban Mae Sariang
3. Chom Chaeng
4. Ban Dong
5. Na Khao
6. Ban Phae'
7. Ban Pong
8. Ban Thung Phrao

Lowland Karen villages
9. Mae Tia

10. Ban Phae' (Phaekho)
11. Phamalaw

Upland Karen villages
12. Ban Hak Mai (six hamlets)
13. Ban Huai Pyng (five hamlets)
14. Mae Umlong Luang (three hamlets)
15. Mae Umlong Noi (two hamlets including Laykawkey)

Upland Lua' villages
16. Ban Dong
17. La'up
18. Ban Pa Pae

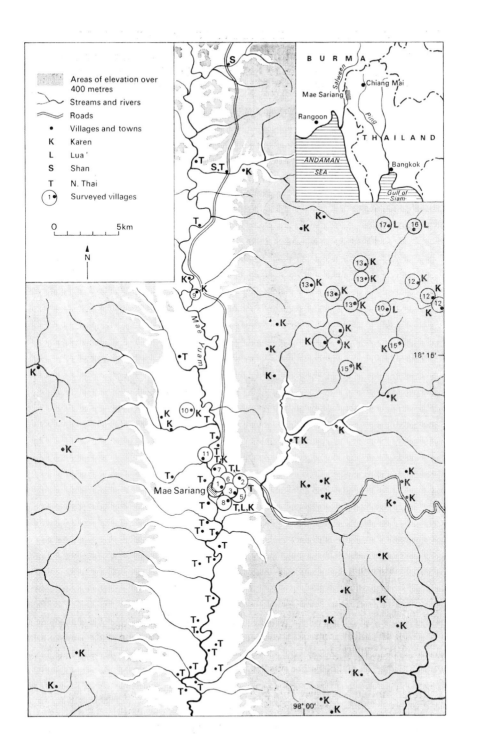

Areas of elevation over
400 metres

Streams and rivers

Roads

• Villages and towns

K Karen

L Lua'

S Shan

T N. Thai

① Surveyed villages

0   5km

N

Irrigated agriculture was introduced into this area within the past 40 or 50 years, and now provides up to half of the rice yield in some of the more favourably located upland villages. Lowland Lua' and Karen villages are

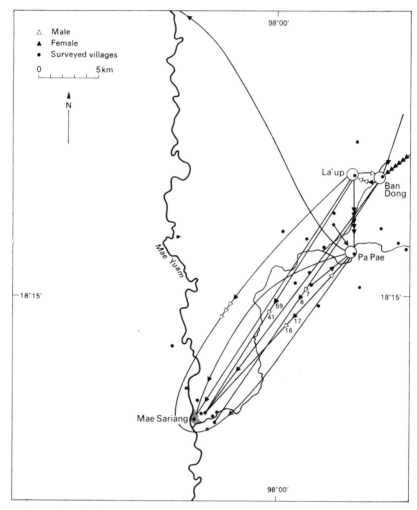

FIG. 16.3. Migration into and out of three upland Lua' villages: Ban Dong, La'up, and Pa Pae. Migration is movement from place of birth to place of residence at time of census (1968–70). Migration from these villages has been shown to those other communities which have been censused. Triangles point direction of movement and indicate numbers of males and females who have moved. Total censused population of Ban Dong was 537 of La'up was 473, and of Pa Pae was 226.

scattered among Northern Thai and Shan villages. The lowlanders are characteristically farmers of irrigated rice, with some supplementary swiddening in the nearby foothills. The introduction of irrigated farming in the hill areas has undoubtedly increased the carrying capacity of the land, but it has not taken care of the population increase within the older hill communities.

The basic approaches of Karen and Lua' in relations with members of other

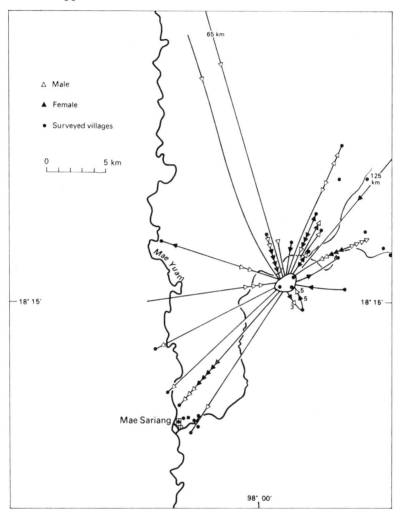

FIG. 16.4. Migration into and out of Mae Umlong Luang, a Karen village with three hamlets. Migration is movement from place of birth to place of residence at time of census. (1968–70). Migration from this village has been shown only to those other communities which have been censused. Triangles point direction of movement and indicate number of males and females who have moved. Total censused population of Mae Umlong Luang was 289.

ethnic groups show many contrasts, indicated in attitudes toward language, settlement patterns, patterns of work in outside labour markets, and reactions to the introduction of new religious ideologies. Probably as a result of the *laissez-faire* attitude of the Thai, the Lua' have adopted an attitude of accommodation in their relations with the Thai. Old Lua' villages in the lowlands have become indistinguishable from Northern Thai villages, and the villagers may have forgotten their ancestors were Lua'. Traditional Lua' culture has been preserved in the upland villages, but the hill villagers are fully aware of the existence of Thai culture in the lowlands, and when people migrate from the hills they recognize that they will become Thai. They feel that Buddhism is more appropriate to life in the valley, and they expect to give up many of their animistic religious beliefs when they become Buddhist Thai.

By contrast, Karens live in a world divided into Karen and non-Karen. This attitude may have developed in Burma in response to persecution at the hands of the Burmese. Although it is not clear what the essence of Karen self-identity contains, beyond recognition of self as Karen, most Karens are determined to maintain their identity, whether they live in the hills or in the valley. Lua' who move to the valley do not consider marriage with Thais to be surprising, and do not make it the subject of negative comment. Lua' who live in the hills do fear that their children might marry Thais if they have too much contact with them in the valley. Their fear is not one of cultural crisis, but that the children might move away from them and not support them in their old age, and not make sacrifices for them after their death. Karens express much stronger sentiments against marriage with Thais on the basis of their desire to maintain Karen identity.

Lua' villages are permanent settlements. Except in very small villages, most marriages are village-endogamous and there is little migration from one Lua' village to another. Migration away from one's village of birth is usually to the valley, and when migration is permanent, it usually implies a decision to 'become Thai'. Marriage is normally patrilocal, and ideally, the youngest son should stay in the house of his parents after he marries, in order to support his parents in their old age, after older sons have married and moved out. Access to swidden land is through patrilineal inheritance of rights to cultivate within communally-held land. These rights are confirmed by village religious leaders who may reallocate land among village members to readjust holdings according to needs of the individual families. Rarely, outside males may marry into the village and receive cultivation rights through their father-in-law. This is an extension of the pattern found in any matrilocal marriage. On occasion in the past, whole groups of Lua' and Karen have been incorporated into Lua' villages under the protection of the chief religious leader. They have been given access to land in return for payment of a standard form of tribute (minor gifts of liquor when they use the land, the leg of any large wild animal they kill, and other payments in recognition of the leader's religious authority).

By contrast with the Lua' situation, most Karen villages are smaller. This is probably a result of Karens having first settled in this area about 120–150 years ago at the pleasure of the Lua', whose claims as landlords were recognized by Northern Thai lowland princes. The Karens settled in the interstices and less-desirable areas between the lands claimed by Lua' villages. Karen villages have expanded and split, expanded and divided, until there is now no more room for additional villages.

Between 10 and 40 per cent of Karen marriages are village-exogamous. Most marriages are between people from nearby villages, but marriages contracted over distances of more than 50 kilometers also occur. Karens also often shift residence from one village to another, parents and siblings may go to join a son or brother who has married in another village, or whole families may move to another location. These moves are usually explained in terms of access to cultivable land, or to an improved labour situation by concentration of a larger group of relatives in a spot where one relative has a good claim on land. As a result of marriages and shifts of residences, Karens have relatives scattered over a wide area, while the relatives of the village-endogamous Lua' are almost entirely concentrated in the village in which they were born (see Figs. 16.3 and 16.4).

Like the Lua', Karens attempt to establish their claims to swidden land on the basis of descent from one of the founding families, but unlike the Lua', there is little agreement (at least in the hills of Mae Sariang District) of the genealogical principles to be followed. There is agreement that cases seem to be settled primarily by weight of numbers of relatives immediately present with genealogical arguments used as rationalizations on both sides, and no strong village leader to adjudicate or to impose religious sanctions (or withhold religious services). These conditions are frequently mentioned by Karens, along with needs for agricultural labour, as motives for high fertility.

The Lua' seem more conscious than do the Karens of the problems of limited land resources and overpopulation. Normally, Lua' marriage requires a bride price, and the young men usually leave their home village to do wage work during the slack agricultural season, or even for several years at a time in order to accumulate the cash needed for a proper wedding. Age at marriage tends to be lower among the more prosperous Lua' villagers, but in general is higher than among the Karen, and natality among Lua' women is consistently lower than among Karen women (see figures or percentages of women married and birth statistics in Table 16.2). Parents in both groups express a desire for large numbers of children. In explaining their desires both Lua' and Karen parents mention the need for assistance in the fields, but Lua' parents anticipate that they will have to split their claims among the adult sons, with only slight flexibility implied by the possibility of reallocation by the religious leader according to need (constraint by community control of resources). Karen parents cite cases where families with many children have concentrated their forces so as to enlarge their claims on swidden land in a situation where there is no outside legal authority to appeal to, and no

TABLE 16.3

Immigrants in different types of communities

Type of community	Male			Female			Total		
	Population	Per cent born elsewhere	Number of other villages represented	Population	Per cent born elsewhere	Number of other villages represented	Population	Per cent born elsewhere	Number of other villages represented
Upland Lua'									
Ban Dong†	250	0·4	1	286	5·9	3	536	3·4	3
Pa Pae	103	1·0	1	123	4·9	3	226	3·1	4
La'up	244	0·8	1	229	0·9	1	473	0·8	1
Upland Karen‡									
Ban Hak Mai (6)	333	36·6	30	332	29·5	22	665	32·9	33
Ban Huai Pyng (5)	245	31·4	19	239	11·7	14	484	21·7	22
Mae Umlong Noi (2)	172	14·0	12	171	17·0	11	343	15·5	14
Mae Umlong Luang (3)	133	15·8	11	156	13·5	6	289	14·5	14
Mae Serayklo	53	26·4	8	44	9·1	4	97	18·6	9
Nolawblekey	52	34·6	8	79	21·5	11	131	26·7	13
Kripu	28	25·0	7	33	9·1	3	61	16·4	5
Lowland Karen									
Mae Tia	174	24·7	26	210	19·5	25	384	21·9	44
Phamalaw	123	15·5	16	105	9·5	9	228	12·7	20
Phaekho	239	12·1	17	246	6·9	8	485	9·5	20
Lowland suburban (mixed ethnic)									
Ban Phae'	454	68·7	62	478	67·6	53	932	68·1	84
Ban Pong	915	58·5	93	870	55·8	84	1785	56·6	105
Ban Thung Phrao	545	35·2	64	549	32·8	63	1094	34·0	83
Lowland urban (mixed ethnic)									
Mae Sariang	762	37·4	93	797	27·7	70	1559	32·5	113

† Includes 2 males and 3 females for whom birthplace was not ascertained.
‡ Upland Karen villages are composed of several neighbouring hamlets, up to 5 kilometres apart, administratively grouped. This table includes four such villages, with the number of hamlets indicated in parentheses. Figures are broken down by hamlet for Mae Umlong Luang, otherwise movements between hamlets of the same village are not counted as migration.

strong authority structure within the village (emphasis of household over community interests). Lua' villages have maintained their solidarity for a hundred years or more, whereas Karen villages in this area, until recently, have split repeatedly, sending out colonies to as yet unoccupied swidden areas. Lua' view village land resources conservatively, as bounded; Karens view land resources as something to be looked for—first at home, and then wherever they may be available (Kunstadter 1971).

The patterns described above relate to swidden land, and apply only indirectly to irrigated land, before it has been levelled, ditched, and cultivated. Irrigated land is individually owned, and is used annually. Claims to irrigated land are legally recognized by the Thai government, and are rarely in dispute.

Lua' social structure is well adapted to maintain permanent villages which are swidden land holding units, and which have no built-in tendency to fission. Title to swidden land traditionally resides in the village as a whole, and is administered for the village by a religious official who has inherited his position patrilineally, within what the Lua' speak of as a royal or princely lineage. If the lineage dies out (as it once did at Ban Pa Pae), villagers may request a member of a related princely lineage from another village to assume the office. Lua' are attached to the place of their parents because of their belief in the power and importance of ancestral spirits, which may give health or illness, and also can assist in giving bountiful harvests. Ancestral spirits are fed once at planting time and once at harvest by each household, and once at the time of burning the fields and again during the weeding season in communal ceremonies. Ancestral spirits are believed to live in the cemetery, and they are summoned from the cemetery, near the village, when their assistance is needed. Lua' are further tied to their home village by a feeling that it is unpleasant to be alone, or to work in fields without neighbouring Lua' fields. Lua' from a single village try to cut their swiddens in contiguous blocks in any one year, moving the blocks from place to place in an orderly pattern of field rotation. Lua' farmers have been observed to withdraw a claim from a swidden if they have no Lua' fields adjacent, and allow Karens to use the land. This is one of the ways in which Karens, little by little, have been adding to their land claims at the expense of their Lua' neighbours.

Karens also consider ancestral spirits to be important, but do not associate them with specific locations. Karens call on their ancestral spirits primarily in connection with illness, not agricultural operations, and they are summoned to a main house post from wherever they may dwell. Karens do not associate agricultural success with particular spirits who reside in a particular place. Thus there is no religious restraint on moving away from the place where one's ancestors lived and died. Nor do Karens feel the need for companionship in the same way as do the Lua'. Karens are perfectly willing to make swiddens in sites surrounded by non-Karens, or even to pioneer a site isolated in the old forest—something a Lua' would be loath to do. Lua' land holdings

23

are concentrated and contiguous for any one village; Karen village land holdings may be diffuse, and Karens do not feel the need to cultivate in a contiguous block.

The normal operation of succession to the religious office in upland Karen villages is likely to result in village factionalism, and perhaps fission, since the rule of succession is ambiguous. In the absence of a resident son of the office-holder, there is no general agreement whether a brother's or sister's son of the husband of the office-holder's daughter is the more legitimate heir. There is also danger that the selection of a successor may result in conflict with the paramount rule of Karen socio-religious structure regarding relations between real and classificatory siblings: an older sibling may not accept the authority of a younger real or classificatory sibling, nor of the descendant of a junior line. Classification of relative age is based not only on the absolute chronology of birth order of siblings, but also on the relative birth order of parents and spouses, so that a man married to the elder sister, or even married to the daughter of the elder sister of the religious leader is classed as the leader's elder brother, and cannot accept his authority.

The likelihood that there will be an unambiguously proper heir is reduced by the fact that husbands almost always go to live in the house of their wife, and marriages are frequently village-exogamous. If there is no commonly recognized leader, factions develop around contenders for the position, and these are the bases for village fission.

These social structural conditions, combined with the rapid population growth of the Karens in the hills of Mae Sariang District, make village fission seem much more reasonable and normal to Karens than to Lua'. In the past, Karen villages have characteristically split to send off colonies, or Karens as families or individuals have gone off on their own, pioneering, or have moved to join existing villages where they can establish a claim to swidden land through relatives. Thus Karens continually relocate their population from place to place in response to the availability of land.

Both Lua' and Karen have other customs for redistribution without village fission. Violations of incest and sexual taboos are believed by the Karens to pollute the earth. A sacrifice must be performed to 'cool' the earth spirit, and if the offence is particularly serious or is repeated, the offenders must be driven out of the village, or they may commit suicide.

Two cases of adultery came to public notice within two years in one Karen village. In both cases, a married man was having an affair with his wife's sister; in one case the adulterous sister and her husband moved out of the village; in the other case the adulterous sister committed suicide, and the man attempted suicide unsuccessfully. Three suicides occurred within a year in a nearby village; the victims were young unmarried people whose choices of marital partners or time of marriage were not approved by their parents. Such behaviour is reportedly widespread among Karens. These examples do not necessarily show intention on the part of the individuals or communities to regulate population size, but they do suggest the potential effect of such customs.

The Lua' do not institutionalize suicide, as do the Karens. They accept and respect their parents' decisions regarding marriage partners, and seem less liable to violate taboos on adultery. The Lua' believe that marriage between forbidden classes of relatives may result in the production of malevolent spirits which cause illness and death. The victim of these spirits may be induced to reveal the name of the person who is unconsciously harbouring the spirit, and this person and his partner may then be forced to leave the village. It is difficult to collect specific information on this, and no recent cases are known to me from Ban Pa Pae, but cases are reported from 30 to 40 years ago, and there are unverified suggestions that some of the people who have migrated into the lowlands from other hill villages were forced out of their mountain homes for this reason. It would take a long time and a very broad study to demonstrate that these actions were in response to population pressure, but none the less they have the effect of reducing population in the hill communities. They also tend to reduce close inbreeding in communities where selection of marriage partners is limited.

Today the limits of expansion and new settlement have been reached in many places. No new large patches of unoccupied land are available into which a large segment of a Lua' or Karen village might move if it were to break off from the parent village. Karens have taken up almost all of the available space between Lua' village holdings, and are continually nibbling at the boundaries of their neighbours. Karens are now demographically dominant in the hill area in which they were newcomers only 120–150 years ago, as a result of their extremely rapid population growth, and their pattern of ecological and social adaptation.

The Karens have gained an advantage over the Lua' since the introduction of irrigated agriculture in this area about 45 years ago. About 60 years ago the power of the Northern Thai princes was removed by the central Thai government, and Lua' claims to legal ownership of the upland area were no longer recognized. The Lua' were the first to begin irrigation, employing lowland Northern Thais to come and teach them proper methods. The Karens learned from the Lua', whom they employed and continue to employ to dig ditches and level paddies. Karens now own an increasing proportion of the irrigated fields in the hill area, both because their dispersed settlement pattern has given them better access to small dispersed areas which can be irrigated, and because they have been more successful at capital formation than have the Lua', once the Lua' were deprived of rent payments.

The Lua' recall the days of their parents and grandparents when they were much richer than they are today. The economic disruption which accompanied the end of the Second World War drove many Lua' out of the elephant business at a time when there was little lumber work available and food prices were high. Karens are better able to conserve their capital than are most Lua'. Even rich Karens appear to spend less of their resources on house contruction, on weddings, funerals, and individual and communal ceremonies than do most Lua', who conform more closely to the 'shared poverty' aspect of closed corporate community life. Karens prefer to save their money and invest it in productive goods, for instance elephants (which have become important again with the revival of the lumber industry) or paddy land—rather than to spend it in feasts and celebrations or expensive curing ceremonies. The availablity of elephants in most Karen villages allows Karens to transport their surplus rice for sale in lowland markets, giving then a further advantage over Lua' farmers, who are often reduced to carrying their rice to market on their backs.

One major type of economic strain for the Lua' is the high cost of their traditional religion, perhaps a survival from the days when they collected land rent from the Karens. In the past some Lua' became Karen in order to escape the burden of heavy religious expenses (a further contribution to the growth of the Karen population and stabilization of Lua' population). At present, some Lua' retain their identity as Lua' while saving their economic resources by becoming Christians. The major motive for conversions has been economic necessity, usually as a result of heavy expenses related to unsuccessful treatment of chronic illness by traditional animistic sacrifices.

Karens also convert to Christianity for materialistic reasons, but their reasons are often phrased as a matter of convenience. Karens in this region have two forms of animistic religion. One centres around the feeding of ancestral spirits, and required the assembly of all lineal relatives at the time of the sacrifice (usually for illness); animals must be specially reared for these sacrifices and cannot be used for any other purpose. The other variety of religion involves being tattooed and performing a small sacrifice to 'pay off' the ancestral spirits for evermore. The ancestral cult seems more common in valley Karen settlements, and in Chiang Mai Province, where hill villages are more stable than in the hills of Mae Sariang District. The tattooing cult seems to be commonest in areas which have had rapid population dispersion. It is easier to be tattooed and give up serving the ancestral spirits whose care and feeding is surrounded by a series of taboos which may be inappropriate to the dispersed settlements of Karens in the hills; it may be still easier to become a Christian and give up the feeding of spirits altogether.

The Lua' have relatively few alternatives available when disease or economic disaster strike, or if they find themselves unable to make a living in the natural and cultural environment of their village. When forced by economic necessity to leave their home village and seek their fortune, the usual decision is to move to the valley where it is easier to gain bare subsistence through odd jobs than it is in the hills where wage-labour opportunities are few and surplus food is scarce. Most Lua' do not have close relatives in any mountain village other than the one into which they were born. Their patrilineal–patrilocal system confines their claims on agricultural land to their home village, thus the Lua', unlike the Karen, cannot call on the bonds of kinship to gain access to the resources of another swiddening community. Once forced out of their home village, many Lua' choose to remain in the valley, even when the immediate economic crisis is past, and having chosen to remain, they become assimilated.

Upland Karens have been very successful in their competition with the Lua'. The end of feudalism and changing economic conditions have led to the economic decline of hill Lua', but the Lua' have found it easy to allow themselves to become Thai, and to move entirely out of the hill ecosystem. Karen social structure and attitudes toward the rest of the world have led to the preservation of a separate Karen identity, while at the same time allowing Karens to expand throughout the hill environment, and to achieve moderate success as participants on the margins of the Thai economic system. Their dispersed village settlement pattern has allowed them to increase their total population far beyond what was achieved by the Lua' before the Karens started moving into the area; in part, of course, this has also been due to the fact that both Karens and Lua' now are on the margins of the Thai economic system.

Social structural differences between Lua' and Karen suggest that the tendency to disperse and relocate population, which is characteristic of the Karens is highly beneficial in their use of land resources, given the present state of affairs in northern Thailand. The Lua' form of adaptation (larger, stable villages) probably developed in response to conditions of periodic raiding and warfare, characteristic of the time before 1850. Concentrated villagers could more easily protect themselves and their material possessions, even though this meant they were less well able to protect their land against the slow, peaceful pressure of increasing Karen population.

The current forms of adaptation by Karen and Lua' are clearly related to the existence of outside socio-economic and political systems: the continued existence of Lua' villages in their present form depends on their ability to move surplus populations out (to the valley, into Thai society), as well as their ability to supply themselves with a few manufactured necessities (plough and hoe blades) and their ability to earn small amounts of money for these necessities (through wage labour and sale of agricultural surpluses). The Karen system of adaptation also depends on the external situation. Wage labour as a source of cash, employment for elephants, and markets for sale of agricultural surpluses and purchase of technical necessities are required, as well as the overall peace which has been maintained by the consolidation of the Thai political structure in this area. Wolf (1957) attributes the following characteristics to 'closed corporate peasant communities': maintenance of communal jurisdiction over land, restriction of membership, maintenance of a religious system, enforcement of mechanisms which ensure the redistribution or destruction of surplus wealth. Wolf remarks on the importance of the peasant communities as a labour pool for the entrepreneurial sector, and comments on the need for the closed corporate community to induce the emigration of a portion of its population. The corporate peasant community, according to Wolf, is not necessarily a product of conquest, but is a result of the dualization of the economy into a dominant entrepreneurial sector and a dominated sector of peasants. The Lua' seem clearly to be members of closed corporate peasant communities, but the Mae Sariang District economy has not closely resembled the classic dual economies. The labour market seems more essential to the maintenance of the hill Lua' system than the availability of Lua' labourers is to the lowland-based economy. The Karen are equally involved in the lowland labour market, but show much less tendency to display the characteristics of the closed corporate community. The situation of the Karen in the same environment as the Lua' seems to indicate that it is not the 'several characteristics of the larger society' alone which necessarily produce communities of this type.

Clearly, the Karen strategy of high population growth, dispersed settlements, and maintenance of cultural identity has been effective in increasing the population and dominance of the Karens in this hill area of Mae Sariang District over the past five or six generations, while the Lua' strategy of slightly slower population growth, more conservative use of land, settled permanent non-divisible villages, and change of identity and ecology for surplus population has been unsuccessful in maintaining the dominant position (though it has allowed them to maintain their hill communities). These seem to be relatively short-run phenomena: Karen strategy has led to great population increase (doubling or more every generation), while Lua' population in the hills appears to have remained almost constant. The Karens are now beginning to run out of land resources while the Lua' have managed to hold on to much of their land and maintain it in a regular system of field rotation. Shorter and less regular fallow cycles, representing more intensive and less conservative use of swidden land by Karens will lead to decline in food production. Will the land-ownership situation of Karens vis-à-vis Lua' be stabilized? Or will the Karens continue to take over whatever little bits and pieces of Lua' land they can get each year? This probably depends largely on the actions of the Thai government. Can the Karens adapt their social structure to a stationary and limited land resource base? The situation at present is clearly unstable, and something will have to change in the Karen food-production–birth–death–migration–population size equation.

The variety of Karen forms of adaptation in other nearby areas suggests that they have considerable flexibility in social structure. Lowland Karen villages in Mae Sariang District, based on irrigated agriculture, show no tendency to fission. They are able to grow large and still maintain a stable pattern of political–religious leadership. In Chiang Mai Province, Marlowe (1969) reports a much heavier dependence on trade relationships and wage labour among upland Karen (he describes their agricultural system as 'sub-subsistence'), and apparently they have a much greater pattern of village stability than do the Mae Sariang hill Karen. Thus the structural instability of the Mae Sariang hill Karen may be a temporary adaptation to an incompletely filled niche into which they have expanded rapidly.

Other patterns are possible in nearby environments, and may be summarized briefly. West of Hua Hin, near the Burma border on the Malay Peninsula, there is a group of Karens who have recently moved into a sparsely settled area, with no competitors for swidden land. They believe that the supply of land is unlimited and there is no reason for them to concern themselves with land ownership. They practice shifting cultivation in the sense that they work fields only for one year, and then move on to another convenient unused patch. Their houses are scattered in their field clearings, and are made for only a single year's occupation. They move them each year. General Karen patterns of matrilocal post-marital residence are followed, but religious leadership within the village seems, on brief examination, to be poorly developed. They are subsistence rice cultivators, but recently have begun to cultivate and sell *Cannabis* and chilli peppers as cash crops, directly to retailers in the nearest town, and to buy some rice rather than raising all their own. This group of Karens has probably had one of the closest approaches in Thailand to true nomadic shifting cultivation.

The Akha of Chiang Rai Province, in the extreme north of Thailand, live in a situation of low local population density, but, at least potentially, compete with other nearby ethnic groups. Kickert (1969) states: 'Land as near as possible to the village is preferred for cultivation. Land is not owned; it is used. That the rights are granted simply to cultivate land without any particular regard to area or place may indicate that, for the Akha, land has always been plentiful'. Villages are groups of households which may or may not stay together; they break up and/or move depending on immediate availability of fertile land, sickness in the vicinity, or disputes. Apparently they have not established stable trading or other relationships with neighbouring groups, and in that sense may be even more free of their surrounding social environment than the Hua Hin Karens. Questions of community population limitation are, for the moment, less relevant than optimization of family and household as productive units. Akha settlements have moved into Thailand from Burma only within the past generation or two.

There are a few Meo settlements in the vicinity of the Lua' and Karen villages of Mae Sariang District described above. They have been founded within the past 10 years. Meo have been in northern Thailand for at least 80 to 100 years, and have expanded steadily southward, moving into the high ridges which were usually unoccupied, but where their principal crops (maize and opium) can grow well. By now they have settlements some 400 kilometres south of the area where they first began to settle in Thailand, and where the heaviest Meo concentration still remains in Thailand.

The Meo economy produces part of its own subsistence crops, but also depends heavily on rice from nearby villages. At least in Mae Chaem District of Chiang Mai Province and Mae Sariang District the Meos have apparently located their villages with reference not only to soil types and environment suitable for opium cultivation, but also with reference to availability of labour and rice supplies from non-Meo villages. Opium is the chief cash crop, and requires a very labour-intensive cultivation, especially during the harvest, which comes after the rice harvest in this area. For purposes of opium culti-vation the Meo households (which are the units of production) wish to enlarge their labour supply as much as possible. They do this by hiring wage labour for the periods of most intensive work, by forming extended family house-holds, and in some locations, by adopting children from other ethnic groups, and apparently by having large numbers of their own children. There is no published account of Meo demography, but unpublished data from Bhruk-sasri and Oughton (personal communication) confirm the impression that Meos form large households and have a very rapidly growing population. A survey of three villages in Chiang Dao District, with a total of 462 individuals, gave an average of 7·2 persons per household, and a median age of 15·5 years.

Marketing the opium depends on intensive contacts with other ethnic groups (usually Haw Chinese); but these are independent of the specific location of the Meo village, since the Haw provide their own pack-animal transport. The whole economic system depends on a complex set of inter-relationships and balances between labour and food supply, and between expenses and potential profits from the sale of opium. The Meo system of agriculture requires clean cultivation, and though it allows repeated culti-vation of the same field for a few years, it is ultimately destructive of soil resources. Keen (personal communication), in his analysis of Meo economy in Tak Province, suggests a balance between forest and cultivated land (forest is necessary to restore soil fertility, and this part of the system is usually out of balance thus requiring movement of Meo villages); between cash crops and subsistence crops (these Meo make little use of non-Meo labour, and must feed themselves locally); and between livestock and opium (pigs are necessary for subsistence, but must be kept away from the opium fields, thus requiring an investment of time in keeping either the fields or the livestock far away from the village). Thus the system (at least in this environment) is geographically unstable. Households separate themselves from villages in order to seek better localities, and villages themselves must move as the soil in the surrounding area becomes exhausted. For the Meo the system may be ten times as profitable as the Lua' or Karen agricultural system, but the Meo leave in their wake a swath of despoiled soil and a crew of unemployed, possibly opium-addicted former workers.

Under the circumstances in which the Akha, Meo, and some Karen live, it is extremely difficult to determine details of population growth. We can use inferential evidence. Meo history indicates that the Meo population has been increasing as well as expanding spatially out of its original home in central China, the expansion perhaps triggered by the introduction of maize as an upland subsistence crop. Population expansion is probably both an effect and a cause of their territorial expansion into northern Vietnam, northern Laos, and northern Thailand.

These examples suggest the importance of time perspective in studies which attempt to relate demographic and economic patterns to settlement patterns. Pioneering, expansion, and post-expansion phases are suggested in the Karen examples. A type of homeostasis within a fairly closed resource system is suggested by the Lua' example (but the Lua' are dependent on an outside system for essential tools, a labour market, and a place to dispose of surplus population). The highly productive possibilities of a predatory exploitative system are suggested by the Meo example, as long as resources (including food, labour, soils, and markets) remain plentiful.

Implications of social structural and demographic variables for models of population genetics

A comparison of places of birth and places of residence at time of census in settlements of different ethnic groups, and in rural versus suburban and urban areas suggests major differences between Lua' and Karen patterns of mate selection, as well as major differences between rural and urban patterns (Table 16.3). The upland Lua' system in the simplest. Their villages are predominantly endogamous, and village exogamous marriages are contracted between a relatively small number of nearby villages. When Lua' migrate out of the mountain villages, they separate themselves from the breeding population of the upland villages and join the general Thai breeding population of the lowlands. There is almost no movement in the other direction.

The majority of upland Karen marriages are contracted between residents of the same village, but a sizeable number of residents of any one village were born elsewhere. Mates may be obtained over considerable distances from a substantial number of different upland and lowland villages. Karens moving to the lowlands tend to remain within the Karen breeding population, which is not limited to one ecological zone (upland versus lowland), although most marriages are zone-endogamous. Lowland rural Karen mate-selection patterns resemble those of the upland areas, lowland suburban Karens still tend to select Karen mates, but a few non-Karens are incorporated into the lowland rural and suburban Karen breeding units.

Urban and non-Karen suburban populations come from mixed origins, including ethnic groups from all over Thailand, and some from neighbouring countries. Boundaries of ethnic endogamy which are characteristic of upland areas tend to break down. In some special cases (e.g., 'Indians' or Moslems) cultural boundaries may be maintained, but in the Mae Sariang area the group is so small that it has not been able to provide enough mates, and wives are often selected from other ethnic groups. They and their children are integrated within the cultural group of their husbands or fathers.

This situation has obvious implications for the characteristics of the gene pool and genetic differentiation between sub-populations. Lua' upland villages are likely to resemble small semi-isolated breeding populations with relatively little exchange of genetic material between one another, and with the likelihood that some rare genes may be lost through migration or perhaps through genetic drift. Karen upland villages seem to be only nodes in a very widespread, large, but essentially closed breeding population. Genes are not likely to be lost to the Karen gene pool by migration, since almost all migration and breeding takes place within the 'Karen world', with occasional additions from outside. The size of the gene pool, in the tens or hundreds of thousands, makes genetic drift unlikely.

Urban and suburban populations in northern Thailand are portions of a very large, variable, open, cosmopolitan population, with continual input of migrants from a variety of sources at varying distances.

Thus, within the same geographical space in northern Thailand, there are three distinct patterns of populations and gene pools, with different kinds of environments and social selective pressures, different kinds of assortment of mates, and different kinds of migration. This situation does not fit the usual *Drosophila* model of populations in which probabilities of mating are applied evenly (randomly) to all individuals in a given space. These examples, along with that described by Neel (1970) and Chagnon (in this volume) suggest that concepts of populations as bounded, homogeneous units may be applicable neither to human hunting and gathering populations, nor, in general, to the sort of 'primitive' agricultural populations which are tied in numerous ways to larger-scale societies. Instead of viewing populations as bounded and homogeneous, it might be more accurate and profitable to think in terms of heterogeneity and permeable boundaries, or perhaps in terms of clines of probabilities of breeding between one individual and any other individual within some defined space.

For humans, space is both a geographical and a social concept. One may construct either geographical or sociological models of human breeding populations. Viewed geographically, the assumption is that the predominant factor affecting mate selection is geographical propinquity, given certain minimal appropriate personal attributes, such as that the potential mates be of opposite sex. A map could then be drawn showing clines of probability of obtaining a mate at distance d from place of birth. In the upland Lua' villages, the probabilities of mate selection would be very high (90 per cent or more) within the village of birth, and then drop off very rapidly at the edge of the village, with at most 5 per cent of the population being drawn from a limited number of neighbouring villages. The probability of obtaining a mate from distance d rapidly drops to zero as d approaches 10 kilometres.

In upland Karen villages perhaps 30 per cent of mates are drawn from outside the village of birth, from a large number of neighbouring villages. The probability of obtaining a mate from distance d does not drop to zero for more than 100 kilometres, although selecting a mate at great distance is increasingly improbable. The picture for lowland Karens is similar. In both the hills and the lowlands the selection is confined largely to other people who identify themselves culturally as Karens, if the children of the mating are to remain within the Karen breeding population. For the upland Lua' the geographical model is reasonably accurate if the substantial number of people moving to the lowlands from hill villages is ignored. For the upland Karen the geographical model is accurate only if the large number of non-Karens living within the Karen geographical space is ignored.

When the Lua' move to the lowlands, they immediately broaden the scope of mate selection by tens or even hundreds of kilometres, and by hundreds or thousands of people. In the urban and suburban areas, with mixed populations, propinquity is still a primary factor in mate selection, but the range is increased, and the system is best considered open rather than bounded. Mate selection in the urban areas corresponds neither to the borders of the community nor to the borders of the ethnic groups. This suggests that a sociological rather than a geographical model needs to be constructed to explain or predict the distribution of genes in succeeding generations.

In constructing the sociological model of the mating system, the aim is to establish the probability that person x will mate with person y. A list can be constructed of the sociological variables which might influence the probabilities of mating between any two individuals. Such factors as marital status (unmarried), absolute age (above 15 years), relative age (within 5 years of the same age, with potential husband older than potential wife), ethnic group (within the same ethnic group), and kinship (excluding most first cousins, all siblings, parents, etc.) affect upland Lua' and Karen mate selection in almost the same ways. As already noted, distance between potential mates' places of birth affects them very differently.

In the urban and suburban lowlands the list would include similar factors, but probabilities would be different, and new factors would be added. Marital status, for example, affects mate selection differently in the lowlands, where men are allowed multiple mates, and where divorce is much more frequent than in the hills; age at marriage tends to be later in the urban and suburban areas, and first cousins may not be restricted as potential mates. Socio-economic factors, such as education and occupation, affect mate selection in the urban and suburban lowlands, but are practically irrelevant in the hills. In the lowlands they may begin to establish boundaries between different classes of people (educated versus uneducated, salaried and professional versus wage labourers or farmers), and begin to isolate breeding populations along class lines, whereas this cannot happen in the educationally and occupationally undifferentiated upland populations. Ethnic boundaries of breeding populations are maintained in the hills, but tend to break down in lowland urban and suburban areas.

Thus the list of factors affecting probabilities for selecting a particular mate would look very different for an upland and an urban individual, with the urban individual probably having a much wider range of mate selection. A complete model for the area would have to include probabilities affecting migration (including moving people from rural to urban probability structure).

Conclusion

Primitive societies (and prehistoric populations) are often assumed to have been in homeostasis—they would have to have been, it is argued, in order to have survived so long. The assumption must be correct, in the long run, for the human species as a whole, but it seems unlikely to have been even a good approximation in the short run, and for particular communities, except under special circumstances. I have suggested in this paper, following Malthus, that population growth is the normal condition of mankind. I have also shown some of the methods developed by small communities with relatively primitive communities for dealing with these chronic problems. I have suggested that in small communities neither births nor deaths are likely to be distributed evenly through time, and that in small communities the populations may be expected to oscillate, with the usual state being one of growth. The problems of what to do with the surplus will be chronic. Segmentation (creation of another similar unit) has been one solution; migration to areas of more intense economic activities has been another solution in many parts of the world for several thousands of years; technological (Boserup 1965) and social (Harner 1970) changes are other possibilities, as are changes in birth and death rates.

The figures from Mae Sariang District support the conclusion that it is the technologically least advanced communities (in this case small, semi-isolated villages of upland swiddeners) that are supplying the greatest natural increase, and are thus one of the major sources of population growth for the more advanced lowland areas. If the arguments presented in this paper about the demographic characteristics of small communities are correct, this conclusion may be generally applicable to many areas of the world.

So far, we have not considered life in cities; but it is appropriate to note here that, until recently, despite the fact that they have been centres of innovation, cities have been unhealthy places to live in. Generally their mortality rates have been higher than in the hinterlands, while their reproductive rates have been lower, often well below the level needed for replacement. The figures in Table 16.2 show a similar trend to what has been the world-wide history of growth of cities, although the urban residents in Mae Sariang are already managing to more than replace themselves. Until recently, the growth of all cities has depended on migration (Davis 1965). Looked at another way, fertility and mortality have not been uniformly distributed spatially, and one (presumably unintended and unrecognized) function of cities has been to drain off and destroy surplus population from the countryside. One feature of the current population explosion which differs from past periods of population growth (such as accompanied the agricultural revolution) is that cities now contain a much larger proportion of the population, and are becoming areas of natural population increase (surplus of births over deaths), making the absorption of ever more migrants from the countryside increasingly difficult.

Urban and suburban areas in northern Thailand have been areas of genetic and cultural mixture, where culturally defined boundaries between breeding populations have tended to break down, and perhaps reform along class lines. In a society such as that of Thailand, the class boundaries are quite permeable so that mate selection based on social class factors is unlikely to produce closed breeding units. Geographic mobility in Thailand is now so great that the flow of genes from different parts of the country is rapid, and even remote district centres are experiencing the world-wide phenomenon of an increasingly cosmopolitan gene pool. A few small semi-isolated gene pools remain in villages like those of the upland Lua' described in this chapter, which encourage emigration as a solution to surplus population growth, but which strictly limit immigration. Such populations may continue to undergo evolutionary differentiation from the metropolitan lowland population as long as they maintain their separate social structure.

REFERENCES

BARTLETT, M. S. (1960). The critical community size for measles in the United States. *Jl. R. statist. Soc.* A **48**, 37–44.

BENDER, D. R. (1971). Population and productivity in tropical bush fallow agriculture. In *Carolina Popul. Center Monogr.* **9** (ed. Polgar).

BOSERUP, E. (1965). *The conditions of agricultural growth: the economics of agrarian change under population pressure*. George Allen and Unwin, London.

CARNEIRO, R. L. (1961). Slash-and-burn agriculture: a closer look at its implications for settlement patterns. *Man and cultures* (ed. A. F. C. Wallace). University of Pennsylvania Press, Philadelphia.

COALE, A. J., LEVY, M. J., Jr., FALLERS, L. A., SCHNEIDER, D. M., and TOMKIN, S. S. (eds.) (1966). *Aspects of the analysis of family structure*. Princeton University Press.

DAVIS, K. (1949). *Human society*. Macmillan, New York.

DAVIS, K. (1965). The urbanization of the human population. *Scient. Am.* **213** (Sept.), 40–53.

—— and BLAKE, J. (1956). Social structure and fertility: an analytical framework. *Econ. Devel. Cult. Change* **4**, 211–235.

DUBOS, R. (1965). *Man adapting.* Yale University Press, New Haven.

EARLY, J. D. (1970a). Demographic profile of a Maya community. The Atitecos of Santiago Atitlan. *Milbank meml Fund Q. Bull.* **47**, 167–78.

—— (1970b). The structure and change of mortality in a Maya community. *Milbank meml Fund Q. Bull.* **47**, 179–201.

HARNER, M. J. (1970). Population pressure and the social evolution of agriculturalists. *SWest. J. Anthrop.* **26**, 67–86.

JELIFFE, D. B. (1962). Culture, social change, and infant feeding. *Am. J. clin. Nutr.* **10**, 19–44.

KICKERT, R. W. (1969). Akha village structure. In *Tribesmen and peasants in North Thailand* (ed. P. Hinton). Tribal Research Centre, Chiang Mai.

KUNSTADTER, P. (1965). *The Lua' (Lawa) of Northern Thailand: aspects of social structure, agriculture, and religion.* Princeton University Center of International Studies Research Monograph **21**.

—— (1966a). Residential and social organization of the Lawa of northern Thailand. *SWest. J. Anthrop.* **22**, 61–84.

—— (1966b). Narrow valleys and individual enterprise. Paper presented at the Pacific Science Congress, Tokyo. (Mimeographed.)

—— (1967). The Lua' (Lawa) and S'kaw Karen of Mae Hong Son Province, north-western Thailand. *South-east Asian tribes, minorities, and nations* (ed. P. Kunstadter). Princeton University Press.

—— (1969a). Hill and valley populations in north-western Thailand. In *Tribesmen and peasants in North Thailand* (ed. P. Hinton). Tribal Research Centre, Chiang Mai.

—— (1969b). Socio-cultural change among upland peoples of Thailand: Lua' and Karen— two modes of adaptation. *Proc. VIII Int. Congr. Anthrop. Ethnol. Sci. Tokyo and Kyoto*, Vol. II.

—— (1970). Cultural patterns, social structure, and reproductive differentials in north-western Thailand. *Symp. Culture, Fam. Planning, hum. Fert.* San Diego, California.

—— (1971). Fertility, mortality, and migration of upland and lowland populations in north-western Thailand. *Carolina Popul. Center Monogr.* **9**.

—— (in press). Subsistence agricultural economics of Lua' and Karen hill farmers of Mae Sariang District, north-western Thailand.

—— BUHLER, R., STEPHAN, F. F., and WESTOFF, C. F. (1963). Demographic variability and preferential marriage patterns. *Am. J. phys. Anthrop.* **21**, 511–19.

LEVY, M. J., Jr. (1952). *The structure of society.* Princeton University Press.

—— (1966). Limits of variation of family structure. In *Aspects of the analysis of family structure* (ed. A. J. Coale *et al.*), Princeton University Press.

LIVINGSTONE, F. B. (1958). Anthropological implications of sickle cell distribution in West Africa. *Am. Anthrop.* **60**, 533–62.

MALTHUS, T. R. (1798). *An essay on the principle of populations as it affects the future improvement of society, with remarks on the speculations of Mr. Godwin, M. Condorect, and other writers.* Johnson, London.

MARLOWE, D. H. (1969). Upland-lowland relationships: the case of the S'kaw Karen of central upland western Chiang Mai. *Tribesmen and peasants in North Thailand* (ed. P. Hinton). Tribal Research Centre, Chiang Mai.

MCARTHUR, N. (1961). *Introducing population statistics.* Oxford University Press, Melbourne and New York.

NEEL, J. V. (1970). Lessons from a 'primitive' people. *Science, N.Y.* **170**, 815–22.

NOTESTEIN, F., TAEUBER, I. B., KIRK, D., COALE, A. J., and KISER, L. K. (1944). *The future population of Europe and the Soviet Union, population projections*, 1940–70. League of Nations, Geneva.

POLGAR, S. (1964). Evolution and the ills of mankind. In *Horizons of anthropology* (ed. Sol Tax). Aldine Press, Chicago.

RAPPAPORT, R. A. (1967). *Pigs for the ancestors: ritual in the ecology of a New Guinea people.* Yale University Press, New Haven and London.

SAHLINS, M. D. (1961). The segmentary lineage: an organization of predatory expansion. *Am. Anthrop.* **63**, 322–45.

SCRIMSHAW, N. S. and GORDON, J. E. (eds.) (1968). *Malnutrition, learning, and behavior.* The Massachusetts Institute of Technology Press, Cambridge, Mass.

—— TAYLOR, C. E., and GORDON, J. E. (eds.) (1968). *Interactions of nutrition and infection.* World Health Organization, Geneva.

SKINNER, G. W. (1964). Marketing and social structure in rural China, Part I. *J. Asian Stud.* **24**, 3–44.

WELBOURN, H. F. (1955). The danger period during weaning. *J. trop. Paediat.* **1**, 34–46; **2**, 98–111.

—— (1958). Bottle feeding: a problem of modern civilization. *J. trop. Paediat.* **3**, 157–66.

WOLF, E. R. (1957). Closed corporate peasant communities in Mesoamerica and Java. *SWest. J. Anthrop.* **13**, 1–18.

YENGOYAN, A. A. (1968). Demographic and ecological influences on aboriginal Australian marriage sections. In *Man the hunter* (eds. R. B. Lee and I. De Vore) Aldine Press, Chicago.

·17

DEMOGRAPHIC VARIABLES AS MEASURES OF BIOLOGICAL ADAPTATION: A CASE STUDY OF HIGH ALTITUDE HUMAN POPULATIONS

PAUL T. BAKER *and* JAMES S. DUTT

Introduction

ALL biological differences between human populations are produced by differences in the genetic structure of the populations or by environmental differences which stimulate contrasting ontogenetic processes in the developing organisms. When we attempt to explain the causes of these differences whether they be genetic or ontogenetic, the most tenable answer is usually that they are the product of adaptation to varying environments. Yet it must be admitted that such an explanation is based primarily on non-human evidence and the number of specific examples which can be cited for man are few indeed (Baker 1966).

As an animal for the study of adaptation, man has a few advantages. His memory serves as a source of information, he can be taught to follow complex instructions for experimental work, and he has through migration and cultural development placed himself in a number of unusual environments where the process of adaptation may be studied. Nevertheless, there are some distinct problems. He has a long generation span and resists intentional manipulation of his environment. For these very obvious reasons, many methods which have provided insights into the adaptive process in other animals have not been applicable to man.

The methods applied to man have followed two general lines. The prime method developed by geneticists is based on a demonstration that particular genes confer a selective advantage on their bearers (World Health Organization 1964). This method produced some striking results on the adaptive value of the sickle-cell haemoglobin gene and suggestive results on the relationship between infectious disease and several other human genes. As a measure of adaptation, this method depends on the demonstration that a specific genotype has a reproductive advantage in a specific environment. Because of the long generation time in man, such studies are generally based on reconstructed data.

In the second general method, the differences in population morphology and physiology have been related to specific environmental stresses and the genetic base has been deduced by the exclusion of ontogenetic processes. This method depends upon differences in functional and behavioural capabilities as a measure of adaption (Weiner 1969).

Both methods are subject to serious limitations and have been appropriately criticized. Thus the number of cases required to demonstrate the adaptive advantage of a given gene in relation to a particular environmental stress is so great that it is improbable that the evolutionary causes of population variations in specific gene frequencies can be demonstrated in cases other than extreme selection coefficients (Morton 1968). In the second method the functional differences may be demonstrable; but whether the differences result in a selective advantage remains speculative and if so the result of selection on what must be a complex genetic base cannot be predicted by present techniques (Bressler 1966, Mazess 1970, and Symposium on Human Adaptation 1970). Finally, as Dobzhansky points out in this volume, the search for simple links between specific genes and specific environmental adaptations may be an oversimplification of the problem since a population is the unit of adaptation and populations seem to adapt in part by genetic diversity.

If a population is accepted as a unit for human studies then quite clearly some further methods must be developed for measuring the adaptation and adaptive potential of human populations. While the two prime methods presently used for the study of human adaptation have not been fully explored and will undoubtedly produce further significant results, it is becoming increasingly apparent that these methods are not sufficient, particularly if one's emphasis is on the adaptation of a population as a unit. It would clearly be helpful if some new criteria could be developed for measuring the adaptation and adaptive potential of human populations.

For the evolutionary geneticist who works with non-human animals, a much simpler problem exists since he has a simple and accurate measure of the comparative biological adaptation for populations—*demographic advantage*. If an evolutionary biologist working with *Drosophila* wishes to know whether one population of *Drosophila* is better adapted to a given environment than another, he has only to place both in the same environment and after a few generations he may measure the comparative adaptive capacity of the two populations by their numbers.

Essentially, no such approach has been used for human populations and it is the purpose of this chapter to explore: first, why demographic criteria have not been used and, second, the possibility of using such data as a measure of differences in the biological adaptation of given human populations.

Human demographic variables as adaptive measures

Historically, students of human evolution have had a long-standing concern with demographic data but this concern has been concentrated on how the demographic characteristics of populations and sub-population units such as classes affect the biological characteristics of future populations. In almost no instance has the reverse question of how the biological characteristics affect the demographic structure been examined. This unidirectional interest can be traced from the early concern of geneticists such as Galton through to the publications of H. J. Muller (1960). Yet in the long publishing history of a journal such as *Eugenics Quarterly* (now *Social Biology*), virtually no articles have used demographic data as a measure of a group's adaptation.

The causes of this trend are by no means obscure. Demography, a science based on empirical observation, has shown that most of the variability between recent populations can be explained by reference to social and technological variables, without reference to any biological variable. At a theoretical level many demographers will agree that the nutrition, health, and even genetic differences in populations might affect their fertility or mortality rate but, at the practical level, variability in these population parameters is better predicted by the technological level of the population. Within a population social variables such as class, rural/urban residence, etc. are much more powerful explanations than any known genetic or biological difference. To cite but one example, demographers find it useful to include a question on the race of the individual in the United States census, but the explanatory power of this variable is related to the cultural differences denoted by the social definition of race in the United States. If the racial classification was not confounded by cultural variables, one suspects that group differences in the demographic variables would diminish radically.

The demographic history of Australia during the past 150 years seems a clear example of the futility of attempts to use demographic variables as measures of comparative biological adaptation. A short time ago the continent was occupied by a population which had been resident at least 10 000 years. Within 150 years the indigenous population had been almost entirely replaced by migrants from a drastically different environment. This seeming paradox of evolutionary principles is, of course, explained by the fact that although both the Australian aborigine and the immigrants occupied the same physical space they did not occupy the same environment because of cultural differences. One very much suspects that if the immigrants had been placed in the aborigine's environment then the demographic consequences might have been reversed.

The Australian example demonstrates the problem of using demographic data as a measure of biological adaptation. The fact is, that although man has been a highly migrant animal in recent millennia, the cultural environment which he carried with him means that we do not ordinarily encounter the situation experimentally developed by the evolutionist where two populations are placed in the *same* environment and demographic data are used as a measure of adaptive success. If such situations could be found for human populations, there seems no reason why demographic variables would not be equally good measures of biological adaptation for man.

When viewed from this perspective, the problem may be restated. Thus, while we can probably never hope to find two human populations with different evolutionary histories living in identical environments, the processes of migration do produce some commonalities in environment; and we may explore the question of whether particular demographic variables may give indications of the level of adaptation in particular environmental circumstances. An even more ambitious hope is that it may be possible in the future to remove the culturally produced variance in demographic variables by statistical techniques so that fertility and mortality characteristics can be used as measures of the biological adaptation of a population to a particular environment.

High-altitude population as a test case

Any environmental stress which has direct effects on the fertility or mortality of human populations could be used as a test situation for examining the potential utility of demographic data for measuring adaptation. Superficially, it appears that the best test case might be provided by examining severe chronic disease situations such as malaria or rapid epidemics such as smallpox. While exploration of these cases is worth while, even slight cultural differences make large differences in potential exposure to these diseases and consequently cultural factors have to be very carefully explored and controlled before any conclusions can be drawn.

The study of malaria is a good case in point: a number of genes are presumed to provide a degree of protection against the effects of malaria. Thus it would seem that a test of the protective value of one of the genes could be accomplished by simply finding two populations in a malarial zone one of which had the gene while the other did not. These groups could then be compared for their demographic characteristics, and presumably if the gene did provide some protection it should be evidenced in the lower mortality figures of the gene-bearing group. This simple model has generally not been applicable to malaria research because very subtle cultural differences affect the frequency of malaria exposure in populations. Slight differences in agricultural practices affect the number of mosquitoes, differences in human population density affect the probability of a given mosquito carrying malaria, and even such a small factor as whether a group sleeps near or away from cattle, which mosquitoes apparently prefer, affects infection levels (Livingstone 1958, 1962).

An analysis based on stresses such as heat, cold, or even malnutrition reveals the same difficulties in controlling cultural variables (Dubos 1959). The stress imposed by altitude appears to be one of the more favourable situations for study since cultural factors are of minor importance in modifying the effects of reduced barometric pressure on man. The basic stress is imposed on the organism by the low oxygen pressure and cultural practices do not modify exposure to the stress. It is probable that individuals performing chronic heavy exercise are subject to a different form of the stress than those who exercise less, but failure to perform any work still does not prevent significant effects. Using altitude as a stressor, the general problem may then be subdivided into three questions: (1) why should altitude affect the demographic characteristics of a human population?; (2) is there non-demographic evidence to suggest that populations vary in their degree of altitude adaptation?; and (3) does the demographic data available support the proposition that the natives of high altitude are better adapted than immigrants?

Why altitude should affect demographic variables

This proposition has been so widely discussed in the literature that it is unnecessary to provide the evidence in great detail. However, the following outline indicates the general nature of the evidence and indicates the sources of information.

(a) Altitude and fertility

1. Experimental studies on several animals, particularly rats, indicate that when oxygen tension is sufficiently low spermatogenesis is affected and the female's number of live offspring is reduced (Altland 1949, Altland and Highman 1968, Chiodi 1964, Johnson and Roofe 1965).
2. Studies on men taken to high terrestrial altitudes indicate at least temporary reductions in sperm count and increases in the number of abnormal spermatozoa (Donayre 1966, Donayre, Guerra-Garcia, Moncloa, and Sobrevilla 1968, Sobrevilla 1967).
3. Studies of women at altitude indicate changes in the menstrual cycle (Donayre 1966, Harris, Shields, and Hannon 1966).
4. Present evidence suggests that at least some human populations grow more slowly at high altitudes and the age of menarche is later than that found in most lowland populations (Bouloux 1968, Donayre 1966, Frisancho and Baker 1970, Sobrevilla 1967, Valsik 1965).
5. Studies on non-human animals show increased foetal wastage and stillbirths at altitude. This has not been reported for man, although anecdotal evidence suggests that women going from low to high altitude while pregnant have a high probability of spontaneous abortion (Johnson and Roofe 1965, McClung 1969, Van Liere and Stickney 1963, Weihe 1962).
6. Children born at high altitudes are smaller than those born to genetically similar mothers at low altitude. These differences include a significant increase in the number of children under 2·5 kg birth weight (Acosta Chavez 1964, Grahn and Kratchman 1963, Lichty, Ting, Bruns, and Dyar 1957, McClung 1969).

In sum, the present evidence suggests that the fecundity and ability of human populations to produce live offspring should be lower at high altitude.

(b) *Altitude and mortality*

1. The low oxygen tension at altitude appears to affect directly the frequency of congenital heart defects; possible effects on the frequencies of other congenital defects remain under debate (Espino-Vela 1967, Grabowski and Cavanagh 1966, Ingalls and Curley 1957, Peñaloza, Banchero, Sime, and Gamboa 1963).
2. At least two occasionally fatal diseases are directly attributable to hypoxic effects. These are acute altitude-induced pulmonary oedema and chronic mountain sickness or Monge's disease (Hultgren 1969, Monge and Monge 1966).
3. The multiple physiological and morphological differences found in altitude natives or immigrants probably have many effects on mortality patterns but at present evidence is limited to examples such as the higher haemorrhagic tendency found among altitude natives (Maccagno 1967, Monge and Monge 1966).
4. Altitude affects not only the human organism but also the infectious diseases which attack him. Therefore, the prevalence of infectious diseases is altitude-related in a manner still poorly understood (Buck, Sasaki, and Anderson 1968, Schmidt 1969, Trapani 1969, Weiser, Peoples, Tull, and Morse 1969).

As is the case with fertility, there exists more than adequate evidence to suggest that altitude should have direct effects on the patterns of human mortality, but the nature of this pattern is not clear other than suggesting a high neonatal mortality.

(c) *Evidence for population differences in altitude adaptation*

The non-demographic evidence for suggesting that some human populations are better adapted to high altitudes than others is primarily historical and physiological with as yet no identified genes that confer improved genetic adaptation. On the negative side it can be demonstrated that any gene which produces anaemias is subject to strong negative selection. Thus, migrations of Mediterranean and African populations into the high-altitude areas of South America have failed to leave any discoverable residue of thalassaemia (Matson, Sutton, Swanson, and Robinson 1966, Matson, Swanson, and Robinson 1966, Quilici 1968). The reasons for this are almost certainly related to the pressures put on the haemolytic systems by the oxygen-transport problems associated with high altitude (Aste-Salazar 1966).

In the very broad historical sense, one cannot fail to be impressed by the lack of biological success shown by populations invading altitudes above

3000 metres. While little is known about the migration history of the high Ethiopian areas, the Himalayan and Andean areas above 3000 metres appear to have been successfully invaded only once each. The Tibetan plateau was recently conquered by the Chinese and popular accounts suggest that colonization efforts are being made. Unfortunately, it is at present impossible to know what success these efforts have had. After the Spanish conquest of the Andes, strong efforts at colonization were made but as measured by the genetic markers in the modern population the conquest appears to have had only minor genetic effects in the higher parts of the Andes (Carles-Trochain 1968, Matson et al. 1966a, Quilici 1968). In his historical coverage of the problem, Mongé has made a strong case for accepting biological differences in hypoxic adaptation as a contributory explanation (Mongé 1948).

In morphology and physiology the populations native to altitudes above 2500 metres are significantly different from low-altitude human populations. These differences seem to be paralleled between Andean and Himalayan natives but from the data so far available the high-altitude population of Ethiopia appears different in many morphological features (Baker 1969, 1971, Clegg, Harrison, and Baker 1970, Lahiri 1965, Little 1969, Mazess 1969, Morpurgo, Battaglia, Bernini, Palucci, and Modiano 1970, Pugh 1966).

Among these multiple morphological and physiological differences between native and contrasting human populations, a sorting of those which are adaptive to high altitude versus those which are not is very difficult. As Mazess (1970) has recently pointed out, it is all too easy and often mistaken to assume that all differences are indicative of better functional capacity. The major difference that probably should be considered as an indication that the native has a better level of adaptation is the consistent finding that at high altitudes the native has the ability to utilize a greater amount of oxygen per unit of body weight than the recent migrant (Baker 1969, Velasquez 1970). Present evidence suggests that at the 4000-metre level the average difference in young adult males is in the range of 20 to 25 per cent. This statement is as usual an oversimplification of the problem since the level of difference is affected by physical condition, disease, nutrition, etc., and should not be freely extrapolated to other age groups or to females. Nevertheless, it seems safe to suggest that if new migrant and native populations were tested at altitude the natives would show a higher oxygen-extractive efficiency.

What is much less certain is whether this difference is the product of ontogenetic processes or is in part related to a difference in the genetic structure of the contrasting populations. This question has been widely debated in the literature and will only be resolved by further data collection or new approaches (Hurtado 1966).

Differences in oxygen-extractive efficiency do not cover all aspects of suggested population differences in the level of biological adaptation. However, it is enough to suggest strongly that native lowland and native high-altitude populations do vary in their level of biological adaptation to altitude. We may, therefore, hypothesize that if we could produce the experimental evolutionist manipulation and place the two populations in an altitude chamber we should see in at least the first generation some significant demographic differences.

Demographic evidence on adaptation to altitude

There is a variety of demographic evidence—folklore, historical, and scientific—from the areas with permanent high-altitude populations. The information is of two general classes: macro- or general information about large populations covering large areas, or micro-information referring to detailed studies on small populations. Both types of material, while varying in their relevant detail, offer information and hypotheses of significance to altitude adaptation.

Macro-studies

One type of macro-evidence may be deduced from the analysis of the stories and beliefs of an area. The traditional beliefs and folklore of the inhabitants of the Andean *altiplano* indicate that the residents believe altitude to have deleterious effects on fertility and mortality. For example, women, especially from the upper socio-economic classes, often go to lower altitudes to give birth. The stated reason for this is that spontaneous abortions are more likely to occur and that babies die more frequently in the highlands than they do at the lower elevations. While this may partially be a result of the poor medical facilities in many *altiplano* communities, the pattern is also found among women residing in urban centres where medical facilities are quite adequate. Another common belief is that newcomers to altitude, human and non-human, suffer a decrease in fertility upon arrival. While such stories and beliefs do not constitute scientific proof, their persistence throughout the Andean highlands suggests that they may have a scientific basis.

Demographic evidence is also found in the chronicles of various early historians. Mongé (1948) has searched through the accounts of many early Spanish writers and summarized their comments on fertility and mortality. He notes that both the Indians and the Spanish were cognizant of altitude and its effect on their lives. The Incas, for example, believed that the environmental zones affected populations and acted on this belief in their colonization plans. New settlements were colonized with populations which had been moved from similar altitude zones. The movement of individuals or groups to a different altitude zone was used as punishment.

Altitude had such an effect on the fertility of the Spanish and their animals, that the capital of the Spanish colony was moved from Jauja in the highlands to Lima on the coast and in the case of one high mining community the historical record showed that it took 53 years before the first Spanish child born in this town survived long enough to be baptized.

A third type of macro-demographic evidence has been derived from the analysis of the national censuses in countries with high-altitude residents. Analyses of such data which consider altitude as a variable have been limited to general comparative examinations of fertility and mortality levels.

In a study of the interaction of fertility and culture using data from the 1940 Peruvian national census, Stycos (1963) pointed out that the Indian regions of the country had lower fertility rates than the Spanish areas. He attributed this difference to an assumed later mean age at first marriage among the Indians and suggested that such relationships were not very stable, particularly among the younger people. Stycos also examined the effect of altitude and fertility but concluded that no significant relationship existed between them. Heer (1964) re-examined the problems of differential fertility between the Spanish and Indian elements, increasing the scope of his study by also including the 1950 national censuses of Ecuador and Bolivia. He also found lower fertility rates among the Indian sectors of all three countries but suggested that Indian fertility was lower because the women more often worked and were consequently practising more birth control than the Spanish.

James (1966) re-analysed Heer's data and suggested that although a relationship might exist between fertility and the number of women in the labour force, the real cause for lower fertility might be a third variable, altitude. Using the Peruvian, Ecuadorian, and Bolivian census data, he found that a significant negative relationship between fertility and altitude existed in all three countries. When he controlled the effect of culture statistically by using language as a third variable, altitude still explained a significant amount of variation in fertility in all three countries. James then offered three possible explanations for the results: (1) the lower fertility at altitude was due to seasonal migration of native highlanders to lowland causing temporary azoospermia to males on their return to altitude; (2) the lower fertility at altitude might be related to higher neonatal mortality rates at altitude; (3) there might be higher rates of spontaneous abortion at altitude which would lower the fertility rate.

Heer (1967), in a response to James' paper, examined the relationship of fertility, altitude, the adult sex ratio, and the percentage of women in the labour force of Peru, Bolivia, and Ecuador. He agreed that altitude was the most important variable explaining fertility for Peru, but stated that the adult sex ratio was a more important variable than altitude in Ecuador, and that both the adult sex ratio and the proportion of females in the labour force were more important factors than altitude in Bolivia. Heer concluded that the evidence suggested that altitude was an important determinant of variation in fertility in the Andean region.

In this rather extended game of numbers, the present authors analysed the data from the more recent 1961 Peruvian census and found that a significant negative correlation still exists between fertility and altitude (see Fig. 17.1). For reasons which will be presented later we did not find some of the previous explanations worth testing; but it is the case that a greater number of males than females migrate downwards, so we tested to see whether the correlation could be explained by the adult sex ratio. We did not find the sex ratio an important variable.

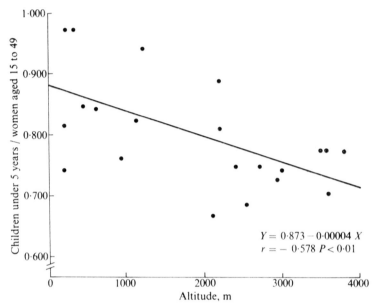

$$Y = 0.873 - 0.00004\ X$$
$$r = -0.578\ P < 0.01$$

FIG. 17.1. Relationship of fertility to altitude for 21 Peruvian Provinces (from Instituto Nacional de Planificacion 1964).

Various national censuses have also been studied for a possible relationship between mortality and altitude. Grahn and Kratchman (1963) analysed data from various low- and high-altitude areas in the United States and reported a highly significant positive correlation between altitude and neonatal mortality. They suggested that the increased neonatal mortality at altitude was a result of lower birth weights and an increased frequency of premature births at altitude (Grahn and Kratchman 1963, McClung 1969).

Similar relationships between neonatal mortality and altitude have also been shown for Peru. Mazess (1965) analysed the 1961 Peruvian vital statistics on mortality and found that the neonatal mortality of areas having a mean altitude above 2000 metres was twice that of the lower departments (he calculated a correlation of +0·70 for 1958 and +0·73 for 1959 between altitude and neonatal mortality). The significant association between altitude and neonatal mortality might be explained by differences in medical care, etc., between the highlands and lowlands. However, when other mortality indices, that tended to remove the effects of differential socio-economic and medical conditions, were considered, the effect of altitude on neonatal mortality was still highly significant although somewhat diminished.

In a study of trends through time of neonatal mortality and birth weight, Frisancho and Cossman (1970) analysed the 1957–67 vital statistics for two low-altitude and five high-altitude United States groups and found that although the percentage of children weighing less than 2·5 kg is still greater at high altitude than at low altitude, infant mortality in the higher groups has declined during the past ten years. The fact that lower birth weights still exist at altitude while mortality has dropped suggests that the lowered neonatal death rates are due to social factors. It is probable that the hospitals and doctors in the high-altitude parts of the United States have become cognizant of the stress that altitude imposes on the newborn infant and have developed specific techniques to care for these neonates.

In evaluating the demographic impact of altitude on human populations the use of census data has many pitfalls caused by the kind of data collected and the ways in which it is analysed. The use of 'the number of live children under five per woman' as an index of fertility may be a good example. Examination of Mazess's results and those of James suggests that the lower fertility reported for the Andean highlands may be a result of a higher infant mortality in these areas rather than the direct effects of altitude on fertility. This possibility has also been suggested by Whitehead (1968) and Bradshaw (1969). Fertility was measured in the 1950 Bolivian and Ecuadorian censuses and the 1961 Peruvian census by compilation of the child–women ratio—the number of children zero to five years of age divided by the number of women fifteen to 45 or 49 years of age. A high infant mortality rate in one area will decrease the number of living children and lead to a lower fertility estimate than that obtained for an area with a lower infant mortality rate although each area has the same fertility. A second problem which the same authors stress is the validity of the census material itself. They feel there is considerable under-enumeration, particularly in the Indian regions of Ecuador and Bolivia.

Thus, we must conclude that while macro-data are useful in generating hypotheses they are most often inadequate to go beyond this level. A major problem is that such data only allow for the compilation of fairly crude estimates of fertility and mortality. Furthermore, it is extremely difficult, if not impossible, to control for various socio-economic, cultural, or medical differences which may obscure any biological relationship that exists. The data are often incomplete, and sizeable sections of the populations may not be included. Finally, the regions covered by the censuses are so large that only general statements about the relationship of altitude, fertility, and mortality can be made. Because of these problems we find ourselves in close agreement with De Jong (1970) who advocated the micro- or detailed study approach to the problem.

Micro-studies

The demographic data available through detailed community studies are quite limited. Some data are available from Vicos, Peru (Alers 1965), Cerro de Pasco, Peru (Centro de Investigaciones Sociales por Muestro 1968), a series of small highland Chilean communities (Cruz-Coke, Cristoffanini, Aspillaga, and Binancani 1966, Cruz-Coke 1967), and Nuñoa, Peru.

Vicos, a district in north central Peru located at an altitude of 2800 m, has a population of about 2000, almost entirely Quechua, and was the focus of an intensive study in cultural anthropology. Cerro de Pasco, the centre of a mining region in north central Peru, is located at 4600 m and has a population of about 30 000, mainly Quecha Indians. It was the centre of a detailed study of fecundity conducted by a Peruvian governmental agency. Cruz-Coke and his co-workers compared census data on low- and medium-altitude Chilean communities with original survey data from a small group of high-altitude natives. The authors recently completed analysis of demographic data collected in a long-term biocultural study of Nuñoa, a Peruvian district located in the southern Peruvian *altiplano* near Puno. Since this study represents the only large-scale study devoted to using demographic data for analysing biological adaptation to altitude we will present this analysis in some detail.

The altitude of the Nuñoa district ranges from 4000 to more than 5000 m with the majority of the 7800 inhabitants living between 4000 and 4500 m. The great majority of the population are Quechua Indians who live on haciendas scattered throughout the district. Most of the residents are pastoralists or subsistence horticulturalists raising potatoes and native grains. The town of Nuñoa, which has about 2000 residents, is the only town in the district and is its social, political, and economic centre.

Health facilities within the district are extremely limited by western standards. There is at present only a *posta medica* or local medical station where first aid and some medicine can occasionally be obtained. The medical station is staffed by a single male nurse. The nearest hospital is located some 50 km from Nuñoa. Because of distance, social tradition, and cost, use of the hospital and trained medical doctors is limited to the small middle and upper class of the district (about 10 per cent of the population).

Since 1930 a district registry of births and deaths has been functioning. For the purpose of our study, we use the data collected by this office from 1940 to 1964. We also used demographic data collected in 1964 and 1965 as part of a biocultural survey of the district. This survey included a detailed demographic questionnaire which was administered to about 10 per cent of the adult population.

Population size and sex–age composition of the population were taken from the 1940 and 1961 national censuses. The presence of only two complete censuses made it necessary to derive the yearly crude death and birth rates based upon estimates of population size. These were made by assuming a simple linear population change based on the points fixed by the censuses. Preliminary analysis as shown in Fig. 17.2 indicated that there was a considerable under-registration of deaths from 1940 to 1950, particularly with respect

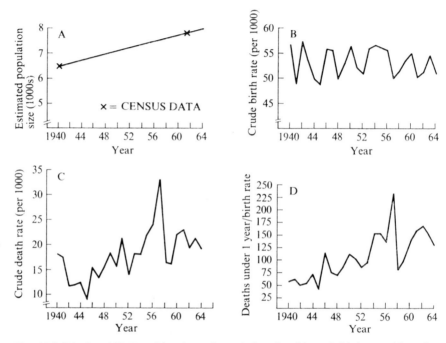

FIG. 17.2. District of Nuñoa: (a) estimated population size, (b) crude birth rate, (c) crude death rate, and (d) infant mortality rate, 1940–64. Based on census and registry data.

to deaths of infants. The analysis of mortality was subsequently limited for most purposes to the 1951–64 period. We believe that there was a considerable amount of emigration, particularly among the young adults. It is difficult, however, to assess the effect, if any, this has had on our fertility or mortality estimates for the district. As a final caution it should be noted that there may be an under-registration of still births and neonatal deaths.

(a) Fertility

The crude birth rate or number of births in a year divided by the total population size and expressed in terms of 1000 persons is often calculated as a general measure of the fertility of a population. Crude birth rates reported for the various high-altitude populations studied, range from 45 to 80 births per thousand (see Table 17.1). While such rates are quite high when compared to those of western countries (about 25 per thousand), they are well within the range found in peasant populations. Yearly rates are available for Nuñoa for a 25-year period and the district has shown a relatively stable rate of between 48 and 56 per thousand.

TABLE 17.1

Comparative fertility and mortality rates for various Andean communities

Place	Mean altitude (M)	Year	Size of population	Crude birth rate (births/1000)	Crude birth rate (deaths/1000)	Infant mortality rate (deaths < 1 year)
Arica, Chile†	100	1965	—	47·9	6·9	24·0
Belen, Chile†	3200	1965	—	46·0	20·7	175·0
Lauca, Chile†	4300	1965	—	82·4	50·0	388·0
Vicos, Peru‡	2800	1952	1798	45·6	14·5	122·0
	2800	1963	2118	56·2	24·6	142·9
Cerro de Pasco, Peru§	4600	1967	30 000	53–54	—	100·0
Nuñoa, Peru	4200	1940	6470	56·6		
	4200	1961	7750	48·6	23·5	164·10

† Cruz-Coke, Cristoffanini, Aspillaga, and Binancani (1966)
‡ Alers (1965).
§ Centro de Investigaciones Sociales por Muestro (1968).

Analysis of average completed family size, i.e., average number of children born to women who have completed the childbearing period, is a more specific measure of fertility. Based on the survey data, an average completed family size of 6·7 appears reasonable for Nuñoa (Hoff 1968). Cruz-Coke *et al.* (1966) reported average completed family sizes of 5·8, 7·3, and 8·5 for three small Aymara communities in Bolivia. These are, again, quite high when compared to the completed family sizes in western countries, which have strong socio-economic pressures for small families and where methods of contraception are well-known and easily available. However, the averages are well below the completed family sizes reported for populations such as the Hutterites who have a completed fertility of over 10 or modern Eskimos who are reported to have a completed fertility of 10·6 (Eaton and Mayer 1953, Milan 1970).

At present, little is known about contraception knowledge or use among Andean Indians. The study in Cerro de Pasco indicated, for that area at least, that knowledge and use of contraceptives is almost wholly limited to the upper socio-economic classes and that few women in the lower socio-economic group practise any form of contraception (see Table 17.2). If the Nuñoa native knows as little about contraceptive methods as the Cerro de Pasco population, it is possible that a completed family size of around seven would be significantly lower than that which would be found in a low-altitude population that also used no methods of contraception. At present, the data are not adequate to support definite conclusions.

TABLE 17.2

Knowledge and use of contraceptive methods in Cerro de Pasco†

Contraceptive methods	Knowledge, per cent						Use, per cent					
		Socio-economic position						Socio-economic position				
	Total	Low	2	3	4	High	Total	Low	2	3	4	High
Douche	38	16	28	38	54	67	17	4	9	20	33	24
Sterilization	32	21	27	28	42	53	5	<0·5	1	1	9	18
Birth-control pills	20	10	18	13	24	45	3	1	1	1	7	10
Rhythm method	19	5	7	11	32	53	2	<0·5	1	<0·5	2	6
Prophylactics	17	3	11	14	28	38	1	<0·5	<0·5	2	2	4
Coitus interruptus	13	5	7	10	22	26	1	<0·5	<0·5	<0·5	3	1
Diaphragm	6	2	4	4	4	4	<0·5	<0·5	<0·5	<0·5	<0·5	1
Intra-uterine device	5	2	4	2	8	12	<0·5	<0·5	<0·5	<0·5	<0·5	1
Jelly	5	2	3	5	7	11	<0·5	<0·5	1	<0·5	<0·5	1
Others	1	<0·5	1	1	<0·5	1	<0·5	<0·5	<0·5	<0·5	<0·5	<0·5
Total percentage of women	58	36	48	58	75	86	23	5	11	22	44	43
Number of cases	583	124	143	128	93	95	583	124	143	128	93	95

† Centro de Investigaciones Sociales por Muestro (1968).

Two other aspects of fertility of possible significance to adaptation are the relationships between pregnancy risk and age, and the sex ratio at birth. Cruz-Coke reported that among his high-altitude population the pregnancy risk rose during the early twenties and remained fairly high until the early forties. A peak occurred during the 25–9 age period while the maximum risk of pregnancy occurred in the 35–45 age category. The distribution of 'the age of mother at birth of child' as recorded in the birth register for Nuñoa is shown in Fig. 17.3. While the maximum number of births was recorded to women between 20 and 24, the data cannot be taken as a true indicator of pregnancy risk, because the total number of women per age grade could not be determined. The number of women in each successive age category is undoubtedly significantly smaller than each preceding one because of emigration, deaths, and a growing population. Data collected during the biocultural survey on a group of women who were post-menopausal is shown in Fig. 17.4. The highest pregnancy risk occurred during the 35–9 age period.

Both the Chilean data and that from Nuñoa fit the general picture of peasant societies where pregnancy risk starts to rise in the late teens, reaches

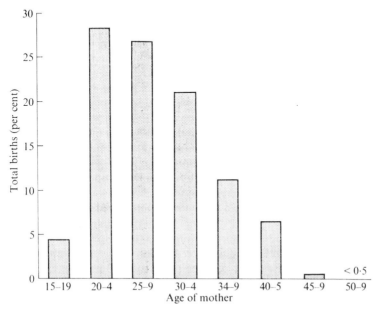

FIG. 17.3. Percentage of births by age of mother. Data from 5111 registered births in the District of Nuñoa, 1940–64.

its peak in the twenties, and remains relatively high during the thirties and early forties (Bogue 1969). In western countries pregnancy risks rise in late teens, reach a peak in early or mid-twenties, drop sharply in thirties and remain low until menopause. Despite these similarities significant differences do exist between the Nuñoa–Chilean pattern and that pattern found in most other peasant societies. Pregnancy risks in Nuñoa and Chile are rather low during the teens and even early twenties, particularly for Cruz-Coke's sample and the maximum peak pregnancy risk occurs quite late in the fertile period. The very low pregnancy risk in the teens is probably explained by the late biological development of the high-altitude female but the reasons for the continued low pregnancy risk during the twenties is not clear. All women contract a sexual partnership by the early twenties and tend to be mated during the entire reproductive span. The Andean area is one of serial monogamy and this raises the possibility that for some reason the pregnancy risk

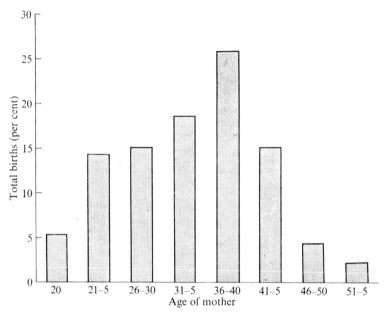

Fig. 17.4. Percentage of births by age of mother as reported by 31 post-menopausal women for 113 births. Data drawn from biocultural survey.

is higher with the second and subsequent mates. This suggestion is supported by the finding in Nuñoa that perhaps more than 50 per cent of all women living through the reproductive span have more than one mate. Furthermore as can be seen in Fig. 17.5, women who had more than one mate had the majority of their children with the second mate.

When one asks why fertility appears to be lower with the first mate, at least three possibilities may be suggested: (1) contraceptive measures are used to a greater extent with the first husband; (2) exposure is lower with the first husband because he is away from the wife more; and (3) first mates separate because of low fertility. Of these suggestions, the first seems improbable because of the lack of contraceptive knowledge. The second may be significant because young men may work away from home more than older men. The third possible explanation is pertinent to biological adaptation since high altitude may reduce the percentage of fertile males in the society and mate-changing based on infertility would in this case be a cultural mechanism for increasing the reproduction of the total group. The present data are not adequate for definite conclusions on the subject but do provide a provocative hypothesis.

The sex ratio at birth may also be affected by altitude. An average birth sex ratio of 105–6 has been reported for most populations (Kirby, McWhirter, Teitelbaum, and Darlington 1967), including the United States. The sex ratio for all births registered in the Nuñoa district for the period from 1940 to 1964 was 111, which is quite high by world standards. While this could be the result of an under-registration of females which happens in some peasant

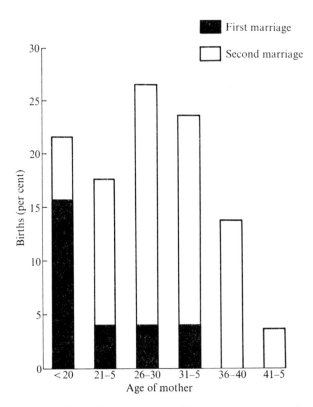

FIG. 17.5. Percentage of births by age as reported by women who entered two marriages. Sample of 16 women reporting 55 births; data drawn from biocultural survey. Not all women included were post-menopausal and additional births from second and subsequent mates would probably be higher for a post-menopausal sample.

societies, examination of the yearly ratios (see Fig. 17.6) demonstrates no apparent pattern. There also does not appear to be any strong cultural reason why this should occur. The survey data that were not affected by the registration factor suggested that in fact the birth sex ratio may actually be somewhat higher than the registration figures indicated (Hoff 1968). At present no specific mechanism whereby altitude would affect sex ratio at birth is known; however, preliminary results of a study on high-altitude cattle inseminated with sperm from low-altitude bulls also reported an elevated sex ratio (Foote and Quevedo 1971).

FIG. 17.6. Annual sex ratio of births for the District of Nuñoa, 1940–64. Based on registry data. Sex ratio for the 26-year period is 1·109.

(b) Mortality

The crude death rate (deaths per year divided by the total population size expressed in terms of 1000 individuals) is a common general measure of the mortality of a population. Crude death rates calculated for the five high-altitude communities ranged from less than 15 to over 25 per thousand with the exception of a Chilean community which had a rate of 50 (see Table 17.1). While these rates are somewhat higher than those found in countries with good medical facilities and adequate care, they are quite typical of mortality rates found in peasant areas. Crude death rates are available for a 15-year period for Nuñoa (see Fig. 17.2) and with the exception of 1957 when an epidemic, possibly scarlet fever, swept through the district, rates have ranged from 15 to 25 deaths per thousand.

Using the age and sex composition of the Province of Melgar (of which Nuñoa is a part) as a base, it was possible to estimate age- and sex-specific mortality rates for the Nuñoan population (see Fig. 17.7). Mortality rates are very high during the first year of life, dropping rapidly during the next 4 years. The lowest rates appear from 5 years to 14, after which time they begin to climb gradually until old age. With the exception of the first year of life when more males die than females, the mortality rates of the two sexes are almost equal.

On the basis of the information provided by analysis of the death register and the estimated age- and sex-specific mortality rates it was possible to construct an approximate survivorship curve for the population (see Fig. 17.8). Fig. 17.8 also presents curves for a primitive agricultural group, the Yạnomamö (compiled from information from Neel (1970), a low-altitude peasant population (United Nations 1967), and a modern western country,

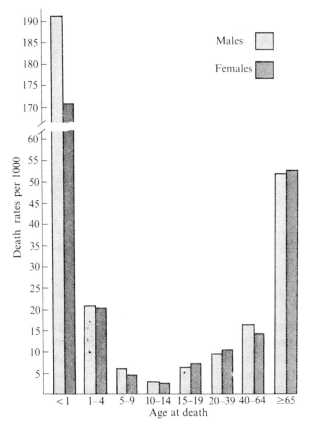

FIG. 17.7. Age- and sex-specific mortality rates for District of Nuñoa. Based on provincial census and data and district registry data, 1940–61.

the United States (Bogue 1969). When the approximate survivorship curve for the Nuñoa population is compared with that typical of the western, peasant, or primitive society it shows substantial differences from any of these. Thus, infant and child mortality is greater than that found in the western and primitive society, but is much less than the mortality common to many peasant societies which lack modern medical care. The reasons for this are undoubtedly complex. One may speculate that while altitude probably increases some kinds of mortality, the hypoxia and cold of this region may also reduce the prevalence and virulence of many diseases found among low-altitude peasants that are fatal to infants. This is partially supported by a recent epidemiological study (Buck *et al.* 1969), which found that the diseases present in a high-altitude area close to Nuñoa are quite different from those found at low elevations on either side of the Andean range.

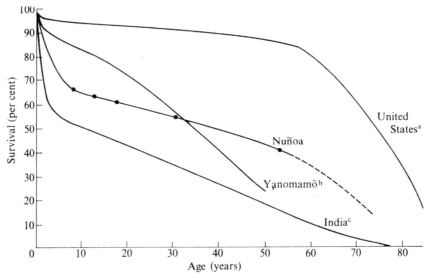

FIG. 17.8. Survivorship estimates for District of Nuñoa compared with other selected populations. (a) estimate for 1965 U.S. population, Bogue (1969); (b) Neel (1970); (c) estimated from 1911 Indian Census, United Nations 1967.

During young adulthood the decline in survivorship shown for Nuñoa in Fig. 17.8 is probably excessive since it could not be corrected for what is undoubtedly a significant emigration. Even considering this factor, it appears that mortality until middle age is much less than among the Yąnomamö and slightly less than the Indian peasant. How it compares with the United States is difficult to judge.

Survivorship after 50 is little better than a guess because most Nuñoans over this age have only a very vague idea of their age. The reported age of death for these individuals must, therefore, be considered to have an error of at least plus or minus ten years. From close questioning of individuals during the course of the survey, it is certain that some individuals do live into the eighties; but we are unable at present to support or reject the claim often made in the Andes that many individuals live to extreme old age.

Conclusions and prospectus

Let us examine now how well the available data have supported our original proposition that high altitude should be the ideal situation for using demographic data as a measure of adaptation.

Fertility as a demographic measure of adaptation could only be partially examined. It has been predicted from non-human animal studies and from physiological studies that native lowlanders who migrate to high altitude should show a significant reduction in fertility. How much loss in fertility or whether it is lower at all cannot be judged at present simply because there is no appropriate material. The census data do suggest that fertility may be reduced in high-altitude natives. The micro-studies provide ambiguous support, since high-altitude Andean populations have rather high fertility. Whether this fertility is below theoretical maximum because of altitude factors hinges on the unknown role of cultural factors such as the use of contraception and coital practice.

The micro-studies provide two other rather interesting suggestions, namely, that there may be a rather high percentage of low-fertility males at altitude and the sex ratio at birth may be elevated among high Andean natives. Both suggestions would require verification by further study.

The mortality impact of altitude provides one clear relationship between hypoxia, biology, and mortality. The newborn at altitude is more likely to have a low birth weight, more likely to have a congenital heart defect, and is more likely to die. In the United States at moderate altitude this relationship is altered probably due to better neonatal health care, but it is interesting that the impact of altitude is apparently greater on the birth weight of the United States newborn than on the Andean Indian child (McClung 1969). One may thus speculate that if the medical-care factors were the same then at high altitudes the Andean neonate might very well show a survival advantage over the infant of a non-altitude native.

Other aspects of mortality and altitude cannot be tested with the present macro- and micro-data. The infant and childhood mortality rates for high Andes natives are not unusual. The measured rates suggest that mortality may, during these ages, be somewhat lower than is common for non-altitude peasants with a comparable level of medical care. This low mortality is not necessarily related to altitude adaptation. It may instead be that better nutrition and less infectious disease in the Andes enhance the survival possibilities of the population compared with peasants in other environments.

The complexities of using demographic variables as adaptation measures for high altitude populations re-emphasize the reasons why human biologists have generally rejected simple indices of fertility and mortality as adaptive measures for human populations. Even where the stress is clearly manifest and is only slightly modified by cultural form it is apparent that these indices cannot be easily interpreted. Of course, the moderate fertility and modest mortality of the Andean native does mean that he has achieved a successful biological adaptation to his environment, but the data are such that we cannot say whether this means he has a higher fertility or lower mortality than a non-native would have in the same environment. Indeed, we cannot even say for certain that his fertility or mortality would be different at sea level.

The limitations encountered in the present analysis do not mean that human demographic data could never be used for the purposes outlined. The scientific method which could provide appropriate data is rather straightforward. Harrison (1966) outlined the method several years ago and we will only briefly restate how this could be applied to the present problems. If, as he proposed, we could find the following four populations, we could use many measures, including demographic ones, to discover how man has adapted to his environment.

1. HAN—A group living at high altitude and native to altitude, in the sense of having a long generational history of high-altitude residence.
2. HAN ↓—A subdivision of group 1, who live under identical conditions but who have migrated down to sea level.
3. LAN—A group living at low altitude with other conditions similar to those of groups 1 and 2.
4. LAN ↑—A subdivision of group 3 which migrated up to the same altitude and conditions of group 1.

With these populations, intergroup comparisons would provide the following information.

HAN–LAN	total differences caused by altitude.
HAN–LAN ↑	genetic features of altitude adaptation.
LAN–LAN ↑	ontogenetic and physiological adaptations to altitude (acclimatization) plus detrimental effects of altitude.
HAN–HAN ↓	ontogenetic and physiological adaptation (acclimatization) to downward migration plus detrimental effects of downward migration.
LAN–HAN ↓	differences in response to sea-level pressure produced by genetic differences.

The major difficulty with the method outlined above is finding populations fulfilling the required conditions. Harrison, Küchemann, Moore, Boyce, Baju, Mourant, Godber, Glasgow, Kopec, Tills, and Clegg (1969) found, in Ethiopia, populations living at 3000 m which contain the HAN and LAN ↑ groups and they have a LAN group for control. These populations which appeared ideal for the analysis did not yield much of the desired information, because of population differences in nutrition and disease. The altitude was also insufficient to demonstrate many hypoxia effects. In the Andean area the HAN– LAN ↑ comparisons are poor because such upward migrants as can be found are in a higher socio-economic position than the peasants who form the major high-altitude group. The HAN–HAN ↓ and LAN–HAN ↓ comparisons show reasonable promise as a research situation. In the United

States the LAN–LAN ↑ comparison could be made but there are essentially no high-altitude natives.

The lack of the ideal natural populations does not mean that the appropriate analysis is impossible, but it does mean that the amount of work required is much greater. In his 1970 paper, De Jong suggested that since it is at least possible to conceptualize and investigate the socio-cultural factors which affect fertility it should be possible to arrive at a reasonable estimate of how much they contributed to the level of population fertility. A comparable structure could be suggested for biological contributions to fertility so that when such a combined research model had been applied to a population of Andean peasants and a population of upward migrant whites in the Andes, we should be able to estimate what would happen to the fertility of either group. By this quite laborious process, it would be possible to use at least some demographic data as a measure of population adaptation to high-altitude stress. If this was all one could derive from such studies the cost and effort would perhaps appear unjustified, but such a method would also provide insights on social accommodations to stress, the effect of other stresses on fertility, and perhaps most importantly how cultural and biological factors interact to foster the survival of human populations when they are subjected to a strong environmental stress.

Almost needless to say, we hope that such integrated studies will, in the future, supplement if not replace the present reductionist approach to the study of human population dynamics.

REFERENCES

ACOSTA CHAVEZ, M. H. (1964). Algunos aspectos del niño primaturo en las alturas; estudio clinico-estadistico realizado en el hospital de Huaron a 4750 metros de altura sobre el nivel del mar. Thesis 5886, Facultad de Medicina, Lima.

ALERS, J. O. (1965). Population and development in a Peruvian community. *J. Int-am. Stud.* **7**, 423–48.

ALTLAND, P. D. (1949). Breeding performance of rats exposed repeatedly to 18 000 feet. *Physiol. Zool.* **22**, 232–46.

—— and HIGHMAN, B. (1968). Sex organ changes and breeding performance of male rats exposed to altitude: effect of exercise and physical training. *J. Reprod. Fert.* **15**, 215–22.

ASTE-SALAZAR, H. (1966). Unpublished work cited in Mongé, C. M. and Mongé, C. C. (1966), *High-altitude diseases: mechanism and management.* Thomas, Springfield.

BAKER, P. T. (1966). Human biological variation as an adaptive response to the environment. *Eugenics Q.* **13**, 81–91.

—— (1969). Human adaptation to high altitude. *Science, N.Y.* **163**, 1149–56.

—— (1971). Adaptation problems in Andean human populations. In *Ongoing evolution of Latin American populations* (ed. F. Salzano). Thomas, Springfield.

BOGUE, D. J. (1969). *Principles of demography.* Wiley, New York.

BOULOUX, C. J. (1968). *Contribution a l'étude biologique des phenomènes pubertaires en très haute altitude.* Monographies du Centre D'hémotypologie, C.H.U. de Toulouse, Hermann.

BRADSHAW, B. S. (1969). Fertility differences in Peru: a reconsideration. *Popul. Stud.* **23**, 5–19.

BRESSLER, J. B. (ed.) (1966). Temperature and the evolution of man. In *Human ecology* (ed. J. B. Bressler). Addison Wesley, Reading, Mass.

BUCK, A., SASAKI, S., and ANDERSON, K. (1968). *Health and disease in four Peruvian villages: contrasts in epidemiology*. Johns Hopkins Press, Baltimore.

CARLES-TROCHAIN, E. (1968). *Étude hémotypologique des pecheurs du lac Titicaca*. Monographies du Centre D'hémotypologie, C.H.U. de Toulouse, Hermann.

CENTRO DE INVESTIGACIONES SOCIALES POR MUESTRO (1968). *Encuesta de fecundidad en la ciudad de Cerro de Pasco*. Ministerio de Trabajo y Communidades, Lima, Peru.

CHIODI, H. (1964). Action of high-altitude chronic hypoxia on newborn animals. In *The physiological effects of high altitude* (ed. W. H. Weihe). Pergamon Press, New York.

CLEGG, E. J., HARRISON, G. A., and BAKER, P. T. (1970). The impact of high altitude on human populations. *Hum. Biol.* **42**, 486–518.

CRUZ-COKE, R. (1967). Genetic characteristics of high-altitude populations in Chile. Paper presented at P.A.H.O., W.H.O., I.B.P. meeting of investigators on population biology of altitude, Washington, D.C., November, 1967.

—— CRISTOFFANINI, A. P., ASPILLAGA, M., and BINANCANI, F. (1966). Evolutionary forces in human populations in an environmental gradient in Arica. *Hum. Biol.* **38**, 421–38.

DE JONG, G. F. (1970). Demography and research with high-altitude populations. *Soc. Biol.* **17**, 114–19.

DONAYRE, J. (1966). Population growth and fertility at high altitude. In *Life at high altitudes*. Pan American Health Organization Sci. Publs. **140**, 74–9.

—— GUERRA-GARCIA, R., MONCLOA, F., and SOBREVILLA, L. A. (1968). Endocrine studies at high altitude: IV. Changes in the semen of men. *J. Reprod. Fert.* **16**, 55–8.

DUBOS, R. (1959). *Mirage of health: utopias, progress, and biological change*. Doubleday, New York.

EATON, J. W. and MAYER, A. J. (1953). The social biology of very high fertility among the Hutterites. *Hum. Biol.* **25**, 206–64.

ESPINO-VELA, J. (1967). Congenital cardiac malformations in high altitude populations. Paper presented at P.A.H.O., W.H.O., I.B.P. meeting of investigators on population biology of altitude, Washington, D.C., November, 1967.

FOOTE, W. D. and QUEVEDO, M. M. (1971). Sex ratio following subjection of semen to reduced atmospheric pressure. *J. Anim. Sci. Suppl. Sex ratio at birth—prospects for control*, 55–58.

FRISANCHO, A. R. and BAKER, P. T. (1970). Altitude and growth: a study of the patterns of physical growth of a high-altitude Peruvian Quechua population. *Am. J. phys. Anthrop.* **32**, 267–78.

—— and COSSMAN, J. (1970). Secular trends in neonatal mortality in the mountain states. *Am. J. Phys. Anthrop.* **33**, 103–6.

GRABOWSKI, D. M. and CAVANAGH, D. (1966). The etiology of hypoxia-induced malformations in the chick embryo. *J. exp. Zool.* **157**, 307–25.

GRAHN, D. and KRATCHMAN, J. (1963). Variation in neonatal death rate and birth weight in the United States and possible relations to environmental radiation, geology, and altitude. *Am. J. hum. Genet.* **15**, 329–52.

HARRIS, C. W., SHIELDS, J. L., and HANNON, J. P. (1966). Acute altitude sickness in females. *Aerospace Med.* **37**, 1163–7.

HARRISON, G. A. (1966). Human adaptability with reference to the I.B.P. proposals for high-altitude research. In *The biology of human adaptability* (eds. P. T. Baker and J. S. Weiner) Clarendon Press, Oxford.

—— KÜCHEMANN, C. F., MOORE, M. A. S., BOYCE, A. J., BAJU, T., MOURANT, A. E., GODBER, M. J., GLASGOW, B. G., KOPEC, A. C., TILLS, D., and CLEGG, E. J. (1969). The effects of altitude variation in Ethiopian populations. *Phil. Trans. R. Soc.* **256**, 147–82.

HEER, D. M. (1964). Fertility differences between Indian and Spanish-speaking parts of Andean countries. *Popul. Stud.* **18**, 71–84.

—— (1967). Fertility differences in Andean countries: a reply to W. H. James. *Popul. Stud.* **21**, 71–3.

HOFF, C. (1968). Reproduction and viability in a highland Peruvian Indian population. In *High altitude adaptation in a Peruvian community*. Occasional Papers in Anthropology No. 1. Department of Anthropology, The Pennsylvania State University.

HULTGREN, H. N. (1969). High altitude pulmonary edema. In *Biomedicine problems of high terrestrial elevations* (ed. A. H. Hegnauer) U.S. Army Research Institute of Environmental Medicine, Natick, Mass. and U.S. Army Medical Research and Development Command, Washington, D.C.

HURTADO, A. (1966). Needs for further research. In *Life at high altitudes. Pan American Health Organization Sci. Publs.* **140**, 80–4.

INGALLS, T. H. and CURLEY, F. J. (1957). Principles governing the genesis of congenital malformations induced in mice by hypoxia. *New Eng. J. Med.* **247**, 758–68.

INSTITUTO NACIONAL DE PLANIFICACION (1964). *Sexto Censo Nacional de Poblacion. Resultados de primera prioridad*. Direccion Nacional de Estadistica y Censos, Lima, Peru.

JAMES, W. H. (1966). The effect of altitude on fertility in Andean countries. *Popul. Stud.* **20**, 97–101.

JOHNSON, D. and ROOFE, P. D. (1965). Blood constituents of normal newborn rats and those exposed to low oxygen tension during gestation; weight of newborn and litter size also considered. *Anat. Rec.* **153**, 303–9.

KIRBY, D. R. S., McWHIRTER, K. G., TEITELBAUM, M. S., and DARLINGTON, C. D. (1967). A possible immunological influence on sex ratio. *Lancet* **2**, 139–40.

LAHIRI, S. (1965). Sherpa physiology. *Nature, Lond.* **207**, 610–12.

LICHTY, J. A., TING, R. Y., BRUNS, P. D., and DYAR, E. (1957). Studies of babies born at high altitudes: 1. Relation of altitude to birth weight. II. Measurement of birth weight, body length, and head size. III. Arterial oxygen saturation and hematocrit values at birth. *Am. med. Assoc. Dis. Child.* **93**, 666–7.

LITTLE, M. A. (1969). Temperature regulation at high altitude: Quechua Indians and U.S. whites during foot exposure to cold water and cold air. *Hum. Biol.* **41**, 519–35.

LIVINGSTONE, F. B. (1958). Anthropological implications of sickle-cell gene distribution in West Africa. *Am. Anthrop.* **60**, 533–62.

—— (1962). Population genetics and population ecology. *Am. Anthrop.* **64**, 44–53.

MACCAGNO, V. (1967). Observaciones sobre ulcera peptica y hemorragia en les grandes alturas. *Proc. V Pan-am. Congr. II Peruvian Congr. Gastroenterol.*

MATSON, G. A., SUTTON, H. E., SWANSON, J., and ROBINSON, A. (1966). Distribution of hereditary blood groups among Indians in South America. II. In Peru. *Am. J. phys. Anthrop.* **24**, 325–49.

—— SWANSON, J., and ROBINSON, A. (1966). Distribution of hereditary blood groups among Indians in South America. III. In Bolivia. *Am. J. phys. Anthrop.* **25**, 13–33.

MAZESS, R. B. (1965). Neonatal mortality and altitude in Peru. *Am. J. phys. Anthrop.* **23**, 209–14.

—— (1969). Exercise performance at high altitude in Peru. *Fed. Proc.* **28**, 1301–6.

—— (1970). Cardiorespiratory characteristics and adaptation to high altitudes. *Am. J. phys. Anthrop.* **32**, 267–78.

McCLUNG, J. (1969). *Effects of high altitude on human birth*. Harvard University Press.

MILAN, F. A. (1970). The demography of an Alaskan Eskimo village. *Arctic Anthrop.* **11**, 26–44.

MONGÉ, C. M. (1948). *Acclimatization in the Andes*. The Johns Hopkins Press, Baltimore.

—— and MONGÉ, C. C. (1966). *High altitude diseases: mechanism and management*. Thomas, Springfield.

MORPURGO, G., BATTAGLIA, P., BERNINI, L., PALUCCI, A. M., and MODIANO, G. (1970). Higher Bohr effect in Indian natives of Peruvian highlands as compared with Europeans. *Nature, Lond.* **227**, 387–8.

MORTON, N. E. (1968). Problems and methods in the genetics of primitive groups. *Am. J. phys. Anthrop.* **28**, 191–202.

MULLER, H. J. (1960). The guidance of human evolution. In *Evolution after Darwin, Vol. 2. The evolution of man* (ed. Sol Tax). University of Chicago Press.

NEEL, J. V. (1970). Lessons from a 'primitive people'. *Science, N.Y.* **170**, 815–22.

PEÑALOZA, D., BANCHERO, N., SIME, F., and GAMBOA, R. (1963). The heart in chronic hypoxia. *Biochem. Clin.* **1**, 283–98.

PUGH, L. G. C. (1966). A programme for physiological studies of high altitude peoples. In *The Biology of Human Adaptability* (eds. P. T. Baker and J. S. Weiner). Clarendon Press, Oxford.

QUILICI, J.-C. (1968). *Les altiplanides du Corridor Interandia.* Centre d'Hémotypologie du Centre National de la Recherche Scientifique, Toulouse.

SCHMIDT, J. P. (1969). Resistance to infectious disease versus exposure to hypobaric pressure and hypoxic, normoxic, or hyperoxic atmospheres. *Fed. Proc.* **29**, 1099–1103.

SOBREVILLA, L. A. (1967). Fertility at high altitude. Paper presented at P.A.H.O., W.H.O., I.B.P. Meeting of investigators on population biology of altitude, Washington, D.C., November, 1967.

STYCOS, J. M. (1963). Culture and differential fertility in Peru. *Popul. Stud.* **16**, 257–70.

SYMPOSIUM ON HUMAN ADAPTATION (1970). Discussion—Session B. *Am. J. phys. Anthrop.* **32**, 315–19.

TRAPANI, I. L. (1969). Environment, infection, and immunoglobulin synthesis. *Fed. Proc.* **28**, 1104–6.

UNITED NATIONS (1967). *Methods of estimating basic demographic measures from incomplete data.* Population Studies No. 42. Department of Economic and Social Affairs. United Nations, New York.

VALSIK, J. A. (1965). The seasonal rhythm of menarche: a review. *Hum. Biol.* **37**, 75–90.

VAN LIERE, E. J. and STICKNEY, J. C. (1963). *Hypoxia.* University of Chicago Press.

VELASQUEZ, T. (1970). Aspects of physical activity in high altitude natives. *Am. J. phys. Anthrop.* **32**, 251–8.

WEIHE, W. H. (1962). Some examples of endocrine and metabolic functions in rats during acclimatization to high altitude. In *The physiological effects of high altitude* (ed. W. H. Weihe). Pergamon Press, New York.

WEINER, J. S. (1969). *Handbook No. 1. A guide to the human adaptability proposals.* F. A. Davis Company, Philadelphia.

WEISER, O. L., PEOPLES, N. J., TULL, A. H., and MORSE, W. C. (1969). Effects of altitude on the microbiota of man. *Fed. Proc.* **29**, 1107–9.

WHITEHEAD, L. (1968). Altitude, fertility, and mortality in Andean countries. *Popul. Stud.* **21**, 71–3.

WORLD HEALTH ORGANIZATION (1964). *Research in population genetics of primitive groups.* Technical Report No. 279. World Health Organization, Geneva.

18

ECOLOGY AND POPULATION STRUCTURE IN THE ARCTIC†

WILLIAM S. LAUGHLIN

THE strategy of my approach to Arctic ecology and population structure is first to examine events within a single population system integrated within a single ecosystem and then to compare these events with those in another population system that is distributed over several ecosystems. The two population systems under examination, Aleut and Eskimo, though diverging from each other for some 10 000 to 15 000 years, have many kinds of traits and habits in common as a consequence of their common ancestry. Other traits are shared as a consequence of gene flow or diffusion engendered by their common ancestry. These common elements provide a basis for meaningful comparisons. The study of the amounts and kinds of genetic, morphological, and behavioural variation in the single Aleutian system provides a new way of approaching variation and structure in the more diverse Eskimo population system. At the same time, the integrity of the configurations of these separate systems provides an indispensable context in which to interpret the events that occur within them (Laughlin 1952, 1968, 1970).

The methodology of this approach requires specification. Among the advantages of testing events within a single population system is the likelihood that various traits will in fact have the same genetic basis. Thus, it is likely, if not certain, that the mandibular torus has the same genetic basis in each of the three Aleutian isolates, all sharing a common origin and all connected by gene flow. At the same time, it is likely that this trait has a different genetic basis and a different origin in Europeans, though it displays sufficient phenotypic similarity to enjoy the same designation.

This may be convincingly illustrated by the use of blood group evidence. Lapps, Eskimos, and Aleuts have varying frequencies of blood group A. However, with the advent of anti-sera for A_1 it became clear that a major difference between these populations lay in the gene for A_2, present in high

† Much of the research referred to here has been supported by the National Science Foundation, the Bureau of Community Environmental Management (H.E.W.), the University of Connecticut Research Foundation, and the Wenner-Gren Foundation for Anthropological Research. Current multidisciplinary investigations are continuing under an International Biological Programme, 'Aleut adaptation to the Bering land-bridge coastal configuration', supported by the National Science Foundation.

frequency in Lapps and absent from Aleut and Eskimo, as well as from Siberian populations.

Looking at traits of social structure and material culture, much the same pattern appears. First, within the Aleut system it seems certain that the kayak, umiak, throwing-board, lamp, backscratcher, and the role of the headman and the summer dispersal carry the same information in all three isolate divisions of the system. These same traits in Greenlandic Eskimos appear to carry essentially the same information, phylogenetically, but with stylistic and functional differences. However, if we take for comparison similar traits in an unrelated population and its cultural system, we are quite certain that the traits are different in their origin as well as in their form, function, use, and meaning. That is, the similarity is phenotypic only, not phyletic. Thus, a throwing board (spear-thrower) in Australia fits the general category in that its form and its use are similar enough to identify it, but if it enjoyed a common origin with that of the Aleuts and Eskimos that common origin is so remote that it cannot be validated simply on the basis of formal similarity.

This methodological approach, the interpretation of events within a single, closed population system, and then the use of these as a yardstick for comparison of events between one population system and another, related, population system and finally for comparisons with unrelated population systems, is a logical extension of the methodology previously described: 'The genetically diverse populations inhabiting similar Arctic habitats, together with the genetically similar populations inhabiting more diverse Arctic habitats constitute in themselves a comparison matrix in which generalizations can be formulated and tested' (Laughlin 1966).

It is all the more important that a rigorous method of analysis be employed where behavioural traits which may have genetic and neurophysiological ingredients are a concern. Thus, 'kayak fear', best known from west Greenland, disabled a significant number of hunters. As a consequence of the seizure and loss of balance, these hunters reduced or gave up their kayak hunting, but they were apparently accommodated in other capacities in land-based activities in the village. 'Kayak fear' as defined in Greenland does not appear to have been a problem in other Eskimo and Aleut populations. Whether other Eskimo and Aleut populations had this trait but gave it a different social treatment remains a research question which must be studied first in the Greenlandic population system. Such behavioural disorders are especially important in the Arctic, for if 10 to 15 per cent of the male hunters are put out of action or impaired, the economy of the community is seriously affected. The same frequency of affliction is even more deleterious in those communities where the food supply is chiefly secured by adult male hunters rather than by a larger proportion of both males and females.

The Aleutian ecosystem

The Aleutian ecosystem differs from most others in that it is geographically coterminous with the Aleuts (Murie 1959, Laughlin 1970). Only Aleuts lived within this area and no Aleuts lived outside it. The shape or configuration of the area plays an important role in determining the richness of the marine ecosystem and in generating variability in the people. The population was arranged linearly and longitudinally over a distance of some 1250 miles, beginning at the Shumagin Islands and Port Moller on the Alaska Peninsula at about the 160° meridian. The nutrient-rich waters of the Pacific Ocean flow into the Bering Sea through the straits between the islands. There is a considerable vertical mixing of the waters and this, with the availability of light (through the absence of winter ice), provides a rich supporting fauna for the larger forms of importance to the people, namely: marine algae, intertidal foods such as sea urchins, octopus, fish, birds, and sea mammals. At the same time, the linear distribution of the Aleuts automatically generated some variability through the inability of people at the opposite ends of the distribution to maintain random mating with each other. In terms of biological distance, the eastern and western Aleuts were more different from each other than are coastal and interior Eskimos of northern Alaska (Jamison, unpublished data) or than are southern and northern Eskimos on the west Greenland coast.

The Aleuts, who are distinct racially and linguistically, are old residents of the area and have, in fact, inhabited the eastern Aleutians for at least 8400 years (Aigner 1970, Laughlin 1967). The high degree of isolation has lasted since they inhabited initially an island (Anangula) which 8400 years ago was a part of the larger Umnak Island and which only a thousand or so years earlier was the terminus of the Bering land-bridge. They appear to have entered this area, overlooking the first channel into the Bering Sea, at a time when an ice sheet covered much of the Alaska Peninsula. It was this ice sheet which inhibited or excluded contact with Eskimos. In later times, the contact border with Eskimos was small and relations between Aleuts and Eskimos were not harmonious.

The population was divided into three major dialectical and breeding groups, western, central, and eastern. Though these dialects were mutually intelligible, they played a prominent role as boundary-maintaining mechanisms in much the same way that the Aleut language inhibited interaction between Aleuts and Eskimos. Though the Aleut and Eskimo languages are historically related they are not mutually intelligible. At the time of discovery in 1741, there were probably some 10 000 eastern Aleuts, 4000 to 5000 central Aleuts, and 1000 to 2000 western Aleuts. These dialect groupings presist today, though the few western Aleut speakers were resettled in the one central dialect village of Atka. The central and western dialects also persist in the Commander Islands of the U.S.S.R. to which Aleuts were transplanted in

1826. The Aleuts of the Pribiloff Islands were drawn from the eastern dialect area.

The diet of the Aleuts provides an inventory of the edible portion of the ecosystem. Subject to regional and annual variation it consisted approximately of one-third pinnipeds, sea otters and whales; one-third fish (salmon, cod, and halibut); and one-third birds and eggs, invertebrates (especially sea-urchins and octopus), marine algae, and land plants. The land plants probably constituted some 5 per cent of the dietary intake. Resident and rookery mammals, such as seals, sea lions, and sea otters, were especially important because of their accessibility. The whales are essentially transient, as are the fur seals, though the chances of intercepting them as they swam through the straits were considerably greater than on a mainland coast.

The population was deployed into exploitation areas consisting of base camps, all-year villages, and satellite villages and camps. In summer-time, the base villages underwent the same dispersal as Eskimo villages, with families moving out to camp at streams or bird-cliffs where annual runs of salmon or nesting birds provided sustenance and an additional increment for winter stores.

It should be noted that when the population was at its maximum, 16 000, the coastline was under almost constant scrutiny. Distances between villages were in many cases less than eight miles, a trip of no more than two hours by kayak. The population as a whole could exercise a tangible effect on the resident sea mammals as well as on the intertidal fauna. Consequently, emphasis was placed on fishing and whaling, which drew on transient populations, and did not diminish the supply.

An interesting question is the extent to which people are affected by the animals they hunt and, in turn, the extent to which they may effect those animals. From the standpoint of Aleuts, Eskimos, and Maritime Chukchi, the use of animal foods provides the primary support of their populations. Conversely, these populations have had little effect on the animal populations. Thus, the populations of whales, walrus, caribou, and bears (polar bears or brown bears) have been little affected by hunting pressure. The majority of animals, fish, and birds are generally non-resident and migratory, and the number of animals taken by hunters is a small proportion with no tangible feedback to the supply of such animals. Hunting pressure may have contributed to the reduction of the musk-ox, especially in Alaska. Generally speaking, however, numbers of animals available are not affected by hunting success in previous years.

A possible exception of considerable value as a model is presented in the triangular relationship of Aleuts, sea otters, and sea-urchins. In this model the sea otter population is a major source of food and fabricational materials and the population of sea otters, owing to its position and habits, responds to the hunting pressure of the Aleuts. The awareness of the Aleuts of their ability to affect the supply of sea otters introduces a new kind of element into the ecological foundations of a climax culture. The essential facts can be sketched out although the assignment of numerical values for systems analysis must await detailed research. Aleuts eat both sea otters and sea-urchins, and sea otters eat sea-urchins.

Sea otters (*Enhydra lutris*) were distributed throughout the Aleutian Islands as well as parts of the Asian and North American coast. Their large numbers provided one of the major reasons for the Russian occupation of the Aleutian Islands; the pelt was valuable then as now. Owing to excessive hunting, the numbers of sea otters were severely reduced to the point where hunting was forbidden by Federal law in 1911. Most of the hunting was done by Aleuts.

When the Russians occupied Alaska they recruited Aleut kayak hunters to hunt sea otters for them. The reason for this is clear. Kayak hunting of sea otters is a complex activity which requires instruction during childhood for maximum efficiency in adults. The tendons of the shoulder, lower back, and knees must be stretched so that the hunter can sit for long hours in his kayak with his legs extended straight in front of him, and be able to cast a harpoon with the aid of a throwing board while in this sitting posture. Thus, the Aleut hunter was given specialized physical training at an early age, instruction in the behaviour of sea otters as well as other animals, a knowledge of operation of the kayak and related gear, including navigation, and the necessary skill for performing simultaneous operations. In contrast, no European ever learned to hunt from a kayak.

Sea otters eat one-fifth of their body-weight each day (Kenyon 1969). They eat a variety of shellfish and fish of which sea-urchins are a major form. Their voracity is aided by their ability to use tools. They can manipulate large stones for use as anvils, and they can grasp objects with dexterity owing to their pronating-supinating forearm in which the ulna and radius are separate. The fingers are carried in a paw but grasp with considerable individual sensitivity. As a consequence of their morphology and habits they are able to overeat their food supply and suffer starvation. Where sea otters clean out the edible beds of molluscs, they must move to another bay or region. They may continue eating younger sea-urchins, but these have little nutritional value and they starve. It appears that there was a limit to the numbers of sea otters, imposed by their own habits and quite apart from the increased pressure placed on them by Aleuts and later by the Russians and Americans who stimulated the Aleuts to overhunt them.

The total marine habitat of the Aleuts and the sea otters was approximately the same, some 5000 square miles. This area corresponds to the coastal area of the islands out to the 30-fathom line or roughly 3 miles from the coast. It is in this same area that the Aleuts secured the larger part of their food. The sea otters were able to secure sea-urchins from greater depths than the

Aleuts and the Aleuts were able to dominate the reefs at low tide for collecting sea-urchins, whelks, limpets, chitons, mussels, octopus, and reef fish.

Viewed from the standpoint of energy flow, an interesting question for systems analysis is whether the Aleuts would have been better advised to kill off all the sea otters and eat the sea-urchins directly. In this way they could have avoided the energy loss attendant upon the conversion of sea-urchins into sea otters. On the other hand, there were fabricational uses of the sea otter which could not be supplied by the sea-urchin: the fur used for clothing, the bones used for tools, and the oesophagus used for leggings or boots or waterproof shirts. There might of course also be some substances in the flesh of the sea otter unavailable in the sea-urchin.

The points to be established from these observations are that the Aleuts had the capability to deplete seriously or even induce the extinction of the sea otter in the Aleutian ecosystem. That they had not done so long before the arrival of the Russians in 1741 may indicate a form of conservation on their part. Another possibility is the probable overhunting of sea otters in the more populated areas and a shift to other foods until the sea otter population recovered. Owing to the fact that all three forms are residents, with the sea-urchins being the least mobile and the Aleuts being the most mobile, and to the fact that the sea-urchins were eaten by both Aleuts and sea otters, there are several points of incompatibility in this shifting triangle.

Another point which directly affects ecology and population structure is that when the total Aleut population system and the total population of sea otters distributed throughout the same islands and peninsular coastline are considered, the sea otters had little refuge. The deployment system of Aleut base villages and satellite camps produced, at the time of maximum population, not only a large number of Aleuts (some 16 000) but also numerous villages or camps of Aleuts on the island perimeters; these increased the scanning capability of the Aleut population system and ensured that more sea otters would be caught.

This Aleut–sea otter–sea-urchin paradigm provides a natural dissection of a basic aspect of ecology and population structure. The supply of sea otters was being reduced by two different kinds of pressure from the Aleut population. First, the kayak hunting was performed only by male hunters. Second, the sea-urchin collecting was nutritionally as important as sea otter hunting and it was practised by a much large proportion of the population, the young and old, males and females, healthy and infirm. In both cases, the absence of winter ice was a major factor in determining the richness of the marine ecosystem and the accessibility of the foods. The high development of kayak hunting in the Aleutian ecosystem is related to the Aleut dependence upon sea-mammal hunting along with fish and birds, and in turn, is related to the absence of winter ice. This illustrates the diverse but related bases for the broad demographic profile of the Aleuts.

In summary, this paradigm, though simplified, is valid because there were no other major predators of sea otters than Aleuts. Killer whales took few sea otters. Each of the forms represents a different point on the food chain culminating in humans. At the bottom of this triangle the sea-urchins are most sensitive to the marine nutrients and provide an index of the basic nutrients—light, and water temperature. The sea-urchins are especially accessible; they can be cropped directly on the reefs by Aleuts of both sexes and of a considerable age range. Thus, the sea-urchin is directly responsible for providing a substantial portion of the food supply to children, as well as aged and infirm persons of both sexes who collect them at low tide on the reefs. How many of these urchins would be collected by sea otters is not known exactly, but it appears that most or all of them would have been eaten by sea otters in the absence of humans. On the other hand, the Aleuts had no way of collecting the deeper sea-urchins and therefore coexistence was possible.

The four complexes of significance in this paradigm are: (1) the habits and distribution of the sea otter, (2) the habits and distribution of the sea-urchin, (3) Aleut kayak hunting of sea otters, and (4) the deployment of the Aleut population system. In quite different ways, the Aleut use of sea-urchins, well attested in archaeological remains for four thousand years, and their kayak hunting of sea otters, also well attested archeologically, contributed to the growth of the Aleut population. The growth of the population led both to greater deployment of Aleuts and therefore more extensive hunting of them in previously inaccessible places, as well as to absolutely larger numbers of people to eat sea otters.

Age at death: longevity and culture climax

An interesting difference between the Aleut population system and those of various Eskimos lies in their longevity. Good data are difficult to find and also to assess. Probably the only data on length of life which do not reflect in some way the effect of European contact are those from skeletal populations. However, these have the drawback that early ages are likely to be under-represented whereas ages above 55 or 60 cannot be reliably assigned to 5- or even 10-year age periods. The study of a large series of Sadlermiut Eskimo skeletons from Native Point, Southampton Island, revealed no person older than age 55 at death (Laughlin 1963).

Two roughly comparable bodies of early data, on Aleuts and Eskimos respectively, indicate better prospects for long life in the Aleutian Islands than in Labrador. The data presented in Figs. 1 and 2 are summarized in Table 18.1.

Forty per cent of the Aleuts died after age 45, whereas only 30 per cent of the Hopedale Eskimos died after the same age. The excess of male deaths in the 25–45-year group among the Aleuts is attributable to death by drowning and other accidents related to marine hunting.

It is known that men of advanced years could not hunt actively from kayaks though they might fish in quiet waters. They could, however, collect intertidal foods and provide some of their own food into extremely advanced ages. They were socially honoured and protected and served as consultants or

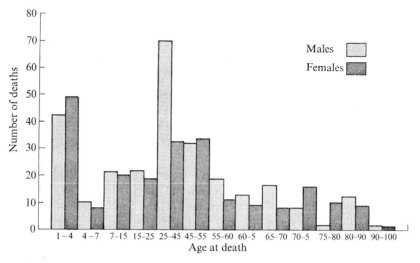

Fig. 18.1. Age at death of the Aleuts at Fox Island (Eastern Aleutians), for the years 1822–36 (except 1824 and 1829). The population numbered 225 females and 266 males. Data from I. Veniaminov (1840).

cultural librarians until they died. Some continued to be used for consultation after they had been converted into mummies and placed in caves where they could be visited. Women, some of whom were specially trained as medical practitioners, continued their diagnostic and advisory services long after they had given up the actual delivery of babies. It is likely that the maintenance

TABLE 18.1

Age at death in the Aleuts of the Aleutian Islands and the Eskimos of Labrador

	Aleut		Eskimo	
	n	*per cent*	*n*	*per cent*
1–15	150	30·55	38	34·55
15–25	41	8·35	10	9·09
25–45	103	20·98	29	26·36
45–65	117	23·83	20	18·18
65–80	58	11·81	13	11·81
80–100	22	4·48	0	0·00

of a sophisticated knowledge of human anatomy and medical practices is related to the length of life and it is possible that this body of knowledge provided some reduction in infant mortality. It seems reasonable to posit a connection between longevity and sophistication in this setting.

Through searching the literature for evidence of longevity in northern Alaska and through personal fieldwork, Stefansson (1958, 1959) was able to find little evidence and few cases of advanced age: 'I cease quoting Murdoch of 1881–3, as I did Simpson of 1852–4, with no precise dating of even one

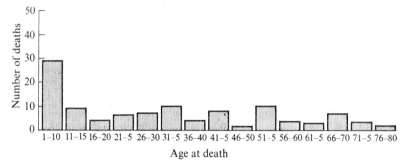

FIG. 18.2. Age at death of the Eskimos at Hopedale, Labrador during the years 1822–36. The total population numbered 110 males and females, and the average age at death was 31·1 years. (Data assembled by F. W. Peacock and forwarded by V. Stefansson.)

instance of great longevity but with the two students agreeing that some persons looked as if they might be past 60, a very few as if past 70, and one or two as if past 80' (Stefansson 1958). To these, he adds one female reported by Jeness, who estimated the age of an Eskimo lady in 1914 as probably not more than 75, though possibly older. Stefansson estimates that the population base on which Simpson's observations were made was composed of some 540 coastal Eskimos plus a similar number of transients during the summer boating and winter sledging seasons. We may use a rough estimate of 1000 for all coastal Eskimos in the Point Lay–Point Barrow–Barter Island coast of north Alaska and possibly as many as half this number for the interior. Assuming that the coastal Eskimos represented the more stable portion of the population system which included the more labile inland Eskimos it would appear that this Eskimo grouping, like that of the Labrador Eskimo of Hopedale, did not maintain the proportion of persons aged 45 and over that is a major feature of the Aleut population.

Relations between dialect isolates

A census of all living Aleuts (Hooper 1897) provides a rich source of information on the integrity of the dialect isolates. A total population of 1140 Aleuts is distributed into one village of western Aleuts (Attu) of 78; one village of central Aleuts (Atka) of 128; and twelve villages of eastern Aleuts numbering 934 altogether. Only 5 persons living in Attu came from the central (3) and eastern (2) dialect groups. Only 13 persons living in Atka came from the eastern (7) and western (6) dialect groups. Only 35 persons living in the eastern area came from the central (25) and western (10) dialect groups (see Table 18.2).

TABLE 18.2

Movement between Aleut dialect groups†

	West (*Attu*)	Central (*Atka*)	East (12 *villages*)	Out-migrants, per cent	
Population	78	128	934		
Sedentes	73	115	899		
Immigrants:					
From *Central*	3	0	25	28	21·9
From *East*	2	7	0	9	1·0
From *West*	0	6	10	16	20·5
Totals	5	13	35	53	
Percentages	6·4	10·2	3·7		

† From Hooper (1897).

These figures, with all their limitations, indicate a high degree of 'ethnic' identity and of dialect integrity or stability. It is interesting that they indicate greater numbers moving to the east and the greatest portion moving into the central area. A breakdown by sex shows that 22 of the 53 migrants were male and 31 were female. Further, more females than males moved into the west and central dialects, whereas more males than females entered the eastern dialect area. The greater mobility of females appears to be a continuing phenomenon (Sternbach 1970).

At a later date, 1948, it was found that a greater proportion of Aleuts (48 out of 144) had parents from two different isolates (Laughlin 1951).

Localization of family names

Another technique for examining relations between isolates is the examination of family names. This technique is subject to error because of adoptions and the fact that females take the name of their husband, but it does indicate a localization of family names. With the advent of Christianity and more particularly with active baptism of Aleuts beginning around 1795, Russian names were uniformly adopted. Of 158 different family names, 144 are uniquely localized in the three dialect isolates, 5 in the west, 14 in the central, and 125 in the eastern isolate. Twelve names are shared between two groups, and 2 names are shared between three dialect groups. Thus, of the 158 names, 144 are not shared and 14 are shared. Considering the historical fact that a little over 100 years had elapsed since these names were assigned, the localization of 144 family names indicates a high degree of stability (see Table 18.3).

TABLE 18.3

Localization of family names

| | Number† | West | Central | East | Shared names | | |
					West and central	West and east	Central and east
West	14	5	1	6	0	0	2
Central	22	1	**14**	5	0	2	0
East	138	6	5	**125**	2	0	0

† Numbers in bold type indicate names that are unique to that isolate; all others are shared.

Some indication of movement can be given in this kind of table by using the number of uniquely localized names expressed as a percentage of the total number of names found in the isolates. An interesting progression results: East 91 per cent, Central 64 per cent, and West 36 per cent. This possibly represents the movement of males carrying their family names, from west to east. In one sense, then, the smallest and most remote isolate is the most isolated by depletion of mobile males. However, immigration of females may actually introduce a high proportion of non-western genes. Until other variables such as family size and sex are introduced, it is probably safest to cite these data as additional evidence of the integrity of the Aleutian isolates.

Accommodation to different ecological zones

Greenland and the Aleutian Islands provide the two best models of closed population systems, in that there was little movement of Eskimos into Greenland after the initial migrations and similarly there was a high degree of isolation of Aleuts. The north to south orientation of the Greenland coasts ranges from the sub-arctic to the high Arctic and therefore includes more environmental differences than are found in the Aleutian ecosystem. A quite different ecological situation and corresponding to it, a quite different population structure, is presented in the north Alaskan coastal and interior population system.

The dichotomous nomenclature of coastal versus inland Eskimos, useful for many purposes, obscures the rotating membership of what is actually a single population system. The Eskimos of Anaktuvuk Pass were found to share many relatives with coastal Eskimos at Wainwright and at Point Barrow and a number were actually born on the coast (Laughlin 1957). The high frequency of blood group B was attributable to founder principle, to one man whose progeny inherited his B gene. It became apparent that some Eskimos did live permanently in the interior though with visits to the coastal populations ranging from rare and brief to frequent and of long duration. Viewed over a period of a few generations, it thus appears that the larger gene pool rotates between the coast and the interior.

This relationship is demonstrated in many other ways than by birthplace and genealogy. In a study of the Eskimo 'trading partnership', another ecologically directed movement of individuals is depicted (Burch 1970). This is a relationship voluntarily established between two Eskimos who are not related on a kinship basis and facilitates the exchange of goods and of services between groups. The coast dwellers have the largest supply of seal oil, seal skins and other marine products such as whale blubber. The inland Eskimos have a much larger supply of caribou skins and therefore have important items for trade with the coastal Eskimos for their oil, skins, and blubber. Owing to their exploitation of marine resources the coastal Eskimos are more numerous, stable, and richer. The situation has been epitomized with precision: ' . . . it was quite possible in the traditional North Alaskan Eskimo system for an intelligent, skilled, and industrious hunter and/or trader who had lots of relatives to become significantly better off than his fellows. Inevitably, such individuals (known as *umialit*, pl.) came from one of the large whaling or trading centres on the coast. It was possible to get rich there, but difficult to get much beyond the subsistence level if one lived far inland. Consequently, virtually all of the richest people in the society came from a single ecological zone' (Burch 1970).

Conclusions

1. There is presumptive evidence that more Aleuts lived longer than Eskimos. It is suggested that skeletal records from pre-contact periods will be valuable in verifying differences seen in early post-contact records. Contemporary demographic data increasingly reflect the effects of introduced diseases, medical attention, new dietary practices, and birth-control measures rather than the original adaptation to ecological zones achieved by the indigenous populations.

2. The Aleuts exercised a tangible feedback in controlling the size of their supporting animal populations. This is best seen in their effect on the residential sea otters which occupied much the same habitat as the Aleuts. The Aleut input was achieved by hunting the sea otters directly and by collecting some of the same foods eaten by sea otters. Only able-bodied males were

kayak hunters, whereas most persons above six years of age collected inter-tidal foods from the reefs.

3. A high degree of localization within the Aleut population system com-posed of population units of varying size was, and to lesser extent still is, manifested in dialect isolates, the localization of family names, and a preference for marrying within dialect communities.

4. The combination of distance and localization contributes to morpho-logical and genetic differences between terminal isolates in spite of a relatively homogenous environment and excellent transport by kayaks and umiaks.

5. A single population system (Aleut) with high boundaries and inhabiting a relatively homogenous ecosystem can generate and maintain more diversity than a single population system inhabiting two distinct ecological zones (North Alaskan Eskimos).

6. A rich and complex culture climax such as that of the Aleuts can be related to its resource base by means of its population structure. The Aleut population was large and geographically deployed to exploit the coastline. The population units were small but diverse in their age and sex composition. A large proportion of the members of each population unit participated directly in hunting and collecting. There was not only comprehensive collec-tion of food and fabricational materials. Thus, the pericardium, oesophagus, and intestines of various sea mammals were regularly used for clothing or for containers. The excellent nutritional base was reflected not only in the population size but in the achievement of considerable longevity. The large size of the population with the presence of many senior people enhanced the complexity of the culture, material and intellectual. Some of the intellectual knowledge, such as the knowledge of human anatomy and health practices, was administered by persons who had been trained by the older and more learned persons. This may have directly reduced infant mortality. Several elements in this kind of interaction matrix are both reflections of the success of the system and causes of it.

REFERENCES

AIGNER, J. S. (1970). Configuration and continuity in Aleut Culture, 1970. Paper presented at A.A.A.S. symposium, *Aleutian ecosystem*, Chicago, 1970.

BURCH, E. S. Jr. (1970). The Eskimo trading partnership in North Alaska. *Anthrop. Papers Univ. Alaska* **15**, 49–80.

HOOPER, C. L. (1897). *A report on the sea-otter banks of Alaska.* Government Printing Office, Washington.

KENYON, K. W. (1969). *The sea otter in the eastern Pacific Ocean.* U.S. Field and Wildlife Service, Division of Wildlife Research, North America Fauna, No. 68.

LAUGHLIN, W. S. (1951). The Alaska Gateway viewed from the Aleutian Islands. In *The physical anthropology of the American Indian.* Viking Fund, New York.

—— (1952). The Aleut-Eskimo community. *Anthrop. Papers Univ. Alaska* **1**, 25–46.

—— (1957). Blood groups of Anaktuvuk Eskimos, Alaska. *Anthrop. Papers Univ. Alaska* **6**, 5–15.

—— (1963). Eskimos and Aleuts: their origins and evolution. *Science, N.Y.* **142**, 633–45.

—— (1966). Genetical and anthropological characteristics of Arctic populations. In *The biology of human adaptability* (eds. P. T. Baker and J. S. Weiner). Clarendon Press, Oxford.

—— (1967). Human migration and permanent occupation in the Bering Sea area. In *The Bering Land Bridge* (ed. D. M. Hopkins). Stanford University Press.

—— (1968). Guide to human population studies. *Arctic Anthrop.* **5**, 32–47.

—— (1970). Aleutian ecosystem. *Science, N.Y.* **169**, 1107–8.

MURIE, O. J. (1959). *Fauna of the Aleutian Islands and Alaska Peninsula.* U.S. Department of the Interior, Fish and Wildlife Service, Washington, D.C.

STEFANSSON, V. (1958). Eskimo longevity in northern Alaska. *Science, N.Y.* **127**, 16–19.

—— (1959). Personal communication, 3 April 1959.

STERNBACH, B. (1970). Demography of Aleut Communities. Paper presented at A.A.A.S. symposium, *Aleutian ecosystem*, Chicago, 1970.

VENIAMINOV, I. (1840). *Notes on the islands of the Unalaska division.* Russian–American Co. St. Petersburg. (In Russian.)

19

TROPICAL ECOLOGY AND POPULATION STRUCTURE

Joseph S. Weiner

'Human ecology is a recognizable discipline or approach within human population biology; it involves a number of different kinds of equilibrium relationships, stable and unstable; various forms of "control" systems are set up in the ecological interrelations; adaptation and selection are expressions of dynamically controlled ecological situations' (Weiner 1968).

To demonstrate convincingly the workings of ecological principles, and particularly to give these a quantitative form, requires an intensive analysis of quite restricted ecological situations; see for example Birdsell's (1953) demonstration of rainfall as a key influence on Australian aboriginal population size, the bioenergetics of rural West Bengal by Parrack, the input–output analysis of Bushman subsistence by Leech, and other examples in Vayda's anthology (1969). The present paper, attempting to cover so many facets of a complex topic, can do no more than present a number of the more important dynamic relationships and generalizations. This paper has drawn heavily on material from Allan (1967), Gourou (1966), and Geertz (1969).

In a study of a major ecosystem such as that of the tropics the material should perhaps be presented at two levels. First there are the 'background' ecological parameters or components which affect the human population—the climate, including rainfall, the soil properties and fertility, the natural vegetation, and disease. The second stage concerns the ecological interactions between population and habitat and their outcome—the modes of agriculture, the carrying capacity of the land, the population density and distribution, the physiological and medical state of the community, and the genetic constitution. Because 'shifting swidden agriculture', historically and today, is the most important tropical mode of existence, most consideration has been given here to this aspect rather than to tropical food gathering or advanced cultivation.

The many disciplines involved in an ecological analysis present a pyramid-like grading of knowledge or rather ignorance. The broad 'base' of ascertained fact is provided by the physical characters of the tropical climate and by the properties of the tropical soil; next above come the characters of the natural biome—the landscape, the vegetation, and fauna. Fairly well understood are the various modes of tropical agriculture, swidden, rotatory, irrigational, and commercial. The products of this agriculture are fairly well documented. The food-value of these products and the nutritional state of the tropical peoples have received less attention but even less is known of the medical and particularly the developmental and physiological state of the populations. Though kinship and mating systems have been subjects of some concern to social anthropologists, demographic data are scarce and uneven. The tip of the pyramid is the meagre information of the genetic constitution of these tropical populations.

The meaning given here to 'population structure' is a biological one covering both the constitution and the functioning of the society. More specifically, it involves the following interconnected topics: (a) the physiological, nutritional, and developmental response to the stresses of life in a tropical ecology, (b) the demographic balance achieved by these adaptations, and (c) the genetic consequences of the demographic structure peculiar to agricultural societies in the tropical milieu. As already remarked, the paucity of information and analysis on all three themes is lamentable; and on the genetic aspects there is nothing comparable to the studies by Neel and Salzano of the seminomadic Xavante marginal agriculturalists.

Climate

The meaning of 'tropics' requires some comment. We may follow the comprehensive definition given by Gourou (1966) as those lands with a hot wet climate having no month with a mean temperature of less than 65°F (18°C), rainfall of above 20 inches annually. Within this wide definition, there would be included three overlapping 'inter-tropical' zones:

1. The humid equatorial jungle regions—the hot wet lands proper, where seasonal variation is small.
2. Forest, woodland, or scrub-savanna regions with a high average rainfall subject to moderate seasonal or monsoonal differences of rainfall and temperature.
3. Regions characterized by well marked hot–dry and hot–wet seasons (this includes the 'Sudanian').

Beyond this last zone is the arid zone of dry heat and desert cold where rainfall is generally too low or unreliable to make cultivation possible. This region provides the conditions for the pastoral way of life.

Some examples of these three tropical climatic zones as encountered in Africa are as follows:

1. The equatorial zone of the Congo Basin is characterized by heavy and continuous rainfall, generally 70 to 120 inches in the year, and constant heat, with temperatures of 80°F (26·5°C) or more day after day; 'there is little relief from steaming conditions, dripping moisture, and the gloom of louring rain-filled clouds' (Allan 1967).

2. In Western Uganda, with an annual rainfall of 35 to 40 inches, the two wet seasons are distinctly separated by dry months; but going north and east into central Uganda the two seasons tend to converge in the mid-months and there is a dry period from December to March, when, although showers occur, temperatures often exceed 90°F (32·5°C).

3. South of the African equatorial climatic zone, starting at about 5° S latitude, is a vast area characterized by a marked dry season throughout May to October and violent alternations of seasons. Annual rainfall commonly ranges from 20 to 50 inches, spread over the months of November or December to March or April, with the wettest months in the southern summer, December to February, and a single rainfall maximum usually in January or February. The winter months, June–August, are dry, humidity is low, and there is considerable diurnal range of temperature with occasional frosts at higher altitudes, while the spring months are very hot and dry. 'Fire blackens the countryside, sweeping through woodland, bush, and grassland, at any time from July to November.' (Allan 1967.) This type of climate extends over much of western and central Tanzania, part of the southern Congo, and most of Zambia, Rhodesia, and Malawi.

Gourou's figure (1966) for the land area of the tropical regions is 16 million square miles; 3 million in Asia and the East Indies, 1 million in Melanesia, Australia, and Oceania, 6·5 million in Africa, and 5·5 million in America. This hot wet belt covers rather more than one-third of the usable portions of the earth's surface.

Soil†

It must not be inferred from the luxuriance of tropical jungle vegetation that the soil in hot, wet lands is generally rich. Tropical soils in fact are usually very poor in soluble elements because the copious warm rains lead to the rapid and deep leaching of the soluble elements in the soil. The warmer the water and the greater its acidity, the greater is its power of hydrolysis. Soils in the rainy tropics are thus usually poor in the mineral matter that can be utilized by plants, such as lime, magnesia, potash, phosphates, and nitrates. Despite this generalization, there exists, of course, a great variety of soil—rich and poor, clay and sandy, thin and deep. The ease of leaching is due in part to the feeble capacity for adsorption of most tropical soils; nor do they easily retain fertilizers because of their poor content of humus. Their clays have an unfavourable structure and have a tendency to accumulate inert lateritic elements.

Tropical soils thus have a tendency to contain a large quantity of inert matter, such as quartz grains and fragments of alumina or of hydroxide of

† Based largely on Gourou (1966) and Geertz (1969).

iron. This material not only contributes very little to the fertility but is not able to prevent the loss by leaching of any fertile elements that are present. Percolating waters will thus soon dissolve and carry away the fertile elements that the deficient clay and the all too rare humus are incapable of holding back. Nevertheless, cultivated tropical plants are adapted to the poor construction and acidity of the soil, provided that they have a suitable physical texture, that is to say, that they are sufficiently friable. When forest cover is cleared the humus will be found only to a depth of a few inches; below this, only sand is present. Once man's exploitation has exposed the underlying sand, the forest may have the greatest difficulty in regenerating.

In the equatorial regions the streams and percolating waters lead to rivers which are very poor in both dissolved and suspended matter, thus confirming the state of exhaustion of the soils from which they have drained. Rivers in equatorial regions are incapable of building great aluvial plains of rich earth.

Forests in the hot belt are rarely virgin. They are mostly secondary, having grown again after being cleared by man. These forests have no more vitality than the temperate forest, because as already mentioned they usually grow in very poor soil. The virgin forest lives in a state of equilibrium with the soil without impoverishing it. Mineral substances extracted from the soil return thereto; organic matter fallen from the trees constitutes the humus. Everything the forest produces goes back to the forest. An enormous amount of dead matter is always accumulating on the forest floor—leaves, branches, vines, whole plants, faunal remains, and wastes—but their rapid decay combined with high absorptive capacity of the luxuriant vegetation means that the nutrients in this dead organic matter are reutilized almost immediately, rather than remaining stored to any great extent or for any great length of time in the soil where they would be liable to the leaching process. This well known paradox of a rich plant and animal life supported on a thin soil is explained by the fact that the cycling of material and energy among the various components of a tropical forest is both so rapid and so nearly closed that only the uppermost layers of the soil are directly and significantly involved.

With the forest destroyed, the soil no longer receives the organic matter necessary for making humus, whilst the processes by which the humus is decomposed continue to act and are even accelerated because lack of cover makes the temperature of the soil rise. Under forest, the temperature of the surface-layer of soil does not exceed 77° or 79°F (25° or 26°C), but after the bush has been removed it may reach 104°F (40°C). The denudation of the soil has yet another disadvantage, for percolation is greater through the bare soil than underneath the forest cover, and the percolating waters leach the nitrates and bases from the soil. There is also much more water available for percolation and leaching in bare ground than under forest.

Tropical soils well protected by a vegetative cover, whether of dense forest or of savanna, are resistent to sheet or gully erosion. The intervention of man, however, may have disastrous consequences; forest clearance, cultivation, over-grazing, and the treading of flocks and herds expose the bare soil to tropical rainstorms, particularly on sloping land. Outside the equatorial belt another factor which limits productivity is the uncertainty of the rainfall.

The ecological equilibrium between the properties of soil and climate on the one hand, and simple cultivation technology on the other finds expression in the subsistence small-economy and the low population densities so characteristic of the tropical world, the Selva of South America, the outer regions of Indonesia, much of New Guinea, Malaya, and Thailand, the Carribean, and parts of western and central Africa. Over this vast area agricultural practice takes the form of swidden and rotatory cultivation of varied kinds. There are of course areas where the combination of soil and water supply provide lands of improvable and permanent agricultural potential.

There are two alternatives to subsistence swidden agriculture. One is the adoption of wet rice cultivation. This is basically a technique for conserving fertility. The other is the institution of cash cropping—banana, coffee, citrus, cocoa, jute, tobacco.

The characteristic agriculture of the tropics†

To put it in oversimplified terms, we may say that tropical agriculture shows a polarization between two very contrasting types of exploitation: the one based on various forms of shifting agriculture and the other on forms of irrigation systems. Both these modes of exploitation represent adaptations at the technological level to the peculiarities of the tropical ecosystem and particularly to the properties of soil structure and fertility.

Shifting cultivation

Over a large part of the rainy tropics agriculture conforms to the same general technological pattern, the system of 'shifting cultivation' without the aid of irrigation, whereby after one or more crop harvests the patch lies fallow and the forest regains control until it is once more cleared. This form of agriculture is known under many different local names: *ladang* (Indonesia), *ray* (Laos), *caingin* (Philippines), *taungya* (Burma), *jhum* (Assam), *bewar* (central India), *podu* (Telugu-speaking parts of India), *milpa* or *coamile* (Mexico), *conuco* (Venezuela), *roca* (Brazil), *masole* (lower Congo).

The undergrowth is cleared and the big trees felled. The biggest trees, and those which yield edible fruits, may be spared, for they are useful for fixing the soil and protecting it from erosion. Usually the trees are felled about six feet from the ground, because in hot lands trees generally have buttresses which widen their bases, and so to cut them off at ground level would be labour wasted. When the trees and branches are dry, they are burnt. The soil is enriched with ashes from the fire. To secure greater fertility in the very poor

† From Gourou (1966) and Geertz (1969).

soils of their open forests the Bembas and Lalas in Zambia pile upon the chosen patch branches collected from all around; in this way they remove the vegetation from an area six or eight times larger than that of the patch. This is known as the citemene system.

Sowing begins after the first rains. A few seeds are put into a hole made with a stick and filled in with the foot. The Kuoys of northern Cambodia have simplified this task by using a tube which allows them to sow the seed without stooping. As a general rule, several kinds of seeds and tubers are planted. Owing to the mixture of crops, the ground is covered over with a thick mantle of cultivated plants, which to some extent protects it from erosion. In forest clearings hoeing is not essential the first year, but becomes so in the second; it is nearly always necessary in savanna clearings. The work of hoeing and weeding is often done communally. Neighbours and relatives assemble and work together, and in Africa south of the Sahara the work is done to the rhythm of drums and songs. The custom was carried by slaves to Haiti, where it is known as *coumbite*. Brazilian cultivators practise the *mutirado*, which is not appreciably different.

If the same patch is cultivated several years in succession, tropical cultivators may employ a system of rotation. After a varying number of years the patch is abandoned and relapses into forest, or into savanna if the area is burnt at the end of every dry season. The promptness with which it is abandoned mainly depends on the rate of reduction of its productivity. After the last harvest, the occupiers having decided not to sow or plant any more crops, the clearing remains fallow. In different regions, depending on the nature of the ground, on the density of population, and on tradition, one finds fallows lasting only 2 or 3 years and others with a duration of 30 years; between 8 and 12 years are necessary to get a good cover of vegetation.

If the *ladang* has been created from forest, the latter very quickly resumes possession of the ground. Colonizing plants come in, and shrubs are succeeded by softwood trees and then by slower-growing species. The forest slowly restocks the soil with organic matter and nitrogen and even mineral substances; and at the same time it hinders soil erosion. The agricultural practices of the American tropical lands differ only slightly from those of the Asiatic and African tropics, even though the plants cultivated are (or were before the Columbian discoveries) different.

Swidden agriculture operates essentially in the same direct cycling manner as does the natural plant life. Swidden farming is aptly described as a system in which 'a natural forest is transformed into a harvestable forest'. The primary function of 'slash and burn' activities is not merely to clear the land but rather the transfer of the rich store of nutrients locked up in the prolific vegetation of the tropical forest to the artificial botanical complex of cultivation. The burning of the slashed plot is a means both of accelerating the process of decay and of directing that process in such a fashion that the nutrients it releases are channelled as fully as possible into certain selected food-producing plants. Since a significant proportion of the mineral energy upon which swidden crops, and especially the grains draw for their growth, comes from the ash remains of the fired forest, rather than from the soil as such, the completeness with which a plot is burnt is a crucial factor in determining its yield. This is a fact of which probably all swidden cultivators are aware. Generally ecological productivity is lower because this transfer is less efficient than that which takes place under natural conditions of decay and regeneration. The result is, of course, the well known drop in fertility on swidden plots; for example, rice output of south Sumatran plots is known to drop as much as 80 per cent between first and second cropping.

The equilibrium of this 'domesticated form of forest system' is a great deal more delicate than that of the natural form and is susceptible to breakdown into an irreversible process of ecological deterioration. Thus forest which is no longer exploited by cultivators and which is simply exposed to bush fires may in due course extend at the expense of the savanna. But a situation may arise in which the patches of exhausted soil are too far from the forest edge for recolonization to occur. The pattern of change may lead not to repeated forest recuperation but to a replacement of tree cover altogether: for example, by the notorious *imperata* savanna grass which has turned so much of southeast Asia into a green desert.

Swidden cultivation may turn out maladaptive in at least three ways: an increase in population may cause old plots to be recultivated too soon; prodigal or inept agricultural practices may sacrifice future prospects to present convenience; or there may be extension into an insufficiently humid environment in which the more deciduous forest has a much slower recovery rate and in which clearing fires are likely to burn off accidentally great stands of timber.

Wet-rice cultivation

'Here we have not the imitation of a tropical forest, but a fabricated aquarium' (Geertz 1969). The supply and control of water is the key factor in wet-rice growing. Excessive flooding is often as great a threat as insufficient inundation; drainage is frequently a more intractable problem than irrigation. The construction and maintenance of even the simplest water-control system, as in rainfall farms, requires much ancillary effort: ditches must be dug and kept clean, sluices constructed and repaired; terraces levelled and dyked; and in more developed true irrigation systems dams, reservoirs, aqueducts, tunnels, wells, and the like become necessary. Even such larger works can be built up slowly, piece by piece over extended periods, and kept in repair by continuous routine care.

In addition to improving the general irrigation system within which a terrace is set, the output of most terraces can be almost indefinitely increased by more careful, fine-comb cultivation techniques; it seems almost always possible somehow to squeeze just a little more out of even a mediocre *sawah* (rice terrace) by working it just a little bit harder. Seeds can be sown in nurseries and then transplanted instead of broadcast; they can even be pre-germinated in the house. Yield can be increased by planting shoots in exactly spaced rows, more frequent and complete weeding, periodic draining of the terrace during the growing season for purposes of aeration, more thorough ploughing, raking, and levelling of the muddy soil before planting, placing selected organic debris on the plot, and so on; harvesting techniques can be similarly perfected, both to reap the fullest percentage of the yield and leave the greatest amount of harvested crop on the field to refertilize it, such as the technique of using the razor-like hand blade found over most of inner Indonesia; double cropping and, in some favourable areas, perhaps triple cropping can be instituted.

Population distribution

General characters

The 'polarization' of the modes of agriculture described above is reflected in the distribution and density of population in the tropical zones. The 13 million square miles of the tropics in Africa, America, Melanesia, Australia, and Oceania contain some 300 million people at a density of 23 per square mile. The 3 million square miles of tropical Asia contain 800 million people, giving a density of 267 per square mile.

This contrast in population distribution is all the more striking when one bears in mind that broadly speaking the Asian and non-Asian tropical regions impose equally stressful climates, that killing or debilitating diseases are wide-spread in all tropical lands, and that the intrinsic poverty of the soil is a general characteristic. The population figures point clearly to the overall importance of the productivity of the two contrasting technical modes of exploiting the tropical habitat.

The population densities should be taken only as indications of the major modes of cultivation involved. Obviously, within each tropical area both high and low population densities are achieved on the basis of the appropriate mode of agriculture. Inner and outer Indonesia provide a very well analysed example (see Geertz 1969). It is of course true that intensive tropical agri-culture is far more developed in tropical Asia than in the non-Asian areas.

While the land-use method and therefore the food supply is the dominant or primary factor in explaining population density and distribution, there are other factors operating to maintain the equilibria in both situations. These, like food availability, are in the nature of density-dependent control factors acting both on population control and on production and distribution re-sources. They would include resources in raw materials for housing, clothing, tools, etc. and liability to infectious diseases. For the complex development of the Maya, Angkor, Anurahapura societies or the major African urban settlements, many other factors are involved including trade, land-use measures, systems of communication, record keeping, etc.

The food–population balance: critical population density

The exploitive factors that determine density of the human occupancy of tropical lands can be specified on a quantitative basis (Allan 1967). For a given territory, the following factors must be taken into account:

1. *The cultivatable proportion (Cp)* is taken as the percentage of the whole territory which can be cultivated *at all*. The uncultivatability of a large proportion of tropical lands is attributable to many causes—past mismanagement and degradation through human occupancy, difficulties of the terrain (slopes, outcrops), the intrinsic lack of fertility of some tropical soils, the high degree of unreliability of rainfall in some places, or to endemic disease (for example, sleeping sickness), which tends to deny access to land, and the lack of resources to bring potential useful areas (such as those needing drainage or heavy manuring) into cultivation. Over a large extent of country in tropical Africa, Allan gives cultivatable percentages ranging from as little as 5 per cent to over 50 per cent, a usual figure being of the order of 25 per cent. He warns against over-optimism as to the availability of readily cultivatable land.

2. *The cultivated area (Ca)* is the area necessary to support one person per year. This may be as low as 0·2 acres or as high as 2 acres, depending on many factors—soil fertility, crop, rainfall, working capacity, farming technique.

3. *The land-use factor (L)* refers to the number of plots necessary to allow a proper ratio of the number of years of 'rest' or non-cultivation (R) to the number of successive years of use (U),

$$L = \frac{R}{U} + 1$$

so that if $U = 3$ and $R = 3$, $L = 2$
$$U = 2 \text{ and } R = 18, L = 10$$

There is a great range of practice in this regard: from the case of a soil which can remain fertile with alternate crop and fallow periods (2 crops areas required)—this is really permanent cultivation land—to the case of a very poor soil, allowing two years cultivation followed by a very long fallow period for full woodland regeneration of 22 years $(L = 12)$. Between this last category of true shifting-cultivation land and true permanent cultivation land are intermediate varieties of recurrent land use, with cultivation periods of, say, 2 years and rest 6 years, requiring 4 plots, or cultivation periods of as much as 6 years with rest periods of as much as 30 years $(L = 6)$.

27

One is here talking of 'obligatory' rather than 'voluntary' shifting culti-vation. The latter is found where land is so abundant in relation to the popu-lation and its requirements that the period of natural soil regeneration has not to be taken into account. Where this obtains, communities (for example, over part of the Congo Basin) are free to move over considerable distances uncontrolled by the cycle of cultivation and soil regeneration.

Taking into account the three factors Cp, Ca, and L, the overall area required per head, that is the *Critical Population Density* (*CPD*) is

$$\frac{100}{Cp} \times Ca \times L.$$

For example: if $Cp = 25$ per cent, $Ca = 0.5$ acres, and $L = 4$ then $CPD = 8$ acres/person or 80 persons/square mile; or if $Cp = 20$ per cent, $Ca = 1.5$ acres, and $L = 10$ then $CPD = 75$ acres/person or 9 persons/square mile.

It is easy to see that in the limiting conditions where Cp is 100 per cent, that is, land is occupied continuously, no rotation occurs, and no land goes out of use ($L = 1$) the density of population will be directly dependent on the acreage required for support. In wet-rice cultivation this could be as little as 0.3 acres/person, so that the CPD is about 1800 persons per square mile.

A fourth factor affecting the ability of the cultivator himself, his 'working capacity', is discussed below.

Shifting cultivation and carrying-capacity

The shifting cultivator has a clear understanding of his environment. He can rate the fertility of a piece of land and its suitability for one or other of his crops by the vegetation which covers it and by the physical properties of the soil. He can also assess the 'staying-power' of a soil, the number of seasons for which it can be cropped with satisfactory results, and the number of seasons for which it must be rested before such results can be obtained again. He takes into account, in fact, the same factors which enter into the calcu-lation of the critical population density. Allan (1967) has shown that the calculated carrying capacity in many situations approximates closely to what is optimally possible as evidenced by the actual practice of the native cultivator.

As the overriding need of cultivation by the rotatory system, enforced by the inherent properties of the soil, is for a large amount of land per person, the outcome is obviously a population of low density made up of scattered and semi-permanent small units or villages. The low density in many cases may in large part result from over-cultivation and the irreversibility of land for further use. Only where cultivation can change to an intensive character technologically, or for other reasons (e.g. trading centres) will larger densities, including small towns, obtain. In the *ladang* system the population is concentrated in hamlets and villages. The dispersal of the dwellings would be pointless, for the instability of the cultivated areas means that no house could remain for long attached to its plot. This does not mean that the villages are firmly fixed; it is sometimes necessary to move a village so as to be nearer to its cultivated patches which are too far from the original site; and the construction of hamlets to be occupied only during the cultivation season may postpone a complete shift. In some instances site changes, particularly over short distances, are for religious rather than agricultural reasons. West African cultivators are much attached to their villages and the associated land, but readily accept the idea of a change of site, provided the necessary formalities are observed.

The pattern of small dispersed settlements is widespread in tropical lands, as the following examples show. The Hanunóo on the slopes of Mount Yagaw (Phillipines) comprise neighbourhood-like unstratified, unsegmented communities of some 6 settlements totalling 128 inhabitants each (60–80 per square mile). The Tsembaga, one of some 20 local groups of Maring speakers in the Simbai and Simi valleys of the Bismark Range in New Guinea, number 204 (the local groups ranging from 100 to 900). The shifting cultivators of the Japura Region of the Western Amazon Forest, the Boro, occupy small clearings in the forest, containing some 50 to 200 individuals; the group occupies a single large house. The Iban of Sarawak with a density of 35–40 per square mile are found only in small village units (Freeman 1955).

The dynamics of group formation in the swidden framework have been described by Vayda and Cook (1964). The Maring and Nataks of Australian New Guinea live in villages or local groups organized into sub-clan and clan clusters, the smallest comprising some 130 persons, the largest about 900 persons. Not only is there change within clan clusters, but there also is movement of groups and individuals from one clan cluster to another, that is, both fission and fusion. Among the immediate causes of these movements are quarrels, wars, fear of retaliation, sorcery accusations, deaths of kinsmen, shortage of men in the unit being joined, and excess of men in the unit from which there is splitting off. There are other and less immediate causes too. Groups that fuse are usually (but not necessarily and not always) connected by affinal, matrilateral, or uterine ties.

There is an alternative to point-settlement concentration and that is a more general household dispersion. In South America the Natuala with a population of 16 000 have a life-centre of church, school, and town hall, but are otherwise altogether dispersed. East Africa also supplies many examples of dispersed settlement.

The great weakness of the swidden system is its inability to keep pace with an increase in population. It works satisfactorily so long as the balance between output and fertility is maintained. If the balance is upset, natural fertility runs the risk of being quickly exhausted. In fact, if the population increases, man either adopts new agricultural methods which give greater yields without harming the soil—as in the case of the flooded rice field—or else he keeps the *ladang*, but reduces the length of the fallow period. If the natural vegetation is not given time enough to replace the thick forest covering, the soil will not be able to repair its fertility satisfactorily. Crops will be less good, and, to ensure his food supply, man will be led to extend his clearings still more. The forest replaces itself less and less well as the soil becomes progressively exhausted, and consequently the soil recovers less and less of its fertility during the fallow periods. Besides, the dangers of erosion and lateritization become more and more pressing. For example, the Ibans of Sarawak grow unirrigated rice in their *ladang* system, and a single harvest followed by long fallow does not exhaust the soil. But if the crops are harvested in successive years, or if the fallow is much reduced, then soil degradation soon occurs. The absolute minimum duration of fallow appears to be four years. The forest can no longer resume possession of some clearings, which are then occupied by tall grasses springing from rhizomes, the most widespread being *Imperata cylindrica* (*alang-alang*). These grasses become highly inflammable straw at the end of the dry season, so that fires used for making clearings easily spread over the grassy areas. The grasses maintain their hold in this way, for if there were no fire, trees would grow again. There are, however, situations where, despite long periods of fallow, the forest sometimes does not regain possession of the cultivated areas; at B'Sar Deung, near Dalat, in the mountains of South Vietnam, even though the fallow period is as long as thirty years, the villagers are faced with a dearth of forest to cut down. Forest has reoccupied only the valley bottoms and the hill-tops, and the slopes are now covered by savanna.

In contrast to the restricted carrying capacity of the swidden is the expansibility of wet-rice cultivation. Demographically, the most significant feature of wet-rice agriculture is its marked capacity to respond to a rising population through intensification; that is, through absorbing increased numbers of cultivators on a unit of cultivated land. Horizontal expansion is, of course, possible for traditional wet-rice agriculturalists, and has to some extent occurred. But the pattern of ecological pressures encourages the opposite practice; working old plots harder rather than establishing new ones.

A wet-rice regime results in the support of an ever-increasing number of people within an undamaged habitat. Restricted areas of Java today—for example, Adiwerna, an alluvial region in the north-central part of the island—reach extraordinary rural population densities of nearly 5000 persons per square mile without any significant decline in per-acre rice production. Nor does there seem to be any region on the island in which the limit for wet-rice growing appears ever to have been reached. Given maintenance of irrigation facilities, and a reasonable level of farming technique, the *sawah* seems virtually indestructible.

Physiological response and health status

In coping with the demands and stresses of the tropical environment, certain biological responses are of special significance for survival and working efficiency. The principal factors of the environment which call for biological adjustments can be summarized as follows.

1. *The nutrients available*, particularly in terms of calorie and protein consumption. The level of growth and development, body composition, and physique attained are of course profoundly influenced. It is not possible to generalise on the adequacy or otherwise of the nutritional status of tropical populations as a whole. The energy and nutrients made available by different forms of swidden cultivation and by wet-rice irrigation merit extended consideration and the energy relationships are discussed further below. In general it seems safe to say that the level of available calories and of protein is low in tropical areas of high rainfall (Vayda 1969). These factors would in turn have an adverse effect on working capacity and increasing the liability to disease.

2. *The intensity of the work* imposed by the terrain and the type of cultivation will demand an appropriate degree of physical fitness as well as manual dexterity. Where malnutrition and poor development obtain, poor physique and low body weight will certainly keep the work capacity at a relatively low level. To work the required acreage and to provide, say, a yield of 12 000 kcals for a 5-family unit, it may be necessary to apply as much as 5000 kcals (extraction ratio of 40 per cent). The most active worker may need to contribute about half this amount, i.e. working on an average ratio of 300 kcals/hr, that is, 5 kcals/min or 1 litre/min. If the maximum working capacity (aerobic power) falls below about 3·0 litres, it would be difficult for this energy output to be achieved. What level of physical fitness tropical cultivators in fact attain is a matter on which we have minimal information.

3. *The intensity of the heat load* will demand an appropriate degree of heat tolerance or acclimatization. This is particularly so if work is to be done efficiently at the temperature levels which prevail at crucial times of the agricultural cycle, when hard work may have to be carried out. The phenomena underlying heat adaptation are well known from laboratory and some field studies (Weiner 1964). To what extent tropical workers use their acclimatizating potential and the factors which may limit full utilization await further study.

4. *The tropical debilitating diseases* such as malaria, hookworm, bilharzia, amoebic dysentry, and gastric enteritis as well as other infectious diseases may also reduce working capacity at critical times of the work cycle. Pregnancy, lactation, and often the need to carry the young infant are additional limiting factors on the mother's working ability.

In calculating critical population densities (see p. 402) it is clear that, strictly, a factor for working capacity should be included. The effect of a working capacity (Wc) falling below its full value (taken as unity) will lead to a reduction in available output and therefore a smaller carrying capacity of the land. With the inclusion of this factor, Wc, we obtain:

$$CPD = \frac{100 \times Ca \times L}{Cp \times Wc}.$$

The energy balance

For a hypothetical family of 5 a daily calorie requirement of 12 000 kcals must be provided. It is said (Hall, quoted in Allan 1947) that an area cropped with maize yields per acre about 3500 kcal/day. Hence for this family, 3·4 acres of maize cultivation is needed; that is 0·7 acres per head. By contrast, 1 acre of wheat yields only 2000 kcals; hence, 6·0 acres or 1·2 acres per head is the required cultivated area. Allan finds that for many hoe cultivation systems in Africa the area of cultivation needed for subsistence is about 1·0 acres per head. It is obvious that the interaction of the factors of soil, water, technique, and physical capacity will determine the cultivated area and this may be as low as 0·4 or as large as 1·5 acres per head.

The input of human energy to provide not only calories but the whole dietary clearly varies a great deal over the tropics as does the yield or output of available energy. But the information on these two prime quantities, which determine the 'extractive ratio' (see Harrison, Weiner, Tanner, and Barnicot 1964) is far from reliable or comprehensive. On the work input side, the inescapable nature of swidden agriculture would seem to require a fairly high level of activity, or more exactly, frequent periods of quite heavy work. Thus, the ratio of input to output would not appear to be that much better than 1:1·5. Amongst the more arduous tasks are the clearing of primary or secondary growth areas, hoeing, planting, harvesting, and cleaning after gleaning. The Hanunóo of the Phillipines put in between 500 to 1000 hours of physical work per year for the average adult person (about 10–20 per cent of their non-sleeping time). This would imply an input expenditure of about 2700 kcals/day. From a direct estimation of food consumption, Rappaport (1969) calculates a calorie expenditure of 2600 kcals/day for adult males and 2200 for adult females in New Guinea.

In some cases the ratio of input to return is higher in New Guinea and, according to Rappaport, much better returns are sometimes obtained—1:10 or even 1:30. These cases imply a low level of activity and the profitable working of a small acreage per person. There are indeed reports which suggest that often the work put in is well below the work capacity of the cultivator. Thus Gourou (1966) writes: 'The time devoted to agricultural operations is often far too short. In the village of Madomale, in the Central African Republic, the men devote only 9·8 per cent of their time to agriculture and the women 13·5 per cent; these percentages are all the more significant since the number of men taking part in the agricultural work is only 72 per cent of the number of women. Amongst the Nsaw tribe of the Bemenda, the aversion of the men to agricultural work is such that they devote only 6 days' labour to the fields, which cover about $1\frac{1}{2}$ acres, whilst the women and girls give 190 days of labour in 6 months. A study of the Zande area in the Wele region of Congo-Leopoldville in 1959–61 showed that the menfolk devoted 19 per cent of their working time to agriculture and the women 27 per cent.' But the calculation suggests that this is in fact a high extractive ratio, namely 1:4.

On the output side again we have a wide range of values; the average yield over the whole agricultural cycle may be as low as 1700 kcals/head/day or as high as 2600 kcals. We read that the cultivated area often yields the barest minimum for subsistence, or, in contrast, that 'in the Banda country of the Central African Republic . . . each cultivator grows more cassava than he needs, so that much remains unharvested, to be uprooted by wart-hogs' (Gourou 1966).

We are therefore faced with a major problem of nutritional ecological dynamics: does the level of calorie expenditure by the community in fact reflect the maximum cultivatable yield? If so, in some soil conditions the work input to produce this maximum yield may need to be high (i.e. a low extractive ratio). In other cases, the work input might be low (i.e. a high extractive ratio) providing a large surplus for non-productive activities.

It is also possible that the energy extracted does not necessarily represent the maximum crop yield even with the available techniques, but that the work is done merely up to a level which will satisfy the basic activity pattern without leaving much surplus. In other words, where the extractive ratio is low (no large surplus produced), we cannot know without direct investigation whether the yield is poor despite hard work or whether a yield is poor because the work input is low. Judging by the frequency with which tropical lands reach critical population densities, by the lack of food surpluses, the extent of malnutrition, the relative reduction in growth and body size, all these strongly suggest that in many, perhaps the majority of, cases the community is subsisting on a maximum yield, despite a large input of work.

The real state of affairs is no doubt much more complex within the shifting cultivating system. The first crops taken may in fact provide a reasonable surplus, but when successive crop yields begin to fall off it would seem that a critical output is being reached and the plot is abandoned.

Tropical ecology and genetic structure

Genetic selection

The question whether various components of the tropical biome have exerted a demonstrable selective advantage in favour of certain bodily characteristics has exercised physical anthropologists for many years. Over the vast areas of the hot wet zones it does seem that certain characters tend to occur in specially high frequency or to a particularly marked degree. A more or less plausible case has been made for the following characters (see also Weiner 1964).

1. Reduction in body weight. Linearity is more a characteristic of hot arid regions; the high area-to-mass ratio would appear to favour heat dissipation (Roberts 1953).
2. Reduction in cutaneous fold thickness which favours heat dissipation (Newman 1956).
3. Increase in nasal index (radio of nasal width to nasal length). A wider nasal passage is thought to be more conductive to cooling of inspired air (Weiner 1964).
4. Increase in skin pigment, as a protection against ultraviolet light damage and carcinogenic effects. Whether this is true of the American tropical peoples remains undecided (Harrison 1961).
5. 'Sticky' rather than 'dry' ear-wax has recently been claimed to be associated with hot climates; the functional value of this is not clear (Matsunaga 1962).
6. Increased frequency of alleles of various polymorphic systems favouring resistance to malaria (Allison 1965).

It may be that qualities such as the above characterized the tropical hunter-gatherer people ancestral to the modern cultivators in these regions. Continuity of affinity between present-day gatherers and hunters, when they still survive, and neighbouring cultivators seems clear but much of this remains to be documented (for further discussion, see Weiner, 1971).

Demographic factors

The genetic structure and dynamics of tropical populations are, of course, conditioned by certain of the demographic characteristics already described as arising from the peculiarities of the tropical way of life, and particularly the subsistence economy. Unfortunately, few examples of 'on the spot' analyses of the interrelation between demographic and genetic characters are available and this topic must largely be presented in general terms. As regards swidden agriculturalists, perhaps the most significant features to be taken into account are the tendency towards population mobility and expansion. The following situations merit consideration.

1. Small breeding units exist as concentrated points of settlement for low-density population. Data on settlement size have been given above. We may suppose, therefore, that much genetic diversity between such settlements will arise through genetic drift.
2. Perhaps equally effective in this regard may be the highly dispersed type of family households, as for example in East Africa (in the Ganda and

Gogo areas) or in the Zandi territory of Ruanda. In this type of settlement distance would presumably restrict the mating opportunities; the size of breeding unit in this pattern of settlement does not, however, seem to have been ascertained.

3. The need to allow long fallow periods leads, as we have seen, to villages moving sooner or later, sometimes over large distances. At the same time, it would seem that new points of settlement must often have arisen by fission from existing villages or lineages when the search for new land necessitates a break-up of the migrating group. Consequently, non-random sampling of the gene pool (the founder effect) must have played a recurrent role in bringing about genetic diversity.

In New Guinea, according to Vayda and Cook (1964), 'specific systems of swidden agriculture under montane conditions apparently make it adaptive in New Guinea to have small local groups and such groups are continually subject to demographic disruptions through disease, crop failures, chance variations in fertility and in male–female ratios, and other factors. Since not all groups within an area have disruptions of the same magnitude and at the same time, it becomes advantageous to have the processes of fission and fusion continually adjusting the local man/land ratios.'

Expansion and migration

The region designated as 'tropical' as we have defined it includes a number of fairly distinct climatic zones and the transitions between them. Historically it would seem inevitable that shifting cultivators would often eventually erupt beyond the boundaries of the zone which they may well have occupied for many hundreds of years and indeed where they may have lived as food gatherers and hunters before adopting agriculture. One may perhaps distinguish two kinds of expansionist process: a slow 'amoeba-like' progression arising from the cyclical nature of land use and abandonment, and a faster, relatively large-scale population movement from a region of high density which has exceeded its critical carrying capacity.

The most significant genetic result would be that characters selected for successful survival in one habitat (for example, in bodily physique) will appear in apparently less-appropriate areas or amongst peoples of very contrasting features: usually, though not invariably, accompanied by hybridization.

The consequences of movement are of course difficult to trace in detail. Hiernaux (1966) has invoked the operation of biological, historical, and demographical factors to account convincingly for the present-day variation and affinities of the Bantu-speaking group of peoples.

Tropical ecology and social structure

No attempt will be made here to discuss this very large and complex subject. In this paper the 'biological structure' of tropical peoples has been presented as causally related to the pecularities and dynamics of tropical agriculture and this in turn to the properties of the soil. These factors are seen as operative also at the sociological level according to the thesis advanced by Meggers (1954). Her thesis is that 'the primary point of interaction between a culture and its environment from the point of view of culture is its suitability for food production.' More explicitly, it is differences of soil fertility, climate, water availability, which 'determine the productivity of agriculture and this in turn regulates population size and concentration and through this influences the socio-political and even the technological development of the culture.'

REFERENCES

ALLAN, W. (1967). *The African husbandman*. Oliver and Boyd, Edinburgh.

ALLISON, A. C. (1965). Population genetics of abnormal haemolobins and glucose-6-phosphate dehydrogenase deficiency. In *Abnormal haemoglobins in Africa* (ed. J. H. P. Jonxis). Blackwell, Oxford.

BIRDSELL, J. B. (1953). Some environmental and cultural factors influencing the structuring of Australian aboriginal society. *Am. Nat.* **87**, 169–207.

GEERTZ, C. (1969). Two types of ecosystem. *Environmental and cultural behaviour* (ed. A. P. Vayda). Natural History Press, New York.

GOUROU, P. (1966). *The tropical world*. Longmans Green, London.

HARRISON, G. A. (1961). Pigmentation. In *Genetical variation in human populations* (ed. G. A. Harrison). Pergamon Press, Oxford.

—— WEINER, J. S., TANNER, J. M., and BARNICOT, N. A. (1964). *Human biology*. Clarendon Press, Oxford.

HIERNAUX, J. (1966). Human biological diversity in Central Africa. *Man, Jl. R. anthrop. Inst.* **1**, 287–306.

MATSUNAGA, E. (1962). The dimorphism in human normal cerumen. *Ann. hum. Genet.* **25**, 273–286.

MEGGERS, B. J. (1954). Environmental limitation on the development of culture. *Am. Anthrop.* **56**, 801–24.

NEWMAN, R. W. (1956). Skinfold measurements in young American males. *Hum. Biol.* **28**, 154–64.

RAPPAPORT, R. A. (1969). Ritual regulation of environmental relations among New Guinea peoples. *Enviromental and cultural behaviour* (ed. A. P. Vayda). Natural History Press, New York.

ROBERTS, D. F. (1953). Bodyweight, race, and climate. *Am. J. phys. Anthrop.* **11**, 533–58.

VAYDA, A. P. (ed.) (1969). *Environmental and cultural behaviour*. Natural History Press, New York.

—— and COOK, E. A. (1964). Structural variability in the Birmarck Mountain Culture of New Guinea: a preliminary report. *Trans. N.Y. Acad. Sci.* **26**, 798–803.

WEINER, J. S. (1964). Human ecology. In *Human biology* (G. A. Harrison, J. S. Weiner, J. M. Tanner and N. A. Barnicot). Clarendon Press, Oxford.

—— (1968). Review of *Human ecology* (ed. J. B. Bresler). *Hum. Biol.* **40**, 280.

—— (1971). *Man's natural history*. Weidenfeld and Nicolson, London.

20

ECOLOGY IN RELATION TO URBAN POPULATION STRUCTURE

STEPHEN BOYDEN

THE term 'human ecology' has an interesting variety of meanings. To one author, at least, it encompasses almost all aspects of science that have any-thing to do with *Homo sapiens*, including human physiology, genetics, embry-ology, evolution, psychology, and sociology (Bews 1935). Others use it in a much more narrow sense, although their specific interpretations of the term vary remarkably according to their academic backgrounds. Thus, when soci-ologists speak of the 'Chicago school of human ecology', they are referring to work which began in the 1920's and which was concerned with the distribu-tion in space within cities of different social groups. The search for some general laws that could be found to apply to the geographical distribution of such groups led, for example, to the 'concentric-zone hypothesis' of Burgess (1925), which sees this distribution in modern cities in terms of a series of concentric zones around the central business district. A fairly extensive literature has now developed in this field of 'human ecology' and active con-troversies have followed the extension and diversification of the studies of the Chicago school (e.g. Shevky and Williams 1949, Shevky and Bell 1955, Abu-Lughod 1969). To another group of workers, human ecology is concerned almost solely with the interaction between the human species and pathogenic micro-organisms, and when used in this sense it would seem to be more or less synonymous with the epidemiology of infectious diseases (Banks 1950). A considerable number of books have appeared with the title 'Human Ecology' and, as would be anticipated, their contents vary considerably. One of the most pleasing is a small book by the late Sir George Stapledon (1964); it is of a somewhat philosophical bent and is full of lively and penetrating comment on human behaviour in a rapidly changing environment; but the only feature it shares with some of the other books with the same title is its concern with human beings.

It would not be sensible to enter here into a lengthy discussion and criti-cism of the various meanings of 'human ecology', or of the expression 'urban ecology', which is used synonymously by some authors. The subject has been well discussed by Bates (1953) and in more detail, but less clearly, by Quinn (1950) (see also Shephard 1967). Suffice it to say that some of the special uses of these terms come as something of a surprise to many biologists who are familiar with the word 'ecology' more or less as it was defined by Haeckel,† its originator. My own view coincides with that of Bates, who thinks that it is better that 'human ecology' be left with a general and rather vague meaning. However, it should be more generally appreciated among those who do use the term in a restricted sense that it has quite different meanings to other groups of workers.

In spite of the diversity of approaches to the study of the relationship of man to his environment, the sum total of work in this area still suffers from one serious deficiency. I do not wish to become involved here in the traditional conflict between biologists and sociologists, but I would like to make the point that one cannot peruse the literature on human ecology (in all its different senses) without being struck by the sparsity of intelligent and constructive co-operation between these two academic disciplines. Biologists who have turned to the subject of human ecology have been accused by sociologists of neglecting 'completely the factor of culture, which makes human ecology differ in certain fundamental ways from plant and animal ecology' (Quinn 1950); and there is ample ground for biologists to make the same sort of accusation in reverse with respect to the sociological ecologists.

It was only very recently, on the biological time scale, that cultural processes first began to appear in the biosphere and superimpose themselves, as it were, on the processes of life which gave rise to them. Since that time, the two sets of processes have not ceased to interact in countless significant ways, and as culture has continued to evolve, the intensity of this interaction has increased enormously; indeed, it is essentially the rapid intensification of this interplay that is responsible for the so-called 'environmental crisis' which is causing so much concern among biological ecologists today. Our understanding of the human situation in scientific terms must surely remain dangerously incomplete so long as we fail to make a deliberate and serious study of this interaction between cultural and natural processes in its own right, and so long as our academic institutions neglect this area of knowledge that lies in the no-man's-land between the natural sciences on the one hand and the social sciences and the humanities on the other.

There is no aspect of human ecology where the importance of this interplay between the processes of culture and of nature is more evident than that which is the main subject of this book. In fact, more effort has probably been made in the fields of demography and human fertility than in any other, to

---

† 'By *ecology*, we understand the study of the economy, of the household, of animal organisms. This includes the relationships of animals with both the inorganic and the organic environments, above all the beneficial and inimical relations with other animals and plants, whether direct or indirect' (Haeckel 1870). The definition of the term 'ecology' as given in Webster's *Collegiate Dictionary* puts the biologist's understanding of the term in a nutshell: 'Biology dealing with the mutual relations between organisms and their environment'.

consider both sides of the picture at the same time, and this volume itself represents further progress in this direction; but even in this area we have a long way to go before the full significance of the interaction between social and biological processes is properly appreciated and understood.

In this paper, I shall attempt to discuss in a few pages the extraordinarily complex topic of fertility and mortality patterns in urban communities, and the ways in which these differ from the patterns in rural areas. I shall also comment briefly on two other aspects: (a) the ecology of cities in terms of one of the dominant themes in classical biological ecology, namely, the question of energy flow and biogeochemical cycles as applied to urban communities; and (b) the need for more work on the biology of modern man.

FERTILITY AND MORTALITY IN URBAN AND RURAL AREAS†

Patterns of fertility and mortality are determined, of course, by the influence of environmental conditions (including social pressures) on genetically determined characteristics of populations. Thus any differences which can be demonstrated between these patterns in different regions (e.g. between urban and rural areas) are due mainly to differences in the environmental conditions in these areas. One of the tasks of the human biologist concerned with these matters is to attempt to recognize and define the various environmental factors which determine these patterns.

† Terminology. Attempts to define the terms 'urban' and 'rural' are fraught with many difficulties and the matter is discussed fully by Petersen (1969). In fact, it has been pointed out that the straight rural–urban comparison in the modern world is not very meaningful and it is suggested that we should recognize four categories in our classification as follows: (1) pre-industrial rural (peasants); (2) pre-industrial urban; (3) industrial rural (including so-called suburban); (4) industrial urban (Baker and Baker 1970). However, in view of the fact that the rural–urban classification has been used by most authors quoted in this paper, it is not possible to adopt the four-category classification here. Nor is it feasible to try to define the term 'urban' in precise terms each time it is used, since we shall be referring to work done by many different demographers in many different lands. In each case it should be assumed that the term 'urban' in this text is being used in the same sense as it is used by the author of the work which is being discussed. It is hoped that this variable will not destroy the validity of any broad conclusions we may reach (Davis 1965). Perhaps the most generally useful definition of an urban community is one which consists of a population of one hundred thousand or more.

The term 'urbanization' is also used by different authors in slightly different senses. Kingsley Davis (1965) uses it to refer to 'the proportion of the total population concentrated in urban settlements, or else to a rise in this proportion' and he states that 'the common mistake is to think of urbanization as simply the growth of cities'. He points out that a distinction between urbanization (in the sense that he uses the term) and the growth of cities is that the former has a beginning and an end, but the latter has no inherent limit. (This is not strictly true, in that in the long run there obviously is a limit to the growth of cities.) Petersen (1969) uses the term 'urbanization' to mean 'the development of large concentrated aggregates of human beings, and the rise of new culture patterns, new ways of thinking and behaviour, characteristic of these cities'. Thus to him urbanization is the 'process or state of population concentration' and he distinguishes between this process and 'urbanism' which is, he says, 'the way of life of the city dwellers'.

Mortality

Although there are numerous causes of death and only one cause of birth, it is considerably easier to explain mortality differences between populations than it is to explain differences in fertility. And it is certainly easier to recognize some of the influences accounting for rural–urban mortality differentials than it is to explain differences in fertility rates.

Historical aspects

One of the most important and clear-cut biological consequences of civilization has been the increase in population densities which began with the Neolithic development and which increased markedly with the appearance and growth of cities. These developments produced profound changes in the patterns of interaction between the human species and its microbiological parasites, with important effects on mortality patterns. Three factors arising out of this increase in population density were particularly important in influencing these relationships. They were: (1) the great increase in the *number* of social contacts experienced by the individual each day, (2) the increased *closeness* of these contacts (because of crowded living conditions and poor ventilation), and (3) the greatly increased possibility of contact with human excreta either directly or indirectly (i.e. through contamination of food and drink).

The effects of these environmental changes on host–parasite relationships were: (a) to increase greatly the chances of an individual coming in contact with human pathogens and (b) to improve greatly the chances of a given pathogenic micro-organism spreading and surviving in the human population. This situation created new opportunities for the evolution of disease-producing bacteria and viruses, because when new strains of pathogens appeared in human populations (whether by cross-infection from other species or as a result of mutation) they stood a much better chance of indefinite survival.

Apart from these relatively obvious and straightforward environmental changes that influenced host–parasite relationships, there were also other more subtle factors that tended to increase the incidence of infectious diseases by affecting the degree of resistance of individual human organisms. Most notable among these was malnutrition, due both to undernutrition and to specific dietary deficiencies, such as ascorbic acid or protein-calorie deficiency.

As a result, therefore, of the increase in density of human populations, infectious diseases became (in the absence at first of new standards of hygiene appropriate to the new host–parasite situation) a most important cause of mortality. An increase in population density occurred, of course, not only within cities, but also in all other areas affected by the Neolithic development; but the effect was obviously more marked in cities, and consequently it was urban populations that were most severely affected by the changes in host–parasite relationships.

Although there is ample justification on epidemiological and anthropological grounds for the view that it was environmental changes associated with the development of civilization that caused contagious diseases, such as plague, cholera, typhoid, dysentery, and tuberculosis to become important causes of death in human populations, it is surprising how many authorities apparently fail to appreciate this fact. So often it is assumed that pestilence, and indeed also malnutrition, had always been a feature of human existence until, in the case of Western society, the advances of medicine in the past half century or so removed them. In fact, for well over 90 per cent of man's time on earth, before the Neolithic development, neither pestilence nor malnutrition is likely to have been a common cause of ill-health or death.

The changes in host–parasite relationships resulting from the new population conditions apply not only to diseases due to bacteria but also to those associated with animal parasites (e.g. helminths) and viruses. It is of interest to note that in the case of viruses, the new standards of hygiene and advances in medical science have not, except in a few instances, produced any noticeable impact on the spread of the infectious agents. The sole tool of medicine against virus infections has been vaccination, which has been effectively introduced against only a small number of particularly serious diseases. Procedures for detecting and identifying separate viruses are a very recent development, and it is therefore not possible to make any definitive statements relating to the number of different viruses which have affected human populations at different times in the past. These techniques have indicated, however, that there are now at least 150 to 200 different viruses at present circulating in modern urban communities, most of them causing relatively mild and short-term disorders. The significant point is that very few of the common virus diseases of today could have existed in human populations prior to the advent of civilization, because the size of contiguous human groups was simply not large enough to sustain the infectious agents (Fenner 1970). It has been estimated, for example, that measles requires a population of at least half a million people in order to maintain itself (Black 1966). The existence, therefore, of the large number of viruses at the present time circulating in human populations must be a new biological development—a consequence of the creation, through the great increase in the human population, of a situation which is permitting a sort of explosive adaptive radiation among viruses capable of multiplying in the tissues of man.

Because the disorders caused by these viruses are mostly mild, they do not appear at first sight to have any significant effect on mortality; however, we are essentially ignorant of the long-term cumulative effects, physiological or mental, of numerous repeated virus infections in the human organism. Certainly, the increasing number of virus infections is a striking feature of the ecology of modern urban man; and on the basis of existing knowledge, the hypothesis that they might collectively contribute to some of the so-called degenerative diseases characteristic of modern society cannot be rejected. If, at some point of time in the future, society decides that this burden is too heavy to carry, it may have to introduce further new standards of hygiene to cope with the situation. (One effective, if somewhat improbable course of action, would be for the World Health Organization to provide the whole population of the world with 'virus' masks, insisting that, for a period of one month simultaneously throughout the world, everyone wear his mask each time he is in the company of others except, his own immediate family.) This would probably result in the virtual elimination of the great majority of these infective agents; the common cold, influenza, and other virus infections of the respiratory and alimentary tracts would, for a while, become things of the past. The exercise would have to be repeated every fifty years or so.

Although, as we have seen, the settled life which followed the Neolithic development and the later growth of cities introduced new threats to human health in the form of contagious disease and malnutrition, the effects of these forms of biological maladjustment on mortality were more than compensated for by the protection afforded by civilization against the environmental hazards of the pre-Neolithic period. Consequently, there occurred a steady growth in world population, so that by 1750 it had probably increased at least one hundredfold since the beginning of the Neolithic period. At about the time of the beginning of the industrial revolution and the period of rapid urbanization in Western Europe there occurred a new spurt in population growth, the actual causation of which is still a matter of debate. It is said that an appreciable fall in the death rate began in Britain around 1780 and continued through the nineteenth century (except, perhaps, for a brief period from about 1811 to 1830, although there is some disagreement about this). It has been suggested that this fall in mortality was due to environmental changes associated with improved conditions of living rather than to advances in medicine (McKeown and Brown 1955), and Petersen (1969) believes that the most important contributory factor was improved nutrition, resulting in a higher resistance to infectious disease. However, this view is difficult to reconcile with the writings of some other authors, including Drummond and Wilbraham (1939), who refer to the last part of the eighteenth century as a 'terrible period of dearth and starvation' (see also Sigsworth 1966).

Although there has been a considerable increase of interest among demographers in recent years in the factors affecting both mortality and fertility in Europe during recent centuries, it seems probable that we will never have a clear and definite picture of what really happened. We can hope, however, for a somewhat better understanding of the demographic events during the early period of urbanization associated with the industrial revolution when the parish registers of that time have been more completely analysed (Eversley 1965).

Thus, the changes in mortality patterns in Western society during the past few centuries have been due basically to two factors: (1) changes in environmental conditions resulting from socio-economic developments, and giving rise to different forms of biological maladjustment contributing to death rates, and (2) the coming into play, after varying lag periods, of the processes of cultural adaptation, including the introduction of new standards of hygiene and also the antidotal measures of modern medicine. (It is true that natural selection probably played a role in rendering human populations somewhat more resistant to the various infective agents, but there can be no doubt that the main factors ultimately reducing mortality from infectious disease and malnutrition were social ones.)

Needless to say, in view of the ever-accelerating rate at which the social and biological environment is changing, we have every reason to anticipate the appearance of further signs of biological maladjustment. In fact, while in Western society cultural adaptive procedures have countered fairly successfully some of the more alarming disorders such as plague and diphtheria, there now appears to be a significant increase in the incidence of cardiovascular disease, which is widely accepted among medical scientists to be associated in some way with modern conditions of life. Moreover, it is not impossible, on the basis of existing evidence, that malignant neoplastic conditions, including leukaemia, may also be in the main pathological responses to fairly recently introduced biological factors. Similarly, suicide, which is the largest single cause of death in some age groups in certain countries, would seem to be especially characteristic of modern Western society.

These new influences have not, for various reasons, brought about a return to the high mortality rate of two hundred or even one hundred years ago. However, there has recently been a slight increase in mortality in some Western countries, although it is too early at present to determine the significance of this development in terms of environmental influences (Krohn and Weber 1967).

Present variability in urban mortality patterns

The mortality rates in different urban communities throughout the world today are extremely variable, and there can be little doubt that the largest single cause of this variation lies in differences in levels of sanitation and general hygiene. The main causes of death in cities where mortality is still high are basically the same as those of the urban areas in Western Europe and North America 100 to 200 years ago, namely, contagious diseases. Although the important principles relating to the control of these conditions, which were learned a century or so ago in Western society, are now appreciated throughout the world, they have yet to be applied effectively in all the developing countries. It has been pointed out that the mistake is made in some developing areas to legislate for standards of housing and sanitation similar to those of modern Western society—standards which, for economic and organizational reasons, are clearly unrealistic in these areas of extremely rapid urbanization. The result is that we tend to find a small 'Westernized' area within such a city with standards as high as those in the modern European-type community, while the authorities turn a blind eye to the rest and greater part of the city, because of the utter impossibility of its reaching required standards. Oram (1965, 1970) has argued that this policy is unwise, and that a great deal more could be achieved if legislative bodies would settle for somewhat lower standards than those typical of modern affluent societies, while insisting on the widespread application of these new standards in all sections of the community.

A striking example of different mortality patterns occurring in the same city and due to different biological conditions prevailing in its different parts, is seen in Johannesburg. The Bantu population in this city is, in terms of its state of biological maladjustment and cultural adaptation, more akin to urban populations in nineteenth-century Britain than it is to the European community. In 1965 the death rate among Bantus (per 100 000 population) from tuberculosis was given as 48; from gastro-enteritis, 102; and from arteriosclerotic and degenerative heart disease, 15. In contrast the 'European' death rate in Johannesburg from tuberculosis was 4 per 100 000; from gastro-enteritis, 7; and from arteriosclerotic and degenerative heart disease, 221 (Smith 1965). It appears that the processes of cultural adaptation have effectively countered tuberculosis in the European segment of the community, but not among the African population, in spite of the fact that the knowledge necessary for successful cultural adaptation is available. Nevertheless, a new form of biological maladjustment has appeared among the Europeans due to the introduction of further new conditions of life which presumably have not yet pervaded the Bantu community to any extent. Of course, in this instance there are clear genetic differences between the two populations, but it is highly unlikely that the big differences in mortality rates from these two conditions could be due to genetic factors. (Another difficulty in the interpretation of these figures lies in the fact that the death rate from 'senility and ill-defined conditions' was 88 in Europeans and 1168 among the Bantus.)

Mortality rates also differ from one part to another of modern Western cities. Sometimes these differences may be due to different conditions of life, but they are more often the consequence of differential distribution within the city areas of groups differing by age and according to marital status.

In summary, there is much variation in urban mortality rates today, ranging, for example, from a rate of 2 per thousand in Canada to 6·9 per thousand in Chad in Africa. At the present time, infant mortality in the cities with the high mortality rate is the main factor responsible for these differences.

Thus, in the urban areas in the United Arab Republic (in 1960), the number of deaths of infants less than one year old was greater than for the age group 1-to-4 or for any later 10-year age group and it was close to twice the figure for the age group 65-plus. In the urban areas in the United Kingdom (in 1966), the figure for the first year of life was about 1/20 of the figure for the 65-plus age group (United Nations 1967). High infant mortality is often taken, with justification, as a general indicator of the level of hygiene and consequently of economic status of a community.

Rural–urban mortality differentials

A study of the literature relating to rural–urban differentials in mortality rates leads us to the conclusion, similar to that which we shall draw in the case of fertility, that, while differentials certainly exist, there seems to be no general law or rule that is applicable to all parts of the world. In the words of one author: 'Mortality levels as indicated by expectation of life at birth and infant mortality rates do not vary systematically with rural–urban residence in those developing countries for which data have been examined, although there is a tendency for mortality to be lower in the principal city than elsewhere in Latin-American countries.' (Johnson 1967.) The failure to find a systematic difference, however, may in some cases be due to the quality of available data.

Woytinsky and Woytinsky (1953) state that death rates in cities are 'generally higher than in rural areas' and cite Great Britain, Denmark, Austria, Australia, and New Zealand as examples. Nevertheless, they point out that the difference is neither consistent nor very large, and they note that France, Switzerland, Spain, Hungary, the Netherlands, and Sweden show the opposite tendency (i.e. higher mortality rates in the rural areas). More recent figures for Western countries show similar small differences, but no constant pattern is discernible and some of the above-mentioned countries have changed places on the two lists (United Nations 1967). Although the rural–urban mortality differential is at present small in Western countries, it is noteworthy that mortality due to one of the most important causes of death in these regions, cardiovascular disease, is higher in urban than in rural areas (Furnass 1970).

In general, the tendency in developing countries is for mortality rates to be somewhat higher in rural areas than in cities (Chandrasekhar 1967, World Health Organization 1967, Petersen 1969). Since in these developing countries infant mortality is still an important cause of death, one of the factors tending to reduce the mortality rates in cities is the fact that in many areas an increasing number of confinements is now taking place in hospitals. For example, 80 per cent of births in Madras city now take place in hospitals (Chandrasekhar 1967).

Until recently, malaria has been another important factor in mortality, and in many areas in many parts of South East Asia, for example, the prevalence of malaria has been higher in rural areas than in the cities (Wiesler 1967). We can anticipate, therefore, that in malaria-infected areas differences in mortality rates between rural and urban areas will tend to decrease with the introduction of malaria control based on the use of insecticides. However, the question of the extent to which malaria control *per se* has in fact contributed to recent sharp falls in mortality (e.g. in Ceylon) is a matter of controversy. While some authorities maintain that the great reduction in the prevalence of malaria has been mainly responsible for the fall in death rates, others hold that the effects have been due rather to general improvement of health services in the affected areas. The debate is an important one in view of its relevance to future trends; for malaria control is more or less complete in many of these areas, while the spread of general health services is only just beginning (Titmuss, Abel-Smith, and Lynes 1961, *Lancet* 1969).

Fertility

Fertility rates in human populations vary widely from time to time and from place to place. While we cannot rule out the possibility that genetic factors play some role, there can be little doubt that these differences are, in the main, due to environmental influences. Basically, there are only three categories of factors which can influence fertility, and any differences that may exist in the birth rates in different communities must be attributed to one or more of these factors. They are:

1. The frequency and distribution in time of heterosexual intercourse during the reproductive period of the females in the population. This factor is to some extent a matter of choice (and as such may be influenced by cultural forces, taboos, and socio-economic aspirations); but it is also affected by external pressures such as levels of fatigue, mood, the quality of personal relationships, and so on.
2. The extent to which the population makes use of culturally-determined artificial means of interfering with conception or with the development of the foetus to full term.
3. Physiological factors influencing the rate of conception and the viability of the foetus. These include not only forms of biological maladjustment interfering with health, but also such physiological regulatory mechanisms as the inhibitory effect of lactation on ovulation.

While all three of these categories of influence play a role, the second group (the use of artificial means of interfering with conception and pregnancy) is at present by far the most important one in accounting for the differences that exist between fertility rates in different communities throughout the world.

Historical aspects

As mentioned above, there has been a good deal of discussion concerning the underlying causes of the increase in population growth that occurred during the period of rapid urbanization associated with the early stages of the industrial revolution in Britain (i.e. from about 1760 to 1840). While it is generally accepted now that these changes were mainly the result of a decrease in mortality due to improved living conditions (McKeown and Brown 1955, Petersen 1969), an increase in the birth rate may also have played some part (Habakkuk 1958, Eversley 1965). If so, this may have been a direct influence of certain social pressures, such as the employment of child labour, which may have tended to promote an increase in birth rates in industrial cities. In fact the influence of economic conditions on fertility in the last century appears to have been extremely complex, just as it is today. While there has been a tendency for periods of poor economic conditions to be associated with periods of relatively low fertility (in both nineteenth and twentieth centuries), when fertility rates are examined in terms of social stratification, at any given point of time, it is often found that the lowest fertility rates occur in the more privileged economic groups.

It is important to appreciate that the fertility patterns characteristic of Western Europe, and particularly of Britain, during the industrial revolution were not only unique in the world at that time, but were also quite different from those seen in developing communities today. Thus, European birth rates before the spread of birth control appear rarely to have exceeded 38 per thousand, whereas in the developing countries today they are almost always over 40 and often over 45 per thousand (Hajnal 1965, Petersen 1969). In other words, the trend towards industrialization and urbanization does not *per se* give rise to low levels of fertility. This point is obviously important in relation to our attempts to predict future trends, because it is often assumed that the increasing urbanization of communities will inevitably lead to the lowering of fertility (Dubos 1965, Smith 1958).

Present variability in urban fertility patterns

Substantial differences exist in fertility rates between cities in different parts of the world, and there are also distinct rural–urban differentials in some regions. However, as in the case of mortality rates, there is no constant relationship between urban and rural rates. Before giving a few examples to illustrate this point, it would be appropriate at this juncture to list some of the factors which are known, or are thought to influence fertility rates; for it is the multiplicity of these factors and the complex and as yet poorly understood interactions between them that account for the lack of uniformity in patterns throughout the world, and from one culture to another.

1. *Age at puberty*. The age of menarche in girls has been found to vary considerably from one part of the world to another, and the indications are

that it has dropped some 4 to 5 years in many Western communities during the past hundred years (Tanner 1962). At the present time the average age of menarche in many Western countries is about 13 years, while in parts of New Guinea it is about 18·5 years (Wark and Malcolm 1969). The possibility exists that genetic factors contribute to such differences in age of puberty between populations and even to the secular trends in growth rates (Tanner 1965), but it would seem that the major effect accounting for these differences is an environmental one, and it is usually assumed that diet is the important factor (Kumar 1967). Since the age of the menopause appears to vary within only very narrow limits (MacMahon and Worcester 1966), this variation in age at menarche might well be an important factor influencing the average completed family size in populations. In view of the fact that diet may be an important environmental influence affecting age at menarche, differences between rural and urban diets might, through this mechanism, influence the rate of natural increase in the respective populations. Some data supporting this suggestion have been published from Yugoslavia, where girls with high protein diets were found to reach menarche 1 to 2 years before those with low protein, high carbohydrate diets; and menarche is said to occur earlier in urban than rural areas in that country (Kralj-Cercek 1956).

2. *Age at marriage.* The age of marriage, in Western countries at least, is said to be one of the most sensitive indicators of economic fluctuations (Eversley 1965), and variation in age of marriage may thus represent one of the ways through which economic changes can influence fertility. There are, of course, big variations in age at marriage in different parts of the world and also between different socio-economic or ethnic groups within urban communities. Moreover, significant changes are occurring at the present time and it is said, for example, that the average age of marriage of urban girls in India has risen since the beginning of the century from 13 to 16 years, and the likelihood is that it will continue to rise for some time (Raina 1967). However, any effects of such trends may to some extent be countered by changes in attitudes towards pre-marital sexual relations and illegitimate birth. In any case, not all authorities agree that differences in average age at marriage in communities form an important factor influencing total fertility, at least in Western societies.

3. *The availability of advice on methods of fertility control, and the accessibility of the means to make use of these methods.* Clearly, both advice on family planning and the means for following such advice are likely to be more readily available in some areas of the world and in some sections of the population than in others. In developing countries especially there is likely to be an important difference between rural and urban areas in this respect. This factor is one of great importance; but it is so obvious that there is no need to elaborate on it here.

4. *The availability of facilities for abortion, and its legality.* The opportunities

for deliberate abortion vary greatly from place to place, and this may be expected to be an important influence affecting differential fertility. However, even this factor cannot be assumed in all circumstances to have a marked effect on birth rates, and Klinger (1967) has suggested that in Hungary, where abortion has been legal since 1956, it is not the basis for, but only a measure of birth control; in other words, if abortion were not available, fertility would be lowered by some other means. However, in Japan, the legalization of abortion is considered to have been a most important influence in the marked decline in fertility that has occurred since its introduction in 1948 (Muramatsu 1960). Since, in areas where abortion becomes legalized, it is more likely to be practised in urban areas than in country districts, especially in developing countries, it may become a factor contributing to rural–urban fertility differentials.

5. *Traditional, moral, and religious attitudes towards fertility control.* The influence of religious dogma on fertility is well recognized, and it no doubt contributes considerably to differences in birth rate in different urban or rural communities. As far as rural–urban differentials are concerned, religion would be anticipated to be a factor only if differences existed between the religious practices and beliefs of the urban and rural peoples. It is interesting that in Australia and in the United States, while the fertility rates among Catholics are higher in both urban and rural areas than those among non-Catholics in the same areas, the urban fertility rates of Catholics are considerably lower than those of rural Catholics (Day 1964). Incidentally, the influence of religion appears to be much more marked when the religious group in question (i.e. in the case of religions that condemn birth control) is in a minority in the population (Day 1967).

6. *Educational levels.* It is well known that level of education can influence fertility; but the relationship between education and fertility levels is by no means a simple one. The complexity of this relationship, and also of the way in which urban and rural conditions may influence fertility patterns, is illustrated by work carried out on populations in Egypt. In one study (El-Badry and Rizk 1967) women were divided into the following educational categories: (a) illiterates, (b) those who could just read and write, (c) those with elementary certificates, (d) those with secondary school certificates, and (e) university graduates. In non-urban (rural) areas the highest fertility was among groups (b) and (c)—that is, among women who could just read and write and those with elementary school certificates. In urban communities, however, the pattern was somewhat different, in that the illiterate women had the highest fertility rates and they were followed, in order of decreasing fertility levels, by those who could just read and write, those with elementary school certificates, those with secondary school certificates, and finally those with university degrees. Thus, for every 100 children born to the illiterate women in urban areas, 87 were born to women who could just read and write,

82 to holders of elementary certificates, 63 to those with secondary certificates, and 53 to female university graduates. Although there was some difference between age at marriage in the different groups, the investigators did not consider this to be an important factor.

In contrast, it has been reported that fertility rates of better-educated groups in Sweden, England and Wales, and the Netherlands are above the average for the communities as a whole (Johnson 1960).

7. *Socio-economic status.* It is difficult, of course, to separate socio-economic class from educational status. Thus, the general picture that there is no constant relationship between socio-economic class and fertility may simply be another way of saying that there is much variation, from community to community, in the effects of education. However, it does seem that, in Western countries at least, any differences that might have existed between the fertility rates of different socio-economic groups tend now to be disappearing. For example, in a recent study in the city of Melbourne in Australia no difference could be detected in the average size of the families of different economic status (Jones 1969). Similarly, in the United States, differences between socio-economic groups in their fertility rates are diminishing and are much smaller than the differences which exist between ethnic and religious categories (Cook 1964).

8. *Working wives.* There is considerable variation between societies, for economic or traditional reasons, with regard to whether or not wives take on work outside the home; but it is not clear to what extent these differences might influence fertility. It has been suggested that this factor might sometimes affect urban–rural differentials, in view of the fact that a small child interferes less with the work of a farm wife than with that of a female employee of a factory or other organization in the city.

9. *Migration.* Migration can affect the fertility rate of a community through its influence on both the age structure and the sex distribution within the population. However, patterns of rural–urban migration vary from one part of the world to another, thus affecting fertility differentials in different ways. While the general tendency is for young adults of both sexes to move from rural to urban areas (tending to augment the crude fertility rates in the cities), in India rural–urban migration has been predominantly of males who leave wives and children in their home villages (Sovani 1967).

10. *Indefinite cultural factors and attitudes.* Tradition has a great deal to do with family size. In fact, one of the most powerful forces affecting all forms of human behaviour is a strong and apparently innate dislike of ridicule. In a culture in which couples are ridiculed for having few children, the birth rate is likely to be high, and vice versa. But there is no consistent world-wide pattern that distinguishes between urban and rural communities in this respect.

11. *The frequency of coitus.* In the human species, in which there is no oestrus period and in which sexual intercourse is likely to take place at any

time throughout the cycle, the frequency of coitus may become an important factor affecting fertility. It has been calculated that, if the rate of coital activity drops to once per month, the probability of conception resulting from such a single 'unprotected' coitus would be between only 1/50 and 1/25 (Tietze 1960). There are grounds for suspecting that this fact may have formed the basis of an important population-regulating mechanism in pre-Neolithic times, and even in the modern world it may be a more significant factor influencing fertility differentials than is usually appreciated. It might be anticipated, for example, that the frequency of mating would be diminished in urban groups living under extremely crowded conditions, and it may also be affected by the family structure in the society in question. It has been argued that the extended 'joint family', which still persists in both rural and urban areas in India, for example, would tend to show lower fertility through its influence on the rate of frequency of coitus (Nag 1967).

12. *Lactation*. One of the marked changes that civilization has brought about in the biology of *Homo sapiens* has been the abandonment of lactation as the means of feeding the human infant. This move began in Europe in the seventeenth and eighteenth centuries, and although there tended to be a return to breast-feeding during the nineteenth century, the present century has seen its further progressive decline in Western society. This trend is now extending to many other communities outside Europe and America (Jelliffe 1955). In the present context, the importance of this trend lies in the fact that lactation suppresses fertility in women, as it does in many other species of mammals. There are two ways in which this factor might influence urban–rural differentials. In the first place it seems likely that the period of lactation amenorrhoea or sterility appears to be influenced by diet, which in turn may be different in rural and in urban areas. For example, the finding that lactation may suppress menstruation for periods of about one year in districts in India, while only for two or three months in the United States and Europe has been explained in terms of nutritional differences between the two groups (Peters, Israel, and Purshottam 1958). Secondly, social pressures tending to suppress lactation and replace it with artificial bottle-feeding are, in developing countries, often more a feature of urban than of rural communities (Jelliffe 1955).

These various factors that may influence fertility are listed simply to illustrate the complexity of the problem under discussion, and also by way of explanation for the lack of any constant relationship between the fertility levels in urban and rural communities.

Rural–urban fertility differentials

Figures from the following countries indicate higher crude fertility rates in rural than in urban areas: Southern Rhodesia, Canada, Panama, Israel, and the United States (United Nations 1967); Taiwan (Chow 1967); Russia (immediately after the revolution and again recently) (Urlanis 1967); the

Philippines, Pakistan, Puerto Rico, Cuba, Brazil, and Mexico (Concepcion 1967); Hungary (before 1914) (Kiser 1967); and Australia (Borrie 1969).

In the following countries, higher fertility rates have been reported for urban than for rural areas: Congo (Democratic Republic of) (United Nations 1967, Concepcion 1967); Gabon, Mali, Sierra Leone (Western area), and El Salvador (United Nations 1967); and Hungary (after 1945) (Kiser 1967).

Thus, while taking the world as a whole there is certainly a tendency for fertility rates to be higher in rural areas, there are some notable exceptions. For instance, in Monterrey in Mexico the completed family size (estimated from the mean number of live births per number of males aged 51 to 60) is 6·03 (Zarate 1967) which, according to Petersen (1969), is about one child more than the highest completed family size found in other Latin-American studies.

We must take some exception, therefore, to the statement by Woytinsky and Woytinsky (1953) that 'the most striking differential in birth rate, fertility rate, and the number of children per family is probably between rural areas and cities, and between urban communities of various sizes ... As a general rule, the smaller the community, the higher the birth rate among women in all age classes.' However, as these authors point out, we must always be cautious in our interpretations of data from some of the developing countries, especially in view of the great difficulties in obtaining reliable information from remote rural areas.

There is, however, one trend which is almost universal, and that is the tendency for rural and urban fertility differentials gradually to diminish, and in most Western countries there is a negligible difference at the present time. In the United States the difference still exists between 'farm families' on the one hand, and urban families on the other, although 'non-farm families' living in rural areas have fertility rates more like those of the cities (Morris and Farley 1964). The tendency for rural–urban differentials to disappear is perhaps the only trend that is constant and of predictive value at the present time; barring a global catastrophe, communications are likely to improve in all areas, rendering urban and rural populations more similar with regard to attitudes and to facilities and advice relevant to family planning.

Comment

From the biological standpoint, the outstanding feature of the last few hundred generations of the human species has been the extraordinary number of changes that have occurred in the social and environmental conditions of life of the human organism. These changes, on the whole, have been especially marked in urban areas. As would be anticipated, there have been many bio-logically determined responses of the human organism to these changes, some of them with far-reaching effects on patterns of mortality and fertility.

Summarizing the situation as far as mortality is concerned, we can state that the conditions of civilization have tended to protect the human organism from the main causes of death in pre-Neolithic society, such as attack from predators, injury (and subsequent tissue infection) received in hunting, and freak climatic conditions. However, these ancient environmental hazards were to a considerable extent replaced by new ones, including especially various contagious diseases. Since the conditions which tended to promote infectious disease were most extreme in the cities, mortality tended in the early stages of the industrial revolution to be higher in the cities than in rural areas. However, the processes of cultural adaptation eventually came into play, and in Western countries they have brought about a marked reduction in mortality rates; in these regions there is at the present time little difference between the mortality rates or urban and rural areas.

In the developing countries the picture is very different. While on the one hand the conditions in the cities are on the whole conducive to high levels of infectious disease, so that one might expect higher mortality rates than in rural areas, this influence is partially countered by the fact that, unlike the situation in Europe during the last century, the practices of cultural adaptation in the form of sophisticated health services are on the whole more effective in urban areas than in rural areas. The developing countries are also in a different position from that in which the industrial nations were during the last century, in that the authorities are fully aware of the connection between high levels of mortality, especially infant mortality, and the contamination of water supplies and food with human excreta. Consequently, immense efforts are being made, especially in Latin America, to improve water supplies and facilities for the safe disposal of sewage. In Africa (with one or two outstanding exceptions), the standard of city water supplies is lower than in Latin America, and the facilities for the disposal of human excreta are much less satisfactory (Johnson 1967). A critical question is whether the improvements in water supplies and sanitation can keep pace with the population increase. Some authorities are not very hopeful, noting that the urban population of the world is expected to increase sevenfold during the second half of this century (World Health Organization 1968).

Similarly, there have been many environmental changes associated with the processes of civilization that can be expected to influence fertility rates. Apart from the physiological mechanisms already mentioned (changes in lactation patterns, variation in age of menarche, etc.), there have been many other subtle social developments that can be suspected of influencing fertility one way or another. The spread of central heating in urban areas in temperate climates is one such change, for there is evidence that exposure for prolonged periods to high environmental temperatures tends to reduce fertility (Chang, Chan, Low, and Ng 1963). Other social developments may influence fertility rates through their effects on human behaviour. For example, some of the factors in the following list of culturally-induced changes, likely through their effects on behaviour to affect fertility, may be much more important in determining birth rates than is usually appreciated: the greatly increased number of social and visual contacts with members of the opposite sex; the increased levels, particularly in modern urban communities, of sexual stimulation through the mass media; the wearing of clothes and the sexually provocative use of clothing; the introduction of the bed (particularly the double bed); and the declining levels of alternative physical challenge and causes of physical fatigue. (This is not to say that there have not also been other subtle environmental factors or social practices influencing sexual behaviour in simple or non-technological societies.)

This list emphasises the complexity of the multiple environmental changes associated with the processes of civilization and urbanization that are likely to affect fertility patterns. The fact that the influence of some of the items on this list is very hard, if not impossible, to study quantitatively makes the scientific evaluation of their importance exceedingly difficult.

A matter of some importance, and one which seems to receive very little attention, is the question of what fertility-regulating mechanisms may have operated in pre-Neolithic society. It is often assumed that whatever mechanisms existed were entirely culturally determined. However, since it is becoming apparent that innate mechanisms of fertility control (both behavioural and physiological) exist in other species, we may justifiably suppose that at some time such mechanisms operated also in our own evolutionary history. The possibility clearly exists that they may indeed have operated right up to the time of the Neolithic development, although it would seem that since that time, under the changed circumstances, they are no longer effective. Nevertheless, some knowledge of what these mechanisms may have been might contribute usefully to our understanding of the present situation. I will not introduce speculation on this subject at this point, but raise the matter in the hope of stimulating some discussion on what seems to me to be not only an interesting but also rather significant topic.

With regard to the future, the data relating to fertility and mortality patterns and to rural–urban differentials can hardly be said to point to an appreciable decrease in rate of population growth in the world in the near future. If this does come about it will not be the consequence of urbanization, but rather as a result of enlightened thinking spreading rapidly (through formal education and through the mass media) to all sections of the community in all countries. In other words, there is nothing intrinsically hopeful in the process of urbanization *per se*, and there is no real justification for the view sometimes expressed that, because urbanization has been associated with a relatively low rate of population growth in Western Europe and North America during the last hundred years, the same course will necessarily be followed in the developing countries in the near future.

The population structure of the developing areas, both urban and rural, is at the present time a cause for very serious concern. The population pyramids are remarkably flat, and while this may perhaps have been the pattern for a long time, in the presence of the increasingly low mortality rates, further unprecedented population growth can be anticipated. Apart from the chance of the development of new attitudes and a growing social conscience, the possibility exists, of course, that some other as yet unanticipated population-controlling factors may come into play. It has been suggested, for instance, that pollution in urban areas might before long reach levels sufficient to influence mortality and possibly also fertility. If this does happen, it may well not be the first time in history. It has been argued (Gilfillan 1965), for example, that the insidious effects of chronic lead poisoning were at least partly responsible, through their influence on fertility, for the decay of the Roman Empire. Thus, with regard to the present situation, while it is abundantly clear that the growth of the world's population must sooner or later cease, the actual manner in which this will come about must remain, in the present state of our knowledge, a matter for conjecture.

ENERGY FLOW AND BIOGEOCHEMICAL CYCLES IN URBAN COMMUNITIES

Although this topic may not at first sight appear to be quite in tune with the main theme of this volume, I offer the following points by way of justification for including it in my paper:

1. The subject is of overwhelming significance in relation to the problems of man in the modern world, but receives little attention in ecological textbooks and works on 'human ecology'.
2. The important developments in urban ecology (in the biological or metabolic sense of the term) are intimately connected with population changes, including rural–urban migration and the overall increase in population. In other words, these physicochemical and energetic aspects of the total urban situation should not be considered as separate and distinct from the changes in the numbers of human organisms and their state of health.
3. In the long run, the ecological consequences of the growth of cities may well have far-reaching and possibly devastating effects on human populations.

The city is not, of course, an 'ecosystem' in the usual sense of the term, in that it is not self-supporting. No appreciable photosynthesis occurs within the urban area and it depends entirely for its supply of energy and chemical compounds on ecosystems and resources beyond its walls. In fact, although we must be wary of the 'organic analogy' approach, the city is, from the ecological viewpoint, much more like a gigantic, immobile animal than it is like an ecosystem.

Chemical cycles

The gross metabolism of a hypothetical modern Western city of one million people is represented diagrammatically in Fig. 20.1. The figures for fossil fuel, water, and food intake and those for the output of particles, hydro-carbons, carbon monoxide, and sewage have been taken from a paper by Wolman (1965). The figures for oxygen intake, and for the release into the

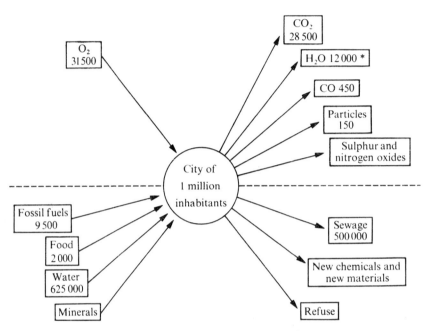

FIG. 20.1. The gross metabolism of a city of one million inhabitants. The figures refer to the number of tons of the substances flowing in and out of the system per day.

atmosphere of carbon dioxide and water have been calculated from these other figures, taking into account also the oxygen utilized and the carbon dioxide exhaled by the human inhabitants of the city. Needless to say, these estimates are crude, and it will be noted, for example, that the input of water does not balance the output. This is because water lost through evaporation and seepage is not represented in the illustration. No attempt has been made to estimate the actual quantities of minerals entering or leaving the city.

The resemblance of the city to a colossal animal lies in its consumption of oxygen, water, and organic matter (in the form of fossil fuels and food substances) and in its release into the atmosphere of carbon dioxide and water vapour, and in its excretion into the surroundings of organic waste material

* This figure of 12 000 tons refers only to the water that is produced in the combustion of fossil fuels.

suspended or dissolved in large volumes of water. However, it differs from an animal in one particularly important respect, namely, that many of its products are quite unlike the products of any biological organism. The metabolism of the city involves the rearrangement of elements to form not only such biologically novel substances as various metal alloys, concrete, and so on, but, more importantly, a vast array of synthetic chemical compounds, many of which, although alien to the biosphere, are nevertheless very potent biologically and therefore likely to cause disturbances in organisms and eco-systems with which they may come in contact. Other products, like plastics and 'hard' detergents are almost undegradable by biological processes. It has been estimated that some half a million different chemical substances, pro-ducts of the metabolism of cities, are released daily into the environment, most of them finding their way eventually into the oceans (Geiling and D'Aguanno 1960, Goldberg 1969).

Apart from the biologically novel products referred to above, the sheer scale of activity of modern cities is causing significant changes in the environ-mental concentration of more 'natural' substances. An increase of 25 per cent in the carbon dioxide content of the total atmosphere of the earth is antici-pated by the year A.D. 2000 (Tukey 1965) and the increasing turbidity of the atmosphere, is causing considerable concern among ecologists.

It does not require much imagination to appreciate that, in view of the quantities involved and the special nature of some of the products, the recent introduction into the biosphere of large and increasing numbers of urban units with these metabolic characteristics is a development of considerable ecological significance.

Energy flow through industrial society

The energy required to maintain the dynamic metabolic processes of the city is at present supplied almost entirely in the form of chemical energy originally trapped from sunlight by plants through photosynthesis; the con-tribution of hydro-electric power and nuclear power is at present negligible. Thus, the energy enters the system in the form of potential chemical energy in fossil fuels and organic matter and it leaves it mainly as heat.

I have not estimated the actual flow of energy through our hypothetical city of one million people, but will refer instead to the figures for the energy utilized by the present world population as a whole. The total amount of energy used by human society and derived from coal, petroleum, natural gas, and electricity in 1966 is given in the *United Nations Statistical Yearbook* of 1967 as the equivalent of 5505×10^6 metric tons of coal. We must add to this, energy provided by pack animals, fuel wood, utilization of wind, and so on, which is estimated to be in the order of 500×10^6 metric tons of coal (Woy-tinsky and Woytinsky 1953). If we convert the sum of these two figures to kilocalories and add to it the energy flow through the individual human organisms (i.e. about $3 \cdot 6 \times 10^{15}$ kcal/yr), we arrive at a total figure of about $4 \cdot 5 \times 10^{16}$ kcal for the year 1966. The present figure (1970) can be expected to exceed this by at least 10 per cent, giving us a value of nearly $5 \cdot 0 \times 10^{16}$ kcal.

It is revealing to compare this figure with estimates that have been made on the total amount of energy captured from sunlight by photosynthesis. One such estimate, cited by Kormondy (1969), is as follows:

Photosynthesis by terrestrial vegetation:

$$4 \cdot 3 - 6 \cdot 3 \times 10^{16} \text{ kcal/yr}$$

Photosynthesis by oceanic vegetation:

$$4 \cdot 3 - 11 \cdot 8 \times 10^{16} \text{ kcal/yr}$$

It is apparent, therefore, that a single species, *Homo sapiens*, now utilizes in its daily activities about as much energy as is fixed by the whole of terrestrial vegetation in the same period of time. Since it is confidently and hopefully predicted by engineers that the rate of energy utilization by mankind will increase some four- to five-fold in the next thirty years, it is clear that before long the energy flow through urban-industrial networks will exceed the total energy consumption by all animals and plants on land and in the sea put together.

These facts are, I believe, helpful in our attempts to view the human situation in biological perspective.

CHANGES IN THE BIOLOGICAL CONDITIONS OF LIFE OF MAN

It is appropriate in the context of this volume to draw attention to the dearth of biologically-oriented studies on man in modern urban society, and to make a few general comments on likely developments in this area.

By far the most outstanding feature of the biology of modern man is the extraordinary degree of change that has occurred in his conditions of life in what has been, in biological perspective, a very short period of time. It is a corollary of Darwinian theory that, if environmental conditions deviate from those to which a species has become genetically adapted through natural selection, signs of biological maladjustment, which may be physiological or behavioural, are likely to occur; and *Homo sapiens* is no exception to this rule. Consequently, the study of the changes in the total environment of man and of his biologically-determined responses to these changes is not only of scientific interest; it is also of great social significance. Oddly enough, however, despite its obvious scientific and social importance, this subject has not attracted the attention of biologists to any extent, and it does not feature prominently either in biological research programmes or in biological education.

It is true, of course, that medical science has made some inroads in this area, but the picture which emerges from this work is incomplete and unbalanced. This is due to the fact that the starting-point in classical medical research is usually an easily recognizable form of biological maladjustment, and the aim is to discover the cause of, or at least a cure for the disorder in question. This approach has led frequently to the labelling of some intermediate factor (e.g. a micro-organism) as the 'cause' of the maladjustment, whereas in fact the underlying cause has often been an ecological one (e.g. crowding, affecting host–parasite relationships or producing new evolutionary possibilities for pathogenic agents). Moreover, the conventional medical approach may fail to pay due attention to some of the reactions of the human organism to environmental change, if these reactions are widespread in a population and not painful or obviously lethal. Such insidious forms of biological maladjustment can easily come to be accepted, even by the medical profession, as 'normal' (e.g. rising blood pressure after the age of 20).

It is clear, therefore, that one of the chief tasks in human biology in the near future must be to increase our understanding of the special biology of man in contemporary society. This work will involve especially: (1) studies aimed at identifying and, where possible, describing in quantitative terms, the biologically significant changes that have occurred and that are occurring in the conditions of life of the human organism and (2) studies aimed at identifying the biologically determined responses, physiological and psychological, to these changes.

To illustrate the complexity and extent of the problem, a list is appended (p. 436) to this article of some of the changes in man's conditions of life imposed on him as a consequence of cultural developments. While some of the items on the list are clear-cut and could easily be analysed quantitatively, others such as the subtle social pressures that affect human behaviour in various ways, are hard to define in scientific terms. Nevertheless, some of the latter group may well be biologically significant and of importance in relation to the health of individuals and of society.

Approaches to the problem

It would be unrealistic and misleading to attempt to study the biology of man in modern society without taking into account the various social and economic factors which influence his conditions of life. In other words, the proper study of the biology of modern man is of necessity multidisciplinary in character, requiring the cooperation of geneticists, ecologists, sociologists, social anthropologists, demographers, social psychologists, medical scientists, economists and others. While the need for such integrative, multidisciplinary work in human biology is clear, it is equally apparent that there are many difficulties to be overcome. These difficulties have no doubt contributed to the delay in the logical development of multidisciplinary studies on man in urban society, but they are not insurmountable and the stage now seems to be set for programmes of research based on this philosophy. In fact, we can recognize several different kinds of multidisciplinary approach to the study of the biology of man in modern society, and it is likely that they will all contribute effectively to progress in this field. The most important of these approaches are as follows.

1. *The integration of existing knowledge*

An unbalanced situation exists in science today, in that massive efforts are aimed, in separate academic disciplines, at seeking new information, while in comparison negligible effort is directed towards the integration of the facts gathered in these different disciplines as they might contribute collectively to the understanding of aspects of the human situation. This situation is regrettable, because data from one discipline will often take on a new significance when viewed alongside data from another, and consequently critical intellectual effort aimed at the synthesis of existing knowledge acquired in different areas of academic endeavour can be expected to give rise to important new concepts, insights, and hypotheses.

Integrative scholarship of this kind could make an effective contribution to human biology, for there already exists a great deal of relevant information scattered in the literature of genetics, anthropology, social anthropology, demography, sociology, social history, psychology, economics, medicine, microbiology, and so on.

2. *The experimental approach*

Although there are obvious limitations to the scope of the experimental method in the study of man, this approach nevertheless has its place in research in human biology. It could be used, for instance, to test a number of simple hypotheses relating to the influence of changes in behaviour patterns on the human organism. To give just one example, the view is often expressed that lack of physical exercise, which is a notable behavioural change associated with our technological society, is detrimental not only to physical fitness but also to mental health. This is an important claim, but on the basis of existing knowledge it can be neither firmly denied nor confirmed. Nevertheless, the hypothesis readily lends itself to testing by the experimental method, for it would be a relatively simple matter to set up a study in which groups of human volunteers would be required to engage in different levels of physical activity for the period of experiment, and in which, at appropriate intervals, measurements would be made to determine the extent to which both physiological and mental processes were influenced by the different regimes.

3. *Large-scale multidisciplinary investigations in human populations*

In view of the limitations of the experimental approach in the study of the responses of the human organism to environmental change, much of the information that we require for a proper scientific description of the situation must be obtained by other methods. Especially important among these are large-scale field studies which are planned and carried out by multidisciplinary research groups and which measure both genetic and environmental (socio-economic and biological) variables on the one hand, and physiological and psychological parameters on the other.

An increasing number of community studies of this kind has been initiated during recent years. Theoretically speaking, they can be of two kinds, and can be referred to as the 'medical approach' and the 'biological approach' respectively. In the case of the former, the study is centred on a particular form of biological maladjustment and the purpose of the investigation is to try to establish links between the disorder in question and environmental or genetic factors. An example of this approach is seen in the Detroit Urban Health Program which was started in 1968. The aim of this study is to appraise the role of stress, socio-economic and psychological factors, race and heredity in the occurrence of hypertension; or, more generally, to assess the contribution of the former variables to variation in blood pressure. The problems posed in both definition and measurement of stress in this study have involved the concerted efforts of demographers, social psychologists, and natural scientists.

In the 'biological approach', the question is posed in the converse manner, by centering the investigation on one or two selected environmental variables, such as degree of crowding, quality of air, or levels of physical work, and aiming to determine the biological responses of the human organism to variations in these environmental factors, measuring a broad range of physiological and psychological parameters.

4. *The study of small groups*

There is also much that can be learned from small-scale and more qualitative non-experimental studies in human populations, particularly in the field of human behaviour. There is a need, for example, for better understanding of the factors influencing the structure and interaction of small human groups, and studies carried out in the manner of the social anthropologist can help to define the basic social parameters of such human groups. Groups are the vehicle for producing, modifying, and transmitting culture; and human cultural adaptation, in all its many variants, is and has been group adaptation. Even in cities, small groups must form, and social isolation (anomie) with its physiological and behavioural consequences, is essentially an urban disease. Comparisons of small groups in societies at all levels of technological development can contribute usefully to our understanding of the social, psychological, and biological determinants and consequences of group behaviour in modern society.

Comparisons may be useful in the study of man not only when made between different contemporary societies, but also when made between societies at different periods of history. It is likely that the injection of an historical dimension into many of the disciplines involved in the study of human biology will contribute substantially to our understanding of the processes by which human society responds to various kinds of environmental influence. Historians themselves may be expected to make an increasing contribution to the understanding of modern man and his biosocial problems, as they tend to abandon their traditional interest in producing an all-embracing 'rational reconstitution of the past' and instead go in for hypothesis-testing and the generation of theory.

Conclusion

Apart from the purely academic arguments, there are also sound practical reasons for encouraging integrative multidisciplinary research on the biology of man in modern society. The survival of the human species and the growth of human populations since the Neolithic development and in the face of changing environmental conditions has been made possible by the processes of cultural adaptation to biological maladjustment. Similarly, the future evolutionary and ecological success of the species in the face of an ever-accelerating rate of environmental change, associated with growing urbanization and industrialization, will depend entirely on the extent to which cultural adaptation continues to be effective. The success of cultural adaptation, in turn, will depend on the level of understanding in society of the increasingly complex interactions between natural processes on the one hand and cultural processes on the other. As pointed out above, the proper study of the biology of modern man is necessarily concerned with these interactions, and human biology may well contribute more than any other established academic discipline to the comprehensive understanding of the human situation and the continued survival and well-being of mankind.

Appendix: List of some of the changes in the biological conditions of life of man
Nutrition

Changes relating to diet and food intake include the introduction of refined carbohydrates in the diet (and the removal from vegetable foodstuffs of non-digestible cellulose); a large increase in fat content of foodstuffs of animal origin; a change in the quality of fat associated with foodstuffs of animal origin (i.e. replacement of poly-unsaturated fatty acids by saturated fatty acids); an increased consumption of sodium chloride; the inclusion of numerous chemical compounds added deliberately to foodstuffs (e.g. colouring or flavouring agents, preservatives, emulsifiers, etc.), or occurring incidentally as contaminants (e.g. herbicides, pesticides, detergents, etc.); the replacement of human milk by cow's milk as a food for the new-born; the addition of sugar and salt to the diet of infants (mainly to satisfy the palate of the mother); a great increase in palatability of foodstuffs through the culinary art and, more recently, through food technology (and the dissociation of palatability from nutritional value); a breakdown of biological (mainly behavioural) regulatory mechanisms for controlling food intake in relation to food requirements. (Note: Specific deficiency diseases, which have been common in earlier phases of civilization, are now relatively unimportant in modern Western society.)

Biologically potent chemicals

Modern urban society renders accessible for consumption a whole range of biologically potent chemical compounds that were not present in the environment of pre-Neolithic man. Broadly speaking, they are of two classes (although the distinction between these two classes is by no means sharp): (1) pleasure-promoting substances (e.g. alcohol, nicotine, marijuana, and L.S.D.), and (2) antidotal substances (e.g. aspirin, antibiotics, countless other drugs used in the treatment of physical sickness, and sedatives, tranquillizers, stimulants, and other psychotropic drugs).

Respiration

Changes have occurred in the quality of the air inhaled by the human organism, primarily as a consequence of the release into the atmosphere of by-products of industrial processes (especially from the combustion of fossil fuels), but also due to the widespread and increasing use of synthteic biocides and the habit of smoking tobacco.

Population, reproduction, and the sexual environment

The human population has increased almost one thousandfold since the beginning of the Neolithic development, and there have been changes in the age structure of society. There has been an increase in life expectancy, due to a fall in mortality rates. There have been major changes in the causes of mortality. There may have occurred a significant change in balance between the level of sexual stimulation and the opportunity for natural sexual outlets in some sections of the community. There has been a substantial increase in the extent of outbreeding.

Host–parasite relationships

As a consequence of greater density of human populations (and of the increase in total population) there has been a marked increase in the number of contacts of the average individual with potentially pathogenic organisms and micro-organisms capable of multiplying in the tissues of the human body. In earlier stages of civilization (and in some parts of the world today), bacterial and protozoal diseases contributed very substantially to mortality in urban populations; these have now become much less important in Western society through fairly successful cultural adaptation. However, the processes of cultural adaptation have so far failed to influence the increasing incidence of infection with viral agents.

Behaviour (and the time budget)

There are a number of clear examples of the influence of cultural developments on the behavioural biology of man. These include: the general regimentation of the time budget; the introduction of regular feeding times; modification of the sleeping pattern (i.e. interference with the opportunity to rest or sleep in response to a feeling of sleepiness, except when it comes on at 'bed-time'); interference with the reaction of mutual (or personal) avoidance in response to personality clashes; a decrease in the level and changes in the nature of physical work (and, in some sections of the community, a substantial increase in time spent more or less immobile, sitting or standing); a decrease in time spent in creative activity and in 'purposeful' activity corresponding to hunting and food-gathering.

The social environment

The numerous biologically significant changes in the social environment of the human organism include: a large increase in the number of daily intraspecific social contacts (but, in some instances, such as the case of the suburban housewife, an opposite effect); the absence of contact and violent interaction with other species; the fragmentation of the life cycle and the appearance of attitudinal barriers between generations; an increased variation in the cultural background of social contacts; an increase in the degree of choice of occupation; a decrease in the amount of freedom of action within an occupation.

The physical environment

Changes in the physical environment, additional to those mentioned above, include an increase in exposure to ionizing radiation and to radio-waves; the frequent application of surface-active agents to the skin; the application to the skin of cosmetics, suntan lotions, etc.; major changes in the aesthetic quality of the environment, and the predominance in the environment of straight lines and rectangles; an increase in hours of exposure to visible light; a decrease in variation in environmental temperature; changes in the level and nature of environmental noises.

Other more general changes

Unlike in pre-Neolithic times, the body of the human organism in modern urban society is usually concealed by clothing, regardless of the environmental temperature. Only the head and hands (and sometimes the arms and legs) are ordinarily exposed. The cover is completely removed only for purposes of ablution, for mating, and sometimes for sleeping, and only extremely rarely in public. Also in contrast to the pre-Neolithic situation, sub-threshold and sub-clinical physiological or behavioural disorders in the human organism are now, under the protective conditions of civilization, of little survival or reproductive disadvantage, and so tend to be allowed to persist in society.

Some other general changes include: an increase in hours spent per day at a single activity or occupation; a decline in enjoyment value of work; separation of work from sense of immediate purpose; a probable decrease in levels of excitement and emotional experience; an increase in the degree of environmental and social change experienced by the individual during his lifetime. There has been an increasing necessity for the exercise of self-discipline and self-restraint for the maintenance of health ('doing what comes naturally' is no longer synonymous with healthy living).

REFERENCES

ABU-LUGHOD, J. O. (1969). Testing the theory of social area analysis: the ecology of Cairo, Egypt. *Am. sociol. Rev.* **34**, 198–212.

BAKER, P. T. and BAKER, T. S. (1970). Biological adaptation in urban man: a methodological approach. In *Man's evolution in the city* (ed. M. Crawford). Chandler, San Francisco

BANKS, A. L. (1950). *Man and his environment.* Cambridge University Press.

BATES, M. (1953). Human ecology. In *Anthropology today* (ed. A. L. Kroeber). University of Chicago Press.

BEWS, J. W. (1935). *Human ecology.* Oxford University Press, London.

BLACK, F. L. (1966). Measle endemicity in insular populations: critical community size and its evolutionary implications. *J. theoret. Biol.* **11**, 207–11.

BORRIE, W. D. (1969). Recent trends and patterns in fertility in Australia. *J. biosoc. Sci.* **1**, 57–70.

BURGESS, E. W. (1925). The growth of the city: an introduction to a research project. In *The city* (eds. R. E. Park, E. W. Burgess, and R. D. McKenzie). University of Chicago Press.

CHANDRASEKHAR, S. (1967). Infant mortality in Madras city. In *World population conference*, 1965 (Vol. 2). United Nations, New York.

CHANG, K. S. F., CHAN, S. T., LOW, W. D., and NG, C. K. (1963). Climate and conception rates in Hong Kong. *Hum. Biol.* **35**, 366–76.

CHOW, L. P. (1967). Evaluation of a family planning programme in China (Taiwan). In *World population conference*, 1965 (Vol. 2). United Nations, New York.

CONCEPCION, M. B. (1967). The effect of current social and economic changes in the developing countries on differential fertility. In *World population conference*, 1965 (Vol. 2). United Nations, New York.

COOK, R. C. (1964). New patterns in U.S. fertility. *Popul. Bull.* **20**, 114–17.

DAVIS, K. (1965). The urbanization of the human population. *Scient. Am.* **213** (Sept.), 41–53.

DAY, L. H. (1964). Fertility differentials among Catholics in Australia. *Milbank meml Fund Q. Bull.* **42**, 57–83.

—— (1967). Catholic teaching and fertility. In *World population conference*, 1965. Vol. 2. United Nations, New York.

DRUMMOND, J. C. and WILBRAHAM, A. (1939). *The Englishman's food.* Jonathan Cape, London.

DUBOS, R. (1965). *Man adapting.* Yale University Press, New Haven.

EL-BADRY, M. A. and RIZK, H. (1967). Regional fertility differences among socio-economic groups in the United Arab Republic. In *World Population Conference*, 1965 (Vol. 2). United Nations, New York.

EVERSLEY, D. E. C. (1965). Population, economy, and society. In *Population in history* (eds. D. V. Glass and D. E. C. Eversley). Arnold, London.

FENNER, F. (1970). The effects of changing social organisation on the infectious diseases of man. In *The impact of civilisation on the biology of man* (ed. S. V. Boyden). Australian National University Press, Canberra.

FURNASS, S. B. (1970). Changes in non-infectious diseases associated with the processes of civilisation. In *The impact of civilisation on the biology of man* (ed. S. V. Boyden). Australian National University Press, Canberra.

GEILING, E. and D'AGUANNO, D. (1960). Our man-made noxious environment. *Fed. Proc.* **19** (Pt.2, Suppl. 4 Sept.), 3–9.

GILFILLAN, S. C. (1965). Lead poisoning and the fall of Rome. *J. occup. Med.* **7**, 53.

GOLDBERG, E. D. (1969). The chemical invasion of the oceans. In *Yearbook of science and technology*. McGraw-Hill, New York.

HABAKKUK, H. J. (1958). The economic history of modern Britain. In *Population in history* (eds. D. V. Glass and D. E. C. Eversley). Arnold, London (1965).

HAECKEL, E. (1870). Ueber Entwicelungsgang und Aufgabe der Zoologie. *Jena. Z. Med. Naturw.* **5**, 353–70. (Cited by Bates 1953.)

HAJNAL, J. (1965). European marriage patterns in perspective. In *Population in history* (eds. D. V. Glass and D. E. C. Eversley). Arnold, London.

JELLIFFE, D. B. (1955). Infant nutrition in the sub-tropics. *World Health Organization Spec. Rept.* No. 529.

JOHNSON, G. Z. (1960). Differential fertility in Europe. In *Demographic and economic change in developed countries*. Princeton University Press.

—— (1967). Public health activities as factors in levels and trends of mortality and morbidity in developing countries. In *World population conference*, 1965 (Vol. 2). United Nations, New York.

JONES, F. L. (1969). *Dimensions of urban social structures*. Australian National University Press, Canberra.

KISER, C. V. (1967). Social, economic and religious factors in the differential fertility of low fertility countries. In *World population conference*, 1965 (Vol. 2). United Nations, New York.

KLINGER, A. (1967). Demographic effects of abortion in some European socialist countries. In *World population conference*, 1965 (Vol. 2). United Nations, New York.

KORMONDY, E. J. (1969). *Concepts of ecology*. Prentice-Hall, Englewood Cliffs.

KRALJ-CERCEK, L. (1956). The influence of food, body build, and social origin on the age at menarche. *Hum. Biol.* **28**, 393–406.

KROHN, E. F. and WEBER, A. (1967). The characteristics of mortality in the European region. In *World population conference*, 1965 (Vol. 2). United Nations New York.

KUMAR, J. (1967). Age at menarche: a comparative study. *Demography* **4**, 333.

LANCET (Leading article) (1969). Malaria and the population explosion. *Lancet* **1**, 899–900.

MACMAHON, B. and WORCESTER, J. (1966). *Age at menopause, United States*, 1960–2. National Center for Health Statistics, Series 11, No. 19. Washington, D.C.

McKEOWN, T. and BROWN, R. G. (1955). Medical evidence related to English population changes in the eighteenth century. *Popul. Stud.* **9**, 119–41.

MORRIS, J. K. and FARLEY, W. R. (1964). Changing patterns of fertility. *Popul. Bull.* **20**, 118–39.

MURAMATSU, M. (1960). Effect of induced abortion on the reduction of birth in Japan. *Milbank meml Fund Q. Bull.* **38**, 153–66.

NAG, M. (1967). Family type and fertility. In *World population conference*, 1965 (Vol. 2). United Nations, New York.

ORAM, N. D. (1965). Health, housing, and urban development. *Papua New Guin. med. J.* **8**, 41–51.

—— (1970). Indigenous housing in Port Moresby. *New Guin. Res. Bull.* (In press.)

PETERS, J., ISRAEL, S., and PURSHOTTAM, S. (1958). Lactation period in Indian women. *Fert. Steril.* **9**, 134–44.

PETERSEN, W. (1969). *Population* (2nd edn.). MacMillan, London.

QUINN, J. A. (1950). *Human ecology*. Prentice-Hall, New York.

RAINA, B. L. (1967). Possible effects of public policy measures on fertility in India. In *World population conference*, 1965 (Vol. 2) United Nations, New York.

SHEPHARD, P. (1967). Whatever happened to human ecology? *Biosci.* **17**, 891–4, 911.

SHEVKY, E. and WILLIAMS, M. (1949). *The social areas of Los Angeles: analysis and typology.* University of California Press, Berkeley.

—— and BELL, W. (1955). *Social areas analysis: theory, illustrative application, and computational procedures.* Stanford University Press.

SIGSWORTH, E. (1966). A provincial hospital in the eighteenth and early nineteenth century. *Coll. Gen. Practrs, Yorkshire Faculty Journal*, 1–8.

SMITH, A. H. (1965). *Report on the health of Johannesburg.* Medical Officer of Health—Annual Report.

SMITH, T. L. (1958). The reproduction rate in Latin America: levels, differentials, and trends. *Popul. Stud.* **12**, 4–16.

SOVANI, N. V. (1967). Internal migration in the future trend of population in India. In *World population conference*, 1965 (Vol. 2). United Nations, New York.

STAPLEDON, G. (1964). *Human ecology.* Faber and Faber, London.

TANNER, J. M. (1962). *Growth at adolescence* (2nd edn). Blackwell, Oxford.

—— (1965). The trend towards earlier physical maturation. In *Biological aspects of social problems* (eds. J. E. Meade and A. S. Parkes). Oliver and Boyd, Edinburgh and London.

TIETZE, C. (1960). Probability of pregnancy resulting from a single unprotected coitus. *Fert. Steril.* **11**, 485–8.

TUKEY, J. W. (Chairman) (1965). *Restoring the quality of our environment.* Pollution Panel, President's Science Advisory Committee, The White House, Washington.

TITMUS, R. M., ABEL-SMITH, B., and LYNES, T. (1961). *Social policies and population growth in Mauritius.* Methuen, London.

UNITED NATIONS (1967). *Demographic Yearbook.* United Nations, New York.

—— (1968). *Statistical Yearbook for 1967.* United Nations, New York.

URLANIS, B. T. (1967). Dynamics of the birth rate in the Union of Soviet Socialist Republics and factors contributing to it. In *World population conference*, 1965 (Vol. 2). United Nations, New York.

WARK, L. and MALCOLM, L. A. (1969). Growth and development of the Lumi child in the Sepik district of New Guinea. *Med. J. Aust.* **2**, 129–36.

WIESLER, H. (1967). Mortality in South-east Asia. In *World population conference*, 1965 (Vol. 2). United Nations, New York.

WORLD HEALTH ORGANIZATION (1967). The world health situation: a statistical review. *W.H.O. Chronicle* **21**, 350–6.

—— (1968). More and safer water for the developing countries. *W.H.O. Chronicle* **22**, 362–71.

WOLMAN, A. (1965). The metabolism of cities. *Scient. Am.* **213** (Sept.), 179–90.

WOYTINSKY, W. S. and WOYTINSKY, E. S. (1953). *World population and production.* The Twentieth Century Fund, New York.

ZARATE, A. O. (1967). Differential fertility in Monterrey, Mexico. *Milbank meml Fund Q. Bull.* **45**, 93–108.

SUBJECT INDEX